Rick Steves'

VENICE

Rick Steves & Gene Openshaw

2014

CONTENTS

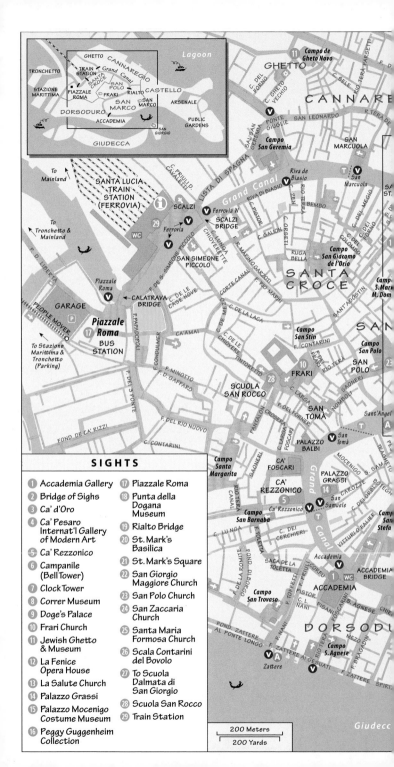

SIGHTS

1. Accademia Gallery
2. Bridge of Sighs
3. Ca' d'Oro
4. Ca' Pesaro Internat'l Gallery of Modern Art
5. Ca' Rezzonico
6. Campanile (Bell Tower)
7. Clock Tower
8. Correr Museum
9. Doge's Palace
10. Frari Church
11. Jewish Ghetto & Museum
12. La Fenice Opera House
13. La Salute Church
14. Palazzo Grassi
15. Palazzo Mocenigo Costume Museum
16. Peggy Guggenheim Collection
17. Piazzale Roma
18. Punta della Dogana Museum
19. Rialto Bridge
20. St. Mark's Basilica
21. St. Mark's Square
22. San Giorgio Maggiore Church
23. San Polo Church
24. San Zaccaria Church
25. Santa Maria Formosa Church
26. Scala Contarini del Bovolo
27. To Scuola Dalmata di San Giorgio
28. Scuola San Rocco
29. Train Station

200 Meters

200 Yards

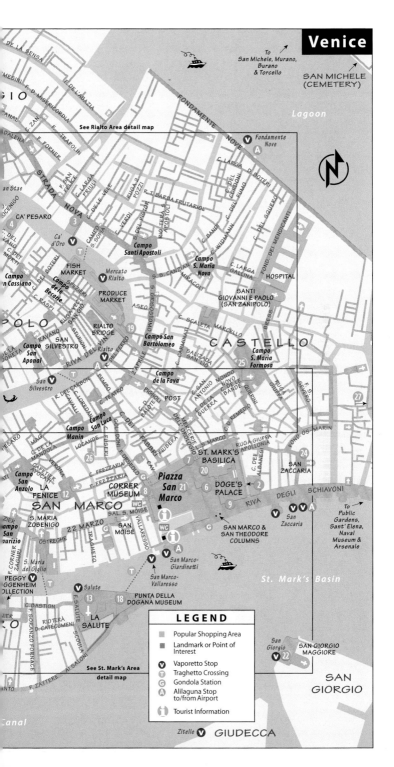

St. Mark's Square Area

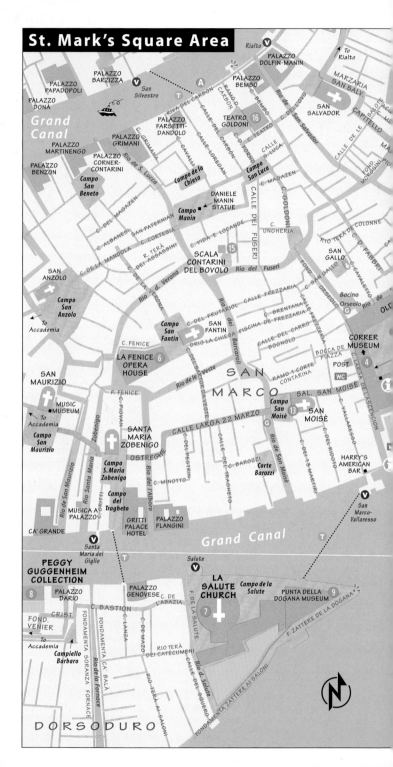

Rialto **V**

To Rialto

PALAZZO DOLFIN-MANIN

PALAZZO BARZIZZA

V San Silvestro **T**

A

RIVA DEL CARBON

C. RAMO D. CARBON

PALAZZO BEMBO

CALLE DEL CARBON

C. DEL'OVO

MARZARIA SAN SALV.

SAN SALVADOR

PALAZZO PAPADOPOLI

PALAZZO DONÀ

Grand Canal

CALLE-LOREDAN

C. CAVALLI

PALAZZO FARSETTI-DANDOLO

TEATRO GOLDONI **16**

C. TEATRO

C. PONTE

C. San Salvador

CALLE S.LUCA

CAPITELLO

BAC C. DE C. ME

PALAZZO MARTINENGO

PALAZZO GRIMANI

C. GRIMANA

Rio de S. Lucca

Campo de la Chiesa

Campo San Luca

C. MAGAZEN

CALLE DE LE

FOND. MOROSINI PIG

PALAZZO BENZON

PALAZZO CORNER-CONTARINI

C. DEL MAGAZEN

C. San Lucca

DANIELE MANIN STATUE

CALLE DEI FUSERI

C. GOLDONI

C. UNGHERIA

MA

Campo San Beneto

C. ALDANESI

SAN PATERNIAN

C. CORTESIA

Campo Manin

VIDA E LOCANDE

RIO TERÀ DE COLONNE

C. D. FABBRI

CA

C. DE LA MANDOLA

R. TERÀ DEI ASSASSINI

SCALA CONTARINI DEL BOVOLO **15**

Rio del Fuseri

FOND. ORSEOLO

C. SAN GALLO

SAN GALLO

C. CAVALETTO

SAN ANZOLO

C. DE LA VERONA

Rio d. Verona

C. DEL FRUTARIOL

CALLE FREZZARIA

C. BRENTANA

PISCINA DE FREZZARIA

Bacino Orseolo **G**

Rio de OLI

Campo San Anzolo

To Accademia

Campo San Fantin

SAN FANTIN

DRIO LA CHIESA Barcaroli

CALLE FREZZARIA

CALLE-DEL-CARRO

BOGNOLO

CORRER MUSEUM

C. FENICE

LA FENICE OPERA HOUSE **6**

C. DELA FENICE

Rio de le Veste

RAMO 1 CORTE CONTARINA

BOCCA DE PIAZZA

POST **4**

SAN MAURIZIO

MUSIC MUSEUM

F. FENICE

C. PIOVAN

SAN MARCO

SAL. SAN MOISÈ

WC

i

To Accademia

Zobenigo

SANTA MARIA ZOBENIGO

CALLE LARGA 22 MARZO

Campo San Moisè **13**

SAN MOISÈ

C. VALLARESSO

C. DEL RIDOTTO

V

Campo San Maurizio

OSTREGHE

Rio dei L'Alboro

C. DEL PESTRIN

CALLE DEL TRAGHETO

G

C. DEI 13 MARTIRI

HARRY'S AMERICAN BAR

i

Rio de San Mauritio

Rio Santa Maria

Campo S.Maria Zobenigo

C. MINOTTO

CALLE DEL TRAGHETO

Corte Barozzi

Rio de San Moisè

Campo del Tragheto

MUSICA A PALAZZO

GRITTI PALACE HOTEL

PALAZZO FLANGINI

San Marco-Vallaresso **V**

CA' GRANDE

V Santa Maria del Giglio

Grand Canal

T

Salute **V**

T

PEGGY GUGGENHEIM COLLECTION **8**

PALAZZO DARIO

PALAZZO GENOVESE

C. DE L'ABAZIA

LA SALUTE CHURCH **7**

Campo de la Salute

PUNTA DELLA DOGANA MUSEUM **9**

FOND. VENIER

CRIST.

C. BASTION

C. LANZA

C. DE MAZO

F. DE LA SALUTE

F. ZATTERE DE LA DOGANA

To Accademia

Campiello Barbaro

FONDAMENTA SORANZA FORNACE

FONDAMENTA CA' BALA

RIO TERÀ DEI CATECUMENI

Rio de la Fornace

RIO TERÀ AI SALONI

CALLE DEL SQUERO

Rio d. Salute

FONDAMENTA ZATTERE AI SALONI

N

DORSODURO

House of Juliet in Verona

Venetian Masks

Gondolas in Venice

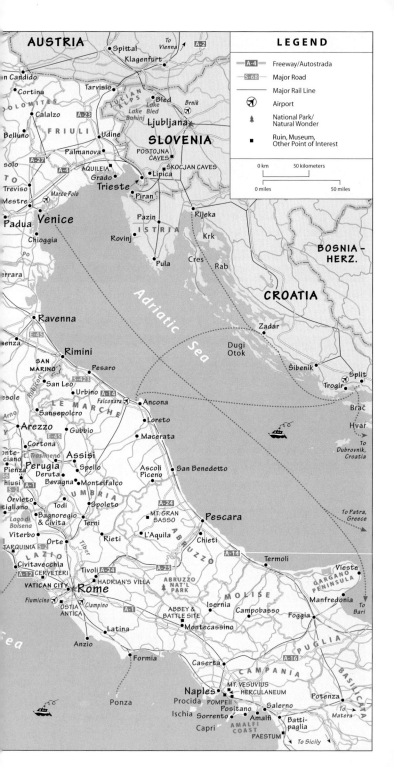

AUSTRIA

Spittal

To Vienna A-2

Klagenfurt

n Candido

Cortina

Tarvisio

Bled

Brnik ✈

OLOMITES

Calalzo

A-23

Lake Bled

Lake Bohinj

Bled

Belluno

FRIULI

Udine

LJUBLJANA ★

JULIAN ALPS

solo

A-27

Palmanova

SLOVENIA

POSTOJNA CAVES

AQUILEIA

ŠKOCJAN CAVES

O

Treviso

A-4

Grado

Lipica

Mestre

✈ *Marco Polo*

Trieste

Padua

Venice

Piran

Pazin

ISTRIA

Rijeka

Chioggia

Rovinj

Krk

Po

BOSNIA–
HERZ.

rrara

Pula

Cres

Rab

CROATIA

Ravenna

Adriatic Sea

Zadar

E-45

Rimini

Dugi
Otok

enza

SAN MARINO

Pesaro

San Leo

S-423

Urbino

A-14

Šibenik

Split ✈

Trogir

esole

Arno

LE MARCHE

Falconara ✈

Ancona

Brač

Sansepolcro

Loreto

Hvar

Arezzo

Gubbio

Macerata

*To
Dubrovnik,
Croatia*

Cortona

onte-
ciano

L. Trasimeno

Assisi

Spello

Ascoli
Piceno

San Benedetto

🚤

Pienza

Perugia

Deruta

hiusi

S-2

Bevagna

Montefalco

A-1

UMBRIA

Orvieto

tigliano

Todi

Spoleto

A-24

MT. GRAN
SASSO

Pescara

*To Patra,
Greece*

Lago di
Bolsena

Bagnoregio
& Civita

Terni

Viterbo

Orte

Rieti

L'Aquila

ABRUZZO

Chieti

A-14

TARQUINIA

S-2

LAZIO

Tiber

Termoli

Vieste

Civitavecchia

CERVETERI

Tivoli

A-24

A-25

A-12

HADRIAN'S VILLA

ABRUZZO
NAT'L
PARK

GARGANO
PENINSULA

VATICAN CITY

Rome ★

MOLISE

Manfredonia

Fiumicino ✈

OSTIA
ANTICA

Ciampino ✈

Isernia

*To
Bari*

A-1

ABBEY &
BATTLE SITE

Campobasso

Foggia

Latina

Montecassino

PUGLIA

Anzio

Caserta

A-16

ea

Formia

CAMPANIA

BASILICATA

Ponza

Naples

MT. VESUVIUS

HERCULANEUM

Potenza

Procida

POMPEII

Positano

Salerno

*To
Matera*

Ischia

Sorrento

Amalfi

Batti-
paglia

Capri

AMALFI
COAST

PAESTUM

To Sicily

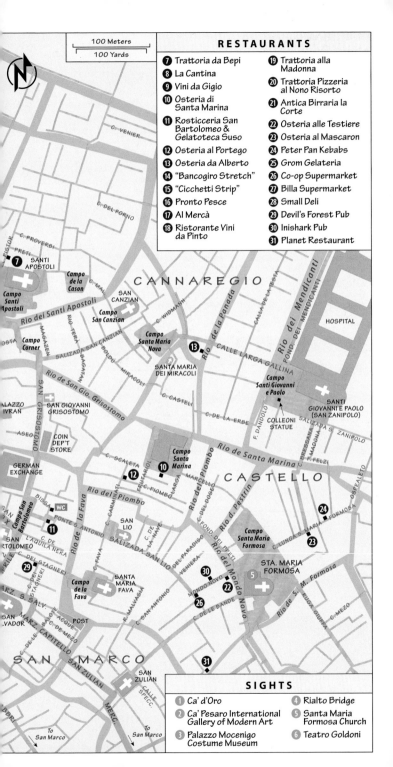

RESTAURANTS

7 Trattoria da Bepi
8 La Cantina
9 Vini da Gigio
10 Osteria di Santa Marina
11 Rosticceria San Bartolomeo & Gelatoteca Suso
12 Osteria al Portego
13 Osteria da Alberto
14 "Bancogiro Stretch"
15 "Cicchetti Strip"
16 Pronto Pesce
17 Al Mercà
18 Ristorante Vini da Pinto

19 Trattoria alla Madonna
20 Trattoria Pizzeria al Nono Risorto
21 Antica Birraria la Corte
22 Osteria alle Testiere
23 Osteria al Mascaron
24 Peter Pan Kebabs
25 Grom Gelateria
26 Co-op Supermarket
27 Billa Supermarket
28 Small Deli
29 Devil's Forest Pub
30 Inishark Pub
31 Planet Restaurant

SIGHTS

1 Ca' d'Oro
2 Ca' Pesaro International Gallery of Modern Art
3 Palazzo Mocenigo Costume Museum
4 Rialto Bridge
5 Santa Maria Formosa Church
6 Teatro Goldoni

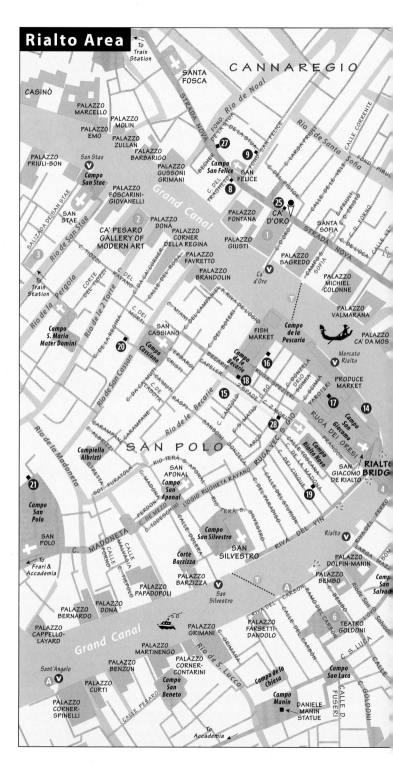

Rialto Area

To Train Station

CANNAREGIO

SANTA FOSCA

CASINÒ

PALAZZO MARCELLO

PALAZZO MOLIN

PALAZZO EMO

PALAZZO ZULLAN

PALAZZO BARBARIGO

PALAZZO PRIULI-BON

San Stae

Campo San Stae

PALAZZO FOSCARINI-GIOVANELLI

PALAZZO GUSSONI GRIMANI

STRADA NOVA

FOND. Rio de Noal

Campo San Felice

SAN FELICE

Rio de Santa Sofia

CALLE CORRENTE

FOND PIRU

27

9

8

C. DEL TRAGHETTO

SAN STAE

SALIZADA DI SAN STAE

Rio de San Stae

Grand Canal

PALAZZO DONÀ

CA' PESARO GALLERY OF MODERN ART

2

PALAZZO CORNER DELLA REGINA

PALAZZO FAVRETTO

PALAZZO BRANDOLIN

PALAZZO FONTANA

25

CA' D'ORO

1

SANTA SOFIA

STRADA NOVA

PALAZZO GIUSTI

PALAZZO SAGREDO

Ca d'Oro

V

PALAZZO MICHIEL COLONNE

PALAZZO VALMARANA

T

3

C. DEL TIOZZI

Rio de la Pergola

CORTE DEL TIOZZI

C. DEL RAVANO

C. DA CA' CORNER

C. DE LA CA' CORNER

CALLE DEL ROSA

Rio de le 2 Torre

C. DE LA REGINA

SAN CASSIANO

C. DEI MORTI

F. MIANI DEL CAMPANIEL

F. RIVA DEL OGIO

C. DEI BOTERI

Campo de la Pescaria

FISH MARKET

PALAZZO CA' DA MOS

Mercato Rialto

V

PRODUCE MARKET

To Train Station

Campo S. Maria Mater Domini

20

Campo Cassiano

ERBARIO

L'ERBARIO

C. DA CA MUTI

CAMUFI

C. DE LA

RASPI

CLAPOTA

C. DE

BECARIE

CAPELER

Campo de le Becarie

16

18

RUGA SPEZIERI

C. DONZELA

C. BO.

GOMMA

SAGREDO

Campo Giacomo

17

14

15

C. LANZOLO

RUGA DEI ORESI

SANSONI

DONZELA

C. SIO MATIO

C. 2 MORI

SPADE

28

PRIANGON

Campo Rialto Novo

SAN GIACOMO DE RIALTO

RIALTO BRIDGE

4

SAN POLO

RIO de le Becarie

GARAMPANE

C. GARAMPANE

Rio de San Cassan

C. DE LA MADONETA

Campiello Albrizti

STRETTA

SOT. FURATOLA

SAN APONAL

Campo San Aponal

C. MADONA

RIO TERÀ S. APONAL

PERDON

C. DE MEZO

C. TODESCHINI

LUGHETA RAVANO

LUGIO

RUGA VECCHIA

C. DEL PARADISO

C. DEL STURION

RIO TERÀ S. SILVESTRO

CALLE DEL CINQUE

CALLE TOSCANA

C. DE LA MADON

19

RIVA DEL VIN

Rialto

V

RIVA DEL FERRO

21

Campo San Polo

SAN POLO

To Frari & Accademia

C. MADONETA

CALLE MANIN

MANIAIA

CALLE FORNO

C. TIEPOLO

Corte Barzizza

Campo San Silvestro

SAN SILVESTRO

Campo Dolera

PALAZZO BERNARDO

PALAZZO CAPPELLO-LAYARD

PALAZZO PAPADOPOLI

PALAZZO DONÀ

PALAZZO BARZIZZA

V

San Silvestro

T

A

PALAZZO GRIMANI

Grand Canal

PALAZZO CORNER-CONTARINI

Rio de S. Lucca

RIVA DEL CARBON

RAMO DEL CARBON

CALLE DEL CARBON

PALAZZO FARSETTI-DANDOLO

PALAZZO DOLFIN-MANIN

PALAZZO BEMBO

Camp San Salva

6

TEATRO GOLDONI

C. S. LUCA

Campo San Luca

CALLE D.

Sant'Angelo

A

V

PALAZZO CURTI

PALAZZO BENZON

PALAZZO MARTINENGO

Campo San Beneto

CALLE PESARO

PALAZZO CORNER-SPINELLI

Campo de la Chiesa

Campo Manin

DANIELE MANIN STATUE

CALLE D. FUSERI

CALLE GOLDONI

To Accademia

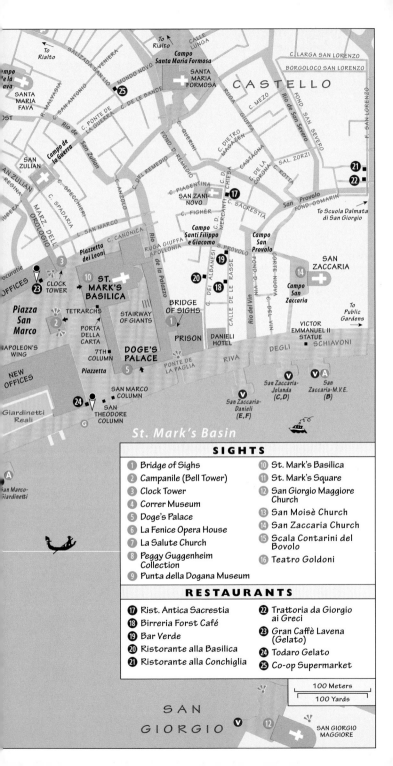

To Rialto
To Rialto

C. LARGA SAN LORENZO
BORGOLOCO SAN LORENZO

Campo Santa Maria Formosa

CASTELLO

SANTA MARIA FORMOSA

C. LARGA SAN LUIO
SALIZADA SAN LUIO
SALIZADA S.LIO VENERA

mpo e la ava

SANTA MARIA FAVA

C. SAN ANTONIO
C. MALVASIA

C. DE LE BANDE
C. PONTE DE LA GUERRA
Rio de San Zulian

C. MEZO
RUGA GIUFFA
FOND. de San Severo

FOND SAN SEVERO

C. LARGA

OST

SAN ZULIAN

Campo de la Guerra

C. ANZOLO

C. DEL REMEDIO

C. QUERINI

C. DIETRO MAGAZEN

SAL. ZORZI

C. DELLA CORONA
C. ROTTA
C. CASTAGNA

F. SAN LORENZO

N ZULIAN

C. SPECCHIERI

REGINA

C. SPADARIA
MARZ. DELL OROLOGIO

C. PIASENTINA

SAN ZANI-NOVO

C.D. CHIESA
C.D. MERCANTI
C. FIGHER

SACRESTIA

San Provolo
FOND. OSMARIN

To Scuola Dalmata di San Giorgio

UBERA

L. SAN MARCO
C. CANONICA

Rio Giuffa de la Palazzo
Ruga Giuffa APOLLONIA

Campo Santi Filippo e Giacomo

S. PROVOLO

Campo San Provolo

SAN ZACCARIA

ocurate

Piazzetta dei Leoni

CLOCK TOWER

ST. MARK'S BASILICA

C. D. ALBANESI

CORTE NUOVA

Campo San Zaccaria

To Public Gardens

FFICES

Piazza San Marco

TETRARCHS

STAIRWAY OF GIANTS

C. DEL ANGELO
C. DE LE RASSE

Rio del Vin

C. DEL VIN
C. DEL VIN

SAN ZACCARIA

NAPOLEON'S WING

PORTA DELLA CARTA

BRIDGE OF SIGHS

PRISON

DANIELI HOTEL

VICTOR EMMANUEL II STATUE

NEW OFFICES

7TH COLUMN

DOGE'S PALACE

Piazzetta

PONTE DE LA PAGLIA

RIVA

DEGLI

SCHIAVONI

SAN MARCO COLUMN

SAN THEODORE COLUMN

San Zaccaria-Jolanda (C,D)

San Zaccaria-M.V.E. (B)

Giardinetti Reali

G

St. Mark's Basin

San Zaccaria-Danieli (E,F)

A
San Marco-Giardinetti

SAN GIORGIO

SAN GIORGIO MAGGIORE

SIGHTS

1. Bridge of Sighs
2. Campanile (Bell Tower)
3. Clock Tower
4. Correr Museum
5. Doge's Palace
6. La Fenice Opera House
7. La Salute Church
8. Peggy Guggenheim Collection
9. Punta della Dogana Museum
10. St. Mark's Basilica
11. St. Mark's Square
12. San Giorgio Maggiore Church
13. San Moisè Church
14. San Zaccaria Church
15. Scala Contarini del Bovolo
16. Teatro Goldoni

RESTAURANTS

17. Rist. Antica Sacrestia
18. Birreria Forst Café
19. Bar Verde
20. Ristorante alla Basilica
21. Ristorante alla Conchiglia
22. Trattoria da Giorgio ai Greci
23. Gran Caffè Lavena (Gelato)
24. Todaro Gelato
25. Co-op Supermarket

100 Meters
100 Yards

Rick Steves'

VENICE

2014

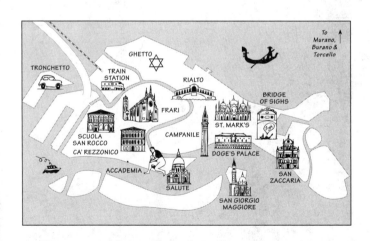

Venice Overview

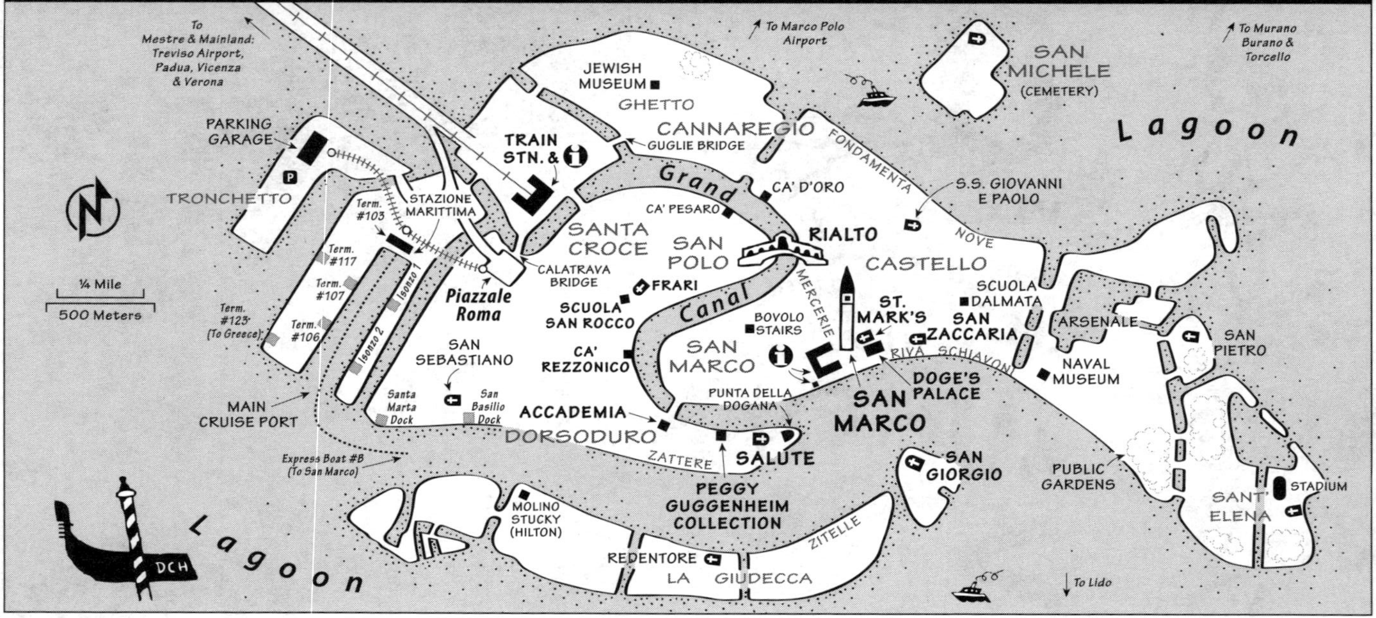

Lagoon

To Murano,
Burano &
Torcello

To Marco Polo
Airport

To Mestre & Mainland:
Treviso Airport,
Padua, Vicenza
& Verona

To Lido

N

¼ Mile
500 Meters

SAN MICHELE
(CEMETERY)

SAN PIETRO

SANT'
ELENA

STADIUM

ARSENALE

NAVAL
MUSEUM

PUBLIC
GARDENS

S.S. GIOVANNI
E PAOLO

SCUOLA
DALMATA

SAN
ZACCARIA

DOGE'S
PALACE

RIVA
SCHIAVONI

SAN
GIORGIO

CASTELLO

NOVE

FONDAMENTA

RIALTO

ST.
MARK'S

SAN MARCO

MERCERIE

CANNAREGIO

GHETTO

GUGLIE BRIDGE

Grand

CA' D'ORO

CA' PESARO

SAN POLO

FRARI

Canal

BOVOLO
STAIRS

SAN MARCO

PUNTA DELLA
DOGANA

SALUTE

ZATTERE

PEGGY
GUGGENHEIM
COLLECTION

ZITELLE

REDENTORE

LA GIUDECCA

JEWISH
MUSEUM

SANTA
CROCE

TRAIN
STN. &

CALATRAVA
BRIDGE

SCUOLA
SAN ROCCO

CA'
REZZONICO

ACCADEMIA

DORSODURO

MOLINO
STUCKY
(HILTON)

PARKING
GARAGE

TRONCHETTO

Piazzale
Roma

STAZIONE
MARITTIMA

Term.
#103

Term.
#117

Term.
#107

Term.
#106

Term.
#123
(To Greece)

SAN
SEBASTIANO

Santa
Marta
Dock

San
Basilio
Dock

MAIN
CRUISE PORT

Express Boat #6
(to San Marco)

Lagoon

DCH

Lagoon

INTRODUCTION

Engineers love Venice—a completely man-made environment rising from the sea, with no visible means of support. Romantics revel in its atmosphere of elegant decay, seeing the peeling plaster and seaweed-covered stairs as a metaphor for beauty in decline. And first-time visitors are often stirred deeply, awaking from their ordinary lives to a fantasy world unlike anything they've ever experienced before.

Those are strong reactions, considering that Venice today, frankly, can also be an overcrowded, prepackaged, tacky tourist trap. But Venice is unique. Built on a hundred islands with wealth from trade with the East, its exotic-looking palaces are laced together by sun-speckled canals. The car-free streets suddenly make walkers feel big, important, and liberated. It's basically one giant amusement park for grown-ups, centuries in the making. And yet, the longer you're here—and the more you explore its back streets—the clearer it becomes that this is also a real, living town, with its own personality and challenges.

By day, Venice is a city of museums and churches, packed with great art. Everything's within a half-hour walk. Cruise the canals on a vaporetto water bus. Climb towers for stunning seascape views. Shop for Venetian crafts (such as glass and lace), high fashions, or tacky souvenirs for your Uncle Eric. Linger over lunch, trying to crack a crustacean with weird legs and antennae. Sip a *spritz* at a café on St. Mark's Square while the orchestra plays "New York, New York."

At night, when the hordes of day-trippers have gone, another Venice appears. Dance across a floodlit square. Glide in a gondola through quiet canals while music echoes across the water. Pretend it's Carnevale time, don a mask—or just a fresh shirt—and become someone else for a night.

Map Legend

⊾	Viewpoint	✈	Airport	🍦	Gelato
↑	Entrance	Ⓣ	Taxi Stand	··········	Pedestrian Zone
⊕	Tourist Info	🇹	Tram Stop	- - - - -	Railway
WC	Restroom	Ⓑ	Bus Stop	··········	Ferry/Boat Route
✡	Synagogue	Ⓟ	Parking		
🏠	Church	)(	Mtn. Pass	⊢—⊢—⊣	Tram
Ⓥ	Vaporetto Dock		Park	▪▪▪▪▪▪▪	Stairs
🇹	Traghetto Crossing	▪	Statue/Point of Interest	· · · · · ·	Walk/Tour Route
Ⓖ	Gondola Station				
Ⓐ	Alilaguna Stop	🏰	Castle	- - - - -	Trail

Use this legend to help you navigate the maps in this book.

About This Book

Rick Steves' Venice 2014 is a personal tour guide in your pocket. Better yet, it's actually two tour guides in your pocket: The co-author of this book is Gene Openshaw. Since our first "Europe through the gutter" trip together as high school buddies in the 1970s, Gene and I have been exploring the wonders of the Old World. An inquisitive historian and lover of European culture, Gene wrote most of this book's self-guided museum tours and neighborhood walks. Together, Gene and I keep this book current (though for simplicity, from this point "we" will shed our respective egos and become "I").

In this book, you'll find the following chapters:

Orientation to Venice includes specifics on public transportation, helpful hints, local tour options, easy-to-read maps, and tourist information. The "Planning Your Time" section suggests a schedule for how to best use your limited time.

Sights in Venice describes the top attractions and includes their cost and hours.

The **Self-Guided Walks** cover Venice's back streets. The walk from St. Mark's to Rialto follows a less touristy route between these two major landmarks, then loops back via Venice's high-end (and tourist-packed) shopping drag. The walk from Rialto to the Frari Church (with its exquisite art) takes you through bustling markets and by a mask-making shop. The walk from St. Mark's to San Zaccaria explores the area behind the basilica, featuring a historic church and a seldom-seen view of the famous Bridge of Sighs.

The **Self-Guided Tours** lead you through Venice's most fascinating museums and sights: the Grand Canal, St. Mark's Square, St. Mark's Basilica, Doge's Palace, Correr Museum, Accademia, Frari Church, Scuola San Rocco, Ca' Rezzonico (Museum of 18th-Century Venice), Peggy Guggenheim Collection, La Salute

Key to This Book

Updates
This book is updated every year—but once you pin down Italy, it wiggles. For the latest, visit www.ricksteves.com/update. For a valuable list of reports and experiences—good and bad—from fellow travelers, check www.ricksteves.com/feedback.

Abbreviations and Times
I use the following symbols and abbreviations in this book:
Sights are rated:

▲▲▲	**Don't miss**
▲▲	**Try hard to see**
▲	**Worthwhile if you can make it**
No rating	**Worth knowing about**

Tourist information offices are abbreviated as **TI,** and bathrooms are **WCs.** To categorize accommodations, I use a **Sleep Code** (described on page 249).

Like Europe, this book uses the **24**-**hour clock.** It's the same through 12:00 noon, then keeps going: 13:00, 14:00, and so on. For anything over 12, subtract 12 and add p.m. (14:00 is 2:00 p.m.).

When giving **opening times,** I include both peak season and off-season hours if they differ. So, if a museum is listed as "May-Oct daily 9:00-16:00," it should be open from 9:00 a.m. until 4:00 p.m. from the first day of May until the last day of October (but expect exceptions).

If you see a ✪ symbol near a sight listing, it means that sight is described in far greater detail elsewhere—either with its own self-guided tour, or as part of a self-guided walk.

For **transit** or **tour departures,** I first list the frequency, then the duration. So, a train connection listed as "2/hour, 1.5 hours" departs twice each hour and the journey lasts an hour and a half.

Church, San Giorgio Maggiore, and the islands in Venice's lagoon (including San Michele, Murano, Burano, and Torcello).

Sleeping in Venice describes my favorite hotels, from good-value deals to cushy splurges. I've focused on hotels conveniently located near St. Mark's Square, the Rialto Bridge, and the Accademia—all handy to the sights in this compact city. I also suggest hotels near the train station and on the mainland, in Mestre.

Eating in Venice serves up a range of options, from inexpensive cafés to fancy restaurants.

Venice with Children includes my top recommendations for keeping your kids (and you) happy.

Shopping in Venice gives you tips for shopping painlessly and enjoyably, without letting it overwhelm your vacation or ruin your budget.

Nightlife in Venice is your guide to after-dark Venice, including gondola rides, concerts, theaters, pubs, and clubs.

Venice Connections lays the groundwork for your smooth arrival and departure, covering transportation by train, bus, car, cruise ship, and plane. It provides detailed information on Venice's two airports (Marco Polo and Treviso), train station (Santa Lucia), and cruise port (Stazione Marittima).

Day Trips include art-filled Padua and romantic Verona.

Venetian History fills you in on the background of this fascinating city.

The **appendix** is a traveler's tool kit, with telephone tips, useful phone numbers and websites, recommended books and films, a festival list, a climate chart, a handy packing checklist, and Italian survival phrases.

Browse through this book and select your favorite sights. Then have a *buono* trip! Traveling like a temporary local, you'll get the absolute most out of every mile, minute, and dollar. As you visit places I know and love, I'm happy that you'll be meeting my favorite Venetians.

Planning

This section will help you get started planning your trip—with advice on trip costs, when to go, and what you should know before you take off.

Travel Smart

Many people travel through Italy thinking it's a chaotic mess. They feel that any attempt at efficient travel is futile. This is dead wrong—and expensive. Italy, which seems as orderly as spilled spaghetti, actually functions well. Only those who understand this and travel smart can enjoy Italy on a budget.

This book can save you lots of time and money. But to have an "A" trip, you need to be an "A" student. Read it all before your trip, noting holidays, specific advice on sights, and days when sights are closed. If you save St. Mark's Basilica for Sunday morning (when it's closed), you've missed the gondola. You can sweat in line at the Doge's Palace, or you can buy your pass at the nearby Correr Museum and zip right through the palace turnstile. Day-tripping to Verona on Monday, when the major sights are closed, is bad news. A smart trip is a puzzle—a fun, doable, and worthwhile challenge.

When you're plotting your itinerary, strive for a mix of intense and relaxed stretches. Every trip—and every traveler—needs slack time (laundry, picnics, people-watching, and so on). Pace yourself. Assume you will return.

Get online at Internet cafés or your hotel, and carry a mobile phone (or use a phone card) to make travel plans: You can find tourist information, learn the latest on sights (special events, tour schedules, etc.), book tickets and tours, make reservations, reconfirm hotels, research transportation connections, and keep in touch with your loved ones.

Enjoy the friendliness of the Venetian people. Connect with the culture. Set up your own quest for the best little square, vaporetto ride, or gelato. Slow down and be open to unexpected experiences. Ask questions—most locals are eager to point you in their idea of the right direction. Keep a notepad in your pocket for noting directions, organizing your thoughts, and confirming prices. Wear your money belt, learn the currency, and figure out how to estimate prices in dollars. Those who expect to travel smart, do.

Trip Costs

Six components make up your trip costs: airfare, surface transportation, room and board, sightseeing/entertainment, shopping/miscellany, and gelato.

Airfare: A basic round-trip flight from the US to Venice (or even cheaper, Milan) can cost, on average, about $800-1,700 total, depending on where you fly from and when (cheaper in winter). If Venice is part of a longer trip, consider saving time and money in Europe by flying into one city and out of another; for instance, into Venice and out of Dubrovnik.

Surface Transportation: Venice's sights are within walking distance of each other, but vaporetto boat rides, while expensive (about $9), are fun and save time. For a one-way trip between Venice's airport and the city, allow about $7 by bus, $20 by Alilaguna water bus, or $145 by water taxi (can be shared by up to 4 people).

The cost of round-trip, second-class train transportation to day-trip destinations is affordable and depends on the speed of the train (about $5 to Padua by slow train, and about $30 to Verona by fast train). For more on public transportation and car rentals, see "Transportation" in the appendix.

Room and Board: You can manage comfortably in Venice in 2014 on $130 a day per person for room and board. This allows $15 for lunch, $25 for dinner, and $90 for lodging (based on two people splitting the cost of a $180 double room that includes breakfast). Students and tightwads can enjoy Venice for as little as $65 a day ($35 for a bed, $30 for meals and snacks).

Sightseeing and Entertainment: Figure about $15-22 per major sight (Accademia, Doge's Palace, Guggenheim), $7-10 for minor ones (climbing church towers), and $25-30 for splurge experiences (such as walking tours and concerts). A gondola ride costs $105 (by day) or $135 (at night); split the cost by going with a pal. An overall average of $40 a day works for most people. Don't skimp here. After all, this category is the driving force behind your trip—you came to sightsee, enjoy, and experience Venice.

Shopping and Miscellany: Figure $3 per postcard (including postage) and $4-5 per coffee, soft drink, or gelato. Shopping can vary in cost from nearly nothing to a small fortune. Good budget travelers find that this category has little to do with assembling a trip full of lifelong and wonderful memories.

When to Go

Venice's best travel months (also its busiest and most expensive) are May, June, September, and October. These months combine the convenience of peak season with pleasant weather.

Summer in Venice is more temperate (high 70s and 80s) than in Italy's scorching inland cities. Most Venetian hotels come with air-conditioning—important in the summer—but it's usually available only from May (at the earliest) through September. Spring and fall can be cool, and many hotels—thanks to a national interest in not wasting energy—are not allowed to turn on their heat until winter.

Between November and April you can usually expect mild winter weather (with lows in the 30s and 40s), occasional flooding, shorter lines, lower prices, and fewer tourists (except during the Carnevale festival, generally in February). While Carnevale comes with high hotel prices, it's a big party, with special concerts, lots of kids' events, fresh pastries, and costumed figures crowding through the city. March and April offer a good balance of low-season prices and comfortable weather. (For specifics, see the climate chart in the appendix.)

Venice has two main weather patterns: Wind from the southeast (the Balkans) brings cold and dry weather, while the sirocco wind from the south (north Africa) brings warm and wet weather, pushing more water into the lagoon and causing flooding *(acqua alta)*. This shouldn't greatly affect your sightseeing plans. *Tabacchi* (tobacco shops) and some souvenir shops sell boots to keep your feet dry. Elevated wooden walkways are sometimes set up in the busier, more flooded squares to keep you above the water. And it's worth a trip to St. Mark's Square to see waiters in fancy tuxes and rubber boots.

Off-Season Travel Tips: Off-season has none of the sweat and stress of the tourist season, but sights may have shorter hours, lunchtime breaks, and fewer activities. Here are several things to keep in mind if you visit Venice off-season, roughly November through March.

• Most sights close early, often at 17:00.

• The orchestras in St. Mark's Square may stop playing at 18:00 (and may not play at all in bad weather or during their annual vacations, usually in March).

• Vaporetto #2 (the Grand Canal fast boat) terminates at the Rialto stop before 9:00 and after 20:00, which means no stops at San Marco and Accademia early in the morning and late in the evening (you can take the slow boat, vaporetto #1, instead).

• Expect occasional flooding, particularly at St. Mark's Square and along Zattere (southern edge of Venice, opposite Giudecca Island).

• Room prices can be about 25-50 percent less than those quoted in this book.

Know Before You Go

Your trip is more likely to go smoothly if you plan ahead. Check this list of things to arrange while you're still at home.

You need a **passport**—but no visa or shots—to travel in Italy. You may be denied entry into certain European countries if your passport is due to expire within three to six months of your ticketed date of return. Get it renewed if you'll be cutting it close. It can take up to six weeks to get or renew a passport (for more on passports, see www.travel.state.gov). Pack a photocopy of your passport in your luggage in case the original is lost or stolen.

Book rooms well in advance if you'll be traveling during peak season (June-Sept, plus Carnevale) or any major holidays (see page 455).

Call your **debit- and credit-card companies** to let them know the countries you'll be visiting, to ask about fees, to request your PIN code (it will be mailed to you), and more. See page 11 for details.

Do your homework if you want to buy **travel insurance.** Compare the cost of the insurance to the likelihood of your using it and your potential loss if something goes wrong. Also, check whether your existing insurance (health, homeowners, or renters) covers you and your possessions overseas. For more tips, see www.ricksteves.com/insurance.

If you're taking an **overnight train** and need a couchette *(cuccetta)* or sleeper—and you *must* leave on a certain day—consider booking it in advance through a US agent (such as www.raileurope.com), even though it may cost more than buying it in Italy. Other Italian trains, like the high-speed Freece trains, require a seat reservation, but for these it's usually possible to make arrangements in Italy just a few days ahead. (For more on train travel, see the appendix.)

If you're planning on **renting a car** in Italy, bring your driver's

INTRODUCTION

license and an International Driving Permit (see page 445). If you drive in restricted areas monitored by cameras, you can be fined without a cop ever stopping you (see page 448).

In Padua, **reservations** are mandatory to visit the Scrovegni Chapel, famous for its frescoes by Giotto, so book well in advance (easily done online; see page 362).

If you plan to hire a **local guide,** reserve ahead by email. Popular guides can get booked up.

If you're bringing a **mobile device,** download any apps you might want to use on the road, such as translators, maps, and transit schedules. Check out **Rick Steves Audio Europe,** featuring audio tours of major sights, hours of travel interviews on Venice, and more (via www.ricksteves.com/audioeurope, iTunes, Google Play, or the Rick Steves Audio Europe smartphone app; for details, see page 21).

Check the **Rick Steves guidebook updates** page for any recent changes to this book (www.ricksteves.com/update).

Because **airline carry-on restrictions** are always changing, visit the Transportation Security Administration's website (www. tsa.gov/travelers) for an up-to-date list of what you can bring on the plane with you...and what you must check.

Practicalities

Emergency and Medical Help: In Italy, dial 113 for English-speaking police help. To summon an ambulance, call 118. If you get sick, do as the Venetians do and go to a pharmacist for advice. Or ask at your hotel for help—they'll know the nearest medical and emergency services. For the hospital, see page 27.

Theft or Loss: To replace a passport, you'll need to go in person to a US embassy (see page 432). If your credit and debit cards disappear, cancel and replace them (see "Damage Control for Lost Cards" on page 13). File a police report either on the spot or within a day or two; you'll need it to submit an insurance claim for lost or stolen railpasses or travel gear, and it can help with replacing your passport or credit and debit cards. For more information, see www.ricksteves.com/help. Precautionary measures can minimize the effects of loss—back up your digital photos and other files frequently.

Time Zones: Italy, like most of continental Europe, is generally six/nine hours ahead of the East/West Coasts of the US. The exceptions are the beginning and end of Daylight Saving Time: Europe "springs forward" the last Sunday in March (two weeks after most of North America), and "falls back" the last Sunday in October (one week before North America). For a handy online time converter, see www.timeanddate.com/worldclock.

Venice Almanac

Population: While there are approximately 270,000 people in greater Venice, only 58,000 people live on the actual islands.

Currency: Euro

Nicknames: La Serenissima and The Queen of the Adriatic

City Layout: The city of Venice is built on more than 100 small islands in the Venetian Lagoon along the Adriatic Sea. The historic center is broken up into six districts that hold the city's main attractions. These *sestieri* include Cannaregio, Castello, Dorsoduro, San Polo, Santa Croce, and San Marco.

Tallest Structure: The Campanile on St. Mark's Square reaches 325 feet and offers a beautiful view of the city. Good news: It has an elevator.

Tourist Tracks: Roughly 22 million tourists flock to Venice each year, with 30,000 roaming the streets each day of the Carnevale festival. St. Mark's Square is the most popular sight and the Rialto Bridge is the top photo spot.

Culture Count: The Venice population has long been almost entirely Italian—but that's changing. You'll notice lots of Asians and Eastern Europeans working in shops and restaurants, as well as lots of Senegalese on the streets selling knockoff bags. While Italian is the official language of Italy, about 2 million people in the Veneto region speak the Venetian dialect. The vast majority of native Venetians are Roman Catholics.

Fun Food Facts: Venice is known for its wine bars (*bacari* or *enoteche*) that serve small bite-sized snacks called *cicchetti*, which are similar to Spanish tapas.

Most Venerable Café: Caffè Florian, on the south side of St. Mark's Square, opened in 1720. Famous visitors have included Lord Byron and Charles Dickens.

Average Venetian: The average Venetian is 46 years old, has 1.4 children, and will live until the age of 82. Half of the Venetian population works in some sector of the tourism industry. Venetians are more likely to have a gondolier license than a driver's license.

Business Hours: Traditionally, Venice uses the siesta plan. People generally work from 9:00 to 13:00 and from 15:30 to 19:00, Monday through Saturday. But many businesses have adopted the government's recommended 8:00 to 14:00 workday, although in tourist areas, shops are open longer (9:00-19:30). Some stores and restaurants close on Sunday. Banking hours are generally Monday through Friday 8:30 to 13:30 and 15:30 to 16:30, but they can vary wildly.

Saturdays are virtually weekdays, with earlier closing hours. Sundays have the same pros and cons as they do for travelers in the US: Sightseeing attractions are generally open, while shops and banks are closed. Rowdy evenings are rare on Sundays.

Watt's Up? Europe's electrical system is 220 volts, instead of North America's 110 volts. Most newer electronics (such as laptops, battery chargers, and hair dryers) convert automatically, so you won't need a converter, but you will need an adapter plug with two round prongs, sold inexpensively at travel stores in the US. Avoid bringing older appliances that don't automatically convert voltage; instead, buy a cheap replacement in Europe.

Discounts: Venice's city museums offer youth and senior discounts to Americans and other non-citizens of the European Union (EU)—bring an ID. These museums include the Doge's Palace, Correr Museum, Clock Tower on St. Mark's Square, Ca' Rezzonico, Ca' Pesaro, Palazzo Mocenigo Costume Museum, Punta della Dogana, Murano's Glass Museum, and Burano's Lace Museum. Italy's national museums generally offer free admission to children under age 18.

Online Translation Tip: You can use Google's Chrome browser (available free at www.google.com/chrome) to instantly translate websites. With one click, the page appears in a (very rough) English translation. You can also paste the URL of the site into the translation window at www.google.com/translate.

Money

This section offers advice on how to pay for purchases on your trip (including getting cash from ATMs and paying with plastic), dealing with lost or stolen cards, VAT (sales tax) refunds, and tipping.

What to Bring

Bring both a credit card and a debit card. You'll use the debit card at cash machines (ATMs) to withdraw local cash for most purchases, and the credit card to pay for larger items. Some travelers carry a third card, in case one gets demagnetized or eaten by a temperamental machine.

For an emergency stash, bring several hundred dollars in hard cash in $20 bills. If you have to exchange the bills, go to a bank; avoid using currency-exchange booths because of their lousy rates and/or outrageous fees.

Cash

Cash is just as desirable in Europe as it is at home. Small businesses (hotels, restaurants, shops, etc.) prefer that you pay your bills with cash. Some vendors will charge you extra for using a credit card, and some won't take credit cards at all. Cash is the best—and sometimes only—way to pay for boats, buses, taxis, and local guides.

Exchange Rate

1 euro (€) = about $1.30

To convert prices in euros to dollars, add about 30 percent: €20 = about $26, €50 = about $65. (Check www.oanda.com for the latest exchange rates.) Just like the dollar, one euro is broken down into 100 cents. You'll find coins ranging from €0.01 to €2, and bills ranging from €5 to €500.

Throughout Europe, ATMs are the standard way for travelers to get cash. But stay away from "independent" ATMs such as Travelex, Euronet, or Forex, which charge huge commissions and have terrible exchange rates.

To withdraw money from an ATM (known as a *bancomat*), you'll need a debit card (ideally with a Visa or MasterCard logo for maximum usability), plus a PIN code. Know your PIN code in numbers; there are only numbers—no letters—on European keypads. Although you can use a credit card for an ATM transaction, it only makes sense in an emergency, because it's considered a cash advance (borrowed at a high interest rate) rather than a withdrawal. Try to withdraw large sums of money to reduce the number of per-transaction bank fees you'll pay.

For increased security, shield the keypad when entering your PIN code, and don't use an ATM if anything on the front of the machine looks loose or damaged (a sign that someone may have attached a "skimming" device to capture account information). It's a good idea to monitor your account while traveling to detect any unauthorized transactions.

Pickpockets target tourists. To safeguard your cash, wear a money belt—a pouch with a strap that you buckle around your waist like a belt and tuck under your clothes. Keep your cash, credit cards, and passport secure in your money belt, and carry only a day's spending money in your front pocket.

Credit and Debit Cards

For purchases, Visa and MasterCard are more commonly accepted than American Express. Just like at home, credit or debit cards work easily at larger hotels, restaurants, and shops. I typically use my debit card to withdraw cash to pay for most purchases. I use my credit card only in a few specific situations: to book hotel reservations by phone, to cover major expenses (such as car rentals, plane tickets, and long hotel stays), and to pay for things near the end of my trip (to avoid another visit to the ATM). While you could use a debit card to make most large purchases, using a credit card offers a greater degree of fraud protection (because debit cards draw funds directly from your account).

Ask Your Credit- or Debit-Card Company: Before your trip, contact the company that issued your debit or credit cards.

• Confirm your **card will work overseas**, and alert them that you'll be using it in Europe; otherwise, they may deny transactions if they perceive unusual spending patterns.

• Ask for the specifics on transaction **fees.** When you use your credit or debit card—either for purchases or ATM withdrawals—you'll typically be charged additional "international transaction" fees of up to 3 percent (1 percent is normal) plus $5 per transaction. If your card's fees seem high, consider getting a different card just for your trip: Capital One (www.capitalone.com) and most credit unions have low-to-no international fees.

• If you plan to withdraw cash from ATMs, confirm your daily **withdrawal limit,** and if necessary, ask your bank to adjust it. Some travelers prefer a high limit that allows them to take out more cash at each ATM stop (saving on transaction fees), while others prefer to set a lower limit in case their card is stolen. Note that foreign banks also set maximum withdrawal amounts for their ATMs.

• Get your bank's emergency **phone number** in the US (but not its 800 number, which isn't accessible from overseas) to call collect if you have a problem.

• Ask for your credit card's **PIN** in case you need to make an emergency cash withdrawal or encounter Europe's "chip and PIN" system; the bank won't tell you your PIN over the phone, so allow time for it to be mailed to you.

Chip and PIN: While much of Europe is shifting to a "chip-and-PIN" security system for credit and debit cards, Italy still uses the old magnetic-swipe technology. (European chip-and-PIN cards are embedded with an electronic security chip, and require the purchaser to punch in a PIN rather than sign a receipt.) If you happen to encounter chip and PIN, it will probably be at automated payment machines, such as those at toll roads or self-serve gas pumps. On the outside chance that a machine won't take your card, find a cashier who can make your card work (they can print a receipt for you to sign), or find a machine that takes cash. But don't panic. Most travelers who are carrying only magnetic-stripe cards never encounter any problems. You can always use an ATM with your magnetic-stripe card, even in countries where people predominantly use chip-and-PIN cards.

Dynamic Currency Conversion: If merchants offer to convert your purchase price into dollars (called dynamic currency conversion, or DCC), refuse this "service." You'll pay even more in fees for the expensive convenience of seeing your charge in dollars.

INTRODUCTION

Damage Control for Lost Cards

If you lose your credit, debit, or ATM card, you can stop people from using your card by reporting the loss immediately to the respective global customer-assistance centers. Call these 24-hour US numbers collect: Visa (tel. 303/967-1096), MasterCard (tel. 636/722-7111), and American Express (tel. 623/492-8427). In Italy, to make a collect call to the US, dial 800-172-444 (press zero or stay on the line for an English-speaking operator). European toll-free numbers (listed by country) can be found at the websites for Visa and MasterCard.

Providing the following information allows for a quicker cancellation of your missing card: full card number, whether you are the primary or secondary cardholder, the cardholder's name exactly as printed on the card, billing address, home phone number, circumstances of the loss or theft, and identification verification (your birth date, your mother's maiden name, or your Social Security number—memorize this, don't carry a copy). If you are the secondary cardholder, you'll also need to provide the primary cardholder's identification-verification details. You can generally receive a temporary card within two or three business days in Europe (see www.ricksteves.com/help for more).

If you report your loss within two days, you typically won't be responsible for any unauthorized transactions on your account, although many banks charge a liability fee of $50.

Tipping

Tipping in Italy isn't as automatic and generous as it is in the US, but for special service, tips are appreciated, if not expected. As in the US, the proper amount depends on your resources, tipping philosophy, and the circumstances, but some general guidelines apply.

Restaurants: A service charge *(servizio)* is usually already included in your bill. If you're pleased with the service, you can round up the bill by a euro or two. For more on tipping in restaurants, see page 278.

Taxis: To tip the cabbie, round up. For a typical ride, round up your fare a bit (for instance, if the fare is €4.50, pay €5). If the cabbie hauls your bags and zips you to the airport to help you catch your flight, you might want to toss in a little more. But if you feel like you're being driven in circles or otherwise ripped off, skip the tip.

Services: In general, if someone in the service industry does a super job for you, a small tip of a euro or two is appropriate...but not required. If you're not sure whether (or how much) to tip for a service, ask your hotelier or the TI.

Getting a VAT Refund

Wrapped into the purchase price of your Italian souvenirs is a Value-Added Tax (VAT) of about 22 percent. You're entitled to get most of that tax back if you purchase more than €155 (about $200) worth of goods at a store that participates in the VAT-refund scheme. Typically, you must ring up the minimum at a single retailer—you can't add up your purchases from various shops to reach the required amount.

Getting your refund is usually straightforward and, if you buy a substantial amount of souvenirs, well worth the hassle. If you're lucky, the merchant will subtract the tax when you make your purchase. (This is more likely to occur if the store ships the goods to your home.) Otherwise, you'll need to:

Get the paperwork. Have the merchant completely fill out the necessary refund document, called a "cheque." You'll have to present your passport. Get the paperwork done before you leave the store to ensure you'll have everything you need (including your original sales receipt).

Get your stamp at the border or airport. Process your VAT document at your last stop in the European Union (such as at the airport) with the customs agent who deals with VAT refunds. Before checking in for your flight, find the local customs office, and be prepared to stand in line. Keep your purchases readily available for viewing by the customs agent (ideally in your carry-on bag—don't make the mistake of checking the bag with your purchases before you've seen the agent). You're not supposed to use your purchased goods before you leave. If you show up at customs wearing your new gondolier outfit, officials might look the other way—or deny you a refund.

Collect your refund. You'll need to return your stamped document to the retailer or its representative. Many merchants work with a service, such as Global Blue or Premier Tax Free, that has offices at major airports, ports, or border crossings (either before or after security, probably strategically located near a duty-free shop). These services, which extract a 4 percent fee, can refund your money immediately in cash or credit your card (within two billing cycles). If the retailer handles VAT refunds directly, it's up to you to contact the merchant for your refund. You can mail the documents from home, or more quickly, from your point of departure (using an envelope you've prepared in advance or one that's been provided by the merchant). You'll then have to wait—it can take months.

Customs for American Shoppers

You are allowed to take home $800 worth of items per person duty-free, once every 30 days. You can also bring in duty-free a liter of alcohol. As for food, you can take home many processed and packaged foods: vacuum-packed cheeses, dried herbs, jams, baked goods, candy, chocolate, oil, vinegar, mustard, and honey. Fresh fruits and vegetables and most meats are not allowed. Any liquid-containing foods must be packed in checked luggage, a potential recipe for disaster. To check customs rules and duty rates, visit http://help.cbp.gov.

Sightseeing

Sightseeing can be hard work. Use these tips to make your visits to Venice's finest sights meaningful, fun, efficient, and painless.

Plan Ahead

Set up an itinerary that allows you to fit in all your must-see sights. For a one-stop look at opening hours, see "Venice at a Glance" (page 46; also see "Daily Reminder" on page 25). Most sights keep stable hours, but you can easily confirm the latest by checking with the TI or visiting museum websites. If you plan to visit Padua's Scrovegni Chapel, make reservations in advance (see page 362).

Don't put off visiting a must-see sight—you never know when a place will close unexpectedly for a holiday, strike, or restoration. Many museums are closed or have reduced hours at least a few days a year, especially on holidays such as Christmas, New Year's, and Labor Day (May 1). A list of holidays is on page 455; check museum websites for possible closures during your trip. In summer, some sights may stay open late. Off-season, many museums have shorter hours.

Going at the right time helps avoid crowds. This book offers tips on the best times to see specific sights. Try visiting popular sights very early or very late. Evening visits are usually peaceful, with fewer crowds. (See the "Venice Early and Late" sidebar on page 50.)

Study up. To get the most out of the self-guided tours and sight descriptions in this book, read them before you visit.

At Sights

Here's what you can typically expect:

Some important sights require you to check daypacks and coats. To avoid checking a small backpack, carry it under your arm like a purse as you enter. From a guard's point of view, a backpack is generally a problem while a purse is not.

Flash photography is often banned to prevent damage to delicate artworks, but taking photos without a flash is usually allowed (look for signs or ask a guard). Even without a flash, a handheld

How Was Your Trip?

Were your travels fun, smooth, and meaningful? If you'd like to share your tips, concerns, and discoveries, please fill out the survey at www.ricksteves.com/feedback. I value your feedback. Thanks in advance—it helps a lot.

camera will take a decent picture (or just buy postcards or posters at the museum bookstore).

You may have to pay cash for the admission fee; some sights don't take credit cards. Museums may show special exhibits in addition to their permanent collection. Some exhibits are included in the entry price, while others come at an extra cost (which you may have to pay even if you don't want to see the exhibit).

Expect changes—artwork can be on tour, on loan, out sick, or shifted at the whim of the curator. To adapt, pick up a floor plan as you enter, and ask museum staff if you can't find a particular item. Say the title or artist's name, or point to the photograph in this book and ask, *"Dov'è?"* (doh-VEH, meaning "Where is?").

Many sights rent audioguides, which generally offer excellent recorded descriptions in English (about €4-7). Bring along your own earbuds to enjoy better sound and avoid holding the device to your ear. To save money, bring a Y-jack and share one audioguide with your travel partner. I've produced free downloadable audio tours of the major sights in Venice; see page 21.

Important sights may have an on-site café or cafeteria (usually a handy place to rejuvenate during a long visit). The WCs at sights are free and generally clean.

Many places sell postcards that highlight their attractions. Before you leave a sight, scan the postcards and thumb through the biggest guidebook (or skim its index) to be sure that you haven't overlooked something that you'd like to see.

Most sights stop admitting people 30 to 60 minutes before closing time, and some rooms may close early (often about 45 minutes before the actual closing time). Guards usher people out, so don't save the best for last.

Every sight or museum offers more than what is covered in this book. Use the information in this book as an introduction—not the final word.

Find Religion

Churches offer some amazing art (usually free), a cool respite from heat, and a welcome seat.

A modest dress code (no bare shoulders or shorts for anyone, even kids) is enforced at larger churches, such as St. Mark's Basilica and the Frari Church, but is often overlooked elsewhere. If you are caught by surprise, you can improvise, using maps to cover your shoulders and a jacket for your knees. (I wear a super-lightweight pair of long pants rather than shorts for my hot and muggy big-city Italian sightseeing.)

Some churches have coin-operated audioboxes that describe the art and history; just set the dial on English, put in your coins, and listen. Other coin boxes illuminate the art (and present a better photo opportunity). I pop in a coin whenever I can. It improves my experience, is a favor to other visitors trying to appreciate a great piece of art in the dark, and is a little contribution to that church and its work. Whenever possible, let there be light.

Traveling as a Temporary Local

We travel all the way to Italy to enjoy differences—to become temporary locals. You'll experience frustrations. Certain truths that we find "God-given" or "self-evident," such as cold beer, ice in drinks, bottomless cups of coffee, and bigger being better, are suddenly not so true. One of the benefits of travel is the eye-opening realization that there are logical, civil, and even better alternatives. A willingness to go local ensures that you'll enjoy a full dose of Italian hospitality.

Europeans generally like Americans. But if there is a negative aspect to the Italians' image of Americans, it's that we are loud, wasteful, ethnocentric, too informal (which can seem disrespectful), and a bit naïve. Think about the rationale behind "crazy" Italian decisions. For instance, many hoteliers turn off the heat in spring and can't turn on air-conditioning until summer. The point is to conserve energy, and it's mandated by the Italian government. You could complain about being cold or hot...or bring a sweater in winter, and in summer, be prepared to sweat a little like everyone else.

While Italians, flabbergasted by our Yankee excesses, say in disbelief, *"Mi sono cadute le braccia!"* ("I throw my arms down!"), they nearly always afford us individual travelers all the warmth we deserve.

Judging from all the happy feedback I receive from travelers who have used this book, it's safe to assume you'll enjoy a great, affordable vacation—with the finesse of an independent, experienced traveler.

Thanks, and *buon viaggio!*

Back Door Travel Philosophy

From *Rick Steves' Europe Through the Back Door*

Travel is intensified living—maximum thrills per minute and one of the last great sources of legal adventure. Travel is freedom. It's recess, and we need it.

Experiencing the real Europe requires catching it by surprise, going casual..."through the Back Door."

Affording travel is a matter of priorities. (Make do with the old car.) You can eat and sleep—simply, safely, and enjoyably—anywhere in Europe for $120 a day plus transportation costs. In many ways, spending more money only builds a thicker wall between you and what you traveled so far to see. Europe is a cultural carnival, and time after time, you'll find that its best acts are free and the best seats are the cheap ones.

A tight budget forces you to travel close to the ground, meeting and communicating with the people. Never sacrifice sleep, nutrition, safety, or cleanliness to save money. Simply enjoy the local-style alternatives to expensive hotels and restaurants.

Connecting with people carbonates your experience. Extroverts have more fun. If your trip is low on magic moments, kick yourself and make things happen. If you don't enjoy a place, maybe you don't know enough about it. Seek the truth. Recognize tourist traps. Give a culture the benefit of your open mind. See things as different, but not better or worse. Any culture has plenty to share.

Of course, travel, like the world, is a series of hills and valleys. Be fanatically positive and militantly optimistic. If something's not to your liking, change your liking.

Travel can make you a happier American, as well as a citizen of the world. Our Earth is home to seven billion equally precious people. It's humbling to travel and find that other people don't have the "American Dream"—they have their own dreams. Europeans like us, but with all due respect, they wouldn't trade passports.

Thoughtful travel engages us with the world. In tough economic times, it reminds us what is truly important. By broadening perspectives, travel teaches new ways to measure quality of life.

Globetrotting destroys ethnocentricity, helping us understand and appreciate other cultures. Rather than fear the diversity on this planet, celebrate it. Among your most prized souvenirs will be the strands of different cultures you choose to knit into your own character. The world is a cultural yarn shop, and Back Door travelers are weaving the ultimate tapestry. Join in!

ORIENTATION TO VENICE

The island city of Venice is shaped like a fish. Its major thoroughfares are canals. The Grand Canal winds through the middle of the fish, starting at the mouth where all the people and food enter, passing under the Rialto Bridge, and ending at St. Mark's Square (Piazza San Marco). Park your 21st-century perspective at the mouth and let Venice swallow you whole.

Venice is a car-less kaleidoscope of people, bridges, and odorless canals. It's made up of more than a hundred small islands—but for simplicity, I refer to the whole shebang as "the island."

There are six districts (*sestieri*, shown on map on page 20): **San Marco** (from St. Mark's Square to the Accademia Bridge), **Castello**

(the area east of St. Mark's Square), **Dorsoduro** (the "belly" of the fish, on the far side the Accademia Bridge), **Cannaregio** (between the train station and the Rialto Bridge), **San Polo** (west of the Rialto Bridge), and **Santa Croce** (the "eye" of the fish, across the canal from the train station).

The easiest way to navigate is by landmarks. Many street corners have a sign pointing you to *(per)* the nearest major landmark, such as San Marco, Accademia, Rialto, and Ferrovia (train station). Obedient visitors stick to the main thoroughfares as directed by these signs...and miss the charm of back-street Venice.

Beyond the city's core lie several other islands, including San Giorgio (with great views of Venice), Giudecca (more views), San Michele (old cemetery), Murano (famous for glass), Burano (lace-

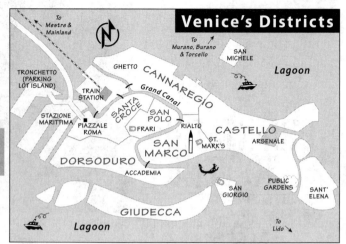

making), Torcello (old church), and the skinny Lido (with Venice's beach).

Planning Your Time

Venice is small. You can walk across it, from head to tail, in about an hour. Nearly all of your sightseeing is within a 20-minute walk of the Rialto Bridge or St. Mark's Square. Remember that Venice itself is its greatest sight. Make time to wander, explore, shop, and simply be. When you cross a bridge, look both ways. You may be hit with a lovely view.

Key considerations: Ninety percent of tourists congregate in a very narrow zone in the center. But even the most touristy stretches of the city are almost ghostly peaceful early and late. Maximize your evening magic, and avoid the midday crowds around St. Mark's Basilica and the Doge's Palace. If you arrive in Venice late in the day, try taking my Grand Canal Cruise and St. Mark's Square Tour. These sights are more romantic and much less crowded after dark—and they provide a wonderful welcome to the city. (Also see "Crowd Control" tips in the "Daily Reminder" sidebar, later.)

Depending on when you visit, you may have to juggle the itineraries below, as sights' visiting hours will vary by season and day of the week.

Venice in One Busy Day

9:00   Take the Grand Canal Cruise, hopping off at the San Tomà stop to tour the Frari Church (except on Sun, when Frari doesn't open until 13:00).

11:00   From Frari Church, take a 20-minute stroll toward

Rick Steves Audio Europe

If you're bringing a mobile device, be sure to check out **Rick Steves Audio Europe,** where you can download free audio tours and hours of travel interviews (via the Rick Steves Audio Europe smartphone app, www.ricksteves.com/audioeurope, iTunes, or Google Play).

My self-guided **audio tours** are user-friendly, easy-to-follow, fun, and informative, covering the Grand Canal, St. Mark's Square, St. Mark's Basilica, and Frari Church. Compared to live tours, my audio tours are hard to beat: Nobody will stand you up, the quality is reliable, you can take the tour exactly when you like, and they're free.

Rick Steves Audio Europe also offers a far-reaching library of intriguing **travel interviews** with experts from around the globe.

ORIENTATION

the Rialto Market, then enjoy the market action and browse for lunch. Catch the vaporetto (boat) to your next stop.

13:00   Tour two of the following three museums: the Accademia (Renaissance Venetian art, closes at

14:00 on Mon), the Peggy Guggenheim Collection (modern art, closed Tue), and Correr Museum (overview of Venetian art and history, ticket bought here includes Doge's Palace).

15:30   Head to—then tour—St. Mark's Basilica (closes at 17:00 in summer, at 16:00 in winter).

17:00   Visit the Doge's Palace (in summer closes at 18:30, last entry at 17:30; closes an hour earlier in winter).

18:00   Tour St. Mark's Square.

19:30   Dinner.

21:00   Gondola ride. If you don't mind eating late, flip-flop this with dinner, as the gondola at sunset is best.

22:00   Enjoy the dueling orchestras with a drink on St. Mark's Square.

Venice in Two or More Days

Day 1

9:00   Take a vaporetto or walk to the train station and over the Calatrava Bridge to Piazzale Roma. Then catch the slow-boat vaporetto (line #1) to take my self-guided Grand Canal Cruise.

10:30   Interrupt the tour, hopping off at Mercato Rialto to explore the market. Eat an early lunch of *cicchetti* (Venetian tapas) at the bars recommended on page 300.

13:00   Continue the Grand Canal Cruise, ending at St. Mark's Square.

13:30   Tour St. Mark's Square.

14:30   Correr Museum (ticket here includes Doge's Palace).

15:30   St. Mark's Basilica (closes at 17:00 in summer, at 16:00 in winter).

17:00   Doge's Palace (closes at 18:30 in summer, last entry at 17:30; closes at 17:30 in winter).

19:00   Go up the Campanile bell tower for the city view (July-Sept only, when it's open until 21:00; in other months, squeeze it in on the afternoon of Day 2).

20:00   Dinner (make a reservation).

22:00   Enjoy the dueling orchestras with a drink on St. Mark's Square.

Day 2

9:00   Shopping or exploring. (My Rialto to Frari Church Walk is a good spine for exploring the market en route to the next sight.)

10:00   Visit the Frari Church. If you like Tintoretto, follow the Frari with the Scuola San Rocco (just behind the church), nudging the rest of your day back an hour.

11:30   Tour Ca' Rezzonico (Museum of 18th-Century Venice, closed Tue).

13:00   Lunch (pizza next to the Accademia Bridge?).

14:00   Your choice: Tour Accademia (closes Mon at 14:00), explore Dorsoduro neighborhood (wander back lanes to the Zattere promenade), or visit La Salute Church (opens for afternoon visits at 15:00) or Peggy Guggenheim Collection (closed Tue).

18:00   Commence pub crawl (perhaps on a pub tour with Alessandro—see page 39).

20:00   Concert and/or gondola ride.

Day 3—Lagoon Tour

10:00	Catch boat at Fondamente Nove to San Michele (old cemetery), then continue to Murano.
11:00	Tour Murano, see glassworks.
13:00	Boat to Burano for lunch and browsing.
15:00	Shuttle boat to Torcello, tour church, back to Burano.
18:00	Zip back to Fondamente Nove in 45 minutes, or—if you'd like to see more of the lagoon—take the long way back by boat via the island of Sant'Erasmo and the Lido (but don't stop there—just enjoy the cruise).
20:00	Dinner and/or concert in Venice.

Day 4 and Beyond

Shop and browse some of Venice's more characteristic areas (such as the zone between Campo Santa Margarita and Campo San Barnaba; the back lanes of Cannaregio, near the Jewish Ghetto; or the sleepy part of Dorsoduro behind the Accademia and Guggenheim).

Take a Venicescapes tour or other tour.

Visit the Church of San Giorgio Maggiore.

Follow additional self-guided neighborhood walks in this book.

Side-trip to Padua (30-50 minutes away by train).

Overview

Tourist Information

With this book, a free city map from your hotel, and the events schedule on the TI's website, there's little need to make an in-person visit to a TI in Venice. That's fortunate, because the city's TIs can be crowded and don't have many free printed materials to hand out. If you need to check or confirm something, try phoning the TI at 041-529-8711 or visit www.turismovenezia.it (click on "Venezia," then the English icon). This website can be more helpful than the actual TI office.

If you must visit a TI, you'll find two convenient branches near **St. Mark's Square** (one in the far-left corner with your back to the basilica, the other next to the Giardinetti Reali park near the San Marco vaporetto stop; both of these are open daily 9:00-19:00). There's also a TI desk at the **airport** (daily 9:00-20:00).

At the **train station,** you'll find TI staffers in a big, white kiosk out front near the vaporetto #2 stop most of the year (from Carnevale—falling sometime in Feb—through Oct daily 9:00-14:30, closed off-season; as this kiosk is shared with the private Alilaguna boat company, be sure to seek out a TI representative). The TI inside the station is open on summer afternoons (daily 13:00-19:00) and all day long in winter (daily 9:00-19:00; likely near track 1, though this may change with station renovation).

Maps: Of all places, you need a good map in Venice. Hotels give away freebies (no better than the small color ones at the front of this book). The TI sells a decent €2.50 map and miniguide—but you can find a wider range at bookshops, newsstands, and postcard stands. The cheap maps are pretty bad, but if you spend €5, you'll get a map that shows you everything. Investing in a good map can be the best €5 you'll spend in Venice. Map lovers should look for the book *Calli, Campielli e Canali,* sold at bookstores for €22.50, with 1:2,000 maps of the whole city.

Also consider a mapping **app** for your smartphone, which uses GPS to pinpoint your location—extremely useful if you get lost in twisty back streets. To avoid data-roaming charges, look for an offline map that can be downloaded in its entirety before your trip. **City Maps 2Go** has a huge number of searchable offline maps, including a fairly good Venice version ($2 pays for any/all of their maps).

Helpful History Timelines: For historical orientation, local guide Michael Broderick (listed later, under "Tours in Venice") has produced three poster-size timelines that cleverly map the city's history and art (sold at local bookstores; see www.venicescapes. org).

Arrival in Venice

For a rundown on Venice's train station, bus station, airport, and cruise terminal, and tips for drivers, see the Venice Connections chapter.

Sightseeing Passes for Venice

Venice offers a dizzying array of combo-tickets and sightseeing passes. Determine roughly what you plan to see, do the math, and pick the pass that suits your plans. For most people, the best choice is the Museum Pass, which covers entry into the Doge's Palace, Correr Museum, and more. Note that some major sights are not covered on any pass, including the Accademia, Peggy Guggenheim Collection, Scuola San Rocco, and Campanile, along with the three sights within St. Mark's Basilica that charge admission.

All of the passes described below are sold at the TI (except for the combo-ticket), and most are also available at participating sights.

Combo-Ticket: A €16 combo-ticket covers both the Doge's Palace and the Correr Museum; to bypass the long line at the Doge's Palace, buy your combo-ticket at the never-crowded Correr Museum. The two sights are also covered by the Museum Pass and Venice Card.

Daily Reminder

Sunday: While anyone is welcome to worship, most churches are closed to sightseers on Sunday morning. They reopen in the afternoon: St. Mark's Basilica (14:00-17:00, until 16:00 Nov-March), Frari Church (13:00-18:00), and the Church of San Zaccaria (16:00-18:00). The Church of San Polo and Naval Museum are closed all day, and the Rialto open-air market consists mainly of souvenir stalls (fish and produce sections closed). It's a bad day for a pub crawl, as most pubs are closed.

Monday: All sights are open except the Rialto fish market, Ca' Pesaro, Palazzo Mocenigo Costume Museum, Lace Museum (on the island of Burano), and Torcello Museum (on the island of Torcello). The Accademia and Ca' d'Oro close at 14:00. Don't side-trip to Verona today, as most sights there are closed in the morning, if not all day.

Tuesday: All sights are open except the Peggy Guggenheim Collection, Ca' Rezzonico (Museum of 18th-Century Venice), and Punta della Dogana.

Wednesday/Thursday/Friday: All sights are open.

Saturday: All sights are open except the Jewish Museum.

Notes: The Accademia is open earlier (daily at 8:15) and closes later (19:15 Tue-Sun) than most sights in Venice. Some sights close earlier off-season (such as the Correr Museum, Campanile bell tower, St. Mark's Basilica, and the Church of San Giorgio Maggiore). Modest dress is recommended at churches and required at St. Mark's Basilica— no bare shoulders, shorts, or short skirts.

Crowd Control: The city is inundated with cruise-ship passengers and tours from mainland hotels daily from 10:00 to about 17:00. While major sights are busiest in the late morning, it's a delightful time to explore the back lanes. The sights that have crowd problems get even more packed when it rains.

To avoid the worst of the crowds at **St. Mark's Basilica,** go early or late. You can bypass the line if you have a bag to check (see page 89).

At the **Doge's Palace,** purchase your ticket at the never-crowded Correr Museum across St. Mark's Square. You can also visit later in the day.

For the **Campanile,** ascend first thing in the morning or go late (it's open until 21:00 July-Sept), or skip it entirely if you're going to the similar San Giorgio Maggiore bell tower.

For the **Accademia,** you'll enjoy fewer crowds by going early or late.

ORIENTATION

Museum Pass: Busy sightseers may prefer this more expensive pass, which covers these museums: the Doge's Palace; Correr Museum; Ca' Rezzonico (Museum of 18th-Century Venice); Palazzo Mocenigo Costume Museum; Casa Goldoni (home of the Italian playwright); Ca' Pesaro (modern art); Museum of Natural History in the Santa Croce district; the Glass Museum on the island of Murano; and the Lace Museum on the island of Burano. At €24, this pass is the best value if you plan to see the Doge's Palace/Correr Museum and even just one of the other covered museums. (Families get a price break on multiple passes—ask.) You can buy it at any of the participating museums.

Chorus Pass: This pass gives church lovers admission to 16 of Venice's churches and their art (generally €3 each)—including the Frari Church—for €10, although the typical tourist is unlikely to see more than two of them.

Venice Card: This pass combines the 11 city-run museums and the 16 churches covered by the Chorus Pass, plus a few minor discounts, for €40. A cheaper variation, the Venice Card San Marco, is more selective: It covers the Correr Museum, Doge's Palace, and your choice of any three churches for €25. But it's hard to make either of these passes pay off.

Rolling Venice: This youth pass offers discounts at dozens of sights and shops, but its best deal is for transit. If you're under 30 and want to buy a three-day transit pass, it'll cost you just €18—rather than €35—with the Rolling Venice pass (€4 for ages 14-29, sold at TIs and HelloVenezia shops).

Transportation Passes: Venice sells transit-only passes that cover *vaporetti* and mainland buses. For a rundown on these, see "Getting Around Venice," later.

Helpful Hints

Theft Alert: The dark, late-night streets of Venice are generally safe. Even so, pickpockets (often elegantly dressed) work the crowded main streets, docks, and *vaporetti*. Your biggest risk of pickpockets is inside St. Mark's Basilica, near the Accademia or Rialto bridges (especially if you're preoccupied with snapping photos), or on a tightly packed vaporetto.

A handy *polizia* station is on the right side of St. Mark's Square as you face the basilica (at #63, near Caffè Florian). To call the police, dial 113. The Venice TI handles complaints—which must be submitted in writing—about local crooks, including gondoliers, restaurants, or hotel rip-offs (fax 041-523-0399, complaint.apt@turismovenezia.it).

It's illegal for street vendors to sell knockoff handbags, and it's also illegal for you to buy them; both you and the vendor can get big fines.

Medical Help: Venice's Santi Giovanni e Paolo hospital (tel. 118) is a 10-minute walk from both the Rialto and San Marco neighborhoods, located behind the big church of the same name on Fondamenta dei Mendicanti (toward Fondamente Nove). You can take vaporetto #4.1 from San Zaccaria, or #5.2 from the train station or Piazzale Roma, to the Ospedale stop.

Be Prepared to Splurge: Venice is expensive for residents as well as tourists, as everything must be shipped in and hand-trucked to its destination. But it's a unique place that's worth paying a premium to fully experience. I find that the best way to enjoy Venice is just to succumb to its charms and blow through a little money.

Take Breaks: Venice's endless pavement, crowds, and tight spaces are hard on tourists, especially in hot weather. Schedule breaks in your sightseeing. Grab a cool place to sit down, relax, and recoup—meditate on a pew in an uncrowded church, or stop in a café.

Etiquette: As ever-growing waves of tourists wash over Venice every year, its residents are struggling to ward off the trash (and trashiness) left in their wake. Picnicking is illegal anywhere on St. Mark's Square, and offenders can be fined. (The only place nearby for a legal picnic is in Giardinetti Reali, the small park along the waterfront west of the Piazzetta near St. Mark's Square. Elsewhere in Venice, picnicking is no problem.) On St. Mark's Square, police admonish snackers and sunbathers. You may see friendly guidelines posted around town discouraging litter, pigeon-feeding, and beachwear (or rather, "encouraging" good behavior, as city officials are hoping that sweet talk will prove more effective).

Dress Modestly: When visiting St. Mark's Basilica or other major churches, men, women, and even children must cover their shoulders and knees (or risk being turned away). Remove hats when entering a church.

Public Toilets: Handy public WCs (€1.50) are near major landmarks, including: St. Mark's Square (behind the Correr Museum and at the waterfront park, Giardinetti Reali), Rialto, and the Accademia Bridge. Use free toilets whenever you can—any museum you're visiting, or any café you're eating in. You could also get a drink at a bar (cheaper) and use their WC for free.

Best Views: A slow vaporetto ride down the Grand Canal on a sunny day—or a misty early morning—is a shutterbug's delight (try to sit in the front seats, available on some older boats; for narration, see my Grand Canal Cruise). On St. Mark's Square, enjoy views from the soaring Campanile or the balcony of St. Mark's Basilica (both require admission). The Rialto and Accademia bridges provide free, expansive views of the Grand Canal, along with a cooling breeze. Or get off the main island for a view of the Venetian skyline: Ascend San Giorgio Maggiore's bell tower, or venture to Giudecca Island to visit the swanky bar of the Molino Stucky Hilton Hotel (free shuttle boat leaves from near the San Zaccaria-M.V.E. vaporetto dock).

Pigeon Poop: If your head is bombed by a pigeon, resist the initial response to wipe it off immediately—it'll just smear into your hair. Wait until it dries, and it should flake off cleanly. But if the poop splatters on your clothes, wipe it off immediately to avoid a stain.

Water: I carry a water bottle to refill at public fountains. Venetians pride themselves on having pure, safe, and tasty tap water piped in from the foothills of the Alps. You can actually see the mountains from Venice's bell towers on crisp, clear winter days.

Updates to This Book: For news about changes to this book's coverage since it was published, see www.ricksteves.com/update.

Services

Internet Access: Almost all hotels have Wi-Fi, many have a computer that guests can use, and most provide these services for free. Otherwise, handy if pricey little Internet places are scattered around town (usually on back streets, marked with an @ sign, and charging €5/hour).

Post Office: Use post offices only as a last resort, as simple transactions can take 45 minutes if you get in the wrong line. You can buy stamps from tobacco shops and mail postcards at any of the red postboxes in town.

The main post office is just north of the Rialto Bridge—on the San Marco side, near the Teatro Malibran on Calle de le Acque (Mon-Fri 8:30-19:10, Sat 8:30-12:30, closed Sun, Castello 5016). You'll find branch offices with shorter hours (generally mornings only) around town, including a handy one right behind St. Mark's Square (near the TI).

Bookstores: In keeping with its literary heritage, Venice has classy and inviting bookstores. The small **Libreria Studium,** a block behind St. Mark's Basilica, has a carefully chosen selection of new English books, including my guidebooks (Mon-Sat 9:00-19:30, Sun 9:30-13:30 & 14:00-18:00, on Calle de la Canon-

ica at #337—see map on page 77, tel. 041-522-2382). Used-bookstore lovers shouldn't miss the funky **Acqua Alta** ("high water") bookstore, whose quirky owner Luigi has prepared for the next flood by displaying his wares in a selection of vessels, including bathtubs and a gondola. Look for the "book stairs" in his back garden (daily 9:00-21:00, large and classically disorganized selection includes prints of Venice, just beyond Campo Santa Maria Formosa on Calle Lunga Santa Maria Formosa at #5176—see map on page 263, tel. 041-296-0841). For a solid selection of used books in English, visit **Marco Polo,** on Calle del Teatro o de l'Opera, close to the St. Mark's side of the Rialto Bridge, just past the Coin department store and behind the church (Mon-Sat 9:30-13:00 & 15:30-19:30, closed Sun, Cannaregio 5886a—see map on page 263, tel. 041-522-6343).

Laundry: You'll find coin-operated launderettes near the train station and off Campo Santa Maria Formosa. I've listed details for a self-service *lavanderia* and a competitively priced full-service laundry near St. Mark's Square (see page 256), and for a self-serve laundry near the train station (page 269). Or ask your hotelier for the nearest launderette.

Travel Agencies: If you need to get train tickets, make seat reservations, or arrange a *cuccetta* (koo-CHET-tah—a berth on a night train), save a time-consuming trip to Venice's crowded train station by using a downtown travel agency. Most trains between Venice, Florence, and Rome require reservations, even for railpass holders. A travel agency can also give advice on cheap flights (book at least a week in advance for the best fares). Both of the following agencies charge a €4-per-ticket fee.

Along the embankment near St. Mark's Square (facing the San Zaccaria vaporetto stop), look for **Oltrex Change and Travel** (daily 9:00-13:00 & 14:00-18:00, closed Sun Nov-April; on Riva degli Schiavoni, one bridge past the Bridge of Sighs—see map on page 77; San Marco 5097b, tel. 041-524-2828, Luca and Beatrice).

Near Rialto, try **Kele & Teo Travel** (Mon-Fri 9:00-18:00, Sat 9:00-12:00, closed Sun; leaving the Rialto Bridge heading for St. Mark's, it's half a block away, tucked down a side street on the right—see map on page 262; tel. 041-520-8722).

English Church Services: San Zulian Church offers a Mass in English (generally May-Sept Mon-Fri at 9:30 and Sun at 11:30, Sun only Oct-April, 2 blocks toward Rialto off St. Mark's Square, tel. 041-523-5383). **St. George's Anglican Church** welcomes all to its English-language Eucharist (Sun at 10:30, located on Campo San Zio in Dorsoduro, midway between Accademia and Peggy Guggenheim Collection, www.stgeorgesvenice.com).

Getting Around Venice
On Foot

The city's "streets" are narrow pedestrian walkways connecting its docks, squares, bridges, and courtyards. To navigate, look for yellow signs on street corners pointing you to *(per)* the nearest major landmark. The first landmarks you'll get to know are San Marco (St. Mark's Square), Rialto (the bridge), Accademia (another bridge), Ferrovia (the train station), and Piazzale Roma (the bus station). Determine whether your destination is in the direction of a major signposted landmark, then follow the signs through the maze.

Dare to turn off the posted routes and make your own discoveries. While 80 percent of Venice is, in fact, not touristy, 80 percent of the tourists never notice. Escape the crowds and explore on foot. Walk and walk to the far reaches of the town. Don't worry about getting lost—in fact, get as lost as possible. Keep reminding yourself, "I'm on an island, and I can't get off." When it comes time to find your way, just follow the arrows on building corners or simply ask a local, *"Dov'è San Marco?"* ("Where is St. Mark's?") People in the tourist business (that's most Venetians) speak some English. If they don't, listen politely, watch where their hands point, say *"Grazie,"* and head off in that direction. If you're lost, refer to your map, or pop into a hotel and ask for their business card—it probably comes with a map and a prominent "You are here."

Every building in Venice has a house number. The numbers relate to the district (each with about 6,000 address numbers), not the street. Therefore, if you need to find a specific address, it helps to know its district, street, house number, and nearby landmarks.

Some helpful street terminology: *Campo* means square, a *campiello* is a small square, *calle* (pronounced "KAH-lay" with an "L" sound) means "street," and a *ponte* is a bridge. A *fondamenta* is the embankment along a canal or the lagoon. A *rio* is a small canal, while a *rio terà* is a street that was once a canal and has been filled in (and a *piscina* is a filled-in former pond). A *sotoportego* is a covered passageway. *Salizzada* means "laid with cobblestones" (indicating it's among the first Venetian streets ever paved). Don't get hung up on the exact spelling of street and square names, which may sometimes appear in the Venetian dialect and other times in standard Italian.

By Vaporetto

Venice's public transit system, run by a company called ACTV, is a fleet of motorized bus-boats called *vaporetti*. They work like city buses except that they never get a flat, the stops are docks, and if you get off between stops, you might drown.

Tickets and Passes

Individual Vaporetto Tickets: A single ticket costs €7. Tickets are good for one hour in one direction; you can hop on and off at stops and change boats during that time. Your ticket (a plastic card embedded with a chip) is refillable—don't toss it after the first use. You can put more money on it at the automated kiosks and avoid waiting in line at the ticket window. The fare is reduced to €4 for a few one-stop runs *(corsa semplice)* that are hard to do by foot, including the route from San Marco to La Salute, from Fondamente Nove to Murano-Colonna, and from San Zaccaria to San Giorgio Maggiore.

Vaporetto Passes: You can buy a pass for unlimited use of *vaporetti:* €18/12 hours, €20/24 hours, €25/36 hours, €30/48 hours, €35/72 hours, €50/7-day pass. All passes must be validated each time you board by touching it to the small white machine on the dock. Because single tickets cost a hefty €7 a pop, these passes can pay for themselves in a hurry. Think through your Venice itinerary before you step up to the ticket booth to pay for your first vaporetto trip. The 48-hour pass pays for itself with five rides (for example: to your hotel, on a Grand Canal joyride, into the lagoon and back, and to the train station). Keep in mind that smaller and/or outlying stops, such as Sant'Elena and Biennale, are unstaffed—another good reason to buy a pass. It's fun to be able to hop on and off spontaneously, and avoid long ticket lines. On the other hand, many tourists just walk and rarely use a boat.

Anyone under 30 years old can get a 72-hour pass for €18 if they also buy a **Rolling Venice** discount card for €4 (see page 26). Those settling in for a longer stay can ride like a local by buying the **Imob** card (€40/5 years, which lets you either ride for €1.30 per trip or buy a *carnet* of 10 rides for €11). See www.actv.it for details.

Passes are also valid on ACTV's mainland buses, including bus #5 to the airport (but not the airport buses run by ATVO, a separate company) and bus #2 to Mestre.

Handy *Vaporetti* from San Zaccaria, near St. Mark's Square

Several *vaporetti* leave from the San Zaccaria docks, located 150 yards east of St. Mark's Square. There are four separate San Zaccaria docks spaced about 70 yards apart, with a total of six different berths, lettered A to E: Danieli (E and F), Jolanda (C and D), M.V.E. (B), and Pietà (A). While this may sound confusing, in practice it's simple: Check the big electronic board (next to the Jolanda C/D dock), which indicates the departure time, line number, destination, and berth letter of upcoming *vaporetti*. Once you've figured out which boat you want, go to that letter berth and hop on. They're all within about a five-minute stroll of each other.

- **Line #1** goes up the Grand Canal, making all the stops, including San Marco, Rialto, Ferrovia (train station), and Piazzale Roma (but it does not go as far as Tronchetto). In the other direction, it goes from San Zaccaria to Arsenale and Giardini before ending on the Lido.
- **Line #2** zips over to San Giorgio Maggiore, the island church across from St. Mark's Square (5 minutes, €4 ride). From there, it continues on to stops on the island of Giudecca, the parking lot at Tronchetto, and then down the Grand Canal. Note: You cannot ride the #2 up the Grand Canal (for example, to Rialto or the train station) directly from this stop—you'll need to walk five minutes along the waterfront, past St. Mark's Square, to the San Marco-Giardinetti dock and hop the #2 from there.
- **Line #4.1** goes to San Michele and Murano in 45 minutes.
- **Line #7** is the summertime express boat to Murano (25 minutes).
- The **Molino Stucky shuttle boat** takes even non-guests to the Hilton Hotel, with its popular view bar (free, 20-minute ride, leaves at 0:20 past the hour from near the San Zaccaria-M.V.E. dock).

Riding the *Vaporetti*

For most travelers, only two vaporetto lines matter: line #1 and line #2. These lines leave every 10 minutes or so and go up and down the Grand Canal, between the "mouth" of the fish at one end and St. Mark's Square at the other. Line #1 is the slow boat, taking 45 minutes and making every stop along the way. Line #2 is the fast boat that zips down the Grand Canal in 25 minutes, stopping only at Tronchetto (parking lot), Piazzale Roma (bus station), Ferrovia (train station), Rialto Bridge, San Tomà (Frari Church), San Samuele (opposite Ca' Rezzonico—an easy *traghetto* ride across), Accademia Bridge, and San Marco (west end of St. Mark's Square, end of the line).

ORIENTATION

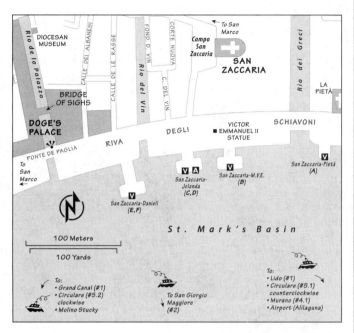

- **Lines #5.1** and **#5.2** are the *circulare* (cheer-koo-LAH-ray), making a loop around the perimeter of the island, with a stop at the Lido—perfect if you just like riding boats. Line #5.1 goes counterclockwise, and #5.2 goes clockwise.
- The **Alilaguna** shuttle to and from the airport stops here as well.

Catching a vaporetto is very much like catching a city bus. You can buy either single-ride tickets (valid for 1 hour) or passes (valid for a variety of durations, from 12 hours to 7 days) from any ticket window or HelloVenezia office. HelloVenezia, run by ACTV, is a string of shops selling tickets and passes at the same prices as ticket windows (www.hellovenezia.com).

Before you board, validate your ticket by holding it up to the small white machine on the dock until you hear a pinging sound. The machine readout shows how long your ticket is valid—and inspectors do come by now and then to check tickets. If you board without a ticket (because ticket windows may be closed at odd hours or small stops), seek out the conductor immediately to buy a single ticket on board (or risk a €50 fine). If you purchase a vaporetto pass, you need to touch the pass to the machine each time you board the boat.

Most stops have at least two docks. Signs on each dock show the vaporetto lines that stop there and the direction they are headed. For example, along the Grand Canal, a #1 or #2 boat might be headed toward St. Mark's Square (signposted *Lido* or *San Marco*), or back toward the mainland (signposted *Ferrovia, Piazzale Roma,* or *Tronchetto*). Helpful electronic boards at most stops display which boats are coming next, and when. Make a point to take advantage of these. Most boats also have electronic boards displaying this information.

Large stops—such as San Marco, San Zaccaria, Rialto, Ferrovia (train station), and Piazzale Roma—have multiple docks. At these, each berth is assigned a letter (clearly marked above the door to the dock, along with the numbers of the vaporetto lines that use that dock). Electronic boards will direct you to the letter of the dock you want.

Sorting out the different directions of travel can be confusing. Some boats have circular routes traveling in one direction only (true for lines #5.1 and #5.2, plus the non-Murano sections of lines #4.1 and #4.2). Be careful of the otherwise-handy express line #2, which runs in both directions and is almost, but not quite, a full loop. The #2 boat leaving from the San Marco stop goes in one direction (up the Grand Canal), while from the San Zaccaria stop—just a five-minute walk away—it goes in the opposite direction (around the tail of the "fish"). Make sure you use the correct stop to avoid taking the long way around to your destination.

You may notice some *vaporetti* sporting a *corsa bis* sign, indicating that it's running a shortened or altered route, and that riders may have to hop off partway and wait for the next boat. If you see a *corsa bis* sign, before boarding ask the conductor whether it's going to your desired destination.

To clear up any confusion, ask a ticket-seller or conductor for help (sometimes they're stationed on the dock to help confused tourists), or look at the most current ACTV timetable (in English and Italian, free at ticket booths but often unavailable—can be downloaded from the ACTV website, www.actv.it).

ORIENTATION

More Vaporetto Tips

For fun, take the Grand Canal Cruise (see that chapter). But be warned: Grand Canal *vaporetti* in particular can be absolutely jam-packed, especially during the tourist rush hour (during mornings heading in from Piazzale Roma, and in evenings heading out to Piazzale Roma). Riding at night, with nearly empty boats and chandelier-lit palace interiors viewable from the Grand Canal, is an entirely different experience.

Vaporetto dell'Arte: Twice hourly, these specially designated *vaporetti* (marked *VA*) go up and down the Grand Canal. They use the same docks as public boats, but are gussied up to impress the discerning tourist (with audioguide commentary, video screens, more comfortable seats, Wi-Fi, and so on); they're also limited to only stops handy to major sights (such as Accademia and San Marco). If you want to ride these, you'll pay an extra €10 above the pass prices listed earlier. If you believe that tourists should be sorted into higher and lower classes—and that it's worth paying extra for elite status—be my guest (see www.vaporettoarte.com)... but I'll save my euros and stick with the public *vaporetti*, which reach all the same places and run far more often. Because the Vaporetto dell'Arte tickets also cover regular *vaporetti*, which run more frequently, many an impatient dell'Arte passholder winds up just hopping on the normal boats anyway.

By *Traghetto*

Only four bridges cross the Grand Canal, but *traghetti* (shuttle gondolas) ferry locals and in-the-know tourists across the Grand Canal at seven handy locations (marked on the color map of Venice at the front of this book). Just step in, hand the gondolier €2,  and enjoy the ride—standing or sitting. Note that some *traghetti* are seasonal, some stop running as early as 12:30, and all stop by 18:00. *Traghetti* are not covered by any transit pass.

By Water Taxi

Venetian taxis, like speedboat limos, hang out at busy points along the Grand Canal. Prices are regulated and listed on the TI's website: €15 for pickup, then €2 per minute; €5 per person for more than four passengers; and €10 between 22:00 and 6:00. Extra bags cost €3 apiece. (For information on taking the water taxi to/from the airport, see the Venice Connections chapter.) Despite regulation, prices can be soft; negotiate and settle on the price or

Is Venice Sinking?

Venice has battled rising water levels since the fifth century. But today, the water seems to be winning. Several factors, both natural and man-made, cause Venice to flood about 100 times a year—usually from October until late winter—a phenomenon called the *acqua alta*.

On my last trip I asked a Venetian how much the city is sinking. He said, "Less than the sea is rising." Venice sits atop sediments deposited at the ancient mouth of the Po River, which are still compacting and settling. Early industrial projects, such as offshore piers and the railroad bridge to the mainland, affected the sea floor and tidal cycles in ways that made the city more vulnerable to flooding. Twentieth-century industry worsened things by pumping massive amounts of groundwater out of the aquifer beneath the lagoon for nearly 50 years before the government stopped the practice in the 1970s. In the last century, Venice has sunk by about nine inches.

Meanwhile, the waters around Venice are rising, a phenomenon that's especially apparent in winter. The highest so far was in November 1966, when a huge storm (the same one that famously flooded Florence) raised Venice's water level to more than six feet above the norm. The notorious *acqua alta* happens when an unusually high tide combines with strong sirocco winds and a storm. Although tides are minuscule in the Mediterranean, the narrow, shallow Adriatic Sea has about a three-foot tidal range. When a storm—an area of low pressure—travels over a body of water, it pulls the surface of the water up into a dome. As strong sirocco winds from Africa blow storms north up the Adriatic, they push this high water ahead of the front, causing a surging storm tide. Add to that the worldwide sea-level rise that's resulted from recent climate change (melting ice caps, thermal expansion of the water, more frequent and more powerful storms) and it makes a high sea that much higher.

rate before stepping in. For travelers with lots of luggage or small groups who can split the cost, taxi boat rides can be a worthwhile and time-saving convenience—and skipping across the lagoon in a classic wooden motorboat is a cool indulgence. For a little more than €100 an hour, you can have a private, unguided taxi-boat tour. You may find more competitive rates if you prebook through

ORIENTATION

If the *acqua alta* appears during your visit, you'll see the first puddles in the center of paved squares, pooling around the limestone grates at the square's lowest point. These grates cover cisterns that long held Venice's only source of drinking water. That's right: Surrounded by the lagoon and beset by con-

stant flooding, this city had no natural source of fresh water. For centuries, residents carried water from the mainland with much effort and risk. In the ninth century, they devised a way to collect rainwater by using paved, cleverly sloped squares as catchment systems, with limestone filters covering underground clay tubs. Venice's population grew markedly once citizens were able to access fresh water by simply dropping buckets down into these "wells." Several thousand cisterns provided the city with drinking water up until 1886, when an aqueduct was built (paralleling the railroad bridge) to bring in water from nearby mountains. Now the wells are capped, the clay tubs are rotted out, and rain drains from squares into the lagoon—or up from it, as the case may be.

So what is Venice doing about the flooding? Since the 1966 flood, officials knew something had to be done, but it took about four decades to come up with a solution. In 2003, a consortium of engineering firms began construction on the MOSE Project. Named for the acronym of its Italian name, *Modulo Sperimentale Elettromeccanico*, it's also a nod to Moses and his (albeit temporary) mastery over the sea.

Underwater "mobile" gates are being installed on the floor of the sea at the three inlets where the open sea enters Venice's lagoon. When the seawater rises above a certain level, air will be pumped into the gates, causing them to rise and shut out the Adriatic. The first gates are already installed, and the project is scheduled to finish by 2016. Will it work? There are many doubters.

the Consorzio Motoscafi water taxi association (tel. 041-522-2303, www.motoscafivenezia.it).

By Gondola

If you're interested in hiring a gondolier for your own private cruise, see the Nightlife in Venice chapter.

Tours in Venice

Avventure Bellissime Venice Tours

This company offers several English-only two-hour walks, including a basic St. Mark's Square introduction called the "Original Venice Walking Tour" (€22, includes church entry, most days at 11:00, Sun at 14:00; 45 minutes on the square, 15 minutes in the church, one hour along back streets), a 70-minute private boat tour of the Grand Canal (€43, daily at 16:30, eight people maximum), a "Hidden Venice" tour (€22, in summer 3/week at 11:30, fewer off-season), and excursions on

the mainland (10 percent discount for Rick Steves readers, see descriptions at www.tours-italy.com, tel. 041-970-499, info@tours-italy.com, Monica or Jonathan).

Classic Venice Bars Tour

Debonair guide Alessandro Schezzini is a connoisseur of Venetian *bacari*—classic old bars serving wine and traditional *cicchetti* snacks. He organizes two-hour Venetian pub tours (€30, any night on request at 18:00, depart from top of Rialto Bridge, better to book by email—alessandro@schezzini.it—than by phone, mobile 335-530-9024, www.schezzini.it). Alessandro's tours include sampling *cicchetti* with wines at three different *bacari*. (If you think of this tour as a light dinner with a local friend, it's a particularly good value.)

Artviva Tours

This company offers a comprehensive program of tours, including Venice in a day, five themed tours (Grand Canal, Venice Walk, Doge's Palace, Gondola Tour, Food and Wine Tour with a sommelier), and a "Learn to Be a Gondolier" tour (for details, see www.italy.artviva.com).

Venicescapes

Michael Broderick's private, themed tours of Venice are intellectually demanding and beyond the attention span of most mortal tourists. But travelers with a keen interest and a desire to learn find him passionate and engaging. Your time with Michael is like a rolling, graduate-level lecture (see his website for various 4-to 6-hour itineraries, 2 people-$250-290 or the euro equivalent, $60/person after that, admissions and transport not included, book in advance, tel. 041-850-5742, mobile 349-479-7406, www.venicescapes.org, info@venicescapes.org).

Local Guides

Plenty of licensed, trained guides are available. If you organize a small group from your hotel at breakfast to split the cost (figure on €70/hour with a 2-hour minimum), the fee becomes more reasonable. The following guides work with individuals, families, and small groups:

Walks Inside Venice is a dynamic duo of women—and their tour-guide colleagues—enthusiastic about teaching (€225/3 hours per group of up to 6 with this book, 3-hour minimum; Roberta: mobile 347-253-0560; Sara: mobile 335-522-9714; www.walksinsidevenice.com, info@walksinsidevenice.com). Roberta has been a big help in the making of this book. They also do side-trips to outlying destinations, and offer regularly scheduled small-group, English-only walking tours (€62.50, departs daily at 14:30, 2.5 hours).

Alessandro Schezzini, mentioned earlier for his Classic Venice Bars Tour, isn't a licensed guide, so he can't take you into sights. But his relaxed, 1.5-hour back-streets tour gets you beyond the clichés and into offbeat Venice (€15/person, departs daily at 16:30, mobile 335-530-9024, www.schezzini.it, alessandro@schezzini.it). He also does lagoon tours in the morning.

Tour Leader Venice, a.k.a. **Treviso Car Service,** offers small-group tours beyond Venice to 16th-century villas, wine-and-cheese tastings, and the Dolomites. Within Venice, their guided excursions include visits to "Venice off the beaten path," the Rialto produce market, the lagoon, and artisan shops (also provides airport transfers—see page 344, mobile 348-900-0700 or 333-411-2840; in Venice: www.tourleadervenice.com, info@tourleadervenice.com; beyond Venice: www.trevisocarservice.com, tvcarservice@gmail.com; Igor, Andrea, and Marta).

Another good option is **Venice with a Guide,** a co-op of 10 good guides (www.venicewithaguide.com), including **Corine Govi** (mobile 347-966-8346, corine_g@libero.it), and **Elisabetta Morelli** (€70/hour, 2-hour minimum, tel. 041-526-7816, mobile 328-753-5220, bettamorelli@inwind.it).

Weekend Tour Packages for Students

Andy Steves (my son) runs Weekend Student Adventures, offering active and experiential three-day weekend tours from €199, designed for American students studying abroad (www.wsaeurope.com for details on tours of Venice and other great cities).

SIGHTS IN VENICE

Venice's greatest sight is the city itself. As well as seeing world-class museums and buildings, make time to wander narrow lanes, linger over a meal, or enjoy evening magic on St. Mark's Square. One of Venice's most delightful experiences—a gondola ride, worth ▲▲▲—is covered in the Nightlife in Venice chapter.

In this chapter, don't judge a listing by its length. Some of Venice's most important sights have the shortest listings and are marked with a ✪. These sights are covered in much greater detail in the individual tour chapters later in this book.

For information on sightseeing passes, see page 24. Venice's city museums offer youth and senior discounts to Americans and other non-EU citizens; see page 10.

Also, be sure to check www.ricksteves.com/update for any significant changes that may have occurred since this book was printed.

San Marco District

▲▲▲St. Mark's Square (Piazza San Marco)

This grand square is surrounded by splashy, historic buildings and sights: St. Mark's Basilica, the Doge's Palace, the Campanile bell tower, and the Correr Museum. The square is filled with music, lovers, pigeons, and tourists by day, and is your private rendezvous with the Venetian past late at night, when Europe's most magnificent dance floor is *the* romantic place to be.

For a slow and pricey evening thrill, invest €12-22 (including the cover charge for the music) for a drink at one of the elegant cafés with the dueling orchestras (see "Cafés on St. Mark's Square," page 81). For an unmatched experience that offers the best people-watching, it's worth the small splurge.

The **Clock Tower** (Torre dell'Orologio), built during the Renaissance in 1496, marks the entry to the main shopping drag, called the Mercerie (or "Marzarie," in Venetian dialect), which connects St. Mark's Square with the Rialto Bridge. From the piazza, you can see the bronze men (Moors) swing their huge clappers at the top of each hour. In the 17th century, one of them knocked an unsuspecting worker off the top and to his death—probably the first-ever killing by a robot. Notice one of the world's first "digital" clocks on the tower facing the square (with dramatic flips every five min-

utes). You can go inside the Clock Tower with a pre-booked guided tour that takes you close to the clock's innards and out to a terrace with good views over the square and city rooftops (€12.50 combo-ticket includes Correr Museum—where the tour starts—but not Doge's Palace; €7 for the tour if you already have a Museum Pass or Correr/Doge's Palace combo-ticket; tours in English Mon-Wed at 10:00 and 11:00, Thu-Sun at 14:00 and 15:00; no kids under age 6). While reservations are required for the Clock Tower tour, you have a decent chance of being able to "reserve" on the spot—try dropping by the Correr Museum for same-day (or day-before) tickets. To ensure a spot in advance, reserve by calling 848-082-000, or book online at http://torreorologio.visitmuve.it.

For more about the square, ✪ see the St. Mark's Square Tour chapter.

▲▲▲St. Mark's Basilica (Basilica di San Marco)

Built in the 11th century to replace an earlier church, this basilica's distinctly Eastern-style architecture underlines Venice's connection with Byzantium (which protected it from the ambition of Charlemagne and his Holy Roman Empire). It's decorated with booty from returning sea captains—a kind of architectural Venetian trophy chest. The interior glows mysteriously with gold mosaics and colored marble. Since about A.D.

830, the saint's bones have been housed on this site.

Cost and Hours: Basilica entry is free, three interior sights charge admission (see below), open Mon-Sat 9:45-17:00, Sun 14:00-17:00 (Sun until 16:00 Nov-March), interior brilliantly lit daily 11:30-12:30, St. Mark's Square, vaporetto: San Marco or

SIGHTS

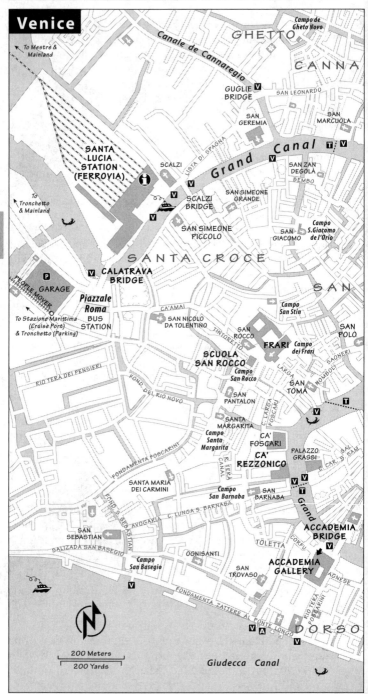

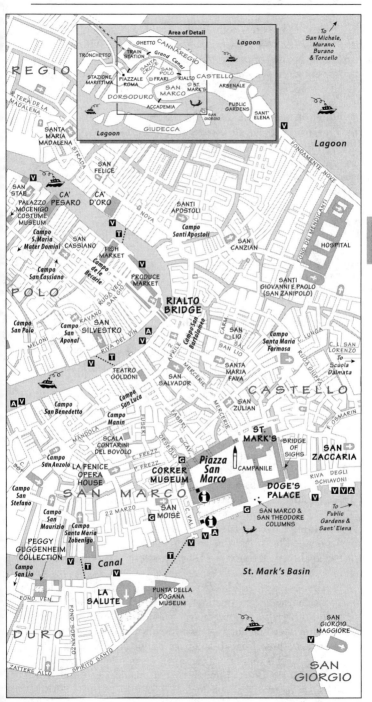

San Zaccaria. The dress code is strictly enforced for everyone (no bare shoulders or bare knees). Lines can be long, and bag check is mandatory, free, and can save you time in line; for details, see the "Orientation" section in the St. Mark's Basilica Tour chapter. No photos are allowed inside. Tel. 041-270-8311, www.basilicasanmarco.it.

Three separate exhibits within the church charge admission: the **Treasury** (€3, includes free audioguide), **Golden Altarpiece** (€2), and **San Marco Museum** (€5). The San Marco Museum has the original bronze horses (copies of these overlook the square), a balcony offering a remarkable view over St. Mark's Square, and various works related to the church.

○ See the St. Mark's Basilica Tour chapter.

▲▲▲Doge's Palace (Palazzo Ducale)

The seat of the Venetian government and home of its ruling duke, or *doge,* this was the most powerful half-acre in Europe for 400 years. The Doge's Palace was built to show off the power and wealth of the Republic. The doge lived with his family on the first floor up, near the halls of power. From his once-lavish (now sparse) quarters, you'll follow the one-way tour through the public rooms of the top floor, finishing with the Bridge of Sighs and the prison. The place is wallpapered with masterpieces by Veronese and Tintoretto. Don't worry too much about the great art. Enjoy the building.

Cost and Hours: €16 combo-ticket includes Correr Museum, also covered by Museum Pass—see page 26, daily April-Oct 8:30-18:30, Nov-March 8:00-17:30, last entry one hour before closing, café, no photos inside, next to St. Mark's Basilica, just off St. Mark's Square, vaporetto stops: San Marco or San Zaccaria, tel. 041-271-5911, http://palazzoducale.visitmuve.it.

Avoiding Lines: If the line is long at the Doge's Palace, buy your combo-ticket at the Correr Museum across the square; then you can go directly through the Doge's turnstile without waiting in line.

Tours: The audioguide costs €5. For a 1.25-hour live guided tour, consider the Secret Itineraries Tour, which takes you into palace rooms otherwise not open to the public (€20, includes Doge's Palace admission but not Correr Museum admission; €14 with combo-ticket; three English-language tours each morning). Reserve ahead for this tour in peak season—it can fill up as much as a month in advance. Book online (http://palazzoducale.visitmuve.it, €0.50 fee), or reserve by phone (tel. 848-082-000, from the US dial

011-39-041-4273-0892), or you can try just showing up at the info desk.

✪ See the Doge's Palace Tour chapter.

▲▲Correr Museum (Museo Correr)

This uncrowded museum gives you a good overview of Venetian history and art. The doge memorabilia, armor, banners, statues (by Canova), and paintings (by the Bellini family and others) re-create the festive days of the Venetian Republic. There are English descriptions and breathtaking views of St. Mark's Square throughout the museum.

Cost and Hours: €16 combo-ticket also includes the Doge's Palace; daily April-Oct 10:00-19:00, Nov-March 10:00-17:00, last entry one hour before closing; no photos, elegant café, enter at far end of square directly opposite basilica, tel. 041-240-5211, http://correr.visitmuve.it.

✪ See the Correr Museum Tour chapter.

▲Campanile (Campanile di San Marco)

This dramatic bell tower replaced a shorter tower, part of the original fortress that guarded the entry of the Grand Canal. That tower crumbled into a pile of bricks in 1902, a thousand years after it was built. Today you'll see construction work being done to strengthen the base of the rebuilt tower. Ride the elevator 325 feet to the top of the bell tower for the best view in Venice (especially at sunset). For an ear-shattering experience, be on top when the bells ring. The golden archangel Gabriel at the top always faces into the wind. Beat the crowds and enjoy the crisp morning air at 9:00 or the cool evening breeze at 18:00.

Cost and Hours: €8, daily Easter-June and Oct 9:00-19:00, July-Sept 9:00-21:00, Nov-Easter 9:30-16:45, tel. 041-522-4064, www.basilicasanmarco.it.

For more on the Campanile, see page 82 of the St. Mark's Square Tour chapter.

La Fenice Opera House (Gran Teatro alla Fenice)

During Venice's glorious decline in the 18th century, this was one of seven opera houses in the city, and one of the most famous in Europe. For 200 years, great operas and famous divas debuted here, applauded by ladies and gentlemen in their finery. Then in 1996,

Venice at a Glance

▲▲▲**St. Mark's Square** Venice's grand main square. **Hours:** Always open. See page 40.

▲▲▲**St. Mark's Basilica** Cathedral with mosaics, saint's bones, treasury, museum, and viewpoint of square. **Hours:** Mon-Sat 9:45-17:00, Sun 14:00-17:00 (until 16:00 Nov-March). See page 41.

▲▲▲**Doge's Palace** Art-splashed palace of former rulers, with prison accessible through Bridge of Sighs. **Hours:** Daily April-Oct 8:30-18:30, Nov-March 8:00-17:30. See page 44.

▲▲▲**Rialto Bridge** Distinctive bridge spanning the Grand Canal, with a market nearby. **Hours:** Bridge—always open; market—souvenir stalls open daily, produce market closed Sun, fish market closed Sun-Mon. See page 53.

▲▲**Correr Museum** Venetian history and art. **Hours:** Daily April-Oct 10:00-19:00, Nov-March 10:00-17:00. See page 45.

▲▲**Accademia** Venice's top art museum. **Hours:** Mon 8:15-14:00, Tue-Sun 8:15-19:15. See page 49.

▲▲**Peggy Guggenheim Collection** Popular display of 20th-century art. **Hours:** Wed-Mon 10:00-18:00, closed Tue. See page 50.

▲▲**Frari Church** Franciscan church featuring Renaissance masters. **Hours:** Mon-Sat 9:00-18:00, Sun 13:00-18:00. See page 53.

▲▲**Scuola San Rocco** "Tintoretto's Sistine Chapel." **Hours:** Daily 9:30-17:30. See page 54.

▲**Campanile** Dramatic bell tower on St. Mark's Square with elevator to the top. **Hours:** Daily Easter-June and Oct 9:00-19:00, July-Sept 9:00-21:00; Nov-Easter 9:30-16:45. See page 45.

▲**Bridge of Sighs** Famous enclosed bridge, part of Doge's Palace, near St. Mark's Square. **Hours:** Always viewable. See page 48.

▲**La Salute Church** Striking church dedicated to the Virgin Mary. **Hours:** Daily 9:00-12:00 & 15:00-17:30. See page 51.

▲**Ca' Rezzonico** Posh Grand Canal palazzo with 18th-century Venetian art. **Hours:** April-Oct Wed-Mon 10:00-18:00, Nov-March Wed-Mon 10:00-17:00, closed Tue year-round. See page 51.

▲**Punta della Dogana** Museum of contemporary art. **Hours:** Wed-Mon 10:00-19:00, closed Tue. See page 51.

▲**Ca' Pesaro** International Gallery of Modern Art in a canalside palazzo. **Hours:** April-Oct Tue-Sun 10:00-18:00, Nov-March Tue-Sun 10:00-17:00, closed Mon year-round. See page 52.

▲**Scuola Dalmata di San Giorgio** Exquisite Renaissance meeting house. **Hours:** Mon 14:45-18:00, Tue-Sat 9:15-13:00 & 14:45-18:00, Sun 9:15-13:00. See page 58.

Church of San Zaccaria Final resting place of St. Zechariah, plus a Bellini altarpiece and an eerie crypt. **Hours:** Mon-Sat 10:00-12:00 & 16:00-18:00, Sun 16:00-18:00. See page 49.

Church of San Polo Ninth-century church with works by Tintoretto, Veronese, and Tiepolo. **Hours:** Mon-Sat 10:00-17:00, closed Sun. See page 54.

Nearby Islands
▲**San Giorgio Maggiore** Island facing St. Mark's Square, featuring church with Palladio architecture, Tintoretto paintings, and fine views back on Venice. **Hours:** April-Oct Mon-Sat 9:00-19:00, Sun 9:00-11:00 & 12:00-19:00; Nov-March daily 9:00-17:30. See page 49.

San Michele Cemetery island on the lagoon. **Hours:** Daily April-Sept 7:30-18:00, Oct-March 7:30-16:30. See page 60.

▲**Murano** Island famous for glass factories and glassmaking museum. **Hours:** Glass Museum open daily April-Oct 10:00-18:00, Nov-March 10:00-17:00 (may be under renovation when you visit). See page 60.

▲▲**Burano** Sleepy island known for lacemaking and a lace museum. **Hours:** Lace Museum open April-Oct Tue-Sun 10:00-18:00, Nov-March Tue-Sun 10:00-17:00, closed Mon year-round. See page 60.

▲**Torcello** Near-deserted island with old church, bell tower, and museum. **Hours:** Church open daily March-Oct 10:30-18:00, Nov-Feb 10:00-17:00, museum closed Mon. See page 61.

SIGHTS

an arson fire completely gutted the theater. But La Fenice ("The Phoenix") has risen from the ashes, thanks to an eight-year effort to rebuild the historic landmark according to photographic archives of the interior. To see the results at their most glorious, attend an evening **performance** (theater box office open daily 10:00-17:00, tel. 041-2424, www.teatrolafenice.it).

During the day, you can take an **audioguide tour** of the opera house. All you really see is the theater itself; there's no "backstage" tour of dressing rooms, or an opera museum, and the dry 45-minute guide mainly recounts two centuries of construction. But the auditorium, ringed with box seats, is impressive: pastel blue with sparkling gold filigree, muses depicted on the ceiling, and a starburst chandelier. It's also a bit saccharine and brings sadness to Venetians who remember the place before the fire. Other than a minor exhibit of opera scores and Maria Callas memorabilia, there's little to see from the world of opera.

For more on the opera house, see page 227 of the St. Mark's to Rialto Loop Walk chapter.

Cost and Hours: €8.50 audioguide tours, generally open daily 9:30-18:00, but can vary wildly, depending on the performance schedule—to confirm, call box office number (listed above) or check www.festfenice.com. La Fenice is on Campo San Fantin, between St. Mark's Square and the Accademia Bridge.

Palazzo Grassi

This former palace, gleaming proudly on the San Marco side of the Grand Canal, holds a branch of the Punta della Dogana contemporary art museum (for details, see "Punta della Dogana," later).

Behind St. Mark's Basilica
▲Bridge of Sighs

This much-photographed bridge connects the Doge's Palace with the prison. Travelers popularized this bridge in the Romantic 19th century. Supposedly, a condemned man would be led over this bridge on his way to the prison, take one last look at the glory of Venice, and sigh. Though overhyped, the Bridge of Sighs is undeniably tingle-worthy—especially after dark, when the crowds have dispersed and it's just you and floodlit Venice.

Getting There: The Bridge of Sighs is around the corner from the Doge's Palace. Walk toward the waterfront, turn left along the water, and look up the first canal on your left. You can walk across the bridge (from the inside) by visiting the Doge's Palace.

See the ❷ St. Mark's to San Zaccaria Walk chapter and the ❷ Doge's Palace Tour chapter.

Church of San Zaccaria

This historic church is home to a sometimes-waterlogged crypt, a Bellini altarpiece, a Tintoretto painting, and the final resting place of St. Zechariah, the father of John the Baptist.

Cost and Hours: Free, €1 to enter crypt, €0.50 coin to light up Bellini's altarpiece, Mon-Sat 10:00-12:00 & 16:00-18:00, Sun 16:00-18:00 only, two canals behind St. Mark's Basilica.

❷ See the St. Mark's to San Zaccaria Walk chapter.

Across the Lagoon from St. Mark's Square

▲San Giorgio Maggiore

This is the dreamy church-topped island you can see from the waterfront by St. Mark's Square. The striking church, designed by Pal-

ladio, features art by Tintoretto, a bell tower, and good views of Venice.

Cost and Hours: Free entry to church; April-Oct Mon-Sat 9:00-19:00, Sun 9:00-11:00 & 12:00-19:00; Nov-March daily 9:00-17:30. The bell tower costs €6 and is accessible by elevator (runs until 30 minutes before the church closes).

Getting There: To reach the island from St. Mark's Square, take the five-minute ride on vaporetto #2 (€4, 6/hour, ticket valid for one hour; leaves from San Zaccaria stop—check the reader-board to see which dock/berth it leaves from, direction: Tronchetto).

❷ See the San Giorgio Maggiore Tour chapter.

Dorsoduro District

▲▲Accademia (Galleria dell'Accademia)

Venice's top art museum, packed with highlights of the Venetian Renaissance, features paintings by the Bellini family, Titian, Tintoretto, Veronese, Tiepolo, Giorgione, Canaletto, and Testosterone. It's just over the wooden Accademia Bridge from the San Marco action.

Cost and Hours: €9, dull audioguide-€6, Mon 8:15-14:00, Tue-Sun 8:15-19:15, last entry 45 minutes before closing, no photos allowed. At Accademia Bridge, vaporetto: Accademia, tel. 041-522-2247, www.gallerieaccademia.org.

❷ See the Accademia Tour chapter.

SIGHTS

Venice Early and Late

Most sightseeing in Venice is restricted to the hours between 10:00 and 18:00. Here are some exceptions:

Sights Open Early

Accademia: Daily at 8:15.

Doge's Palace: Daily April-Oct at 8:30, Nov-March at 8:00.

Naval Museum: Mon-Sat at 8:45.

Campanile: Daily Easter-Oct at 9:00, Nov-Easter at 9:30.

Frari Church: Mon-Sat at 9:00.

La Salute Church: Daily at 9:00.

San Giorgio Maggiore: Daily at 9:00.

Scuola Dalmata di San Giorgio: Tue-Sun at 9:15.

Scuola San Rocco: Daily at 9:30.

St. Mark's Basilica: Mon-Sat at 9:45.

San Marco Museum: Mon-Sat at 9:45.

Sights Open Late

Doge's Palace: April-Oct daily until 18:30.

Correr Museum: April-Oct daily until 19:00.

Punta della Dogana: Wed-Mon until 19:00.

Jewish Museum: June-Sept Sun-Fri until 19:00.

Campanile: Daily Easter-June and Oct until 19:00, July-Sept until 21:00.

Accademia: Tue-Sun until 19:15.

Ca' d'Oro: Tue-Sat until 19:15.

Always Open

St. Mark's Square and the Rialto Bridge are always open, uncrowded in the early morning, and magical at night.

▲▲Peggy Guggenheim Collection

The popular museum of far-out art, housed in the American heiress' former retirement palazzo, offers one of Europe's best reviews of the art of the first half of the 20th century. Stroll through styles represented by artists whom Peggy knew personally—Cubism (Picasso, Braque), Surrealism (Dalí, Ernst), Futurism (Boccioni), American Abstract Expressionism (Pollock), and a sprinkling of Klee, Calder, and Chagall.

Cost and Hours: €14, usually includes temporary exhibits, audioguide-€7, Wed-Mon 10:00-18:00, closed Tue, pricey café, vaporetto: Accademia or Salute, tel. 041-240-5411, www.guggenheim-venice.it.

✪ See the Peggy Guggenheim Collection Tour chapter.

▲La Salute Church (Santa Maria della Salute)

This impressive church with a crown-shaped dome was built and dedicated to the Virgin Mary by grateful survivors of the 1630 plague.

Cost and Hours: Free entry to church, €3 to enter the Sacristy; daily 9:00-12:00 & 15:00-17:30. It's a 10-minute walk from the Accademia Bridge; the Salute vaporetto stop is at its doorstep, tel. 041-241-1018, www.seminariovenezia.it.

○ See the La Salute Church Tour chapter.

▲Ca' Rezzonico (Museum of 18th-Century Venice)

This grand Grand Canal palazzo offers the most insightful look at the life of Venice's rich and famous in the 1700s. Wander under ceilings by Tiepolo, among furnishings from that most decadent century, enjoying views of the canal and paintings by Guardi, Canaletto, and Longhi.

Cost and Hours: €8, audioguide-€4; April-Oct Wed-Mon 10:00-18:00, Nov-March Wed-Mon 10:00-17:00, closed Tue year-round; ticket office closes one hour before museum does, no photos, café, at Ca' Rezzonico vaporetto stop, tel. 041-241-0100, http://carezzonico.visitmuve.it.

○ See the Ca' Rezzonico Tour chapter.

▲Punta della Dogana

This museum of contemporary art, opened in 2009, makes the Dorsoduro a major destination for art lovers. Housed in the former Customs House at the end of the Grand Canal, it features cutting-edge 21st-century art in spacious rooms. This isn't Picasso and Matisse, or even Pollock and Warhol—those guys are ancient history. But if you're into the likes of Jeff Koons, Cy Twombly, Rachel Whiteread, and a host of newer artists, the museum is world-class. The displays change completely about every year, drawn from the museum's large collection—so large it also fills Palazzo Grassi, farther up the Grand Canal.

Cost and Hours: €15 for one locale, €20 for both; Wed-Mon 10:00-19:00, closed Tue, last entry one hour before closing; audioguide-€5 or €8 for both museums, small café, tel. 199-139-139, www.palazzograssi.it.

Getting There: Punta della Dogana is near La Salute Church (Dogana *traghetto* or vaporetto: Salute). Palazzo Grassi is a bit upstream, on the east side of the Grand Canal (vaporetto #2: San Samuele, or vaporetto #1 to Ca' Rezzonico then *traghetto* across the canal).

SIGHTS

Billboards

As part of Venice's ongoing reno- vation, you will see scaffolding covering major monuments—and advertising covering the scaffold- ing. Cash-strapped Venice is seek- ing funding from corporations in exchange for advertising space. Might there be Coca-Cola ads cov- ering St. Mark's Square? The mayor of Venice said of the possibility of more billboards: "It's not beautiful. It's not ugly. It's necessary."

Santa Croce District
▲Ca' Pesaro International Gallery of Modern Art

This museum features 19th- and early 20th-century art in a 17th-century canalside palazzo. The collection is strongest on Italian (especially Venetian) artists, but also presents a broad array of other well-known artists. While the Peggy Guggenheim Collection is Venice's undisputedly best modern collection, Ca' Pesaro comes in a clear second—and features a handful of recognizable masterpieces (most notably Klimt's *Judith II*).

Cost and Hours: €8; April-Oct Tue-Sun 10:00-18:00, Nov-March Tue-Sun 10:00-17:00, closed Mon year-round, last entry one hour before closing, two-minute walk from San Stae vaporetto stop, tel. 041-524-0695, http://capesaro.visitmuve.it.

Visiting the Museum: After buying your tickets, head upstairs, then turn right into the central hall, which displays works first shown at Venice's illustrious Biennale art show—including virtually all of the museum's highlights. In the very center of the room, beneath a Calder mobile, is Kandinsky's *White Zig Zags* (plus other recognizable shapes). At the right end of the hall (from where you entered) are three more masterpieces, side by side: the colorful *Nude in the Mirror*, by Bonnard, which flattens the 3-D scene into a 2-D pattern of rectangles; Chagall's surprisingly realistic portrait of his hometown rabbi, *Rabbi #2* (a.k.a. *The Rabbi of Vitebsk*); and Klimt's beautiful/creepy *Judith II*, with eagle-talon fingers.

To see the rest of the collection, head back out to the landing at the top of the stairs and turn right to go through nine roughly chronological rooms—from Venetian and Italian artists of the 19th century, with an emphasis on sculptor Medardo Rosso (Rooms 1 and 2); to the early 20th-century Milanese sculptor Adolfo Wildt (Room 3); to international modernists, including some pieces that were first exhibited right here in the Ca' Pesaro when it was a cradle of Modern art (Rooms 4-6, look for works by Miró and Kandinsky in Room 4); to Italian art from the 1930s through post-WWII (Rooms 7-9). Forgotten on the top floor is the museum's skippable collection of Oriental art.

Palazzo Mocenigo Costume Museum

The Museo di Palazzo Mocenigo offers a walk through six rooms of a fine 17th-century mansion with period furnishings, family portraits, ceilings painted (c. 1790) with family triumphs (the Mocenigos produced seven doges), Murano glass chandeliers *in situ,* and a paltry collection of costumes with sparse descriptions.

Cost and Hours: €5; April-Oct Tue-Sun 10:00-17:00, Nov-March Tue-Sun 10:00-16:00, closed Mon year-round, last entry one hour before closing, a block in from San Stae vaporetto stop, tel. 041-721-798, http://mocenigo.visitmuve.it.

San Polo District

▲▲▲Rialto Bridge

One of the world's most famous bridges, this distinctive and dramatic stone structure crosses the Grand Canal with a single con-

fident span. The arcades along the top of the bridge help reinforce the structure...and offer some enjoyable shopping diversions, as does the **market** surrounding the bridge (produce market closed Sun, fish market closed Sun-Mon).

For more on the Rialto Bridge, see the ✪ St. Mark's to Rialto Loop Walk chapter. For more on the markets, see the ✪ Rialto to Frari Church Walk chapter.

▲▲Frari Church
(Basilica di Santa Maria Gloriosa dei Frari)

My favorite art experience in Venice is seeing art in the setting for which it was designed—as it is at the Frari Church. The Franciscan

"Church of the Brothers" and the art that decorates it are warmed by the spirit of St. Francis. It features the work of three great Renaissance masters: Donatello, Giovanni Bellini, and Titian—each showing worshippers the glory of God in human terms.

Cost and Hours: €3, audioguide-€2, Mon-Sat 9:00-18:00, Sun 13:00-18:00, last entry 30 minutes before closing, modest dress recommended, no photos, on Campo dei Frari, near San Tomà vaporetto and *traghetto* stops, tel. 041-272-8618, www.basilicadeifrari.it.

✪ See the Frari Church Tour chapter.

A Dying City?

Venice's population (58,000 in the historic city) is half what it was just 30 years ago, and people are leaving at a rate of a thousand a year. Of those who stay, 25 percent are 65 or older.

Sad, yes, but imagine raising a family here: Apartments are small, high up, and expensive. Humidity and occasional flooding make basic maintenance a pain. Home-improvement projects require navigating miles of red tape, and you must follow regulations intended to preserve the historical ambience.

Everything is expensive because it has to be shipped in from the mainland. You can easily get glass and tourist trinkets, but it's hard to find groceries or get your shoes fixed. Running basic errands involves lots of walking and stairs—imagine crossing over arched bridges while pushing a child in a stroller and carrying a day's worth of groceries.

With millions of visitors a year (150,000 a day at peak times), on any given day Venetians are likely outnumbered by tourists. Despite government efforts to subsidize rents and build cheap housing, the city is losing its residents. The economy itself is thriving, thanks to tourist dollars and rich foreigners buying second homes. But the culture is dying. Even the most hopeful city planners worry that in a few decades Venice will not be a city at all, but a museum, a cultural theme park, a decaying Disneyland for adults.

▲▲Scuola San Rocco

Sometimes called "Tintoretto's Sistine Chapel," this lavish meeting hall (next to the Frari Church) has some 50 large, colorful Tintoretto paintings plastered to the walls and ceilings. The best paintings are upstairs, especially the *Crucifixion* in the smaller room. View the neck-breaking splendor with the mirrors available in the Grand Hall.

Cost and Hours: €10, includes audioguide, daily 9:30-17:30, last entry 30 minutes before closing, no photos, tel. 041-523-4864, www.scuolagrandesanrocco.it.

 See the Scuola San Rocco Tour chapter.

Church of San Polo

This nearby church, which pales in comparison to the two sights just listed, is only worth a visit for art lovers. One of Venice's oldest churches (from the ninth century), San Polo features works by

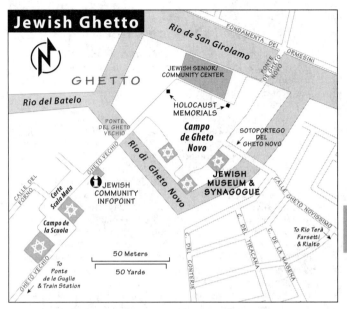

Jewish Ghetto

GHETTO

Rio de San Girolamo

FONDAMENTA DEI ORMESINI

PONTE DEL GHETO NOVO

JEWISH SENIOR/ COMMUNITY CENTER

Rio del Batelo

HOLOCAUST MEMORIALS

Campo de Gheto Novo

SOTOPORTEGO DEL GHETO NOVO

PONTE DEL GHETO VECHIO

GHETO VECHIO

Rio di Gheto Novo

CALLE DEL FORNO

Corte Scala Mata

JEWISH COMMUNITY INFOPOINT

JEWISH MUSEUM & SYNAGOGUE

CALLE GHETO NOVISSIMO

Campo de la Scuola

C. DEL CONTERIE

C. DEL TIRACANA

C. DE LA MASENA

To Rio Terà Farsetti & Rialto

GHETO VECHIO

To Ponte de le Guglie & Train Station

50 Meters

50 Yards

SIGHTS

Tintoretto, Veronese, and Tiepolo and son. For more information, see page 238 of the Rialto to Frari Church Walk chapter.

Cost and Hours: €3, Mon-Sat 10:00-17:00, closed Sun.

Cannaregio District

Jewish Ghetto

Tucked away in the Cannaregio District is the ghetto where Venice's Jewish population once lived, segregated from their non-

Jewish neighbors. While today's Jewish population is dwindling, the neighborhood still has centuries of history, not to mention Jewish-themed sights and eateries.

Getting There: From either the San Marcuola vaporetto stop or the train station, walk five minutes to the Ponte de Guglie bridge that crosses the Cannaregio Canal. Cross the bridge and turn left. About 50 yards north of the bridge, a small covered alleyway (Calle del Gheto Vechio) leads between the *farmacia* and the Gam-Gam Kosher Restaurant, through a newer Jewish section, across a bridge, and into the historic core of the ghetto at Campo de Gheto Novo.

Jews in Venice's Ghetto

In medieval times, Jews were grudgingly allowed to do business in Venice, but they weren't permitted to live here until 1385 (subject to strict laws and special taxes). Anti-Semitic forces tried to oust them from the city, but in 1516, the doge compromised by restricting Jews to a special (undesirable) neighborhood. It was located on an easy-to-isolate island near the former foundry *(geto)*. In time, the word "ghetto" caught on across Europe as a term for any segregated neighborhood.

The population swelled with immigrants from elsewhere in Europe, reaching 5,000 in the 1600s, the Golden Age of Venice's Jews. Restricted within their tiny neighborhood (the Gheto Novo—"New Ghetto"), they expanded upward, building six-story "skyscrapers" that still stand today. The community's five synagogues were built atop the high-rise tenements. (As space was very tight and you couldn't live above a house of worship, this was the most practical use of precious land.) Only two synagogues are still active. You can spot them (with their five windows) from the square, but to visit them you have to book a tour through the Jewish Museum.

Relations with the non-Jewish community were complex: While Jewish moneylenders were treated harshly, Jewish merchants were more valued and treated with more respect. The island's two bridges were locked at night, when only Jewish doctors—coming to the aid of Venetians—were allowed to come and go. Eventually the ghetto community was given more land and spread to adjacent blocks.

In 1797, Napoleon opened the ghetto gates and ended its isolation. Complete emancipation for Venice's Jews came with the founding of the Italian republic in the 1860s.

Visiting the Jewish Ghetto: Campo de Gheto Novo must have been quite a scene in the 17th century, ringed by 70 shops and with all of Venice's Jewish commerce compressed into this one spot. Today there are only about 500 Jews in all of Venice—and only a few dozen live in the actual ghetto. The square is still surrounded by the six-story "skyscrapers" that once made this a densely packed neighborhood.

Today the square, with its three cistern wells, is quiet. The Jewish people you may see here are likely tourists. Look for the large Jewish senior center/community center (Casa Israelitica di Riposo), flanked by two different Holocaust memorials by the Lithuanian artist Arbit Blatas. The barbed wire and bronze plaques remind us that it was on this spot that the Nazis rounded up 200 Jews for deportation (only 8 returned).

The **Jewish Museum** (Museo Ebraico), at #2902b, is small, but modern and well-presented—a worthwhile stop. Exhibits include silver menorahs, cloth covers for Torah scrolls, and a concise bilingual exhibit on the Venetian Jewish community (€4, June-Sept Sun-Fri 10:00-19:00, Oct-May Sun-Fri 10:00-17:30, closed Jewish holidays and Sat year-round, bookstore, small café, Campo de Gheto Novo, tel. 041-715-359, www.museoebraico.it). You can see three of the ghetto's five **synagogues** with the 45-minute English tour (€10, includes museum admission, tours run hourly on the half-hour June-Sept Sun-Fri 10:30-17:30, Oct-May Sun-Fri 10:30-16:30, no tours Sat and Jewish holidays). Group sizes are limited (the 11:30 and 12:30 tours are the most popular), so show up 20 minutes early to be sure you get in.

Backtrack across the bridge that you came in on, and look on the left for the **information point** run by the Jewish community, at #1222, where Anat Shriki answers questions about ghetto history in fluent English (Mon-Fri 10:00-13:30, Wed until 17:00, closed Sat-Sun, on Calle del Gheto Vechio, tel. 041-523-7565, www.jvenice.org).

Return to the square and exit through Sotoportego del Gheto Novo for the best view of the "fortress ghetto," with tall tenement buildings rising from the canal and an easy-to-lock-up little bridge and gateway.

Calatrava Bridge (a.k.a. Ponte della Costituzione)
This controversial bridge, designed by Spanish architect Santiago Calatrava, is just upstream from the train station. Only the fourth

bridge to cross the Grand Canal, it carries foot traffic between the train station and bus terminal at Piazzale Roma.

The bridge draws snorts from Venetians. Its modern design is a sore point for a city with such rich medieval and Renaissance architecture. With an original price tag of €4 million, the cost rose to around €11 million by the time it finally opened, after lengthy delays, in 2008. Then someone noticed that people in wheelchairs couldn't cross, so the bridge was retrofitted with a special carriage on a track. And, to add practical insult to aesthetic injury, critics say the heavy bridge is crushing the centuries-old foundations at either end, threatening nearby buildings.

Ca' d'Oro
This "House of Gold" palace, fronting the Grand Canal, is quintessential Venetian Gothic (Gothic seasoned with Byzantine and Islamic accents—see "Ca' d'Oro" on page 69). Inside, the permanent collection includes a few big names in Renaissance paint-

ing (Ghirlandaio, Signorelli, and Mantegna), a glimpse at a lush courtyard, and a grand view of the Grand Canal.

Cost and Hours: €6, dry audioguide-€4, Mon 8:15-14:00, Tue-Sat 8:15-19:15, Sun 10:00-18:00, free peek through hole in door of courtyard, Cannaregio 3932, vaporetto: Ca' d'Oro, www. cadoro.org.

Castello District

▲Scuola Dalmata di San Giorgio

This little-visited *scuola* (which can mean either "school," or as in this case, "meeting place") features an exquisite wood-paneled chapel decorated with the world's best collection of paintings by Vittorio Carpaccio (1465-1526).

The Scuola, a reminder that cosmopolitan Venice was once Europe's trade hub, was one of a hundred such community centers for various ethnic, religious, and economic groups, supported by the government partly to keep an eye on foreigners. It was here that the Dalmatians (from a region of Croatia) worshipped in their own way, held neighborhood meetings, and preserved their culture.

Cost and Hours: €5, Mon 14:45-18:00, Tue-Sat 9:15-13:00 & 14:45-18:00, Sun 9:15-13:00, on Calle dei Furlani at #3259a, tel. 041-522-8828.

Getting There: The Scuola is located midway between St. Mark's Square and the Arsenale. Go north from Campo San Provolo (by the Church of San Zaccaria), following the street as it changes names from L'Osmarin to St. George to Greci. At the second bridge, turn left on Fondamenta dei Furlani.

Visiting the Scuola: The chapel on the ground floor is one of the best-preserved Renaissance interiors in Venice. Ringing the room is the cycle of paintings that Carpaccio was hired to paint (1502-1507). For more information, you can buy an English booklet for €5.

The scenes run clockwise around the room, telling the story of St. George (Dalmatia's patron saint), who slew a dragon and metaphorically conquered paganism. Carpaccio cuts right to the climax. In the first panel on the far left, George meets the dragon on the barren plain, charges forward, and jams his spear through the dragon's skull, to the relief of the damsel in distress (in red). George gets there a bit too late—notice half a damsel on the ground. This painting is one of Carpaccio's masterpieces. He places George and the dragon directly facing each other. Meanwhile, the center of the composition—where George meets dragon—is also the "vanishing point" that draws your eye to the distant horizon. Very clever.

The story of St. George continues in the next panel, as George leads the bedraggled dragon (spear still in his head) before the thankful, wealthy pagan king and queen. Next, they kneel before George (now with a red sash, far right) as he holds a pan of water, baptizing them.

The rest of the panels (about St. Jerome and St. Tryphone) are also by Carpaccio. In the last panel on the right, St. Augustine pauses while writing. He hears something. The dog hears it, too. It's the encouraging voice of St. Jerome, echoing mysteriously through the spacious room. Carpaccio sweated small details like the scattered books and the shadow cast by the statue of Christ.

In the adjoining room, see the cross and censers (incense burners) used by the community in religious processions. Upstairs is another paneled room with more depictions of St. George (but not by Carpaccio).

Naval Museum and Arsenale

The mighty Republic of Venice was home to the first great military-industrial complex: a state-of-the-art shipyard that could build a powerful warship of standardized parts in an assembly line (and did so to intimidate visiting heads of state). While the Arsenale is still a military base and is therefore closed to the public, its massive and evocative gate, the Porta Magna, is worth a look (to see the gate, turn left at the Naval Museum and follow the canal). At the waterfront end of the canal, in front of the Arsenale, stands the Naval Museum (Museo Storico Navale). It's very old-school and military-run, but anyone into maritime history or sailing will find its several floors of exhibits interesting. You'll see the evolution of warships, displays on old fishing boats, and gondolas (all described in English).

Cost and Hours: Museum—€1.55, Mon-Sat 8:45-13:30, closed Sun, Castello 2148, tel. 041-244-1399.

Getting There: From the Doge's Palace, hike six bridges east along the waterfront to the Naval Museum. To see the gate, turn left at the museum and follow the canal.

Sant'Elena

For a pleasant peek into a completely non-touristy, residential side of Venice, walk or catch vaporetto #1 from St. Mark's Square to the neighborhood of Sant'Elena (at the fish's tail). This 100-year-old suburb lives as if there were no tourism. You'll find a kid-friendly park, a few lazy restaurants, and beautiful sunsets over San Marco.

La Biennale

From roughly June through November, Venice hosts an annual world's fair—contemporary art in odd years, modern architecture in even years—in buildings and pavilions scattered throughout Giardini park and the Arsenale. The festival is an excuse for temporary art exhibitions, concerts, and other cultural events around the city (for more information, see page 456; www.labiennale.org).

Venice's Lagoon

With more time, venture to some nearby islands in Venice's lagoon. While still somewhat touristy, they offer an escape from the crowds, a chance to get out on a boat, and some enjoyable diversions for fans of glassmaking and lace.

The islands are listed in order of proximity to Venice, from nearest to farthest. For more information, ☉ see the Venice's Lagoon Tour chapter.

San Michele (a.k.a. Cimitero)

This island is the final resting place of Venetians and a few foreign VIPs, from poet Ezra Pound to composer Igor Stravinsky (cemetery open daily April-Sept 7:30-18:00, Oct-March 7:30-16:30).

▲Murano

Famous for its glassmaking, this island is home to several glass factories and the **Glass Museum** (Museo Vetrario), which traces the history of this delicate art (€8, daily April-Oct 10:00-18:00, Nov-March 10:00-17:00, last entry 30 minutes before closing, tel. 041-739-586, http://museovetro.visitmuve.it).

▲▲Burano

This island's claim to fame is lacemaking, and (along with countless lace shops) it offers a delightful pastel village alternative to big, bustling Venice. Its **Lace Museum** (Museo del Merletto di Burano) shows the island's lace heritage (€5, April-Oct Tue-Sun 10:00-18:00, Nov-March Tue-Sun 10:00-17:00, closed Mon year-round, tel. 041-730-034, http://museomerletto.visitmuve.it).

▲Torcello

This sparsely populated island features Venice's oldest church. With impressive mosaics, a climbable bell tower, and a modest museum of Roman sculpture and medieval sculpture and manuscripts, the church is worth a wander (€5; church open daily March-Oct 10:30-18:00, Nov-Feb 10:00-17:00, museum and campanile close 30 minutes earlier, museum closed Mon; last entry to all sights 30 minutes before closing; museum tel. 041-730-761, church/bell tower tel. 041-730-119).

GRAND CANAL CRUISE

Canal Grande

Take a joyride and introduce yourself to Venice by boat. Cruise the Canal Grande all the way to San Marco, starting at the train station (Ferrovia) or the bus station (Piazzale Roma).

If it's your first trip down the Grand Canal, you might want to stow this book and just take it all in—Venice is a barrage on the senses that hardly needs narration. But these notes give the cruise a little meaning and help orient you to this great city.

This tour is designed to be done on the slow boat #1 (which takes about 45 minutes). The express boat #2 travels the same route, but it skips many stops and takes only 25 minutes, making it hard to sightsee.

To help you enjoy the visual parade of canal wonders, I've organized this tour by boat stop. I'll point out both what you can see from the current stop, and what to look forward to as you cruise to the next stop. If you download my free audio tour, you won't even have to look at the book (see "Audio Tour," later).

Orientation

Length of This Tour: Allow 45 minutes (25 minutes for an express version on vaporetto #2). With limited time, take the 25-minute express vaporetto #2. Or only do half the trip—choose either Ferrovia-to-Rialto or Rialto-to-San Marco.

Cost: €7 for a one-hour vaporetto ticket, or covered by a pass—best choice if you want to hop on and off (see page 31).

When to Go: Boats run every 10 minutes or so. Enjoy the best light and the fewest crowds by riding late in the day. Avoid the morning rush hour (8:00-10:00), when local workers and tourists commute into town (from Ferrovia to San Marco—in the same direction as this tour). In the evening, the crowds head the opposite way, and boats to San Marco are less crowded. Sunset bathes the buildings in gold (particularly on the left side, which is the San Marco side); after dark, chandeliers light up building interiors.

Seating Strategies: As the *vaporetti* can be jammed, strategize about where to sit—then, when the boat pulls up, make a bee-line for your preference. Some *vaporetti* have seats in the bow (in front of the captain's bridge), which is the perfect vantage point for spotting sights left, right, and forward. However, many boats lack these seats, so you have to settle for another option: Sit inside (and view the passing sights through windows); stand in the open middle deck (you can try to move back and forth—almost impossible if the boat is crowded); or sit outside in the back (where you'll miss the wonderful forward views).

If you have to commit to one side, consider this: The left side has a slight edge, with more sights and the best light late in the day. You're more likely to find an empty seat if you catch the vaporetto at Piazzale Roma—the stop *before* Ferrovia.

Because it's hard to see it all in one go, you may want to do this tour twice (perhaps once in either direction).

Getting There: This tour starts at the Ferrovia vaporetto stop (at Santa Lucia train station). It also works—and the boat can be less crowded—if you board upstream from Ferrovia at Piazzale Roma, a short walk from Ferrovia over the Calatrava Bridge. At Piazzale Roma, check the electronic boards to see which dock the next #1 or #2 is leaving from, hop on board to get your pick of seats, and start reading the tour when your vaporetto reaches Ferrovia.

Stops to Consider: You can break up the tour by hopping on and off at various sights described in greater depth elsewhere in this book (but remember, a single-fare vaporetto ticket is good for just one hour; passes let you hop on and off all day).

These are all worth considering as hop-off spots: San Marcuola (Jewish Ghetto), Mercato Rialto (fish market and famous bridge), Ca' Rezzonico (Museum of 18th-Century Venice), Accademia (art museum and the nearby Peggy Guggenheim Collection), and Salute (huge and interesting church and nearby Punta della Dogana contemporary art museum).

Information: Some city maps (on sale at postcard racks) have a handy Grand Canal map on the back.

Audio Tour: You can download this chapter as a free Rick Steves audio tour (see page 21).

Starring: Palaces, markets, boats, bridges—Venice.

GRAND CANAL

Grand Canal

Vaporetto Stops

1. Ferrovia
2. Riva de Biasio
3. San Marcuola
4. San Stae
5. Ca' d'Oro
6. Mercato Rialto
7. Rialto
8. San Silvestro
9. Sant'Angelo
10. San Tomà
11. Ca' Rezzonico
12. Accademia
13. Santa Maria del Giglio
14. Salute
15. San Marco
16. San Zaccaria

GRAND CANAL

Background

While you wait for your boat, here's some background on Venice's "Main Street."

At more than two miles long, nearly 150 feet wide, and nearly 15 feet deep, the Grand Canal is the city's largest canal, lined with its most impressive palaces. It's the remnant of a river that once spilled from the mainland into the Adriatic. The sediment it carried formed barrier islands that cut Venice off from the sea, forming a lagoon.

Venice was built on the marshy islands of the former delta, sitting on wood pilings driven nearly 15 feet into the clay (alder was the preferred wood). About 25 miles of canals drain the city, dumping like streams into the Grand Canal. Technically, Venice has only three canals: Grand, Giudecca, and Cannaregio. The 45 small waterways that dump into the Grand Canal are referred to as rivers (e.g., Rio Novo).

Venice is a city of palaces, dating from the days when the city was the world's richest. The most lavish palaces formed a grand architectural cancan along the Grand Canal. Once frescoed in reds and blues, with black-and-white borders and gold-leaf trim, they made Venice a city of dazzling color. This cruise is the only way to truly appreciate the palaces, approaching them at water level, where their main entrances were located. Today, strict laws prohibit any changes in these buildings, so while landowners gnash their teeth, we can enjoy Europe's best-preserved medieval city—slowly rotting. Many of the grand buildings are now vacant. Others harbor chandeliered elegance above mossy, empty (often flooded) ground floors.

The Tour Begins

❶ Ferrovia

The **Santa Lucia train station,** one of the few modern buildings in town, was built in 1954. It's been the gateway into Venice since 1860, when the first station was built. "F.S." stands for "Ferrovie dello Stato," the Italian state railway system.

More than 20,000 people a day commute in from the mainland, making this the busiest part of Venice during rush hour. The **Calatrava Bridge,** spanning the Grand Canal between the train station and Piazzale Roma upstream, was built in 2008 to alleviate some of the congestion and make the commute easier (for more about the bridge, see page 57).

Opposite the train station, atop the green dome of **San Simeon Piccolo** church, St. Simeon waves *ciao* to whoever enters or leaves the "old" city. The pink church with the white Carrara-marble facade, just beyond the train station, is the **Church of the Scalzi** (Church of the Barefoot, named after the shoeless Carmelite monks), where the last doge (Venetian ruler) rests. It looks relatively new because it was partially rebuilt after being bombed in 1915 by Austrians aiming (poorly) at the train station.

❷ Riva de Biasio

Venice's main thoroughfare is busy with all kinds of **boats:** taxis, police boats, garbage boats, ambulances, construction cranes, and

even brown-and-white UPS boats. Somehow they all manage to share the canal in relative peace.

About 25 yards past the Riva de Biasio stop, look left down the broad **Cannaregio Canal** to see what was the **Jewish Ghetto** (described on page 55). The twin, pale-pink, six-story "skyscrapers"—the tallest buildings you'll see at this end of the

canal—are reminders of how densely populated the world's original ghetto was. Set aside as the local Jewish quarter in 1516, this area became extremely crowded. This urban island developed into one of the most closely knit business and cultural quarters of all the Jewish communities in Italy, and gave us our word "ghetto" (from *geto,* the copper foundry located here).

❸ San Marcuola

At this stop, facing a tiny square just ahead, stands the unfinished Church of San Marcuola, one of only five churches fronting the Grand Canal. Centuries ago, this canal was a commercial drag of expensive real estate in high demand by wealthy merchants. About 20 yards ahead on the right (across the Grand Canal) stands the stately gray

Turkish "Fondaco" Exchange, one of the oldest houses in Venice. Its horseshoe arches and roofline of triangles and dingleballs are reminders of its Byzantine heritage. Turkish traders in turbans docked here, unloaded their goods into the warehouse on the bottom story, then went upstairs for a home-style meal and a place to sleep. Venice in the 1500s was very cosmopolitan, welcoming every religion and ethnicity, so long as they carried cash. (Today the building contains the city's Museum of Natural History—and Venice's only dinosaur skeleton.)

Just 100 yards ahead on the left, Venice's **Casinò** is housed in the palace where German composer Richard *(The Ring)* Wagner died in 1883. See his distinct, strong-jawed profile in the white plaque on the brick wall. In the 1700s, Venice was Europe's Vegas, with casinos and prostitutes everywhere. *Casinòs* ("little houses" in Venetian dialect) have long provided Italians with a handy escape from daily life. Today they're run by the state to keep Mafia influence at bay. Notice the fancy front porch, rolling out the red carpet for high rollers arriving by taxi or hotel boat.

❹ San Stae

The San Stae Church sports a delightful Baroque facade. Opposite the San Stae stop is a little canal opening—on the second building to the right of that opening, look for the peeling plaster that once made up **frescoes** (you can barely distinguish the scant remains of little angels on the lower floors). Imagine the facades of the Grand Canal at their finest. Most of them would have been covered in frescoes by the best artists of the day. As colorful as the city is today, it's still only a faded, sepia-toned remnant of a long-gone era, a time of lavishly decorated, brilliantly colored palaces.

Just ahead, jutting out a bit on the right, is the ornate white facade of **Ca' Pesaro** (which houses the International Gallery of Modern Art—see page 52). *"Ca'"* is short for *casa* (house). Because only the house of the doge (Venetian ruler) could be called a palace *(palazzo),* all other Venetian palaces are technically *"Ca'."*

In this city of masks, notice how the rich marble facades along the Grand Canal mask what are generally just simple, no-nonsense brick buildings. Most merchants enjoyed showing off. However, being smart businessmen, they only decorated the side of the buildings that would be seen and appreciated. But look back as you pass Ca' Pesaro. It's the only building you'll see with a fine side facade. Ahead, on the left, with its glorious triple-decker medieval arcade (just before the next stop) is Ca' d'Oro.

❺ Ca' d'Oro

The lacy **Ca' d'Oro** (House of Gold) is the best example of Venetian Gothic architecture on the canal. Its three stories offer dif-

ferent variations on balcony design, topped with a spiny white roofline. Venetian Gothic mixes traditional Gothic (pointed arches and round medallions stamped with a four-leaf clover) with Byzantine styles (tall, narrow arches atop thin columns), filled in with Islamic frills. Like all the palaces, this was originally painted and gilded

to make it even more glorious than it is now. Today the Ca' d'Oro is an art gallery (described on page 57).

Look at the Venetian chorus line of palaces in front of the boat. On the right is the arcade of the covered **fish market,** with the open-air **produce market** just beyond. It bustles in the morning but is quiet the rest of the day. This is a great scene to wander through—even though European Union hygiene standards have made it cleaner but less colorful than it once was.

Find the *traghetto* gondola ferrying shoppers—standing like Washington crossing the Delaware—back and forth. There are

seven *traghetto* crossings along the Grand Canal, each one marked by a classy low-key green-and-black sign. Driving a *traghetto* isn't these gondoliers' normal day jobs. As a public service, all gondoliers are obliged to row the *traghetto* a few days a month. Make a point to use them. At €2 a ride, *traghetti* offer the cheapest gon-

dola ride in Venice (but at this price, don't expect them to sing to you).

❻ Mercato Rialto

This stop was opened in 2007 to serve the busy market (boats only stop here between 8:00 and 20:00). The long and officious-looking building at this stop is the Venice

courthouse. Straight ahead in the distance, rising above the huge post office, is the tip of the Campanile (bell tower), crowned by its golden angel at St. Mark's Square, where this tour will end. The **German Exchange** (100 yards directly ahead, on left side) was the trading center for German metal merchants in the early 1500s (once a post office, it will soon be a shopping center).

You'll cruise by some trendy and beautifully situated wine bars on the right, but look ahead as you round the corner and see the impressive Rialto Bridge come into view.

A major landmark of Venice, the **Rialto Bridge** is lined with shops and tourists. Constructed in 1588, it's the third bridge built

on this spot. Until the 1850s, this was the only bridge crossing the Grand Canal. With a span of 160 feet and foundations stretching 650 feet on either side, the Rialto was an impressive engineering feat in its day. Earlier Rialto Bridges could open to let big ships in, but not this one. When this new bridge was completed, much of the Grand Canal was closed to shipping and became a canal of palaces.

When gondoliers pass under the fat arch of the Rialto Bridge, they take full advantage of its acoustics: *"Volare, oh, oh..."*

❼ Rialto

Rialto, a separate town in the early days of Venice, has always been the commercial district, while San Marco was the religious and governmental center. Today, a winding street called the Mercerie connects the two, providing travelers with human traffic jams and a mesmerizing gauntlet of shopping temptations. This is the only stretch of the historic Grand Canal with landings upon which you can walk. They unloaded the city's basic necessities here: oil, wine, charcoal, iron. Today, the quay is lined with tourist-trap restaurants.

Venice's sleek, black, graceful **gondolas** are a symbol of the city (for more on gondolas, see page 331). With about 500 gondoliers joyriding amid the churning *vaporetti,* there's a lot of congestion on the Grand Canal. Pay attention—this is where most of the gondola and vaporetto accidents take place. While the Rialto is the highlight of many gondola rides, gondoliers understandably prefer the quieter small canals. Watch your vaporetto driver curse the better-paid gondoliers.

Ahead 100 yards on the left, two gray-colored **palaces** stand side by side (the City Hall and the mayor's office). Their horseshoe-shaped, arched windows are similar and their stories are the same height, lining up to create the effect of one long balcony.

❽ San Silvestro

We now enter a long stretch of important **merchants' palaces,** each with proud and different facades. Because ships couldn't

navigate beyond the Rialto Bridge, the biggest palaces—with the major shipping needs—line this last stretch of the navigable Grand Canal.

Palaces like these were multi-functional: ground floor for the warehouse, offices and showrooms upstairs, and the living quarters above the offices on the "noble floors" (with big windows designed to allow in maximum light). Servants lived and worked on the top floors (with the smallest windows). For fire-safety reasons, the kitchens were also located on the top floors. Peek into the noble floors to catch a glimpse of their still-glorious chandeliers of Murano glass.

❾ Sant'Angelo

Notice how many buildings have a foundation of waterproof white

stone *(pietra d'Istria)* upon which the bricks sit high and dry. Many canal-level floors are abandoned as the rising water level takes its toll.

The **posts**—historically painted gaily with the equivalent of family coats of arms—don't rot underwater. But the wood at the waterline, where it's exposed to oxygen, does. On the smallest canals, little blue gondola signs indicate that these docks are for gondolas only (no taxis or motor boats).

⑩ San Tomà

Fifty yards ahead, on the right side (with twin obelisks on the rooftop) stands **Palazzo Balbi,** the palace of an early-17th-century captain general of the sea. These Venetian equivalents of five-star admirals were honored with twin obelisks decorating their palaces. This palace, like so many in the city, flies three flags: Italy (green-white-red), the European Union (blue with ring of stars), and Venice (a lion on a field of red and gold). Today it houses the administrative headquarters of the regional government.

Just past the admiral's palace, look immediately to the right, down a side canal. On the right side of that canal, before the bridge, see the traffic light and the **fire station** (the 1930s Mussolini-era building with four arches hiding fireboats parked and ready to go).

The impressive **Ca' Foscari,** with a classic Venetian facade (on the corner, across from the fire station), dominates the bend in the canal. This is the main building of the University of Venice, which has about 25,000 students. Notice the elegant lamp on the corner—needed in the old days to light this intersection.

The grand, heavy, white **Ca' Rezzonico,** just before the stop of the same name, houses the Museum of 18th-Century Venice (❂ described in the Ca' Rezzonico Tour chapter). Across the canal is the cleaner and leaner **Palazzo Grassi,** the last major palace built on the canal, erected in the late 1700s. It was purchased by a French tycoon and now displays part of Punta della Dogana's contemporary art collection.

⑪ Ca' Rezzonico

Up ahead, the Accademia Bridge leads over the Grand Canal to the **Accademia Gallery** (right side), filled with the best Venetian paintings (❂ described in the Accademia Tour chapter). The bridge was put up in 1934 as a temporary structure. Locals liked it, so it stayed. It was rebuilt in 1984 in the original style.

⑫ Accademia

From here, look through the graceful bridge and way ahead to enjoy a classic view of **La Salute Church,** topped by a crown-shaped dome supported by scrolls (❂ described in the La Salute Church

Tour chapter). This Church of St. Mary of Good Health was built to thank God for delivering Venetians from the devastating plague of 1630 (which had killed about a third of the city's population).

The low, white building among greenery (100 yards ahead, on the right, between the Accademia Bridge and the church) is the **Peggy Guggenheim Collection.** The American heiress "retired" here, sprucing up a palace that had been abandoned in mid-construction. Peggy willed the city her fine collection of modern art (✪ described in the Peggy Guggenheim Collection Tour chapter).

As you approach the next stop, notice on the right how the fine line of higgledy-piggledy palaces evokes old-time Venice. Two

doors past the Guggenheim, Palazzo Dario has a great set of characteristic **funnel-shaped chimneys.** These forced embers through a loop-the-loop channel until they were dead—required in the days when stone palaces were surrounded by humble, wooden buildings, and a live spark could make a merchant's workforce homeless. Notice this early Renaissance building's flat-feeling facade with "pasted-on" Renaissance motifs. Three doors later is the **Salviati building,** which once served as a glassworks. Its fine mosaic, done by Art Nouveau in the early 20th century, features Venice as a queen being appreciated by the big shots of society.

⓭ Santa Maria del Giglio

Back on the left stands the fancy Gritti Palace hotel. Hemingway and Woody Allen both stayed here (but not together).

Take a deep whiff of Venice. What's all this nonsense about stinky canals? All I smell is my shirt. By the way, how's your captain? Smooth dockings? To get to know him, stand up in the bow and block his view.

⓮ Salute

The huge La Salute Church towers overhead as if squirted from a can of Catholic Reddi-wip. Like Venice itself, the church rests upon pilings. To build the foundation for the city, more than a

million trees were piled together, reaching beneath the mud to the solid clay. Much of the surrounding countryside was deforested by Venice. Trees were imported and consumed locally—to fuel the furnaces of Venice's booming glass industry, to build Europe's biggest merchant marine, to form light and flexible beams for nearly all of the buildings in town, and to prop up this city in the mud.

As the Grand Canal opens up into the lagoon, the last building on the right with the golden ball is the 17th-century **Customs House,** which now houses the Punta della Dogana contemporary art museum (listed on page 51). Its two bronze Atlases hold a statue of Fortune riding the ball. Arriving ships stopped here to pay their tolls.

⓯ San Marco

Up ahead on the left, the green pointed tip of the Campanile marks **St. Mark's Square,** the political and religious center of Venice...

and the final destination of this tour. You could get off at the San Marco stop and go straight to St. Mark's Square. But I'm staying on the boat for one more stop, just past St. Mark's Square (it's a quick walk back).

Survey the lagoon. Opposite St. Mark's Square, across the water, the ghostly white church with the pointy bell tower is **San Giorgio Maggiore,** with great views of Venice (❂ see the San Giorgio Maggiore Tour chapter). Next to it is the residential island Giudecca, stretching from close to San Giorgio Maggiore past the Venice youth hostel (with a nice view, directly across) to the Hilton Hotel (good nighttime view, far right end of island).

Still on board? If you are, as we leave the San Marco stop, prepare for a drive-by view of St. Mark's Square. First comes the bold white facade of the old mint (marked by a tiny cupola, where Venice's golden ducat, the "dollar" of the Venetian Republic, was made) and the library facade. Then come the twin columns topped by St. Theodore and St. Mark, who've welcomed visitors since the 15th century. Between the columns, catch a glimpse of two giant figures atop the **Clock Tower**—they've been whacking their clappers every hour since 1499. The domes of **St. Mark's Basilica** are soon eclipsed by the lacy facade of the **Doge's Palace.** Next you'll see the **Bridge of Sighs** (leading from the palace to the prison—check out the maximum-security bars), many gondolas with their green breakwater buoys, and then the grand harborside promenade—the **Riva.**

Follow the Riva with your eye, past elegant hotels to the green area in the distance. This is the largest of Venice's few **parks,** which hosts the annual Biennale festival (see page 456). Much farther in the distance is the **Lido,** the island with Venice's beach. Its sand and casinos are tempting, but its car traffic disrupts the medieval charm of Venice.

⑯ San Zaccaria

OK, you're at your last stop. Quick—muscle your way off this boat! (If you don't, you'll eventually end up at the Lido.)

At San Zaccaria, you're right in the thick of the action. A number of other *vaporetti* depart from here (see page 32). Otherwise, it's a short walk back along the Riva to St. Mark's Square. Ahoy!

GRAND CANAL

ST. MARK'S SQUARE TOUR

Piazza San Marco

Venice was once Europe's richest city, and Piazza San Marco was its center. As middleman in the trade between Asia and Europe, wealthy Venice profited from both sides. In 1450, Venice had 180,000 citizens (far more than London) and a gross "national" product that exceeded that of entire countries.

The rich Venetians taught the rest of Europe about the good life—silks, spices, and jewels from the East, crafts from northern Europe, good food and wine, fine architecture, music, theater, and laughter. Venice was a vibrant city full of painted palaces, glittering canals, and impressed visitors. Five centuries after its power began to decline, Venice still has all of these, with the added charm of romantic decay. In this tour, we'll spend an hour in the heart of this Old World superpower.

Orientation

Getting There: Signs all over town point to *San Marco*—meaning both the square and the basilica—located where the Grand Canal spills out into the lagoon. Vaporetto stops: San Marco or San Zaccaria.

Campanile: If you ascend the bell tower, it'll cost you €8 (daily Easter-June and Oct 9:00-19:00, July-Sept 9:00-21:00; Nov-Easter 9:30-16:45).

Clock Tower: To see the interior, you need to book a spot on a tour through the Correr Museum (see page 45 for specifics).

Information: There are two TIs near St. Mark's Square. One is in the southwest corner of the square; the other is along the waterfront at the San Marco-Vallaresso vaporetto dock.

Audio Tour: You can download this chapter as a free Rick Steves audio tour (see page 21).

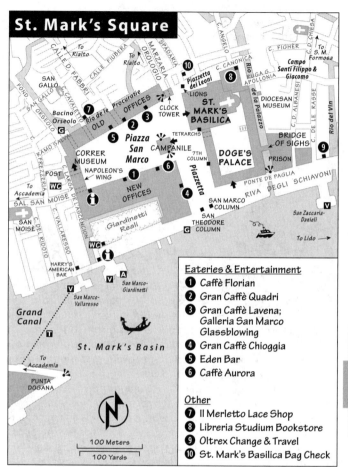

St. Mark's Square

Eateries & Entertainment
1 Caffè Florian
2 Gran Caffè Quadri
3 Gran Caffè Lavena;
   Galleria San Marco
   Glassblowing
4 Gran Caffè Chioggia
5 Eden Bar
6 Caffè Aurora

Other
7 Il Merletto Lace Shop
8 Libreria Studium Bookstore
9 Oltrex Change & Travel
10 St. Mark's Basilica Bag Check

ST. MARK'S SQUARE

Services: Handy public WCs (€1.50) are behind the Correr Museum and also at the waterfront park, Giardinetti Reali (near the TI and San Marco-Vallaresso vaporetto dock).

Eating: Cafés with live music provide an engaging soundtrack for St. Mark's Square (see "Cafés on St. Mark's Square" sidebar, later). The Correr Museum (at the end of the square opposite the basilica) has a quiet upstairs coffee shop overlooking the crowded square. For a list of restaurants in the area, see page 303.

Necessary Eyesores: Expect scaffolding and advertising billboards to cover parts of the square and its monuments when you visit.

Cardinal Points: The square is aligned (roughly) east-west. So, facing the basilica, north is to your left.

Starring: Byzantine domes, Gothic arches, Renaissance arches... and the wonderful, musical space they enclose.

The Tour Begins

• *For an overview of this grand square and the buildings that surround it, view it from the west end of the square (away from St. Mark's Basilica).*

The Piazza

St. Mark's Basilica dominates the square with its Eastern-style onion domes and glowing mosaics. Mark Twain said it looked

like "a vast warty bug taking a meditative walk." (I say it looks like tiara-wearing ladybugs copulating.) To the right of the basilica is its 325-foot-tall Campanile. Behind the Campanile, you can catch a glimpse of the pale-pink Doge's Palace. Lining the square are the former government offices *(procuratie)* that managed the treasury of St. Mark's, back when the church and state were one, and administered the Venetian empire's vast network of trading outposts, which stretched all the way to Turkey.

The square is big, but it feels intimate with its cafés and dueling orchestras. By day, it's great for people-watching and pigeon-chasing. By night, under lantern light, it transports you to another century, complete with its own romantic soundtrack. The piazza draws Indians in saris, English nobles in blue blazers, and Nebraskans in shorts. Napoleon called the piazza "the most beautiful drawing room in Europe." Napoleon himself added to the intimacy by building the final wing, opposite the basilica, that encloses the square.

For architecture buffs, here are three centuries of styles, bam, side by side, *uno-due-tre*, for easy comparison:

1. On the left side (as you face the basilica) are the "old" offices, built about 1500 in solid, column-and-arch Renaissance style.

2. The "new" offices (on the right), in a High Renaissance style from a century later (c. 1600), are a little heavier and more ornate. This wing mixes arches, the three orders of columns from bottom to top—Doric, Ionic, and Corinthian—and statues in the Baroque style.

3. Napoleon's wing, at the opposite end from the basilica, is later (c. 1800) and designed to fit in. The dozen Roman emperors decorating the parapet were once joined by Napoleon in the

middle, but today the French emperor is gone.

The arcade ringing the square, formerly lined with dozens of fine cafés, still provides an elegant promenade—complete with drapery that is dropped when necessary to provide relief from the sun.

Imagine this square full of water, with gondolas floating where people now sip cappuccinos. That happens every so often at very high tides *(acqua alta),* a reminder that Venice and the sea are intertwined. (Now that one is sinking and the other is rising, they are more intertwined than ever.)

Venice became Europe's richest city from its trade with northern Europeans, Ottoman Muslims, and Byzantine Christians. Here in St. Mark's Square, the exact center of this East-West axis, we see both the luxury and the mix of Eastern and Western influences.

Watch out for pigeon speckle. The pigeons are not indigenous to Venice (they were imported by the Habsburgs) nor loved by residents. In fact, Venetians love seagulls because they eat pigeons. In 2008, Venice outlawed the feeding of pigeons. But tourists—eager for a pigeon-clad photo op—haven't gotten that message, so at least some pigeons persist. Vermin are a problem on this small island, where it's said that each Venetian has two pigeons and four rats. (The rats stay hidden, except when high tides flood their homes.)

• *Now approach the basilica. If it's hot and you're tired, grab a shady spot at the foot of the Campanile.*

St. Mark's Basilica

The facade is a wild mix of East and West, with round, Roman-style arches over the doorways, golden Byzantine mosaics, a roofline

ringed with pointed Gothic pinnacles, and Muslim-shaped onion domes (wood, covered with lead) on the roof. The brick-structure building is blanketed in marble that came from everywhere—columns from Alexandria, capitals from Sicily, and carvings from Constantinople. The columns flanking the doorways show the facade's variety—purple, green, gray, white, yellow, some speckled, some striped horizontally, some vertically, some fluted—all topped with a variety of different capitals.

What's amazing isn't so much the variety as the fact that the whole thing comes together in a bizarre sort of harmony. St. Mark's remains simply the most interesting church in Europe, a church that (to paraphrase Goethe) "can only be compared with itself."

For more on the basilica, inside and out, see the ✪ St. Mark's Basilica Tour chapter.

• *Facing the basilica, turn 90 degrees to the left to see the...*

Clock Tower (Torre dell'Orologio)

Any proper Renaissance city wanted to have a fine, formal entry and a clock tower. In Venice's case, its entry was visible from the

sea and led from the big religious and governmental center to the rest of the city. The Clock Tower retains some of its original blue and gold pigments, a reminder that, in centuries past, this city glowed with bright color.

Two bronze "Moors" stand atop the Clock Tower (built originally to be Caucasian giants, they only switched their ethnicity when their metal darkened over the centuries). At the top of each hour they swing their giant clappers. The clock dial shows the 24 hours, the signs of the zodiac, and in the blue center, the phases of the moon—important information, as a maritime city with a shallow lagoon needs to know the tides. Above the dial is the world's first digital clock, which changes every five minutes.

An alert winged lion, the symbol of St. Mark and the city, looks down on the crowded square. He opens a book that reads *"Pax Tibi Marce,"* or "Peace to you, Mark." As legend goes, these were the comforting words that an angel spoke to the stressed evangelist, assuring him he would find serenity during a stormy night that the saint spent here on the island. Eventually, St. Mark's body

found its final resting place inside the basilica, and now his winged-lion symbol is everywhere. (Find four in 20 seconds. Go.)

Venice's many lions express the city's various mood swings through history—triumphant after a naval victory, sad when a favorite son has died, hollow-eyed after a plague, and smiling when the soccer team wins.

Cafés on St. Mark's Square

In Venice's heyday, it was said that the freedoms a gentleman could experience here went far beyond what any one person could actually indulge in. But one extravagance all could enjoy was the ritual of publicly consuming coffee: showing off with an affordable luxury, doing something trendy, while sharing the ideas of the Enlightenment.

Exotic coffee was made to order for the fancy café scene. Traders introduced coffee, called the "wine of Islam," from the East. The first coffeehouses opened in the 17th century, and by 1750 there were dozens of cafés lining Piazza San Marco and 200 operating in Venice.

Today, several fine old cafés survive and still line the square. Those with live music feature similar food, prices, and a three- to five-piece combo playing a selection of classical and pop hits, from Brahms to "Bésame Mucho." If you sit outside and get just a drink, expect to pay €12-22, including a €6 cover charge when the orchestra is playing (no cover charge otherwise). A coffee—your cheapest option—costs about €6 if you sit at an outside table, plus the €6 cover charge when the music plays, bringing it to €12 total (the venerable Caffè Florian charges a little more). It's perfectly acceptable to nurse a cappuccino for an hour—you're paying for the music with the cover charge. Do remember that a law limits what a café can charge for coffee at the bar—no matter how fancy the place or how high the demand. So, you can sip your coffee at the bar at a nearly normal price—even with the orchestra playing.

Caffè Florian (on the right as you face the church) is the most famous Venetian café and one of the first places in Europe to serve coffee (daily 10:00-24:00, shorter hours in winter). It's been a popular spot for a discreet rendezvous in Venice since 1720. The orchestra here plays a more classical repertoire than at the other cafés. The outside tables are the main action, but do walk inside through the richly decorated, old-time rooms where Casanova, Lord Byron, Charles Dickens, and Woody Allen have all paid too much for a drink.

Gran Caffè Quadri, opposite the Florian, has an equally illustrious roster of famous clientele, including the writers Stendhal and Dumas, and composer Richard Wagner.

Gran Caffè Lavena, near the Clock Tower, is newer and less storied. Drop in to check out its dazzling but politically incorrect chandelier.

Gran Caffè Chioggia, on the Piazzetta facing the Doge's Palace, charges slightly less, with one or two musicians, usually a pianist, playing cocktail jazz.

Eden Bar and **Caffè Aurora** are less expensive and don't have live music.

The pair of lions squatting between the Clock Tower and basilica have probably been photographed being ridden by every Venetian child born since the dawn of cameras.

Campanile

The original Campanile (cam-pah-NEE-lay, bell tower) was an observation tower and a marvel of medieval and Renaissance ar-

chitecture until 1902, when it toppled into the center of the piazza. It had groaned ominously the night before, sending people scurrying from the cafés. The next morning... crash! The golden angel on top landed right at the basilica's front door, standing up.

The Campanile was rebuilt 10 years later complete with its golden archangel Gabriel, who always faces the breeze. You can ride a lift to the top for the best view of Venice. It's crowded at peak times, but well worth it.

Because St. Mark's Square is the first place in town to start flooding, there are tide gauges at the outside base of the Campanile (near the exit, facing St. Mark's Square) that show the current sea level *(livello marea).* Find the stone plaque (near the exit door) that commemorates the high-water 77-inch level from the disastrous floods of 1966. In December of 2008, Venice suffered another terrible high tide, cresting at 61 inches.

If the tide is mild (around 20 inches), the water merely seeps up through the drains. But when there's a strong tide (around 40 inches), it looks like someone's turned on a faucet down below. The water bubbles upward and flows like a river to the lowest points in the square, which can be covered with a few inches of water in an hour or so. When the water level rises one meter above mean sea level, a warning siren sounds, and it repeats if a serious flood is imminent.

Many doorways have three-foot-high wooden or metal barriers to block the high water *(acqua alta),* but the seawater still seeps in through floors and drains, rendering the barriers nearly useless. (For background on what causes the flooding, see the sidebar on page 36.)

You might see stacked wooden benches in the square; during floods, the benches are placed end-to-end to create elevated sidewalks. If you think the square is crowded now, when it's flooded it turns into total gridlock, as all the people normally sharing the whole square jostle for space on the narrow wooden walkways.

In 2006, the pavement around St. Mark's Square was taken

Escape from St. Mark's Square

Crowds getting to you? Here are some relatively quiet areas on or near St. Mark's Square.

Correr Museum: Sip a cappuccino in the café of this uncrowded history museum in a building that overlooks St. Mark's Square (enter at the far end of the piazza). ✪ See the Correr Museum Tour chapter.

Giardinetti Reali: The small park is along the waterfront, west of the Piazzetta (facing the water, turn right—it's next to the TI and the only place near the square for a legal picnic).

San Giorgio Maggiore: This is the fairy-tale island you see from the Piazzetta (catch vaporetto #2 from the San Zaccaria stop, past the Bridge of Sighs). ✪ See the San Giorgio Maggiore Tour chapter.

Il Merletto: This lace shop is in a small, decommissioned chapel near the northwest corner of St. Mark's Square (daily 10:00-17:00, go through Sotoportego del Cavalletto and across the little bridge on the right).

La Salute Church: This cool church in a quiet neighborhood is a short hop on vaporetto #1 from the San Marco-Vallaresso stop; or you can ride the nearby *traghetto*. ✪ See the La Salute Church Tour chapter.

Caffè Florian: The plush interior of this luxurious 18th-century café, located on St. Mark's Square, is generally quiet and nearly empty. A coffee here can be a wonderful break (see "Cafés on St. Mark's Square," earlier).

up, and the entire height of the square was raised by adding a layer of sand and then replacing the stones. If the columns along the ground floor of the Doge's Palace look stubby, it's because this process has been carried out many times over the centuries, buying a little more time as the sea slowly swallows the city.

• *The small square between the basilica and the water is the...*

Piazzetta

This "Little Square" is framed by the Doge's Palace on the left, the library on the right, and the waterfront of the lagoon. In former days, the Piazzetta was closed to the public

for a few hours a day so that government officials and bigwigs could gather in the sun to strike shady deals.

The pale-pink **Doge's Palace** is the epitome of the style known as Venetian Gothic. Columns support traditional, pointed Gothic  arches, but with a Venetian flair—they're curved to a point, ornamented with a trefoil (three-leaf clover), and topped with a round medallion of a quatrefoil (four-leaf clover). The pattern is found on buildings all over Venice and on the formerly Venetian-controlled Croatian coast, but nowhere else in the world (except Las Vegas).

The two large 12th-century **columns** near the water were looted from Constantinople. Mark's winged lion sits on top of one. The lion's body (nearly 15 feet long) predates the wings and is more than 2,000 years old. The other column holds St. Theodore (battling a crocodile), the former patron saint who was replaced by Mark. I guess stabbing crocs in the back isn't classy enough for an upwardly mobile world power. Criminals were executed by being hung from these columns in the hopes that the public could learn its lessons vicariously.

Venice was the "Bride of the Sea" because she depended on sea trading for her livelihood. This "marriage" was celebrated annually by the people on Ascension Day. The doge, in full regalia, boarded a ritual boat (his Air Force One equivalent) here at the edge of the Piazzetta and sailed out into the lagoon. There a vow was made, and he dropped a jeweled ring into the water to seal the marriage.

In the distance, on an island across the lagoon, is one of the grandest views in the city, of the Church of San Giorgio Maggiore. With its four tall columns as the entryway, the church, designed by the late-Renaissance architect Andrea Palladio, influenced the appearance of future government and bank buildings around the world.

Palladio's sober classical lines are pure and intellectual, but with their love of extravagance, Venetians wanted something more

ST. MARK'S SQUARE

Venetian Gothic

∧ + ⌂ + ⌂ + ✿ =

exuberant. More to local taste was the High Renaissance style of Jacopo Sansovino, who (around 1530) designed the library (here on the Piazzetta) and the delicate Loggetta at the base of the Campanile (destroyed by the collapse of the tower in 1902 and then pieced back together).

Tetrarchs and the Doge's Palace's Seventh Column

Where the basilica meets the Doge's Palace is the traditional entrance to the palace, decorated with four small Roman statues—

the **Tetrarchs.** No one knows for sure who they are, but I like the legend that says they're the scared leaders of a divided Rome during its fall, holding their swords and each other as all hell breaks loose around them. Some believe that they are the leaders of the Eastern and Western empires (the bearded ones) with their chosen successors (the clean-shaven, younger ones). Whatever the legend, these statues—made of precious purple porphyry stone—are symbols of power. They were looted, likely from Constantinople, and then placed here proudly as spoils of war. How old are they? They've guarded the palace entrance since the city first rose from the mud.

About two-thirds of the way down the Doge's Palace, look for a **column** that's slightly shorter and fatter than the rest (it's the seventh from the water). Its carved capital tells a story of love, romance, and tragedy: 1) In the first scene (the carving facing the Piazzetta), a woman on a balcony is wooed by her lover, who says, "Babe, I want *you!*" 2) She responds, "Why, little ol' *me?*" 3) They get married. 4) Kiss. 5) Hit the sack—pretty

racy for 14th-century art. 6) Nine months later, guess what? 7) The baby takes its first steps. 8) And as was all too common in the 1300s...the child dies.

• *Continue down the Piazzetta to the waterfront. Turn left and walk (east) along the water. At the top of the first bridge, look inland at the...*

Bridge of Sighs

In the Doge's Palace (on your left), the government doled out justice. On your right are the prisons. (Don't let the palatial facade

fool you—see the bars on the windows?) Prisoners sentenced in the
palace crossed to the prisons by way
of the covered bridge in front of you.
This was called the Prisons' Bridge
until the Romantic poet Lord Byron
renamed it in the 19th century. From
this bridge, the convicted got their

final view of sunny, joyous Venice before entering the black and
dank prisons. According to the Romantic legend, they sighed.

Venice has been a major tourist center for four centuries. Any-
one who's ever come here has stood on this very spot, looking at the
Bridge of Sighs. Lean on the railing leaned on by everyone from
Casanova to Byron to Hemingway.

> *I stood in Venice, on the Bridge of Sighs,*
> *a palace and a prison on each hand.*
> *I saw, from out the wave, her structures rise,*
> *as from the stroke of the enchanter's wand.*
> *A thousand years their cloudy wings expand*
> *around me, and a dying glory smiles*
> *o'er the far times, when many a subject land*
> *looked to the Winged Lion's marble piles,*
> *where Venice sat in state, throned on her hundred isles!*

> —from Lord Byron's *Childe Harold's Pilgrimage*

ST. MARK'S BASILICA TOUR

Basilica di San Marco

Among Europe's churches, St. Mark's is peerless. From the outside, it's a riot of domes, columns, and statues, completely unlike the towering Gothic churches of northern Europe or the heavy Baroque of much of the rest of Italy. Inside is a decor of mosaics, colored marbles, and oriental treasures that's rarely seen elsewhere. The Christian symbolism is unfamiliar to Western eyes, done in the style of Byzantine icons and even Islamic designs. Older than most of Europe's churches, it feels like a remnant of a lost world.

This is your best chance in Italy (outside of Ravenna) to glimpse a forgotten and somewhat mysterious part of the human story—Byzantium.

Orientation

Cost: Entering the church is free. Three separate, optional sights inside require paid admission: the Treasury (€3, includes audioguide), Golden Altarpiece (€2), and San Marco Museum—the sight most worth its entry fee (€5, enter museum up stairs from atrium either before or after you tour the church).

Hours: The church and its museums are open Mon-Sat 9:45-17:00, Sun 14:00-17:00 (Sun until 16:00 Nov-March). The interior is brilliantly lit daily from 11:30 to 12:30; although this also coincides with an especially busy time, it may be worth it for the additional lighting, which brings the otherwise dim gold-leaf domes and mosaics to glowing life.

Lines: There's almost always a long line to get into St. Mark's; try going early or late. (It's very smart to check your day bag at the nearby church, which allows you to skip to the front of the line—see "Bag Check," later.) If you wind up in a long line, don't fret; it gives you time to enjoy one of Europe's fin-

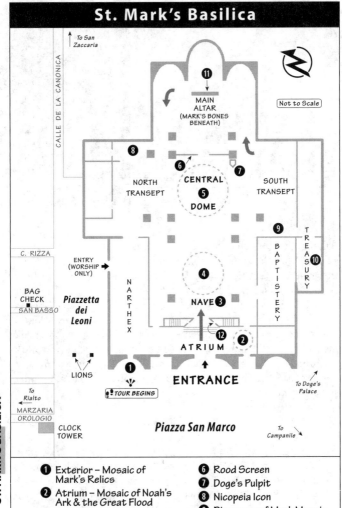

St. Mark's Basilica

To San Zaccaria

CALLE DE LA CANONICA

Not to Scale

MAIN ALTAR (MARK'S BONES BENEATH) ⑪

⑧

⑥ **CENTRAL DOME** ⑤ ⑦

NORTH TRANSEPT

SOUTH TRANSEPT

⑨

C. RIZZA

ENTRY (WORSHIP ONLY) ➤

BAG CHECK
SAN BASSO

Piazzetta dei Leoni

NARTHEX

BAPTISTERY

TREASURY ⑩

④

NAVE ③

To Rialto

MARZARIA
OROLOGIO

LIONS

① ⑫ ② **ATRIUM**

ENTRANCE

To Doge's Palace

▼ **TOUR BEGINS**

CLOCK TOWER

Piazza San Marco

To Campanile

ST. MARK'S BASILICA

① Exterior – Mosaic of Mark's Relics
② Atrium – Mosaic of Noah's Ark & the Great Flood
③ Nave – Mosaics & Greek-Cross Floor Plan
④ Pentecost Mosaic
⑤ Central Dome – Ascension Mosaic

⑥ Rood Screen
⑦ Doge's Pulpit
⑧ Nicopeia Icon
⑨ Discovery of Mark Mosaic
⑩ Treasury
⑪ Golden Altarpiece
⑫ Stairs up to Loggia: San Marco Museum & Bronze Horses

est squares as you read ahead in this chapter—and besides, the line moves pretty fast. Once inside, it can be packed, and you just have to shuffle through on a one-way system (another good reason to read this chapter before you enter).

Dress Code: Modest dress (no bare knees or bare shoulders) is strictly enforced, even for kids. Shorts are OK if they cover the knees.

Theft Alert: St. Mark's Basilica is the most dangerous place in Venice for pickpocketing—inside, it's always a crowded jostle.

Getting There: Signs throughout Venice point to *San Marco*, meaning both the square and the church (vaporetto: San Marco or San Zaccaria).

Information: Guidebooks are sold at the bookstand in the basilica's atrium. Tel. 041-270-8311, www.basilicasanmarco.it.

Church Services: Experience the church in its uncrowded glory at any Mass outside of visiting hours (e.g., daily at 8:00 or 18:45; see www.basilicasanmarco.it for full schedule). Enter through the "worship only" door around the left side of the basilica.

Tours: Free, hour-long English **tours** (heavy on the mosaics' religious symbolism) are offered many days at 11:00 (meet in atrium, schedule varies, see schedule board just inside entrance). You can download this chapter as a free Rick Steves **audio tour** (see page 21).

Length of This Tour: Allow one hour. If you have less time, forgo one (or all) of the basilica's three museums. The most skippable is the Golden Altarpiece (elaborate gold altarpiece near Mark's burial place), followed by the Treasury (fascinating but obscure old objects).

Bag Check (and Skipping the Line): Small purses and shoulder-slung bags are allowed inside, but larger bags and backpacks are not. Check them for free for up to one hour at the nearby church called Ateneo San Basso, 30 yards to the left of the basilica, down narrow Calle San Basso (see map page 88; daily 9:30-17:00). Note that you can't check small bags that would be allowed inside.

Those with a bag to check actually get to skip the line, as do their companions (up to three or so). Leave your bag at Ateneo San Basso and pick up your claim tag. Take your tag to the basilica's tourist entrance. Keep to the left of the railing where the line forms and show your tag to the gatekeeper. He'll let you in, ahead of the line. After touring St. Mark's, come back and pick up your bag.

Services: A free WC is inside the San Marco Museum.

Photography: Although officially forbidden inside the church, it is allowed on the balcony of the San Marco Museum, which has great views overlooking the square.

ST. MARK'S BASILICA

Eating: No food is allowed inside the church. For suggestions nearby, see page 303.

Starring: St. Mark, Byzantium, mosaics, and ancient bronze horses.

The Tour Begins

❶ Exterior—Mosaic of Mark's Relics

• *Start outside in the square, far enough back to take in the whole facade. Then zero in on the details.*

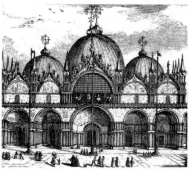

St. Mark's Basilica is a treasure chest of booty that was looted during Venice's glory days. That's most appropriate for a church built on the stolen bones of a saint.

The **mosaic over the far left door** shows the theft that put Venice on the pilgrimage map. Two men (in the center, with crooked staffs) enter the church bearing a coffin with the body of St. Mark, who looks pretty grumpy from the long voyage.

St. Mark was the author of one of the Gospels, the four Bible books telling the story of Jesus' life (Matthew, Mark, Luke, and John). Seven centuries after his death, his holy body was in Muslim-occupied Alexandria, Egypt. In A.D. 828, two visiting merchants of Venice "rescued" the body from the "infidels," hid it in a pork barrel (which was unclean to Muslims), and spirited it away to Venice.

The merchants presented the body—not to a pope or bishop—but to the doge (with white ermine collar, on the right) and his wife, the dogaressa (with entourage, on the left), giving instant status to Venice's budding secular state. They built a church here over Mark's bones and made him the patron saint of the city. You'll see his symbol, the winged lion, all over Venice.

The original church burned down in A.D. 976. Today's structure was begun in 1063. The mosaic, from 1260, shows that the church hasn't changed much since then—you can see the onion domes and famous bronze horses on the balcony.

The St. Mark's you see today, mostly from the 11th century,

St. Mark's...Cathedral, Church, or Basilica?

All three are correct. The church is also a cathedral, because it's the home church of the local bishop. It's a basilica, be-

cause it's the home of a patriarch and because the meaning of "basilica" evolved into an honorary title conferred on select churches by the pope. Coincidentally, it's also a basilica in the architectural sense. Its floor plan (if you ignore the transepts) has a central nave with flanking side aisles, a layout patterned after the ancient Roman public buildings called "basilicas." The transepts turn the

basilica plan into a cross—in this case, a Greek cross, as it has four equal arms.

was modeled after a great fourth-century church in Constantinople (Istanbul), the Church of the Holy Apostles (now long gone). Venice needed roots. By building a retro church, the city could imply that it had been around for longer than it actually had been. (Throughout European history, upstarts loved to fake deep roots this way. Germany embraced mystic, medieval lore as it emerged as a modern nation in the 19th century, England cooked up the King Arthur legend, and so on.)

In subsequent centuries, the church was encrusted with materials looted from buildings throughout the Venetian empire (see sidebar on page 98). Their prize booty was the four bronze horses that adorn the balcony, stolen from Constantinople during the Fourth Crusade (these are copies, as the originals are housed inside the church museum); the atrium you're about to enter was added on to the church as their pedestal. Later, it was decorated with a mishmash of plundered columns. The architectural style of St. Mark's has been called "Early Ransack."

• *Enter the atrium (entrance hall) of the basilica, through a sixth-century, bronze-paneled Byzantine door—which likely once swung in Constantinople's Hagia Sophia church. Immediately after being admitted by the dress-code guard, look up and to the right into an archway decorated with fine mosaics.*

ST. MARK'S BASILICA

Christ as Pantocrator

Most Eastern Orthodox churches have at least one mosaic or painting of Christ in a standard pose—as "Pantocrator," a Greek word meaning "Ruler of All." St. Mark's features several images of Christ as Pantocrator (for example, over the altar, in the central dome, and over the entrance door). The image, so familiar to Orthodox Christians, may be a bit foreign to Protestants, Catholics, and secularists.

As King of the Universe, Christ sits (usually on a throne) facing directly out, with penetrating eyes. He wears a halo divided with a cross. In his left hand is a Bible, while his right hand blesses, with the fingers forming the Greek letters chi and rho, the first two letters of "Christos." The thumb touches the fingers, symbolizing how Christ unites both his divinity and his humanity. On either side of Christ's head are the Greek letters "IC XC," short for "IesuC XristoC."

❷ Atrium—Mosaic of Noah's Ark and the Great Flood

St. Mark's famous mosaics, with their picture symbols, were easily understood in medieval times, even by illiterate masses. Today's literate masses have trouble reading them, so let's practice on these, some of the oldest (13th century), finest, and most accessible mosaics in the church. In the scene to the right of the entry door, Noah and sons are sawing logs to build a boat. Venetians—who were great ship builders—related to the story of Noah and the Ark. At its peak, Venice's Arsenale warship-building plant employed several thousand.

ST. MARK'S BASILICA

Below that are three scenes of Noah putting all species of animals into the Ark, two by two. (Who's at the head of the line? Lions.) Across the arch, the Flood hits in full force, drowning the wicked. Noah sends out a dove twice to see whether there's any dry land where he can dock. He finds it, leaves the Ark with a gorgeous rainbow overhead, and offers a sacrifice of thanks to God. Easy, huh?

Venture past Noah under the Creation Dome

(if it's not blocked off), which tells the entire story of Genesis, including Adam and Eve and the original sin. In a scene-by-scene narration, we see Adam lonely in the garden, the creation of Eve, the happy couple in Eden, and then trouble: from apple to fig leaf to banishment.

• *Now that our medieval literacy rate has risen, rejoin the slow flow of people. Notice the entrance to the San Marco Museum (Loggia dei Cavalli). You could follow the rest of this tour in a number of ways: For example, you can visit the San Marco Museum now or save it until after you've toured the main part of the church. Survey the lay of the (holy) land and consider the flow of the masses.*

Assuming you're following the tour as written, climb seven steps, pass through the doorway, and enter the nave. Loiter somewhere just inside the door (crowd permitting) and let your eyes adjust.

❸ The Nave— Mosaics and Greek-Cross Floor Plan

The initial effect is dark and unimpressive (unless they've got the floodlights on). But as your pupils slowly unclench, notice that the

entire upper part is decorated in mosaic—nearly 5,000 square yards (imagine paving a football field with contact lenses). These golden mosaics are in the Byzantine style, though many were designed by artists from the Italian Renaissance and later. The often-overlooked lower walls are covered with green-, yellow-, purple-, and rose-colored marble slabs, cut to expose the grain, and laid out in geometric patterns. Even the floor is mosaic, with mostly geometrical designs. It rolls like the sea. Venice is sinking and shifting, creating these cresting waves of stone.

The church is laid out with four equal arms, topped with domes, radiating out from the center to form a Greek cross (+). Those familiar with Eastern Orthodox churches will find familiar elements in St. Mark's: a central floor plan, domes, mosaics, and iconic images of Mary and Christ as Pantocrator—ruler of all things. As your eyes adjust, the mosaics start to give off a "mystical, golden luminosity," the atmosphere of the Byzantine heaven. The air itself seems almost visible, like a cloud of incense. It's a subtle effect, one that grows on you as the filtered light changes. There are more beautiful, bigger, more overwhelming, and even holier churches, but none is as stately.

• Find the chandelier near the entrance doorway (in the shape of a Greek cross cathedral space station), and run your eyes up the support chain to the dome above.

❹ Pentecost Mosaic

In a golden heaven, the dove of the Holy Spirit shoots out a pin-wheel of spiritual lasers, igniting tongues of fire on the heads of the 12 apostles below, giving them the ability to speak other languages without a Rick Steves phrase book. You'd think they'd be amazed, but their expressions are as solemn as... icons. One of the oldest mosaics in the church (c. 1125), it has distinct "Byzantine" features: a gold background and apostles with halos, solemn faces, almond eyes, delicate blessing hands, and rumpled robes, all facing forward.

This is art from a society still touchy about the Bible's commandment against making "graven images" of holy things. Byzantium had recently emerged from two centuries of Iconoclasm, in which statues and paintings were broken and burned as sinful "false gods." The Byzantine style emphasizes otherworldliness rather than literal human detail.

• Shuffle along with the crowds up to the central dome.

❺ Central Dome—Ascension Mosaic

Gape upward to the very heart of the church. Christ—having lived his miraculous life and having been crucified for man's sins—ascends into the starry sky on a rainbow. He raises his right hand and blesses the universe. This isn't the dead, crucified, mortal Jesus featured in most churches, but a powerful, resurrected God, the ruler of all.

Christ's blessing radiates, rippling down to the ring of white-robed apostles below. They stand amid the trees of the Mount of Olives, waving good-bye as Christ ascends. Mary is with them, wearing blue with golden Greek crosses on each shoulder and looking ready to play patty-cake. From these saints, goodness descends, creating the Virtues that ring the base of the dome between the windows. In Byzantine churches, the window-lit dome represented heaven, while the dark church below represented earth—a microcosm of the hierarchical universe.

Beneath the dome at the four corners, the four Gospel writers ("Matev," "Marc," "Luca," and "Ioh") thoughtfully scribble down the heavenly events. This wisdom flows down like water from the

Mosaics

St. Mark's mosaics are designs or pictures made with small cubes of colored stone or glass pressed into wet plaster. An-

cient Romans paved floors, walls, and ceilings with them. When Rome "fell," the art form died out in the West but was carried on by Byzantine craftsmen. They perfected the gold background effect by baking gold leaf into tiny cubes of glass called *tesserae* (tiles). The surfaces of the tiles are purposely cut unevenly to capture light and give off a shimmering effect. The reflecting gold mosaics helped to light thick-walled, small-windowed, lantern-lit Byzantine churches, creating a golden glow that symbolized the divine light of heaven.

St. Mark's mosaics tell the entire Christian history from end to beginning. Entering the church, you're greeted with scenes from the end of the world (Apocalypse) and the Pentecost. As you approach the altar, you walk backward in time to the source, experiencing Jesus' Passion and crucifixion, his miraculous life, and continuing back to his birth and Old Testament predecessors. Over the altar at the far end of the church (and over the entrance door at the near end) are images of Christ—the beginning and the end, the Alpha and Omega of the Christian universe.

symbolic Four Rivers below them, spreading through the church's four equal arms (the "four corners" of the world), and baptizing the congregation with God's love. The church building is a series of perfect circles within perfect squares—the cosmic order—with Christ in the center solemnly blessing us. God's in his heaven, saints are on earth, and all's right with the world.

Under the Ascension Dome— The Church as Theater

Look around at the church's furniture and imagine a service here. The ❻ **rood screen,** topped with 14 saints, separates the congrega-

tion from the high altar, heightening the "mystery" of the Mass. The ❼ **pulpit on the right** was reserved for the doge, who led prayers and made important announcements.

The Venetian church service is a theatrical multimedia spectacle, combining words (prayers, biblical passages, Latin and Greek phrases), music (chants, a choir, organ, horns, strings), images (mosaics telling Bible stories), costumes and props (priests' robes, golden reliquaries, candles, incense), set design (the mosaics, rood screen, Golden Altarpiece), and even stage direction (processionals through the crowd, priests' motions, standing, sitting, kneeling, crossing yourself). The symmetrical church is itself part of the set design. The Greek-cross floor plan symbolizes perfection, rather than the more common Latin cross of the crucifixion (emphasizing man's sinfulness). Coincidentally or not, the first modern opera—also a multimedia theatrical experience—was written by St. Mark's *maestro di cappella*, Claudio Monteverdi (1567-1643).

North Transept

In the north transept (the arm of the church to the left of the altar), today's Venetians pray to a painted wooden icon of Mary and baby Jesus known as ❽ **Nicopeia,** or "Our Lady of Victory" (on the east wall of the north transept, it's a small painting crusted over with a big stone canopy). In its day, this was the ultimate trophy—the actual icon used to protect the Byzantine army in war, looted by the Crusaders. Supposedly painted by the evangelist Luke, it was once enameled with bright paint and precious stones, and Mary was adorned with a crown and necklace of gold and jewels (now on display in the Treasury). Now the protector of Venetians, this Madonna has helped the city persevere through plagues, wars, and crucial soccer games.

• *In the south transept (to the right of main altar), find the dim mosaic high up on the wall above the entrance to the treasury.*

❾ Discovery of Mark Mosaic

This mosaic isn't a biblical scene; it depicts the miraculous event that capped the construction of the present church.

It's 1094, the church is nearly complete (see the domes shown in cutaway fashion), and they're all set to re-inter Mark's bones under the new altar. There's just one problem: During the decades of construction, they forgot where they'd stored his body!

So (in the left half of the mosaic), all of Venice gathers inside the church to bow down and pray for help finding the bones. The doge (from the Latin *dux,* meaning leader) leads them. Soon after (the right half), the patriarch (far right) is inspired to look inside a hollow column where he finds the relics. Everyone turns and applauds, including the womenfolk (left side of scene), who stream in from the upper-floor galleries. The relics were soon placed under the altar in a ceremony that inaugurated the current structure.

The door under the rose window, with the green curtain, leads directly from the Doge's Palace. On important occasions, the doge entered the church through here, ascended the steps of his pulpit, and addressed the people.

St. Mark's Three Museums

Inside the church are three sights, each requiring a separate admission. These provide an easy way to experience the richness of Byzantium. The San Marco Museum also gives you access to great views over the inside of the church, as well as to St. Mark's Square outside.

⑩ Treasury (Tesoro)

• *The two-room Treasury is in the south transept. The admission fee includes an audioguide.*

If you're not into metalworking or religious objects, you may find the Treasury's cramped collection somewhat underwhelming, but the objects become more interesting when you consider their illustrious past. These rooms hold an amazing collection of precious items, most of them stolen from Constantinople: Byzantine chalices, silver reliquaries, monstrous monstrances (for displaying the Communion wafer), and icons done in gold, silver, enamels, gems, and semiprecious stones. These pieces, highlighting finely worked and translucent material, are the ones that show up in art textbooks as the finest surviving Byzantine treasures (assuaging any Venetian guilt). As Venice thought of itself as the granddaughter of Rome and the daughter of Byzantium, Venetians consider these treasures not stolen, but inherited—rock crystal, jasper, alabaster, and marble that was rightfully theirs. Less sophisticated thieves would have smelted these pieces, but the Venetians safely stored them here for posterity.

Some of the items represent the fruits of labor by different civilizations over a thousand-year period. For example, an ancient rock-crystal chalice made by the Romans might have been decorated centuries later with Byzantine enamels and then finished still later with gold filigree by Venetian goldsmiths. This is marvelous handiwork, but all the more marvelous for having been done when Western Europe was still mired in mud.

• *Enter the main room, to the right. Start with the large glass case in the center of the room.*

Main Room: This display case holds the most precious Byzantine objects (mostly war booty brought here during the Fourth Crusade). The hanging lamp with the protruding fish features

Byzantium, the Fourth Crusade, and Venice

The Byzantine Empire was the eastern half of the ancient Roman Empire that *didn't* "fall" in A.D. 476. It remained Christian, Greek-speaking, and enlightened for another thousand years.

In A.D. 330, Constantine, the first Christian emperor, moved the Roman Empire's capital to the newly expanded city of Byzantium, which he humbly renamed Constantinople. With him went Rome's best and brightest. When the city of Rome decayed and fell, plunging Western Europe into its "Dark Ages," Constantinople lived on as the greatest city in Europe.

Venice had strong ties with Byzantium from its earliest days. In the sixth century, Byzantine Emperor Justinian invaded northern Italy, briefly reuniting East and West, and making Ravenna his regional capital. In 800, Venetians asked the emperor in Constantinople to protect them from Charlemagne's marauding Franks.

Soon Venetian merchants were granted trading rights to Byzantine ports in the Adriatic and eastern Mediterranean. They traded raw materials from Western Europe for luxury goods from the East. By the 10th century, about 10,000 Venetian merchants lived and worked in Constantinople. Meanwhile, relations between Byzantine Christians and Roman Catholics were souring across Europe over religious grounds—and because Constantinople's local merchants felt crowded out by the powerful Venetians, the corporate titans of the day. In 1171, the Byzantine emperor had the Venetian merchants expelled from the city; after a decade of more conflict, the entire Roman Catholic population—about 60,000 people—was either slaughtered or expelled from Constantinople.

Powerful, rich Venice wasn't about to stand for it—the Venetians had virtually no economy without trade. Two decades later, they saw their chance: The pope was organizing a Crusade to "save" the Holy Land from Muslim influence. Venice offered her ships to transport more than 30,000 Crusaders. They set out bound for Jerusalem...but the ships, led by the Venetian doge, diverted to Constantinople. The Crusaders sacked the Byzantine capital and occupied it from 1204 to 1261, turning the city into a quarry—one wide open for plunder. During that period, any ship traveling from Constantinople to Venice was

fourth-century Roman rock crystal framed in 11th-century Byzantine metalwork.

Just behind the lamp, a black bucket, carved with scenes of satyrs chasing nymphs, epitomizes the pagan world that was fading as Christianity triumphed. Also in the case are blue-and-gold lapis lazuli icons of the Crucifixion and of the Archangel

required to bring with it a souvenir for the Venetian Republic. Eventually the riches of Constantinople ended up in Venice—much of it here, in St. Mark's Basilica.

You can still see much of what the Venetians carried home: the bronze horses, bronze doors of Hagia Sophia, Golden Altarpiece enamels, the Treasury's treasures, the Nicopeia icon, and much of the marble that now covers the (brick) church. A good portion of the artistic riches adorning the church and filling its treasury was 700 years old when it was brought here...800 years ago.

The Venetians were clearly thieves, albeit thieves with good taste. While you could say the treasures belong in Turkey today, a good Venetian would argue that had they not "rescued" it, much of it (especially anything made from precious metal) never would have survived the centuries.

After the Fourth Crusade, Venice rose while the Byzantine Empire faded. Then both civilizations nose-dived when Constantinople finally fell to the Ottomans in 1453, severely damaging Venice's trading empire and ending Byzantium entirely. Constantinople, however, soon began to thrive again—once a bustling Christian city of a thousand churches, it flourished again as the newly Islamic city of Istanbul.

ST. MARK'S BASILICA

Michael—standing like an action hero, ready to conquer evil in the name of Christ. This features a Byzantine specialty: enamel work (more on that craft at the Golden Altarpiece). See various chalices (cups used for the bread and wine during Mass) made of onyx, agate, and rock crystal, and an incense burner shaped like a domed church.

• *Along the walls, find the following displays (working counterclockwise around the room).*

The first three glass cases have bowls and urns made of glass or rock crystal, gold and silver, and precious stones, and laced with elaborate filigree (twisted wires). The styles blend elements from the three medieval cultures that cross-pollinated in the Eastern Mediterranean: Venetian, Byzantine, and Islamic.

Next, on a wooden pedestal, comes the Urn of Artaxerxes I (next to the window in the right wall), an Egyptian-made object that once held the ashes of the great Persian king who ruled 2,500 years ago (r. 465-425 B.C.).

The next cases hold religious paraphernalia used for High Mass—chalices, reliquaries, candlesticks, bishops' robes, and a 600-year-old crosier (ceremonial shepherd staff) still used today by the chief priest on holy days.

Next is the Ciborio di Anastasia (far left corner), a small marble canopy that once arched over the blessed communion wafer during Mass. The object may be a gift from "Anastasia," the name carved on it in Greek. She was a lady-in-waiting in the court of the emperor Justinian (483-565). Christian legend has it that she was so beautiful that Justinian (a married man) pursued her amorously, so she had to dress like a monk and flee to a desert monastery.

Moving to the next wall, you'll see two large golden panels that once fronted an altar; flanking the panels are two golden candlesticks. What detail! The smiling angels at the top, the literary lion, the man with the weight on his shoulders, the row of queens... all the way down to the roots. Continuing counterclockwise, see a photo of a Madonna adorned with jewels, gold, and enamel.

Next to the Madonna, notice the granite column that extends below current floor level—you can see how the floor has risen as things have settled in the last 1,000 years.

Relics/Sanctuary Room: Straight ahead, the glass case over the glowing alabaster altar contains elaborate gold-and-glass reliquaries holding relics of Jesus' Passion—his torture and execution. The reliquary showing Christ being whipped (from 1125) holds a stone from the column he was tied to. You may scoff, but of Europe's many "Pieces of the True Cross" and "Crown of Thorns" relics, these have at least some claim of authenticity. Legend has it that Christ's possessions were gathered up in the fourth century by Constantine's mother and taken to Constantinople. During the Crusade heist of 1204, Venetians brought them here. They've been paraded through the city every Good Friday for 800 years.

Back by the room's entrance is a glass reliquary with the bones of Doge Orseolo (r. 976-978), who built the church that preceded the current structure. Another contains the bones of St. George, legendary dragon slayer.

The Legend (Mixed with a Little Truth) of Mark and Venice

Mark (died c. A.D. 68) was a Jewish-born Christian, and he might have actually met Jesus. He traveled with fellow convert

Paul, eventually settling in Alexandria as the city's first Christian bishop. On a trip to Rome, Peter—Jesus' right-hand man—asked him to write down the events of Jesus' life. This became the Gospel of Mark.

During his travels, Mark stopped in the lagoon (in Aquileia on the north coast of the Adriatic), where he dreamed of a Latin-speaking angel who said, *"Pax tibi Marce, evangelista meus"* ("Peace to you, Mark, my evangelist"), promising him rest after death. Back in Alexandria, Mark was attacked by an anti-Christian mob. They tied him with ropes and dragged his body through the streets until he died.

Eight centuries later, his body lay in an Alexandrian church that was about to be vandalized by Muslim fanatics. Two Venetian traders on a business trip saved the relics from desecration by hiding them in a basket of pork—a meat considered unclean by Muslims—and quickly setting sail. The perilous voyage home was only completed after many more miracles. The doge received the body, and in 828 they built the first church of St. Mark's to house it. During construction of the current church (1094), Mark's relics were temporarily lost, and it took another miracle to find them, hidden inside a column. Today, Venetians celebrate Mark on the traditional date of his martyrdom, April 25.

The events of Mark's life are portrayed vividly in many mosaics throughout the basilica. Unfortunately, most of them are either off-limits to tourists or in the dim reaches of the church. You can enjoy them by paging through a St. Mark's guidebook with photos.

⓫ Golden Altarpiece (Pala d'Oro)

• *The Golden Altarpiece is located behind the main altar. Join the line to pay, and then go through the turnstile.*

Under the green marble canopy, supported by four intricately carved alabaster columns, sits the **high altar.** Inside the altar is an urn (not visible) with the mortal remains of Mark, the Gospel writer. (Look through the grate of the altar to read *Corpus Divi Marci Evangelistae,* or "Body of the Evangelist Mark.") He rests in peace, as an angel had promised him. Shh.

As you shuffle along, notice the marble canopy's **support columns** carved with New Testament scenes.

The **Golden Altarpiece** itself is a stunning golden wall made of 250 blue-backed enamels with religious scenes, all set in a gold frame and studded with 15 hefty rubies, 300 emeralds, 1,500 pearls, and assorted sapphires, amethysts, and topaz. The Byzantine-made enamels were part of the Venetians' plunder of 1204, subsequently pieced together by Byzantine craftsmen specifically for St. Mark's high altar. It's a bit  much to take in all at once, but get up close and find several details you might recognize:

In the center, Jesus as Ruler of the Cosmos sits on a golden throne, with a halo of pearls and jewels. Like a good Byzantine Pantocrator, he dutifully faces forward and gives his blessing while stealing a glance offstage at Mark ("Marcus") and the other saints.

Along the bottom row, Old Testament prophets show off the books of the Bible they've written. With halos, solemn faces, and elaborately creased robes, they epitomize the Byzantine icon style.

Follow Mark's story in the panels along the sides. In the bottom left panel, Mark meets Peter (seated) at the gates of Rome. It was Peter (legend has it) who gave Mark the eyewitness account of Jesus' life that Mark wrote down in his Gospel. Mark's story ends in the bottom right panel with the two Venetian merchants returning by ship, carrying his coffin here to be laid to rest.

Byzantium excelled in the art of *cloisonné* enameling. A piece of gold leaf is stamped with a design, then filled in with pools of enamel paint, which are baked on. Look at a single saint to see the detail work: The gold background around the saint is the gold-leaf medallion that gets stamped. The golden folds in the robe are the raised edges of the impression. The different colors of the robe are different-colored paints in the recessed areas, each color baked on in a separate firing. Some saints even have pearl crowns or jewel collars pinned on. This kind of craftsmanship—and the social infrastructure that could afford it—made Byzantium seem like an enchanted world during Europe's dim Middle Ages.

After you've looked at some individual scenes, back up as far as this small room will let you and just let yourself be dazzled by the whole picture—this "mosaic" of Byzantine greatness—and marvel at the fact that it's still here. While the altarpiece contains 30 pounds of gold, Napoleon's men thought it was just gold leaf, so they didn't bother melting it down. And during World War II, the altarpiece almost certainly would have been snatched by the Nazis, had it not been hidden away in an Umbrian villa.

This magnificent altarpiece sits on a swivel (notice the mechanism at its base) and is swung around on festival Sundays so the entire congregation can enjoy it, as Venetians have for so many centuries.

⑫ San Marco Museum (Museo di San Marco)— Mosaics, Bronze Horses, View of the Piazza, and More

• *The staircase up to the museum is in the atrium near the main entrance. The sign says* Loggia dei Cavalli, Museo. *Ascend the steps, buy your ticket, and enter. In the first room, you'll see several models of the church at various stages of its history. Notice how the original domes, once squat, were made taller in the 13th century, leaving today's church with a dome-within-a-dome structure. Notice also the historic drawings here.*

Next are the museum's three highlights: view of the interior (right), view of the square (out the door to the left), and bronze horses (directly ahead). Belly up to the stone balustrade (on the right) to survey the interior.

View of Church Interior

Scan the church, with its thousands of square meters of mosaics, then take a closer look at the Pentecost Mosaic (first dome above you, described earlier). The unique design at the very top signifies the Trinity: throne (God), Gospels (Christ), and dove (Holy Spirit). The couples below the ring of apostles are the people of the world (I can find Judaea, Cappadocia, and Asia), who, despite their different languages, still understood the Spirit's message.

If you were a woman in medieval Venice, you'd enjoy this same close-up view, because in the Middle Ages, women climbed the same stairs you just did and found a spot along the balconies at your feet. The balcony was for women, the nave for men, and the altar for the priests. Back then the rood screen (the fence with the 15 figures on it) separated the priest from the public. The doge was also allowed to address his public from the pulpit, thereby amplifying the power of his political speeches with the force of God.

Appreciate the patterns of the mosaic floor—one of the finest in Italy—that covers the floor like a Persian carpet.

• *From here, the museum loops you along the left gallery to the far (altar) end of the church, then back to the bronze horses. Along the way, you'll see...*

Mosaic Fragments

These mosaics once hung in the church, but when they became damaged or aesthetically old-fashioned, they were replaced by new and more fashionable mosaics. These few fragments avoided the garbage can. You'll see mosaics from the church's earliest days (and most "Byzantine" style, c. 1070) to more recent times (1700s, more realistic and detailed). Many are accompanied by small photos that show where the fragment used to fit into a larger scene.

The mosaics—made from small cubes of stone or colored glass pressed into wet clay—were assembled on the ground, then cemented onto the walls. Artists draw the pattern on paper, lay it on the wet clay, and slowly cut the paper away as they replace it with cubes. The first mosaic on your left as you enter shows a reproduction of a paper "cast" of a mosaic.

Continuing on, down a set of stairs, you'll see other artwork and catch glimpses of the interior of the church from the north transept. Here you get a close-up view of the **Tree of Jesse mosaic,** showing Jesus' distant ancestor at the root and his mom at the top. This mosaic is from 1540, during the High Renaissance—it's much more modern than those decorating the domes, which date mostly from the 1200s.

• *Take this opportunity to compare the styles, then continue on to the Sala dei Banchetti (WCs near the room's entrance).*

Sala dei Banchetti

This large, ornate room—once the doge's banquet hall—is filled with religious objects, tapestries, and carpets that once adorned the church, Burano-made lace vestments, illuminated music manuscripts, a doge's throne, and much more.

Try reading some music. The manuscripts date from the 16th century—before the age of treble and bass clefs. You'll see a C clef along the left margin of each staff (which could slide along the staff to locate middle C). From this, you could chant notes in proper relationship to each other, following the rhythm indicated.

In the center of the hall stands the most prestigious artwork here, the *Pala Feriale,* by Paolo Veneziano (1345). On ordinary workdays, these 14 scenes painted on wood covered the basilica's golden Pala d'Oro. The top row is seven saints (including crucified Christ). Below are seven episodes in Mark's life. In the first panel, Mark kneels before a red-robed Saint Peter and receives his calling. Next, he arrives in Alexandria and makes his first convert. Then Jesus appears to Mark. Mark is beaten to death and dragged through the streets. The panel of the sailboat tells the story of the Venetian merchants' trip home with Mark's relics. A storm at sea billows their sails, ripples the flag, churns the waves, and scares the crew as the ship heads toward the rocks. But then Mark himself appears miraculously at the stern and calms the storm, bringing the ship (and his own body) safely to Venice. Paolo proudly signed his name (along the bottom) and the names of his two assistants, his sons Luca and Giovanni. In the next panel, Mark's long-lost body is rediscovered hidden in a column. Finally, worshippers gather at Mark's tomb by the altar of the basilica.

• *Now double back toward the museum entrance, through displays of stone fragments from the church, finally arriving at...*

The Bronze Horses (La Quadriga)

Stepping lively in pairs and with smiles on their faces, they exude energy and exuberance. Art historians don't know how old they

are—they could be from ancient Greece (fourth century B.C.) or from ancient Rome, during its Fall (fourth century A.D.). Professor Carbon Fourteen says they're from around 175 B.C. Originally, the horses pulled a chariot driven by an emperor, *Ben-Hur* style. These bronze statues were not hammered and bent into shape by metalsmiths, but were cast from clay molds by using the lost-wax technique. The heads are detachable and adjustable—even swappable. The bronze is high quality, with 97 percent copper. Originally, gilded, they still have some streaks of gold. Long gone are the ruby pupils that gave the horses the original case of "red eye." While four-horse statues were once relatively common, this is the only intact group of four horses to survive from ancient times. That they survived at all is amazing, as bronze work like this almost always ends up being smelted down by conquerors.

Megalomaniacs through the ages have coveted these horses not only for their artistic value, but because they symbolize Apollo, the Greco-Roman god of the sun...and of secular power. Legend says they were made in the time of Alexander the Great, then taken by Nero to Rome. Constantine took them to his new capital in Constantinople to adorn the chariot racecourse. The Venetians then stole them from their fellow Christians when they sacked the city in 1204 and brought them here to St. Mark's in 1255. The doge spoke to his people while standing between the horses when they graced the balcony atop the church's facade (where the copies—which you'll see next—stand today).

What goes around comes around, and Napoleon came around and took the horses when he conquered Venice in 1797. They stood atop a triumphal arch in Paris until Napoleon's empire was "blown-aparte" and they were returned to their "rightful" home. Their expressive faces seem to say, "Oh boy, Wilbur, have we done some travelin'."

The horses were again removed from their spot when they were attacked by their most dangerous enemy yet—modern man. The threat of oxidation from pollution sent them galloping for cover inside the church in 1975.

• *The visit ends outside on the balcony overlooking St. Mark's Square.*

ST. MARK'S BASILICA

The Loggia and View of St. Mark's Square

You'll be drawn repeatedly to the viewpoint of the square, but remember to look at the facade to see how cleverly all the looted ar-chitectural elements blend together. Ramble among the statues of water-bearing slaves that serve as drain spouts. The horses are modern copies (note the 1978 date on the hoof of the horse to the right).

Be a doge, and stand between the bronze horses overlooking St. Mark's Square. Under the gilded lion of St. Mark, in front of the four great Evangelists (who once stood atop the columns), and flanked—like Apollo—by the four glorious horses, he inspired the Venetians in the square below to great things.

Admire the mesmerizing, commanding view of the center of this city, which so long ago was Europe's only superpower, and today is just a small town with a big history—one that's filled with tourists.

DOGE'S PALACE TOUR

Palazzo Ducale

Venice is a city of beautiful facades—palaces, churches, carnival masks—that can cover darker interiors of intrigue and decay. The Doge's Palace, with its frilly pink exterior, hides the fact that the "Most Serene Republic" (as Venice called itself—"serene" meaning stable) was far from serene in its heyday.

The Doge's Palace housed the fascinating government of this rich and powerful empire. It also served as the home for the Venetian ruler known as the doge (pronounced "dohzh"), or duke. For four centuries (about 1150-1550), this was the most powerful half-acre in Europe. The rest of Europe marveled at the way Venice could govern itself without a dominant king, bishop, or tyrant. The doges wanted their palace to reflect the wealth and secular values of the Republic, impressing visitors and serving as a reminder that the Venetians were Number One in Europe.

Orientation

Cost: €16 combo-ticket also includes the Correr Museum.

Hours: Daily April-Oct 8:30-18:30, Nov-March 8:00-17:30, last entry one hour before closing.

Crowd Control: To avoid the long peak-season line at the Doge's Palace, you have several options (the first is best).

• Buy your combo-ticket at the Correr Museum. Or if you're purchasing a Museum Pass (which covers the Doge's Palace—see page 26), get it at one of the less-crowded museums covered by the pass. Then go straight to the Doge's Palace turnstile, skirting along to the right of the long ticket-buying line and entering at the "prepaid tickets" entrance.

• Pay €0.50 extra to buy your ticket online—at least 48 hours

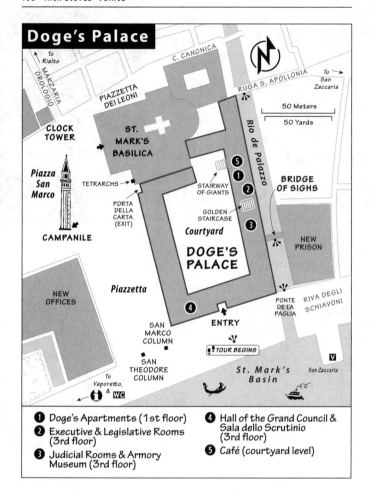

Doge's Palace

To Rialto

C. CANONICA

RUGA S. APOLLONIA

To San Zaccaria

PIAZZETTA DEI LEONI

50 Meters

50 Yards

CLOCK TOWER

ST. MARK'S BASILICA

Rio de palazzo

Piazza San Marco

TETRARCHS

❺
❶
❷

BRIDGE OF SIGHS

STAIRWAY OF GIANTS

PORTA DELLA CARTA (EXIT)

GOLDEN STAIRCASE

❸

CAMPANILE

Courtyard

DOGE'S PALACE

NEW PRISON

NEW OFFICES

Piazzetta

❹

PONTE DE LA PAGLIA

RIVA DEGLI SCHIAVONI

SAN MARCO COLUMN

ENTRY

SAN THEODORE COLUMN

🛈 TOUR BEGINS

St. Mark's Basin

San Zaccaria

To Vaporetto, & 🛈 WC

V

❶ Doge's Apartments (1st floor)

❷ Executive & Legislative Rooms (3rd floor)

❸ Judicial Rooms & Armory Museum (3rd floor)

❹ Hall of the Grand Council & Sala dello Scrutinio (3rd floor)

❺ Café (courtyard level)

DOGE'S PALACE

in advance—on the museum website (http://palazzoducale. visitmuve.it).

• In peak season, visit the palace at about 17:00, when the line diminishes.

• Book a guided Secret Itineraries Tour (see "Tours," below).

Getting There: The palace is next to St. Mark's Basilica, on the lagoon waterfront, and just off St. Mark's Square. Vaporetto stops: San Marco or San Zaccaria.

Information: There are some English descriptions, and guidebooks are on sale in the bookshop. Tel. 041-271-5911, http:// palazzoducale.visitmuve.it.

Tours: The fine **Secret Itineraries Tour** follows the doge's footsteps through rooms not included in the general admission price. Though the tour skips the palace's main hall, you're welcome to visit the hall afterward on your own. Three 1.25-hour English-language tours run each morning. Reserve ahead, as tours fill up—although you can try just showing up at the information desk (€20, includes Doge's Palace admission but not Correr Museum; €14 with combo-ticket; to reserve from the US dial 011-39-041-4273-0892, within Italy call 848-082-000, or reserve online for €0.50 extra at http://palazzoducale.visitmuve.it).

The **audioguide** tour is dry but informative (€5, 1.5 hours, need ID or credit card for deposit). Pick it up after you pass through the turnstile after the ticket counter.

Length of This Tour: Allow 1.5 hours. If you need to shave some time off your visit, head straight to the third floor (the Square Room) and follow the tour from there to the Hall of the Grand Council. Skip the prisons.

Services: Some WCs are in the courtyard; more are halfway up the stairs to the balcony level. An elevator (off the courtyard) is available for those who have difficulty climbing stairs. Any bag bigger than a large purse must be checked (free) in the courtyard.

Photography: Not allowed inside.

Cuisine Art: A pricey sandwich-and-salad café is in the palace courtyard (€7 *panini,* €10-13 salads, €4 cappuccino; it's tucked in the gallery behind the Stairway of Giants, and the tour route also deposits you there). Nearby are expensive cafés on St. Mark's Square and good sandwich bars on Calle de le Rasse (two blocks behind the palace—see page 303).

Starring: Big rooms bare of furnishings but crammed with history, Tintoretto masterpieces, and the doges.

The Tour Begins

Exterior

"The Wedding Cake," "The Tablecloth," or "The Pink House" is also sometimes known as the Doge's Palace. The style is called Ve-

netian Gothic—a fusion of Italian Gothic with a delicate Islamic flair. The columns originally had bases on the bottoms, but these were covered over as the columns sank, and the square was built up over the centuries. If you compare this lacy, top-heavy structure with the massive fortress palaces of Florence, you realize the wisdom of building a city in the middle of the sea—you have no natural enemies except

DOGE'S PALACE

gravity. This unfortified palace in a city with no city wall was the doge's way of saying, "I am an elected and loved ruler. I do not fear my own people."

The palace was originally built in the 800s, but most of what we see came after 1300, as it was expanded to meet the needs of the empire. Each doge wanted to leave his mark on history with a new wing, but so much of the city's money was spent on the palace that finally a law was passed levying an enormous fine on anyone who even mentioned any new building. That worked for a while, until one brave (and wealthy) doge proposed a new wing, paid his fine... and started building again.

• *Enter the Doge's Palace from along the waterfront. After you pass through the turnstile, ignore the signs and cross the courtyard, noticing the two fine wellheads (the courtyard once functioned as a cistern), and stand at the foot of the grand staircase topped by two statues.*

Courtyard and Stairway of Giants (Scala dei Giganti)

Imagine yourself as a foreign dignitary on business to meet the doge. In the courtyard, you look up a grand staircase topped with

two nearly nude statues of, I think, Moses and Paul Newman (more likely, Neptune and Mars, representing Venice's prowess at sea and at war). The doge and his aides would be waiting for you at the top, between the two statues and beneath the winged lion. No matter who you were—king, pope, or emperor—you'd have to hoof it up. The powerful doge would descend the stairs for no one.

Many doges were crowned here, between the two statues. The doge was something like an elected king—which makes sense only in the dictatorial republic that was Venice. Technically, he was just a noble selected by other nobles to carry out their laws and decisions. Many doges tried to extend their powers and rule more as divine-right kings. Many others just put on their funny hats and accepted their role as figurehead and ceremonial ribbon-cutter. Because doges served a lifelong term, most were geezers, elected in their 70s and committed to preserving Venetian traditions.

The palace is attached to the church, symbolically welding church and state. Both buildings have ugly brick behind a painted-lady veneer of marble. In this tour, we'll see the similarly harsh inner workings of an outwardly serene, polished republic.

The courtyard is a hodgepodge of architectural styles, as the palace was refurbished over the centuries. There are classical statues in Renaissance niches, shaded by Baroque awnings, topped by Flamboyant Gothic spires, and crusted with the Byzantine onion domes of St. Mark's Basilica.

• *Cross back to near the entrance and follow the signs up the tourists' staircase to the first-floor balcony (loggia), where you can look back down on the courtyard. From this point on, it's hard to get lost. It's a one-way system, so just follow the arrows.*

Midway along the balcony, you'll find a face in the wall, the...

Mouth of Truth

This fierce-looking androgyne opens his/her mouth, ready to swallow a piece of paper, hungry for gossip. Letterboxes like this (some with lions' heads) were scattered throughout the palace. Originally, anyone who had a complaint or suspicion about anyone else could accuse him anonymously *(denontie secrete)* by simply dropping a slip of paper in the mouth. This set the blades of justice turning inside the palace.

• *Toward Paul Newman is the entrance to the...*

Golden Staircase (Scala d'Oro)

The palace was architectural propaganda, designed to impress visitors. This 24-karat gilded-ceiling staircase was something for them to write home about. As you ascend the stairs, look back at the floor below and marvel at its 3-D pattern.

• *Start up the first few steps of the Golden Staircase. Midway up, at the first landing, turn right, which takes you up into the...*

Doge's Apartments (Appartamento del Doge)

The dozen or so rooms on the first floor are where the doge actually lived. The blue-and-gold-hued Sala dei Scarlatti (Room 5) is typical of the palace's interior decoration: gold-coffered ceiling, big stone fireplace, silky walls with paintings, and a speckled floor. There's very little original furniture, as doges were expected to bring their own. Despite his high office, the doge had to obey several rules that bound him to the city. He couldn't leave the palace unescorted, he couldn't open official mail in private, and he and his family had to leave their own home and live in the Doge's Palace.

The large Room 6, the Sala dello Scudo (Shield Hall), is full

Paintings by Titian, Veronese, and Tintoretto

The doge had only the top Venetian painters decorate his palace. While the palace was once rich in Titians, fires in the late 1500s destroyed nearly all the work by the greatest Venetian master. As the palace was hastily reconstructed, the Titians were replaced with works by Veronese and Tintoretto. (Most of these canvases were painted in workshops, and quickly patched in to fill empty spaces.)

Veronese used the best pigments available—from precious stones, sapphires, and emeralds—and his colors have survived vividly. These Veronese paintings are by his hand and are fine examples of his genius. Tintoretto, on the other hand, didn't really have his heart in these commissions, and the pieces here were done by his workshop.

The paintings of the Doge's Palace are a study of old Venice, with fine views of the old city and its inhabitants. The extravagant women's gowns in the paintings by Veronese show off a major local industry—textiles. While the paintings are not generally of masterpiece quality, they're historically interesting. They prove that in the old days, Venice had no pigeons.

of maps and globes. The main map illustrates the reach of Venice's maritime realm, which stretched across most of the eastern Mediterranean. The Venetian Republic was a mighty trading empire, built not on vast land holdings but upon a network of ports and a mastery of the sea. With the maps in this room you can trace the eye-opening trip across Asia—from Italy to Greece to Palestine, Arabia, and "Irac"—of local boy Marco Polo (c. 1254-1325). Finally, he arrived at the other side of the world. This last map (at the far end of the room) is shown "upside-down," with south on top, giving a glimpse of the Venetian worldview circa 1550. It depicts China, Taiwan (Formosa), and Japan (Giapan), while America is a nearby island with California and lots of Terre Incognite.

In Room 7, the Sala Grimani, are several paintings of the lion of St. Mark, including the famous one by Vittore Carpaccio of a smiling lion (on the long wall). The lion holds open a book with these words, *"Pax Tibi Marce..."* ("Peace to you, Mark"), which according to legend were spoken by an angel welcoming

DOGE'S PALACE

Executive & Legislative Rooms

ROOM 11
COLLEGIO HALL

ROOM 12
SENATE HALL

Courtyard

(Not to scale)

ROOM OF THE 4 DOORS

SQUARE ROOM

GOLDEN STAIRCASE

HALL OF THE COUNCIL OF 10

❶ TINTORETTO – Justice Presenting the Sword and Scales

❷ TITIAN – Doge Kneeling

❸ TIEPOLO – Venice Receiving Neptune

❹ VERONESE – The Rape of Europa

❺ TINTORETTO – Bacchus and Ariadne

❻ VERONESE – Discussion

❼ VERONESE – Mars and Neptune with Campanile and Lion

❽ TINTORETTO – Triumph of Venice

❾ Clocks

St. Mark to Venice. In the background is the Doge's Palace and the Campanile.

When you reach Room 10, the Sala dei Filosofi (Philosophers' Hall), look for the first doorway on the right, pop up the humble stairway, and look back at a Titian quickie, painted in just three days. This fresco of St. Christopher carrying the Christ child across the lagoon was made for a doge who believed that if you looked at St. Christopher, you wouldn't die that day.

• *After browsing the dozen or so private rooms of the Doge's Apartments, continue up the Golden Staircase to the third floor, which was the "public" part of the palace. The first room at the top of the stairs is the...*

Square Room (Atrio Quadrato)

The ceiling painting, ***Justice Presenting the Sword and Scales to Doge Girolamo Priuli,*** is by Tintoretto. (Stand at the top of the painting for the full 3-D effect.) It's a late-Renaissance masterpiece. So what? As you'll soon see, this palace is wallpapered with Titians, Tintorettos, and Veroneses. Many have the same theme you see here: a doge, in his ermine cape, gold-brocaded robe, and funny one-horned hat with earflaps, kneeling in the presence of saints, gods, or mythological figures.

• *Enter the next room.*

DOGE'S PALACE

Room of the Four Doors
(Sala delle Quattro Porte)

This was the central clearinghouse for all the goings-on in the palace. Visitors presented themselves here and were directed to their destination—the courts, councils, or the doge himself.

The room was designed by Andrea Palladio, the architect who did the impressive Church of San Giorgio Maggiore, across the Grand Canal from St. Mark's Square. On the intricate stucco ceiling, notice the feet of the women dangling down below the edge (above the windows), extending the illusion.

On the wall to the left of the door you entered from is a painting by (ho-hum) Titian, showing a **doge kneeling** with great piety before a woman embodying Faith holding the Cross of Jesus. Notice old Venice in the misty distance under the cross. This is one of many paintings you'll see of doges in uncharacteristically humble poses—paid for, of course, by the doges themselves.

G. B. Tiepolo's well-known *Venice Receiving Neptune* is now displayed on an easel, but it was originally hung on the wall above the windows where they've put a copy (you'll get a closer look at the painting when you loop back through this room in a few minutes). The painting shows Venice as a woman—Venice is always a woman to artists—reclining in  luxury, dressed in the ermine cape and pearl necklace of a doge's wife (dogaressa). Crude Neptune, enthralled by the First Lady's beauty, arrives bearing a seashell bulging with gold ducats. A bored Venice points and says, "Put it over there with the other stuff."

• *Enter the small room with the big fireplace and several paintings.*

Ante-Collegio Hall (Sala dell'Anticollegio)

It took a big title or bribe to get in to see the doge. Once accepted for a visit, you would wait here before you entered, combing your hair, adjusting your robe, popping a breath mint, and preparing the gifts you'd brought. While you cooled your heels and warmed your  hands at the elaborate fireplace, you might look at some of the paintings—among the finest in the palace, worthy of any museum in the world.

The Rape of Europa (on the wall opposite the fireplace), by Paolo Veronese, most likely shocked many small-town visitors with its risqué subject matter. Here Zeus, the king of the Greek gods, appears in the form of a bull with a foot fetish, seducing a beautiful earthling, while cupids spin playfully overhead. The Venetian Renaissance looked back to pagan Greek and Roman art, a big change from the saints and crucifixions of the Middle Ages. This painting doesn't portray the abduction in a medieval condemnation of sex and violence, but rather as a celebration in cheery pastel colors of the earthy, optimistic spirit of the Renaissance.

Tintoretto's ***Bacchus and Ariadne*** (to the right of the fireplace) is another colorful display of Venice's sensual tastes. The God of Wine seeks a threesome, offering a ring to the mortal Ariadne, who's being crowned with stars by Venus, who turns slowly in zero gravity. The ring is the center of a spinning wheel of flesh, with the three arms like spokes.

But wait, the doge is ready for us. Let's go in.

• *Enter the next room and approach your imaginary doge.*

Collegio Hall (Sala del Collegio)

Flanked by his cabinet of six advisers—one for each Venetian neighborhood—the doge would sit on the wood-paneled platform at the far end to receive ambassadors, who laid their gifts at his feet and pleaded their countries' cases. All official ceremonies, such as the ratification of treaties, were held here.

At other times, it was the "Oval Office" where the doge and his cabinet (the executive branch) met privately to discuss proposals to give to the legislature, pull files from the cabinets (along the right wall) regarding business with Byzantium, or rehearse a meeting with the pope. The wooden benches around the sides (where they sat) are original. The clock on the wall is a backward-running 24-hour clock with Roman numerals and a sword for hands.

The **ceiling** is 24-karat gold, with paintings by Veronese. These are not frescoes (painting on wet plaster), like those in the Sistine Chapel, but actual canvases painted in Veronese's studio and then placed on the ceiling. Within years, Venice's humidity would have melted frescoes like mascara.

The T-shaped painting of the woman with the spider web (on the ceiling, opposite the big window) represents the Venetian symbol of ***Discussion.*** You can imagine the webs of truth and lies woven in this room by the doge's scheming advisers.

In ***Mars and Neptune with Campanile and Lion*** (the ceiling painting near the entrance), Veronese presents four symbols of the Republic's strength—military, sea trade, city, and government (plus a cherub about to be circumcised by the Campanile).

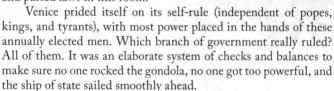

• *Enter the large Senate Hall.*

Senate Hall (Sala del Senato)

While the doge presided from the stage, senators mounted the podium (middle of the wall with windows) to address their 120 colleagues. The legislators, chaired by the doge, debated and passed laws in this room.

Venice prided itself on its self-rule (independent of popes, kings, and tyrants), with most power placed in the hands of these annually elected men. Which branch of government really ruled? All of them. It was an elaborate system of checks and balances to make sure no one rocked the gondola, no one got too powerful, and the ship of state sailed smoothly ahead.

Tintoretto's large *Triumph of Venice* on the ceiling (central painting, best viewed from the top) shows the city in all its glory. Lady Venice is up in heaven with the Greek gods, while barbaric lesser nations swirl up to give her gifts and tribute. Do you get the feeling the Venetian aristocracy was proud of its city?

On the wall are two large clocks, one of which has the signs of the zodiac and phases of the moon. And there's one final oddity in this room, in case you hadn't noticed it yet. In one of the wall paintings (above the entry door), there's actually a doge...not kneeling.

• *Exiting the Senate Hall, pass again through the Room of the Four Doors, then around the corner into a hall with a semicircular platform at the far end.*

Hall of the Council of Ten (Sala del Consiglio dei Dieci)

By the 1400s, Venice had a worldwide reputation for swift, harsh, and secret justice. The dreaded Council of Ten—10 judges, plus the doge and his six advisers—met here to dole out punishment to traitors, murderers, and "morals" violators. (Note the 17 wood panels where they presided.)

Slowly, they developed into a CIA-type unit with their own force of police officers, guards, spies, informers, and even assassins.

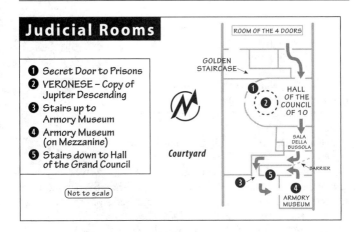

They had their own budget and were accountable to no one, soon making them the de facto ruling body of the "Republic." It seemed no one was safe from the spying eye of the "Terrible Ten." You could be accused anonymously (by a letter dropped into a Mouth of Truth), swept off the streets, tried, judged, and thrown into the dark dungeons in the palace for the rest of your life without so much as a Miranda warning.

It was in this room that the Council decided who lived or died, and who was decapitated, tortured, or merely thrown in jail. The small, hard-to-find **door** leading off the platform (the fifth panel to the right of center) leads through secret passages to the prisons and torture chambers.

The large, central, oval ceiling painting by Veronese (a copy of the original stolen by Napoleon and still in the Louvre) shows *Jupiter Descending from Heaven to Strike Down the Vices,* redundantly informing the accused that justice in Venice was swift and harsh. To the left of that, Juno showers Lady Venice with coins, crowns, and peace.

Though the dreaded Council of Ten was eventually disbanded, today their descendants enforce the dress code at St. Mark's Basilica.

• *Pass through the next room, turn right, and head up the stairs to the Armory Museum.*

Armory Museum (L'Armeria)

The aesthetic of killing is beyond me, but I must admit I've never seen a better collection of halberds, falchions, ranseurs, targes, morions, and brigandines in my life. The weapons in these three rooms make you realize the important role the military played in keeping the East-West trade lines open.

Room 1: In the glass case on the right, you'll see the suit of

DOGE'S PALACE

armor worn by the great Venetian mercenary general, Gattamelata (far right, on horseback), as well as "baby's first armor" (how soon they grow up!). A full suit of armor could weigh 66 pounds. Before gunpowder, crossbows (look up) were made still more lethal by turning a crank on the end to draw the bow with extra force.

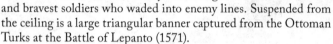

Room 2: In the thick of battle, even horses needed helmets. The hefty broadswords were brandished two-handed by the strongest and bravest soldiers who waded into enemy lines. Suspended from the ceiling is a large triangular banner captured from the Ottoman Turks at the Battle of Lepanto (1571).

Room 3: At the far (left) end of the room is a very, very early (17th-century) attempt at a 20-barrel machine gun. On the walls and weapons, the "C-X" insignia means that this was the private stash of the "Council of Ten."

Room 4: In this room, rifles and pistols enter the picture. Don't miss the glass case in the corner, with a tiny crossbow, some torture devices (including an effective-looking thumbscrew), the wooden "devil's box" (a clever item that could fire in four directions at once), and a nasty, two-holed chastity belt. These disheartening "iron breeches" were worn by the devoted wife of the Lord of Padua. Out the windows are fine views of San Giorgio Maggiore.

• *Exit the Armory Museum (after enjoying a closer look at that early machine gun). Go downstairs, turn left, and pass through the long hall that's lined with wood-carved benches and has a wood-beam ceiling. Now turn right and open your eyes as wide as you can to see the...*

Hall of the Grand Council (Sala del Maggiore Consiglio)

It took a room this size to contain the grandeur of the Most Serene Republic. This huge room (175 by 80 feet) could accommodate up to 2,600 people at one time. The engineering is remarkable. The ceiling is like the deck of a ship—its hull is the rooftop, creating a huge attic above that.

The doge presided from the raised **dais,** while the nobles—the backbone of the empire—filled the center and lined the long walls. Nobles were generally wealthy men over 25, but the title had less to do with money than with long bloodlines. In theory, the doge, the Senate, and the Council of Ten were all subordinate to the Grand Council of nobles who elected them.

On the wall over the doge's throne is Tintoretto's monsterpiece, **_Paradise,_** the largest oil painting in the world. At 570 square

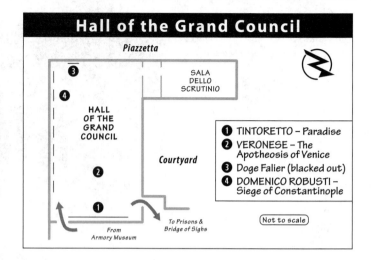

Hall of the Grand Council

Piazzetta

SALA DELLO SCRUTINIO

HALL OF THE GRAND COUNCIL

Courtyard

1 TINTORETTO – Paradise
2 VERONESE – The Apotheosis of Venice
3 Doge Falier (blacked out)
4 DOMENICO ROBUSTI – Siege of Constantinople

Not to scale

To Prisons & Bridge of Sighs

From Armory Museum

---

feet, it could be sliced up to wallpaper an apartment with enough left over for placemats.

Christ and Mary are at the top of heaven, surrounded by 500 people. It's rush hour in heaven, and all the good Venetians made it. The painting leaves you feeling that you get to heaven not by being a good Christian, but by being a good Venetian. Tintoretto worked on this in the last years of his long life. On the day it was finished, his daughter died. He got his brush out again and painted her as saint number 501. She's dead center with the blue skirt, hands clasped, getting sucked up to heaven. (At least, that's what an Italian tour guide told me.)

Veronese's *The Apotheosis of Venice* (on the ceiling at the Tintoretto end—view it from the top) is a typically unsubtle work showing Lady Venice being crowned a goddess by an angel.

Ringing the top of the hall are portraits, in chronological order, of the first 76 doges. The one at the far end that's blacked out (in the left corner) is the notorious **Doge Marin Falier,** who opposed the will of the Grand Council in 1355. He was tried for treason, beheaded, and airbrushed from history.

Along the entire wall to the right of Paradise, the *Siege of Constantinople* (by Tintoretto's son, Domenico Robusti) shows Venice's greatest military (if not moral) victory, the conquest of the fellow-Christian city of Constantinople during the Fourth Crusade (1204, see sidebar on page 98). The mighty walls of Constantinople

DOGE'S PALACE

repelled every attack for nearly a thousand years. But the sneaky Venetians (in the fifth painting) circled around back and attacked where the walls rose straight up from the water's edge. Skillful Venetian oarsmen cozied their galleys right up to the dock, allowing soldiers to scoot along crossbeams attached to the masts and on to the top of the city walls. In the foreground, an archer cranks up his crossbow. The gates are opened,

the Byzantine emperor parades out to surrender, and tiny Doge Dandolo says, "Let's go in and steal some bronze horses."

But soon Venice would begin its long slide into historical oblivion. One by one, the Ottomans gobbled up Venice's trading outposts. In the West, the rest of Europe ganged up on Venice to reduce her power. By 1500, Portugal had broken Venice's East-West trade monopoly by finding a sea route to the East around the southern tip of Africa. To top it off, despite winning a famous victory in the bloody Battle of Lepanto in 1571 (depicted in paintings in the adjoining Sala dello Scrutinio), Venice's reputation as a naval power began to suffer; their ships could not compete with Spain's more modern, more effective armada. Over the centuries, Venice remained a glorious city, but not the world power she once was. Finally, in 1797, the French general Napoleon marched into town shouting, *"Liberté, égalité, fraternité."* The Most Serene Republic was finally conquered, and the last doge was deposed in the name of modern democracy.

Out the windows (if they're open) is a fine view of the domes of the basilica, the palace courtyard below, and Paul Newman.

The adjoining **Sala dello Scrutinio** features paintings bursting with action. This room overlooks the Piazzetta; from its balcony, a newly elected doge was presented to the people of Venice. A noble would announce, "Here is your doge, if it pleases you." That was fine, until one time when the people weren't pleased. From then on they just said, "Here is your doge."

• *Consider reading about the prisons here in the Grand Council Hall, where there are more benches and fewer rats.*

To reach the prisons, exit the Grand Hall by squeezing through the door to the left of Tintoretto's monsterpiece. Follow signs for Prigioni/ Ponte dei Sospiri, *passing through several rooms. In a room adjoining Room 31, you'll find a narrow staircase going down, following signs to the prisons. (Don't miss it, or you'll miss the prisons altogether and end up at the bookshop near the exit.) Then cross the covered Bridge of Sighs over the canal to the prisons. Start your visit in the cells to your left.*

Prisons

The palace had its own dungeons. In the privacy of his own home, a doge could oversee the sentencing, torturing, and jailing of political

cal opponents. The most notorious cells were "the wells" in the basement, so-called because they were deep, wet, and cramped.

By the 1500s, the wells were full of political prisoners. New prisons were built across the canal (to the east of the palace) and connected with a covered bridge.

Medieval justice was harsh. The cells consisted of cold stone with heavily barred windows, a wooden plank for a bed, a shelf, and a bucket. (My question: What did they put on the shelf?) You can feel the cold and damp.

Circle the cells. Notice the carvings made by prisoners—from olden days up until 1930—on some of the stone windowsills of the cells, especially in the far corner of the building.

While a small taste of the prisons is enough for most visitors, if you have more time and interest, explore the rest of the prisons (following signs for *Complete Tour*). You can descend lower to the cells known as "the wells." Or stay on this floor, where there's a room displaying ceramic shards found in archaeological digs. Adjoining that are more cells, including the farthest cell, where you can see the bored prisoners' compelling and sometimes artistic graffiti. The singing gondoliers outside are a reminder of how tantalizingly close these pitiful prisoners were to one of the world's finest cities.

• *Wherever you roam, you'll end up where you entered. Now recross the...*

Bridge of Sighs

According to romantic legend, criminals were tried and sentenced in the palace, then marched across the canal here to the dark prisons. On this bridge, they got one last look at Venice. They gazed out at the sky, the water, and the beautiful buildings.

• *As you cross the Bridge of Sighs, pause to look through the marble-trellised windows at all the tourists and the heavenly Church of San Giorgio Maggiore. Heave one last sigh and leave the palace.*

CORRER
MUSEUM TOUR

Museo Correr

A doge's hat, gleaming statues by Canova, and paintings by the illustrious Bellini family—for some people, that's a major museum; for others, it's a historical bore. But the Correr Museum has one more thing to offer, and that's a quiet refuge—a place to rise above St. Mark's Square when the piazza is too hot, too rainy, or too overrun with tourists. Besides, the museum is included if you've bought a ticket to the Doge's Palace...whether you want it or not. Those who enter are rewarded with an easy-to-manage overview of Venice's art and history.

Orientation

Cost: €16 combo-ticket also includes the Doge's Palace and the two lesser museums inside the Correr (National Archaeological Museum and the Monumental Rooms of the Marciana National Library—described briefly in this chapter).

Tickets to tour the Clock Tower include admission to the Correr but not the Doge's Palace (€12.50, requires reservation, see page 40).

Hours: Daily April-Oct 10:00-19:00, Nov-March 10:00-17:00, last entry one hour before closing.

Getting There: The entrance is on St. Mark's Square in Napoleon's wing—the building at the far end of the square, opposite the basilica. Climb the staircase to the first-floor ticket office and bookstore.

Information: English descriptions are provided throughout. Tel. 041-240-5211, http://correr.visitmuve.it.

Length of This Tour: Allow one hour. With less time, stick to the first floor (Rooms 2-18 only), and skip the second-floor paintings.

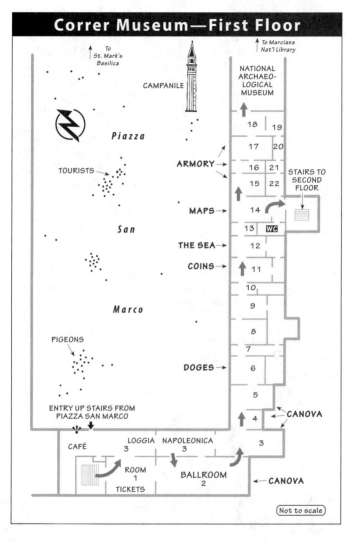

Correr Museum—First Floor

To St. Mark's Basilica

To Marciana Nat'l Library

CAMPANILE

NATIONAL ARCHAEO-LOGICAL MUSEUM

Piazza

TOURISTS →

ARMORY →

18   19
17   20
16   21
15   22

STAIRS TO SECOND FLOOR

San

MAPS →

14

13   WC

THE SEA →

12

COINS →

11

Marco

10
9
8
7

PIGEONS

DOGES →

6

5

ENTRY UP STAIRS FROM PIAZZA SAN MARCO

4   ← CANOVA

LOGGIA 3   NAPOLEONICA 3

CAFÉ

3

ROOM 1

BALLROOM 2

TICKETS

← CANOVA

Not to scale

Baggage Check: Free and mandatory for bags bigger than a large purse.

Photography: Not allowed.

Cuisine Art: The elegant museum café has good sandwiches and a few tables with outstanding views of St. Mark's Square (€7 *panini*, €10-13 salads, €4 cappuccino).

Starring: Canova statues, Venetian historical artifacts, the Bellini family, and a Carpaccio.

CORRER

The Tour Begins

The Correr Museum gives you admission and access to three connected museums—the Correr proper (which we'll see), the National Archaeological Museum, and the Marciana National Library.

The Correr itself is on three long, skinny floors that parallel St. Mark's Square. This tour covers the first two floors: The first floor contains Canova statues and Venetian history; the second floor displays a chronological overview of Venetian paintings. In this museum in particular, many paintings can rotate places or be out on loan at any given time. Don't get flustered if you can't find a described work of art—just keep on browsing through the Correr's halls.

First Floor

• *Buy your ticket. After entering, you'll likely find yourself in the long, skinny Room 3, the Loggia Napoleonica. From there, turn right into the large ballroom (Room 2). Note that, because of temporary exhibits, you may end up entering Room 2 directly from the bookshop—or Room 2 may be closed altogether.*

Room 2 (Ballroom)

Canova—*Orpheus and Eurydice*
(*Orfeo*, 1775-1776; *Euridice*, 1775)

Orpheus is leading his beloved back from hell when she is tugged from behind by the cloudy darkness. She calls for help. Orpheus

looks back and smacks his forehead in horror...but he can do nothing to help, and he has to hurry on.

In this youthful work, Venice's greatest sculptor, Antonio Canova, already shows elements of his later style: high-polished, slender, beautiful figures; an ensemble arrangement, with more than one figure; open space between the figures that's almost as compelling as the figures themselves; and a statue group that's interesting from many angles.

Carved by a teenage Canova, this piece captures the Rococo spirit of Venice in the late 1700s—elegant and beautiful, but tinged with bittersweet loss. Even Canova's later works—which were more sober, minimalist, and emotionally restrained—retained the elegance and romantic sentiment of the last days of the Venetian Republic.

Antonio Canova (1757-1822)

Son of a Venetian stonemason, Canova grew up with a chisel in his hand in a studio along the Grand Canal, precociously

mastering the sentimental, elegant Rococo style of the late 1700s. At 23, he went to Rome and beyond, studying ancient statues at the recently discovered ruins of Pompeii. These archaeological finds inspired a new Renaissance-style revival of the classical style. Canova's pure, understated elegance and "neo"-classical style soon became the rage all over Europe.

Called to Paris, Canova became Napoleon's court sculptor and carved perhaps his best-known work: Napoleon's sister as Venus, reclining on a couch (now in the Borghese Gallery, in Rome). Canova combined Rococo sentiment and elegance with the cool, minimal lines of classicism.

• *Enter the long hallway known as the Loggia Napoleonica, and admire its views over St. Mark's Square.*

Room 3 (Loggia Napoleonica)

Find Canova's pyramid-shaped model of the **Monument to Titian** *(Monumento a Tiziano, 1795).* Canova intended this design (based on the pyramid of Gaius Cestius in Rome) for a tomb for the painter Titian. But it was used instead for the tomb of an Austrian princess in Vienna, as well as for Canova's own memorial in the Frari Church (for more on Titian's and Canova's monuments, see page 155).

• *Continue on into Room 4.*

Room 4

Canova—*Daedalus and Icarus* (*Dedalo e Icaro*, 1778-1779)

Serious Daedalus straps wax-and-feather wings, which he's just crafted, onto his son's shoulders. The boy is thrilled with the new toy, not knowing what we know—that the wax in the wings will soon melt in the sun and plunge him to his death. Daedalus' middle-aged, sagging skin contrasts with Icarus'

supple form. Canova, a stonemason's son, displays the tools of the family trade on the base.

Canova was only 20 when Venice's procurator commissioned this work from the hometown prodigy. It was so realistic that it caused a stir—skeptics accused Canova of not really sculpting it, but making it from plaster casts of live humans.

Room 5

Canova—*Cupid and Psyche* (*Amore e Psiche*, c. 1787)

Though not a great painting, this is Canova's 2-D version of a famous scene he set in stone (now in the Louvre). The two lovers spiral around each other in the never-ending circle of desire. The two bodies and Cupid's two wings form an X. But the center of the composition is the empty space that separates their hungry lips.

Canova—*Paris* (*Paride*, 1807)

The guy with black measles is not a marble statue of Paris; it's a plaster of Paris, a life-size model that Canova used in carving the real one in stone. The dots are sculptor's "points," which tell the sculptor how far into the block he should chisel to establish the figure's rough outline.

Other Canovas

The other large statues in the Canova rooms are either lesser works or more plaster *(gesso)* studies for works later executed in marble. You'll also see small clay models in which Canova worked out ideas before chiseling into an expensive block of marble.

• *Enter the world of Venice's doges. On an easel in Room 6, find a doge portrait.*

Room 6: The Doge

Lazzaro Bastiani—*Portrait of Francesco Foscari* (*Ritratto di Francesco Foscari*, c. 1460)

Foscari, dressed in the traditional brocaded robe and cap with cloth earflaps, introduces us to the powerful, regal world of the doges, the "elected princes" who served as ceremonial symbols of the glorious Republic of Venice.

CORRER

The Doge's World

While some doges were powerful dictators, and others merely doddering figureheads, all of Venice's rulers were expected to put on a good show at official events. St. Mark's Square was the site of many ceremonial parades. At the head came flag bearers and trumpet players sounding a fanfare. Next came the bigwigs, the archbishop, the bearer of the doge cap, the doge's chair, and finally Il Serenissimo himself, under an umbrella. Noble ladies looked on from the windows above—the very windows of today's Correr Museum.

The process of electing a new doge was weirdly complicated: Thirty nobles were chosen by casting lots, then 21 of them were eliminated by lots. The remaining 9 elected 40 nobles, whose number was whittled down to 25 by lots...and so on through several more steps, until, finally, 41 electors—chosen by their peers and by chance—selected the next doge. It's all as baffling as...well, the American Electoral College.

Foscari (1373-1457, buried in the Frari Church) became doge when Venice was at its historical peak as a prosperous sea-trading empire, with peaceful ties to eastern Ottomans and mainland Europeans. He has a serene look of total confidence...a look that would slowly melt as he led Venice on a 31-year war of expansion that devastated northern Italy, embroiled Venice in messy European politics, and eventually drained the city's coffers. Meanwhile, the Ottomans captured Constantinople. By the time the Venetian Senate "impeached" Foscari, forcing his resignation, Venice was sapped, soon to be surpassed by the new maritime powers of Spain and Portugal.

In the glass case, find doge memorabilia, including the funny **doge cap** with a single horn at the back, often worn over a cloth cap with earflaps.

• *High on the wall opposite the room's entrance, find the large painting by...*

CORRER

Andrea Michieli—*Arrival at San Marco of Dogaressa Morosina Grimani* (*Sbarco a San Marco della Dogaressa Morosina Grimani*, c. 1597)

Although doges were men, several wives were crowned with ceremonial titles. This painting shows coronation ceremonies along the water by the Piazzetta. The lagoon is jammed with boats. Notice the Doge's Palace on the right, the Marciana National Library on the left (designed by Jacopo Sansovino), and the Campanile and Clock Tower in the distance. The dogaressa (left of center, in yellow, wearing her doge cap tilted back) arrives to receive the front-door key to the Doge's Palace.

The doge's private boat, the *Bucintoro* (docked at lower left, with red roof), has brought the First Lady and her entourage of red-robed officials, court dwarves, musicians, dancers, and ladies in formal wear. She walks toward the World Theater (on the right, in the water), a floating pavilion used for public ceremonies.

• *The displays in Rooms 7-10 change often. Browse the exhibits, but also appreciate the fact that these rooms were once government offices.*

Rooms 7-10: Government Offices

Some of the rich furnishings in these rooms—pictures of doge processions (often in Room 7); rare books in walnut bookcases and a Murano chandelier under a wood-beamed ceiling (Room 8); and portraits of political bigwigs—are reminders that this wing once housed the administrative offices of a wealthy, sophisticated, trade-oriented republic.

• *Move to Room 11 to view Venetian coins. The collection runs chronologically clockwise around the room.*

Room 11: Coins and the Treasury

The Venetian ducat weighed only a bit more than a US penny, but was mostly gold (by decree, 99 percent pure gold, weighing 3.5

grams). First minted around 1280 (find Giovanni Dandolo's *zecchino*, or "sequin," in the first glass case to the right of the door that leads into the next room), it became the strongest currency in all Europe for nearly 700 years, eventually replacing the Florentine florin. In Renaissance times, 100 ducats would be an excellent salary for a year, with a single ducat worth about $1,000. The most common design shows Christ on the "heads" side, standing in an oval of stars. "Tails" features the current doge kneeling before St. Mark and the inscription "sacred money of Venice" *(SM Veneti)*.

Hanging above the newest coins, find **Tintoretto's painting** of three red-robed treasury officials who handled ducats in these offices (*St. Justina and the Treasurers*, 1580). The richness of their fur-lined robes suggests the almost religious devotion that officials were expected to have as caretakers of the "sacred money" of Venice.

Room 12: Venice and the Sea

Venice's wealth came from its sea trade. Raw materials from Europe were exchanged for luxury goods from eastern lands controlled by Muslim Ottomans and Byzantine Christians.

Models of Galleys *(Modello di Galera)*

These fast oar- and wind-powered warships rode shotgun for Venice's commercial fleets plying the Mediterranean. With up to 150 men (four per oar, some prisoners, mostly proud professionals) and three horizontal sails, they could cruise from Venice to Constantinople in about a month. In battle, they specialized in turning on a dime to aim cannons, or in quickly building up speed to ram other ships with their formidable prows. Also displayed are large lanterns from a galley's stern.

• *Find two similar paintings depicting...*

The Battle of Lepanto (Battaglia di Lepanto, c. 1571)

The two paintings (flanking the door behind the galleys, by unknown Venetian artists) capture the confusion of a famous battle

fought off the coast of Greece in 1571 between Muslim Ottomans and a coalition of Christians. This battle ended Ottoman dominance at sea. Sort it out by their flags. The turbaned Ottomans fought under the crescent moon. On the Christian side, Venetians had the winged lion, the pope's troops flew the cross, and Spain was marked with the Habsburg eagle.

The fighting was fierce and hand-to-hand as the combatants boarded each other's ships and cannons blasted away point-blank. Miguel de Cervantes fought in this battle; he lost his hand and had to pen *Don Quixote* one-handed.

The Christians won, sinking 113 enemy ships and killing up to 30,000. It was a major psychological victory, as it was a turning point in the Ottoman threat to Europe.

But for Venice, it marked the end of an era. The city lost 4,000 men and many ships, and never fully recovered its trading empire in Ottoman lands. Moreover, Spain's cannon-laden sailing ships proved to be masters of the waves, making Spain the next true naval power. Venice's shallow-hulled galleys, so swift in the placid Mediterranean, were no match on the high seas.

Room 13: The Arsenale

The Arsenale shipbuilding center, located near the tail of Venice, was a rectangular, artificial harbor surrounded by workshops where

ships could be mass-produced as though on a modern assembly line (but it was the workers who moved). If needed, they could crank out a galley a day. Look for various sketches and paintings of the Arsenale, including a 17th-century pen-and-ink plan *(Pianta dell'Arsenale)* by Antonio di Natale showing a bird's-eye view. The Arsenale's entrance (lower left of Natale's painting) is still guarded today by the two lions.

Room 14: The Map Room (Venezia Forma Urbis)

Old maps show a city relatively unchanged over the centuries, hemmed in by water. Find your hotel on Jacopo de' Barbari's big

black-and-white map from 1500. There's the Arsenale in the fish's tail. There's Piazza San Marco with a church standing where the Correr Museum entrance is today. The Accademia Bridge hadn't been built yet (nor had the modern train station). We'll see more about Barbari's impressive map upstairs.

Rooms 15-18: Armory

You'll find weapons from medieval times to the advent of gunpowder—maces, armor, swords, Ottoman pikes, rifles, cannons, shields, and a teeny-tiny pistol hidden in a book (in a glass case in Room 17).

• *Those interested in visiting the National Archaeological Museum (Greek and Roman statues) and the impressive Marciana National Library can reach them from Rooms 18 and 19 (included with Correr Museum admission). It's a bit of a detour to the library, and some may wish to skip ahead to "Venetian Painting."*

National Archaeological Museum and Marciana National Library

In the archaeological museum, you pass through room after room of ancient statues (mostly copies that aren't that ancient). You eventually reach the library, famous in Renaissance times because Venice was a major center of printing and secular knowledge. The library displays antique globes and manuscripts. On the ceiling are *tondi* (round) paintings of virtues and allegories of the liberal arts, such as mathematics, geometry, and music. The three *tondi* immediately above where you enter are by Paolo Veronese. The walls are richly decorated with portraits of renowned scholars and ancient philosophers who twist and turn in their niches in classical Baroque style. The smaller room at the end of the hall features Roman copies of Greek statuary and a trompe l'oeil ceiling that makes the wood-beam ceiling appear even higher. The painting in the center of the ceiling by Titian shows Lady Wisdom seated in the clouds reading a book and a scroll.

• *Backtrack to Room 14 (WCs nearby), then head upstairs to the second floor, following signs to* La Quadreria—Picture Gallery. *Enter Room 25.*

Second Floor

Venetian Painting

The painting highlights (the Bellinis) are located at the far end of this wing, and you have permission to hurry there. But along the way, trace the development of Venetian painting from golden Byzantine icons to Florentine-inspired 3-D to the natural beauty of Bellini and Carpaccio.

Room 25

Paolo Veneziano—
Six Saints (Sei Santi, 1340s)

Gold-backed saints combine traits from Venice's two stylistic sources: Byzantine (serene, elongated, somber, and iconic, with gold background, like the mosaics in St. Mark's) and the Gothic of mainland Europe (curvy, expressive bodies posed at a three-quarter angle, colorful robes, and individualized faces).

Room 26

Lorenzo Veneziano—*Figures and Episodes of Saints (Figure e Storie di Santi, second half of 14th century)*

Influence from the mainland puts icons in motion, adding drama to the telling of the lives of the saints (here, in the small scenes above

CORRER

BELLINI PAINTINGS → 36 | 34 ← MESSINA'S PIETÀ

33 ← BREUGHEL

BARBARI WOODCUT
32
31

CARPACCIO → 38

29

Piazza San Marco
27 | 28

26

25 PAOLO VENEZIANO

STAIRS FROM FIRST FLOOR

(Not to scale)

the three saints). St. Nicholas grabs the executioner's sword and lifts him right off the ground before he even knows what's happening.

Room 27: Flamboyant Gothic

Architectural fragments of Gothic buildings remind us that Venice's distinctive architecture is Italian Gothic, filtered through Eastern exoticism. You'll see examples, in both paint and stone, of pointed arches decorated with the flame-like curlicues that gave the Flamboyant Gothic style its name.

Room 29: International Gothic

Master of the Jarves Cassoni—*Story of Alatiel* (*Storie di Alatiel*, first half of 15th century)

As humanism spread, so did art that was not exclusively religious. These scenes, painted on the panels of a chest, depict a story from Boccaccio's bawdy *Decameron*. Done in the elegant, detailed naturalism of the International Gothic style, the painting emphasizes decorative curves—curvy filigree patterns in clothes, curvy boats, curvy sails, curvy waves, curvy horses' rumps—all enjoyed as a pleasing pattern.

Room 31: Ferrarese Painters

Baldassare Estense—*Portrait of a Young Man* (*Ritratto di Gentiluomo*, c. 1475)

The young man in red is not a saint, king, or pope, but an ordinary citizen painted, literally, wart and all. On the window ledge is a

CORRER

strongly foreshortened book. And behind the young man, the curtain opens to reveal a new world—a spacious 3-D vista courtesy of the Tuscan Renaissance.

Room 32

Jacopo de' Barbari—
Perspective View of Venice
(*Veduta Prospettica di Venezia*, 1500)

How little Venice has changed in 500 years! Barbari's large, intricately detailed woodcut of the city put his contemporaries in a unique position—a mile up in the air, looking down on the rooftops. He chronicles nearly every church, alleyway, and gondola. Both the final product and the carved wood block from which it was printed are on display, a tribute to Barbari's painstaking labor.

Room 33: Flemish Artists

Pieter Brueghel II—
Adoration of the Magi
(*Adorazione dei Magi*, 1617-1633)

The detailed, everyday landscapes of Northern masters strongly influenced Venetian artists. Lost in this snowy scene of the secular working world is Baby Jesus in a stable (lower left), worshipped by the Magi. Venetians learned that landscape creates its own mood, and humans don't have to be the center of every painting.

Room 34

Antonello da Messina—*Pietà*
(*La Pietà*, c. 1475)

The Sicilian painter Messina wowed Venice with this work when he visited in 1475, bringing a Renaissance style and new painting techniques. After a thousand years of standing rigidly on medieval crucifixes, the body of Christ finally softens into a natural human posture. The scene is set in a realistic, distant landscape.

Remember this work, as I'll refer to it later.

Room 36: The Bellini Family (I Bellini)

One family single-handedly brought Venetian painting into the Renaissance—the Bellinis.

Jacopo Bellini—*Crucifixion* (*La Crocifissione*, c. 1450)

Father Jacopo (c. 1400-1470) had studied in Florence when Donatello and Brunelleschi were pioneering 3-D naturalism.

Daughter Cecilia (not a painter) married the painter Mantegna, whose precise lines and statuesque figures influenced his brothers-in-law.

Gentile Bellini—*Portrait of Doge Mocenigo* (*Ritratto del Doge Mocenigo*, c. 1478-1485)

Elder son Gentile (c. 1429-1507) took over the family business and established a reputation for documenting Venice's rulers and official ceremonies. His straightforward style and attention to detail capture the ordinary essence of this doge.

Giovanni Bellini—*Crucifixion* (*La Crocifissione*, c. 1453-1455)

Younger son Giovanni (c. 1430-1516) became the most famous Bellini, the man who pioneered new techniques and subject matter, trained Titian and Giorgione, and almost single-handedly invented the Venetian High Renaissance.

Compare this early *Crucifixion* (young Giovanni's earliest documented work) with his father's version. Young Giovanni weeds out all the crowded, medieval mourners, leaving only Mary and John. Behind, he paints a spacious (Mantegnesque) landscape, with a lake and mountains in the distance. Our eyes follow the winding road from Christ to the airy horizon, ascending like a soul to heaven.

Giovanni Bellini—*The Dead Christ Supported by Two Angels* (*Cristo Morto Sorretto da Due Angeli*, 1453-1455)

In another early work, Giovanni explores human anatomy, with exaggerated veins, a heaving diaphragm, and even a hint of pubic hair. Mentally compare this stiff, static work with Antonello da Messina's far more natural *Pietà*, done 20 years later, to see how far Giovanni still had to go. In fact, Giovanni was greatly influenced by Antonello, appreciating the full potential of the new invention of oil-based paint. Armed with this more transparent paint, he could add subtler shades of color and rely less on the sharply outlined forms we see here.

Giovanni Bellini— *Madonna and Child* (*Madonna col Bambino*, c. 1470-1475)

Though the canvas is a bit wrinkled, its subject is one Giovanni would paint again and again— lovely, forever-young Mary (often shown from the waist up) holding rosy-cheeked Baby Jesus. He portrayed the holiness of mother and child with a natural-looking, pastel-colored, soft-focus beauty.

Room 38

Vittore Carpaccio—*Two Venetian Gentlewomen* (*Due Dame Veneziane*, c. 1490)

Two well-dressed Venetians look totally bored, despite being surrounded by a wealth of exotic pets and amusements. One lady absentmindedly plays with a dog, while the other stares into space. Romantics imagined them to be kept ladies awaiting lovers, but the recent discovery of the once-missing companion painting tells us they're waiting for their menfolk to return from hunting. If you like Carpaccio, the Scuola Dalmata di San Giorgio (between St. Mark's Square and Arsenale) has the world's best collection; see page 58.

The colorful details and love of luxury are elements that would dominate the Venetian High Renaissance. Fascinating stuff, but my eyes—like theirs—are starting to glaze...

ACCADEMIA TOUR

Galleria dell'Accademia

The Accademia (ack-ah-DAY-mee-ah) is the greatest museum anywhere for Venetian Renaissance art and a good overview of painters whose works you'll see all over town. Venetian art is underrated and, I think, misunderstood. It's nowhere near as famous today as the work of the florescent Florentines, but—with historical slices of Venice, ravishing nudes, and very human Madonnas—it's livelier, more colorful, and simply more fun.

Orientation

Cost: €9.

Hours: Mon 8:15-14:00, Tue-Sun 8:15-19:15, last entry 45 minutes before closing.

Avoiding Lines: Just 360 people are allowed into the gallery at one time, so you may have to wait. It's most crowded on Monday mornings and whenever it rains; it's least crowded Tue-Sun mornings (before about 10:00) and late afternoons (after about 17:00). While it's possible to book tickets in advance (€1.50/ticket surcharge; either book online at www.gallerieaccademia.org or call 041-520-0345), it's generally not necessary if you avoid the busiest times.

Getting There: The museum faces the Grand Canal, just over the Accademia Bridge (vaporetto stop: Accademia). It's a 15-minute walk from St. Mark's Square—just follow the signs to *Accademia*.

Information: Some of the Accademia's rooms have information in English. The dull audioguide costs €6, and the bookshop sells guidebooks for €14. Tel. 041-522-2247, www.gallerieaccademia.org.

Renovation: This museum seems to be in a constant state of disar-

Accademia

ACCADEMIA

HIGH RENAISSANCE ROOM 10

ROOM 11

⓫ ⓾

To Zattere

To Eateries & Zattere

Camp. Calbo

⑧

⑨

ROOM 9

ROOM 6

ROOM 8

ROOM 7

Courtyard

(Not to Scale)

ROOM 12

RIO TERÀ ANTONIO FOSCARINI

ROOM 13

ROOM 5 ⑦

ROOM 2

EARLY REN.

④

ROOM 14

ROOM 4 ⑥ ⑤

ROOM 3

RIO TERÀ DE LA CARITÀ

ELEGANT DECAY

ROOM 16

ROOM 15

⓬ ROOM 20

⓭ ⑭

ROOM 17

Courtyard

MEDIEVAL ROOM 1

③

ROOM 19

ROOM 21

WC

To Cafés, Peggy Guggenheim Collection & La Salute

ROOM 18

ROOM 22

ROOM 24 ①

②

ROOM 23 "DISPLACED HIGHLIGHTS"

STAIRS

ENTRANCE (BELOW)

CAFE

To Frari & Ca' Rezzonico

■ PIZZA

WC

Campo de la Carità

To San Marco & Rialto

ACCADEMIA BRIDGE

Ⓥ Accademia

Grand Canal

① TITIAN – Presentation of the Virgin

② VENEZIANO – Madonna and Child with Two Donors

③ JACOBELLO – Coronation of the Virgin in Paradise

④ GIOVANNI BELLINI – Enthroned Madonna with Child

⑤ MANTEGNA – St. George

⑥ GIO. BELLINI – Madonna and Child between St. Catherine and Mary Magdalene

⑦ GIORGIONE – The Tempest

⑧ VERONESE – Feast in the House of Levi

⑨ TITIAN – Pietà

⑩ TINTORETTO – The Removal of St. Mark's Body

⑪ TIEPOLO – Discovery of the True Cross

⑫ CANALETTO – Perspective with Portico

⑬ GUARDI – San Giorgio Maggiore and the Giudecca

⑭ GENTILE BELLINI – Procession in St. Mark's Square

ray. A major expansion and renovation has been dragging on for years. Paintings come and go, and the actual locations of the pieces described here are likely to be way off. Still, the museum contains sumptuous art—the best in Venice. Be flexible: You'll probably just end up wandering around and matching descriptions to blockbuster paintings when you find them. If you don't find a particular piece where I've described it, check Room 23 (at the end of the tour), which seems to be their catchall holding pen for displaced art.

Length of This Tour: Allow one hour.

Baggage Check: You must use a locker for large bags (€1 deposit).

Photography: Not allowed.

Cuisine Art: For forgettable food at inflated prices but priceless Grand Canal views, **Bar Foscarini** is right next door (at the base of the Accademia Bridge); for a less expensive, far more characteristic Venetian experience, walk less than five minutes to the delightful **Enoteca Cantine del Vino Già Schiavi** *cicchetti* bar (both described on page 305, along with other options nearby). A cheap café is at the opposite end of the embankment from Bar Foscarini, and a handful of cafés line Calle Nuova Sant'Agnese, which connects this area to the Peggy Guggenheim Collection.

Nearby: While you're in the Accademia neighborhood, consider visiting the ✪ Ca' Rezzonico, ✪ Peggy Guggenheim Collection, historic ✪ La Salute Church, and Punta della Dogana contemporary art museum (see page 51).

Starring: Titian, Veronese, Giorgione, Bellini, and Tintoretto.

The Tour Begins

Venice—Swimming in Luxury

The Venetian love of luxury shines through in Venetian painting. We'll see grand canvases of colorful, spacious settings peopled with happy locals in extravagant clothes having a great time. The museum proceeds chronologically from the Middle Ages to the 1700s. But before we start at the medieval beginning, let's sneak a peek at a work by the greatest Venetian Renaissance master, Titian.

• *Buy your ticket, check your bag, and head upstairs to a large hall filled with gold-leaf altarpieces. At the top of the stairs, turn left and enter the small Room 24.*

Titian (Tiziano Vecellio)—*Presentation of the Virgin* (*Presentazione della Vergine*, 1534-1538)

A colorful crowd gathers at the foot of a stone staircase. A dog eats a bagel, a mother handles a squirming baby, an old lady sells eggs, and onlookers lean out the windows. Suddenly the crowd turns and

points at something. Your eye follows up the stairs to a larger-than-life high priest in a jeweled robe.

But wait! What's that along the way? In a pale blue dress that sets her apart from all the other colored robes, dwarfed by the enormous staircase and columns, the tiny, shiny figure of the child Mary almost floats up to the astonished priest. She's unnaturally small, easily overlooked at first glance. When we finally notice her, we realize all the more how delicate she is amid the bustling crowd, hard stone, and epic grandeur. Venetians love this painting and call it, appropriately enough, the "Little Mary."

The painting is a parade of colors. Titian (TEESH-un) leads your eyes from the massive buildings to the deep blue sky and mountains in the background to the bright red robe of the man in the crowd to glowing Little Mary. Titian painted the work especially for this room, fitting it neatly around the door on the right. The door on the left was added later, cutting into Titian's masterpiece.

This work is typical of Venetian Renaissance art. Here and throughout this museum, you will find: 1) bright, rich color; 2) big canvases; 3) Renaissance architectural backgrounds; 4) slice-of-life scenes of Venice; and 5) 3-D realism. It's a religious scene, yes, but it's really just an excuse to display secular splendor—Renaissance architecture, colorful robes, and human details.

Now that we've gotten a taste of Renaissance Venice at its peak, let's backtrack and see some of Titian's predecessors.

• *Return to Room 1, stopping at a painting (near the stairs) of Mary and Baby Jesus.*

Medieval Art

Paolo Veneziano—*Madonna and Child with Two Donors (Madonna col Bambino e Due Committenti, c. 1325)*

Mary sits in heaven. The child Jesus is a baby in a bubble, a symbol of his "aura" of holiness.

Notice how two-dimensional

and unrealistic this painting is. The sizes of the figures reflect their religious importance—Mary is huge, being the mother of Christ as well as the "Holy Mother Church." Jesus is next in size, then the two angels who crown Mary. Finally, in the corner, are two mere mortals kneeling in devotion. The golden halos let us know who's holy and who's not. Medieval Venetian artists, with their close ties to the East, borrowed techniques such as gold-leafing, frontal poses, and "iconic" faces from the religious icons of Byzantium (modern-day Istanbul).

Most of the paintings in Room 1 are altarpieces, intended to sit in the center of a church for the faithful to meditate on during services. Many feature the Virgin Mary being crowned in triumph. Very impressive. But it took Renaissance artists to remove Mary from her golden never-never land, clothe her in human flesh, and bring her down to the real world we inhabit.

• *On the left side of the room, you'll find...*

Jacobello del Fiore—*Coronation of the Virgin in Paradise* (*Incoronazione della Vergine in Paradiso*, 1438)

This swarming beehive of saints and angels is an attempt to cram as much religious information as possible into one space. The architectural setting is a clumsy try at three-dimensionality (the railings of the wedding-cake structure are literally glued on). The color-coordinated saints are simply stacked one on top of the other, rather than receding into the distance as they would in real life.

• *Enter Room 2 at the far end of this hall.*

Early Renaissance (1450-1500)

Only a few decades later, artists rediscovered the natural world and ways to capture it on canvas. With this Renaissance, or "rebirth," of the arts and attitudes of ancient Greece and Rome, painters took a giant leap forward. They weeded out the jumble of symbols, fleshed out cardboard characters into real people, and placed them in spacious 3-D settings.

Giovanni Bellini—*Enthroned Madonna with Child*, a.k.a. *San Giobbe Altarpiece* (*Madonna in Trono col Bambino*, c. 1480)

Mary and the Baby Jesus meet with saints beneath an arched half-dome, engaging in a sacred conversation (*sacra conversazione*). A trio of musician angels jams at her feet. In its original church setting, the painting's pillars and arches matched the real ones around it, as though Bellini had blown a hole in the wall and built another chapel, allowing us mortals to mingle with holies.

Giovanni Bellini (bell-EE-nee) takes only a few figures, places them in this spacious architectural setting, and balances them, half on one side of Mary and half on the other. Left to right, you'll find St. Francis (medieval founder of an order of friars), John the Baptist, Job, St. Dominic (founder of another order of monks), St. Sebastian, and St. Louis.

The painting has a series of descending arches. At the top is a Roman arch. Hanging below that is a triangular canopy. Then comes a pyramid-shaped "arch" formed by the figures themselves, with Mary's head at the peak, echoed below by the pose of the three musicians. Subconsciously, this creates a mood of serenity, order, and balance, not the hubbub of the *Coronation*. Look at St. Sebastian—even arrows can't disturb his serenity.

In Bellini's long career, he painted many altarpieces in the *sacra conversazione* formula: The Virgin and Child surrounded by

saints "conversing" informally about holy matters while listening to some tunes. The formula, developed in the 1430s and 1440s by Fra Angelico (1400-1455) and other Florentine artists, became a common Renaissance theme. Compare this painting with other *sacras* by Bellini in the Frari Church (see page 153) and the Church of San Zaccaria (see page 243).

• *Climb the small staircase and pass through Room 3 into the small Room 4.* **Note:** *Particularly after this point, some of the paintings described here may be missing. If you can't find them, look for them at the end of our tour, in Room 23.*

Andrea Mantegna—*St. George* (*San Giorgio*, c. 1460)

This Christian dragon slayer is essentially a Greek nude sculpture with armor painted on. He rests his weight on one leg in the same asymmetrical pose *(contrapposto)* as a classical sculpture, Michelangelo's *David*, or an Italian guy on the street corner. The doorway he stands in resembles a niche designed for a classical statue.

Mantegna (mahn-TAYN-yah) was trained in the Tuscan tradition, in which painters were like sculptors, "carving" out figures (like this) with sharp outlines, filling them in with color, and setting them in distant backdrops like the winding road behind George. When Mantegna married Giovanni Bellini's sister, he brought Florentine realism and draftsmanship to his in-laws.

St. George radiates Renaissance optimism—he's alert but relaxed, at rest but ready to spring into action, humble but confident. With the broken lance in his hand and the dragon at his feet, George is the strong Renaissance Man slaying the medieval dragon of superstition and oppression.

• *Find three women and a baby on a black background.*

Giovanni Bellini—*Madonna and Child between St. Catherine and Mary Magdalene* (*Madonna col Bambino tra Sta. Caterina e Maria Maddalena*, c. 1490)

In contrast to Mantegna's sharp-focus 3-D, this painting features three female heads on a flat plane with a black-velvet backdrop. Their features are soft, hazy, and atmospheric, glowing out of the darkness as though lit by soft candlelight. It's not sculptural line that's important here, but color—warm, golden, glowing flesh tones. The faces emerge from the canvas like cameos.

Bellini painted dozens of Madonna and Childs in his day. (Others are nearby.) This Virgin Mary is pretty, but she's upstaged by the sheer idealized beauty of Mary Magdalene (on the right). Mary Magdalene's hair is down, like the prostitute that legend says she was, yet she has a childlike face, thoughtful and repentant. This is the perfect image of the innocent woman who sinned by loving too much.

Bellini was the teacher of two more Venetian greats, Titian and Giorgione, schooling them in the new medium of oil painting. Mantegna painted *St. George* using tempera paint (pigments dissolved in egg yolk), while Bellini pioneered oils (pigments in vegetable oil)—a more versatile medium. Applying layer upon transparent layer, Bellini painted creamy complexions with soft outlines, bathed in an even light. His gift to the Venetian Renaissance was the "haze" he put over his scenes, giving them an idealized, glowing, serene, and much-copied atmosphere. (You can see more of Bellini's work at the Correr Museum, Frari Church, and the Church of San Zaccaria.)

• *Around the partition (in Room 5), you'll find...*

Giorgione (Giorgio da Castelfranco)—*The Tempest* (*La Tempesta*, c. 1505)

It's the calm before the storm. The atmosphere is heavy—luminous but ominous. There's a sense of mystery. Why is the woman nursing

her baby in the middle of the countryside? And the soldier—is he ogling her or protecting her? Will lightning strike? Do they know that the serenity of this beautiful landscape is about to be shattered by an approaching storm?

The mystery is heightened by contrasting elements. The armed soldier contrasts with the naked mother and her baby. The austere, ruined columns contrast with the lusciousness of Nature. And, most important, the stillness of the foreground scene is in direct opposition to the threatening storm in the background. The landscape itself is the main subject, creating a mood, regardless of what the painting is "about."

Giorgione (jor-JONE-ay) was as mysterious as his few paintings, yet he left a lasting impression. A student of Bellini, he learned to use haziness to create a melancholy mood of beauty. But nothing beautiful lasts—flowers fade, Mary Magdalenes grow old, and Giorgione died at 33. In *The Tempest*, the fleeting stillness is about to be shattered by the slash of lightning, the true center of the composition.

• *Exit and browse through several rooms. Continue up the five steps to the large Room 10.*

Venetian High Renaissance (1500-1600)— Titian, Veronese, and Tintoretto

Paolo Veronese—*Feast in the House of Levi* (*Convito in Casa di Levi*, 1573)

Parrrrty!! Stand about 10 yards away from this enormous canvas, to where it just fills your field of vision...and hey, you're invited. Venice loves the good life, and the celebration is in full swing. You're in a huge room with a great view of Venice. Everyone's dressed to kill in colorful silk and velvet robes. Conversation roars, and the servants bring on the food and drink.

This captures the Venetian attitude (more love, less attitude) as well as the style of Venetian Renaissance painting. Remember:

1) bright colors, 2) big canvases, 3) Renaissance architectural settings, 4) scenes of Venetian life, and 5) 3-D realism. Painters had mastered realism and now gloried in it.

The *Feast in the House of Levi* is, believe it or not, a religious work painted for a convent. The original title was *The Last Supper*. In the center of all the wild goings-on, there's Jesus, flanked by his disciples, sharing a final meal before his crucifixion.

This festive feast captures the optimistic spirit of Renaissance Venice. Life was a good thing and beauty was to be enjoyed. Renaissance men and women saw the divine in the beauties of Nature and glorified God by glorifying man.

Uh-uh, said the Church. In its eyes, the new humanism was the same as the old hedonism. The false spring of the Renaissance froze quickly after the Reformation, when half of Europe left the Catholic Church and became Protestant.

Veronese (vayr-oh-NAY-zay) was hauled before the Inquisition, the Church tribunal that punished heretics. What did he mean by painting such a bawdy Last Supper? With dwarf jesters? And apostles picking their teeth (between the columns, left of center)? And dogs and cats? And a black man, God forbid? And worst of all, some German soldiers—maybe even Protestants!—at the far right?

Veronese argued that it was just artistic license, so they asked to see his—it had expired. But the solution was simple. Rather than change the painting, just fine-tune the title. *Sì, no problema*. Veronese got out his brush, and *The Last Supper* became the *Feast in the House of Levi*, written in Latin on the railing to the left: *"FECIT D. COVI. MAGNV. LEVI"*.

Titian—*Pietà* (c. 1573)
Jesus has just been executed, and his followers grieve over his body before burying it. Titian painted this to hang over his own tomb.

Titian was the most famous painter of his day—perhaps even more famous than Michelangelo. He excelled in every subject: portraits of dukes, kings, and popes; racy nudes for their bedrooms; solemn altarpieces for churches; and pagan scenes from Greek mythology. He was cultured and witty, a fine musician and businessman—an all-around Renaissance kind of guy.

Titian was old when he painted this. He had seen the rise and decline of the Renaissance and had experienced much sadness in his own life. Unlike Titian's colorful and exuberant "Little Mary," done at the height of the Renaissance, this canvas is dark, the mood more somber.

The dead Christ is framed by a Renaissance arch like the one in Bellini's *Enthroned Madonna,* but here the massive stones overpower the figures, making them look puny and helpless. The lion statues are downright scary. Instead of the clear realism of Renaissance paintings, Titian uses rough, messy brushstrokes, a technique that would be picked up by the Impressionists three centuries later. Titian adds a dramatic compositional element—starting with the lion at lower right, a line of motion sweeps up diagonally along the figures, culminating in the grief-stricken Mary Magdalene, who turns away, flinging her arm and howling out loud.

The kneeling figure of an old, bald man is a self-portrait of the aging Titian, tending to the corpse of Jesus, who symbolizes the once powerful, now dead Renaissance Man. In the lower right, a painting-within-the-painting shows Titian and his son kneeling, asking the Virgin to spare them from the plague of 1576. Unfortunately, first the son and then the father succumbed.

• *On the opposite wall, find...*

Tintoretto (Jacopo Robusti)—*The Removal of St. Mark's Body (Trafugamento del Corpo di San Marco,* 1562-1566)

The event that put Venice on the map is frozen at its most dramatic moment. Muslim fundamentalists in Alexandria are about to burn St. Mark's body (there's the smoke from the fire in the center), when suddenly a hurricane appears miraculously, sending them running for cover. (See the wisps of baby-angel faces in the storm, blowing on the infidels? Look hard, on the left-hand side.) Meanwhile, Venetian merchants whisk away the body.

Tintoretto makes us part of the action. The square tiles in the courtyard run straight away from us, an extension of our reality, as though we could step right into the scene—or the merchants could carry Mark into ours.

Tintoretto would have made a great black-velvet painter. His colors burn with a metallic sheen, and he does everything possible to make his subject popular with common people.

In fact, Tintoretto was a common man himself, self-taught, who apprenticed only briefly with Titian before striking out on his own. He sold paintings in the marketplace in his youth and insisted on living in the poor part of town, even after he became famous.

Tintorettos abound here, in the next room, and throughout Venice. Look for these characteristics, some of which became stan-

ACCADEMIA

dard features of the Mannerist and Baroque art that followed the Renaissance: 1) heightened drama, violent scenes, strong emotions; 2) elongated bodies in twisting poses; 3) strong contrasts between dark and light; 4) bright colors; and 5) diagonal compositions.

(Tintoretto fans will want to see his "Sistine Chapel"; see the ✪ Scuola San Rocco Tour chapter.)

• *Spend some time in this room, the peak of the Venetian Renaissance and the climax of the museum. After browsing, enter Room 11 and find a large, round painting. Stand underneath it for the full effect.*

Elegant Decay (1600-1800)

Giovanni Battista Tiepolo—*Discovery of the True Cross* (*La Scoperta della Vera Croce*, c. 1745)

Tiepolo blasts open a sunroof and we gaze up into heaven. We (the viewers) stand in the hole where they've just dug up Christ's cross,

looking up dresses and nostrils as saints and angels cavort overhead.

Tiepolo was the last of the great colorful, theatrical Venetian painters. He took the colors, the grand settings, and the dramatic angles of previous Venetian masters and plastered them on the ceilings of Europe's Baroque palaces, such as the Royal Palace in Madrid, Spain; the Residenz in Würzburg, Germany; and the Ca' Rezzonico in Venice (✪ see the Ca' Rezzonico Tour chapter). This piece is from a church ceiling.

Tiepolo's strongly "foreshortened" figures are masterpieces of technical skill, making us feel as if the heavenly vision is taking place right overhead. Think back on those clumsy attempts at three-dimensionality we saw in the medieval room, and realize how far painting has come. The fresco fragments hanging around the corners of this room were salvaged from a church bombed in World War I.

• *Along the long corridor to your left, in Room 17, you'll find works of the later Venetians. (If this wing is closed, loop back the way you came and step through Room 24—with the giant Titian canvas we saw at the beginning of this tour—to reach Rooms 23 and 20.)*

Canaletto and Guardi: Views of Venice

By the 1700s, Venice had retired as a world power and become Europe's number-one tourist attraction. Wealthy offspring of the nobility traveled here to soak up its art and culture. They wanted souvenirs, and what better memento than a picture of the city itself?

Guardi and Canaletto painted "postcards" for visitors who lost their hearts to the romance of Venice. The city produced less art as it became art itself. Here are some familiar views of a city that has aged gracefully.

Canaletto (Giovanni Antonio Canal)— *Perspective with Portico (Prospettiva con Portico, 1765)*

Canaletto gives us a sharp-focus, wide-lens, camera's-eye perspective on the city. Although this view of a portico looks totally realistic, Canaletto has compressed the whole scene to allow us to see more than the human eye could realistically take in. We see the portico as though we were standing underneath it, yet we also see the entire portico at one glance. The pavement blocks, the lines of columns, and the slanting roof direct our eye to the far end, which looks very far away indeed. Canaletto even paints a coat of arms (at right) at a very odd angle, showing off his mastery of 3-D perspective.

Francesco Guardi—*San Giorgio Maggiore and the Giudecca (San Giorgio Maggiore e Giudecca, c. 1774)*

Unlike Canaletto, with his sharp-focus detail, Guardi sweetens Venice up with a haze of messy brushwork. In this familiar view across the water from St. Mark's Square, he builds a boatman with a few sloppy smudges of paint. Guardi catches the play of light at twilight, the shadows on the buildings, the green of the water and sky, the pink light off the distant buildings, the Venice that exists in the hearts of lovers—an Impressionist work a century ahead of its time.

• *At the end of the corner, turn left. Or, if the corridor is closed, circle back through Room 24. Either way, you'll wind up in a hallway; on the Grand Canal side is Room 23 (with "displaced highlights," explained next); and on the inland side is a WC and a smaller hallway leading to Room 20.*

Room 23: Displaced Highlights

This giant hall, divided by partitions, is where the Accademia tends to shuffle the items that have been pulled from their regular spots during the ongoing renovation. If you missed any of the works described up until now, use this book's photos to see if you can track them down now.

• *To wrap up the tour, go down the little hallway (between the WC and the stairs down to Room 24), then turn left into Room 20.*

Gentile Bellini—*Procession in St. Mark's Square (Processione in Piazza San Marco*, 1496)

A fitting end to our tour is a look back at Venice in its heyday. Painted by Giovanni's big brother, this wide-angle view—more than any human eye could take in at once—reminds us how little Venice has changed over the centuries. There is St. Mark's gleaming gold with mosaics, the four bronze horses, the three flagpoles out front, the old Campanile on the right, and the

Doge's Palace. There's the guy selling 10 postcards for a dollar. (But there's no Clock Tower with the two bronze Moors yet, the pavement's different, the church is covered with gold, and there are no café orchestras playing "New York, New York.") Every detail is in perfect focus, regardless of its distance from us, presented for our inspection. Take some time to linger over this and the other views of old Venice in this room. Then get outta here and enjoy the real thing.

FRARI CHURCH TOUR

Basilica di Santa Maria Gloriosa dei Frari

For me, this church offers the best art-appreciation experience in Venice, because so much of its great art is in situ—right where it was designed to be seen, rather than hanging in museums. Because Venice's spongy ground could never support a real stone Gothic church (such as those you'd find in France), the Frari is made of light and flexible brick. As with Venetian architecture in general, the white limestone foundation insulates the building from the wet soil.

The church was built by the Franciscan order, which arrived in Venice around 1230 (the present building was consecrated in 1492). Franciscan men and women were inspired by St. Francis of Assisi (c. 1182-1226), who dedicated himself to a non-materialistic lifestyle—part of a reform movement that spread across Europe in the early 1200s. The Roman Church felt distant and corrupt, and there was a hunger for religious teaching that connected with everyday people. While some of these movements were dubbed heretical (like that of the Cathars in southern France), the Franciscans (and Dominicans) eventually earned the Church's blessing.

The spirit of St. Francis of Assisi warms both the church of his "brothers" *(frari)* and the art that decorates it. The Franciscan love of all of creation—Nature and Man—later inspired Renaissance painters to capture the beauty of the physical world and human emotions, showing worshippers the glory of God in human terms.

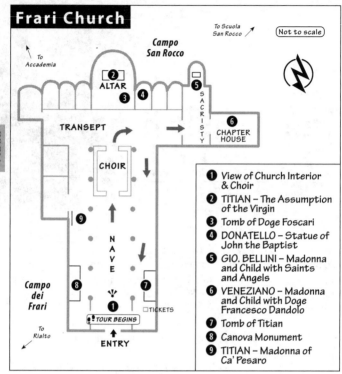

Frari Church

To Scuola
San Rocco

Not to scale

To
Accademia

Campo
San Rocco

ALTAR ❷

❸ ❹

❺
SACRISTY

❻
CHAPTER
HOUSE

TRANSEPT

CHOIR

❾

N
A
V
E

Campo
dei
Frari

❽

❼

❶

TICKETS

To
Rialto

🎧 TOUR BEGINS

ENTRY

❶ View of Church Interior
& Choir

❷ TITIAN – The Assumption
of the Virgin

❸ Tomb of Doge Foscari

❹ DONATELLO – Statue of
John the Baptist

❺ GIO. BELLINI – Madonna
and Child with Saints
and Angels

❻ VENEZIANO – Madonna
and Child with Doge
Francesco Dandolo

❼ Tomb of Titian

❽ Canova Monument

❾ TITIAN – Madonna of
Ca' Pesaro

Orientation

Cost: €3.

Hours: Mon-Sat 9:00-18:00, Sun 13:00-18:00, last entry 30 minutes before closing.

Dress Code: Modest dress is recommended.

Getting There: It's on Campo dei Frari, near the San Tomà vaporetto and *traghetto* stops. From the dock, follow signs to *Scuola Grande di San Rocco*. For a pleasant stroll from the Rialto Bridge, ✪ take the Rialto to Frari Church Walk.

Information: Tel. 041-272-8618, www.basilicadeifrari.it.

Audioguides: You can rent an audioguide for €2. Or you can download this chapter as a free Rick Steves audio tour (see page 21).

Length of This Tour: Allow one hour. Don't miss Titian's *Assumption*, Donatello's statue, or Bellini's altarpiece.

Photography: Prohibited.

Eating: The church square is ringed with small, simple, reasonably priced cafés. The recommended Grom *gelateria* has a branch right on the square, facing the left side of the church at #3006.

Concerts: The church occasionally hosts evening concerts and small theatrical performances (usually around €15, buy tickets at church, for details see www.basilicadeifrari.it).

Nearby: For efficient sightseeing, combine your visit with the ✪ Scuola San Rocco, located behind the Frari Church. The ✪ Ca' Rezzonico is a seven-minute walk away.

Starring: Titian, Giovanni Bellini, Paolo Veneziano, and Donatello.

The Tour Begins

• *Enter the church, let your eyes adjust, and stand just inside the door with a good view down the long nave toward the altar.*

❶ Church Interior and Choir (1250-1443)

The simple, spacious (110-yard-long), well-lit Gothic church—with rough wood crossbeams and a red-and-white color scheme—is truly a remarkable sight in a city otherwise crammed with exotic froufrou. Traditionally, churches in Venice were cross-shaped, but because the Franciscans were an international order, they weren't limited to Venetian tastes. This new T-shaped footprint featured a long, lofty nave—flooded with light and suited to large gatherings—where common people heard sermons. The T, or tau, is the symbol of the Franciscan order. St. Francis chose the tau as his personal symbol, wearing it on his clothes and using it in place of his signature.

The wooden choir area in the center of the nave allowed friars to hold smaller, more intimate services. From the early 16th century, as worshippers entered the church and looked down the long nave to the altar, they were greeted by Titian's glorious painted altarpiece—then, as now, framed by the arch of the choir entrance.

Walk prayerfully toward the Titian, stopping in the gorgeously carved 1480s choir. Notice the fine inlay above the chairs, showing the Renaissance enthusiasm for Florentine-style depth and perspective. Surviving choirs such as this are rare. (In response to Luther's challenge, Counter-Reformation churches discarded the idea of the choirs and altar screens in order to get priests closer to their flocks.)

• *Approach Titian's heavenly vision.*

❷ Titian (Tiziano Vecellio)—
The Assumption of the Virgin (1516-1518)

Glowing red and gold like a stained-glass window, this altarpiece sets the tone of exuberant beauty found in this church. At the end of her life (though looking 17 here), Mary was miraculously "assumed" into heaven. As cherubs lift her up to meet a Jupiter-like

God, the stunned apostles on earth reach up to touch the floating bubble of light.

Look around. The church is littered with chapels and tombs "made possible by the generous financial support" of rich people who donated to the Franciscans for the good of their souls (and usually for tomb-topping statues of themselves, as well). But the Franciscans didn't sell their main altar; instead they hired the new whiz artist, Titian, to create a dramatic altar painting.

Unveiled in 1518, the work scandalized a Venice accustomed to simpler, more contemplative church art. The rich colors, twisting poses, and mix of saccharine angels with blue-collar apostles were unheard of. Most striking, this Virgin is fully human, not a stiff icon on a throne. The Franciscans thought this Mary aroused excitement rather than spirituality. They agreed to pay Titian only after the Holy Roman Emperor offered to buy the altar if they refused.

In a burst of youthful innovation, Titian (1488-1576) had rewritten the formula for church art, hinting at changes to come with the Mannerist and Baroque styles. He energized the scene with a complex composition, overlapping a circle (Mary's bubble) and a triangle (draw a line from the apostle reaching up to Mary's face and down the other side) on three horizontal levels (God in heaven, Man on earth, Mary in between). Together, these elements draw our eyes from the swirl of arms and legs to the painting's focus—the radiant face of a triumphant Mary, "assumed body and soul into heaven."

• *Flanking the painting are marble tombs lining the walls. On the wall to the right of the altar is the...*

❸ Tomb of Doge Foscari (15th Century)

This heavy, ornate tomb marks the peak of Venice's worldly power. Doge Francesco Foscari (1373-1457) assumed control of the city's powerful seafaring empire and then tried to expand it onto the mainland, battling Milan in a 31-year war of attrition that swept through northern Italy. Meanwhile, on the unprotected eastern front, the Ottomans took Constantinople (1453) and scuttled Venice's trade. Venice's long slide into historical oblivion had begun. Financially drained city fathers forced Foscari to resign, turn in his funny hat, and hand over the keys to the Doge's Palace.

• In the first chapel to the right of the altar, you'll find...

❹ Donatello—*Statue of John the Baptist* (1438)

In the center of the altarpiece, the cockeyed prophet of the desert—emaciated from his breakfast of bugs 'n' honey and dressed

in animal skins—freezes mid-rant when he spies something in the distance. His jaw goes slack, he twists his face and raises his hand to announce the coming of...the Renaissance.

The Renaissance began in the Florence of the 1400s, where Donatello (1386-1466) created realistic statues with a full range of human emotions. This warts-and-all John the Baptist contrasts greatly with, say, Titian's sweet Mary. Florentine art (including painting) was sculptural, strongly outlined, and harshly realistic, with muted colors. Venetian art was painterly, soft focus, and beautiful, with bright colors.

Florentine expatriates living in Venice commissioned Donatello to make this wooden statue for their local chapel.

• Enter the sacristy through the door at the far end of the right transept. You'll bump into an elaborate altar crammed with reliquaries. Opposite that (near the entrance door) is a clock, intricately carved from a single piece of wood. At the far end of the room, you'll find Bellini's glowing altarpiece.

❺ Giovanni Bellini—*Madonna and Child with Saints and Angels* (1488)

The Pesaro family, who negotiated an acceptable price and place for their family tomb, funded this delightful chapel dominated by a Bellini masterpiece.

Mary sits on a throne under a half-dome, propping up Baby Jesus (who's just learning to stand), flanked by saints and serenaded by musician angels. Giovanni Bellini (c. 1430-1516), the father of the Venetian Renaissance, painted fake columns and a dome to match the real ones in the gold frame, making the painting seem to be an extension of the room. He completes the illusion with glimpses of open sky in the background. Next, he fills the artificial niches with symmetrically posed, thoughtful saints—left to right, find Saints Nicholas, Peter, Mark, and Sean Connery (Benedict).

Bellini combined the meditative poses of the Venetian Byzantine tradition with Renaissance improvements in modern art. He made the transition from painting with medieval tempera (egg yolk-based) to painting in oil (pigments dissolved in vegetable oil). Oils allowed a subtler treatment of colors because artists could apply them in successive layers. And because darker colors aren't so muddy when painted in oil, they "pop," effectively giving the artist a brighter palette.

Bellini virtually invented the formula (later to be broken by his precocious pupil, Titian) for Venetian altarpieces. This type of holy conversation *(sacra conversazione)* between saints and Mary can also be seen in Venice's Accademia and Church of San Zaccaria.

Renaissance humanism demanded Madonnas and saints that were accessible and human. Bellini delivers, but places them in a physical setting so beautiful that it creates its own mood of serene holiness. The scene is lit from the left, but nothing casts a harsh shadow—Mary and the babe are enveloped in a glowing aura of reflected light from the golden dome. The beauty is in the details, from the writing in the dome, to the red brocade backdrop, to the swirls in the marble steps, to the angels' dimpled legs.

• *In the adjoining room, find a painting in the shape of a Gothic arch.*

❻ Paolo Veneziano—*Madonna and Child with Doge Francesco Dandolo* (c. 1339)

Bellini's Byzantine roots can be traced to Paolo Veneziano (literally, "Paul the Venetian"), the first "name" artist in Venice, who helped shape the distinctive painting style of his city. In turn, Veneziano was inspired by Byzantine artists who had come to Venice in search of greater freedom of expression. They had chafed under strict societies (Byzantine and, in some locales, Islamic) that frowned on painting figurative images. In Venice, these expats found an eager community of  rich patrons who indulged their love of deeper color, sentiment, movement, and decoration. (Venice clung to this style to the point that it eventually lagged behind Western Europe.)

In this altarpiece, Veneziano paints Byzantine icons, then sets them in motion. Baby Jesus turns to greet a kneeling Doge Dandolo, while Mary turns to acknowledge the doge's wife. None other than St. Francis presents "Francis" (Francesco) Dandolo to the Madonna. Both he and St. Elizabeth (on the right) bend at the waist and gesture as naturally as 14th-century icons can.

• *Return to the nave and head left, toward the door you entered through. Turn around and face the altar. The Tomb of Titian is in the second bay on your right.*

❼ Tomb of Titian (1852)

The enormous carved marble monument is labeled "Titiano Ferdinandus MDCCCLII." The tomb celebrates both the man (the center statue shows Titian with a beard and crown of laurels) and

his famous paintings (depicted in the background reliefs).

Titian was the greatest Venetian painter, excelling equally in inspirational altarpieces, realistic portraits, joyous mythological scenes, and erotic female nudes.

He moved to Venice as a child, studied first as a mosaic-maker and then under Giovanni Bellini and Giorgione, before establishing his own bold style, which featured teenage Madonnas (see a relief of *The Assumption of the Virgin* behind Titian). He became wealthy and famous, traveling Europe to paint stately portraits of kings and nobles, and colorful, sexy works for their bedrooms. Titian resisted the temptation of big money that drew so many of his contemporary Venetian artists to Rome. Instead he always returned to his beloved Venice (see winged lion on top)...and favorite Frari Church.

In his old age, Titian painted dark, tragic masterpieces, including the *Pietà* (see relief in upper left) that was intended for his tomb but ended up in the Accademia (see page 144). Nearing 90, he labored to finish the *Pietà* as the plague enveloped Venice. One in four people died, including Titian's son and assistant, Orazio. Heartbroken, Titian died soon afterward, probably of the plague, although his death was officially chalked up to influenza (to keep his body from being burned—a requirement for plague victims). His tomb was built three centuries later to remember and honor this great Venetian.

• *On the opposite side of the nave is the pyramid-shaped...*

❽ Canova Monument (1827)

Antonio Canova (1757-1822, see his portrait above the door) was

Venice's greatest sculptor. He created gleaming white, highly polished statues of beautiful Greek gods and goddesses in the Neoclassical style. (See several of his works at the Correr Museum.)

The pyramid shape is timeless, suggesting pharaohs' tombs and the Christian Trinity. Mourners, bent over with grief, shuffle up to pay homage to the master artist. Even the winged lion is choked up.

Follow me here. Canova himself designed this pyramid-shaped tomb, not for his own use, but as the tomb of an artist he greatly admired: Titian. But the Frari picked another design for Titian's tomb, so Canova used the pyramid for an Austrian princess...in Vienna. After his death, Canova's pupils copied the design here to honor their master. In fact, Canova isn't buried here—he lies in southern Italy. But inside the tomb's open door, you can (barely) see an urn, which contains his heart.

• *Head back toward the altar. Halfway up the left wall is...*

❾ Titian—*Madonna of Ca' Pesaro* (1519-1526)

Titian's second altarpiece for the Frari Church displays all his many skills. Following his teacher Bellini, he puts Mary (seated)

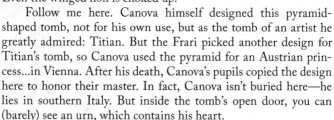

and baby (standing) on a throne, surrounded by saints having a holy conversation. And, like Bellini, he paints fake columns that echo the church's real ones.

But wait. Mary is off-center, Titian's idealized saints mingle with Venetians sporting five o'clock shadows, and the stairs run diagonally away from us. Mary sits not on a throne, but on a pedestal. Baby Jesus is restless. The precious keys of St. Peter seem to dangle unnoticed. These things upset traditional Renaissance symmetry, but they turn a group of figures into a true scene. St. Peter (center, in blue and gold, with book) looks down at Jacopo Pesaro, who kneels to thank the Virgin for his recent naval victory over the Ottomans (1502). A flag-carrying lieutenant drags in a turbaned captive. Meanwhile, St. Francis talks to Baby Jesus while gesturing down to more members of the Pesaro family. The little guy looking out at us (lower right) is the Pesaro descendant who administered the trust fund to keep prayers coming for his dead uncle.

Titian combines opposites: a soft-focus Madonna with photo-realistic portraits, chubby winged angels with a Muslim prisoner, and a Christian cross with a battle flag. In keeping with the spirit of St. Francis' humanism, Titian lets mere mortals mingle with saints. And we're right there with them.

• *While this church is a great example of art* in situ, *in a sense, all of Venice is art* in situ. *At the Frari, you're away from the touristy center. Before returning to the mobs, why not explore some back lanes and lonely canals from here and enjoy a softer, more meditative side of town?*

FRARI

SCUOLA SAN ROCCO TOUR

Scuola Grande di San Rocco

The 50-plus paintings in the Scuola Grande di San Rocco—often called "Tintoretto's Sistine Chapel"—present one man's very personal vision of Christian history. Tintoretto spent the last 20 years of his life working practically for free, driven by the spirit of charity that the Scuola, a Christian organization, promoted. For Tintoretto fans, this is the ultimate. Even for the art-weary, his large, colorful canvases, framed in gold on the walls and ceilings of a grand upper hall, are an impressive sight.

Orientation

Cost: €10, includes a fine audioguide.

Hours: Daily 9:30-17:30, last entry 30 minutes before closing.

Getting There: It's next to the Frari Church (vaporetto: San Tomà). For an easy route on foot from the Rialto Bridge, ✪ take the Rialto to Frari Church Walk, following signs to *Scuola Grande di San Rocco*.

Information: Tel. 041-523-4864, www.scuolagrandesanrocco.it.

Mirrors: Use the mirrors scattered about the museum's Grand Hall, because much of this art is on the ceiling and a pain in the neck.

Length of This Tour: Allow one hour. If you have less time, skip the ground floor, and focus on the Great Upper Hall and Albergo Hall.

Photography: Prohibited.

Services: WCs are on the ground floor (through the bookstore).

Nearby: Right next door is the Church of San Rocco, featuring still more Tintorettos (free, same hours as the Scuola).

Starring: Tintoretto, Tintoretto, and Tintoretto.

Scuola San Rocco

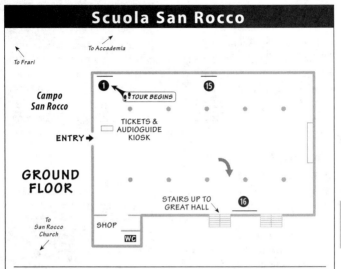

To Frari

To Accademia

Campo
San Rocco

❶ **!TOUR BEGINS**

❶❺

TICKETS &
AUDIOGUIDE
KIOSK

ENTRY →

**GROUND
FLOOR**

STAIRS UP TO
GREAT HALL

❶❻

To
San Rocco
Church

SHOP

WC

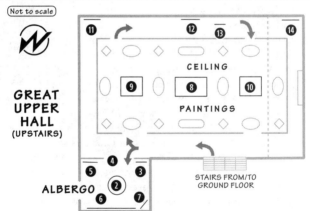

(Not to scale)

**GREAT
UPPER
HALL**
(UPSTAIRS)

❶❶   ❶❷ ❶❸   ❶❹

CEILING

❾   ❽   ❿

PAINTINGS

STAIRS FROM/TO
GROUND FLOOR

❹
❺   ❸
❷
ALBERGO
❻   ❼

SCUOLA SAN ROCCO

❶ The Annunciation
❷ St. Roch in Glory
❸ Christ Before Pilate
❹ Christ Crowned
with Thorns
❺ The Way to Calvary
❻ The Crucifixion
❼ Three Apples
❽ The Miracle of the
Bronze Serpent

❾ Moses Strikes Water
from the Rocks
❿ The Fall of Manna in the Desert
⓫ The Adoration of
the Shepherds
⓬ The Resurrection
⓭ Tintoretto's Carved Face
⓮ The Last Supper
⓯ The Flight into Egypt
⓰ The Circumcision

The Tour Begins

The art of the Scuola is contained in three rooms—the Ground Floor Hall (where you enter) and two rooms upstairs, including the Great Upper Hall, with the biggest canvases. Your ticket also admits you to the Scuola's small and skippable treasury (one more flight up).

• *Enter on the ground floor, which is lined with big, colorful Tintoretto canvases. Begin with the first canvas on the left.*

Ground Floor Hall

❶ The Annunciation

An angel swoops through the doorway, dragging a trail of naked baby angels with him, to tell a startled Mary she'll give birth to Jesus. This canvas has many of Tintoretto's typical characteristics:

- **The miraculous and the everyday mingle side by side.** Glorious angels are in a broken-down house with stacks of lumber and a frayed chair.
- **Bright light and dark shadows.** A bright light strikes the brick column, highlighting Mary's face and the angel's shoulder, but casting dark shadows across the room.
- **Strong 3-D sucks you into the scene.** Tintoretto literally tears down Mary's wall to let us in. The floor tiles recede sharply into the distance, making Mary's room an extension of our real space.
- **Colors that are bright, almost harsh,** with a metallic "black-velvet" sheen, especially when contrasted with the soft-focus haze of Bellini, Giorgione, Veronese, and (sometimes) Titian.
- **Twisting, muscular poses.** The angel turns one way, Mary turns the other, and the baby angels turn every which way.
- **Diagonal composition.** Shadows run diagonally on the floor as Mary leans back diagonally.
- **Rough brushwork.** The sketchy pattern on Mary's ceiling contrasts with the precise photo-realism of the brick column.

And finally, *The Annunciation* exemplifies the general theme of the San Rocco paintings—God intervenes miraculously in our everyday lives in order to save us.

• *We'll return to the ground floor later, but let's get right to the highlights. Climb the staircase (taking time to admire the plague scenes that are not by Tintoretto) and enter the impressive Great Upper Hall.*

Wow! Before we tackle the big canvases in this huge room, let's start where Tintoretto did, in the Albergo Hall—the small room in the left

Jacopo Tintoretto (1518-1594)

The son of a silk dyer ("Tintoretto" is a nickname meaning "little dyer"), Tintoretto applied a blue-collar work ethic to painting, becoming one of the most prolific artists ever. He trained briefly under Titian, but their egos clashed. He was influenced more by Michelangelo's recently completed *Last Judgment,* with its muscular, twisting, hovering nudes and epic scale.

By age 30, Tintoretto was famous, astounding Venice with the innovative *St. Mark Freeing the Slave* (now in the Accademia). He married, had eight children (three of whom became his assistants), and dedicated himself to work and family, shunning publicity and living his whole life in his old Venice neighborhood.

Twenty years of his life were spent decorating the Scuola di San Rocco. It was a labor of love, showing his religious faith, his compassion for the poor, and his artistic passion.

corner of the Great Upper Hall. On the ceiling of the Albergo Hall is an oval painting of St. Roch, best viewed from the doorway.

Albergo Hall (Sala d'Albergo)— Christ's Passion

❷ *St. Roch in Glory* (1564)

Start at the feet of St. Roch (San Rocco), a French medical student in the 1300s who dedicated his short life to treating plague victims. The Scuola di San Rocco was a kind of Venetian "Elks Club" whose favorite charity was poor plague victims.

This is the first of Tintoretto's 50-plus paintings in the Scuola. It's also the one that got him the job, beating entries by Veronese and others.

Tintoretto amazed the judges by showing the saint from beneath, as though he hovered above in a circle of glory. This Venetian taste for dramatic angles and illusion would later become standard in Baroque ceilings. Tintoretto trained by dangling wax models from the ceiling and lighting them from odd angles.

• *On the walls are scenes of Christ's trial, torture, and execution. Work counterclockwise around the room. Start with the one to the right of the door (as you face it).*

• *Let's look at a few pieces in depth. Start with the largest painting, in the center of the ceiling. View it from the top (the Albergo end), not directly underneath.*

❽ The Miracle of the Bronze Serpent

The tangle of half-naked bodies (at the bottom of the painting) represents the children of Israel, wrestling with poisonous snakes and writhing in pain. At the top of the pile, a young woman gestures toward Moses (in pink), who points to a pole carrying a bronze serpent sent by God. Those who looked at the statue were miraculously healed. His work all done, God (above in the clouds) high-fives an angel.

This was the first of the Great Hall panels Tintoretto painted in response to a terrible plague that hit Venice in 1576. One in four died. Four hundred a day were buried. Like today's Red Cross, the Scuola sprang into action, raising funds, sending doctors, and giving beds to the sick—and aid to their families. Tintoretto saw the dead and dying firsthand. While capturing their suffering, he gave a ray of hope that help is on the way: Turn to the cross, and be saved by your faith.

There are dozens of figures in the painting, shown from every conceivable angle. Tintoretto was well aware of where it would hang and how it would be viewed. Walk around beneath it and see the different angles come alive. The painting becomes a movie, and the children of Israel writhe like snakes.

• *The rectangular panel at the Albergo end of the hall is...*

❾ Moses Strikes Water from the Rocks

Moses (in pink, in the center) hits a rock in the desert with his staff, and it miraculously spouts water, which the thirsty Israelites

catch in jars. The water spurts like a ray of light. Moses is a strong, calm center to a spinning wheel of activity.

Tintoretto worked fast, and, if nothing else, his art is exuberant. He trained in fresco painting, which must be finished before the plaster dries. With these paintings, he sketched an outline right onto the canvas, then improvised details as he went.

The sheer magnitude of the San Rocco project is staggering.

This canvas alone is 300 square feet—like painting a bathroom with an artist's tiny brush. The whole project, counting the Albergo Hall, Great Upper Hall, and the Ground Floor Hall together, totals some 8,500 square feet—more than enough to cover a typical house, inside and out. (The Sistine Chapel ceiling, by comparison, is 5,700 square feet.)

• *The rectangular panel at the altar end of the hall is...*

⓾ *The Fall of Manna in the Desert*

It's snowing bread, as God feeds the hungry Israelites with a miraculous storm. They stretch a blanket to catch it and gather it up

in baskets. Up in the center of the dark cloud is a radiant, almost transparent God, painted with sketchy brushstrokes to suggest he's an unseen presence.

Tintoretto tells these Bible stories with a literalness that was very popular with the poor, uneducated sick who sought help from the Scuola. He was the Spielberg of his day, with the technical know-how to bring imagination to life, to make the miraculous tangible.

• *You could grow old studying all the art here, so we'll select just a couple of the New Testament paintings on the walls. Start at the Albergo end, on the right, with...*

⓫ *The Adoration of the Shepherds*

Christ's glorious life begins in a straw-filled stable with cows, chickens, and peasants who pass plates of food up to the new par-

ents. It's night, with just a few details lit by phosphorescent moonlight: the kneeling shepherd's forehead and leggings, the serving girl's shoulders, the faces of Mary and Joseph...and little baby Jesus, a smudge of light.

Notice the different points of view. Tintoretto clearly has placed us on the lower floor, about eye level with the cow, looking up through the roof beams at the night sky. But we also see Mary and Joseph in the loft above as though they were at eye level. By using multiple perspectives (and ignoring the laws of physics), Tintoretto could portray every detail at its perfect angle.

• *In the middle of the long wall, on the same side, find...*

⑫ The Resurrection

Angels lift the sepulchre lid, and Jesus springs forth in a blaze of light. The contrast between dark and light is extreme, with great dramatic effect.

• *Head for* The Last Supper, *in the corner to the left of the altar. On the way there, look on the wall for a* **wood carving of Tintoretto** *(⑬ third statue from altar, directly opposite entry staircase). The artist holds the tools of his trade. His craggy, wrinkled face peers out from under a black cap and behind a scraggly beard.*

⑭ The Last Supper

A dog, a beggar, and a serving girl dominate the foreground of Christ's final Passover meal with his followers. More servants work

in the background. The disciples themselves are dining in the dark, some with their backs to us, with only a few stray highlights to show us what's going on. Tintoretto emphasizes the human, everyday element of that gathering, in contrast to, say, Leonardo da Vinci's more stately version. And he sets the scene at a diagonal for dramatic effect.

The table stretches across a tiled floor, a commonly used device to create 3-D space. But Tintoretto makes the more distant tiles unnaturally small to exaggerate the distance. Similarly, the table and the people get proportionally smaller and lower until, at the far end of the table, tiny Jesus (with glowing head) is only half the size of the disciple at the near end.

Theatrically, Tintoretto leaves it to us to piece together the familiar narrative. The disciples are asking each other, "Is it I who will betray the Lord?" Jesus, meanwhile, unconcerned, hands out Communion bread.

• *Browse the Great Upper Hall and notice the various easel paintings by other artists. Contrast Titian's placid, evenly lit, aristocratic An-nunciation (displayed on an easel by the altar) with the blue-collar Tintoretto version downstairs. After you've gotten your fill of the Great Upper Hall, head back downstairs for Tintoretto's last works. The first one is directly across from the foot of the stairs.*

Ground Floor Hall—The Life of Mary
⑮ The Flight into Egypt

There's Mary, Joseph, and the baby, but they're dwarfed by palm trees. Tintoretto, in his old age, returned to composing a Venetian

specialty—landscapes—after years as champion of the Michelangelesque style of painting beefy, twisting nudes. The leafy greenery, the still water, the supernatural sunset, and the hut whose inhabitants go about their work tell us better than any human action that the holy family has found a safe haven.

• *Over your right shoulder, above the door, is...*

⓰ *The Circumcision*

This painting, bringing the circumcision of the Baby Jesus into sharp focus, is the final canvas that Tintoretto did for the Scuola.

He collaborated on this work with his son Domenico, who carried on the family business.

In his long and prolific career, Tintoretto saw fame and many high-paying jobs. But at the Scuola, the commission became an obsession. It stands as one man's very personal contribution to the poor, to the Christian faith, and to art.

CA'REZZONICO TOUR

*Museum of 18th-Century Venice
(Museo del Settecento Veneziano)*

*Endowed by nature with a pleasing physical appearance, a
confirmed gambler, a great talker, far from modest, always
running after pretty women...I was certain to be disliked.
But, as I was always willing to take responsibility for my actions, I decided I had a right to do anything I pleased.*
—*The Memoirs of Giacomo Casanova*

Venice in the 1700s was the playground for Europe's aristocrats,
including the wealthy Rezzonico (ret-ZON-ee-koh) family, who
owned this palace. Today, the Ca' Rezzonico (a.k.a. the Museo del
Settecento Veneziano) contains furniture, decoration, and artwork
from the period. This grand home on the Grand Canal is the best
place in town to experience the luxurious, decadent spirit of Venice
in the Settecento (the 1700s).

Orientation

Cost: €8.

Hours: April-Oct Wed-Mon 10:00-18:00, Nov-March Wed-Mon
10:00-17:00, closed Tue year-round, ticket office closes one
hour before museum does.

Getting There: The museum is located in Dorsoduro, on the west
bank of the Grand Canal at the Ca' Rezzonico vaporetto
stop. While the Accademia and Rialto bridges are a 10- or
20-minute walk respectively, the San Samuele *traghetto* takes
you across the Grand Canal right to the museum (daily 8:30-
12:30, €2).

Information: Tel. 041-241-0100, http://carezzonico.visitmuve.it.

Audioguide: The audioguide costs €4 (€6/2 people) and lasts 1.5
hours.

Length of This Tour: Allow one hour, or more if you want to explore the third floor on your own. If you have less than an hour, focus on Rooms 1-7 on the first floor, with their Tiepolo ceilings and ambience.

Baggage Check: Required and free.

Services: The Ca' Rezzonico has a bookstore and WCs.

Photography: Prohibited.

Cuisine Art: The museum's café has simple fare (€4-5 *panini*). The delightful Campo San Barnaba is just a three-minute walk away; for eateries on and near that square, see page 306.

Starring: A beautiful palace with 18th-century furnishings and paintings by G. B. Tiepolo, Canaletto, and Guardi.

The Tour Begins

Our Ca' Rezzonico tour covers two floors. The first floor has rooms decorated with period furniture and ceiling frescoes by G. B. Tiepolo. The second floor dis-plays paintings by Canaletto, Guardi, G. D. Tiepolo, Longhi, and others. (The third floor painting gallery—which we won't visit—shows lots of flesh in lots of rooms.)

First, step onto the dock on the Grand Canal and admire Ca' Rezzonico's heavy stone facade. This dock was, of course, the main entrance back in the 1700s. Next, admire the 1700s-era covered gondola in the courtyard. Picture this arriving at the Ca's dock for a party during Carnevale. A charcoal heater inside kept the masked and caped passengers warm, as they sipped Prosecco and chatted in French, enjoying their winter holiday away from home...

First Floor

• *Buy tickets on the ground floor, then ascend the grand staircase to the first floor (where you show your ticket), entering the ballroom. From here, simply follow the one-way route through the numbered rooms.*

Room 1: Ballroom

A great place for a wedding reception. At 5,600 square feet, it could be the biggest private venue in the city. Stand in the center, and the room gets even bigger, with a ceiling painting that opens up to the heavens and painted, trompe l'oeil (optical illusion) columns and arches that open onto fake alcoves.

Imagine dancing under candlelit chandeliers to Vivaldi's *Four Seasons*. Servants glide by with drinks and finger foods. The gentlemen wear powdered wigs, silk shirts with lacy sleeves, tight velvet coats and breeches, striped stockings, and shoes with big buckles. They carry snuffboxes with dirty pictures inside the lids. The ladies powder their hair, pile it high, and weave in stuff—pictures of their children or locks of a lover's hair. And everyone carries a mask on a stick to change identity in a second.

The chandeliers of gold-covered wood are original. But while most of the furniture we'll see is from the 1700s, it's not from the Rezzonico family collection.

• *Promenade across the floor, bearing right into the next room.*

Room 2: Nuptial Allegory Room

In fact, there *was* a wedding here—see the happy couple on the ceiling, arriving in a chariot pulled by four white horses and serenaded by angels, cupids, and Virtues. In 1757, Ludovico Rezzonico exchanged vows with Faustina Savorgnan in this room, under the bellies of the horses painted for the occasion by Giovanni Battista ("John the Baptist") Tiepolo. G. B. Tiepolo (1696-1770), the best-known decorator of Europe's palaces, was at the height of his fame and technique. He knocked this off in 12 days. His bright colors, mastery of painting figures from every possible angle, wide knowledge of classical literary subjects, and sheer, unbridled imagination made his frescoes blend seamlessly with ornate Baroque and Rococo furniture.

The Rezzonico were a family of *nouveaux riches* who bought their way into the exclusive club of Venetian patrician families. The state, which needed money for its military adventures, actually sold noble status to parvenu families like the Rezzonico. These upwardly mobile families then followed a strategy to be accepted by the old nobility. Over the course of several generations, the Rezzonico bought and decorated this fancy palace, married into high society, managed to secure a prestigious Venetian office, and even put one of their relatives on the papal throne. In early times, art was about scoring religious points to gain the way to heaven. In the 18th cen-

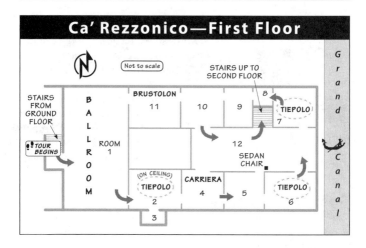

Ca' Rezzonico—First Floor

tury, wealthy people commissioned art like the works in this palace simply to gain respect.

The *Portrait of Clement XIII*, pink-cheeked and well-fed, shows the most famous Rezzonico. As pope (elected in 1758), Clement spent his reign defending the Jesuit society from anti-Catholic European nobles. A **prayer kneeler** (in the tiny adjoining chapel, Room 3) looks heavily used, dating from the sin-and-repent era of Settecento Venice.

Room 4: Pastel Room

Europe's most celebrated painter of portraits in pastels was a Venetian, Rosalba Carriera (1675-1757). Wealthy French and English tourists on holiday wanted a souvenir of Venice, and Carriera obliged, with miniature portraits on ivory rather than the traditional vellum (soft animal skin). These were products of narcissism—the Facebook photos of the 18th century that proclaimed, "Look how charming/interesting I am."

She progressed to portraits in pastel, a medium that caught the luminous, pale-skin, white-haired, heavy-makeup look that was considered so desirable. Still, her *Portrait (Ritratto) of Sister Maria Caterina* has a warts-and-all realism that doesn't hide the nun's heavy eyebrows, long nose, and forehead vein, which only intensifies the spirituality she radiates.

At age 45, Carriera was invited by tourists

whom she'd befriended to visit them in Paris. There she became the toast of the town. Returning triumphantly to Venice, she settled into her home on the Grand Canal and painted until her eyesight failed.

Also in the room is the **portrait of Cecilia Guardi Tiepolo:** wife of famous painter Giovanni Battista Tiepolo, sister of famous painter Francesco Guardi, and mother of not-very-famous painter Lorenzo Tiepolo, who painted this when he was 21.

Room 5: Tapestry Room

Tapestries, furniture, a mirror, and a door with Asian themes that shows an opium smoker on his own little island paradise (lower panel) give a sense of the Rococo luxury of the wealthy. In a century dominated by the French court at Versailles, Venice was one of the few cities that could hold its own. The furniture ensemble of gilded wood chairs, tables, and chests hints at the Louis XIV (claw-foot) style, but the pieces were made in a Venetian workshop.

Despite Venice's mask of gaiety, in the 1700s it was a poor, politically bankrupt, dirty city. Garbage floated in the canals, the streets were either unpaved or slippery with slime, and tourists could hardly stand visiting St. Mark's Basilica or the Doge's Palace because of the stench of mildew. But its reputation for decay and sleaze was actually romanticized into a metaphor for adventures into shady morality. With licensed casinos and thousands of courtesans (prostitutes), it was a fun city for foreigners freed from hometown blinders.

Room 6: Throne Room

"Nowhere in Europe are there so many and such splendid fêtes, ceremonies, and public entertainments of all kinds as there are in Venice," wrote a visitor from France. As you check out the view of the Grand Canal, imagine once again that you're attending a party here. You could watch the *Forze d'Ercole* (Force of Hercules) acrobats, who stood in boats and kept building a human pyramid—of up to 50 bodies—until they tumbled, laughing, into the Grand Canal. At midnight the hosts would dim the mirrored candleholders on the walls, so you could look out on a fireworks display over the water.

Carnevale, Venice's prime party time, stretched from the

Famous 18th-Century Venetians

Canaletto (Giovanni Antonio Canal): Painter of Venice views
Antonio Canova: Neoclassical sculptor
Giacomo Casanova: Gambler, womanizer, revolutionary
Carlo Goldoni: Playwright of realistic comedies
Francesco Guardi: Painter of romantic Enlightened ideas
Giovanni Battista (G. B.) Tiepolo: Painter of Rococo ceilings
Giovanni Domenico (G. D.) Tiepolo: Painter son of famous Tiepolo

day after Christmas to Lent. Everyone wore masks. Frenchmen, dressed as turbaned Ottoman Turks, mingled with Turkish traders dressed as harlequins. Fake Barbary pirates fought playfully with skin-blackened "Moors." And long-nosed Pulcinella clowns were everywhere, reveling in the time when all social classes partied as one because "the mask levels all distinctions."

The **ceiling fresco,** again by Giovanni Battista Tiepolo, certainly trompes my oeil. (It's best viewed from the center.) Tiepolo

opens the room's sunroof, allowing angels to descend to earth to pick up the Rezzonico clan's patriarch. The old, bald, bearded fellow is crowned with laurels and begins to rise on a cloud up to the translucent temple of glory. The angels hold Venice's Golden Book, where the names of the city's nobles were listed. In 1687, the Rezzonico family bought their way into the exclusive club. Tiepolo captures the moment just as the gang is exiting through the "hole" in the ceiling. The leg of the lady in blue hangs over the "edge" of the fake oval. Tiepolo creates a zero-gravity universe that must have astounded visitors. Walk in circles under the fresco, and watch the bugling angel spin.

• *Pass through the large next room and into...*

Room 7: Tiepolo Room

The ceiling painting by G. B. Tiepolo depicts Nobility and Virtue as a kind of bare-breasted, Thelma-and-Louise duo defeating Treachery, who tumbles down.

CA'REZZONICO

The painting—which is on canvas, not a fresco like the others—was moved here from another palazzo.

Portraits around the room are by Tiepolo and his sons, Lorenzo and Giovanni Domenico. The paintings are sober and

down-to-earth, demonstrating the artistic range of this exceptional family. G. B. was known for his flamboyance, but he passed to his sons his penchant for painting wrinkled, wizened old men in the Rembrandt style. In later years, G. B. had the pleasure of traveling with his sons to distant capitals, meeting royalty, and working on palace ceilings. Giovanni Domenico (G. D.) contributed some of the minor figures in the Ca' Rezzonico ceilings and went on to a successful artistic career of his own. (We'll see his work upstairs.)

This was the game room, and you can see a card table in the center. The big walnut cabinet along the wall is one of the few original pieces of furniture from the Rezzonicos' collection.

Room 9: Library
Ca' Rezzonico was the home of the English poet Robert Browning (1812-1889) in his later years. Imagine him here in this study, in a melancholy mood after a long winter, reading a book and thinking of words from a poem of his: "Oh to be in England, now that April's there...."

Room 10: Lazzarini Room
The big, colorful paintings are by Gregorio Lazzarini (1655-1730), Tiepolo's teacher. Tiepolo took Lazzarini's color, motion, and twisted poses and suspended them overhead.

Room 11: Brustolon Room
Andrea Brustolon (1662-1732) carved Baroque fantasies into the custom-made tables, chairs, and vase stands that he crafted in his Venice workshop. In black ebony, reddish boxwood, and brown walnut, they overwhelm with the sheer number of figures, yet each carving is a gem worth admiring. The big vase stand is a harmony of different colors: a white vase supported by ebony slaves in chains

Giacomo Casanova (1725-1798)

I began to lead a life of complete freedom, caring for nothing except what pleased me.
                            —*The Memoirs of Giacomo Casanova*

Casanova, a real person who wrote an exaggerated autobiography, typifies the Venice that so entranced the rest of Europe. In his life, he adopted many personae, worked in a number of professions, and always took the adventurous path.

Casanova was born just across the Grand Canal from the Ca' Rezzonico. The son of an actor, Casanova trained to be a priest, but was expelled for seducing nuns. To Venetians he was first known as a fiery violinist at fancy parties in palaces such as the Ca' Rezzonico. He would later serve time in the Doge's Palace prison, accused of being a magician.

As a professional gambler and charmer, he roamed Europe's capitals seducing noblewomen, dueling with fellow men of honor, and impressing nobles with his knowledge of Greek literature, religion, politics, and the female sex. His memoirs, published after his death, cemented his reputation as a genial but cunning rake, rogue, and rapscallion.

and a brown boxwood Hercules. The slaves' chains are carved from a single piece of wood—a racist motif, but an impressive artistic feat.

The room's flowery Murano glass chandelier—of pastel pinks, blues, and turquoise—is original.

• *Backtrack to Room 10, then turn right into the large, sparsely decorated room called the...*

Room 12: Portego

That funny little cabin in the room is a **sedan chair,** a servant-powered taxi for Venice's nobles. Four strong-shouldered men ran poles through the iron brackets on either side, then carried it on their shoulders, while the rich rode in red-velvet luxury above the slimy streets.

• *The staircase to the second floor is here in Room 12, in the middle of the long wall. On the second floor, you emerge into Room 13 and find the two Canaletto paintings on the opposite wall.*

Second Floor

The first floor showed the rooms and furniture of the 1700s. The second-floor paintings depict the people who sat in those chairs.

Room 13: Painting Portego—Canaletto

Rich tourists wanting to remember their stay in Venice sought out Canaletto (1697-1768) for a "postcard" view. The ***Grand Canal from***

Palazzo Balbi to Rialto (by Giovanni Antonio Canal, called Il Canaletto) captures the view you'd see from the palazzo two doors down. With photographic clarity, Canaletto depicts buildings, boats, and shadows on the water, leading the eye to the tiny, half-hidden Rialto Bridge on the distant horizon.

The ***View of Rio dei Mendicante*** chronicles every chimney, every open shutter, every pair of underwear hanging out to dry.

Canaletto was a young theater-set painter working on Scarlatti operas in Rome when he decided his true calling was painting reality, not Baroque fantasy. He moved home to Venice, set up his easel outside, and painted scenes like these two, directly from nature. It was considered a very odd thing to do in his day.

Despite the seeming photorealism and crystal clarity, these wide-angle views are more than any human eye could take in without turning side to side. Canaletto, who meticulously studied the mathematics of perspective, was not above tweaking those rules to compress more of Venice into the frame.

In the *Grand Canal from Palazzo Balbi to Rialto,* notice there are shadows along both sides of the canal—physically impossible, but more picturesque. His paintings still have a theater-set look to them, but here, the Venice backdrop is the star.

To meet the demand for postcard scenes of Venice, Canaletto resorted in later years to painting from engravings or following formulas. But these two early works reflect his pure vision to accurately paint the city he loved.

Grand Tour visitors routinely reported that Venice pleased the eye but not the heart or mind. Just as they experienced the city without feeling any real passion, these paintings let you see it, marvel, and move on.

CA'REZZONICO

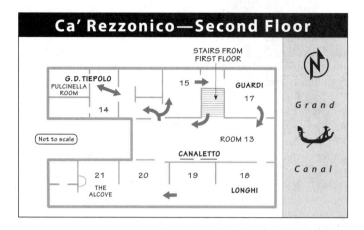

Ca' Rezzonico—Second Floor

STAIRS FROM
FIRST FLOOR

G. D. TIEPOLO
PULCINELLA
ROOM

14

15

GUARDI

17

Grand

Not to scale

ROOM 13

CANALETTO

21

20

19

18

THE
ALCOVE

LONGHI

Canal

• *From here, we'll move roughly clockwise around the second floor. Head for the door behind your right shoulder. Room 14 is actually a maze of several rooms.*

Room 14: G. D. Tiepolo's Frescoes from the Villa in Zianigo

The son of G. B. Tiepolo decorated the family villa with frescoes for his own enjoyment. They're far more down-to-earth than G. B.'s

high-flying fantasies. **New World** features butts, as ordinary folk crowd around a building with a peep-show window. The only faces we see are the two men in profile— Giovanni Domenico Tiepolo (far right, with eyeglass) and his father, G. B. (arms folded)—and baby brother Lorenzo (center). The **Pul-**

cinella Room (far right corner) has several scenes (including one overhead) of the hook-nosed, white-clothed, hunchbacked clown

who, at Carnevale time, represented the lovable country bumpkin. But here, he and his similarly dressed companions seem tired, lecherous, and stupid. The decadent gaiety of Settecento Venice was at odds with the *Liberté, Egalité,* and *Fraternité* erupting in France.

The 18th century was a time of great change. The fresh ideas and innovations of the Enlightenment swept more adaptable societies upward into a thriving new modern age. Meanwhile, a Venice in denial declined.

Venetians bought into their own propaganda. The modern ideas coming out of France threatened the very foundation of what La Serenissima was all about. Over time Venetians stopped trading, stopped traveling, and became stuck in the mud. Like Marie Antoinette retreating into her little hamlet at Versailles, the aristocracy of Venice withdrew into their palaces. Insisting their city remained exceptional, Venetian society chose to dance rather than to adapt. As Venice fell, its appetite for decadence grew. Through the 18th century, the Venetians partied and partied, as if drunk on the wealth accumulated through earlier centuries as a trading power.

• *Backtrack through the maze of Room 14, winding your way into a room with a harpsichord, or spinet, cleverly named the...*

Room 15: Spinet Room

The 1700s saw the development of new keyboard instruments that would culminate by century's end in the modern piano. This particular specimen has strings that are not hammered (like a piano) but plucked. At this point, a pluck was just a pluck—always the same volume. When hammers were introduced shortly after this, the novelty of being able to play both soft and loud sounds prompted Italians to name the instrument the *pianoforte* (the soft-loud).

Room 17: Parlor Room

Francesco Guardi (1712-1793), like Canaletto, supplied foreigners with scenes of Venice. But Guardi uses rougher brushwork that casts a romantic haze over the decaying city.

The Parlor (Il Parlatorio delle Monache di S. Zaccaria) is an

interior landscape featuring visiting day at a convent school. The girls, secluded with their servant girls behind grills, chat and have tea with family members, friends, ladies with their pets, and potential suitors. Convents were like finishing schools for aristocratic girls, where they got an education and learned manners before re-entering the world. Note the puppet show (starring spouse-abusing Pulcinella).

Guardi's **Il Ridotto di Palazzo Dandolo** shows partygoers in masks at a Venetian palace licensed for gambling. Casanova and others claimed that these casino houses had back rooms for the private use of patrons and courtesans. The men wear the traditional *bautta*—a three-piece outfit consisting of a face mask, three-cornered hat, and cowl. This getup was actually required by law in certain seedy establishments to ensure that every sinner was equally anonymous. The women wear Lone Ranger masks, and parade a hint of cleavage to potential customers.

• *Continuing along, you'll pass back through the Painting Portego and into...*

Room 18: Longhi Room

There is no better look at 1700s Venice than these genre scenes by Pietro Longhi (1702-1785), depicting everyday life among the upper classes. See ladies and gentlemen going to the hairdresser or to the dentist, dressed in the finery that was standard in every public situation. These small easel works provide a psychoanalytic insight into society. They come with an overwhelming sense of boredom. There's no dynamism. There aren't even any windows. It's a society closed to the world, without initiative, and—it seems—with no shortage of leisure time.

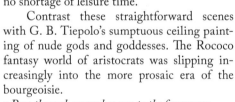

Contrast these straightforward scenes with G. B. Tiepolo's sumptuous ceiling painting of nude gods and goddesses. The Rococo fantasy world of aristocrats was slipping increasingly into the more prosaic era of the bourgeoisie.

• *Pass through several rooms to the far corner.*

Room 21: The Alcove

Casanova daydreamed of fancy boudoirs like this one, complete with a large bed (topped with a Madonna by Rosalba Carriera), a walnut dresser, Neoclassical wallpaper, and silver toiletries. Even the presence of the baby cradle would not have dimmed his ardor.

the garden (at the left end of the café/shop building as you face it; enter from side courtyard).

Photography: Permitted only in garden and terrace.

Cuisine Art: I'd skip the pricey café on site (€6-14 sandwiches, €12-14 pastas, big €16-20 salads). Instead, see page 305 in the Eating in Venice chapter for recommendations in the Dorsoduro neighborhood. Also consider the options noted for the Accademia Tour, as that museum is just a five-minute walk away, along a street lined with many eateries.

Nearby: If you like contemporary art, this is your neighborhood. Browse the art galleries, and visit the Punta della Dogana museum (next to La Salute, see page 51).

Starring: Picasso, Kandinsky, Mondrian, Dalí, Pollock...and Peggy herself.

The Tour Begins

After passing through a garden courtyard sprinkled with statues, you enter the palazzo. There's a wing to the left and a wing to the right, plus a modern annex. The collection is (very) roughly chronological, starting to the left with Cubism and ending to the right with post-World War II artists.

The collection's strength is its Abstract, Surrealist, and Abstract-Surrealist art. The placement of the paintings may change, so use this chapter as an overview, not a painting-by-painting tour. What makes this collection unique is that it hangs here in Peggy's home, much as it did in her lifetime.

• *Walk through Peggy's collection and her life. From the sculpture garden, head into the...*

Entrance Hall: Meet Peggy Guggenheim

Picture Peggy Guggenheim greeting guests here—standing before the **trembling-leaf mobile by Alexander Calder,** flanked by two Picasso paintings, surrounded by her yapping dogs and meowing cats, and wearing her Calder-designed earrings, Mondrian-print dress, and "Catwoman" sunglasses.

During the 1950s and 1960s, this old palazzo on the Grand Canal was a mecca for "Moderns," from composer Igor Stravinsky to actor Marlon Brando, from painter Mark Rothko to writer Truman Capote, from choreographer George Balanchine to Beatle John Lennon and performance artist Yoko Ono. They came to sip cocktails, tour the great art, talk about ideas, and meet the woman who had become a living legend.

Pablo Picasso—*On the Beach* (1937)

Curious, balloon-animal women play with a sailboat while their friend across the water looks on. Of all of Peggy's many paintings, this was her favorite.

By the time Peggy Guggenheim first became serious about modern art (about the time this was painted), Pablo Picasso—the most famous and versatile 20th-century artist—had already been through his Blue, Rose, Fauve, Cubist, Synthetic Cubist, Classical, Abstract, and Surrealist phases, finally arriving at a synthesis of these styles. Peggy had some catching up to do.

• *Enter the first room to the left, and you'll see a dining-room table in the center.*

1900-1920: Cubists in the Dining Room

Peggy's **dining-room table** reminds us that this museum was, indeed, her home for the last 30 years of her life. Most of the furniture is now gone, but the walls are decorated much as they were when she lived here, with paintings and statues by her friends, colleagues, and mentors. Here, she entertained countless artists and celebrities (more name-dropping), from actor Paul Newman to poet Allen Ginsberg, from sculptor Henry Moore to playwright Tennessee Williams, from James Bond creator Ian Fleming to glass sculptor Dale Chihuly.

Most of the art in the dining room dates from Peggy's childhood, when she was raised in the lap of luxury in New York, oblivious to the artistic upheavals going on in Europe.

In 1912, the *Titanic* went down, taking Peggy's playboy tycoon father with it...and leaving his 14-year-old daughter with a small but comfortable trust fund and a man-sized hole in her life.

Approaching adulthood, Peggy rejected her traditional American upbringing. She started hanging out at a radical bookstore, got a nose job (a botched operation, leaving her with a rather bulbous schnozz)...and began planning a trip to Europe.

In 1920, 21-year-old Peggy arrived in Paris, where a revolution in art was taking place.

• *Find the following early 20th-century art (or similar pieces) in the Dining Room. (These and other items sometimes move around—if you don't see them where I mention them, keep looking.)*

Pablo Picasso—*The Poet* (1911)

Picasso, a Spaniard living in Paris, shattered the Old World into brown shards ("cubes") and reassembled it in Cubist style. It's a vaguely recognizable portrait of a man from the waist up—tapering to a head at the top, smoking a pipe (?), and cradling the traditional lyre of a poet. While the newfangled motion-picture camera could capture a moving image, Picasso suggests motion with a collage of stills.

Marcel Duchamp—*Nude (Study), Sad Young Man on a Train* (1911-1912)

In a self-portrait, Duchamp poses gracefully with a cane, but the moving train jiggles the image into a blur of brown. Duchamp is best known not for paintings like this, but for his outrageous conceptual pieces: his urinal-as-statue *(Fountain)* and his moustache on the *Mona Lisa* (titled *L.H.O.O.Q.*, which—when spoken aloud in French—is a pun that translates loosely as "she has a hot ass"). In a 2004 poll of British artists, Duchamp's urinal was named the most influential modern artwork of all time.

Constantin Brancusi—*Maiastra* (c. 1912)

For the generation born before air travel, flying was magical. This high-polished bird is the first of many by Brancusi, who dreamed of flight. But this bronze bird just sits there. For centuries, a good sculptor was one who could capture movement in stone. Brancusi reverts to the essential forms of "primitive" African art, in which even the simplest statues radiate mojo.

• *Head next door, into the Kitchen.*

Marc Chagall—*Rain* (1911)

The rain clouds gather over a farmhouse, the wind blows the trees and people, and everyone prepares for the

storm. Quick, put the horse in the barn, grab an umbrella, take a leak, and round up the goats in the clouds.

Marc Chagall, a Russian living in France, reinvented scenes from his homeland with a romantic, weightless, childlike joy in topsy-turvy Paris.

1920s: Abstraction and Various "-Isms"

In the Roaring Twenties, Peggy spent *her* twenties right in the center of avant-garde craziness: Paris. For the rest of her life, Europe—not America—would be her permanent address.

In Paris, trust-funded Peggy lived the bohemian life. Post-WWI Paris was cheap and, after the bitter war years, ready to party. Days were spent drinking coffee in cafés, talking ideas with the likes of activist Emma Goldman, writer Djuna *(Nightwood)* Barnes, and photographer Man Ray. Nights were spent abusing the drug forbidden in America (alcohol), dancing to jazz music into the wee hours, and talking about Freud and s-e-x.

One night, at the top of the Eiffel Tower, a dashing artist and intellectual nicknamed "The King of Bohemia" popped the question. Peggy and Laurence Vail soon married and had two children, but the partying only slowed somewhat. This thoroughly modern couple dug the wild life and the wild art it produced.

Vassily Kandinsky—*White Cross* (1922)

I see white, I see crosses, but where's the white cross? Oh, there it is on the right, camouflaged among black squares.

Like a jazz musician improvising from a set scale, Kandinsky plays with new patterns of related colors and lines, creating something that's simply beautiful, even if it doesn't "mean" anything. As Kandinsky himself would say, his art was like "visual music—just open your eyes and look."

• *Continue across the hall, into the Living Room.*

Piet Mondrian—*Composition with Red* (1938-1939)

Like a blueprint for Modernism, Mondrian's T-square style boils painting down to its basic building blocks—black lines, white canvas, and the three primary colors (red, yellow, and blue) arranged in orderly patterns. This stripped-down canvas even omits yellow and blue.

Mondrian started out painting realistic landscapes of the orderly fields in his native Holland. Increasingly, he simplified things into horizontal and vertical grids, creating rectangles of different proportions. This one has horizontal lines to the left, vertical ones to the right. The horizontals appear to dominate, until we see that they're balanced by the tiny patch of red.

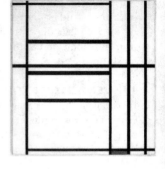

For Mondrian, who was heavily into Eastern mysticism, up vs. down and left vs. right were metaphors for life's ever-shifting dualities: good vs. evil, man vs. woman, fascism vs. communism. The canvas is a bird's-eye view of Mondrian's personal landscape.

• *Head next door, into the Library.*

1930s: Abstract Surrealists

In 1928, Peggy's marriage to Laurence Vail ended, and she entered into a series of romantic attachments. Though not stunningly attractive, she was easy to be with, and she truly admired artistic men.

In 1937, she began an on-again, off-again sexual relationship with playwright Samuel *(Waiting for Godot)* Beckett. Beckett steered her toward Modern painting and sculpture—things she'd never paid much attention to.

She started hanging out with the French Surrealists, from artist Marcel Duchamp to writer André Breton to filmmaker/artist Jean *(Beauty and the Beast)* Cocteau. Duchamp, in particular, mentored her in modern art, encouraging her to use her money to collect and promote it. Nearing 40, she moved to London and launched a new career.

Yves Tanguy—*The Sun in Its Jewel Case* (1937)

In May of 1938, this painting was featured at Guggenheim Jeune, the art gallery Peggy opened in London. Tanguy's painting sums

up the turbulent art that shocked a sleepy London during that first season.

Weird, phallic, tissue-and-bone protuberances cast long shadows across a moody, dreamlike landscape—the landscape of the mind. (Peggy said the picture "frightened" her, but added, "I got over my fear...and now I own it.") The figures are Abstract (unrecognizable), and the mood is Surreal, producing the style cleverly dubbed Abstract Surrealism.

Peggy was drawn to Yves Tanguy and

Abstract Art

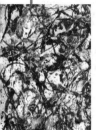

Abstract art simplifies. A man becomes a stick figure. A squiggle is a wave. A streak of red expresses anger. Arches make you want a cheeseburger. These are universal symbols that everyone from a caveman to a banker understands. Abstract artists capture the essence of reality in a few lines and colors, even things a camera can't—emotions, theoretical concepts, musical rhythms, and spiritual states of mind.

Most 20th- and 21st-century paintings are a mix of the real world ("representation") and the colorful patterns of "abstract" art. An abstract artist purposely "abstracts" only some elements of camera-eye reality to make the resulting canvas more provocative, expressive, or challenging.

had a short but intense affair with the married man. Tanguy, like his art, was wacky and spontaneous, occasionally shocking friends by suddenly catching and gobbling up a spider and washing it down with white wine. The Surrealists saw themselves as spokesmen for Freud's "id," the untamed part of the personality that thinks dirty thoughts when the "ego" goes to sleep.

The Guggenheim Jeune gallery exhibited many of the artists we see in this museum, including Kandinsky, Mondrian, and Calder. Guggenheim Jeune closed as a financial flop after just two years, but its shocking paintings certainly created a buzz in the art world, and as the years passed the gallery's failure gained a rosy glow of success.

Salvador Dalí—*The Birth of Liquid Desires* (1931-1932)

Salvador Dalí could draw exceptionally well. He painted "unreal" scenes with photographic realism, making us believe they could

truly happen. This air of mystery—the feeling that anything is possible—is both exciting and unsettling. His men explore the caves of the dream world and morph into something else before our eyes.

Personally, Peggy didn't like Dalí or his work, but she dutifully bought this canvas (through his wife, Gala) to complete her collection.

GUGGENHEIM

1939-1940: Peggy's Shopping Spree in Paris

Peggy moved back to Paris and rented an apartment on the Ile St. Louis. In September, Nazi Germany invaded Poland, sparking World War II. All of France waited...and waited...and waited for the inevitable Nazi attack on Paris.

Meanwhile, Peggy spent her days shopping for masterpieces. Using a list compiled by Duchamp and others, she personally visited artists in their studios—from Brancusi to Dalí to Giacometti—often negotiating directly with them. (Picasso initially turned Peggy down, thinking of her as a gauche, bargain-hunting housewife. When she entered his studio he said, "Madame, you'll find the lingerie department on the second floor.") In a few short months, she bought 37 of the paintings now in the collection, perhaps saving them from a Nazi regime that labeled such art "decadent."

In 1941, with the Nazis occupying Paris and most of Europe, Peggy fled her adopted homeland. With her stash of paintings and a new companion—painter Max Ernst—she sailed from Lisbon to safety in New York.

• *Pass back through the Entrance Hall—where Peggy welcomed celebrity guests, from writer Somerset Maugham to actor Rex Harrison to painter Marc Chagall—and into the east wing. The right entryway leads to a room filled with Surrealist canvases.*

GUGGENHEIM

1941-1945: Surrealists Invade New York

Trees become women, women become horses, and day becomes night. Balls dangle, caves melt, and things cast long shadows across film-noir landscapes—Surrealism. The world was moving fast, and Surrealists caught the jumble of images. They scattered seemingly unrelated things on the canvas, leaving us to trace the connections in a kind of connect-the-dots game without numbers.

Peggy spent the war years in America. She married Max Ernst, and their house in New York City became a gathering place for exiled French Surrealists and young American artists.

In 1942, she opened a gallery/museum in New York called Art of This Century that featured, well, essentially the collection we see here in Venice. But patri-  otic, gung-ho America was not quite ready for the nonconformist, intellectual art of Europe.

Max Ernst—*The Antipope* (c. 1942)

The horse-headed nude in red is a portrait of Peggy—at least, that's what she thought when she saw it. She loved the painting and insisted that Max give it to her as a wedding present, renamed *The Mystic Marriage*.

Others read more into it. Is the horse-headed warrior (at right) Ernst himself? Is he being wooed by one of his art students? Is that Peggy's daughter, Pegeen (center), watching the scene, sadly, from a distance? And is Peggy turning toward her beloved Max, subconsciously suspicious of the young student...who would (in fact) soon steal Max from her? Ernst uses his considerable painting skill to bring to light a tangle of secret urges, desires, and fears—hidden like the grotesque animal faces in the reef they stand on.

Paul Delvaux—*The Break of Day* (1937)

Full-breasted ladies with roots cast long shadows and awaken to a mysterious dawn. If you're counting boobs, don't forget the one reflected in the nightstand mirror.

René Magritte—*Empire of Light* (1953-1954)

Magritte found that, even under a sunny blue sky, suburbia has its dark side.

• *Across the hall is the Guest Bedroom, with a fireplace and works by Pollock.*

1945-1948: The Postwar Years: Pollock in the Guest Bedroom

Certain young American painters—from Mark Rothko to Robert Motherwell to Robert De Niro Sr. (the actor's father)—were strongly influenced by Peggy's collection. Adopting the Abstract style of Kandinsky, they practiced Surrealist spontaneity to "express" themselves in the physical act of putting paint on canvas. The resulting style (duh): Abstract Expressionism.

Jackson Pollock—*Enchanted Forest* (1947)

"Jack the Dripper" attacked America's postwar conformity with a can of paint, dripping and splashing a dense web onto the canvas. Picture Pollock in his studio, jiving to the hi-fi, bouncing off the walls, throwing paint in a moment of alcohol-fueled enlightenment.

Peggy helped make Pollock a celebrity. She bought his earliest works (which show

Abstract-Surrealist roots), exhibited his work at her gallery, and even paid him a monthly stipend to keep experimenting.

By the way, if you haven't yet tried the Venetian specialty *spaghetti al nero di seppia* (spaghetti with squid in its own ink), it looks something like this.

In 1946, Peggy published her memoirs, titled *Out of This Century: The Informal Memoirs of Peggy Guggenheim*. The front cover was designed by Max Ernst, the back by Pollock. Peggy herself was now a celebrity.

• *The room on the other side of the fireplace was Peggy's Bedroom.*

1950s: Peggy in the Bedroom

As America's postwar factories turned swords into kitchen appliances, Peggy longed to return "home" to Europe. The one place that kept calling to her was Venice, ever since she visited here with Laurence Vail in the 1920s. "I decided Venice would be my future home," she wrote. "I felt I would be happy alone there."

In 1947, after a grand finale exhibition by Pollock, she closed the Art of This Century gallery, crated up her collection, and moved to Venice. In 1948, she bought this palazzo and moved in.

This was Peggy's bedroom. She painted it turquoise. She commissioned the **silver headboard by Alexander Calder** for her canopy bed, using its silver frame to hang her collection of earrings, handmade by the likes of Calder and Tanguy. Venetian mirrors hung on the walls, along with a sentimental portrait of herself and her sister as children. Ex-husband Laurence Vail's collage-decorated bottles sat on the nightstand.

The same year she moved in, Peggy showed her collection in its own pavilion at the Biennale, Venice's world's fair of art, and it was the hit of the show. Europeans were astounded and a bit dumbfounded, finally seeing the kind of "degenerate" art forbidden during the fascist years, plus the radical new stuff coming out of New York City.

In 1951, Peggy met the last great love of her life, an easygoing, blue-collar Italian with absolutely no interest in art. She was 53, Raoul was 30. When Raoul died in 1954 in a car accident, Peggy comforted herself with her pets.

• *The tiny corner room adjoining the bedroom displays paintings by Pegeen.*

Pegeen

Peggy's daughter, Pegeen, inherited some of Laurence Vail's artistic talent, painting childlike scenes of Venice, populated by skinny Barbie dolls with antennae.

The guest bedroom (where the Pollocks are) was a busy place. Pegeen and her brother, Sinbad, visited their mother in Venice, as did Peggy's ex-husbands and their new loves. Other overnight guests ranged from sculptor Alberto Giacometti (who honeymooned here), to author and cultural explorer Paul Bowles, to artist Jean Arp.

• *Return to the Entrance Hall, then go out onto the Terrace, overlooking the Grand Canal.*

Exhibitionists on the Terrace

> *You fall in love with the city itself. There is nothing left over in your heart for anyone else.*
>
> —Peggy Guggenheim

The obviously exuberant figure in Marino Marini's equestrian statue, *The Angel of the City* (1948), faces the Grand Canal, spreads

his arms wide, and tosses his head back in sheer joy, with an eternal hard-on for the city of Venice. Every morning, Peggy must have felt a similar exhilaration as she sipped coffee while taking in this unbelievable view.

Marini originally designed his bronze rider with a screw-off penis (which sounds dirtier than it is) that could be removed for prudish guests or by curious ones. Someone stole it for some unknown purpose, so the current organ is permanently welded on.

The palazzo—formally Palazzo Venier dei Leoni—looks modern but is old. Construction began in 1748, but only the ground floor was completed. Legend has it that members of a rival family across the canal squelched plans for the upper stories so their home wouldn't be upstaged. The palazzo remained unfinished until Peggy bought it in 1948 and spruced it up. She added the annex in 1958. The **lions** *(leoni)* of the original palace still guard the waterfront entrance.

Peggy's outlandish and rather foreign presence in Venice—drinking, dressing up outrageously, and sunbathing on her rooftop for all to see—was not immediately embraced by the Venetians. But for artists in the 1950s and 1960s, Peggy's palazzo was *the* place to be, especially when the Biennale brought the jet set. Everyone from actor Alec Guinness, to political satirist Art Buchwald, to gossip columnist Hedda Hopper signed her guest book. Picture Peggy and guests, decked out in evening clothes, hopping into her custom-built gondola (nicknamed *La Barchessa,* after the doge's private boat) to ride slowly down the canal for a martini and a Bellini at Harry's Bar.

GUGGENHEIM

The Rest of the Museum

• We've seen the core of Peggy's collection (and home). But the museum complex also houses two other collections donated by Peggy's fellow art lovers, as well as a fine garden.

Schulhof and Mattioli Collections

The recently acquired **Schulhof Collection,** most likely exhibited in the wing perpendicular to the palazzo (which you can enter from near Peggy's Bedroom), brings the museum into the late 20th century.

Increasingly, you'll have to focus your eyes to look *at* the canvases, not *through* them. In the 1950s and '60s, the trend was toward bigger canvases, abstract designs, and experimentation with new materials and techniques.

Enjoy the simple lines and colors of big, empty canvases by Americans such as Ellsworth Kelly, Barnett Newman, and Mark Rothko. They were following in the footsteps of Abstract artists such as Mondrian and Kandinsky (whose work they must have considered busy). Calder's mobiles are like hanging Kandinskys brought to life by a gust of wind. The geometrical forms here reflect the same search for order, but these artists painted to the 5/4 asymmetry of Dave Brubeck's jazz classic, "Take Five."

Other painters explored a new dimension: texture. Some works (such as those by de Kooning) have very thick paint piled on. Some (by Dubuffet or Tapies) applied material such as real dirt and organic waste to the canvas. Fontana punctured the canvas so that the fabric itself (and the hole) becomes the subject. The canvas is a tray, serving up a delightful array of substances with interesting colors, patterns, shapes, and textures.

In the psychedelic '60s, Pop Art (Warhol) raised pop-ular cultural icons to the level of high art, and Op Art (Riley) featured optical illusions that mess with your mind when you stare at them. Cy Twombly added crayon-scribbled doodles to the canvas, suggesting handwritten messages with mysterious meanings. Also in the collection are a number of sculptures by Chillida, Calder, Hepworth, and Arp. By the way, many of the Schulhof artists—Calder, Fontana, Chillida, Riley, and Twombly—were first introduced to the world at the Venice Biennale.

The **Mattioli Collection,** most likely housed in the café/shop building across the garden from the main palazzo, features paintings and sculptures by well-known Italians, as well as the less-famous postwar generation of young Italians who were strongly influenced by Peggy's collection.

You'll see a lone canvas by Modigliani, pieces by the Futurists, and some fine sculptural works by the father of Futurism, **Umberto Boccioni.** His *Dynamism of a Speeding Horse + Houses* (1915), assembled from wood, cardboard, and metal, captures the blurred motion of a modern world—accelerated by technology, then shattered by World War I, which would leave nine million Europeans dead and everyone's moral compass spinning. (In fact, this statue was shattered by the destructive force of Boccioni's own kids, who scattered the cardboard "houses" while using it as a rocking horse.)

Boccioni's *Unique Forms of Continuity in Space* (1913, one of a dozen authorized bronze casts in the world's museums) seems inspired by the flowing works by Picasso and Duchamp we saw earlier. The energetic cyborg speeds forward, rippled by the winds of history, as it strides purposefully into the future. This work may look familiar—check your pocket for one of Italy's €0.20 coins and compare.

Peggy sponsored young artists, including **Tancredi**—just one name, back when that was odd—who was given a studio in the palazzo's basement. Tancredi had a relationship with daughter Pegeen, with her mother's blessing. (Pegeen died in 1967 of a barbiturates overdose.)

Sculpture Garden

Peggy opened her impressive collection of sculpture to the Venetian public for free. It features first-rate works by all the greats, from Brancusi to Giacometti. After so much art already, you might find the trees—so rare in urban Venice—more interesting.

If, after your visit here, you still don't like modern art, think of what Peggy used to tell puzzled visitors: "Come back again in 50 years."

Café/Shop and More Exhibitions

The long building facing the main palazzo from across the garden houses the overpriced **café, shop, WCs,** and (in the back) halls for the **Mattioli Collection** (described earlier) and **temporary exhibits.** Step into the café just to peruse the fascinating black-and-white photos of Peggy standing alongside her art, taken in the very same rooms in which the paintings now hang.

• *Finally, in the southwest corner of the garden (along the brick wall), find...*

Peggy's Grave and Her Dogs' Graves

"Here Lie My Beloved Babies," marks the grave of Peggy's many dogs, her steady companions as she grew old. Note the names of some of these small, long-haired Lhasa Apsos.

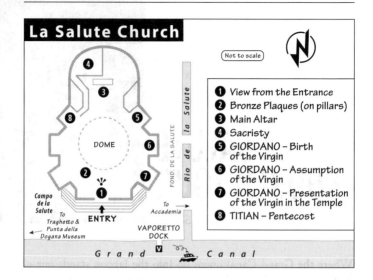

La Salute Church

Not to scale

DOME

Campo
de la
Salute
To
Traghetto &
Punta della
Dogana Museum

ENTRY

To
Accademia

FOND. DE LA SALUTE

Rio de la Salute

VAPORETTO
DOCK

Grand Canal

❶ View from the Entrance
❷ Bronze Plaques (on pillars)
❸ Main Altar
❹ Sacristy
❺ GIORDANO – Birth
    of the Virgin
❻ GIORDANO – Assumption
    of the Virgin
❼ GIORDANO – Presentation
    of the Virgin in the Temple
❽ TITIAN – Pentecost

The Tour Begins

Exterior

The white stone church has a steep dome that rises above the octagonal structure. It's encrusted with Baroque scrolls, leafy Corinthian columns, and 125 statues, including the lovely ladies lounging over the central doorway. The architect conceived of the church in the shape of a crown.

During the bitter plague of 1630, the Virgin Mary took pity on the city of Venice, miraculously allowing only one in three Venetians (46,000 souls) to die. During this terrible time, Venetians built this church in honor of Our Lady of Health. Her statue tops the lantern, and she's dressed as an admiral, hand on a rudder, welcoming ships to the Grand Canal.

Even today, Mary's intercession is celebrated every November 21, when a floating bridge is erected across the Grand Canal so Venetians can walk from San Marco across the water and right up the seaweed-covered steps to the front door.

At age 32, architect Baldassare Longhena (1598-1682) supported the city's heaviest dome by sinking countless pilings (locals claim over a million) into the sandy soil to provide an adequate foundation. The 12 Baroque scrolls at the dome's base function as buttresses to help support the mammoth structure.

Interior

❶ View from the Entrance

The church has a bright, healthy glow, with white stone (turned gray because of a fungus) illuminated by light filtering through the dome's windows. The nave is circular, surrounded by chapels. In contrast to the ornate Baroque exterior, the inside is simple, with only Corinthian columns and two useless balcony railings up in the dome. The red, white, and yellow marble of the floor adds a cheerful note.

Longhena focuses our immediate attention on the main altar. Every other view is blocked by heavy pillars. A master of "theatrical architecture," Longhena reveals the side chapels only one by one, as we walk around and explore. Viewed from the center of the church, the altar and side chapels are framed by arches.

Some of the "marble" is actually brick covered with marble dust. The windows, with clear glass in a honeycomb pattern, bring in maximum light.

• *Look at the pillars near the entrance, opposite the altar, to find the...*

❷ Bronze Plaques

The church is dedicated not just to physical health but to spiritual health as well. The plaques relate that on September 16, 1972, Albino Luciani, the future Pope John Paul I, visited here and paid homage to the Virgin of Health (six years later, he fell sick and died after only 30 days in office).

❸ Main Altar

The marble statues on the top of the main altar tell the church's story: The Virgin and Child (center) are approached for help by a kneeling, humble Lady Venice (left). Mary shows compassion and sends an angel baby (right) to drive away Old Lady Plague.

The icon of a black, sad-eyed Madonna with a black baby (12th-century Byzantine) is not meant to be ethnically accurate. Here, a "black" Madonna means an otherworldly one.

• *Find the entrance to the Sacristy, if it's open (entry location varies). It costs €3 to get in, but cheapskates can get a glimpse of the paintings for free by standing outside the entry.*

❹ Sacristy

Along one wall is Tintoretto's big and colorful *Marriage at Cana* (1551). The receding dinner table leads the eye to Jesus, who is surrounded by the bustle of the wedding feast. On the right, the host (in gray) orders the servant to bring more wine. The apostles at

LA SALUTE

the table portray leading Venetian artists of the day. On the ceiling are three ultra-dramatic paintings by Titian, with gruesome subjects: *Cain Clubbing Abel, Abraham Sacrificing His Son,* and *David Slaying Goliath* (c. 1543-1544). The panels—featuring stormy clouds, windblown hair, flat tones, and overwrought poses—date from Titian's "Mannerist crisis." After visiting Rome and seeing the work of Michelangelo in the Sistine Chapel, Titian abandoned his standard, sweet, and tested style to paint epic, statuesque, and dramatic works in the Mannerist style. To appreciate his range of styles, contrast the ceiling panels with the painting over the altar, Titian's stately *St. Mark Enthroned with Saints* (c. 1511).

• *Back in the circular nave, there are six side chapels—three to the left, three to the right. Start near the main altar, on the right side (to your right as you face the altar).*

Side Chapel Paintings

Luca Giordano (1632-1705) celebrates the Virgin in three paintings with similar compositions—heaven and angels above, dark earth below.

Giordano, a prolific artist from Naples, was known as "Luca fa presto" (Fast Luke) for the speed (some would say sloppiness) with which he dashed off his paintings.

• *In the chapel to the right of the altar is...*

❺ Giordano—*Birth of the Virgin* (1674)

Little baby Mary in her mom's arms seems like nothing special. But God the Father looks down from above and sends the dove of the Holy Spirit.

• *In the middle chapel (on the right side), look for...*

❻ Giordano—*Assumption of the Virgin* (1667)

Mary, at the end of her life, is being taken gloriously, by winged babies, up from the dark earth to the golden light of heaven. The apostles cringe in amazement. A later artist thought his statue was better and planted it right in our way.

• *In the chapel closest to the entrance, see...*

❼ Giordano—*Presentation of the Virgin in the Temple* (early 1670s)

Notice how the painting fits the surrounding architecture. It's great to enjoy art *in situ*. The child Mary (in blue, with wispy halo) ascends a staircase that goes diagonally "into" the canvas. Giordano places us viewers at the foot of the stairs. The lady in the lower left asks her kids, "Why can't you be more like her?!"

• *From here, look directly across to the other side of the nave at Titian's* Pentecost, *in the chapel closest to the main altar. The painting looks its best from this distance and angle.*

❽ Titian—*Pentecost* (1546)

The dove of the Holy Spirit sends spiritual rays that fan out to the apostles below, giving them tongues of fire above their heads. They

 gyrate in amazement, each one in a different direction. Using floor tiles and ceiling panels, Titian has created the 3-D illusion of a barrel-arched chapel, with the dove coming right into the church through a fake window. But the painting was not designed for this location and, up close, the whole fake niche looks...fake.

SAN GIORGIO MAGGIORE TOUR

San Giorgio Maggiore is the dreamy church-topped island you see across the lagoon from St. Mark's Square. It's just a five-minute vaporetto ride away. Even if you're not interested in Palladio's influential architecture, Tintoretto's famous *Last Supper*, or the stunning bell-tower views of Venice and the lagoon, it's worth a trip just to escape from tourist-mobbed St. Mark's Square.

Orientation

Cost: Admission to the church is free. It costs €6 to go up the bell tower. Bring €0.50 coins to light the artwork.

Hours: Both the church and tower are open April-Oct Mon-Sat 9:00-19:00, Sun 9:00-11:00 & 12:00-19:00; Nov-March daily 9:00-17:30. The last ascent in the tower elevator is 30 minutes before closing time.

Avoiding Crowds: The church is never crowded, but the bell tower and elevator can be. Come early or late to have it to yourself.

Getting There: The only way to reach the church is by taking a five-minute ride on vaporetto #2, which leaves near St. Mark's Square from the San Zaccaria stop, located east of the Bridge of Sighs (€4, 6/hour, ticket valid for one hour, direction: Tronchetto, stop: San Giorgio). You can't ride to San Giorgio from the San Marco stop—only from San Zaccaria. To get back to St. Mark's Square, take the #2 headed the opposite way (direction: San Zaccaria).

Mass: Mass is held on Sundays at 11:00, when the church is closed to sightseers. To attend Mass, held in the Conclave, ring the bell at the door to the right of the main entrance. In the winter, when it's too cold inside the church, Mass is held in the adjacent chapel.

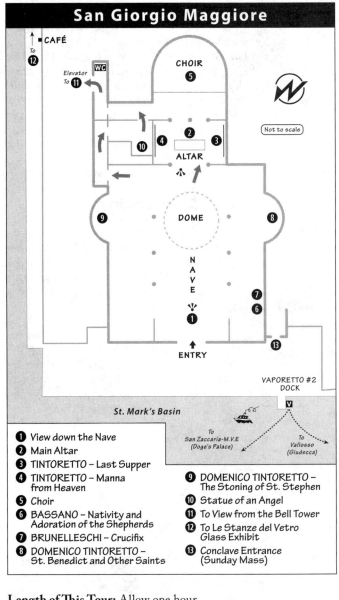

San Giorgio Maggiore

CAFÉ

To ⑫

CHOIR ⑤

Elevator
To ⑪

WC

Not to scale

② ③
④
⑩
ALTAR

DOME

N
A
V
E

⑨   ⑧

⑦
⑥

①

⑬

ENTRY

VAPORETTO #2
DOCK

St. Mark's Basin

V

To
San Zaccaria–M.V.E
(Doge's Palace)

To
Vallosso
(Giudecca)

① View down the Nave
② Main Altar
③ TINTORETTO – Last Supper
④ TINTORETTO – Manna
   from Heaven
⑤ Choir
⑥ BASSANO – Nativity and
   Adoration of the Shepherds
⑦ BRUNELLESCHI – Crucifix
⑧ DOMENICO TINTORETTO –
   St. Benedict and Other Saints

⑨ DOMENICO TINTORETTO –
   The Stoning of St. Stephen
⑩ Statue of an Angel
⑪ To View from the Bell Tower
⑫ To Le Stanze del Vetro
   Glass Exhibit
⑬ Conclave Entrance
   (Sunday Mass)

SAN GIORGIO MAGGIORE

Length of This Tour: Allow one hour.

WCs: A pay WC is at the base of the elevator, inside the church (€0.50).

Photography: Permitted (a rarity in Venice).

Eating: A fine little harborside café, rarely used by tourists, is about 150 yards around the left of the church. Its terrace is peaceful—except at lunchtime, when it's mobbed by librarians (€4 *panini*, €8.50 pastas and salads, €10 *secondi*, daily 10:00-20:00, off-season 11:00-15:00).

The Rest of the Island: You can walk along the left side of the church to the café and view the pleasure boats in the marina. Inside the pink building just beyond the café is **Le Stanze del Vetro,** a super-modern space with rotating exhibits relating to glass. Typically their spring exhibition features contemporary glass art, while their fall show highlights a historic Venetian maestro (free entry, Thu-Tue 10:00-19:00, closed Wed, www.lestanzedelvetro.it).

Starring: Palladio, Tintoretto, and views of Venice.

The Tour Begins

Exterior

The facade looks like a Greek temple, a style well-known today because of its architect, Andrea Palladio (1508-1580). Palladio's

hugely influential treatise on architecture inspired centuries of architects in England and America with its expert application of Greco-Roman styles. Countless villas, palaces, and churches look like this. They are "Palladian."

Palladio's ingenious facade overlaps two temple fronts. Four tall columns, topped by a triangular pediment resembling a Greek porch, mark the entryway to the tall, central nave. This is superimposed over the facade of the lower side aisles. Behind the facade rises a dome topped with a statue of St. George (the Christian slayer of medieval dragons) holding a flag. The whole complex is completed by the bell tower, which echoes the Campanile in St. Mark's Square across the water.

This church feels so striking because it just doesn't fit with old-school Venice. Palladio makes no concession to the Byzantine legacy of Venice that you see across the water at the Doge's Palace.

• *Walk into the interior of the church.*

Interior

❶ View down the Nave, then up the Nave

The interior matches the outer facade, with a high nave flanked by lower side aisles. The walls are white (Palladio's favorite color); the windows

have clear, rather than stained, glass; and the well-lit church has the clarity, orderliness, and mathematical perfection of the classical world. In keeping with Palladio's classical sensitivity, all decor is in harmony (compared to the relative chaos of, say, the Frari Church). Oh, the stout, stony symmetry and mathematical purity—with light spilling in from the canal—it's enough to give a Renaissance architect a...never mind.

• *Head down the nave to the...*

❷ Main Altar

The altar is topped with a bronze globe of the world. When this place was being built, Church doctrine was being challenged by the discovery of the New World, the founding of secular societies, and the groundbreaking scientific advancements of the Enlightenment. With this altar, the globe is embraced as if to declare the universality of the Christian message. God, overhead, is wearing a triangular halo, reminding us he's part of the Trinity.

• *On the wall to the right of the altar is...*

❸ Tintoretto—*Last Supper*, 1592-1594

This is the last of several versions of the *Last Supper* by Tintoretto (1518-1594) that decorate Venice, each one different and inven-

tive (compare it with the Scuola San Rocco version, pictured on page 166). Here, the table stretches diagonally away from us on a tiled floor. The convincing perspective effect is theatrical, engaging the viewer. The scene is crowded—servants and cats mingle with wispy angels. A blazing lamp, radiating supernatural light, illuminates the otherwise dark interior. At the far left, a beggar is fed, illustrating Christ's concern for the poor. The devilish guy on the right rejects a basket of communion wafers while eyeing a more hedonistic banquet. Your eyes go straight to a well-lit Christ, serving his faithful with both hands—wholeheartedly.

San Giorgio was the church for a Benedictine monastery, an order that stressed a simple lifestyle and concern for the poor. They hired Tintoretto (a common-man's painter) and worked closely with him to hone the message that all are welcome— saints, servants, beggars, sinners—into the Christian faith. The monks appreciated Tintoretto's jumble of the spiritual with the mundane, proclaiming that God works miraculously with us on an everyday level.

This canvas works together theologically with the other canvas flanking the altar.

• *On the wall to the left of the altar is...*

❹ Tintoretto—*Manna from Heaven*, 1591-1592

This painting illustrates the Benedictine motto: Work and pray. Here we see the sunny morning after the storm, when God rained bread down on the hungry Israelites. Some work, others relax prayerfully, and others gather the heavenly meal in baskets, basking in the glow of the miracle. The message: Work and pray, and God will take care of you.

• *Behind the altar is the...*

❺ Choir

This beautiful space features 82 stalls elaborately carved in walnut. Here, monks stood and sang, carrying on the prayers, chants, and traditions of the Benedictine order, whose relationship with the island stretched back to A.D. 982 (the monastery closed in 1807). The choir was designed with acoustics in mind, and the barrel-vault ceiling is backed up with a woofer-shaped apse—all to amplify the Gregorian chants that still fill this church on occasion. (Suddenly I feel a cough coming on...my, the echoes.)

More Art Inside the Church

As long as you're here, check out a few more works. They're minor pieces in art-drenched Venice, but they'd be stars in any American museum.

Back near the entrance, in the first chapel on the right as you face the altar, is Jacopo Bassano's ❻ *Nativity and Adoration of the Shepherds,* where a radiant Baby Jesus lights the dim canvas. In the next chapel is a carved ❼ *Crucifix* by Florentine dome-builder Filippo Brunelleschi.

In the transepts are two works by Jacopo Tintoretto's son, Domenico. In the right transept, the static ❽ *St. Benedict and Other Saints* shows the early monk (to left, in black, bald and bearded) along with Pope Gregory (who wrote about him) having a heavenly vision. ❾ *The Stoning of St. Stephen* (left transept) shows that Domenico had his father's raw talent, but not his flair for dramatic compositions that recede into the distance.

On your way to the bell tower, you'll pass the original ❿ **statue of an angel** that once stood atop the tower (a copy stands there today). Made in the 18th century of laminated wood covered in lead, it was destroyed by lightning in 1993. Restorers have done their best to piece it back together.

• *You'll find the elevator to the top of the bell tower in the far left corner of the church.*

⓫ View from the Bell Tower

The bell tower has no grille (unlike the Campanile at St. Mark's, which has one to keep suicidal people from jumping) and gives a grand view in all directions. Start by looking at the city (to the north), and go clockwise:

Facing North (toward the city): This is the famous view of Venice's skyline, dominated by St. Mark's Campanile. The big,

long, brick church farther inland is Santi Giovanni e Paolo. Farther to the right (east) is the barely visible basin of the Arsenale, the former shipyard, which in its medieval heyday bragged that it was capable of producing a ship a day. Farther still is the green parkland where the Venice Biennale international exhibition is held annu-

ally (alternating each year between art and architecture). North of Venice, in the hazy distance (just to the right of Santi Giovanni e Paolo), you can glimpse several islands. Tiny San Michele (with cypress trees) is the city's cemetery—from here, the island looks connected to Venice. Murano, the next closest, appears to be an extension of the forested cemetery. Burano is to the distant right, with its leaning bell tower. And Torcello (trust me) is just beyond Burano.

Facing East and South: Look out at the lagoon, which leads to the open Adriatic. This tower was once used to spot approaching enemy boats. The lagoon is too shallow for serious shipping; posts mark the channels dredged to let boats pass through. There's a strict speed limit: 5 knots per hour (kph) on the small canals, 7 kph on the Grand Canal, and 11 kph around the perimeter of the island city.

The long, narrow island of Lido in the distance is six miles

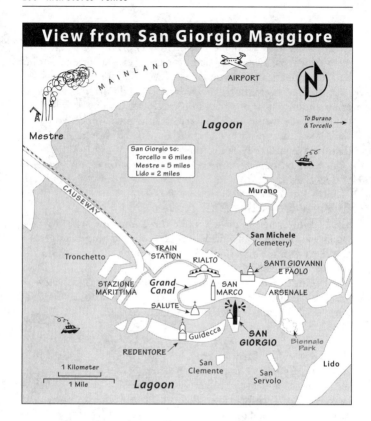

View from San Giorgio Maggiore

MAINLAND

AIRPORT

Lagoon

To Burano
& Torcello →

Mestre

San Giorgio to:
Torcello = 6 miles
Mestre = 5 miles
Lido = 2 miles

Murano

CAUSEWAY

San Michele
(cemetery)

Tronchetto

TRAIN
STATION

RIALTO

SANTI GIOVANNI
E PAOLO

STAZIONE
MARITTIMA

Grand
Canal

SAN
MARCO

ARSENALE

SALUTE

REDENTORE

Guidecca

SAN
GIORGIO

Biennale
Park

Lido

1 Kilometer

San
Clemente

San
Servolo

1 Mile

Lagoon

long and only a half-mile wide (with cars and ferry service to the mainland). The green dome on the island marks the Lido's town center, home to modern hotels and beaches. The Lido serves as a natural breakwater against the wind and waves of the Adriatic Sea, helping create the placid waters of the Venetian lagoon. At the right end of the Lido (visible from here, but not obvious) is the narrow opening to the Adriatic, where the long-delayed underwater flood barriers are being built. Designed to block the *acqua alta* flooding, the multibillion-dollar project involves the construction of a series of hinged barriers that will rise up to block high tides threatening the lagoon.

Once a year, the mayor of Venice sails to the opening of the Adriatic to celebrate the ritual marriage of Venice and the sea—the same ritual performed centuries ago by the doges in their gold-leaf boat.

Between the Lido and San Giorgio are several smaller islands,

which have been home over the centuries to monasteries and hospitals. The plain, rectangular white building on San Servolo, the little island just before the Lido, was a hospital for the insane in the 18th century and now houses a university.

At your feet are the green gardens and the cloisters of the former abbey of San Giorgio.

Facing West: Below is the church, with its dome topped by a green St. George carrying a flag (or is his arm still missing?). You

can see the back sides of the white statues atop Palladio's facade. Arcing gracefully to the left is the island of Giudecca, which is oh-so-close to the island you're on, but must be reached by a short swim or vaporetto #2. The Giudecca, which has always been isolated from the rest of the city, was a popular place to build villas in Venice's heyday. The island's separation also made it a perfect place for exiles such as Michelangelo, who found refuge and peace here between commissions. Today, except for a few churches, a youth hostel, and a couple of luxury hotels, the Giudecca is home to locals going about their quiet lives, oblivious to the tourism that dominates the rest of Venice. You can see the swimming pool of the jet-setty Ciprani Hotel, the domes of other Palladian churches (the only sights on this otherwise residential island), and, at the far end, the Molino Stucky, an old, industrial flour mill that reopened in 2007 as the Hilton Hotel.

Directly across from you is the grand dome of La Salute Church. At the head of the Grand Canal stands the golden globe of the old Customs House, now the Punta della Dogana contemporary art museum. Looming beyond La Salute's dome, and a bit to the right, is Venice's cruise port. How many megaships are in town today? And in the far distance, through the smog, are the burning smokestacks and cranes of lovely Mestre, on the mainland.

Looking Up: The bells chime the hours and ring especially loudly at noon. Try being here then, and when people ask you, "How did you enjoy San Giorgio Maggiore?" you can say, "What?"

VENICE'S LAGOON TOUR

San Michele • Murano • Burano • Torcello

Fascinating islands hide out in Venice's lagoon, a calm section of the Adriatic protected from wind and waves by the natural breakwater of the Lido. The brackish marsh—a mix of fresh water and silt from the mainland's rivers, plus the tide-driven saltwater of the Adriatic—is set among a maze of sandbars. The lagoon is big (212 square miles) and so shallow that you could walk across most of it without getting your hair wet. Centuries ago, the shallow water and treacherous sandbars made the Isle of Venice safe from attack by land or sea. Venice is the only great medieval city that never needed a wall.

Cradled by the lagoon, north of the city, are four islands easily laced together in a pleasant day trip, a nice escape from the hubbub of Venice. Though they're all basically satellites of Venice, each one has its own personality and claims to fame: Murano is known for glass; Burano for lace and photogenic, exuberantly colorful houses; and tranquil Torcello for its antique church's fine mosaics. San Michele is the cemetery island, the last stop for its residents, but the first stop for the vaporetto from Venice. The lagoon is home to many more islands, but these four are the most worthwhile for visitors.

We'll sail first from Venice to Murano (stopping at San Michele on the way), and then to Burano, from where we'll make a side-trip to Torcello before returning to Venice.

Orientation

Transportation: We'll travel by vaporetto, but there are other options (see sidebar in this chapter). Since single vaporetto tickets (€7) expire after one hour, getting a vaporetto pass for this

lagoon excursion makes more sense (such as a 12-hour pass for €18; see page 31 for more on vaporetto tickets).

Sightseeing Costs: Murano's Glass Museum costs €8 (may be undergoing renovation when you visit), Burano's Lace Museum is €5, and Torcello's main attraction—its church—costs €5 (its other sights cost a few euros each).

When to Go: If you want to visit all of the lagoon sights, keep in mind that Burano's good Lace Museum and Torcello's dull church museum are closed Mondays.

Avoiding Crowds: You aren't the only tourist in Venice spending your day seeing these sights, in this same order. *Vaporetti* can be very crowded; if you want a seat for the longer rides, consider showing up at the boat dock a bit early to get in line.

Information: Pick up a free map of the lagoon and its islands from any TI. Two words you'll see all day: *vetri* (glass, Murano's specialty) and *merletti* (lace, Burano's specialty).

Length of This Tour: Since it takes a minimum of three hours round-trip from St. Mark's to Torcello, allow at least six hours to blitz all four islands. Eight hours (or more) lets you slow down, browse, and enjoy. For an hour-by-hour itinerary, see page 20. If you only have a few hours to spare, stick to visiting either Murano (for glass; it's also much closer to reach) or Burano/Torcello (for small-town, rustic ambience).

Starring: World-famous Venetian glass and lace, the mosaics of the oldest Venetian church, outrageously colorful fishermen's villages, and the quieter side of Venice.

Where to Start

You can start from St. Mark's Square, from the train station or bus station, or from the Fondamente Nove vaporetto stop (15 minutes' walk from Rialto or San Marco). Wherever you start, your first goal is to locate a vaporetto heading to the Colonna stop on the island of Murano (listed on signs and schedules as Murano-Colonna).

From Fondamente Nove: The Fondamente Nove stop is on the north shore of Venice (the "back" of the fish, an enjoyable 15-minute walk from the Rialto or San Marco area—see directions below). Lines #4.1 and #4.2 converge here before heading out to Murano. Catch either one (every 10 minutes). From Fondamente Nove the boats cross to San Michele (whose stop is called Cimitero) in six minutes, then continue another three minutes to Murano-Colonna.

Walking to Fondamente Nove is easy and scenic, passing through two of Venice's most pleasant squares: First head for Campo Santa Maria Formosa (north of St. Mark's), then navigate north to Campo San Zanipolo/Santi Giovanni e Paolo (with its hulking church). Behind the church is Venice's gigantic, brick hospital *(ospedale);* walk between that building and the canal (on Fondamenta dei Mendicanti) until you reach the lagoon; turn left and walk a few more minutes to the vaporetto stops.

From St. Mark's Square: From the San Zaccaria stop, catch vaporetto #4.1, which leaves every 20 minutes (check the readerboard to find the right dock to wait at). It travels around the "tail" of fish-shaped Venice, making several stops before reaching Murano-Colonna after 45 minutes. (During the summer, you can also take the express #7 vaporetto directly to Murano in 25 minutes, but you'll miss the cemetery.)

From the Train Station or Bus Station: Catch vaporetto #4.2, which leaves every 20 minutes and takes 40 minutes to reach Murano-Colonna. (You can also take the express #3 vaporetto, which goes directly to Murano-Colonna twice an hour, but then you'll have to skip the cemetery.)

The Route

Here's the plan: On the way to Murano, you can make a quick visit to the cemetery on San Michele (Cimitero stop). On Murano, you'll arrive at the Colonna stop, but leave the island from a different stop (Murano-Faro). At Murano-Faro, board vaporetto #12 for the 30-minute trip to Burano. From Burano, you can side-trip to Torcello on vaporetto #9 (5-minute trip each way). To make a quick return to Venice from Burano, hop on vaporetto #12, which arrives at Fondamente Nove (45 minutes). For a longer, more scenic return, see the end of this chapter.

The Tour Begins

• *After leaving Fondamente Nove, the next stop of the #4.1 and #4.2 vaporetto lines is Cimitero. Hop off here for a short visit to...*

San Michele

The cemetery island's location—directly across the water from the emergency room of Venice's Santi Giovanni e Paolo hospital—is

just a coincidence. The stopover is easy, since boats come every 10 minutes. If you even half-enjoy wandering through old cemeteries, you'll dig this one—it's full of flowers, trees, scurrying lizards, and birdsong, and has an intriguing chapel (cemetery open daily April-Sept 7:30-18:00, Oct-March 7:30-16:30; reception to the left as you enter, free WC to the right, no picnicking).

The island, which is dedicated to St. Michael and holds a Renaissance church, became Venice's cemetery in 1806 when Napoleon decreed that it was unhygienic to bury bodies within a city. As a result, Venice's coffins were shipped out to San Michele, and since then, Venetians have been buried here. You'll find the dearly departed (many with their photos) sorted into sections *(campi)* of priests *(preti)*, nuns *(suore)*, monks *(frati)*, children *(bambini)*, civilian victims of war, soldiers, military sailors *(marinai)*, and so on. The cemetery is divided into numbered zones called *recinti*.

Foreign Romantics and artists who made Venice their adopted hometown have also chosen this spot as their final resting place. Because many came from other cultures and weren't Catholic, you'll find them in the Evangelico (Protestant) section, Recinto XV; and the Greco (Orthodox) section, Recinto XIV. To find both of these sections—with the graves of the most famous foreigners—go basically straight ahead from the entrance to the far end, following the maps and signs.

In Recinto XV lies Idaho-born poet **Ezra Pound.** While his

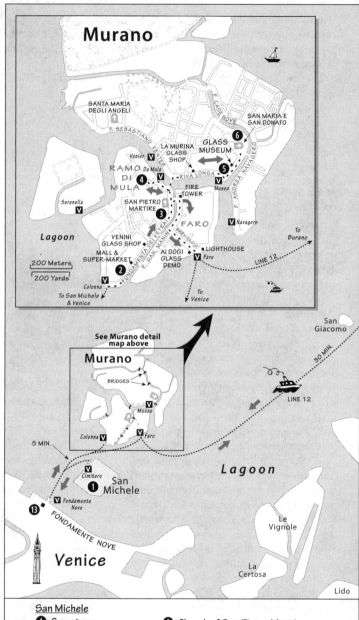

San Michele
1 Cemetery

Murano
2 Fondamenta dei Vetrai

3 Church of San Pietro Martire
4 Residential Murano: Ramo da Mula
5 Glass Museum
6 Santa Maria e San Donato Church

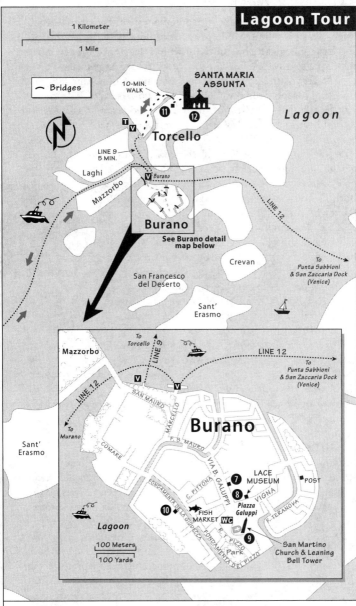

Lagoon Tour

1 Kilometer

1 Mile

~ Bridges

SANTA MARIA
ASSUNTA

10-MIN.
WALK

Lagoon

11

12

Torcello

LINE 9
5 MIN.

Laghi

V *Burano*

LINE 12

Mazzorbo

Burano

See Burano detail
map below

Crevan

San Francesco
del Deserto

*To
Punta Sabbioni
& San Zaccaria Dock
(Venice)*

Sant'
Erasmo

*To
Torcello*

LINE 9

LINE 12

LINE 12

*To
Punta Sabbioni
& San Zaccaria Dock
(Venice)*

Mazzorbo

SAN MAURO

Sant'
Erasmo

*To
Murano*

COMARE

F. S. MAURO

MARCELLO

VIA B. GALUPPI

C. PIZTONA

FONDAMENTA DE LA GIUDECCA

Burano

7 LACE
MUSEUM

8

*Piazza
Galuppi*

VIGNA

POST

F. TERANOVA

FISH
MARKET

WC

R. T. PIZZO

FONDAMENTA DEL PIZZO

Park

9

San Martino
Church & Leaning
Bell Tower

Lagoon

100 Meters

100 Yards

Burano
7 Merletti d'Arte dalla Lidia
Lace Shop
8 Lace Museum
9 Bell Tower
10 Trat. al Gatto Nero da Ruggero

Torcello
11 Locanda Cipriani Hotel
12 Santa Maria Assunta Church

Eating near Fondamente Nove
13 Ristorante Algiubagió

LAGOON

works are less familiar than his contemporaries', he was a huge influence on his fellow Modernists, most notably T. S. Eliot (from the Evangelico gate, he's in the near-left quarter of the section—look for a small stone in a large plot, with three large bushes).

Nearby is the grave of Nobel Laureate and onetime US Poet Laureate **Joseph Brodsky** (1940-1996), who was expelled from Soviet Russia, lived the rest of his life in America, and asked to be buried here in Venice. It's in the far-left quarter, facing the gravel path and Ezra Pound.

Recinto XIV (the "Greco" section) is nearby: Exit the Evangelico gate and turn left, following the wall until you reach the gate marked *Rec. Greco*. Inside, find Russian-born Modernist composer **Igor Stravinsky** (far right corner, alongside his wife) and the Russian dancer/choreographer **Diaghilev** (the canopied tomb along the far wall, piled with ballet slippers left in homage by his admirers).

• *Return to the dock and catch any #4.1 or #4.2 vaporetto heading toward the right (boats leave every 10 minutes). While you're waiting, look for the blue funeral boat with a rack on wheels for the coffin. It's usually moored next to the vaporetto.*

It's just a three-minute crossing to the Murano-Colonna stop. (If the vaporetto's too crowded, you could just swim it.) As you approach the island of Murano, you'll see its ghostly lighthouse (faro) *off to the right. In centuries past, the* faro *guided boats from the open sea into town. Near the lighthouse is the stop where you'll leave Murano for the island of Burano.*

▲Murano

Murano is famous for its glass factories. A 1292 Venetian law restricted glass production (and its dangerous furnaces) to the isle of Murano to prevent fires on the main island...and to protect the secrets of Venetian glassmaking. Originally, glassmakers made mosaic tiles, later branching out to produce the ornate vases, beaded necklaces, glass sculptures, and wine decanters you'll see here today.

Murano may seem dominated by glassworks and the glass shops that line its main canal, but there's much more to the island. If you take time to wander, you'll find impressive churches, scenically situated restaurants, and untouristed residential areas.

LAGOON

From the Colonna vaporetto stop, skip the glass shops in front of you, walk to the right, and wander up the street along the

canal, **Fondamenta dei Vetrai** (Glassmakers' Embankment). The Faro district of Murano, on the other side of the canal, is packed with factories *(fabriche)* and their furnaces *(fornaci)*. The brick buildings give Murano a 19th-century, Industrial Age look and feel. At #14 is the entry to the island's small indoor **shopping mall,** with a free WC and a Despar supermarket on the upper floor (closed Sun).

You'll pass dozens more **glass shops** along the canal. Window-shopping here can be as much fun as buying—the personality, style, and prices of wares varies wildly from place to place. Early along this promenade, at #47, is the venerable **Venini** shop, with glass that's a cut above much of what else is on offer here, and with an interior showing off the ultimate in modern Venetian glass design (Mon-Sat 9:30-18:00, closed Sun). The storefronts along here display everything from knickknacks (glass menageries) to vases to decorative items to, well, glasses. If a window display grabs your attention, step inside; you might even see a glass maestro working on small-scale works in one corner of a showroom. Note that the really cheap places likely aren't selling authentic Murano glass; if that matters to you, ask before you buy. (Several shops sport signs pointedly reminding potential customers that their glass may be a bit more expensive...because it's not made in China.) If your browsing starts turning to buying, be sure to read my tips on page 327.

Continue up Fondamenta dei Vetrai until you see a tower on your right and a church on your left. The **tower** was built as a fire

lookout in this city of furnaces. The **Church of San Pietro Martire** (free but donations appreciated, open erratic hours with demand, possibly closed 12:00-15:00 when it's not busy, www.sandonatomurano. it) features Giovanni Bellini's solid-color *Virgin Enthroned with Mark and a Kneeling Doge*

(right wall of the nave in the center). This votive painting—showing a doge being introduced to the Virgin Mary by St. Mark—was the doge's way of thanking Mary for his position of power. The doge wears a luxurious ermine cloak (a symbol of royalty) and a ducal crown hat. The sacristy/museum has ornately carved caryatids (human pillars, c. 1660) with expressive faces and arms posed every which way (€1.50 admission). The carved panels between the caryatids depict scenes from the life of John the Baptist, culminating in his beheading in the far corner. In the next rooms, see ceremonial religious objects and statues, then check out the photos (at the landing midway up the steps) of these objects being used in modern-day Venetian parades. Upstairs are piles of relics in glass cases.

For a slice of **residential Murano,** continue past the church along the canal, bending left and passing the big, green metal bridge. Keep going as the promenade bears left and feeds you down the street called Ramo da Mula, and wander this very tidy "subdivision." In this old shell there's a new vibrancy, as tourist-swamped Venice's high rents and real-estate prices have driven locals to the outlying islands. Behind the glass shops, Murano is a workaday community of 6,000 residents. It has real neighborhoods, with moms shopping at markets, schools filled with noisy children, bikes in the front yards, and benches warmed by Venetian old-timers.

Backtrack to the embankment, and use the green bridge to cross the Grand Canal of Murano. Once across, turn right. Just after the first side street, you'll pass another unique shop, **La Murina,** with elegant and modern home-decor items (such as striking chandeliers; Riva Longa 17, tel. 041-527-4605).

Continue past the shop, then pass a smaller Co-op supermarket and the Murano-Museo vaporetto stop. Where the canal bends left, look for Murano's **Glass Museum** *(Museo Vetrario).* The museum may be undergoing a major renovation during your visit, but you'll likely at least find a historical exhibit about glassmaking here. The museum emphasizes ancient glass and glassmaking techniques in order to illustrate how Venice has carried on making the same colors and using the same techniques from its earlier days. Also on display, of course, are the very best examples of 500 years of Venetian glassmaking (details may change during or after renovation—but likely €8, daily April-Oct 10:00-18:00, Nov-March 10:00-17:00, last entry 30 minutes before closing, Fondamenta Giustinian 8, tel. 041-739-586, http://museovetro.visitmuve.it).

One hundred yards farther along the canal is **Santa Maria e San Donato Church,** the architectural highlight of Murano (free, erratic opening hours, www.sandonatomurano.it). Before entering, note the fine Byzantine Romanesque exterior—especially the stonework of its apse, facing the canal. At the base of the towering campanile is an elaborate memorial to residents of the Veneto (the region surrounding Venice) who have been lost fighting in all wars. Now head inside (free entry but donations appreciated, same iffy hours as the other church). The interior takes you back to the 12th century. Built when St. Mark's Basilica was under construction, the highlights are its inlaid stone floor and the gorgeous mosaic

Guided Tours to Murano

I recommend the self-guided tour in this chapter. But if you'd like to test your ability to resist a smooth-talking Italian glass salesman, or if you'd like to join a group for your trip out to Murano, consider these two other ways to get there.

By Speedboat Tour: The easiest—and priciest—way to see Murano, Burano, and Torcello is to pay €20 for a rushed and touristy four-hour speedboat tour by Alilaguna. They leave three times a day in summer from the San Marco-Giardinetti dock; look and listen for guides calling out for potential passengers (April-Oct usually at 9:30, 11:00, and 14:30, fewer cruises Nov-March, tel. 041-240-1711). The tours are speedy indeed—live guides race through the commentary in up to five languages—and boats stop for roughly 40 minutes at each island. The stops are for glassblowing and lacemaking demonstrations followed by sales spiels, leaving no time left to explore on your own.

A Free Ride with a Sales Pitch: You can also get to Murano for free on a speedboat. Tourists are practically kidnapped from St. Mark's Square by the aggressive sales reps who approach them and ferry them out to the island (35-minute ride). Your only obligation is to sit through a fairly interesting 20-minute glassmaking demonstration and sales pitch. After that, you're on your own. (In fact, they don't promise you a trip back to Venice.)

During the demonstration, the glassblower typically sticks a rod with raw glass on the end into a furnace, melts the glass, and expands it by blowing through the hollow rod. Then he shapes it with tongs into a vase, a glass, or a piece of art. This is followed by an almost comically high-pressure sales pitch in the showroom. (The spiel is brief, and there really is no obligation to buy anything.) If you do buy something, see page 327 for tips on having a purchase shipped home.

If you just want to see a glassblower in action, you don't need to go out to Murano—visit Galleria San Marco, at #139 on St. Mark's Square (see Shopping in Venice chapter). But if you do visit Murano, you'll likely be approached by a local salesman trying to lure you into his shop for a free demo. If you'd rather see a similar demo in a lower-pressure environment, just drop into the Ai Dogi shop near the Murano-Faro vaporetto stop, at the end of my Murano tour (see page 218).

above the altar. It features Mary as God's mother, gliding in from heaven on her carpet, blessing the faithful with two open hands.

When you're ready to leave Murano, find your way back to the green bridge and cross back toward San Pietro Martire. Near the church, cross the narrow canal to Fondamenta Daniele Manin. Before the next bridge, turn left on the street called Bressagio, which

LAGOON

takes you toward the white-stone lighthouse *(faro)* and its Murano-Faro vaporetto dock.

To your right are some of Murano's actual glass factories and their showrooms. At #25, the **Ai Dogi** factory's showroom has an open kiln area where you can watch a glassblower at work. While most such demos on Murano come with a pushy sales pitch, Ai Dogi just lets you watch a maestro work his magic (Mon-Sat roughly 9:30-15:30—often with a lunch break, no activity on Sun or on particularly hot days).

• *To continue our tour, walk over to the Murano-Faro vaporetto stop and catch the #12 vaporetto to* **Burano** *(2/hour, 30 minutes, usually at :19 and :49 past the hour, boat destination may say* Treporti *or* Punta Sabbioni*). If you'd prefer to head straight back to Venice, take either the #3 vaporetto (for the train station and bus station), the #4.2 (for Fondamente Nove and St. Mark's Square), or the #12 or #13 (to Fondamente Nove). The #4.1 is a much slower way back, as it loops around Murano before heading back to Fondamente Nove, then to the train and bus stations.*

▲▲Burano

Burano has three vaporetto docks: Docks B and C (side by side) are for boats to/from Murano and Venice, while dock A (set apart,

to the right as you step off the boat) is for the shuttle to Torcello. Upon arrival, note departure times—most boats leave twice an hour, and are more or less coordinated. (For example, if you want to go from Murano straight to Torcello, you should be able to change easily in Burano.)

Famous for its lace and outlandishly colorful houses, Burano is a sleepy island with a sleepy community (pop. 2,700)—village Venice without the glitz. Its vibrantly painted homes look like Venice before the plaster peeled off. Each adjoining townhouse is painted its own color. While Venice is a showy city of merchants, Burano is a humble town of fishermen. Though the island's main drag is mobbed with tourists by day, at night it's quiet. Laundry hangs over alleyways, and sunshades (typical of the area) cover the doors of residents' homes. The church's bell tower leans at a five-degree angle...the same as Pisa's.

This town's history is ancient, dating back to when the island was, like Torcello, a haven for mainlanders fleeing from barbarian invasions. "Burano" likely comes from "Porta Boreana"—the city gate from the settlers' hometown that faced the bracing Bora

Boating in Venice

Italian law stipulates that a luxury tax is levied on all boats—except in Venice, where they're considered a necessity. Vene-tians go everywhere by boat. Calling a taxi? A boat comes. Going to the hospital to have a baby? Just hop on the vaporetto. Garbage day? You put your bag on the canal edge, and a garbage boat mashes it and takes it away.

Many residents own a boat, though it's not always practical for everyday activities. If you want to cruise to the grocery store, you first have to check the tide table to make sure your boat can fit beneath certain bridges. And parking is always a huge problem everywhere—either you know a friend nearby with a grandfathered parking space, or your partner has to "circle the block" while you shop.

Locals rely more on the public *vaporetti* and *traghetti*. While tourists pay plenty for these boats, Venetians ride cheap and easy. An all-year pass costs less than €1 a day.

Gondolas are strictly for tourists these days, but in earlier times, these flat-bottomed boats were the only way to negotiate the tricky, shallow lagoon. The oarsman had to stand up in the back of the boat to see oncoming sandbars. Today, boats ply confidently between the shifting sandbanks of the lagoon, thanks to thoroughfares defined by modern pilings.

While many Venetians own a car for driving on the isle of Lido or the mainland, they admit they're "not very much beloved on the road."

wind. It's that same wind that meant survival on the lagoon. It kept away the malaria-carrying mosquitoes that made other places (like Torcello) less habitable, and whisked sailing fishermen away from the stagnant waters nearby. (Nevertheless, Burano is often engulfed in the fog that's so common on the lagoon—the island's vividly painted facades helped those fishermen find their way home in the mist.)

Burano can be covered in a 10-minute stroll. From the vaporetto dock, follow the crowds into the center. The tight **main drag** is packed with tourists and lined with shops, some of which sell Burano's locally produced white wine. Soon you'll hit the first of many picture-perfect Burano canals; turn left and follow it straight ahead to a bridge, which deposits you on the main square, **Piazza Galuppi**—jammed with lace shops, restaurants, and happy shutterbugs.

Most tourists visit Burano for its lace, and they're not disap-

pointed. Lace is cheaper in Burano than in Venice, and serious shoppers should comparison-shop in Venice before visiting Burano. Of the many lace shops, I like **Merletti d'Arte dalla Lidia** for its fine private museum (in the rear of the shop and upstairs). Paola, who speaks English, gives visitors a warm welcome as she shows off the masterpieces of lace from all over Europe. Use a magnifying glass to marvel at the intricate knots, and be sure to go upstairs (daily 9:30-18:00, just off the big square opposite the leaning tower at Via Baldassarre Galuppi 215, tel. 041-730-052, www.dallalidia.com).

Lace fans enjoy the **Lace Museum** (Museo del Merletto di Burano), with a small but modern and well-presented exhibit about Burano's favorite product. The visit begins on the ground floor, with a 20-minute film telling the history of Burano and the significance of lace during Venice's golden age. You'll learn how the intricate patterns of lace were inspired by the ornate Gothic facades of Venice, the city where they claim the craft was invented, or at least perfected. Then you'll head upstairs to see lots of actual antique lace (slide the drawers to see more samples) as well as some actual, antique lacemakers, squinting at the windows while they work (€5, April-Oct Tue-Sun 10:00-18:00, Nov-March Tue-Sun 10:00-17:00, closed Mon year-round, some English descriptions, tel. 041-730-034, http://museomerletto.visitmuve.it).

Back outside, at the far end of the piazza (near the far tip of this little island) is Burano's famous leaning church **bell tower.** The Church of San Martino Vescovo has a fine, restored Tiepolo painting of the Crucifixion (along the left wall of the nave, near the back; free entry but donations appreciated, typically closed 12:00-15:00).

Burano holds many back lanes and Technicolor tranquil canals beyond its touristy core. Wander to the far side of the island, and the mood shifts. Explore to the right of the leaning tower for a peaceful yet intensely colorful, small-town lagoon world. Benches lining a little promenade at the water's edge make for a pretty picnic spot.

Eating at Burano: The park next to Burano's only vaporetto dock is another good picnic option. You'll find plenty of touristy eateries on Burano, all enthusiastic about their fish. While you have plenty of options for a quick bite, if you want to dine, con-

LAGOON

sider **Trattoria al Gatto Nero da Ruggero.** They serve pricey, good traditional dishes outside overlooking the peaceful canal or in the dressy interior (€16-20 pastas, €20-35 *secondi,* closed Mon, crisp service, 5-minute walk from the ferry dock and from the thriving main tourist drag at Fondamenta de la Giudecca 88, tel. 041-730-120).

• *To reach our tour's next stop,* **Torcello,** *take the shuttle boat (Line #9) that runs twice hourly (likely at :05 and :35 past each hour; five-minute trip). If you want to skip Torcello and head right back to Venice, see the end of this chapter.*

▲Torcello

This is the birthplace of Venice, where some of the first mainland refugees settled, escaping the barbarian hordes. Yet today,

it's the least-developed island (pop. 20) in the most natural state, marshy and shrub-covered. There's little for tourists to see except the church (a 10-minute walk from the dock), the oldest in Venice, and still sporting some impressive mosaics.

From the vaporetto dock, walk along the canal through a salty landscape and think of the original inhabitants. Romanized farmers came here, escaping the Germanic barbarians who started streaming through the mainland in the fifth century. By the 11th century, the teeny island had 11 churches. But one look around makes it easy to understand why this place was inhospitable—the farming was poor, there was no fresh water, and mosquitoes and malaria were big problems. Even though residents diverted the flow of mainland rivers, the lagoon silted up around them anyway, and the island was slowly abandoned.

Approaching the church, you'll pass by the remote yet fancy **Locanda Cipriani Hotel** next door. With just five rooms, it's hosted Thomas Mann, Queen Elizabeth II, and Princess Diana.

The **Santa Maria Assunta Church** complex consists of three sights: the church itself, the bell tower (behind the church, climb a ramped stairway for great lagoon views), and a small museum (facing the church, in two separate buildings, but with little to see—mainly just sparsely described old artifacts, including a few sixth-century

LAGOON

mosaic fragments). The church is the only one of these really worth paying to visit (€5), but various combo-tickets, which include an audioguide, let you get into the other sights as you like (church open daily March-Oct 10:30-18:00, Nov-Feb 10:00-17:00; museum and campanile close 30 minutes earlier, museum closed Mon; last entry to all sights 30 minutes before closing; museum tel. 041-730-761, church/bell tower tel. 041-730-119). There's a pay WC between the museum's two buildings.

The circular ruins in front of the church used to be a baptistery from the ninth century; in those days, you couldn't enter a church until you were baptized.

Inside the church, the brick walls and wood-beam ceiling are classically Venetian building materials—that is, flexible, to accommodate the ever-shifting sands underneath.

The **altar** has the relics of St. Heliodorus (d. 390), a local-born bishop who was the travel partner of the famed St. Jerome on a trip to the Holy Land. The columns of the rood screen (separating the altar area from the congregation) were obviously scavenged from elsewhere—note the variety of capitals.

The **apse mosaic** (over the altar) shows Mary and baby Jesus above and the 12 apostles below. Her three stars symbolize her virginity: before, during, and after giving birth to Jesus.

In the **right apse,** with its sumptuous vault, find Christ Pantocrator, ruler of all, flanked by archangels Michael and Gabriel. On the ceiling, Christ is represented by the sacrificial lamb.

The mosaic on the **back wall** is justifiably famous and worth examining. Six horizontal bands depict the Last Judgment (and other scenes). From top to bottom, see:

1. The Crucifixion.

2. A striding Christ pulling an elderly, bearded Adam (with Eve behind him) out from Limbo while stepping on a devil.

3. Christ, in an almond-shaped bubble, as the Creator, flanked by John the Baptist, Mary, and other holy souls in Paradise. From the bottom of the bubble pours a river of fire, which runs down the wall to hell.

4. Angels preparing the Throne of Judgment—empty except for a book (whose seven seals, it was predicted, will be broken during Judgment Day). Note Adam and Eve kneeling below.

5 and 6. Archangel Michael (over the door) weighing souls on a scale, while mischievous devils try to tip the scales in their favor.

On the right are the fires of hell, where sinners—many of them turbaned Muslims—are tormented by black-skinned demons. A crude display of the seven deadly sins appears at the lower right: pride (crowned heads in flames), lust (bodies in flames), gluttony (guys eating even their fingers), envy (skulls with worms eating out their coveting eyes), anger (men waist-deep in cold water to cool down), greed (fancy earrings), and laziness (useless hands and cut-off feet).

• *Avoid the eighth deadly sin—missing your vaporetto—by allowing at least 10 minutes to get from the church back to the boat dock. Boats to Burano generally depart at :10 and :40 past the hour (5 minutes).*

To get back to Venice from Burano, catch the #12 vaporetto to Fondamente Nove (2/hour at :26 and :56, 45 minutes). From Fondamente Nove, if you need to get to St. Mark's, you can take the #4.2 vaporetto to San Zaccaria (an additional 30 minutes).

If you feel like taking a longer boat ride from Burano, you can take the #12 in the other direction. It runs once an hour from Burano to Punta Sabbioni on the peninsula of Cavallino, where you connect to the #14, which takes you to the San Zaccaria–Pietà dock and St. Mark's Square. This route is more complicated, but will give you a fine lagoon cruise experience.

LAGOON

ST. MARK'S TO RIALTO LOOP WALK

Two rights and a left (simple!) can get you from St. Mark's Square to the Rialto Bridge via a completely different route from the one most tourists take. Along the way, take in some lesser sights in the area west of St. Mark's Square. Then we'll return to St. Mark's along the tourist's main drag, the Mercerie.

Orientation

Length of This Walk: Allow one hour for a leisurely walk.
San Moisè Church: Free, Mon-Sat 9:30-12:30, Sun Mass only at 11:00, tel. 041-296-0630.
La Fenice Opera House: €8.50 for dry 45-minute audioguide tour, generally open daily 9:30-18:00, theater box office open daily 10:00-17:00.
Rialto Market: The souvenir stalls are open daily; the produce market is closed on Sunday; and the fish market is closed on Sunday and Monday. The market is lively only in the morning.

The Walk Begins

Start at St. Mark's Square

• *From the square, walk to the waterfront and turn right. You're walking on recently raised Venice—in 2006, the stones were taken up and six inches of extra sand put down, to minimize flooding. Continue along the water toward the white TI pavilion.*

Along the waterfront, you'll see the various boats that ply Venice's waters. Hiring a gondola here is often more expensive than elsewhere in Venice. Classic wooden motorboats operating as water taxis are pricey (about €60 from here to the train station), but they are a classy splurge if you split the fare with others. Hotel shuttle

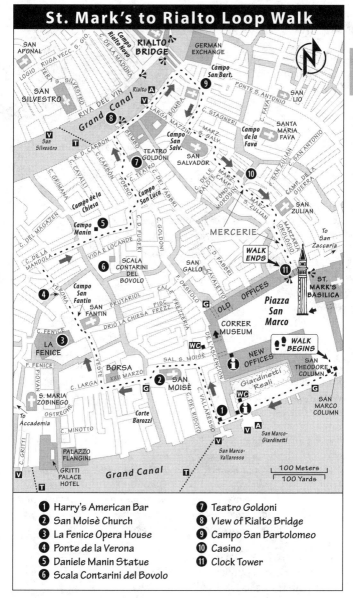

St. Mark's to Rialto Loop Walk

1. Harry's American Bar
2. San Moisè Church
3. La Fenice Opera House
4. Ponte de la Verona
5. Daniele Manin Statue
6. Scala Contarini del Bovolo
7. Teatro Goldoni
8. View of Rialto Bridge
9. Campo San Bartolomeo
10. Casino
11. Clock Tower

boats bring guests here from distant, $700-a-night hotels.

Run the gauntlet of souvenir stands to the entrance to the **Giardinetti Reali** (Royal Gardens, once the site of a huge grain-storage depot that was destroyed by Napoleon). The grounds (with ample benches) offer some precious greenery in a city built of stone on mud.

After the park entrance, the walkway runs right into the **TI**, in a cute 18th-century former coffeehouse pavilion. Go around the left side of the TI pavilion and—from atop the bridge—look across the mouth of the Grand Canal to view the big dome of La Salute Church. The guy balancing a bronze ball on one foot is on top of the old Customs House, which now houses the Punta della Dogana contemporary art museum.

• *Twelve steps down and 20 yards ahead on the right is...*

❶ Harry's American Bar

Hemingway put this bar on the map by making it his hangout in the late 1940s. If Brad and Angelina are in town, this is where they'll be. If they're not, you'll see plenty of dressed-up Americans looking around for celebrities. The discreet (and overpriced) restaurant upstairs is where the glitterati hang out. The street-level bar is for gawkers. If you wear something a bit fancy (or artsy bohemian), you can pull up a stool at the tiny bar by the entrance and pay too much for a Bellini (Prosecco and peach puree), which was invented right here.

• *Head inland down Calle Vallaresso, one of Venice's most exclusive streets, past fancy boutiques such as Emilio Pucci, Brunello Cucinelli, Roberto Cavalli, and Bruno Magli. At the T intersection, turn left and head west on Salizada San Moisè (which becomes Calle Larga XXII Marzo). Continue to the first bridge and a square dominated by the fancy facade of a church. Climb the bridge, and against a soundtrack of tourists negotiating with hustling gondoliers, look back at the ornate...*

❷ San Moisè Church

This is the parish church for St Mark's; because of tourist crowds at the basilica, this is where the community actually worships. While it's one of Venice's oldest churches, dating from the 10th century (note the old tower on the right), its busy facade is 17th-century Baroque. This was an age when big shots who funded such projects expected to see their faces fea-

tured (see the bust of Mr. Fini in the center). Moses (Moisè) caps the facade.

Inside, the altarpiece depicts Mount Sinai, with Moses (kneeling) receiving the two tablets with the Ten Commandments. The alcove to the left of the altar has Tintoretto's 16th-century *Christ Washing the Disciples' Feet.*

The modern building on the right is the ritzy, five-star **Bauer Hotel,** originally an 18th-century palace. While it was closed throughout the 1940s, the owners added this Fascist-deco wing, defying Italian historical-preservation codes. Its facade still gives locals the Mussolini-creeps. Now it's one of the few modern buildings in town. You can take a few minutes to wander through the hotel for a James Bond-meets-Mussolini architectural experience.

• *Continue past the bridge, down Calle Larga XXII Marzo, a big street that seems too wide and large for Venice. It was created during the 19th century by filling in a canal. You can make out the outline of the sidewalks that once flanked the now-gone canal. Pass by the Vivaldi lookalikes selling concert tickets and (mostly Senegalese) immigrants illegally selling knockoffs of Prada bags.*

Halfway down the street, after passing the grand Borsa, turn right on tiny Calle del Sartor da Veste. Go straight, crossing a bridge. At the next square, you'll find...

❸ La Fenice Opera House (Gran Teatro alla Fenice)

Venice's famed opera house, built in 1792 (read the MDCCXCII on the facade), was started as a business venture by a group of no-

bles who recognized that Venice was short on entertainment opportunities for the well-heeled set. (In the 18th century, aristocrats strolled around several months out of the year with little to do.)

La Fenice was reduced to a hollowed-out shell by a disastrous fire in 1996. After a vigorous restoration campaign, "The Phoenix"—true to its name—has risen again from the ashes. La Fenice resumed opera productions in 2004, opening with *La Traviata.* The theater is usually open daily to the public (for information, see page 45).

Venice is one of the cradles of the art form known as opera. An opera is a sung play and a multimedia event, blending music, words, story, costume, and set design. Some of the great operas were first performed here in this luxurious setting. Verdi's *Rigoletto* (1851) and *La Traviata* (1853) were actually commissioned by La Fenice. The man who put words to some of Mozart's opera tunes was a Venetian, Lorenzo da Ponte, who drew inspiration from the city's libertine ways and joie de vivre. In recent years, La Fenice's musical standing was overshadowed by its reputation as a place for the wealthy to parade in furs and jewels.

• *Passing La Fenice, continue north along the same street (though its name is now Calle de la Verona), to a small bridge over a quiet canal.*

❹ Ponte de la Verona

Pause atop this bridge, where reflections can make you wonder which end is up. Looking above you, see bridges of stone propping

up leaning buildings, and there's a view of the "Leaning Tower" of San Stefano.

People actually live in Venice. Notice their rooftop gardens, their laundry, their plumbing, electricity lines snaking into their apartments, and the rusted iron bars and bolts that hold their crumbling homes together. On one building, find centuries-old relief carvings—a bearded face and a panel of an eagle with its prey.

While many Venetians own (and love) their own boats, parking watercraft is a huge problem. Getting a spot is tough, and when you finally find one, it's very expensive and rarely near your apartment. (For more on boating in Venice, see page 219.)

People once swam freely in the canals. Find the sign that reads *Divieto di Nuoto* ("swimming not allowed").

• *Continue north. At the T intersection, turn right on Calle de la Mandola. You'll cross over a bridge into a spacious square dominated by a statue and an out-of-place modern building.*

❺ Campo Manin

The centerpiece of the square is **a statue of Daniele Manin** (1804-1857), Venice's fiery leader in the battle for freedom from Austria and eventually a united Italy (the Risorgimento). The statue faces the red house Manin lived in. Chafing under Austrian rule, the Venetians rose up in 1848. The Austrians laid siege to the city (1849) and bombarded it into surrender. Manin was banished and spent his final years in Paris, still proudly drumming up support for modern Italy. In a rare honor, he's buried in St. Mark's Basilica.

• *Scala Contarini del Bovolo is a block south of*

here, with yellow signs pointing the way. Facing the Manin statue, turn right and exit the square down an alley. Turn left with the street, then immediately follow yellow signs to the right, into a courtyard with one of Venice's hidden treasures...

❻ Scala Contarini del Bovolo

The Scala is a cylindrical brick tower with five floors of spiral staircases faced with white marble banisters (probably closed for renovation during your visit).

Built in 1499, it was the external staircase of a palace (external stairs saved interior space for rooms). Architecture buffs admire the successful blend of a Gothic building with a Renaissance staircase.

If the tower is open, you can pay a small fee to wind your way up the "snail shell" (*bovolo* in the local dialect). It's 113 steps to the

top, where you're rewarded with views of the Venetian skyline.

• *Unwind and return to the Manin statue. Continue east, circling around the right side of the big Cassa di Risparmio bank, marveling at its Modernist ugliness. At Campo San Luca, walk halfway through the square, then turn left (north) on Calle del Forno. Note the 24-hour pharmacy vending machine (on the right) that dispenses shower gel, Band-Aids, bug repellant, toothbrushes, toothpaste, condoms, and other after-hours necessities. Heading north, glance 20 yards down the street to the right at the flag-bedecked...*

❼ Teatro Goldoni

Though this theater dates from the 1930s, there's been a theater here since the 1500s, when Venice was at the forefront of secular entertainment. Many of Carlo Goldoni's (1707-1793) groundbreaking comedies were first performed here. Before Goldoni's time, most Italian theater was formulaic and somewhat contrived, but Goldoni portrayed real-life situations of the new middle class—and with a refreshing sense of humor and honesty. Thanks in part to his ample use of the Venetian dialect, he remains especially popular in his native city, and the theater was renamed in his honor. Today, Teatro Goldoni is still a working theater of mainly Italian productions.

• *Continue north on Calle del Forno. You're very close to the Grand Canal. Keep going north, angling to the right through the small square (Corte del Teatro) and down a teeny-tiny alleyway. Pop! You emerge on the Grand Canal, about 150 yards downstream from the...*

❽ Rialto Bridge

Of Venice's more than 400 bridges, only four cross the Grand Canal. Rialto was the first among these four.

The original Rialto Bridge, dating from 1180, was a platform supported by boats tied together. It linked the political side (Palazzo Ducale) of Venice with the economic center (Rialto). Rialto, which takes its name from *riva alto* (high bank), was one of the earliest Venetian settlements. When Venice was Europe's economic superpower, this was where bankers, brokers, and merchants conducted their daily business.

Rialto Bridge II was a 13th-century wooden drawbridge. It was replaced in 1588 by the current structure, with its bold single arch (spanning 160 feet) and arcades on top designed to strengthen the stone span. Its immense foundations stretch 650 feet on either side. Heavy buildings were then built atop the foundations to hold everything in place. The Rialto remained the only bridge crossing the Grand Canal until 1854.

Marking the geographical center of Venice (midway down the Grand Canal), the Rialto is the most sensible location for retail shops. The government built it with the (accurate) expectation that it'd soon pay for itself with rent from the shops built into it. Like the (older) Ponte Vecchio in Florence, the Rialto was originally lined with luxury gold and jewelry shops. The bridge is cleverly designed to generate maximum rent: three lanes, two rows of 12 shops each, with a warehouse area above each shop under the lead-and-timber roof.

Reliefs of the Venetian Republic's main mascots, St. Mark and St. Theodore, crown the arch. Barges and *vaporetti* run the busy waterways below, and merchants vie for tourists' attention on top.

The Rialto has long been a symbol of Venice. Aristocratic inhabitants built magnificent palaces just to be near it. The poetic Lord Byron swam to it all the way from Lido Island. And thousands of marriage proposals have been sealed right here, with a kiss, as the moon floated over La Serenissima.

• *From here, you can continue this walk and return to St. Mark's Square or pick up my Rialto to Frari Church Walk (next chapter). Either way, you might want to take a break to check out the fish and produce market that lies just over the bridge. To continue this walk, follow me along the Mercerie, the most direct (and tourist-clogged) route back to St. Mark's. From the base of the Rialto Bridge (on the San Marco side), go 100 yards directly to...*

❾ Campo San Bartolomeo

This square is one of the city's main crossroads. Locals routinely meet at the statue of Carlo Goldoni, the beloved and innovative 18th-century playwright for whom Teatro Goldoni, which we saw earlier, was named. The pharmacy on this square (marked by a green cross) keeps an electronic counter in its window, ticking down the population of Venice as it shrinks.

• *Head to the right 100 yards, down Via 2 Aprile, setting your sights on the green and red umbrellas on the corner. They mark a stretch of town once famous for selling umbrellas and handbags. From there, turn left and follow the crowds 100 yards more along Marzaria San Salvador, a.k.a. the...*

Mercerie

You're in the city's high-rent district. The Mercerie (or "Marzarie," in Venetian dialect) is a string of connecting streets lined mostly with big-name chain and luxury stores. Much of the glass displayed here is Chinese, not Venetian. (If you're shopping for glass that's actually made in Venice, look for the Murano symbol.)

• *When you get to the yellow two-way arrow "directing" you to San Marco, head right and then follow the flow left another 100 yards until you reach a bridge, which makes for a fun gondola viewing perch. At the top of the bridge, belly up to the railing on the left. Above the arcade on your left is the little iron balcony of the city's best-preserved...*

❿ Casino

While humble from the outside, the interior is a great example of a classic Venetian space. If the windows are open, spy the lacy pastel and stucco ceilings inside. Though only a few of Venice's casinos still exist, the city once had several hundred of these "little houses"—city-center retreats for the palazzo-dwelling set. For many patricians, they served as 17th-century man caves, used for entertaining, gambling, and/or intimate encounters. For well-to-do women, casinos provided a different kind of escape: Inspired by Madame de Pompadour (Louis XV's mistress), ladies would hold court with writers, artists, and avant-garde types.

• *Cross the bridge and continue straight for 100 yards along Marzaria San Zulian. On the way, notice the metal two-foot-high flood barrier braces at shop doors—and how merchandise is elevated in anticipation of high water (local insurance doesn't cover floods).*

When you hit the next schizophrenic Per S. Marco *arrow (in front of the church), go right a few steps, then left onto Marzaria dell'Orologio, a street named for where you're heading: the Clock Tower. You're approaching St. Mark's Square (back where you started this walk) and the city's front door. Overhead at the end of the street, you'll see the Renaissance* **⓫ Clock Tower,** *built when it was considered important that cities have a proper main gate and a grand clock. This city door leads from the grand center clustered around St. Mark's Square, into the city through which you've just walked.*

RIALTO TO FRARI CHURCH WALK

Cross the Rialto Bridge, and dive headlong into Venice's thriving market area. The area west of the Grand Canal is less touristy—a place where "real" Venetians live. This 20-minute walk is the most direct route from the Rialto Bridge to the Frari Church and Scuola San Rocco. This chapter is less a collection of sights than it is a tour of the Rialto market area, followed by a convenient, easy-to-follow route through the San Polo area. After exploring the lively produce and stinky fish markets, you'll see pubs and squares that are at least a bit off the tourist path.

Orientation

Length of This Walk: Allow a leisurely hour.

When to Go: The markets are lively only in the morning. The produce market is closed on Sunday, and the fish market is closed on Sunday and Monday.

Ancient Musical Instruments Collection (in the Church of San Giacomo de Rialto): Free, Mon-Sat 9:00-17:00, Sun 11:00-19:00.

Church of San Polo: €3, Mon-Sat 10:00-17:00, closed Sun.

Tragicomica Mask Shop: Daily 10:00-19:00, at Calle dei Nomboli 2800, tel. 041-721-102. The owners are generally happy to show their workshop to customers who buy a mask.

Eateries: Many pubs and restaurants in the Rialto area are recommended in the Eating in Venice chapter.

The Walk Begins

• *From the top of the Rialto Bridge, walk down the bridge (heading away from the St. Mark's side) and about 50 yards onward until you see an old square on your right. Go to its fountain.*

❶ Campo San Giacomo

This square, named for the church that faces it, looks today much like it did in the 16th century. The buildings lining the square are

High Renaissance, mostly built after a 1514 fire devastated this area. Find the MDXX date on the arcade: It was built in 1520. Only the church predates that fire. The square is designed to collect rainwater and store it in a cistern that once fed this fountain (for more on this system, see page 36).

Back when the Rialto Bridge was a drawbridge (until the 1590s), big ships would dock alongside this historic market. Imagine the commotion as ships tied up to load and unload their spices, oil, wine, and jewels. The line of buildings between Campo San Giacomo and the canal was once a strip of banks. It's still called Bancogiro, which means the place where letters of credit were endorsed. Back when carrying cash meant carrying gold and silver—heavy and dangerous—letters of credit were a godsend. Today you'll find a line of popular eateries here (described on page 300). Behind the trashy jewelry stands are real jewelry shops. In fact, the street across from the market has been called "Street of Jewelers" for more than 500 years.

Opposite the church, a granite hunchback supports steps leading to a column. Until the 1550s, when a financial crisis knocked it for an economic loop, Venice was Europe's trading capital. You could call this neighborhood the "Wall Street" of medieval Europe. In those days, this column was the closest thing they had to a *Wall Street Journal*. Someone climbed the stair each noon and stood on the column to read aloud the daily news from the doge: which ships had docked, which foreign ambassadors were in town, the price of pepper, and so on. Behind the hunchback, the lane Calle de la Sicurtà is named for the maritime insurance companies that once did business here.

The church facade is one of the oldest in town. Back before clocks had minute hands, its porch was a shelter for the poor. The spirit of St. James the Minor, for whom the church is named, watched over the business community, encouraging honesty in a time when banking regulations were nonexistent. Today the church's tranquil interior hosts an exhibition of historical musical instruments.

Walk along the canal side of the church. The large white building behind the church was and still is the city's fiscal administration building. Walk left, out to the canal, and look back at the structure. Notice how it tilts out (probably because the bridge's huge foundation is compressing the mud beneath it).

Now turn right and walk along the canal to a little canalside dead-end that's as close as you can get to the Rialto Bridge. Take in the great view of the bridge. The former post office (directly across from you) was originally the German merchants' hall (see the seal). It's about to be reincarnated as a Benetton-owned shopping center.

You're standing under a former prison. Study the iron grills over the windows. Notice the interlocking pipes with alternating joints—you couldn't cut just one and escape.

• *From the prison, walk back along the canal, proceed through the triple archway, cross the square, and enter the square named Casaria (for the historic cheese market). Today, this is Venice's...*

❷ Produce Market (Erberia)

Colorful stalls offer fresh fruit and vegetables, some quite exotic. Nothing is grown on the island of Venice, so everything is shipped

in daily from the mainland. The Mercato Rialto vaporetto stop is a convenient place for boats to unload their wares, here in the heart of fish-shaped Venice. At #203-204 (halfway down the first set of stalls, on the left), the shop called Macelleria Equina sells horse *(cavallo)* and donkey *(asino)* meat. Continue along the canal, exploring all the produce stalls.

• *Follow your nose straight ahead (passing six alleyways on your left) until you see* Mercato del Pesce *on the brick wall of the open-air arcade that houses the...*

❸ Fish Market (Pescaria)

This market is especially vibrant and colorful in the morning. The open-air stalls have the catch of the day—Venice's culinary spe-

Rialto to Frari Church Walk

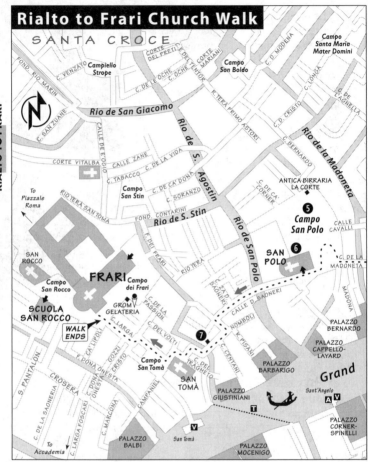

cialty. Find eels, scallops, crustaceans with five-inch antennae, and squid destined for tonight's risotto soaking in their own ink. This is the Venice that has existed for centuries: Workers toss boxes of fish from delivery boats while shoppers step from the *traghetto* (gondola shuttle) into the action. It's a good peek at workaday Venice. Shoppers are exacting and expect to know if the fish is fresh or frozen, farmed

or wild. Local fish are small and considered particularly tasty because of the high concentration of salt at this end of the Adriatic.

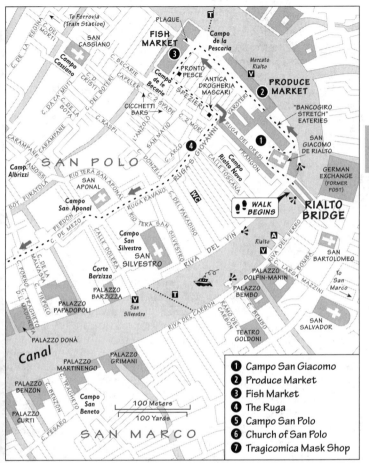

1 Campo San Giacomo
2 Produce Market
3 Fish Market
4 The Ruga
5 Campo San Polo
6 Church of San Polo
7 Tragicomica Mask Shop

Any salmon you see are farmed, mostly from northern Europe. It's not unusual to pay €30 per kilo (about 2.2 pounds) for the best fish.

In the courtyard between market buildings, locate a square, white Istrian stone on the wall between two arches. It lists the minimum length permitted for a fish to be sold. Sardines must be seven centimeters; *peocio* (mussels) must be three centimeters. (Below that, someone has added a penis joke.)

Now walk away from the water to the end of the fish market. You're on **Campo de la Becarie** ("Butchers' Square"). If the market has you ready for a fishy nibble, you'll find many good options near here (listed on page 301 of the Eating in Venice chapter). Several of my favorite local bars serving the Venetian version of tapas, *cicchetti*, line up along Calle de le Do Spade (we'll pass it in just a moment). If it's lunchtime, consider dropping by one or more of these for a progressive feast: Bar all'Arco, Osteria ai Storti, Cantina Do Mori, and Cantina Do Spade. Or, for something a bit more upscale, pop into the hole-in-the-wall Pronto Pesce for tasty fish hors d'oeuvres (just steps away, facing the side of the fish market at #319).

When you're ready, follow Ruga dei Spezieri ("Spicers' Road") back toward the Rialto. Along the way, pop into Antica Drogheria Mascari (on the right at #380), which hides a vast enoteca holding 600 different Italian wines arranged by region, plus spices and lots of gifty edibles.

• *At the end of Ruga dei Spezieri, you'll see a sign for Ruga Vechia San Giovanni. Turn right along it. (The second street you pass on the right, Sotoportego dei Do Mori, leads in just a block to the* cicchetti *bars mentioned earlier.)*

❹ The Ruga

This busy street is lined with shops that get progressively less touristy and more practical. As you walk, you'll see fewer trinkets and more clothes, bread, shoes, watches, shampoo, and underwear.

• *The Ruga changes names as you go. Just keep heading basically straight (little jogs are OK). When in doubt, follow signs pointing to* Ferrovia *(train station). You'll pass straight through Campo San Aponal, then cross a wide bridge, and later a narrow one, soon after arriving at...*

❺ Campo San Polo

One of the largest squares in Venice, Campo San Polo is shaped like an amphitheater, with its church tucked away in the corner (just ahead of you). Antica Birraria la Corte, a fine and family-friendly pizzeria/ristorante, is located at the far side (see listing under "Other Good Eateries near the Rialto Market," page 301). The square's amphitheater shape was determined by a curved canal at the base of the buildings. Today, the former canal is now a *rio terà*—a street made of landfill. A few rare trees grace the square, as do rare benches occupied by grateful locals. In the summer, bleachers and a screen are erected for open-air movies.

• *On the square is the...*

❻ Church of San Polo (S. Paolo Apostolo)

This church, one of the oldest in Venice, dates from the ninth century (English description at ticket desk). The wooden, boat-shaped ceiling recalls the earliest basilicas built after Rome's fall. While the church is skippable for many, art enthusiasts visit to see

Tintoretto's *Last Supper,* Giovanni Battista Tiepolo's *Virgin Appearing to St. John of Nepomuk* and his son Domenico's *Stations of the Cross,* and Veronese's *Betrothal of the Virgin with Angels.*

• *From the Church of San Polo, continue about 200 yards (following* Ferrovia *signs). You'll cross a bridge, jog left when you have to, then right, onto Calle dei Nomboli. On the right at #2800, directly across the alley from the Casa Goldoni museum, you'll see the...*

❼ Tragicomica Mask Shop

One of Venice's best mask stores, Tragicomica is also a workshop that offers a glimpse into the process of mask-making. Venice's

masks have always been a central feature of the celebration of Carnevale—the local pre-Lent, Mardi Gras-like blowout. (The translation of Carnevale is "goodbye to meat," referring to the lean days of Lent.) You'll see Walter and Alessandra hard at work.

Many masks are patterned after standard characters of the theater style known as commedia dell'arte: the famous trickster Harlequin, the beautiful and cunning Columbina, the country bumpkin Pulcinella (who later evolved into the wife-beating Punch of marionette shows), and the solemn, long-nosed Doctor *(dottore).*

• *Continuing along, cross the bridge and veer right, passing San Tomà Church and its square. You'll soon see purple signs directing you to* Scuola Grande di San Rocco. *Follow these until you bump into the back end of the Frari Church, with Scuola San Rocco next door.*

♻ *See the Frari Church Tour chapter; also see the* ♻ *Scuola San Rocco Tour chapter.*

ST. MARK'S TO SAN ZACCARIA WALK

San Zaccaria, one of the oldest churches in Venice, is just a few minutes on foot from St. Mark's Square. The church features a Bellini altarpiece and a submerged crypt that might be the oldest place in Venice. This short walk gets you away from the bustle of St. Mark's, includes a stroll along the waterfront, and brings you right back where you started.

Orientation

Length of This Walk: Allow about an hour for a leisurely walk (though the actual distance is short).

Church of San Zaccaria: Free, €1 to enter crypt, €0.50 coin to illuminate Bellini's altarpiece, Mon-Sat 10:00-12:00 & 16:00-18:00, Sun 16:00-18:00 only. Mass is held daily at 18:30 and Sun also at 10:00 and 12:00.

The Walk Begins

❶ Start at St. Mark's—Piazzetta dei Leoni

Facing St. Mark's Basilica, start in the small square to the left of the church (Piazzetta dei Leoni), with the 18th-century stone lions that kids love to play on. See those drains in the pavement? You're standing on a cistern, fed by four drains.

Notice the nicely restored north side of the basilica, with fine 14th-century reliefs. Notice also the prayer entrance below the exquisite Porta dei Fiori. To the left, high above the tomb of Daniele Manin, the great 19th-century Italian and Venetian patriot, is a statue with baby Jesus on his shoulder. That's St. Christopher, patron saint of us travelers.

The white Neoclassical building at the far east end of the

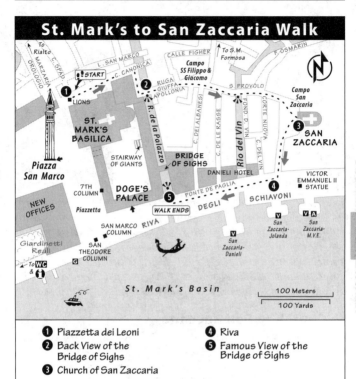

St. Mark's to San Zaccaria Walk

❶ Piazzetta dei Leoni
❷ Back View of the Bridge of Sighs
❸ Church of San Zaccaria
❹ Riva
❺ Famous View of the Bridge of Sighs

square (built in 1834, when Venice was under Austrian rule) houses the offices of Venice's "patriarch," the special title given to the local bishop. In the 1950s, this is where the future Pope John XXIII presided as Venice's patriarch and cardinal. The popular, warm-hearted cardinal went on to become the "Sixties Pope," who oversaw major reforms in the Catholic Church (Vatican II). Locals still refer to him as "Il Papa Buono" (the good pope). You'll see a plaque dedicated to "Papa Giovanni XXIII" on this building.

• *Head east along Calle de la Canonica, past a fine English-language bookstore, then turn right and circle behind the basilica. Passing some of the sexiest gondoliers in town, you'll reach a bridge with a...*

❷ View of the Bridge of Sighs

This lesser-known view of the Bridge of Sighs also lets you see the tourists who are ogling it, with cameras cocked. You can just see the Lady Justice relief (centered above the windows), with her sword and scales—a reminder that the courts were to the right and the prison to the left.

On the basilica side of the bridge is a common sight in neighborhood Venice: a street-side altarpiece and donation box. As the street signs tell you, the bridge you're on marks the boundary between two traditional neighborhoods, the *sestiere* (district) of San Marco and that of Castello. Throughout this walk, you'll pass relics of a fast-fading era: newspaper stands, public telephones, and a 24-hour cigarette vending machine.

• *Continue east, passing through a lively, small square. You'll cross another bridge with a view of a "Modern Bridge of Sighs," which connects two wings of the exclusive Danieli Hotel. Continue east another 50 yards, through the Gothic gate of what was once a cloistered Benedictine convent, and into a square where you see the...*

❸ Church of San Zaccaria

Back in the ninth century, when Venice was just a collection of wooden houses and before there was a St. Mark's Basilica, a stone

church and convent stood here. This is where the doges worshipped, public spectacles occurred, and sacred relics were kept. Today's structure dates mostly from the 15th century.

The tall facade by Mauro Codussi (who also did the Clock Tower in St. Mark's Square) and others is early Renaissance. The "vertical" effect produced by the four support pillars that rise up to an arched crown is tempered by the horizontal, many-layered stories and curved shoulders.

In the northwest corner of Campo San Zaccaria (near where you entered) is a plaque from 1620 listing all the things that were

prohibited "in this square" *(in questo campo),* including games, obscenities, dishonesty, and robbery, all "under grave penalty" *(sotto gravis pene).*

• *Enter the church. The second chapel on the right holds the...*

Body of Zechariah (S. Zaccaria)

Of the two bodies in the chapel, the lower one in the glass case is the reputed body of Zechariah, the father of John the Baptist. Back when mortal remains were venerated and thought to bring miracles to the faithful, Venice was proud to own the bones of St. Zechariah ("San Zaccaria," also known as Zacharias).

• *The church is blessed with fine art. On the opposite side of the nave (second chapel on the left), you'll find...*

Giovanni Bellini—*Madonna and Child with Saints* (1505)

Mary and the baby, under a pavilion, are surrounded by various saints interacting in a so-called *sacra conversazione* (holy conversation), which in this painting is more like a quiet meditation. The saints' mood is melancholy, with lidded eyes and downturned faces. A violinist angel plays a sad solo at Mary's feet.

This is one of the last of Bellini's paintings in the *sacra conversazione* formula, the newer type of altarpiece that liberated the Virgin, Child, and saints from the separate cells of the older triptych style. Compare this to his other variations on this theme in the Accademia (see Accademia Tour chapter) and Frari Church (see Frari Church Tour chapter). The life-size saints stand in an imaginary extension of the church—the pavilion's painted columns match those of the real church. We see a glimpse of trees and a cloudy sky beyond. Bellini establishes a 3-D effect using floor tiles. The four saints pose symmetrically, and there's a harmony in the big blocks of richly colored robes—blue, green, red, white, and yellow. A cool white light envelops the whole scene, creating a holy ambience. (To add even more light, drop a €0.50 coin in the box in front of the altar.)

The ever-innovative Bellini was productive until the end of his long life—he painted this masterpiece at age 75. The German artist Albrecht Dürer said of him: "He is very old, and still he is the best painter of them all."

• *On the right-hand side of the nave is the entrance (€1 entry fee) to the...*

Crypt

Before you descend into the crypt, the first room (Chapel of Sant'Atanasio) contains **Tintoretto's** *Birth of John the Baptist* (c. 1560s, on the altar), which tells the back story of Zechariah. In the background, old Zechariah's wife, Elizabeth, props herself up in bed while nurses hold and coo over her newborn son, little John the Baptist. The birth was a miracle, as she was past childbearing age. On the far right, Zechariah—the star of this church—witnesses the heavens opening up, bringing this miracle to earth.

The five **gold thrones** (displayed in this room or one of the next rooms) were once seats for doges. Every Easter, the current doge would walk from St. Mark's Square to this religious center and thank the nuns of San Zaccaria for giving the land for the square.

The small next room contains religious objects as well as an engraving of the doge parading into Campo San Zaccaria.

Next comes the **Chapel of San Tarasio,** dominated by an impressive 15th-century prickly gold altarpiece by Antonio Vivarini. The predella (seven small scenes beneath the altarpiece) may be by Paolo Veneziano, the 14th-century grandfather of Venetian painting. Look down through glass in the floor to see the 12th-century mosaic floor from the original church. In fact, these rooms were parts of the earlier churches.

Finally, go downstairs to the **crypt**—the foundation of a church built in the 10th century. The crypt is low and the water table high, so the room is often flooded, submerging the bases of the columns. It's a weird experience, calling up echoes of the Dark Ages.

• *Emerge from the Church of San Zaccaria into the small campo. Before leaving the campo, check out the small art gallery on the left (free), the thirst-quenching water fountain, and the pink* Carabinieri *police station (a former convent), marked by the Italian flag. Then exit the square at the far end, and head south— past that cigarette machine—until you pop out at the waterfront, right on the...*

❹ Riva

The waterfront promenade known as the "Riva" was built not for tourists but as part of the port of San Marco. Until recently, big ships tied up here. Today it's lined with some of the town's finest hotels and provides a great view of the Church of San Giorgio Maggiore (one stop away on vaporetto #2).

The big equestrian monument depicts **Victor Emmanuel II,** who helped lead Italy to unification and became the country's first king in 1861. Beyond that (over the bridge) is the four-columned **La Pietà Church,** where Antonio Vivaldi once directed the music.

Five bridges farther along (not visible from here) are the Arsenale and Naval Museum (described on page 59).

The Riva is lined with many of Venice's most famous luxury hotels. For a peek at the *most* famous and luxurious, turn right, cross over one bridge, and nip into the **Danieli Hotel.** Tuck in your shirt, stand tall and aristocratic, and (with all the confidence of a guest) be swept by the revolving door into the sumptuous interior of what was once the Gothic Palazzo Dandolo. As you check out the Danieli's restaurant menu (that's why you're there, isn't it?), admire the lobby, the old-style chandeliers, water-taxi drive-up entrance, and the occasional celebrity. Since 1820, the Neo-Gothic Danieli has been Venice's most exclusive hotel. Exquisite as all this is, it still gets flooded routinely in the winter.

• *Facing the water, turn right and head west toward St. Mark's Square. The commotion atop a little bridge marks the...*

❺ Famous View of the Bridge of Sighs

The Bridge of Sighs connects the Doge's Palace (left) with the doge's prison (right). The bridge let justice be very swift indeed, as convicted criminals could, upon sentencing, be escorted directly from the palace's secretive court-room to prison, without being seen in public.

Notice the beefy bars on the prison. There were no windows, so throughout the year it would alternate between very hot and very cold. The top floor, below the lead roof, was nicknamed "The Oven." While designed for 300 people, the prison routinely held 500.

From this historic bridge (according to romantic legend), prisoners took one last look at Venice before entering the dark and unpleasant prisons. And sighed. Lord Byron picked up on the legend in the early 1800s and gave the bridge its famous nickname, making this sad little span a big stop on the Grand Tour. Look high up on your left—although that rogue Casanova wrote of the bridge in his memoirs, he was actually imprisoned here in the Doge's Palace. Check out the carved relief on the palace corner, to your left, showing the biblical scene of drunken Noah spilling his wine but still being thoughtfully cared for by his sons. The message: Even if your superiors don't deserve re-spect because of their actions, cut them some slack, and treat them well.

Nowadays, while the bridge is a human traffic jam of gawking tourists during the day, it remains breathtakingly romantic in the lonely late-night hours.

• *Your tour's over. (By the way, if you need some quick cash, this is a great place to pick a pocket. There's lots of bumping, and everyone's distracted…)*

SLEEPING IN VENICE

For hassle-free efficiency and the sheer magic of being close to the action, I favor hotels that are handy to your sightseeing activities.

I've listed rooms in five neighborhoods: St. Mark's bustle, the Rialto action, the quiet Dorsoduro area behind the Accademia art museum, near the train station, and on the mainland in Mestre (handy for drivers and train travelers, but far from the action). I also mention several apartment rentals, big fancy hotels, cheap dorms, and other places on the mainland beyond the urban center.

A major feature of this book is its extensive listing of good-value rooms. I like places that are clean, central yet not in the tourist flood zone, relatively quiet at night (except for the song of gondoliers), reasonably priced, friendly, small enough to have a hands-on owner and stable staff, run with a respect for Venetian traditions, and not listed in other guidebooks. (In Venice, for me, six out of these eight criteria means it's a keeper.) I'm more impressed by a handy location and a fun-loving philosophy than flat-screen TVs and a pricey laundry service.

Book your accommodations well in advance if you'll be traveling during busy times. See page 455 for a list of major holidays and festivals in Venice; for tips on making reservations, see page 250.

Note that hotel websites are particularly valuable for Venice, because they often include detailed directions that can help you get to your rooms with a minimum of wrong turns in this navigationally challenging city.

Rates and Deals

I've described my recommended accommodations using a Sleep Code (see sidebar). Prices listed are for one-night stays in peak season (April, May, June, Sept, and Oct) and assume you're booking directly (not through a TI or online hotel-booking engine). Booking services extract a commission from the hotel, which logically closes the door on special deals. Book direct.

The city of Venice levies a tax on hotel rooms to generate income for infrastructure and restoration projects. This tax is generally not included in the prices in this book, and must be paid in cash at checkout. It varies from €1 to €4 per person, per night, depending on how many stars the hotel has.

Prices can spike during festivals. Almost all places drop prices from November through March (except during Christmas and Carnevale—Feb 22-March 4 in 2014) and in July and August. A €180 double can cost €80-90 in winter. Off-season, don't pay the rates I list.

Over the past decade, Venice has seen the opening of several big new hotels, countless little boutique hotels, and the conversion of many private homes to short-term rental apartments, nearly doubling Venice's hotel capacity. Now the city is overbuilt for hotels. Demand is soft and, therefore, so are the prices.

These days, it seems no Venetian hotel expects to actually get its published "rack rate." While I wish I could promise a set price or a discount for readers of this book, it's a pricing free-for-all; most hotels change prices from day to day, according to demand. I'd suggest emailing several hotels to ask for their best price. Comparison-shop and make your choice.

As you look over the listings, you'll notice that some accommodations promise special prices to Rick Steves readers who book directly with the hotel. To get these rates, you must mention this book when you reserve, and then show the book upon arrival. Rick Steves discounts apply to readers with ebooks as well as printed books. Because we trust hotels to honor this, please let me know if you don't receive a listed discount. Note, though, that discounts understandably may not be applied to promotional rates.

In general, prices can soften if you do any of the following: offer to pay cash, stay at least three nights, or mention this book. You can also try asking for a cheaper room or a discount, or offer to skip breakfast.

To save money during a relatively slow time, consider arriving without a reservation and dropping in at the last minute. Big, fancy hotels put empty rooms on an aggressive push list, offering great prices. Many hotels in Venice list rooms on www.venere.com, especially for last-minute vacancies (two to three weeks before the date). Before you bite, check to see if rates are lower than the prices in this book.

Sleep Code

(€1 = about $1.30, country code: 39)

Price Rankings

To help you easily sort through these listings, I've divided the accommodations into three categories based on the price for a double room with bath during high season:

$$$ **Higher Priced**—Most rooms €180 or more.
  $$ **Moderately Priced**—Most rooms between €130-180.
   $ **Lower Priced**—Most rooms €130 or less.

I always rate hostels as $, whether or not they have double rooms, because they have the cheapest beds in town. Prices can change without notice; verify the hotel's current rates online or by email. For the best prices, always book direct.

Abbreviations

To give you maximum information in a minimum of space, I use the following code to describe the accommodations in this book. Prices listed are per room, not per person. When a price range is given for a type of room (such as double rooms listing for €100-150), it means the price fluctuates with the season, size of room, or length of stay; expect to pay the upper end for peak-season stays.

S = Single room (or price for one person in a double).
D = Double or twin room. "Double beds" can be two twins sheeted together, and are usually big enough for nonromantic couples.
T = Triple (generally a double bed with a single).
Q = Quad (usually a double bed and 2 small singles; adding an extra child's bed to a T is usually cheaper).
b = Private bathroom with toilet and shower or tub.
s = Private shower or tub only (the toilet is down the hall).

According to this code, a couple staying at a "Db-€140" hotel would pay a total of €140 (about $180) for a double room with a private bathroom. Unless otherwise noted, breakfast is included, hotel staff speak basic English, and credit cards are accepted. Venice charges a hotel tax of €1-4 per person, per night. This tax is typically not included in the prices I've listed here.

There's almost always Wi-Fi and/or a guest computer available, either free or for a fee.

Making Hotel Reservations

Reserve your rooms several weeks in advance—or as soon as you've pinned down your travel dates—particularly if you'll be traveling during peak times. Note that some national holidays jam things up and merit making reservations far in advance (see "Holidays and Festivals" on page 455).

Requesting a Reservation: It's usually easiest to book your room through the hotel's website. Many have a reservation-request form built right in. (For the best rates, be sure to use the hotel's official site and not a booking agency's site.) Just type in your preferred dates, and the website will automatically display a list of available rooms and prices. Simpler websites will generate an email to the hotelier with your request. If there's no reservation form, or for complicated requests, send an email (see next page for a sample request). Most recommended hotels are accustomed to guests who speak only English.

The hotelier wants to know:
- the number and type of rooms you need
- the number of nights you'll stay
- your date of arrival
- your date of departure
- any special needs (such as bathroom in the room or down the hall, twin beds vs. double bed, air-conditioning, quiet, view, ground floor, etc.)

If you request a room by email, use the European style for writing dates: day/month/year. For example, for a two-night stay in July of 2014, ask for "1 double room for 2 nights, arrive 16/07/14, depart 18/07/14." Make sure you mention any discounts—for Rick Steves readers or otherwise—when you make the reservation.

Confirming a Reservation: When the hotel replies with its room availability and rates, just email back to confirm your reservation. Most places will request a credit-card number to hold your room. While you can email it (I do), it's safer to share that confidential info via a phone call, two emails (splitting your number between them), or the hotel's secure online reservation form. On the small chance that a hotel loses track of your reservation, bring along a hard copy of their confirmation.

Canceling a Reservation: If you must cancel your reservation, it's courteous—and smart—to do so with as much advance notice as possible, especially for smaller family-run places. Simply make a quick phone call or send an email. Request confirma-

Sample Hotel Reservation Request

From:	rick@ricksteves.com
Sent:	Today
To:	info@hotelcentral.com
Subject:	Reservation request for 19-22 July

Dear Hotel Central,

I would like to reserve a double room for 2 people for 3 nights, arriving 19 July and departing 22 July. If possible, I would like a quiet room with a bathroom inside the room.

Please let me know if you have a room available and the price.

Thank you!
Rick Steves

tion of your cancellation in case you are accidentally billed.

Be warned that cancellation policies can be strict; read the fine print or ask about these before you book. For example, if you cancel on short notice, you could lose your deposit, or be billed for one night or even your entire stay. Internet deals may require prepayment, with no refunds for cancellations.

Reconfirming Your Reservation: Call to reconfirm your room reservation a few days in advance. Smaller hotels appreciate knowing your estimated time of arrival. If you'll be arriving late (after 17:00), let them know.

Reserving Rooms as You Travel: You can make reservations as you travel, calling hotels a few days to a week before your arrival. If you'd rather travel without any reservations at all, you'll have greater success snaring rooms if you arrive at your destination early in the day. When you anticipate crowds (weekends are worst), call hotels at about 9:00 or 10:00 on the day you plan to arrive, when the receptionist knows who'll be checking out and just which rooms will be available. If you encounter a language barrier, ask the fluent receptionist at your current hotel to call for you.

Phoning: For tips on how to call hotels overseas, see page 425.

Types of Accommodations

Hotels

The double rooms in Venice listed in this book will range from about €90 (very simple, toilet and shower down the hall) to €400 (plush Grand Canal views and maximum plumbing), with most clustered around €130-180 (with private bathrooms).

Solo travelers find that the cost of a *camera singola* (single room) is often only 25 percent less than a *camera doppia* (double room). Three or four people can economize by requesting one big room. (If a Db is €110, a Qb would be about €150.) Most listed hotels have rooms for any size party, from one to five people. If there's room for an extra cot, they'll cram it in for you (charging you around €25). English works in all but the cheapest places.

Nearly all places offer private bathrooms. Generally rooms with a bath or shower also have a toilet and a bidet (which Italians use for quick sponge baths). The cord that dangles over the tub or shower is not a clothesline. You pull it when you've fallen and can't get up.

Double beds are called *matrimoniale,* even though hotels aren't interested in your marital status. Twins are *due letti singoli.* Even if a single or triple room isn't listed, ask—they can accommodate you.

When you check in, usually the receptionist will ask for your passport and may want to keep it for anywhere from a couple of minutes to a couple of hours. Hotels are legally required to register each guest with the police. Relax. Americans are notorious for making this chore more difficult than it needs to be.

Assume that breakfast is included in the prices I've listed, unless otherwise noted. If breakfast is included but optional, you may want to skip it. While convenient, it's usually expensive—€5-8 per person for a simple continental buffet with ham, cheese, yogurt, and unlimited *caffè latte.* A picnic in your room followed by a coffee at the corner café can be cheaper.

More pillows and blankets are usually in the closet or available on request. In Italy, towels and linens aren't always replaced every day. Hang your towel up to dry. Some hotels use lightweight "waffle" or very thin, tablecloth-type towels; these take less water and electricity to launder and are preferred by many Italians.

Most hotel rooms have a TV, phone, and Wi-Fi; sometimes there's a guest computer in the lobby. Simpler places rarely have a room phone, but often have Wi-Fi. Pricier hotels are more likely to have elevators and small stocked mini-fridges in the rooms called *frigo bars* (FREE-goh; pay for what you use). Elevators are often very small—pack light, or you may need to send your bags up separately.

SLEEPING

Chill Out

All but the cheapest hotels have air-conditioning. Because Europeans are generally careful with energy use, you'll find government-enforced limits on air-conditioning and heating. There's a one-month period each spring and fall when neither is allowed. Air-conditioning sometimes costs an extra per-day charge, is worth seeking out in summer (though it may be on only at certain times of the day), and is rarely available from fall through spring.

Most hotel rooms with air conditioners come with a control stick (like a TV remote) that generally has the same symbols and features: fan icon (click to toggle through wind power, from light to gale); louver icon (choose steady airflow or waves); snowflake and sunshine icons (cold air or heat, depending on season); clock ("O" setting: run x hours before turning off; "I" setting: wait x hours to start); and the temperature control (21 degrees Celsius is comfortable).

If you're arriving early in the morning, your room probably won't be ready. You can drop your bag safely at the hotel and dive right into sightseeing.

Hoteliers can be a great help and source of advice. Most know Venice well, and can assist you with everything from public transit and airport connections to finding a good restaurant, the nearest launderette, or an Internet café. But even at the best places, mechanical breakdowns occur: Air-conditioning malfunctions, sinks leak, hot water turns cold, and toilets gurgle and smell. Report your concerns clearly and calmly at the front desk. For more complicated problems, don't expect instant results.

If you suspect night noise will be a problem, ask for a quiet room in the back or on an upper floor. In Venice, a canalside room sounds romantic, but in reality you might be sleeping next to a busy, noisy, boat- and gondola-clogged "street." The quietest Venetian rooms will probably face a courtyard.

To guard against theft in your room, keep valuables out of sight. Some rooms come with a safe, and other hotels have safes at the front desk. I've never bothered using one.

Checkout can pose problems if surprise charges pop up on your bill. If you settle up your bill the afternoon before you leave, you'll have time to discuss and address any points of contention (before 19:00, when the night shift usually arrives).

Above all, keep a positive attitude. Remember, you're on vacation. If your hotel is a disappointment, spend more time out enjoying the city you came to see.

Hostels

You'll pay about €25 per bed to stay at a hostel. Travelers of any age are welcome if they don't mind dorm-style accommodations and meeting other travelers. Most hostels offer kitchen facilities, guest computers, Wi-Fi, and a self-service laundry. Nowadays, concerned about bedbugs, hostels are likely to provide all bedding, including sheets.

Independent hostels tend to be easygoing, colorful, and informal (no membership required); hostelworld.com is the standard way backpackers search and book hostels these days, but also try www.hostelz.com, www.hostels.com, and www.hostelbookers.com.

Official hostels are part of Hostelling International (HI) and share an online booking site (www.hihostels.com). HI hostels typically require that you either have a membership card or pay extra per night.

Apartments

Many Venetians rent out their apartments, which can be a great value for families or multiple couples traveling together. Rentals are generally by the week, with prices starting around €100 per day. A bigger place for a family of four to five rents for around €200 per day. Apartments typically offer a couple of bedrooms, a sitting area, and a teensy *cucinetta* (kitchenette), usually stocked with dishes and flatware. After you check in, you're basically on your own. While you won't have a doorman to carry your bags or a maid to clean your room each day, you will get an inside peek at a Venetian home, and you can save lots of money—especially if you take advantage of the cooking facilities—with no loss of comfort.

Several of these recommended hotels, all listed later in this chapter, rent apartments (with small kitchens) on the side: **$$$ Hotel Campiello,** east of St. Mark's Square, has three modern, upscale, and quiet family apartments for up to six people, just steps away from their hotel. Nearby, **$$ Locanda al Leon** has a pair of two-bedroom, two-bathroom apartments with kitchens. **$$$ Hotel Flora,** west of St. Mark's Square, has a great family-size apartment. **$$ Pensione Guerrato,** west of the Rialto Bridge, has apartments for four to eight people. East of the Rialto Bridge, **$$ Locanda la Corte** has two quads for up to eight (in hotel, no kitchen), and **$ Albergo Doni** has three basic apartments.

Websites such as HomeAway.com and its sister site VRBO.com let you correspond directly with European property owners or managers. Airbnb.com makes it reasonably easy to find a place to sleep in someone's home. Beds range from air-mattress-in-living-room basic to plush-B&B-suite posh. If you want a place to sleep that's free, Couchsurfing.com is a vagabond's alternative to Airbnb.

Flexible Floors

All over town, from palaces to cheap, old hotels, you'll find speckled floors *(pavimento alla Veneziana)*. While they might look like cheap linoleum, these are historic—protected by the government and a pain for Venetian landlords to maintain. As Venice was built, it needed flexible flooring to absorb the inevitable settling of the buildings. Through an expensive and laborious process, several layers of material were built up and finished with a broken marble top that was shaved and polished to what you see today. While patterns were sometimes designed into the flooring, it's often just a speckled hodgepodge. Keep an eye open for this. Once a year, the floor is rubbed with natural oil to maintain its flexibility, and craftspeople still give landlords fits when repairs are needed.

SLEEPING

It lists millions of outgoing members, who host fellow "surfers" in their homes.

Another worthwhile option is **Cross-Pollinate.com,** an online booking agency representing B&Bs and apartments in a handful of European cities, including Venice. Unlike huge aggregator websites like HomeAway or VRBO, Cross-Pollinate handpicks its listings, selectively presenting each one as if recommending it to a friend. Search their website for a listing you like, then submit your reservation online. If the place is available, you'll be charged a small deposit and emailed the location and check-in details. Policies vary from owner to owner, but in most cases you'll pay the balance on arrival in cash. Venice listings range from a Lido B&B room for two for €60 per night to a two-bedroom San Marco apartment sleeping seven for €270 per night. Minimum stays vary from one to three nights (US tel. 800-270-1190, Italy tel. 06-9936-9799, www. cross-pollinate.com, info@cross-pollinate.com).

Accommodations

Hotels in Venice can be tricky to locate. Use the maps in this book and you'll be fine. If necessary, ask locals for help when you get close. Most hotel websites have a good map designed for clients to print out. The website www.veniceexplorer.net allows you to search using a hotel's address number and district (I've included these in my listings; click "Venice Civic Number" to open the search window); it's better than other map websites, which often choke on Venetian addresses. Remember that Venice has six districts: San Marco, Castello, Cannaregio, San Polo, Santa Croce, and Dorsoduro.

For romantic splurges, consider Hotel al Ponte Antico, Hotel Flora, Pensione Accademia, or Locanda la Corte—in that order of price and experience.

Big church-run institutional places cost about the same as a modest hotel, but come with a pristine lack of stress that some prefer. The best ones, well-located and a good value, are Casa per Ferie Santa Maria della Pietà, Don Orione Religious Guest House, Istituto Ciliota, Foresteria della Chiesa Valdese, and Foresteria Levi.

For those on a tight budget, Venice's little, relatively dumpy hotels and youth hostel are cheapest.

All of the preceding accommodations are fully described later in this chapter.

Near St. Mark's Square

To get here from the train station or Piazzale Roma bus station, ride the vaporetto to San Zaccaria—either the slow #1 or the fast #2 (from the Tronchetto parking lot, it's #2 only). Consider using your ride to follow my tour of the Grand Canal (❂ see Grand Canal Cruise chapter); to make sure you arrive via the Grand Canal, confirm that your boat goes "*via Rialto.*"

Nearby Laundries: Lavanderia Gabriella offers full service a few streets north of St. Mark's Square (€15/load includes wash, dry, and fold; drop off Mon-Fri 8:00-12:30, closed Sat-Sun; pick up 2 hours later or next working day, on Rio Terà de le Colonne, look for #985, tel. 041-522-1758, Elisabetta).

Effe Erre, a modern self-service *lavanderia,* is near the recommended Hotel al Piave on Ruga Giuffa at #4826 (€12/load, daily 6:30-24:00, mobile 349-058-3881, Massimo).

East of St. Mark's Square

Located near the Bridge of Sighs, just off the Riva degli Schiavoni waterfront promenade, these places rub drainpipes with Venice's most palatial five-star hotels. To locate the following hotels, see the map on page 258.

$$$ Hotel Campiello, lacy and bright, was once part of a 19th-century convent. Ideally located 50 yards off the waterfront on a tiny square, its 16 rooms offer a tranquil, friendly refuge for travelers who appreciate comfort and professional service (Sb-€130, Db-€180, bigger "superior" rooms €20-30 more, 10 percent discount with this book if you reserve direct and pay cash on arrival, air-con, elevator, free Wi-Fi; just steps from the San Zaccaria vaporetto stop, Castello 4647; tel. 041-520-5764, www.hcampiello.it, campiello@hcampiello.it; family-run for four generations, currently by Thomas, Nicoletta, and Marco). They also rent three modern family apartments, under rustic timbers just steps away (up to €380/night).

$$$ Hotel Fontana, two bridges behind St. Mark's Square, is a pleasant family-run place with 15 sparse but classic-feeling rooms overlooking a lively square (Sb-€120, Db-€180, family rooms, 10 percent cash discount, quieter rooms on garden side, 2 rooms have terraces for €20 extra, air-con, elevator, free Wi-Fi in common areas, on Campo San Provolo at Castello 4701, tel. 041-522-0579, www.hotelfontana.it, info@hotelfontana.it, cousins Diego and Gabriele).

$$$ Hotel la Residenza is a grand old palace facing a peaceful square. It has 16 small rooms on three levels (with no elevator) and a huge, luxurious lounge that comes with a piano and a stingy breakfast. This is a good value for romantics—you'll feel like you're in the Doge's Palace after hours (Sb-€105, Db-€205, view Db-€215, air-con, free Wi-Fi, on Campo Bandiera e Moro at Castello 3608, tel. 041-528-5315, www.venicelaresidenza.com, info@venicelaresidenza.com, Giovanni).

$$ Locanda al Leon, which feels a little like a medieval tower house, is conscientiously run and rents 13 reasonably priced rooms just off Campo Santi Filippo e Giacomo (Db-€160, Db with square view-€180, Tb-€200, Qb-€240, these prices with cash and this book, air-con, free Wi-Fi, 2 apartments with kitchens, Campo Santi Filippo e Giacomo, Castello 4270, tel. 041-277-0393, www.hotelalleon.com, leon@hotelalleon.com, Giuliano and Marcella). Their down-the-street annex, **B&B Marcella,** has three newer, classy, and spacious rooms for the same rates (check in at main hotel).

$ Albergo Doni, situated along a quiet canal, is dark and quiet. This time-warp—with 13 well-worn, once-classy rooms up a creaky stairway—is run by friendly Tessa and her brother, an Italian stallion named Nikos (S-€70, D-€105, Db-€130, T-€135, Tb-€170, €5 discount in 2014 with this book, ceiling fans, three Db rooms have air-con, free Wi-Fi in common areas, 3 nice overflow apartments are same price but no breakfast, on Fondamenta del Vin at Castello 4656, tel. 041-522-4267, www.albergodoni.it, albergodoni@hotmail.it).

$ Casa per Ferie Santa Maria della Pietà is a wonderful church-run facility renting 53 beds in 15 rooms just a block off the Riva, with a fabulous lagoon-view roof terrace that could rival those at the most luxurious hotels in town. Institutional, with generous public spaces and dorm-style comfort, there are no sinks, toilets, or showers in any of its rooms, but there's plenty of plumbing down

SLEEPING

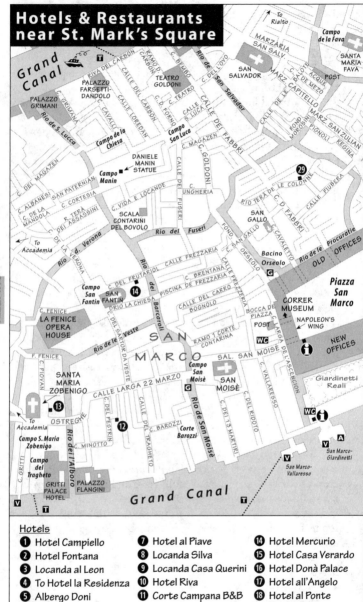

Hotels & Restaurants near St. Mark's Square

Hotels

1. Hotel Campiello
2. Hotel Fontana
3. Locanda al Leon
4. To Hotel la Residenza
5. Albergo Doni
6. Casa per Ferie Santa Maria della Pietà
7. Hotel al Piave
8. Locanda Silva
9. Locanda Casa Querini
10. Hotel Riva
11. Corte Campana B&B
12. Hotel Flora
13. Hotel Bel Sito
14. Hotel Mercurio
15. Hotel Casa Verardo
16. Hotel Donà Palace
17. Hotel all'Angelo
18. Hotel al Ponte dei Sosperi
19. Hotel Ca' Dei Conti

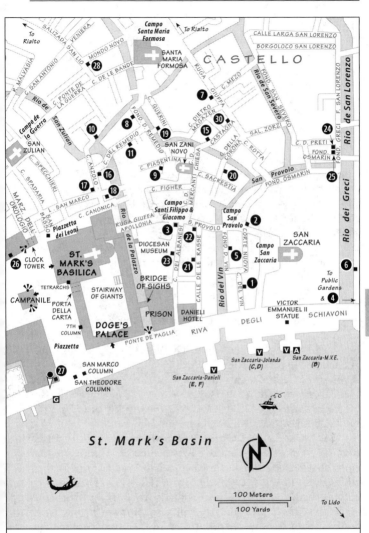

Eateries & Other

- 20 Ristorante Antica Sacrestia
- 21 Birreria Forst Café
- 22 Bar Verde
- 23 Ristorante alla Basilica
- 24 Ristorante alla Conchiglia
- 25 Trattoria da Giorgio ai Greci
- 26 Gran Caffè Lavena (Gelato)
- 27 Todaro Gelateria
- 28 Co-op Supermarket
- 29 Lavanderia Gabriella
- 30 Lavanderia Effe Erre

the hall (€40 beds in 4- to 8-bed dorms, S-€55, D-€100, straight price all year, only twin beds, reserve with credit card but pay cash, air-con, free Wi-Fi, profits go to church care for poor, 100 yards from San Zaccaria-Pietà vaporetto dock, down Calle de la Pietà from La Pietà Church at Castello 3701, take elevator to third floor, tel. 041-883-0111, www.bedandvenice.it, info@bedandvenice.it).

North of St. Mark's Square

To locate the following hotels, see the map on page 258.

$$ Hotel al Piave, with 28 fine, air-conditioned rooms above a bright and classy lobby, is fresh, modern, and comfortable. You'll enjoy the neighborhood and always get a cheery welcome (Db-€155, larger "superior" Db-€200, Tb-€200, Qb-€260; family suites-€280 for 4, €300 for 5, or €310 for 6; €10 Rick Steves discount when you book directly and pay in cash, free Wi-Fi, on Ruga Giuffa at Castello 4838, tel. 041-528-5174, www.hotelalpiave.com, info@hotelalpiave.com; Mirella, Paolo, Ilaria, and Federico speak English).

$$ Locanda Silva is a big, basic, beautifully located hotel with a functional 1960s feel, renting 23 decent old-school rooms that are particularly worth considering if you're willing to share a bathroom to save some money (S-€70, Sb-€85, D-€85, D with toilet but shared shower-€90, Db-€140, Tb-€160, Qb-€180, book direct and request 10 percent Rick Steves discount, another 10 percent off if you stay at least 2 nights, discounts valid only with cash, closed Dec-Jan, air-con, lots of stairs, pay Wi-Fi, on Fondamenta del Remedio at Castello 4423, tel. 041-522-7643, www.locandasilva.it, info@locandasilva.it; Sandra, Katia, and Massimo).

$$ Locanda Casa Querini rents six bright, high-ceilinged rooms on a quiet square tucked away behind St. Mark's. You can enjoy your breakfast or a sunny happy-hour picnic sitting at their tables right on the sleepy little square (Db-€155, Tb-€180, one cheaper small double, these prices promised in 2014 for Rick Steves readers who book direct and pay cash, €5 additional discount if you book on their website, air-con, free Wi-Fi, halfway between San Zaccaria vaporetto stop and Campo Santa Maria Formosa at Castello 4388 on Campo San Zaninovo/Giovanni Novo, tel. 041-241-1294, www.locandaquerini.com, info@locandaquerini.com; Silvia, Patrizia, and Caterina).

$ Hotel Riva, with gleaming marble hallways, big exposed beams, fine antique furnishings, and lots of stairs, is romantically situated on a canal along the gondola serenade route. This has long been a standby in this book, but how it'll stack up when it reopens after a major renovation remains to be seen (see website for latest prices, on Ponte de l'Anzolo at Castello 5310, tel. 041-522-7034, www.hotelriva.it, info@hotelriva.it, Daniella).

$ Corte Campana B&B, run by enthusiastic and helpful Riccardo, rents three quiet and characteristic rooms up a few flights of stairs just behind St. Mark's Square. One room has a private bath down the hall (Db-€125, Tb-€165, Qb-€190, prices are soft, cash only, 2-night minimum, at least €10/night less for stays of 4 nights, air-con, pay Wi-Fi but free guest computer, on Calle del Remedio at Castello 4410, tel. 041-523-3603, mobile 389-272-6500, www.cortecampana.com, info@cortecampana.com).

Near Campo Santa Maria Formosa

A bit farther north of the options listed above, these are in a pleasant, somewhat less touristy neighborhood near the inviting Campo Santa Maria Formosa. For locations, see the map on page 263.

$$ Locanda la Corte is perfumed with elegance without being snooty. Its 17 attractive, high-ceilinged, wood-beamed rooms—Venetian-style, done in earthy pastels—circle a small, quiet courtyard (standard Db-€150, deluxe Db-€170, 10 percent discount with cash and this book, suites and family rooms available, air-con, free Wi-Fi, on Calle Bressana at Castello 6317, tel. 041-241-1300, www.locandalacorte.it, info@locandalacorte.it, Marco and Tommy the cat).

$ Alloggi Barbaria rents eight backpacker-type rooms on one floor around a bright but institutional-feeling common area. Beyond Campo San Zanipolo/Santi Giovanni e Paolo, it's a long walk from the action, in a residential neighborhood, and only a step above a youth hostel (Db-€90-100, third or fourth person-€25 each, pay cash for best price, family deals, limited breakfast, air-con, free Wi-Fi, on Calle de le Capucine at Castello 6573, tel. 041-522-2750, www.alloggibarbaria.it, info@alloggibarbaria.it, Giorgio and Fausto).

West of St. Mark's Square

To locate the following hotels, see the map on page 258.

$$$ Hotel Flora sits buried in a sea of fancy designer boutiques and elegant hotels almost on the Grand Canal. It's formal, with uniformed staff and grand public spaces, yet the 40 rooms have a homey warmth and the garden oasis is a sanctuary for well-heeled, foot-weary guests (generally Db-€260, check website for special discounts or email Sr. Romanelli for 10 percent Rick Steves discount off standard prices, air-con, elevator, free Wi-Fi, fitness room, family apartment, on Calle Bergamaschi at San Marco 2283a, tel. 041-520-5844, www.hotelflora.it, info@hotelflora.it).

$$$ Hotel Mercurio, a lesser value a block in front of La Fenice Opera House, offers 29 peaceful, comfortable rooms (Sb-€180, Db-€240, Tb-€290, Qb-€320, about €30 extra for a canal view, €10 discount on any room when booked direct and paid in

SLEEPING

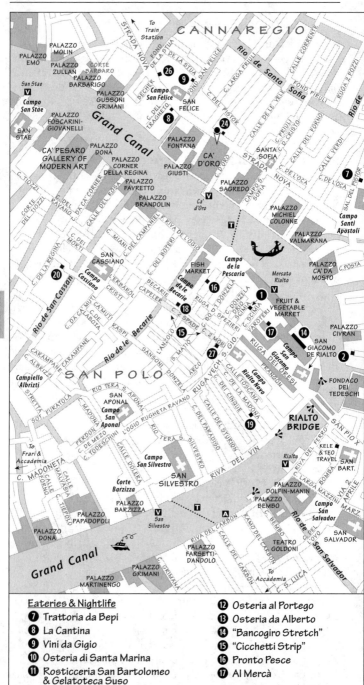

Eateries & Nightlife

7 Trattoria da Bepi
8 La Cantina
9 Vini da Gigio
10 Osteria di Santa Marina
11 Rosticceria San Bartolomeo & Gelatoteca Suso

12 Osteria al Portego
13 Osteria da Alberto
14 "Bancogiro Stretch"
15 "Cicchetti Strip"
16 Pronto Pesce
17 Al Mercà

Hotels & Restaurants near the Rialto Bridge

Hotels
1. Pensione Guerrato
2. Hotel al Ponte Antico
3. Locanda la Corte
4. To Alloggi Barbaria
5. Hotel Giorgione
6. Foresteria della Chiesa Valdese

18. Ristorante Vini da Pinto
19. Trattoria alla Madonna
20. Trattoria Pizzeria al Nono Risorto
21. Osteria alle Testiere
22. Osteria al Mascaron
23. Peter Pan Kebabs

24. Grom Gelateria
25. Co-op Supermarket
26. Billa Supermarket
27. Small Deli
28. Devil's Forest Pub
29. Inishark Pub
30. Planet Restaurant

SLEEPING

cash, air-con, lots of stairs, free Wi-Fi, on Calle del Fruttariol at San Marco 1848, tel. 041-522-0947, www.hotelmercurio.com, info@hotelmercurio.com; Monica, Vittorio, Natale, and Giacomo).

$$$ **Hotel Bel Sito** offers pleasing yet well-worn Old World character, 34 rooms, generous public spaces, a peaceful courtyard, and a picturesque location—facing a church on a small square between St. Mark's Square and the Accademia (Sb-€110, Db-€185, €20 extra for "superior" room with view of canal or square, air-con, elevator, free Wi-Fi; near Santa Maria del Giglio vaporetto stop—line #1, on Campo Santa Maria Zobenigo/del Giglio at San Marco 2517, tel. 041-522-3365, www.hotelbelsitovenezia.it, info@hotelbelsito.info, manager Rossella).

Near the Rialto Bridge

These two places are on opposite sides of the Grand Canal, each within a short walk of the Rialto Bridge. Vaporetto #2 brings you to the Rialto quickly from the train station, the Piazzale Roma bus station, and the parking-lot island of Tronchetto. You can also take the slower vaporetto #1 (but not from Tronchetto). To locate the following hotels, see the map on page 263.

East of the Rialto Bridge: $$$ **Hotel al Ponte Antico** is exquisite, professional, and small. With nine plush rooms, a velvety royal living/breakfast room, and its own dock for water taxi arrivals, it's perfect for a romantic anniversary. Because its wonderful terrace overlooks the Grand Canal, Rialto Bridge, and market action, its non-canal-view rooms may be a better value (Db-€320, "superior" Db-€400, deluxe canal-front Db-€490, air-con, free Wi-Fi, 100 yards from Rialto Bridge at Cannaregio 5768, tel. 041-241-1944, www.alponteantico.com, info@alponteantico.com, Matteo makes you feel like royalty).

West of the Rialto Bridge: $$ **Pensione Guerrato,** above the colorful Rialto produce market and just two minutes from the Rialto Bridge, is run by friendly, creative, and hardworking Roberto and Piero. Their 800-year-old building—with 24 spacious, charming rooms—is simple, airy, and wonderfully characteristic (D-€95, Db-€135, Tb-€155, Qb-€175, Quint/b-€185, these prices with this book and cash, check website for special discounts, Rick Steves readers can ask for €5/night discount below online specials, air-con, free Wi-Fi in lobby, on Calle drio la Scimia at San Polo 240a, tel. 041-528-5927, www.pensioneguerrato.it, info@pensioneguerrato.it, Monica and Rosanna). My tour groups book this place for 60 nights each year. Sorry. The Guerrato also rents family apartments in the old center (great for groups of 4-8) for around €60 per person.

Near the Accademia Bridge

As you step over the Accademia Bridge, the commotion of touristy Venice is replaced by a sleepy village laced with canals. This quiet area, next to the best painting gallery in town, is a 15-minute walk from the Rialto or St. Mark's Square.

The fast vaporetto #2 connects the Accademia Bridge with the train station (15 minutes), Piazzale Roma bus station (20 minutes), Tronchetto parking lot (25 minutes), and St. Mark's Square (5 minutes). For hotels south of the Accademia Bridge, vaporetto #5.1 to Zattere (or the Alilaguna speedboat from the airport to Zattere) is a good option.

To locate the following hotels, see the map on page 267.

South of the Accademia Bridge, in Dorsoduro

$$$ Pensione Accademia fills the 17th-century Villa Maravege like a Bellini painting. Its 27 comfortable, elegant rooms gild the lily. You'll feel aristocratic gliding through its grand public spaces and lounging in its wistful, breezy gardens (Sb-€80-160, standard Db-€145-295, bigger "superior" Db-€210-390, Tb-€340, Qb-€370, 5 percent Rick Steves discount on balance when booked direct and paying in cash—mention when reserving and show this book, air-con, cheap Wi-Fi in rooms, free Wi-Fi in lobby, on Fondamenta Bollani at Dorsoduro 1058, tel. 041-521-0188, www.pensioneaccademia.it, info@pensioneaccademia.it).

$$$ Pensione la Calcina, the home of English writer John Ruskin in 1876, maintains a 19th-century formality. It comes with three-star comforts in a professional yet intimate package. Its 27 nautical-feeling rooms are squeaky clean, with nice wood furniture, hardwood floors, and a peaceful canalside setting facing Giudecca Island (Sb-€140, Sb with view-€170, Db-€150-250, Db with view-€290-330, price depends on size, air-con, free Wi-Fi, rooftop terrace, buffet breakfast outdoors on platform over lagoon, near Zattere vaporetto stop at south end of Rio de San Vio at Dorsoduro 780, tel. 041-520-6466, www.lacalcina.com, info@lacalcina.com).

$$$ Hotel Belle Arti, with a stiff, serious staff, lacks personality but has a grand entry, an inviting garden terrace, and 64 heavily decorated rooms (Sb-€150, Db-€240, Tb-€270, air-con, elevator, pay Wi-Fi in common areas, 100 yards behind Accademia art museum on Rio Terà A. Foscarini at Dorsoduro 912a, tel. 041-522-6230, www.hotelbellearti.com, info@hotelbellearti.com).

$$ Casa Rezzonico, a tranquil getaway far from the crowds, rents seven inviting, nicely appointed rooms with a grassy private garden terrace. All of the rooms overlook either the canal or the garden (Sb-€130, Db-€170, Tb-€200, Qb-€230, ask for Rick Steves discount when you book, air-con, free Wi-Fi, near Ca'

SLEEPING

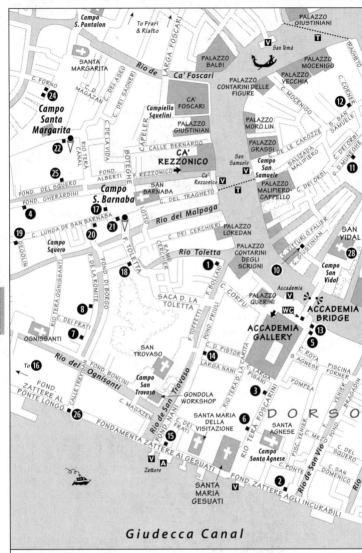

SLEEPING

Giudecca Canal

Hotels
1 Pensione Accademia
2 Pensione la Calcina
3 Hotel Belle Arti
4 Casa Rezzonico
5 Hotel Galleria
6 Don Orione Religious Guest House
7 Ca' San Trovaso
8 Casa di Sara

9 Novecento Hotel
10 Foresteria Levi
11 Istituto Ciliota
12 Albergo San Samuele

Eateries & Nightlife
13 Bar Foscarini
14 Enoteca Cantine del Vino Già Schiavi

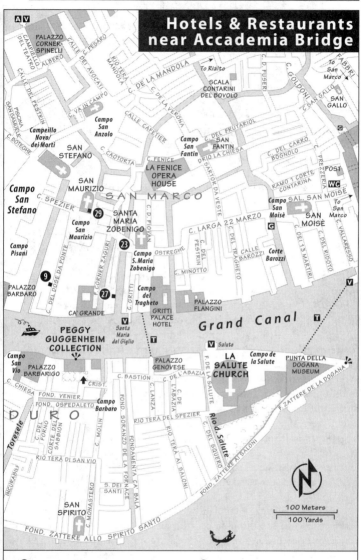

Hotels & Restaurants near Accademia Bridge

SLEEPING

15 Terrazza del Casin dei Nobili
16 To Ae Oche Pizzeria & Billa Supermarket
17 Ristoteca Oniga
18 Osteria Enoteca Ai Artisti
19 Pizzeria al Profeta
20 Enoteca e Trattoria la Bitta
21 Grom Gelateria
22 Il Doge Gelateria

23 Small Deli
24 Caffè Rosso & Pizza al Volo
25 Venice Jazz Club
26 El Chioschetto alle Zattere
27 Musica a Palazzo
28 Interpreti Veneziani Orchestra
29 Music Museum

Rezzonico vaporetto stop—line #1, a few blocks past Campo San Barnaba on Fondamenta Gherardini at Dorsoduro 2813, tel. 041-277-0653, www.casarezzonico.it, info@casarezzonico.it, brothers Matteo and Mattia).

$$ Hotel Galleria has nine tight, old-fashioned, velvety rooms, most with views of the Grand Canal. Some rooms are quite narrow. It's run with a family feel by Luciano and Stefano (S-€85, D-€130, Grand Canal view D-€150, skinny Grand Canal view Db-€160, palatial Grand Canal view Db-€185, breakfast in room, ceiling fans, free mini-bar, free Wi-Fi, 30 yards from Accademia art museum, next to recommended Foscarini pizzeria at Dorsoduro 878a, tel. 041-523-2489, www.hotelgalleria.it, info@hotelgalleria.it).

$$ Don Orione Religious Guest House is a big cultural center dedicated to the work of a local man who became a saint in modern times. With 80 rooms filling an old monastery, it feels cookie-cutter-institutional (like a modern retreat center), but is also classy, clean, peaceful, and strictly run. It's beautifully located, comfortable, and a good value supporting a fine cause: Profits go to mission work in the developing world (Sb-€96, Db-€160, Tb-€207, Qb-€248, groups welcome, air-con, elevator, free Wi-Fi, on Rio Terà A. Foscarini, Dorsoduro 909a, tel. 041-522-4077, www.donorione-venezia.it, info@donorione-venezia.it). From the Zattere vaporetto stop, turn right, then turn left. It's just after the church at #909a.

$ Ca' San Trovaso rents seven simple rooms split between the main building and a nearby annex. The location is peaceful, on a small, desolate-feeling canal (Sb-€90, Db-€115, Db with bigger canal view and air-con-€130, Tb-€145, breakfast in your room, air-con in most rooms, free Wi-Fi, no common space except small roof terrace, near Zattere vaporetto stop, off Fondamenta de le Romite at Dorsoduro 1350/51, tel. 041-277-1146, mobile 339-445-8821, www.casantrovaso.com, info@casantrovaso.com, Mark and Cristina).

$ Casa di Sara, a colorfully decorated B&B, is hidden in a leafy courtyard in a humble back-street area overlooking a canal. Their four quiet rooms and tiny roof terrace offer the maximum in privacy (Sb-€85, Db-€110, Tb-€130, air-con, free Wi-Fi, along Fondamenta de le Romite at Dorsoduro 1330, mobile 342-596-3563, www.casadisara.com, info@casadisara.com, Aniello).

North of the Accademia Bridge

These places are between the Accademia Bridge and St. Mark's Square.

$$$ Novecento Hotel rents nine plush rooms on three floors, complemented by a big, welcoming lounge and an elegant living room. This boutique hotel has a tasteful sense of style, mingling

Art Deco with North African and Turkish decor (Db-€270, bigger "superior" Db-€290, air-con, lots of stairs, free Wi-Fi, on Calle del Dose, off Campo San Maurizio at San Marco 2683, tel. 041-241-3765, www.novecento.biz, info@novecento.biz).

$$$ Foresteria Levi, run by a foundation that promotes research on Venetian music, offers 20 quiet, institutional yet comfortable and spacious rooms (some are lofts). Prices vary wildly—ask for the Rick Steves deal (generally around Db-€190, fans, elevator, free Wi-Fi, family loft rooms, on Calle Giustinian at San Marco 2893, tel. 041-786-711, www.fondazionelevi.it, info@foresterialevi.it).

$$ Istituto Ciliota is a big, efficient, and sparkling-clean place—well-run, well-located, and church-owned—with an Ikea-style charm, 30 dorm-like rooms, and a peaceful garden. If you want industrial-strength comfort at a good price with no stress and little character, this is a fine value. During the school year, half the rooms are used by students (Sb-€90, Db-€130, cheaper with longer stays, air-con, mini-fridges in each room, elevator, free Wi-Fi in some areas, on Calle de le Muneghe just off Campo San Stefano near the Accademia Bridge and vaporetto stop, San Marco 2976, tel. 041-520-4888, www.ciliota.it, info@ciliota.it).

$ Albergo San Samuele is a backpacker place that's dumpy but in a great locale. It rents 10 basic rooms in a crumbling old palace near Campo San Stefano. Sleep here only if their price is far less than what you can get at my other listings (S-€70, D-€90, Db-€115, extra bed-€15, no breakfast, fans, free Wi-Fi, on Salizada San Samuele at San Marco 3358, tel. 041-520-5165, www.hotelsansamuele.com, info@hotelsansamuele.com).

Near the Train Station

I don't recommend the train station area. It's crawling with noisy, disoriented tourists with too much baggage and people whose life's calling is to scam visitors out of their money. It's so easy just to hop a vaporetto upon arrival and sleep in the Venice of your dreams. Still, some like to park their bags near the station, and if so, these places stand out. The farther you get from the station, the more pleasant the surroundings (for locations, see the map on page 270).

Nearby Laundry: The nearest self-service **laundry** is across the Grand Canal from the station (€14/load, daily 7:30-22:30, on Ramo de le Chioverete, Santa Croce 665b).

Close to the Station

$$$ Hotel Abbazia, in the dreary hotel zone near the train station, fills a former abbey with both history and class. The refectory makes a grand living room for guests, a garden fills the old courtyard, and the halls leading to 50 rooms are monkishly wide (Db-€200, larger "superior" Db-€230—choose Venetian or modern style, ask for 10

SLEEPING

Hotels & Restaurants near the Train Station

1. Hotel Abbazia
2. Albergo Marin & Launderette
3. Hotel S. Lucia
4. Hotel Rossi
5. Locanda Ca' San Marcuola
6. Locanda Herion
7. Hotel Henry
8. To Osteria L'Orto dei Mori
9. To Osteria Ai 40 Ladroni
10. Timon Enoteca Osteria
11. To Osteria al Bacco
12. Pizzeria Vesuvio
13. Enoteca Cicchetteria Do Colonne
14. Antica Birraria la Corte
15. Brek Cafeteria
16. Grom Gelateria

Road to Mestre & Mainland

To Road to Mestre & Mainland

To Tronchetto

SANTA LUCIA TRAIN STATION (FERROVIA)

FOND. DE

C. DE LA 2 CORTI

C. DE LA CORTI

RAMO DEI SCALZI

C. PRIULI DEI CAVALETTI

PHARMACY

SCALZI

Ferrovia W

Ferrovia Scalzi

Ferrovia

SCALZI BRIDGE

SAN SIMEONE PICCOLO

CAMP DE LE CHIOVERETE

C. DEI BERGAMASCHI

WC

To Stazione Marittima & Tronchetto

R.AMPA SAN BASILIO

PEOPLE MOVER

Canale de la Liberta

PONTE DELLA Santa Chiara

CO-OP SUPER-MARKET

Piazzale Roma

CALATRAVA BRIDGE

FOND. DE LA CROCE

FOND. DE SAN SIMEONE PICCOLO

CALLE NOVA DE S.

F. DEI TOLENTINI

CASE NOVE

CAMPO D. LA

PARKING GARAGE

P

RIO TERA SAN ANDREA

Piazzale Roma

BUS STATION

Giardino Papadopoli

RIO Novo

Campiello de Lana

F. CONDULMER

SAN NICOLO DA TOLENTINO

PHARMACY

Canale de Santa Maria Maggiore

S A N T A   C R O C E

FONDAMENTA DEL 3 PONTE

F. DEL PASSAMONTE

F. MINOTTO

F. D. GAFFARO

C. DE CA'AMAI

C. DE S. BIACA

GALLO

C. BASEGO

F. DEL RIO NUOVO

Rio de la Cazziola

100 Meters
100 Yards

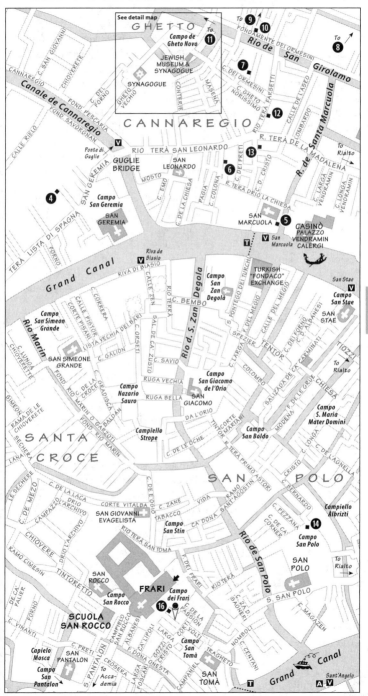

See detail map

GHETTO

To 9 10

To
8

Campo de
Gheto Nova 11

JEWISH
MUSEUM &
SYNAGOGUE

7

Fondamente dei Ormesini

Rio de San

C. dei Ormesini

Girolamo

SYNAGOGUE

GHETTO
VECHIO

C. GHETO
NORISSIMO

RIO TERA FARSETTI

Calle de l'Aseo

Lombardo

CONTERIE

MASENA

12

Calle de Santa Marcuola

Canale de Cannaregio

CANNAREGIO

FOND. DEL FORNO

FOND. SAXORGNAN

CALLE RIELO

To
Rialto

Ponte di
Guglie

V

RIO TERA SAN LEONARDO

R. TERA DE LA MADALENA

GUGLIE
BRIDGE

SAN
LEONARDO

C. DEI PRETI

C. CRISTO

13

R. de Santa Marcuola

MOSTO

6

RIO TERA DRIO LA CHIESA

C. LARGA
VENDRAMIN

C. LONGA
VENDRAMIN

SAN GEREMIA

C. EMO

C. DE LA PIAGIA

C. COLONA

SAN
MARCUOLA

5

CASINÒ
PALAZZO
VENDRAMIN
CALERGI

4

Campo
San Geremia

TERA LISTA DI SPAGNA

FOND. DEL FORNO

Riva de
Biasio

V

RIVA DI BIASIO

T

V San
Marcuola

San Stae

V

Grand Canal

CALLE ZEN

RIO TERA

C. BEMBO

Campo
San Zan
Degola

S. PONTEGO DEI TURCHI

TURKISH
"FONDACO"
EXCHANGE

F. E DEL MEGIO

CALLE DEL MEGIO

Campo
San Stae

Campo
San Simeon
Grande

CORRERA

CALLE PISTOR

CORTE PISANI

LISTA VECHIA DEI BARI

RIO D. S. ZAN Degola

SAN
STAE

V

Rio Marin

C. LUNGA
CHIOVERETE

SAN SIMEONE
GRANDE

C. DE LA CROCE

C. GALION

SAL. DE CA. SAVIO

SPEZIER

TENTOR

COLOMBO

C. LARGA

C. DEL FORNO

S. D. C. CARMINATI

SALIZADA DE CA. CAVANELI

CHIESA

SAN
GIACOMO

CHIESA

To
Rialto

TIOZZI

SANTA

RAMA DE LE
CHIOVERETE

FOND. RIO MARIN G. GARZOTI

C. DE LA GRADISCA

Campo
Nazario
Sauro

RUGA VECHIA

RUGA BELLA

DA L'ORIO

Campo
San Giacomo
de l'Orio

MODENA

C. DE LE GRIE

Campo
S. Maria
Mater Domini

C. LONGA

SIMEON DE LE
SECHERE

FOND. RIO MARIN

C. DE LE OCHE

Campo
San Boldo

CRISTO

C. DE L'AGNELLA

CROCE

LE SECHERE

LANA

C. DE MEZO

Campiello
Strope

X. TERA PRIMO ASTORI

TINTOR. MARIANI

X. TINTOR

SAN

POLO

C. BERNARDO

C. DE LA LACA

CAMPAZZO L'ARCHIVO

DRIO

DE L'ARCHIVO

CORTE VITALBA

C. ZANE

VIDA

RAMO
SANT'AGOSTIN

CA' DONA

C. DE CA'
CORNER

C. PEZZANA

Campiello
Albrizti

CHIOVERE

TINTORETTO

RAMO CIMESIN

SAN GIOVANNI
EVAGELISTA

CORTE
TABACCO

Campo
San Stin

F. DEI FRARI

14

Campo
San Polo

SAN
ROCCO

RIO TERA SAN TOMA

CA' DONA

RIO TERA

SAN
POLO

To
Rialto

DE CA.
FALIER

SAN
ROCCO

FRARI

Campo
dei Frari

16

RIO DE SAN POLO

S. POLO

C. MAGAZEN

Campo
San Rocco

Campiello
San Rocco

C. DE LA
PASSION

C. DONA ONESTA

RAMO
SAONERI

NOMBOLI

SCUOLA
SAN ROCCO

C. PRETI

PANTALON

CAMPIELD
ALBANESI

GOZZI

C. CA TIPOLI

C. DE LA PASSION

C. C VOLTI

Campo
San
Tomà

C. CENTANI

TRAGHETO

Capielo
Mosca

SAN
PANTALON

CROSERA

FOSCARI

LARGA

F. DONA ONESTA

SAN
TOMÀ

Grand Canal

Campo
San
Pantalon

C. VINANTI

FORNO

PANTALON

To
Accademia

CAMPANIEL

T

A V

Sant'Angelo

SLEEPING

percent Rick Steves discount when you book direct, air-con, no elevator but plenty of stairs, free Wi-Fi, fun-loving staff, 2 blocks from the station on the very quiet Calle Priuli dei Cavaletti, Cannaregio 68, tel. 041-717-333, www.abbaziahotel.com, info@abbaziahotel.com).

$ Albergo Marin has a humdrum lobby, but its 19 rooms are a good value. It's across the Grand Canal from the train station— close enough to be convenient, but far enough to be quiet, sane, and residential (Sb-€120, D-€110, Db-€130, big "superior" Db with fancy showers-€160, Tb-€160, 5 percent discount if you pay cash, air-con, free Wi-Fi, on Ramo de le Chioverete at Santa Croce 670b, tel. 041-718-022, www.albergomarin.it, info@albergomarin. it, brothers Giacomo and Filippo).

$ Hotel S. Lucia, 150 yards from the train station, is oddly modern and sterile, with bright and spacious rooms and tight showers. Its 13 rooms are simple and clean. Guests enjoy their sunny garden area out front (S-€60, D-€90, Db-€110, Tb-€130, 5 percent discount if you pay cash, breakfast-€5, air-con, free Wi-Fi, closed Nov-Feb, on Calle de la Misericordia at Cannaregio 358, tel. 041-715-180, www.hotelslucia.com, info@hotelslucia.com, Gianni and Alessandra).

$ Hotel Rossi, sitting quietly at the end of a dead-end street, rents 14 tired, well-worn rooms that are cheap in every sense (S-€59, D-€83, Db-€98, Tb-€118, air-con, free Wi-Fi in common areas, a short walk from the station and a block off the main street at Lista di Spagna, Cannaregio 262, tel. 041-715-164, www.hotelrossi.ve.it, into@hotelrossi.ve.it).

Farther from the Station, Toward the Jewish Ghetto and Rialto

While still walkable from the station, these listings are just outside the chaotic station neighborhood, in a far more pleasant residential zone close to the former Jewish Ghetto. The nearest Grand Canal vaporetto stop is San Marcuola.

$$ Locanda Ca' San Marcuola is a peaceful, characteristic, good-value oldie-but-goodie renting 14 fine rooms a few steps from the Grand Canal (Db-€140, €10 more for slightly bigger room overlooking small canal, air-con, elevator, pay Wi-Fi, next to San Marcuola vaporetto stop on Campo San Marcuola, Cannaregio 1763, tel. 041-716-048, www.casanmarcuola.com, info@ casanmarcuola).

$ Locanda Herion, tucked down a sleepy lane just off a busy shopping street, rents 15 beige-tiled, homey rooms (Db-€130, larger rooms available at higher rates, 10 percent discount if you book direct, air-con, pay Wi-Fi in lobby, a few shared terraces, on Campiello Augusto Picutti, Cannaregio 1697a, tel. 041-275-9426, www.locandaherion.com, info@locandaherion.com).

$ Hotel Henry, a tiny, family-owned hotel, rents 15 simple, flowery, nicely maintained rooms with few public spaces. It's in a sleepy residential neighborhood near the Jewish Ghetto, a 10-minute walk from the train station (D-€80, Db-€95, Tb-€130, Qb-€160, these prices good with cash and this book through 2014, breakfast-€10, air-con, free Wi-Fi, on Calle Ormesini at Campiello Briani, Cannaregio 1506e, tel. 041-523-6675, www.alloggi-henry.com, info@alloggihenry.com, Manola and Henry).

More Hotels in Venice

Big, Fancy Hotels that Discount Shamelessly: Several big, plush, **$$$** places with greedy, sky-high rack rates (around Db-€300-350) frequently have steep discounts (often around Db-€220-250, and as low as Db-€120 or less off-season) if you book through their websites. All of the ones I've listed here are on the map on page 258, except Hotel Giorgione. If you want sliding-glass-door, uniformed-receptionist kind of comfort and formality in the old center, these are worth considering: **Hotel Giorgione** (big, garish, shiny, near Rialto Bridge—see map on page 263; www.hotelgiorgione.com); **Hotel Casa Verardo** (elegant and quietly parked on a canal behind St. Mark's, more stately, 22 rooms, www.casaverardo.it); **Hotel Donà Palace, Hotel all'Angelo,** and **Hotel al Ponte dei Sosperi** (three sister hotels sitting like Las Vegas in the touristy zone a few blocks behind St. Mark's Basilica, with stiff service and renting a total of 100 overpriced rooms that are getting a bit long in the tooth, all on Calle Larga San Marco, www.donapalace.it); and **Hotel Ca' Dei Conti** (5 minutes northeast of St. Mark's Square, palatial and perfectly located but €500 rooms are worth it only when deeply discounted, www.cadeiconti.com).

Other Options: If all my other listings are full, try one of the following hotels. Rates for these places vary widely with the season and demand (generally around Db-€160-190 for a standard double room in high season): **Hotel Violino d'Oro** is a beautiful boutique hotel (Via XXII Marzo, San Marco 2091, tel. 041-277-0841, www.violinodoro.com). Its sister hotel, **Hotel Anastasia,** is more modest, with limited reception staff (San Marco 2141, tel. 041-277-0776, www.hotelanastasia.com). **Hotel American Dinesen** offers 30 plush rooms with all comforts (near Peggy Guggenheim Collection at Fondamenta Bragadin, Dorsoduro 628, tel. 041-520-4733, www.hotelamerican.com). **Hotel La Fenice et des Artistes** has 68 classy but unpretentious rooms on a sleepy square (near opera house at Campiello della Fenice, San Marco 1936, tel. 041-523-2333, www.fenicehotels.it). **Hotel dei Dragomanni** is modern, stylish, and pricey (facing Grand Canal at San Marco 2711, tel. 041-277-1300, www.hoteldragomanni.com).

SLEEPING

Cheap Dormitory Accommodations

$ **Foresteria della Chiesa Valdese** is ramshackle, chilly, and run-down yet charming. It rents 70 beds—mostly in tight (6- to 10-bed) dorms, but with nine fine doubles and some larger private rooms sleeping up to six. It comes with generous public spaces and classic paintings on the walls and ceilings. Its profits support the charity work of the Methodist Church. They take reservations for the rooms, but only accept walk-ins for the dorms (dorm bed-€35, Db-€105-140, Tb-€120-140, Qb-€155-170, Quint/b-€185-220, €5/person less for multi-night stays; includes breakfast, sheets, towels, and lockers; must check in and out when office is open—8:30-19:30, no air-con, elevator, near Campo Santa Maria Formosa on Fondamenta Cavagnis at Castello 5170, see map on page 263, tel. 041-528-6797, www.foresteriavenezia.it, info@foresteriavenezia.it).

$ **Venice's youth hostel,** on Giudecca Island with 260 beds and grand views across the Bay of San Marco, is a godsend for back-packers shell-shocked by Venetian prices. Though the facility was recently renovated, at heart it's a classic hostel—big rooms stacked with bunk beds (€27 beds with sheets and breakfast in 8- to 20-bed dorms, €2 extra the first night for nonmembers, free Wi-Fi, lockers, towels-€5, room lock-out 10:00-13:30, office open 24 hours, Fondamenta Zitelle 86, tel. 041-523-8211, www.ostellovenezia.it, info@ostellovenezia.it). Take vaporetto #4.1 from the bus or train stations (from the Tronchetto parking lot, take vaporetto #2) to the Zitelle stop, then walk right along the embankment to #86.

On the Mainland, in Mestre

Venice's causeway meets the mainland at a gloomy, industrial, concrete burg called Mestre (MEH-streh). The streets surrounding the Mestre station are a stark contrast to Venice: big, dingy buildings and modern roads buzzing with traffic. It's hard to justify sleeping here when the magic of Venice is so close. But for some, bunking here may make sense: Your money buys far more comfort and amenities; it's very handy for side-tripping by rail to other towns (such as Padua, Vicenza, and Verona); and it's more likely to have affordable rooms when Venice proper is chockablock with festivals. Drivers wanting to do a one-day blitz of Venice can park right at their Mestre hotel.

Mestre is very easily connected to Venice. From its big station, trains depart about every 10 minutes, zipping to Venezia Santa Lucia Station (right on the Grand Canal) in about 10 minutes for €1.20 (buy tickets at machines). Alternatively, you can catch bus #2, right in front of Mestre's train station, and ride it to Venice's Piaz-zale Roma (also right on the Grand Canal, across from the train station) in 15 minutes (€1.30, also covered by Venice's transit passes).

These hotels all charge around €100 for a double in peak season, but rates are extremely soft. In slow times, you can get a much better deal. All of these are quite modern when compared to the typically musty, Old World options in Venice. My Mestre recommendations all have air-conditioning, free Wi-Fi, and pay parking—either on-site or discounted at the big Parcheggio Stazione garage across from the station (figure €10-16/day; request when you reserve).

Right in Front of the Station

$ Hotel Tritone, a high-rise with 60 rooms, has the most convenient location, facing Mestre's train station (leaving the station, cross the street, turn right, and walk to the end of the block). With friendly service, a very Italian borderline-gaudy lobby, and lots of little extras, it's a fine mix of convenience and comfort (Db-€100, elevator, parking at adjacent lot-€14/day, Viale Stazione 16, tel. 041-538-3125, www.hoteltritonevenice.com, info@hoteltritonevenice.com).

$ Hotel Paris, a lesser value, is close to the station and worth considering if you can get a deal. It has 18 small, modern, modestly stylish rooms (Db-€105, on-site parking, Via Venezia 11, tel. 041-926-037, www.hotelparis.it, info@hotelparis.it). It's hiding in a drab sea of apartment blocks: Leaving the station, cross the street, turn left along Viale Stazione, and turn right after one block up Via Venezia.

A Bit Farther, but Still Walkable

While slightly less handy to the station (requiring about a 10-minute walk), these options are a better value and get you a bit outside the gloomy concrete. To reach them from the station, exit straight ahead and go up Via Piave. After about four blocks, turn left for Hotel Villa Costanza or Hotel Cris, or (soon after) right for Hotel Aaron. For these hotels, the bus (which stops along Via Piave) can be a faster and easier way to reach Venice than the train (and lets you skip the station-area chaos).

$ Hotel Villa Costanza is the nicest place I saw in Mestre. This stylish, professional-feeling boutique hotel fills an old villa on a sleepy residential street with 26 classy rooms, an inviting modern lounge, and a covered terrace (Db-€120, elevator, on-site parking, Via Monte Nero 25, tel. 041-932-624, www.hotelvillacostanza.com, info@hotelvillacostanza.com).

$ Hotel Cris, a simpler option up the street from Hotel Villa Costanza, has 18 nondescript rooms (Db-€99 but often much cheaper with online deals, on-site parking, Via Monte Nero 3a, tel. 041-926-773, www.hotelcris.it, hotelcris@tiscali.it).

$ Hotel Aaron oozes modern artistic style, with 20 sleek, good-value rooms on a pleasant street just off Viale Piave (Db-€75 on weekdays, €100 on weekends, breakfast-€5, elevator, Via Felisati 187, tel. 041-538-5868, www.hotelaaron.com, info@hotelaaron.com).

Behind Mestre Station, in Marghera

If you leave the station through its back door (follow the underground tunnel connecting platforms to the end beyond tracks 12/13), you'll pop out into Marghera: a much more pleasant, residential-feeling area, with freestanding homes, gardens, and trees. Exiting the station, turn left down the first street, then right onto Via Rizzardi. This main drag is lined with lots of big tour hotels (where cut-rate tours shoehorn their groups at Venice's doorstep), as well as this smaller, charming option.

$ **Casa Villa Gardenia,** just before the roundabout on the right (about a 10-minute walk from the station's tracks), is sweetly run by Lorenza, who rents six rooms in a pleasant old villa (Db-€92, free on-site parking, Via Rizzardi 36c, Marghera, tel. 041-930-207, www.casavillagardenia.it).

Other Mainland Options

Beyond the urban core of Mestre described above, these two places combine fine prices with easy bus links into Venice.

$ **Villa Dolcetti** is a 1635 building with six comfortable rooms in a suburb of Venice. Art lovers Diego and Tatiana provide a buffet breakfast, free parking, and lots of sightseeing advice (Db-€80, "superior" Db-€90, Tb-€110, these prices for Rick Steves readers booking direct, air-con, tel. 041-563-1077, www.villadolcetti.com, info@villadolcetti.com). It's in the town of Oriago di Mira, at Via Venezia 85. Steps away is a bus stop on the Venice-Padua line that connects you to Venice's Piazzale Roma (2/hour, 25 minutes).

$ **Villa Mocenigo Agriturismo,** about 10 miles from Marco Polo Airport, is a working, family-run farm in a peaceful rural location between Venice and Padua. Its 10 rooms are furnished with antiques, and regional specialties are served for dinner (Sb-€40-55, Db-€60-74, extra bed-€20-25, dinner about €20/person, air-con, free parking, Via Viasana 59 in Mirano-Venezia, tel. 041-433-246, mobile 335-547-4728, www.villamocenigo.com, info@villamocenigo.com). Email for directions. Buses to Venice leave directly from the villa (3/hour, 45 minutes).

EATING IN VENICE

The Italians are masters at the art of fine living. That means eating long and well. Lengthy, multicourse meals and endless hours sitting in outdoor cafés are the norm. Americans eat on their way to an evening event and complain if the check is slow in coming. For Italians, dining is an end in itself, and only rude waiters rush you. When you want the bill, mime-scribble on your raised palm or request it: *"Il conto, per favore."* You may have to ask for it more than once. If you're in a hurry, request the check when you receive the last item you've ordered.

A highlight of your Italian adventure will be this country's cafés, cuisine, and wines. Trust me: This is sightseeing for your palate. Even if you liked dorm food and are sleeping in cheap hotels, your taste buds will relish an occasional first-class splurge. You can eat well without going broke. But be careful: You're just as likely to blow a small fortune on a disappointing meal as you are to dine wonderfully for €25.

In general, Italians eat meals a bit later than we do. At 7:00 or 8:00 in the morning, they have a light breakfast (coffee and a roll, often standing up at a café). Lunch, which is usually the main meal of the day, begins around 13:00 and can last for a couple of hours. Then they eat a late, light dinner (around 20:00-21:30, or maybe earlier in winter). To bridge the gap, people drop into a bar in the late afternoon for a *spuntino* (snack) and aperitif.

Don't expect all-day service at restaurants. Most kitchens close between their lunch and dinner service. Good restaurants don't reopen for dinner before 19:00.

Breakfast

Italian breakfasts, like Italian bath towels, are small: The basic, traditional version is coffee and a roll with butter and marmalade.

These days, many places also have juice, yogurt, maybe cereal, possibly cold cuts and sliced cheese, and sometimes eggs (typically hard-boiled; scrambled or fried eggs are rare). Small budget hotels may leave a basic breakfast in a fridge in your room (stale croissant, roll, jam, yogurt, coffee). In general, the pricier the hotel, the bigger the breakfast.

The strong coffee at breakfast is often mixed about half-and-half with heated milk. At your hotel, refills are usually free. The delicious red orange juice *(spremuta di arance rosse)* is made from Sicilian blood oranges.

If you want to skip your hotel breakfast, consider browsing for a morning picnic at a local open-air market. Or do as the Italians do: Stop into a bar or café to drink a cappuccino and munch a *cornetto* (croissant) while standing at the bar. While the *cornetto* is the most common pastry, you'll find a range of *pasticcini* (pastries, sometimes called *dolci*—"sweets"). Look for *otto* ("8"-shaped pastry, often filled with custard, jam, or chocolate), *sfoglia* (can be fruit-filled, like a turnover), or *ciambella* (doughnut filled with custard or chocolate)—or ask about local specialties.

Restaurants

While *ristorante* is self-explanatory, you'll also see other types of Italian eateries: A *trattoria* and an *osteria* (which can be more casual) are generally family-owned places serving home-cooked meals, often at moderate prices. A *locanda* is an inn, a *cantina* is a wine cellar, and a *birraria* is a brewpub. *Pizzerie, rosticcerie* (delis), *tavola calda* bars, *enoteche* (wine bars), and other alternatives are explained later.

Looking for an "untouristy restaurant" in Venice is like looking for the same thing at Disneyland. Venice restaurants exist to feed tourists. Still, some cater to groups and sloppy big spenders, while others respect their clientele—both locals and travelers. Avoid places with big signs boasting, "We Speak English and Accept Credit Cards." High-rent restaurants parked on famous squares or canals generally serve tourists bad food at high prices. The natives eat better at low-rent holes-in-the-wall, which need to be good to be known. While Venetians still eat out and have their favorites, a restaurateur once confided in me that no restaurant in Venice can be truly untouristy: They all want and need the tourist euro.

Cover and Tipping

Before you sit down, look at a menu to see what extra charges a restaurant tacks on. Two different items are routinely factored into your bill: the *coperto* and the *servizio*.

The **coperto** (cover charge), sometimes called *pane e coperto*

Eating with the Seasons

Italian cooks love to serve you fresh produce and seafood at its tastiest. If you must have porcini mushrooms outside of fall,

they'll be frozen. Each region in Italy has its specialties, which you'll see displayed in open-air markets. To get a plate of the freshest veggies at a fine restaurant, request "*Un piatto di verdure della stagione, per favore.*"

Here are a few examples of what's fresh when:

April-May:	Calamari, squid, green beans, asparagus, artichokes, and zucchini flowers
April-May and Sept-Oct:	Black truffles
May-June:	Mussels, asparagus, zucchini, cantaloupe, and strawberries
May-Aug:	Eggplant
Oct-Nov:	Mushrooms, white truffles, and chestnuts
Nov-Feb:	Radicchio
Fresh year-round:	Clams, meats, and cheese

EATING

(bread and cover), offsets the overhead expenses from the basket of bread on your table to the electricity running the dishwasher. It's not negotiable, even if you don't eat the bread. Think of it as covering the cost of using the table for as long as you like. (Italians like to linger.) Most restaurants add the *coperto* onto your bill as a flat fee (€1-3.50 per person; the amount should be clearly noted on the menu).

The ***servizio*** (service charge) of about 10 percent pays for the waitstaff. At most legitimate eateries, the words *servizio incluso* are written on the menu and/or the receipt—indicating that the listed prices already include the fee. You can add on a tip, if you choose, by including a euro or two for each person in your party. While Italians don't think about tips in terms of percentages—and many don't tip at all—this extra amount usually comes out to about 5 percent (10 percent is excessive for all but the very best service).

If you see the words *servizio non incluso* on the menu or bill, you are expected to add a tip of about 10 percent. A few trendy restaurants don't include the service in the menu prices—but will automatically tack on a 10 percent *servizio* charge to your bill. Most good-value eateries have a cover charge, and the service is already included in the menu prices (i.e., *servizio incluso*). Places with *both* a cover and a tacked-on service charge are best avoided—that's a clue that a restaurant is counting on a nonlocal clientele who can't gauge value. The same goes for the opposite: Places that advertise "no cover, no service charge" to attract tourists are likely raising their prices to compensate.

Courses: Antipasto, *Primo,* and *Secondo*

A full Italian meal consists of several courses:

Antipasto (usually €5-10): An appetizer such as bruschetta, grilled veggies, deep-fried tasties, thin-sliced meat (such as prosciutto or carpaccio), or a plate of olives, cold cuts, and cheeses. A plate of *antipasti misti* ("mixed"—an assortment) could make a light meal in itself.

Primo piatto (usually €7-15): A "first dish" generally consisting of pasta, rice, or soup. If you think of pasta when you think of Italy, you can dine well here without ever going beyond the *primo*.

Secondo piatto (usually €10-25): A "second dish," equivalent to our main course, of meat or fish/seafood. Italians freely admit the *secondo* is the least interesting part of their cuisine.

A vegetable side dish *(contorno)* may come with the *secondo* but more often must be ordered separately (€5-6).

The euros can add up in a hurry, and for most travelers, a complete meal with all three courses (plus *contorni*, dessert, and wine) is simply too much food. To avoid overeating (and to stretch your budget), share dishes. A good rule of thumb is for each person to order any two courses. For example, a couple can order and share one antipasto, one *primo*, one *secondo,* and one dessert; or two *antipasti* and two *primi*; or whatever combination appeals.

Another good option is sharing an array of *antipasti*—either by ordering several specific dishes or, at restaurants that offer self-serve buffets, by choosing a variety of cold and cooked appetizers from an *antipasti* buffet spread out like a salad bar. At buffets, you pay per plate; a typical serving costs about €8 (generally Italians don't treat buffets as all-you-can-eat, but take a one-time moderate serving; watch others and imitate).

To maximize the experience and flavors, small groups can mix *antipasti* and *primi* family-style (skipping *secondi*). If you do this right, you can eat well in better places for less than the cost of a tourist menu in a cheap place.

Ordering Tips

Seafood and steak may be sold by weight (priced by the kilo—1,000 grams, or just over two pounds; or by the *etto*—100 grams). The abbreviation *s.q. (secondo quantità)* means an item is priced "according

ives, and artichokes), *funghi* (mush-
auce, oregano, garlic, no cheese), *napo-
es, and tomato sauce), *vegetariana* or or-
with vegetables), *quattro formaggi* (four
tro stagioni (different toppings on each
se who can't choose just one menu item).
your pizza, you'll get *peperoni* (green or
request *diavola* or *salsiccia piccante* in-
taly to American pepperoni). Kids like
o sauce, mozzarella, and basil—the red,
ian flag). *Pizza bianca* (or *pizza ciaccina*)
matoes.

ns, but inexpensive cafés. These neigh-
ffee, mini-pizzas, premade sandwiches,
Many dish up plates of fried cheese and
glass counter, ready to reheat. This bud-
iivalent of English pub grub. Unique to
alize in finger foods and appetizers that
ick and tasty meal (see "The Stand-Up
Crawl Dinner" sidebar on page 302).

s, bars usually have trays of cheap, pre-
on a baguette; *piadini*, on flatbread; or
iite bread)—some are delightful grilled.
1ayo.) To save time for sightseeing and
bar for a light lunch, such as a ham-and-
ast); have it grilled twice if you want it
go," say, "*da portar via*" (for the road), or
anal). Many bars are small—if you can't
stand up or find a ledge to sit on outside.
e service (see next). All bars have a WC
k, and customers—and the discreet pub-

ou'll notice a two- or three-tiered pric-
1p of coffee while standing at the bar is
at an indoor table (you'll pay still more
y places have a *lista dei prezzi* (price list)
ar and *al tavolo* (table)—posted some-
register. If you're on a budget, don't sit
ng out the financial consequences. Ask,
nd?" by saying, "*Costa uguale al tavolo o
-GWAH-lay ahl TAH-voh-loh oh ahl
Italy, you can get cheap coffee at the bar
matter how fancy, and pay the same low,
ce (generally only a euro if you stand).

to quantity." Unless the menu indicates a fillet *(filetto)*, fish is usually served whole with the head and tail. However, you can always ask your waiter to select a small fish for you. Sometimes, especially for steak, restaurants require a minimum order of four or five *etti* (which diners can share). Make sure you're really clear on the price before ordering.

Some special dishes come in larger quantities meant to be shared by two people. The shorthand way of showing this on a menu is "X2" (for two), but the price listed generally indicates the cost per person.

If you order a pasta dish and a side salad but no main course, the waiter will ask when you want the salad served (Italians prefer it after the pasta, believing that it enhances digestion). If you want the salad with your pasta, specify *insieme* (een-see-YEH-meh, "together").

Because pasta and bread are both starches, Italians consider them redundant. If you order only a pasta dish, bread may not come with it; you can request it, but you may be charged extra. On the other hand, if you order a vegetable antipasto or a meat *secondo*, bread is provided to balance the ingredients.

At places with counter service—such as at a bar or a freeway rest-stop diner—you'll order and pay at the *cassa* (cashier). Take your receipt over to the counter to claim your food.

EATING

Fixed-Price Meals

You can save by getting a fixed-priced meal, which is frequently exempt from cover and service charges. Avoid the cheapest ones (often called a *menù turistico*), which tend to be bland and heavy, pairing a very basic pasta with reheated schnitzel and roast meats.

MENU TURISTICO € 19,00
ANTIPASTO di MARE
PRIMI PIATTI
RISOTTO alla PESCATORA
SPAGHETTI alla MARINARA
SPAGHETTI allo SCOGLIO
TRENETTE al PESTO
SECONDI PIATTI
PESCE ai FERRI
FRITTO MISTO
GRIGLIATA di CARNE
CONTORNI
PATATE FRITTE o INSALATA

Look instead for a genuine *menù del giorno* (menu of the day), which offers diners a choice of appetizer, main course, and dessert. It's worth paying a little more for an inventive fixed-price meal that shows off the chef's creativity.

While fixed-price meals can be easy and convenient, galloping gourmets order à la carte with the help of a menu translator. (The *Rick Steves' Italian Phrase Book & Dictionary* has a menu decoder with enough phrases for intermediate eaters.)

When going to an especially good restaurant with an approachable staff, I like to find out what they're eager to serve, or I'll simply say, "*Mi faccia felice*" (Make me happy) and set a price limit.

Pasta, Pasta!

Italy is famous for its cuisine, but above all, it's known for pasta. Each of the more than 600 varieties of Italian pasta has its reason for being—usually as the perfect platform for highlighting the sauce, meat, or regional ingredients of a particular dish. While we think of pasta as a main dish, in Italy it's considered a *primo piatto*—first course. Italian pasta falls into two broad categories: long and short.

Long pasta (pasta lunga) is long enough to twist around a fork. Aside from the universally familiar spaghetti, you'll find *capellini* (thin "little hairs"); *vermicelli* (slightly thicker "little worms"); and long, hollow *bucatini*. Flattened versions of *pasta lunga* include *linguine* (narrow "little tongues"), *fettuccine* (wider "small ribbons"), *tagliatelle* (even wider), and *pappardelle* (very wide, best with meat sauces).

Short pasta (pasta corta) can be speared or scooped with a fork. The most common *pasta corta* are short tubes, such as *penne, rigatoni, ziti, manicotti,* and *cannelloni*; they come either *lisce* (smooth) or *rigate* (grooved—better to catch and cling to sauce). Many short pastas are named for their unique shapes: *conchiglie* (shells), *farfalle* (butterflies), *cavatappi* (corkscrews), *ditali* (thimbles), *gomiti* ("elbow" macaroni), *lumache* (snails), *marziani* (spirals resembling "Martian" antennae), and even *strozzapreti* (priest stranglers)...to name just a few.

The short pastas are almost always made fresh and often are designed to be filled *(ripieni)*. Aside from the familiar ravioli and tortellini, this category includes *gnocchi* (shell-shaped, hand-rolled dumplings usually made from potatoes), *tortelli* (C-shaped, stuffed ravioli), and *agnolotti* or *mezzelune* (stuffed pasta shaped like "priest's hats" or "half-moons").

Most types of pasta can come in slight variations: If it's a bit thicker, *-one* is added to the end; if it's a bit thinner, *-ine, -ette,* or *-elle* is added. For example, *tortellini* are smaller *tortelli*, while *tortelloni* are bigger.

Budget Eating

Italy offers many budget options for hungry travelers, but beware of cheap eateries that sport big color photos of pizza and piles of different pastas. They have no kitchens and simply microwave disgusting prepackaged food.

The keys to eating affordably in Venice are pizza, *döner kebabs*, bars/cafés, self-service cafeterias, and picnics. Sandwiches *(panini, piadini,* and *tramezzini*; described on page 294) are sold fast and cheap at bars everywhere and can stave off midmorning hunger. There's a great "sandwich row" of cheap cafés near St. Mark's Square (see page 303). For speed, value, and ambience, you can get a filling plate of typically Venetian appetizers at nearly any bar. I like small, fun, stand-up mini-meals at *cicchetti* bars best (many are

---

prosciutto, mushrooms, rooms), *marinara* (tomato *letana* (mozzarella, anchov *tolana* ("greengrocer-style, different cheeses), and *qu* of the four quarters, for th If you ask for pepperoni o red peppers, not sausage) stead (the closest thing in the bland *margherita* (toma white, and green of the Ita is "white" pizza, with no t

Bars/Cafés

Italian "bars" are not tave borhood hangouts serve c and drinks from the coole vegetables from under the get choice is the Italian e Venice, *cicchetti* bars spe can combine to make a q Progressive Venetian Pub

Food: For quick mea made sandwiches *(panin tramezzini,* on crustless w (Others have too much room for dinner, stop by a cheese sandwich (called really hot. To get food "to *"da portar canale"* (for the find a table, you'll need to Most charge extra for tal *(toilette, bagno)* in the ba lic—can use it.

Prices and Paying: ing system. Drinking a cheaper than drinking it at an outdoor table). Ma with two columns—*al* where by the bar or cash down without first check "Same price if I sit or st *al banco?"* (KOH-stah o BAHN-koh). Throughou of any establishment, no government-regulated pr

to quantity." Unless the menu indicates a fillet *(filetto),* fish is usually served whole with the head and tail. However, you can always ask your waiter to select a small fish for you. Sometimes, especially for steak, restaurants require a minimum order of four or five *etti* (which diners can share). Make sure you're really clear on the price before ordering.

Some special dishes come in larger quantities meant to be shared by two people. The shorthand way of showing this on a menu is "X2" (for two), but the price listed generally indicates the cost per person.

If you order a pasta dish and a side salad but no main course, the waiter will ask when you want the salad served (Italians prefer it after the pasta, believing that it enhances digestion). If you want the salad with your pasta, specify *insieme* (een-see-YEH-meh, "together").

Because pasta and bread are both starches, Italians consider them redundant. If you order only a pasta dish, bread may not come with it; you can request it, but you may be charged extra. On the other hand, if you order a vegetable antipasto or a meat *secondo,* bread is provided to balance the ingredients.

At places with counter service—such as at a bar or a freeway rest-stop diner—you'll order and pay at the *cassa* (cashier). Take your receipt over to the counter to claim your food.

EATING

Fixed-Price Meals

You can save by getting a fixed-priced meal, which is frequently exempt from cover and service charges. Avoid the cheapest ones (often called a *menù turistico*), which tend to be bland and heavy, pairing a very basic pasta with reheated schnitzel and roast meats.

MENU € 19,00
TURISTICO
ANTIPASTO di MARE
PRIMI PIATTI
RISOTTO alla PESCATORA
SPAGHETTI alla MARINARA
SPAGHETTI allo SCOGLIO
TRENETTE al PESTO
SECONDI PIATTI
PESCE ai FERRI
FRITTO MISTO
GRIGLIATA di CARNE
CONTORNI
PATATE FRITTE o INSALATA

Look instead for a genuine *menù del giorno* (menu of the day), which offers diners a choice of appetizer, main course, and dessert. It's worth paying a little more for an inventive fixed-price meal that shows off the chef's creativity.

While fixed-price meals can be easy and convenient, galloping gourmets order à la carte with the help of a menu translator. (The *Rick Steves' Italian Phrase Book & Dictionary* has a menu decoder with enough phrases for intermediate eaters.)

When going to an especially good restaurant with an approachable staff, I like to find out what they're eager to serve, or I'll simply say, *"Mi faccia felice"* (Make me happy) and set a price limit.

Pasta, Pasta!

Italy is famous for its cuisine, but above all, it's known for pasta. Each of the more than 600 varieties of Italian pasta has its reason for being—usually as the perfect platform for highlighting the sauce, meat, or regional ingredients of a particular dish. While we think of pasta as a main dish, in Italy it's considered a *primo piatto*—first course. Italian pasta falls into two broad categories: long and short.

Long pasta *(pasta lunga)* is long enough to twist around a fork. Aside from the universally familiar spaghetti, you'll find *capellini* (thin "little hairs"); *vermicelli* (slightly thicker "little worms"); and long, hollow *bucatini*. Flattened versions of *pasta lunga* include *linguine* (narrow "little tongues"), *fettuccine* (wider "small ribbons"), *tagliatelle* (even wider), and *pappardelle* (very wide, best with meat sauces).

Short pasta *(pasta corta)* can be speared or scooped with a fork. The most common *pasta corta* are short tubes, such as *penne*, *rigatoni*, *ziti*, *manicotti*, and *cannelloni*; they come either *lisce* (smooth) or *rigate* (grooved—better to catch and cling to sauce). Many short pastas are named for their unique shapes: *conchiglie* (shells), *farfalle* (butterflies), *cavatappi* (corkscrews), *ditali* (thimbles), *gomiti* ("elbow" macaroni), *lumache* (snails), *marziani* (spirals resembling "Martian" antennae), and even *strozzapreti* (priest stranglers)...to name just a few.

The short pastas are almost always made fresh and often are designed to be filled *(ripieni)*. Aside from the familiar ravioli and tortellini, this category includes *gnocchi* (shell-shaped, hand-rolled dumplings usually made from potatoes), *tortelli* (C-shaped, stuffed ravioli), and *agnolotti* or *mezzelune* (stuffed pasta shaped like "priest's hats" or "half-moons").

Most types of pasta can come in slight variations: If it's a bit thicker, *-one* is added to the end; if it's a bit thinner, *-ine*, *-ette*, or *-elle* is added. For example, *tortellini* are smaller *tortelli*, while *tortelloni* are bigger.

Budget Eating

Italy offers many budget options for hungry travelers, but beware of cheap eateries that sport big color photos of pizza and piles of different pastas. They have no kitchens and simply microwave disgusting prepackaged food.

The keys to eating affordably in Venice are pizza, *döner kebabs*, bars/cafés, self-service cafeterias, and picnics. Sandwiches *(panini, piadini,* and *tramezzini;* described on page 294) are sold fast and cheap at bars everywhere and can stave off midmorning hunger. There's a great "sandwich row" of cheap cafés near St. Mark's Square (see page 303). For speed, value, and ambience, you can get a filling plate of typically Venetian appetizers at nearly any bar. I like small, fun, stand-up mini-meals at **cicchetti bars** best (many are

As for what to put on that pasta, the options are almost as endless as the shapes. The following terms are usually preceded by *alla* (in the style of) or *in* (in):

aglio e olio: garlic and olive oil

alfredo: butter, cream, and parmesan

amatriciana: pork cheek, pecorino cheese, and tomato

arrabbiata: "angry," spicy tomato sauce with chili peppers

bolognese: meat and tomato sauce

boscaiola: mushrooms and sausage

burro e salvia: butter and sage

carbonara: bacon, egg, cheese, and pepper

carrettiera: spicy and garlicky, with olive oil and little tomatoes

diavola: "devil-style," spicy hot

funghi: mushrooms

frutti di mare: seafood

genovese: pesto (basil ground with parmigiano cheese, garlic, pine nuts, and olive oil)

gricia: cured pork and pecorino romano cheese

marinara: usually tomato, often with garlic and onions, but can be a seafood sauce ("sailor's style")

norma: tomato, eggplant, and ricotta cheese

pajata (or *pagliata*): calf intestines

pescatora: seafood ("fisherman-style")

pomodoro: tomato only

puttanesca: "harlot-style" tomato sauce with anchovies, olives, and capers

ragù: meaty tomato sauce

scoglio: mussels, clams, and tomatoes

sorrentina: "Sorrento-style," with tomatoes, basil, and mozzarella (usually over gnocchi)

sugo di lepre: rich sauce made of wild hare

tartufi (or *tartufate*): truffles

umbria: sauce of anchovies, garlic, tomatoes, and truffles

vongole: clams and spices

recommended in this chapter). Those on a hard-core budget equip their room with a pantry stocked at the market (fruits and veggies are remarkably cheap) or pick up a kebab (or the equivalent), then dine in at picnic prices. Bars and cafés, described in detail later, are another good place to grab a meal on the go.

Pizzerias

Pizza, readily available, is cheap if you avoid the most crowded areas. A pizza at a sit-down place will run about €6-12, plus drinks and cover. If you want a killer canalside setting without a killer price, stick to pizza. Even at a tourist trap, pizza is fun and relatively inexpensive. See the "Pizza in Venice?" sidebar for tips.

Key pizza vocabulary: *capricciosa* ("chef's choice," generally prosciutto, mushrooms, olives, and artichokes), *funghi* (mushrooms), *marinara* (tomato sauce, oregano, garlic, no cheese), *napoletana* (mozzarella, anchovies, and tomato sauce), *vegetariana* or *ortolana* ("greengrocer-style," with vegetables), *quattro formaggi* (four different cheeses), and *quattro stagioni* (different toppings on each of the four quarters, for those who can't choose just one menu item). If you ask for pepperoni on your pizza, you'll get *peperoni* (green or red peppers, not sausage); request *diavola* or *salsiccia piccante* instead (the closest thing in Italy to American pepperoni). Kids like the bland *margherita* (tomato sauce, mozzarella, and basil—the red, white, and green of the Italian flag). *Pizza bianca* (or *pizza ciaccina*) is "white" pizza, with no tomatoes.

Bars/Cafés

Italian "bars" are not taverns, but inexpensive cafés. These neighborhood hangouts serve coffee, mini-pizzas, premade sandwiches, and drinks from the cooler. Many dish up plates of fried cheese and vegetables from under the glass counter, ready to reheat. This budget choice is the Italian equivalent of English pub grub. Unique to Venice, **cicchetti bars** specialize in finger foods and appetizers that can combine to make a quick and tasty meal (see "The Stand-Up Progressive Venetian Pub-Crawl Dinner" sidebar on page 302).

Food: For quick meals, bars usually have trays of cheap, premade sandwiches (*panini,* on a baguette; *piadini,* on flatbread; or *tramezzini,* on crustless white bread)—some are delightful grilled. (Others have too much mayo.) To save time for sightseeing and room for dinner, stop by a bar for a light lunch, such as a ham-and-cheese sandwich (called *toast*)*;* have it grilled twice if you want it really hot. To get food "to go," say, *"da portar via"* (for the road), or *"da portar canale"* (for the canal). Many bars are small—if you can't find a table, you'll need to stand up or find a ledge to sit on outside. Most charge extra for table service (see next). All bars have a WC *(toilette, bagno)* in the back, and customers—and the discreet public—can use it.

Prices and Paying: You'll notice a two- or three-tiered pricing system. Drinking a cup of coffee while standing at the bar is cheaper than drinking it at an indoor table (you'll pay still more at an outdoor table). Many places have a *lista dei prezzi* (price list) with two columns—*al bar* and *al tavolo* (table)—posted somewhere by the bar or cash register. If you're on a budget, don't sit down without first checking out the financial consequences. Ask, "Same price if I sit or stand?" by saying, *"Costa uguale al tavolo o al banco?"* (KOH-stah oo-GWAH-lay ahl TAH-voh-loh oh ahl BAHN-koh). Throughout Italy, you can get cheap coffee at the bar of any establishment, no matter how fancy, and pay the same low, government-regulated price (generally only a euro if you stand).

Pizza in Venice?

While not the home of pizza, Venice is enthusiastic about it. For tourists, a great way to enjoy a delightful Venetian setting at a painless price is to have a pizza with a beer or carafe of house wine at a canalside restaurant. Pizza ranges from €4 for take-out to €6 in a cheap restaurant to €12 in a high-quality restaurant. Personally, I like to go top-end on pizza: Invest the extra euros, and enjoy a great setting, classy service, and the best quality. If you're in the mood for pizza, consider one of these places (all described in more detail earlier in this chapter):

Several fun-loving, youthful pizzerias feature inexpensive and good pizzas, big pizza parlor-type interiors, and relaxing outdoor seating, such as **Pizzeria al Profeta** (with a leafy garden, near Campo San Barnaba), **Ae Oche Pizzeria** (with casual tables overlooking the Giudecca Canal), **Antica Birraria la Corte** (on a big, breezy neighborhood square), and **Trattoria Pizzeria al Nono Risorto** (near the Rialto Bridge with a garden full of tables).

For basic pizza with one of the city's most picturesque settings—on the Grand Canal under the Accademia Bridge—check out **Bar Foscarini.**

For top-shelf pizza served in a more formal restaurant setting, consider **Terrazza del Casin dei Nobili** (with elegant seating overlooking the Giudecca Canal), **Ristorante Antica Sacrestia** (in a classy restaurant near St. Mark's Square), and **Pizzeria Vesuvio** (with fine outdoor seating too, near the Jewish Ghetto).

If you prefer takeout, try one of the hole-in-the-wall shops that bake huge, round, family-size pizzas (about 20 inches across) or "normal" ones (12 inches); *pizza al taglio* means "by the slice." While many shops sell individual slices of round, Naples-style pizza, you may also see *pizza rustica*—thick pizza baked in a large rectangular pan and sold by weight. If you simply ask for a piece, you may be handed a gigantic slab and charged top euro. Instead, clearly indicate how much you want: 100 grams, or *un etto*, is a hot and cheap snack; 200 grams, or *due etti*, makes a light meal. Or show the size with your hands—*tanto così* (TAHN-toh koh-ZEE) means "this much." Just remember that picnicking isn't allowed on St. Mark's Square.

EATING

If the bar isn't busy, you can probably just order and pay when you leave. Otherwise: 1) Decide what you want; 2) find out the price by checking the price list on the wall, the prices posted near the food, or by asking the barista; 3) pay the cashier; and 4) give the receipt to the barista (whose clean fingers handle no dirty euros) and tell him or her what you want.

For more on drinking, see "Beverages," later.

Kebab Shops

Perhaps the best value in town for a cheap, hot meal is a *döner kebab*. Look for little hole-in-the-wall kebab shops, where you can get a hearty takeaway dinner wrapped in pita bread for €3.50. Pay an extra euro to super-size it, and it'll feed two. Ask locally for the favorite place in your neighborhood, as the quality can vary substantially.

Tavola Calda Bars and *Rosticcerie*

For a fast and cheap lunch, find an Italian variation on the corner deli: a *rosticceria* (specializing in roasted meats and accompanying *antipasti*) or a *tavola calda* bar ("hot table" point-and-shoot cafeteria with a buffet spread of meat and vegetables; sometimes called *tavola fredda*, or "cold table," in the north). For a healthy light meal, ask for a mixed plate of vegetables with a hunk of mozzarella *(piatto misto di verdure con mozzarella)*. Don't be limited by what's displayed. If you'd like a salad with a slice of cantaloupe and a hunk of cheese, they'll whip that up for you in a snap. Belly up to the bar and, with a pointing finger and key words in the chart in this chapter, you can get a fine mixed plate of vegetables. If something's a mystery, ask for *un assaggio* (oon ah-SAH-joh) to get a little taste.

Wine Bars

Wine bars (*enoteche;* sometimes called *bacari* in Venice) are a popular, fast option for lunch. Surrounded by the office crowd, you can get a fancy salad, a plate of meats and cheeses, and a glass of fine wine (see blackboards for the day's selection and price per glass—and go for the top end). A good *enoteca* aims to impress visitors with its wine, and will generally choose excellent-quality ingredients for the simple dishes it offers with the wine (though prices can add up quickly—be careful with your ordering to keep this a budget choice).

Groceries and Delis

Another budget option is to drop by an *alimentari* (neighborhood grocery) or *salumeria* (delicatessen) to pick up some cold cuts, cheeses, and other supplies for a picnic. Some *salumerie*, and any *paninoteca* or *focacceria* (sandwich shop), can make you a sandwich to order. Just point to what you want, and they'll stuff it into a *panino* (baguette); if you want it heated, say, *"scaldare, per favore"* (skahl-DAH-ray pehr fah-VOH-ray). To get a sampler plate of cold cuts and cheeses in a restaurant, ask for *affettato misto* (mixed cold cuts) or *antipasto misto* (cold cuts, cheeses, and marinated vegetables).

Salumi ("salted" meats), also called *affettati* ("cut" meats), are an Italian staple. While most American cold cuts are cooked, in Italy they're far more commonly cured by air-drying, salting, and

Ordering Food at *Tavola Calda* Bars and *Rosticcerie*

plate of mixed veggies	*piatto misto di verdure*	pee-AH-toh MEE-stoh dee vehr-DOO-ray
Heated, please.	*Scaldare, per favore.*	skahl-DAH-ray, pehr fah-VOH-ray
A taste, please.	*Un assaggio, per favore.*	oon ah-SAH-joh, pehr fah-VOH-ray
artichoke	*carciofi*	kar-CHOH-fee
asparagus	*asparagi*	ah-spah-RAH-jee
beans	*fagioli*	fah-JOH-lee
breadsticks	*grissini*	gree-SEE-nee
broccoli	*broccoli*	BROH-koh-lee
cantaloupe	*melone*	may-LOH-nay
carrots	*carote*	kah-ROT-ay
green beans	*fagiolini*	fah-joh-LEE-nee
ham	*prosciutto*	proh-SHOO-toh
mushrooms	*funghi*	FOON-ghee
potatoes	*patate*	pah-TAH-tay
rice	*riso*	REE-zoh
spinach	*spinaci*	spee-NAH-chee
tomatoes	*pomodori*	poh-moh-DOH-ree
zucchini	*zucchine*	zoo-KEE-nay

(Excerpted from *Rick Steves' Italian Phrase Book & Dictionary*)

EATING

smoking. (Don't worry; these so-called "raw" meats are safe to eat, and you can really taste the difference.)

The two most familiar types of *salumi* are *salame* and prosciutto. **Salame** is an air-dried, sometimes spicy sausage that comes in many varieties, including *finocchiona* (with fennel seeds), *salame piccante* (spicy hot, similar to pepperoni), and *salame di Sant'Olcese* (what we'd call "Genoa salami"). When Italians say **prosciutto**, they usually mean *prosciutto crudo*—the "raw" ham that air-cures on the hock and is then thinly sliced. Produced mainly in the north of Italy, prosciutto can be either *dolce* (sweet) or *salato* (salty). Purists say the best is *prosciutto di Parma*.

Other *salumi* may be less familiar. Air-cured pork variations include *culatello* (prosciutto made with only the finest cuts of meat), *capocollo* (or *coppa*; peppery pork shoulder), *speck* (smoked pork shoulder), *guanciale* (tender pork cheek), and *lonzino* (cured pork loin). *Pancetta*—which can be eaten raw or added to cooked dishes—is salt-cured, peppery pork belly meat (similar to bacon). *Mortadella*, a finely ground pork loaf, is similar to our baloney, and *bresaola* is air-cured beef. But look out for *testa in cassetta* (head-cheese—organs in aspic) and *lampredotto*—cow stomach that resembles a lamprey (eel), a traditional budget food in Tuscany.

As for **formaggio** (cheese), you're probably already familiar with several Italian favorites: *asiago* (hard cow cheese that comes either *mezzano*—young, firm, and creamy; or *stravecchio*—aged, pungent, and granular); *fontina* (semi-hard, nutty, Gruyère-style mountain cheese); *gorgonzola* (pungent, blue-veined cheese, either *dolce*—creamy, or *stagionato*—aged and hard); *mascarpone* (sweet, buttery, spreadable dessert cheese); *parmigiano-reggiano* (hard, crumbly, sharp, aged cow cheese with more nuanced flavor than American "parmesan"; *grana padano* is a less expensive variation); *pecorino* (either *fresco*—fresh, soft, and mild; or *stagionato*—aged and sharp, sometimes called *pecorino romano*); *provolone* (rich, firm, aged cow cheese), *ricotta* (soft, airy cheese made by "recooking" leftover whey), and, of course, mozzarella. The best mozzarella is *mozzarella di bufala*, made from the milk of water buffaloes; other variations include *burrata* (a creamy mozzarella) and *scamorza* (similar to mozzarella, but often smoked).

Picnic Tips

Picnicking saves lots of euros and is a great way to sample regional specialties. A typical picnic for two might be fresh rolls, 100 grams (*un etto*, EH-toh, plural *etti*, EH-tee—about a quarter pound) of cheese, 100 grams of meat (sometimes ordered by the slice—*fetta*—or piece—*pezzi;* for two people, I might get *cinque pezzi*—five pieces—of prosciutto). Add two tomatoes, three carrots, two apples, yogurt, and a liter box of juice. Total cost: about €10.

In the process of assembling your meal, you get to deal with the Italians in the market scene. For a colorful experience, gather your ingredients in the morning at a produce market (most fun at and around the big Rialto Market); you'll probably need to hit several stalls to put together a complete meal (note that many close in the early afternoon). While it's fun to visit the small

specialty shops, an *alimentari* is your one-stop corner grocery store (most will slice and stuff your sandwich for you if you buy the ingredients there). The rare *supermercato* (look for the Conad, Despar, and Co-op chains) gives you more efficiency with less color for less cost. At busier supermarkets you'll need to take a number for deli service.

Juice lovers can get a liter of O.J. for the price of a Coke or coffee. Look for "100% *succo*" (juice) on the label or be surprised by something diluted and sugary sweet. Hang on to the half-liter mineral-water bottles (sold everywhere for about €1). Buy juice in cheap liter boxes, then drink some and store the extra in your water bottle. (I refill my water bottle with tap water—*acqua del rubinetto*.)

Picnics can be adventures in high cuisine. Be daring. Try the fresh mozzarella, *presto* pesto, shriveled olives, and any UFOs the locals are excited about. If ordering *antipasti* (such as grilled or marinated veggies) at a deli counter, you can ask for *una porzione* in a plastic take-away container *(contenitore)*. Use gestures to show exactly how much you want. The word *basta* (BAH-stah)— "enough"—works as a question or as a statement.

Shopkeepers are happy to sell small quantities of produce, but it's customary to let the merchant choose for you. Say *"per oggi"* (pehr OH-jee; "for today") and he or she will grab you something ready to eat. To avoid being overcharged, know the cost per kilo and study the weighing procedure as if you're doing the arithmetic.

EATING

Gelato

Gelato is an edible art form—and it's one souvenir that can't break and won't clutter your luggage. While American ice cream is made with cream and has a high butterfat content, Italian gelato is made with milk. It's also churned more slowly, making it denser. Connoisseurs believe that because gelato has less air and less fat (which coats the mouth and blocks the taste buds), it's more flavorful than American-style ice cream.

Stop by a *gelateria* and survey your options. A key to gelato appreciation is sampling liberally and choosing flavors that go well together. Ask, as Italians do, for *"Un assaggio, per favore?"* (A taste, please?; oon ah-SAH-joh pehr fah-VOH-ray) and *"Quali gusti stanno bene insieme?"* (What flavors go well together?; KWAH-lee GOO-stee STAH-noh BEH-nay een-see-EH-may).

Not all *gelaterie* are created equal. The best ones display signs reading *artiginale, nostra produzione,* or *produzione propia,* meaning the gelato is made on the premises. Seasonal flavors are also a good sign. Gelato stored in covered metal tins (rather than white plastic) is more likely to be homemade. Gelato aficionados avoid colors that don't appear in nature; for fewer chemicals and real flavor, go for mellow hues.

As far as flavors, the sky's the limit. Most *gelaterie* label each tub with the flavor (in Italian and, often, in English) and, sometimes, a little picture to help identify it. Aside from the typical *crema* (vanilla), *cioccolato* (chocolate), and *fragola* (strawberry), here are a few flavors worth trying: After Eight (chocolate and mint), *bacio* (chocolate hazelnut, named for Italy's popular "kiss" candies), *croccantino* ("crunchy," with toasted peanut bits), *cassata* (with dried fruits), *fior di latte* (sweet milk), *macedonia* (mixed fruits), *riso* (with actual bits of rice mixed in), *malaga* (similar to rum raisin), *tartufo* (super chocolate), *zuppa inglese* (sponge cake, custard, chocolate, and cream), and the popular *stracciatella* (vanilla with chocolate chips). Flavors named Snickers, Lion, and Bounty resemble their namesake candy bars.

Gelato variations or alternatives include *sorbetto* (sorbet—made with fruit, but no milk or eggs); *granita* or *grattachecca* (a cup of slushy ice with flavored syrup); and *cremolata* (a gelato-*granita* float).

Most *gelaterie* clearly display prices and sizes. In the textbook *gelateria* scam, the tourist orders two or three flavors—and the clerk selects a fancy, expensive chocolate-coated waffle cone, piles it high with huge scoops, and cheerfully charges the tourist €10. To avoid rip-offs, point to the price or say what you want: *"Una coppetta da tre euro"* (OO-nah koh-PEH-tah dah tray eh-OO-roh; a €3 cup).

Beverages

Italian bars serve great drinks—hot, cold, sweet, caffeinated, or alcoholic. Chilled bottled water, still *(naturale)* or carbonated *(frizzante)*, is sold cheap in stores. Coffee and wine—two Italian specialties—are covered in greater depth later.

Juice: *Spremuta* means freshly squeezed, as far as *succo* (fruit juice) is concerned (order *una spremuta*—don't confuse it with *spumante*, sparkling wine). It's usually orange juice *(arancia)*, and February through April it's almost always made from blood oranges *(arance rosse)*.

Beer: Beer on tap is *alla spina*. Get it *piccola* (33 cl, 11 oz), *media* (50 cl, about a pint), or *grande* (a liter). Italians drink mainly lager beers. You'll find local brews (Peroni and Moretti) and imports such as Heineken as well. A *lattina* (lah-TEE-nah) is a can and a *bottiglia* (boh-TEEL-yah) is a bottle.

Cocktails and Spirits: Italians appreciate both *aperitivi* (palate-stimulating cocktails) and *digestivi* (after-dinner drinks designed to aid digestion). Popular *aperitivo* options include Campari (dark-colored bitters with herbs and orange peel), Americano (vermouth with bitters, brandy, and lemon peel), Cynar (bitters flavored with artichoke), and Punt e Mes (sweet red vermouth and red wine). Widely used vermouth brands include Cinzano and Martini. *Digestivo* choices are usually either a strong herbal bitters or something sweet. Many restaurants have their own secret recipe for a bittersweet herbal brew called *amaro;* popular commercial brands are Fernet Branca and Montenegro. If your tastes run sweeter, try *amaretto* (almond-flavored liqueur), Frangelico (hazelnut liqueur), *limoncello* (lemon liqueur), *nocino* (dark, sweet walnut liqueur), and *sambuca* (syrupy, anise-flavored liqueur; *con moscha* adds "flies"— three coffee beans). *Grappa* is a brandy distilled from grape skins and stems; *stravecchio* is an aged, mellower variation.

Coffee and Other Hot Drinks

The espresso-based style of coffee so popular in the US was born in Italy. If you ask for *"un caffè,"* you'll get a shot of espresso in a little cup—the closest to American-style drip coffee is a c*affè Americano.* Most Italian drinks begin with espresso, to which is added varying amounts of hot water and/or steamed or foamed milk. Milky drinks, like cappuccino or *caffè latte,* are served to locals before noon and to tourists any time of day (to an Italian, cappuccino is a breakfast drink). If they add any milk after lunch, it's just a splash, in a *macchiato* (mah-kee-AH-toh). Italians like their coffee only warm—to get it very hot, request *"Molto caldo, per favore"* (MOHL-toh KAHL-doh pehr fah-VOH-ray). Any coffee drink is available decaffeinated—ask for it *decaffeinato:* deh-kah-feh-ee-NAH-toh.

Experiment with a few of the options:
- **Cappuccino:** Espresso with foamed milk on top
- **Caffè latte:** Espresso mixed with hot milk, no foam, in a tall glass (ordering just a "latte" gets you only milk)
- **Caffè macchiato:** Espresso "marked" with just a splash of milk, in a small cup
- **Latte macchiato:** Layers of hot milk and foam, "marked" by an espresso shot, in a tall glass
- **Caffè corto/lungo:** Concentrated espresso diluted with a tiny bit of hot water, in a small cup
- **Caffè americano:** Espresso diluted with even more hot water, in a larger cup
- **Caffè corretto:** Espresso "corrected" with a shot of liqueur (normally grappa, amaro, or Sambuca)
- **Marocchino:** "Moroccan" coffee with espresso, foamed milk, and cocoa powder; the similar *mocaccino* has chocolate instead of cocoa

- *Caffè freddo:* Sweet and iced espresso
- *Cappuccino freddo:* Iced cappuccino
- *Caffè hag:* Instant decaf

Notice that there's a big difference between *caffè macchiato* and *latte macchiato*. If you order simply a *"macchiato,"* you'll probably get the coffee version...and have to get your milk fix elsewhere.

More Hot Drinks: *Cioccolato* is hot chocolate. *Tè* is hot tea. *Tè freddo* (iced tea) is usually from a can—sweetened and flavored with lemon or peach.

Wine

The ancient Greeks who colonized Italy more than 2,000 years ago called it Oenotria—land of the grape. Centuries later, Galileo wrote, "Wine is light held together by water." Wine *(vino)* is certainly a part of the Italian culinary trinity—the grape, olive, and wheat. (I'd add gelato.) Ideal conditions for grapes (warm climate, well-draining soil, and an abundance of hillsides) make the Italian peninsula a paradise for grape growers, winemakers, and wine drinkers. Italy makes and consumes more wine per capita than any other country. For regional wines produced near Venice, see "Top Local Wines," later.

To order a glass *(bicchiere;* bee-kee-EH-ree) of red *(rosso)* or white *(bianco)* wine, say, *"Un bicchiere di vino rosso/bianco."* *Corposo* means full-bodied. House wine *(vino della casa)* comes in a carafe; choose from a quarter-liter pitcher (8.5 oz, *un quarto*), half-liter pitcher (17 oz, *un mezzo*), or one-liter pitcher (34 oz, *un litro*). In Venice you can also order an *ombra* ("shadow"), a mini-glass often offered with *cicchetti*.

Wine Labels and Lingo

Even if you're clueless about wine, the information on an Italian wine label can help you choose something decent. Terms you may see on the bottle include *classico* (from a defined, select area), *annata* (year of harvest), *vendemmia* (harvest), and *imbottigliato dal produttore all'origine* (bottled by producers). To figure out what you like—and what suits your pocketbook—visit an *enoteca* (wine bar) and sample wines side-by-side. In general, Italy designates its wines by one of four official categories:

Vino da Tavola (VDT) is table wine, the lowest grade, made from grapes grown anywhere in Italy. It's inexpensive, but Italy's wines are so good that, for many people, a basic *vino da tavola* is just fine with a meal. Many restaurants, even modest ones,

Describing Wine in Italian

As you can see from many of the words listed below, adding a vowel to the English word often gets you close to the Italian one. Have some fun, gesture like a local, and you'll have no problems speaking the language of the *enoteca*. *Salute!*

dry	*secco*	SEH-koh
sweet	*dolce*	DOHL-chay
earthy	*terroso*	teh-ROH-zoh
tannic	*tannico*	TAH-nee-koh
young	*giovane*	JOH-vah-nay
mature	*maturo*	mah-TOO-roh
sparkling	*spumante, frizzante*	spoo-mahn-tay, freed-ZAHN-tay
fruity	*fruttato*	froo-TAH-toh
full-bodied	*corposo, pieno*	kor-POH-zoh, pee-EH-noh
elegant	*elegante*	eh-leh-GAHN-tay

take pride in their house wine *(vino della casa)*, bottling their own or working with wineries.

EATING

Denominazione di Origine Controllata (DOC) meets national standards for high-quality wine. It's made from grapes grown in a defined area, is usually quite affordable, and can be surprisingly good. Hundreds of wines have earned the DOC designation. In Tuscany, for example, many such wines come from the Chianti region, located between Florence and Siena.

Denominazione di Origine Controllata e Guarantita (DOCG), the highest grade, meets national standards for the highest-quality wine (made with grapes from a defined area whose quality is "guaranteed"). These wines can be identified by the pink or green label on the neck...and the scary price tag on the shelf. Only a limited number of wines in Italy can be called DOCG. They're generally a good bet if you want a quality wine, but you don't know anything else about the winemaker. (*Riserva* indicates a DOC or DOCG wine matured for a longer, more specific time.)

Indicazione Geographica Tipica (IGT) is a broad group of wines that range from basic to some of Italy's best. These wines don't follow the strict "recipe" required for DOC or DOCG status, but give local vintners creative license. This category includes the Super Tuscans, wines made from a mix of international grapes (such as cabernet sauvignon) grown in Tuscany and aged in small oak barrels for only two years. The result is a lively full-bodied wine that dances all over your head...and is worth the steep price for aficionados.

Other terms you may see on the bottle include *classico* (from a defined, select area), *annata* (year of harvest), *vendemmia* (harvest), and *imbottigliato dal produttore all'origine* (bottled by producers).

Venetian Cuisine

Even more so than the rest of Italy, Venetian cuisine relies heavily on fish, shellfish, risotto, and polenta. Along with the usual pizza-and-pasta fare, here are some typical foods you'll encounter.

Bar Snacks

Venetians often eat a snack—*cicchetti* or *panini*—while standing at a bar. (Remember, you'll usually pay more if you sit, rather than stand.)

Cicchetti: Generic name for various small finger foods served in some pubs—like appetizers or tapas, Venetian-style. Designed as a quick meal for working people, the selection and ambience are best on workdays (Mon-Sat lunch and early dinner). See "The Stand-Up Progressive Venetian Pub-Crawl Dinner," later.

Panini: Sandwiches made with rustic bread, filled with meat, vegetables, and cheese, served cold or toasted—*riscaldato* (ree-skahl-DAH-toh). *Piadini* are flatbread or wrap-like sandwiches. You can eat your sandwich at the bar or take it with you.

Tramezzini: Crustless, white bread sandwiches served cold and stuffed with a variety of fillings (e.g., egg, tuna, or shrimp), mixed with a mayonnaise dressing. The selection is best in the morning and skimpy by afternoon.

Appetizers *(Antipasti)*

Antipasto di mare: A marinated mix of fish and shellfish served chilled.

Asiago cheese: The Veneto region's specialty, a cow's-milk cheese that's either *mezzano*—young, firm, and creamy; or *stravecchio*—aged, pungent, and granular.

Sarde in saor: Sardines marinated with onions.

Rice *(Riso)*, Pasta, and Polenta

Risotto: Short-grain rice, simmered in broth and often flavored with fish and seafood. For example, *risotto nero* is risotto made with squid and its ink, and *risotto ai porcini* contains porcini mushrooms.

Risi e bisi: Rice and peas.

Pasta e fagioli: Bean and pasta soup.

Bigoli in salsa: A long, fat, whole-wheat noodle (one of the few traditional pastas) with anchovy sauce.

Other pasta dishes: While the basic choice here remains **pasta** *al pomodoro* (simple tomato sauce), you'll also see **pasta** *alla buzzara* (in a rich seafood-tomato sauce, generally with shrimp and often topped with a giant shrimp cut in half lengthwise) and *al vongole* (with clams).

Polenta: Cornmeal boiled into a mush and served soft or cut into firm slabs and grilled. Polenta is a standard accompaniment with cod *(baccalà)*, or calf liver and onions *(fegato alla veneziana)*.

Seafood *(Frutti di Mare)*

Some sea creatures found in the Adriatic are slightly different from their American cousins. Generally, Venetian fish are smaller than American salmon and trout (think sardines and anchovies). The shellfish are more exotic. The most common fish on Venetian plates—such as sea bass, bream, salmon, and turbot—are farmed, not wild. The weirder the animal (eel, octopus, frogfish), the more local it is.

Baccalà: Dried Atlantic salt cod that's rehydrated and served with polenta; or chopped up and mixed with mayonnaise as a topping for *cicchetti* (appetizers), called *baccalà mantecato*.

Branzino: Sea bass, grilled and served whole (with head and tail).

Calamari: Squid, usually cut into rings and either deep-fried or marinated.

Cozze: Mussels, often steamed in an herb broth with tomato.

Gamberi: The generic name for shrimp. *Gamberetti* are small shrimp, and *gamberoni* are large shrimp.

Moleche col pien: Fried soft-shell crabs.

Orata: Sea bream, a common European game fish that is now widely farmed.

Pesce fritto misto: Assorted deep-fried seafood (often calamari and prawns).

Pesce spada: Swordfish.

Rombo: Turbot, a flatfish similar to flounder.

Rospo: Frogfish, a small marine fish.

Salmone: Salmon, farm-raised in northern Europe and shipped in.

Seppia: Cuttlefish, a squid-like creature that sprays black ink

EATING

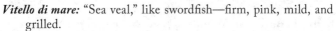

when threatened. *Seppia al nero* is the squid in its own ink, often served over spaghetti. It's sweet and tender when grilled—either *grigliata* or *alla griglia* (without its ink).

Sogliola: Sole, served poached or oven-roasted.

Vitello di mare: "Sea veal," like swordfish—firm, pink, mild, and grilled.

Vongole: Small clams, often steamed with fresh herbs and wine, or served as a first course, such as *spaghetti alle vongole.*

Zuppa di pesce: Seafood stew.

Desserts *(Dolci)*

Tiramisù: Spongy ladyfingers soaked in coffee and Marsala, layered with mascarpone cheese and bitter chocolate. Arguably Venetian in origin, the literal meaning of the word is "pick-me-up."

Venetian cookies: There are numerous varieties, due perhaps to Venice's position in trade (spices) and the Venetians' love of celebrations. Many treats were created for certain feast days and religious holidays. *Pinza,* a sweet made with corn, wheat flour, and raisins (and sometimes figs, almonds, and lemon), is made for Epiphany, January 6. *Fritole* are tiny doughnuts associated with Carnevale (Mardi Gras). *Bussola* rings are made for Easter. Other popular treats are *bisse* (seahorse-shaped cookies) and *croccante* (made with toasted corn and almonds, similar in texture to peanut brittle).

Cocktails

Spritz: The dominant predinner drink *(aperitivo)* among Venetians is the *spritz.* This refreshing *aperitivo* mixes white wine, soda, and ice with a liquor of your choice and is garnished with an olive or skewer of fruit. When you order, you'll be asked if you'd like your *spritz con Campari* (bitter—traditionally the man's choice) or *con Aperol* (sweeter, a supposedly feminine choice). Between 18:00 and 20:00, this happy pink drink dominates Venice's watering holes.

Bellini: Cocktail of Prosecco and white-peach puree; invented (and drunk by Hemingway) at the pricey Harry's American Bar (near San Marco-Vallaresso vaporetto stop).

Tiziano: Grape juice and Prosecco.

Sgroppino: Traditional drink of squeezed lemon juice, lemon gelato, and vodka, designed to finish off a meal.

Top Local Wines

Prosecco: Sparkling wine, usually a predinner drink, but can be ordered any time. It's neutral-tasting, making it easy to drink too much. Connoisseurs say the best hails from Valdobbiadene.

Soave: Crisp, dry white (great with seafood) from near Verona. "Soave Classico" designates a higher quality. Other whites from the Veneto include Pinot Grigio and Bianco di Custoza.

Valpolicella: Light, dry, fruity red from the hills north of Verona. If you ordered the house wine *(vino della casa),* you're likely drinking Valpolicella.

Bardolino: Beaujolais-like picnic wine that's also made from Valpolicella grapes.

Amarone: Rich, intense red, with alcohol content at about 16 percent, made from partially dried—*passito*—Valpolicella grapes then aged for at least four years in oak.

Recioto: Sweet dessert wine made with high-sugar Valpolicella grapes that are also dried and aged.

Fragolino: A sweet, slightly fizzy dessert wine made from a strawberry-flavored grape.

Restaurants

While touristy restaurants are the scourge of Venice, the following places are popular with actual Venetians and respect the tourists who happen in. First trick: Walk away from triple-language menus. Second trick: For freshness, eat fish. Most seafood dishes are the catch-of-the-day. Third trick: Eat later. A place may feel really touristy at 19:00, but if you come back at 21:00, it can be filled with locals. Tourists eat barbarically early, which is fine with the restaurants because they fill tables that would otherwise be used only once in an evening.

Near the Rialto Bridge

For locations, see the map on page 263.

North of the Bridge

These restaurants are located beyond Campo Santi Apostoli, on or near the Strada Nova, the main drag going from Rialto toward the train station.

Trattoria da Bepi, bright and alpine-paneled, feels like a classic, where Loris carries on his mother's passion for good, traditional Venetian cuisine. Ask for the seasonal specialties: The seafood appetizer plate and crab dishes are excellent. There's good seating inside and out. If you trust Loris, you'll walk away with a wonderful dining memory (€7-12 pastas, €14-20 *secondi*, Fri-Wed 12:00-

14:30 & 19:00-22:00, closed Thu, half a block off Campo Santi Apostoli on Salizada Pistor at #4550, tel. 041-528-5031).

La Cantina is an elegant *enoteca*, both rustic and sophisticated—you won't find a menu here. Rather than cook (there's no kitchen), Francesco and Andrea prepare wonderful gourmet cold plates of meat, cheese, and fish. Though it's not cheap (meat-and-cheese plates-€15/person, seafood plates-€30/person), you'll enjoy the very best ingredients paired with fine wines. You can sit inside and watch the preparation scene, or enjoy the parade of passersby from great seats right on the Strada Nova. For a budget alternative, have a *cicchetto* at the bar with a glass of fine wine (€1.50 for ham-and-cheese *cicchetti*, €2.50 for seafood; Mon-Sat 10:00-22:00, closed Sun, facing Campo San Felice on Strada Nova near Ca' d'Oro, Cannaregio 3688, tel. 041-522-8258).

Vini da Gigio has an enthusiasm for good food and a traditional Venetian menu, with a classy but un-snooty setting that's a pleasant mix of traditional and contemporary (€13-18 pastas, €19-24 *secondi*, Wed-Sun 12:00-14:30 & 19:00-22:30, closed Mon-Tue, 4 blocks from Ca' d'Oro vaporetto stop on Fondamenta San Felice at #3628a—behind the church on Campo San Felice, tel. 041-528-5140).

East of the Rialto Bridge

The next few places hide away in the twisty lanes between the Rialto Bridge and Campo Santa Maria Formosa. Osteria da Alberto is a tad farther north of the others, in Cannaregio.

Osteria di Santa Marina, serving pricey, near-gourmet cuisine in a dressy dining room, is highly regarded by Venetians. The presentation is impressive, but you feel there's more pretense than love of food. Cheap-eating tricks are frowned on in this elegant, borderline stuffy restaurant (€16 pastas, €27-30 *secondi*, €75-80 fixed-price meals, Mon-Sat 12:30-14:30 & 19:30-22:00, closed Sun, reserve for dinner, eat indoors or outdoors on pleasant Campo Marina at #5911, between Rialto Bridge and Campo Santa Maria Formosa, tel. 041-528-5239, www.osteriadisantamarina.com).

Rosticceria San Bartolomeo is a cheap—if confusing—self-service diner. This throwback budget eatery has a surly staff: Don't take it personally. Notice that the different counters serve up different types of food—pastas, *secondi*, fried goodies, and so on. You can get it to go, grab one of the few tiny tables, or munch at the bar—but I'd skip their upper-floor restaurant option (€7-8 pastas, great fried *mozzarella al prosciutto* for €1.60, fruit salad, €2 glasses of wine, prices listed on wall behind counter, no cover and no service charge, daily 9:00-21:30, San Marco 5424, tel. 041-522-3569). To find it, imagine the statue on Campo San Bartolomeo walking backward 20 yards, turning left, and going under a passageway—now, follow him.

Osteria al Portego is a friendly neighborhood eatery. Carlo serves good meals and excellent €1-3 *cicchetti*—best enjoyed early, around 18:00 (from 19:00 to 21:00, their six tables are reserved for those ordering from the menu; the *cicchetti* are picked over by 21:00). The *cicchetti* here can make a great meal, but consider sitting down for a dinner from their fine menu. Reserve ahead if you want a table (€13 pastas, €1 glasses of house wine, daily 10:30-15:00 & 18:00-22:00, near Campo Santa Marina at #6015 on Calle de la Malvasia, tel. 041-522-9038). From Rosticceria San Bartolomeo (listed above), continue over a bridge to Campo San Lio, turn left, and follow Calle Carminati straight 50 yards over another bridge.

Osteria da Alberto, up near Campo Santa Maria Novo, is one of my standbys. They offer up excellent daily specials, €11-18 seafood dishes, €9-12 pastas, and a good house wine in a woody and characteristic interior (although it's set along a canal, you can't see it from the dining area). It's smart to reserve at night—I'd request a table in front (Mon-Sat 12:00-14:30 & 18:30-22:30, closed Sun; on Calle Larga Giacinto Gallina, midway between Campo Santi Apostoli and Campo San Zanipolo/Santi Giovanni e Paolo, and next to Ponte de la Panada bridge at #5401; tel. 041-523-8153, www.osteriadaalberto.it, run by Graziano and Giovanni).

Rialto Market Area

As with market neighborhoods anywhere, you'll find lots of hard-working hole-in-the-walls with a line on the freshest of ingredients and catering to local shoppers needing a quick, affordable, and tasty bite. This area is very crowded by day, nearly empty early in the evening, and packed with young Venetian clubbers later.

Most of these places are informal, serving *cicchetti* and/or light meals. At each place, look for the list of snacks and wine by the glass at the bar or on the wall. When you're ready for dessert, try dipping a Burano biscuit in a glass of strawberry-flavored *fragolino* or another sweet dessert wine. Most bars are closed 15:00-18:00, and offer glasses of house wine for under €1, better wine for around €2.50, and *cicchetti* for €1-2.

My listings below include a strip of trendy places fronting the Grand Canal, a stretch of dark and rustic pubs serving regional tapas, a few little places on the market, a venerable old Venetian diner, and a couple of solid places for pasta and pizza. Most of these eateries are within 200 yards of the market and each other.

EATING

The Bancogiro Stretch: Five Places Overlooking the Grand Canal

Just past the Rialto Bridge, between Campo San Giacomo and the Grand Canal, this strip of five popular places has some of the best canalside seating in Venice. I call this the "Bancogiro Stretch" (Bancogiro is the strip of old banking buildings they front).

Each place has a unique character and formula. Unless otherwise noted, all of these are open daily; while you can get a drink anytime, dinner is typically served only after 19:00 or 19:30. During meals, they charge more and limit table seating to those ordering full lunches or dinners; but between mealtimes you can enjoy a drink or a snack at fine prices. After dinner hours, the Bancogiro Stretch—and especially in the surrounding alleys that house low-rent bars—becomes a youthful and trendy nightspot. Before or after dinner, this strip is one of the best places in town for a *spritz*.

Here's the rundown (in the order you'll reach them from the Rialto Bridge): **Bar Naranzaria** serves Italian dishes with a few Japanese options (€12-14 pastas, €17-23 *secondi*). **Caffè Vergnano**, your cheapest option—especially during mealtimes—is just a café with no cover (€10-12 salads, pizzas, and pastas—and a busy microwave oven). **Osteria al Pescador** is a more serious restaurant (€13-18 pastas, €23-27 *secondi*). **Bar Ristorante Bancogiro** is really good, with romantic dining upstairs (no canal views), a passion for the best cheese, and good *cicchetti* options at the bar (€15-18 pastas, €22-26 *secondi*, nice €15 cheese plate, closed Mon, tel. 041-523-2061). The more modern **Bar Ancòra** seems to be most popular with the local bar crowd, with a live piano player crooning lounge music during busy times (€13 pastas, €17 *secondi*, *cicchetti* at the bar).

The *Cicchetti* Strip: Four Venetian Tapas Bars

The 100-yard-long stretch starting two blocks inland from the Rialto Market (along Sotoportego dei Do Mori and Calle de le Do Spade) is beloved among Venetian *cicchetti* enthusiasts for its delightful bar munchies, good wine by the glass, and fun stand-up conviviality. These four places serve food all day, but the spread is best at around noon (generally open daily 12:00-15:00 & 18:00-20:00 or 21:00; two of the places I list are closed Sun). While each place offers a fine bar-and-stools scene, you might instead choose to treat one like a restaurant, order from their rustic menu, and grab a table. Scout these four places in advance (listed in the order you'll reach them, if coming from the Rialto Bridge) to help decide which ambience is right for the experience you have in mind. Then pick one, dig in, and drink up.

Bar all'Arco, a bustling one-room joint, is particularly enjoyable for its tiny open-face sandwiches (closed Sun, San Polo 436; Francisco, Anne, Matteo).

Cantina Do Mori has been famous with locals (since 1462) and savvy travelers (since 1982) as a convivial place for fine wine. They serve a forest of little edibles on toothpicks and *francobolli* (a spicy selection of 20 tiny, mayo-soaked sandwiches nicknamed "stamps"). Go here to be abused in a fine atmosphere—the frowns are part of the shtick (closed Sun, San Polo 430).

Osteria ai Storti, with a cool photo of the market in 1909, is run by Alessandro, who speaks English and enjoys helping educate travelers, and his sister Baby—pronounced "Bobby" (€8 pastas, €12-13 *secondi*, daily except closed Sun off-season, around the corner from Cantina Do Mori on Calle San Matio—follow signs, San Polo 819).

Cantina Do Spade is expertly run by Francesco, who clearly lists the *cicchetti* and wines of the day (also good for sit-down meals, 30 yards down Calle de le Do Spade from Osteria ai Storti at San Polo 860, tel. 041-521-0583).

Other Good Eateries near the Rialto Market

Pronto Pesce is the perfect place to sample fish while watching the market action. Umberto and his staff speak English and like to explain what's good. They serve a €10 mixed fish plate with bread (daily from 13:00 until it's sold out) that locals plan their day around. Consider their "express plates" of pasta (€12-15, served daily 12:45-14:15), fish risotto specials, artful fish hors d'oeuvres, and many other fresh fish tidbits. This fancy hole-in-the-wall is fun for a quick bite—eat standing up or take it to go (Mon 11:30-15:00, Tue-Sat 10:00-15:00, closed Sun, generally open in the evenings only for groups, facing the fish market on Calle de le Becarie o Panataria, San Polo 319, tel. 041-822-0298).

Al Mercà ("At the Market"), a few steps away and off the canal, is a lively little nook with a happy crowd, where law-office workers have lunch and young locals gather in the evening for drinks and little snacks. The price list is clear, and I've found the crowd to be welcoming to tourists interested in connecting (stand at the bar or in the square—there are no tables and no interior, Mon-Sat 9:30-14:30 & 18:00-21:00, closed Sun, on Campo Cesare Battisti, San Polo 213).

Ristorante Vini da Pinto is a cheap, tourist-friendly eatery with a basic menu and forgettable food at decent prices. It has good service and relaxing outdoor seating (€8-12 pastas, €9-19 *secondi*, €13 fixed-price meal, open long hours daily, facing the fish market, San Polo 367a, tel. 041-522-4599).

Trattoria alla Madonna is a big, bustling, classic Italian eatery with old-school formal waiters, a huge menu, and about

The Stand-Up Progressive Venetian Pub-Crawl Dinner

My favorite Venetian dinner is a pub crawl *(giro d'ombra)*—a tradition unique to Venice, where no cars means easy crawling. *(Giro* means stroll, and *ombra*—slang for a glass of wine—means shade, from the old days when a portable wine bar scooted with the shadow of the Campanile bell tower across St. Mark's Square.)

Venice's residential back streets hide plenty of characteristic bars *(bacari)* with countless trays of interesting toothpick munchies *(cicchetti)* and blackboards listing the wines that are uncorked and served by the glass. This is a great way to mingle and have fun with the Venetians. Bars don't stay open very late, and the *cicchetti* selection is best early, so start your evening by 18:00. Most bars are closed on Sunday. For a stress-free pub crawl, consider taking a tour with the charming Alessandro Schezzini (see page 38).

Cicchetti bars have a social stand-up zone and a cozy gaggle of tables where you can generally sit down with your *cicchetti* or order from a simple menu. In some of the more popular places, the crowds happily spill out into the street. Food generally costs

a hundred tables. Tour groups find it efficient, and local families have come here for lunch after church for generations. There's no romance—just solid, reliable, traditional food from a menu that hasn't changed since World War II (€11-13 pastas, €13-16 *secondi*, closed Wed, tucked away on Calle della Madonna, 2 minutes west of Rialto Bridge, San Polo 594, tel. 041-522-3824).

Farther West, Toward Ca' Pesaro: **Trattoria Pizzeria al Nono Risorto** is unpretentious, inexpensive, youthful, and famous for serving good pizza in a nice setting. You'll sit in a gravelly garden under a leafy canopy, surrounded by Italians enjoying huge €8-10 salads, €9-12 pastas and pizzas, and €12-18 grilled meat or fish dishes (Thu 19:00-22:30, Fri-Tue 12:00-14:30 & 19:00-22:30, closed Wed, reservations smart on weekends; from Rialto fish market, get out your map and walk 3 minutes away from the Rialto to Campo San Cassiano—it's just over the bridge on Sotoportego de Siora Bettina at #2338; tel. 041-524-1169).

the same price whether you stand or sit.

I've listed plenty of pubs in walking order for a quick or extended crawl. If you've crawled enough, most of these bars make a fine one-stop, sit-down dinner.

While you can order a plate, Venetians prefer going one-by-one...sipping their wine and trying this...then give me one of those...and so on. Try deep-fried mozzarella cheese, gorgonzola, calamari, artichoke hearts, and anything ugly on a toothpick. *Crostini* (small toasted bread with a topping) are popular, as are marinated seafood, olives, and prosciutto with melon. Meat and fish (*pesce*; PESH-ay) munchies can be expensive; veggies *(verdure)* are cheap, at about €3 for a meal-sized plate. In many places, there's a set price per food item (e.g., €1.50). To get a plate of assorted appetizers for €8 (or more, depending on how hungry you are), ask for *"Un piatto classico di cicchetti misti da €8"* (oon pee-AH-toh KLAH-see-koh dee cheh-KET-tee MEE-stee dah OH-toh ay-OO-roh). Bread sticks (*grissini*) are free for the asking.

Bar-hopping Venetians enjoy an *aperitivo*, a before-dinner drink. Boldly order a Bellini, a *spritz con Aperol*, or a Prosecco, and draw approving looks from the natives.

Drink the house wines. A small glass of house red or white wine (*ombra rosso* or *ombra bianco*) or a small beer (*birrino*) costs about €1. The house keg wine is cheap—€1 per glass, about €4 per liter. *Vin bon*, Venetian for fine wine, may run you from €2 to €6 per little glass. There are usually several fine wines uncorked and available by the glass. A good last drink is *fragolino*, the local sweet wine—*bianco* or *rosso*. It often comes with a little cookie (*biscotti*) for dipping.

EATING

Between the Rialto Bridge and Frari Church: **Antica Birraria la Corte** is an everyday eatery on the delightful Campo San Polo. Popular for its €8-11 pizza, calzones, and wonderful selection of hearty €10-13 salads, it fills the far side of this cozy, family-filled square. While the interior is a sprawling beer hall, it's a joy to eat on the square, where metal tables teeter on the cobbles, the wind plays with the paper mats, and children run free (€11-13 pastas, €12-20 *secondi*, daily 12:00-14:30 & 18:00-22:30, Campo San Polo 2168—see map on page 270, tel. 041-275-0570).

Near St. Mark's Square

While my first listing is a serious restaurant, the other places listed here are cheap-and-cheery options convenient to your sightseeing. For locations, see the map on page 258.

Ristorante Antica Sacrestia is a classic restaurant where the owner, Pino, takes a hands-on approach to greeting guests. His staff serve creative €33-50 fixed-price meals and a humdrum €20 *menù del giorno*. (Be warned: These meals seem designed to overwhelm you with too much food. You will not leave hungry.) You can also order à la carte; try the delightful €21 antipasto spread, which looks like a lagoon aquarium spread out on a plate. The entrance courtyard is a great place to sip a drink if you have to wait for a table. While the food isn't high cuisine, the service is animated and the experience is memorable. My readers are welcome to a free *sgroppino* (lemon vodka after-dinner drink) upon request (€13-18 pastas and pizzas, €20-30 *secondi*, Tue-Sun 11:30-15:00 & 18:00-23:00, closed Mon, behind San Zaninovo/Giovanni Novo Church on Calle Corona at Castello 4463, tel. 041-523-0749).

"Sandwich Row": On Calle de le Rasse, just steps away from the tourist intensity at St. Mark's Square, is a handy strip I call "Sandwich Row." Lined with sandwich bars, it's the closest place to St. Mark's to get a decent sandwich at an affordable price with a place to sit down (most places open daily 7:00-24:00, €1 extra to sit; from the Bridge of Sighs, head down the Riva and take the second lane on the left). I particularly like **Birreria Forst,** a pleasantly unpretentious café that serves a selection of meaty €3 sandwiches with tasty sauce on wheat bread, or made-to-order sandwiches for €4 (daily 9:30-22:00, air-con, rustic wood tables, Castello 4540, tel. 041-523-0557), and **Bar Verde,** a more modern sandwich bar with fun people-watching views from its corner tables (big €4-5 sandwiches, splittable €9 salads, fresh pastries, at the end of Calle de le Rasse at #4526, facing Campo Santi Filippo e Giacomo).

Ristorante alla Basilica, just one street behind St. Mark's Basilica, is a church-run, indoor, institutional-feeling place that serves a solid €14 fixed-price lunch (including water). It's not self-serve—you'll be seated and can choose a pasta, a *secondi*, and a vegetable side dish off the menu (Tue-Sun 11:45-15:00, closed Mon, air-con, on Calle dei Albanesi at #4255, tel. 041-522-0524).

Picnicking: Though you can't picnic on St. Mark's Square, you can legally take your snacks to the nearby Giardinetti Reali, the small park along the waterfront west of the Piazzetta.

North of St. Mark's Square, near Campo Santa Maria Formosa

For a (marginally) less touristy scene, walk a few blocks north to the inviting Campo Santa Maria Formosa. For locations, see the map on page 263.

Osteria alle Testiere is my top dining splurge in Venice. Hugely respected, Luca and his staff are dedicated to quality, serving up creative, artfully presented market-fresh seafood (there's no meat on the menu), homemade pastas, and fine wine in what the chef calls a "Venetian Nouvelle" style. With only 22 seats, it's tight and homey, with the focus on food and service. They have daily specials, 10 wines by the glass, and one agenda: a great dining experience. This is a good spot to let loose and trust your host. They're open for lunch (12:30-14:30), and reservations are a must for their two dinner seatings: 19:00 and 21:30 (€20 pastas, €26 *secondi*, plan on spending €50 for dinner, closed Sun-Mon, on Calle del Mondo Novo, just off Campo Santa Maria Formosa at Castello 5801, tel. 041-522-7220; you can also reserve online at www.osterialletestiere.it).

Osteria al Mascaron is where I've gone for years to watch Gigi, Momi, and their food-loving band of ruffians dish up rustic-yet-sumptuous pastas with steamy seafood to salivating foodies. The seafood pastas seem pricey at €26-36, but they're meant for two (it's OK to ask for single portions). The €16 *antipasto misto* plate—have fun pointing—and two glasses of wine make a terrific light meal (€16-20 main dishes, Mon-Sat 12:00-15:00 & 19:00-23:00, closed Sun, reservations smart Fri-Sat; on Calle Lunga Santa Maria Formosa, a block past Campo Santa Maria Formosa, at #5225; tel. 041-522-5995, www.osteriamascaron.it).

Fast and Cheap Eats: The veggie stand on Campo Santa Maria Formosa is a fixture. For *döner kebabs* (€3.50) and pizza to go (€2/slice), head down Calle Lunga Santa Maria Formosa to **Peter Pan,** at #6249 (daily 11:00-24:00).

In Dorsoduro

All of these recommendations are within a 10-minute walk of the Accademia Bridge (for locations, see the map on page 267). Dorsoduro is great for restaurants and well worth the walk from the more touristy Rialto and San Marco areas. The first two listings are near the Accademia (and best for lunch). The next two are in Zattere, overlooking the Giudecca Canal. And the last four (best for dinner) are near Campo San Barnaba.

Near the Accademia Bridge

Bar Foscarini, next to the Accademia Bridge and Galleria, offers decent €8-15 pizzas and €8-10 *panini* in a memorable Grand Canal-view setting. The food is decent but forgettable, and pricey drinks pad your tab, but you're paying a premium for this premium location. On each visit to Venice, I grab a pizza lunch here while I ponder the Grand Canal bustle. They also serve a €10 breakfast (Wed-Mon 7:00-22:30, until 21:00 Nov-April, closed Tue year-round, on Rio Terà A. Foscarini at #878c, tel. 041-522-7281, Paolo).

Enoteca Cantine del Vino Già Schiavi, with a wonderfully characteristic *cicchetti*-bar ambience, is much loved for its €1 *cicchetti,* €3.50 sandwiches (order from list on board), and €1-2 glass-

EATING

es of wine. You're welcome to enjoy your wine and finger food at the bar or out on the sidewalk. This is primarily a wine shop with great prices for bottles to go—and plastic glasses for picnickers (Mon-Sat 8:00-20:30, closed Sun, 100 yards from Accademia art museum on San Trovaso canal; facing Accademia, take a right and then a forced left at the canal to the second bridge—it's at #992, tel. 041-523-0034).

In Zattere

Terrazza del Casin dei Nobili takes full advantage of the warm, romantic evening sun. They serve finely crafted, regional specialties with creativity at tolerable prices. The canalside seating is breezy and beautiful, but comes with the rumble of *vaporetti* from the nearby stop. The interior is bright and hip (good €8-10 pizzas, €13-15 pastas, €14-18 *secondi*, daily 12:00-23:00 except closed Thu off-season; from Zattere vaporetto stop, turn left to #924; tel. 041-520-6895, Ruggiero and Eleonora). On Wednesday and Sunday evenings in summer, there's live music nearby on the Zattere promenade—see page 267.

Ae Oche Pizzeria is playful, with casual tables on the canal and a sprawling pizza-parlor interior. It's a hit with young Venetians for its fun atmosphere and good prices (daily 12:00-15:00 & 19:00-23:00, a couple of hundred yards from the Zattere vaporetto stop, Dorsoduro 1414, tel. 041-520-6601).

On or near Campo San Barnaba

This small square is a delight—especially in the evening. As these places are within a few steps of each other—and the energy and atmosphere can vary—I like to survey the options before choosing (although reservations may be necessary to dine later in the evening).

Ristoteca Oniga is all about fresh fish, with a chic-and-ship-shape interior, great tables on the square, and the enthusiastic direction of Raffaele. The menu is accessible and always includes a good vegetarian dish (€12-14 pastas, €18-22 *secondi*, Wed-Mon 12:00-14:30 & 19:00-22:30, closed Tue, reservations smart, Campo San Barnaba, Dorsoduro 2852, tel. 041-522-4410, www.oniga.it).

Osteria Enoteca Ai Artisti serves well-presented quality dishes either in its tight little wine-snob interior or at a few petite, romantic canalside tables. They serve good wines by the glass from their prizewinning list (€13-15 pastas, €20-25 *secondi*, closed Sun, Fondamenta de la Toletta, Dorsoduro 1169a, tel. 041-523-8944).

Pizzeria al Profeta is a casual place popular for great pizza and steak. Its large interior seems to stoke conviviality, as does its leafy garden out back (€8-10 pizzas, Wed-Mon 12:00-14:30 & 19:00-23:00, closed Tue; from Campo San Barnaba, walk to the end of Calle Lunga San Barnaba; Dorsoduro 2671, tel. 041-523-7466).

Enoteca e Trattoria la Bitta is dark and woody, with a soft-jazz bistro feel, tight seating, and a small, forgettable back patio. They serve beautifully presented, traditional Venetian food with—proudly—no fish. Their helpful waitstaff and small, handwritten daily menu are clearly focused on quality, with local ingredients and a "slow food" ethic. As it has an avid following, they do two dinner seatings (19:00 and 21:00), reservations are required, and service can be intense (€10-11 pastas, €16-27 *secondi*, dinner only, Mon-Sat 18:30-23:00, closed Sun, cash only, just off Campo San Barnaba on Calle Lunga San Barnaba, Dorsoduro 2753a, tel. 041-523-0531, Debora and Marcellino).

In Cannaregio

Cannaregio, along the fish's "back," offers the classic chance in Venice to get off the beaten path. I've listed restaurants both near the Jewish Ghetto and near a main thoroughfare (see map on page 270; these zones are about a 10-minute walk apart). Also listed here are a few convenient, last-resort options next to the train station.

Behind the Jewish Ghetto

This sleepy neighborhood—more residential than touristic—features a grid layout with straight and spacious canalside walks (part of an expansion from the 1400s). Although it lacks the higgledy-piggledy feel of the older part of town, it's worth the long walk for a look. Rather than come here just for a meal, I'd make time to explore and then grab a bite while in the neighborhood. Cannaregio is most peaceful at sunset.

Osteria L'Orto dei Mori is a chic place serving nicely presented, creative Venetian cuisine. You can eat in the elegant, modern interior or on a great neighborhood square with 10 tables surrounded by a classic scene of wellhead, bridges, and canal (€14 pastas, €19-23 *secondi*, smart to reserve for dinner, Wed-Mon 12:30-15:30 & 19:00-24:00, closed Tue, facing a bridge on Fondamenta dei Mori, on Campo dei Mori, Dorsoduro 3386, tel. 041-524-3677, www.osteriaortodeimori.com).

Osteria Ai 40 Ladroni ("The 40 Thieves") is a characteristic, unpretentious old standby with a few tables on the canal, a rustic interior, and a convivial garden out back. The action is near the bar (€9-12 pastas, €10-15 *secondi*, they're proud of their mixed seafood *antipasti*, Tue-Sun 12:00-14:30 & 19:00-22:00, closed Mon, Fon-

EATING

Romantic Canalside Settings

Of course, if you want a meal with a canal view, it generally comes with lower quality and/or a higher price. But if you're determined to take home a canalside memory, these places can be great.

Near the Rialto Bridge: The five places I call the "Bancogiro Stretch" offer wonderful canalside dining and a great place to enjoy a drink and/or a snack between meals or after dinner (see page 300).

Rialto Bridge Tourist Traps: Venetians are embarrassed by the lousy food and aggressive "service" at the string of joints dominating the best romantic, Grand Canal-fringing real estate in town. Still, if you want to linger over dinner with a view of the most famous bridge and the songs of gondoliers oaring by (and don't mind eating with other tourists), this can be enjoyable. Don't trust the waiter's recommendations for special meals. The budget ideal would be to get a simple pizza or pasta and a drink for €15, and savor the ambience without getting ripped off. But few restaurants will allow you to get off that easy. To avoid a dispute over the bill, ask if there's a minimum charge before you sit down (most places have one).

Near the Accademia: Bar Foscarini, next to the Accademia Bridge, offers decent pizzas overlooking the canal with no cover or service charge (see page 305).

East of St. Mark's Square: Ristorante alla Conchiglia and

damenta de la Sensa at Calle del Capitello, Dorsoduro 3253, tel. 041-715-736).

Timon Enoteca Osteria, while nothing earthshaking, has a relaxing canalside setting with nice wines and *cicchetti* (a block past the Jewish Ghetto on Fondamenta Ormesini at Calle de la Malvasia, Dorsoduro 2754, tel. 041-524-6066).

Osteria al Bacco is simple and rustic, with a typical Venetian menu and a couple of canalside tables (€10 pastas, €16 *secondi*, closed Mon, on Fondamenta Capuzine at Calle Girolamo, Dorsoduro 3054, tel. 041-721-415).

Along the Main Drag

Just a few blocks closer to the Grand Canal from the options listed above, the following places are a few steps from the main drag connecting the train station to the Rialto/San Marco area, near the San Marcuola vaporetto stop.

Pizzeria Vesuvio serves some of the best and most popular

Trattoria da Giorgio ai Greci, several blocks behind St. Mark's, both have a few tables next to one of the smaller canals frequented by gondoliers. While tourist traps, they are lit up like Venetian Christmas trees after dark, and you can't argue with their setting (€17-20 fixed-price meals, €6-17 pastas and pizzas, €10-25 *secondi*, cover and service charge extra; on Fondamenta San Lorenzo near the Ponte dei Greci bridge).

Overlooking the Giudecca Canal: **Terrazza del Casin dei Nobili** is located in Zattere—on the Venice side of the wide Giudecca Canal—and is particularly nice just before sunset (vaporetto: Zattere, see page 306). For a cheaper perch on the same canal, consider **Ae Oche Pizzeria,** described on page 306. **I Figli delle Stelle Ristorante,** on the island of Giudecca, is a classy restaurant offering romantic canalside seating and a wonderful experience (vaporetto: Zitelle, see page 310).

On Fondamente Nove with a View of the Open Lagoon: **Ristorante Algiubagió** offers a good opportunity to eat well while overlooking the north lagoon (see page 310).

On Burano: **Trattoria al Gatto Nero** sits on a tranquil canal under a tilting bell tower in the pastel townscape of Burano. If you're touring the lagoon and want to enjoy Burano without the crowds, go late and consider a dinner here (see page 221).

EATING

pizza in town. A neighborhood favorite, it has classy indoor seating and pleasant tables outside (€6-9 pizzas, daily 9:30-23:30 except closed Tue off-season, on Rio Terà Farsetti, Cannaregio 1837, tel. 041-795-688).

Enoteca Cicchetteria Do Colonne is a local dive with a loyal following and a good spread of *cicchetti* and sandwiches. It's handy for a drink and a snack. While the food is mediocre, the scene (both at the bar and at the tables outside) feels real and is fun (daily 10:00-22:00, on Rio Terà del Cristo, Cannaregio 1814, tel. 041-524-0453).

Near the Train Station

There are piles of eateries near the station. The buffet in the station itself is quite good, with peaceful garden seating out back in summer, big €3-4 sandwiches, and slices of pizza for €3. A block away is a small branch of the efficient and economical **Brek,** a popular self-service cafeteria chain (€6 pastas, €7-12 *secondi*, daily 11:30-

22:00, head left as you leave the station and walk about 50 yards past the bridge along Rio Terà Lista di Spagna to #124).

Splurging on a Water View

On Giudecca Island, with a View of St. Mark's Square: **I Figli delle Stelle Ristorante** offers a delightful dining experience with an excuse to ride the boat from St. Mark's Square across to the island of Giudecca. Simone and his staff artfully serve Venetian classics with a dash of Rome and Puglia and a passion for fish and lamb. While they have inside seating, the reason to venture here is to sit canalside with fine views of Venice across the broad Giudecca Canal and all the water traffic. Reserve ahead to specify "first line" seating along the water, "second line" seating a few steps away, or a table inside (€15 pastas, €22 *secondi*, daily 12:30-14:30 & 19:00-22:30, 50 yards from Zitelle vaporetto dock—from San Marco ride line #4.2 or #2, Giudecca 70/71, tel. 041-523-0004, www.ifiglidellestelle.it).

On Fondamente Nove, with a Lagoon View: **Ristorante Algiubagió,** though not cheap, is a good place to eat well overlooking the northern lagoon. The name is a combination of the owners' four names—Alberto, Giulio, Barbara, and Giovanna—who strive to impress visitors with quality, creative Venetian cuisine made using the best ingredients. Reserve a table on the lagoon facing the island of San Michele or in their classy cantina dining room (€16-19 pastas, €20-28 *secondi*, €35-54 fixed-price meals, daily 12:00-15:00 & 19:00-22:30, between the two sets of vaporetto docks on Fondamente Nove, Cannaregio 5039—see map on page 213, tel. 041-523-6084, www.algiubagio.net). This is a convenient place to eat if you're taking the vaporetto out to the islands in the lagoon.

Picnics

You're legally forbidden from picnicking anywhere on or near St. Mark's Square except for Giardinetti Reali, the waterfront park near the San Marco vaporetto docks. Though it's legal to eat outdoors elsewhere around town, you may be besieged by pigeons.

Venice has one main produce market, and several convenient supermarkets:

Outdoor Market near the Rialto: The **fruit and vegetable market** that sprawls for a few blocks just past the Rialto Bridge is a fun place to assemble a picnic (best Mon-Sat 8:00-13:00, liveliest in the morning, closed Sun). The adjacent **fish market** is wonderfully slimy (closed Sun-Mon). Side lanes in this area are speckled with fine little hole-in-the-wall munchie bars, bakeries, and cheese shops.

Neighborhood Deli near the Rialto: One tiny *alimentari* just around the corner from the Rialto market sells a flavorful concoc-

EATING

tion of cheese, Kalamata olives, sun-dried tomatoes, olive oil, and hot peppers that they call *intruglio*. It goes great with a fresh roll (€2.70). It's at the end of my favorite strip of *cicchetti* bars, near the fruit and vegetable market at the San Polo end of the Rialto Bridge (see map on page 263; Mon-Sat 9:00-20:00, Sun 11:00-19:00, San Polo 414).

Neighborhood Deli near the Accademia Bridge: A small deli hides along the main route between the Accademia and St. Mark's Square (at #2512, on the zigzag bridge near the Church of Santa Maria Zobenigo/del Giglio—see map on page 267).

Produce Stands: Many squares have a dedicated produce stand. To find the one nearest St. Mark's Square, face St. Mark's Basilica, then walk along its left side, heading east down Calle de la Canonica. Cross the bridge and turn left at Campo Santi Filippo e Giacomo. There are also stands on Campo Santa Maria Formosa and Campo Santa Margherita.

Supermarket near St. Mark's Square: A handy (but often mobbed) **Co-op** supermarket is between St. Mark's and Campo Santa Maria Formosa, on the corner of Salizada San Lio and Calle del Mondo Novo at #5817. It has a great selection of picnic supplies, including packaged salads for €3 (daily 8:30-20:30).

Other Supermarkets: The largest supermarket in town is the **Co-op** at Piazzale Roma, next to the vaporetto stop at #504-507 (daily 8:30-20:00). It's an easy walk from the train station, as is the **Billa** supermarket on Campo San Felice (daily 8:00-23:00, along the Strada Nova between the train station and Rialto area, Cannaregio 3660). Another **Billa** supermarket is convenient for those staying in Dorsoduro: It's at #1492, as far west as possible on the Zattere embankment, by the San Basilio vaporetto stop and the cruise-ship docks (Mon-Sat 8:30-23:00, Sun 8:30-21:00).

Good Gelato Spots

You'll find good *gelaterie* in every Venetian neighborhood, offering one-scoop cones for about €1.50. Look for the words *artigianale* or *produzione propria*, which indicates that a shop makes its own gelato. All of these are open long hours daily.

The popular, inventive, upscale **Grom** ice-cream chain has three branches in Venice: on Campo San Barnaba at #2761 (beyond the Accademia Bridge); on the Strada Nova at #3844, not far from the Rialto; and on Campo dei Frari at #3006, facing the Frari Church (all open long hours daily). A competing gourmet gelato shop, **Gelatoteca Suso,** serves up delectable flavors such as fig and nut (next to recommended Rosticceria San Bartolomeo on Calle de la Bissa, San Marco 5453). **Il Doge,** on the big and bustling Campo Santa Margarita, has a wide range of homemade

EATING

flavors, as well as Sicilian-style *granita* (slushy ice flavored with fresh fruit; Dorsoduro 3058a, tel. 041-523-4607).

On St. Mark's Square, two venerable cafés have gelato counters: **Gran Caffè Lavena** (April-Oct daily until 24:00, no gelato Nov-March, at #134) and **Todaro** (on the corner of the Piazzetta at #5, near the water and just under the column topped by St. Theodore slaying a crocodile).

VENICE WITH CHILDREN

Some of the best fun I've had with my kids has been in Venice. The city doesn't need an amusement park...it is one big fantasy world. It's safe, friendly, and like nothing else your kids have ever seen. Though there's lots of pavement and few parks or playgrounds, just being there—and free to wander—can be delightful.

However, while Venice is great for older children and teens, it presents challenges if you're traveling with toddlers or infants. You'll need to keep toddlers safely in hand, as there are rarely any fences or walls between the sidewalk and the water. (Campo Santa Maria Formosa is the rare place in Venice where you'll find railings because a preschool uses it as their playground.) With hundreds of stepped bridges, Venice is a frustrating obstacle course for strollers. But considering the danger of a child falling into a canal or getting lost in a crowd, bringing a stroller—the smallest, lightest umbrella stroller possible—is a good tactic for navigating with a wily pre-schooler. Parents with small babies might find a baby carrier more hassle-free.

Trip Tips

Eating

Venetian fare is different from the "Italian food" you have at home. While there's plenty of pasta, it's often prepared with seafood rather than tomatoes or meat. Picky eaters will want to avoid local seafood dishes such as eel (*anguilla*) and cuttlefish (*seppia*). Try these tips to keep your kids content and well-fed.

- Start the day with a good breakfast (at hotels, kids sometimes eat free).
- For lunch or a snack, it's fun to buy pizza by the slice, fold it in half, and eat it as you stroll...or find a perch on a nearby square.

Favorite pizza choices for kids include *margherita* (tomato sauce, cheese, and basil) and spicy *diavola* or *salame piccante*, which are the closest things on the menu to sliced pepperoni sausage (if you ask for *peperoni*, you'll get bell peppers).

- For ready-made sandwiches and other portable food, drop by an *alimentari* (deli) or a supermarket. Be aware that you can't picnic on St. Mark's Square (but you can at Giardinetti Reali, the nearby waterfront park; see page 83).

- Choose easy eateries. For good old American food, check out one of the American hamburger joints between the Rialto Bridge and St. Mark's Square. A good, safe (though not exotic) bet is the **Brek** self-serve restaurant near the train station (see page 309). Having snacks on hand can avoid meltdowns. Stock your day bag with trail mix or crackers, and plan to buy plenty of gelato.

- Eat dinner early (19:00 at restaurants), and skip the romantic places. Try places on squares where kids can run free while you dine. You can nearly always get some kind of plain noodles.

Sightseeing

The key to a successful Venetian family vacation is to slow down. Tackle one or two key sights each day, mix in a healthy dose of pure fun in a square or on a boat, and take extended breaks when needed. A vaporetto ride is a great way to start your visit. Consider these other tips:

- Incorporate your child's interests into each day's plans. Let your kids make some decisions: choosing lunch spots or deciding when to take a gondola ride. Let them lead you through the maze of Venice's back streets. Get lost together. If your children are old enough, they can be the tour guides and read this book's self-guided tours. (Standard tip for good guides: a two-scoop gelato.)

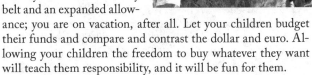

- Give your child a money belt and an expanded allowance; you are on vacation, after all. Let your children budget their funds and compare and contrast the dollar and euro. Allowing your children the freedom to buy whatever they want will teach them responsibility, and it will be fun for them.

- Buy your child a trip journal, and encourage them to write down their observations, thoughts, and favorite memories. This journal will end up being their favorite souvenir.

- While Venice is short on parks, its many small squares have served as playgrounds for local children for centuries. Let your kids run around while you take a seat at a café or bench.

- Seek out museums with kid appeal, such as the Peggy Guggenheim Collection—though be aware that art may feature nudes or erotic themes. If you're visiting art museums with younger children, hit the gift shop first so you can buy postcards; then hold a scavenger hunt to find the pictured artwork.

- Even if you have the best-behaved kids in the world, mix-ups happen. It's good to have a "what if" procedure in place in case something goes wrong, such as getting separated in a crowd. Be sure to give each child a business card from your hotel and your own contact information (if you brought a mobile phone on your trip).

- Italy's national museums generally offer free admission to children under age 18—always ask before buying tickets for your kids.

- If your kids love playing in the sand, consider staying in an apartment near the Lido. Easy beach access offers a convenient daily activity.

- Apartments, typically with multiple bedrooms and kitchen facilities, can save money over hotel rooms and eliminate the stress that can accompany restaurant dining with small children. See page 254 for some options.

- Follow this book's crowd-beating tips. Kids dislike long lines even more than you do.

- Give your kid a cheap camera. Venice turns anyone into a photographer.

- Look for family and child discounts. If buying the Doge's Palace/Correr Museum combo-ticket or a Museum Pass, ask for the family discount. A family ticket is also available for the Chorus Pass, which covers church visits. The Rolling Venice youth discount pass gives discounts on many sights and transportation for travelers under 30 (see page 26).

Top Sights and Activities

Kid-Centric Attractions
St. Mark's Square
This grand square is surrounded by splashy historic buildings and sights: St. Mark's Basilica, the Doge's Palace, the Campanile bell tower, and the Correr Museum. The square is filled with music, lovers, pigeons, and tourists by day. By night, the historical buildings are lit up, small orchestras put on free concerts, and good gelato is only a walk away. Anyone of any age will enjoy the magic of St. Mark's Square day or night.

The **pigeons** on the square offer a new breed of bird-watching. (Though feeding them is now against the law, most tourists don't realize that—and enjoy trying to lure as many birds to drape over their kids as possible.) If you yell, the birds will just ignore you, but tossing a sweater into the air kicks off a pigeon evacuation.

Elevator Ride
Ride the elevator to the top of the Campanile bell tower to enjoy the grand view, and be there as the huge bells whip into ear-shattering action at the top of each hour (see St. Mark's Square Tour, page 76).

Boat Rides
Ride lots of boats (vaporetto, gondola, *traghetto*, or speedboat tours of the lagoon). If you can, try to sit in the front seat of a vaporetto for my Grand Canal Cruise (see page 62). See how many kinds of service boats you can spot while on the canal (UPS, police, fire, garbage, and so on).

Glassblowing Demonstration
For a quick and entertaining demo of Venice's favorite craft, stop by the Galleria San Marco (just off St. Mark's Square, see page 327).

Rialto Bridge and Fish Market
The Rialto fish market is as fishy as they get (closed Sun-Mon, on the canal two blocks west of Rialto Bridge). Get there early in the day to watch people unload the boats at the market. You can leave by *traghetto* and cross the Grand Canal (*traghetto* dock at market).

Museums and Exhibits

CHILDREN

Be choosy when taking kids to museums. The venerable and fascinating (to adults) Accademia will probably bore children. But don't skip art entirely. Kids like holding mirrors to see the ceiling paintings at the Scuola San Rocco. The Peggy Guggenheim Collection has colorful modern art by Picasso and others.

Doge's Palace
The building is more impressive than the art inside. If your children aren't wowed by the architecture, they may enjoy the tour of the dark, dank prison. The dungeon held the notorious lover Giacomo Casanova, sentenced to prison for being a magician. In his memoirs, he describes how he used an iron rod and the help of a fellow prisoner to make his escape (◉ see the Doge's Palace Tour chapter).

Cost and Hours: €16 combo-ticket, €8 for kids ages 6-14 and students ages 15-25, also includes Correr Museum; families with two adults and at least one child get reduced rates; daily April-Oct 8:30-18:30, Nov-March 8:00-17:30, last entry one hour before closing, tel. 041-271-5911, http://palazzoducale.visitmuve.it.

Venetian Adventures

To help your kids realize the magic of Venice, stoke their imagination with some of these recommended books:

This Is Venice by Miroslav Slasek: The classic 1960s picture book captures Venice's charm with witty illustrations.

Kids Go Europe: Treasure Hunt Venice: Tiny, spiral-bound book that takes kids on a scavenger hunt through Venice.

Stravaganza: City of Masks by Mary Hoffman: Third in the time-traveling series set in 16th-century "Talia," an alternate-history Italy.

The Dragon's Pearl by Devin Jordan: The untold early adventures of 16-year-old Venetian Marco Polo.

Daughter of Venice by Donna Jo Napoli: A young girl seeks to free herself from the strictures of 16th-century Venetian society, disguising herself as a beggar boy to avoid entering a convent.

Stones in Water and its sequel, *Fire in the Hills* by Donna Jo Napoli: Young Roberto is caught up in World War II, shipped off to a labor camp by the Nazis, and struggles to return to his beloved Venice.

Venice for Kids by Elisabetta Pasqualin is a great guidebook for tweens and up, available at many museum bookshops.

VivaVenice: A Guide to Exploring, Learning, and Having Fun by Paola Zoffoli is full of interesting facts, and it's sold at many bookstores in the city.

Scuola San Rocco

This museum houses some of the best paintings by Tintoretto, which cover not only the walls, but the ceilings. Your kids may get a kick out of using the provided mirrors to look at the paintings on the ceiling—up close and personal, without straining their necks (❂ see the Scuola San Rocco Tour chapter).

Cost and Hours: €10, includes audioguide, free for those under age 18, daily 9:30-17:30, last entry 30 minutes before closing, tel. 041-523-4864, www.scuolagrandesanrocco.it.

The Peggy Guggenheim Collection

This museum shows major works from the first half of the 20th century, including pieces by Picasso, Pollock, Chagall, Magritte, and Dalí. Your children may not understand Surrealism, Futurism, or Abstract Expressionism, but there's enough variety here that they'll find something "cool." For younger kids, the outdoor sculpture garden is a rare green space in Venice where they can burn off some energy. Free workshops every Sunday at 15:00 give kids ages 4-10 a chance to experiment with techniques; though usually in Italian, the activity is sometimes offered in English (❂ see the Peggy Guggenheim Collection Tour chapter).

CHILDREN

Cost and Hours: €14, €8 for students under age 26, free for kids under age 10, Wed-Mon 10:00-18:00, closed Tue, pricey café, vaporetto: Accademia or Salute, tel. 041-240 5411, www.guggenheim-venice.it.

San Giorgio Maggiore

Located on an island a short boat ride away, this is a great church to visit after battling the hordes of St. Mark's Square. Enjoy a lagoon ride to the island, then take an elevator to the top of the bell tower (❂ see the San Giorgio Maggiore Tour chapter).

Cost and Hours: Free entry to church; €0.50 to light the artwork, elevator to bell tower-€6; April-Oct Mon-Sat 9:00-19:00, Sun 9:00-11:00 & 12:00-19:00; Nov-March daily 9:00-17:30. The last ascent in the tower elevator is 30 minutes before closing time.

Parks

Giardino Papadopoli

This tiny park, near the train station and the Piazzale Roma bus station, has one of Venice's rare playgrounds. Coming from the train station, take the Calatrava Bridge across the Grand Canal, turn left, and take the next bridge over a side canal to the park.

Giardini Pubblici (Public Gardens)

An ideal spot for children who want an American park experience, the Public Gardens have swings, slides, a play area, and big trees (a rarity in Venice). It's about a 20-minute walk along the water from St. Mark's Square, past the vaporetto docks and the Victor Emmanuel II statue, to the Public Gardens.

Parco Delle Rimembranze (Memorial Park)

Located in the Sant'Elena neighborhood beyond the Public Gardens, this park contains a soccer field, along with basketball and tennis courts. It's one of the largest open spaces in Venice.

Beaches and Other Experiences

Lido

The Lido has a fun, free, clean beach that's good for swimming, with an affordable self-service café, a bar, rentable umbrellas, and a well-priced beach-gear shop. Even the ride across the lagoon is enjoyable (vaporetto: Lido, walk 10 minutes on Gran Viale S. Maria Elisabetta to beach entry).

Soccer

Consider attending a soccer game at the stadium located in the Sant'Elena neighborhood. Venice's team is currently in the Pro Seconda Divisione league (not so good), so the crowds aren't as enthusiastic as they might be, but games are fun nonetheless. Matches take place on Sundays from September to June (ask at the TI). Buy a scarf with the team colors—black, orange, and green—and join the fun.

Signor Blum

This shop, on Campo San Barnaba—about a 10-minute walk northwest of the Accademia—has an array of colorfully painted wooden decorations. It's a good place to shop for kid-friendly souvenirs (for details, see page 325 in the Shopping in Venice chapter).

CHILDREN

SHOPPING IN VENICE

The merchants of Venice are abundant, making this a great town for shoppers. Long a city of aristocrats, luxury goods, and trade, Venice was built to entice. While no one claims it's great for bargains, it has a shopping charm that makes paying too much strangely enjoyable. Carnevale masks, lace, glass, antique paper products, designer clothing, one-of-a-kind jewelry, custom-made shoes, fancy accessories, hand-painted or printed velvet and silk tapestries, and paintings are all popular with tourists visiting Venice.

In many areas, Venice feels like one big open-air shopping mall. Trinket stands tuck themselves between internationally famous designers and hole-in-the-wall artisan shops. While there are plenty of temptations, remember: Anything not made locally is brought in by boat—and therefore generally more expensive than elsewhere in Italy. And, given Venice's tourist cachet, even items made here are priced at a premium. The shops near St. Mark's Square charge the most.

In touristy areas, shops are typically open from 9:00 to 19:30 (sometimes with a break from about 13:00 until 15:00 or 16:00), and more stores are open on Sunday here than in the rest of the country. If you're buying a substantial amount from nearly any shop, bargain—it's accepted and almost expected. Offer less and offer to pay cash; merchants are very conscious of the bite taken by credit-card companies.

The first part of this chapter highlights areas of Venice with the best concentration of quality shops; the second part describes some of the items you'll see sold (such as Carnevale masks, glass, jewelry, and lace).

For information on VAT refunds and customs regulations, see page 14.

Where to Shop

Here are a few neighborhoods that are fun to browse—even if you're just window-shopping.

San Marco

The San Marco area—between the back of St. Mark's Square and the Grand Canal—has Venice's highest concentration of shops. The streets closest to St. Mark's Square, and those between St. Mark's and the Rialto Bridge, are also the highest-trafficked, the highest-rent, and the highest-priced. This is where you'll see all of the big international names; it seems you can't be a fashion-world staple until you have a branch in San Marco.

Between St Mark's Square and the Rialto: This predictable Venetian shopping stretch starts on St. Mark's, where you can walk the entire colonnaded square past pricey jewelry, glass, lace, and clothing stores. **Galleria San Marco,** right on the square, sells glass items and does glassblowing demonstrations, while **Il Merletto,** just north of the square, has lace goods (both described later).

The Mercerie is the main street between St. Mark's Square (also labeled as "Marzarie"; leave the square from under the Clock Tower) and the Rialto, noted for its fancy windows and designer labels. You'll wind up at Rialto Bridge, where the streets on either side are a cancan of shopping temptations. (Some quieter options on the other side of the Rialto are described later.) For ordinary clothing and housewares, the best all-purpose department store is the **Coin** store on the St. Mark's Square side of the Rialto Bridge (Mon-Sat 9:30-19:30, Sun 11:00-19:30; from the bridge, head north).

West of St. Mark's Square: A half-block detour out the far end of the square leads to several high-fashion shops along Calle Vallaresso (southwest of St. Mark's, away from the Rialto). For a somewhat lower-roller ambience, the streets and bridges connecting Campo Santa Maria Zobenigo, Campo San Maurizio, and Campo San Stefano (basically parallel to the Grand Canal) are scattered with a few shops that, while not quite "untouristy," are a bit more characteristic and affordable. Interesting places along here include the **Bevilacqua** and **Venetia Studium** textile shops (both described later).

A bit farther west, you'll find a fascinating smattering of mostly cutting-edge art boutiques, in the zone north and west of Campo San Stefano, toward the Grand Canal. From that square, head west on Calle Botteghe, which becomes Crosera before it runs into the skinny square called Salizada San Samuele. Fronting this square are a half-dozen low-profile art galleries worth a browse. Halfway

SHOPPING

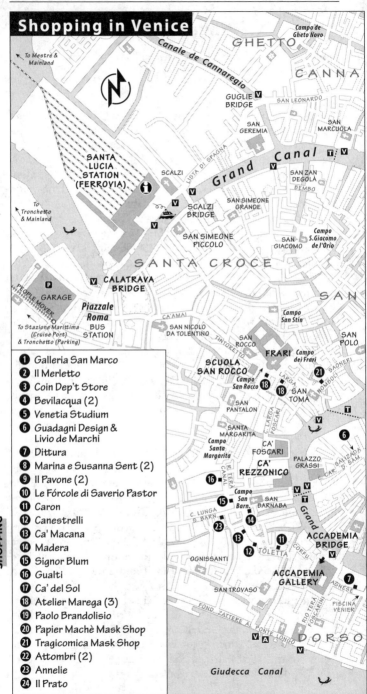

Shopping in Venice

① Galleria San Marco
② Il Merletto
③ Coin Dep't Store
④ Bevilacqua (2)
⑤ Venetia Studium
⑥ Guadagni Design & Livio de Marchi
⑦ Dittura
⑧ Marina e Susanna Sent (2)
⑨ Il Pavone (2)
⑩ Le Fórcole di Saverio Pastor
⑪ Caron
⑫ Canestrelli
⑬ Ca' Macana
⑭ Madera
⑮ Signor Blum
⑯ Gualti
⑰ Ca' del Sol
⑱ Atelier Marega (3)
⑲ Paolo Brandolisio
⑳ Papier Machè Mask Shop
㉑ Tragicomica Mask Shop
㉒ Attombri (2)
㉓ Annelie
㉔ Il Prato

SHOPPING

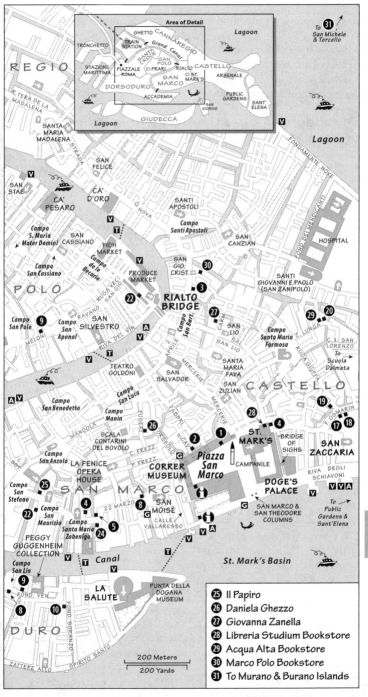

Area of Detail

To San Michele & Torcello

Lagoon

REGIO

TRONCHETTO

GHETTO CANNAREGIO

TRAIN STATION

Grand Canal

SANTA CROCE

FRARI

RIALTO

CASTELLO

STAZIONE MARITTIMA

PIAZZALE ROMA

SAN POLO

SAN MARCO

ST. MARK'S

ARSENALE

DORSODURO

ACCADEMIA

SAN GIORGIO

PUBLIC GARDENS

SANT' ELENA

Lagoon

GIUDECCA

Lagoon

FONDAMENTE NOVE

SAN STAE

CA' PESARO

CA' D'ORO

SAN FELICE

SANTI APOSTOLI

Campo Santi Apostoli

SAN CANZIAN

HOSPITAL

Campo S. Maria Mater Domini

SAN CASSIANO

FISH MARKET

Campo de le Becarie

PRODUCE MARKET

SAN GIO. CRIST.

SANTI GIOVANNI E PAOLO (SAN ZANIPOLO)

Campo San Cassiano

RUGA VECCHIA SAN GIO.

POLO

Campo San Polo

Campo San Aponal

RIALTO BRIDGE

SAN SILVESTRO

RIVA DEL VIN

Campo San Barti.

SAN LIO

SAN LIO

SANTA MARIA FORMOSA

Campo Santa Maria Formosa

RUGA GIUFFA

C. LUNGA

C. L. SAN LORENZO

To Scuola Dalmata

MELONI

APRILE

MERCERIE

SANTA MARIA FAVA

TEATRO GOLDONI

SAN SALVADOR

SAN ZULIAN

CASTELLO

Campo San Benedetto

Campo San Luca

Campo Manin

MERCERIE

F. OSMARIN

SAN ZACCARIA

SCALA CONTARINI DEL BOVOLO

FUSERI

FABBRI

C. FREZZ.

P. FREZZ.

ST. MARK'S

BRIDGE OF SIGHS

MANDOLA

Campo San Anzolo

LA FENICE OPERA HOUSE

CORRER MUSEUM

Piazza San Marco

CAMPANILE

DOGE'S PALACE

RIVA DEGLI SCHIAVONI

Campo San Stefano

SAN MARCO

SAN MOISÈ

SAN MARCO & SAN THEODORE COLUMNS

To Public Gardens & Sant'Elena

Campo San Maurizio

22 MARZO

Campo Santa Maria Zobenigo

CALLE VALLARESSO

PEGGY GUGGENHEIM COLLECTION

Campo San Lio

Canal

St. Mark's Basin

FOND. VEN.

LA SALUTE

FOND. SORANZO

PUNTA DELLA DOGANA MUSEUM

DURO

ZATTERE ALLO

SPIRITO SANTO

200 Meters

200 Yards

SHOPPING

25 Il Papiro
26 Daniela Ghezzo
27 Giovanna Zanella
28 Libreria Studium Bookstore
29 Acqua Alta Bookstore
30 Marco Polo Bookstore
31 To Murano & Burano Islands

down the square, **Guadagni Design** sells sleek and unique house-wares (at #3336, www.guadagnidesign.it). At the bottom, peek into the shop of **Livio de Marchi,** who specializes in outlandish and/or remarkably detailed wood-carvings—from handbags and ballet shoes to gloves and teddy bears to a bizarre phallus-medusa head (at #3157a, www.liviodemarchi.com).

Dorsoduro, Across the Accademia Bridge

Some of the best shopping in Venice is in Dorsoduro. While the area immediately around the Accademia and Peggy Guggenheim Collection is crowded and can feel tacky, within a few blocks things mellow out and feel a bit more local.

Near the Accademia and Guggenheim: For a strip of very touristy (yet still worthwhile) shops—mostly selling glass and/or jewelry with an artistic bent—browse the busy streets connecting those two museums (Calle Nova Sant'Agnese, Piscina del Forner, and Fondamenta Venier). Interesting shops along here are the **Dittura** slipper shop, the **Marina e Susanna Sent** jewelry gallery, and the **Il Pavone** paper shop (all described later).

Nearby, one canal east of the Guggenheim Collection, detour south along Fondamenta Soranzo to reach **Le Fórcole di Saverio Pastor,** the workshop of a local craftsman who carves the uniquely curvy Venetian oarlocks called *fórcole*. You can watch Saverio work, and you can buy a scale model (closed Sun and usually Sat, Fondamenta Soranzo de la Fornace, Dorsoduro 341, www.forcole.com).

Near Campo San Barnaba: The area around Campo San Barnaba, about a 10-minute walk northwest of the Accademia, is a great place to window-shop, as it strikes the right balance between tourist-friendly and local. Crossing the canal west of the Accademia, angle up the street called La Toletta, passing several interesting shops: **Caron** handmade glass jewelry (open daily, at #1195); **Canestrelli,** where soft-spoken Stefano Coluccio makes unique convex mirrors in circular frames, like the ones in old paintings (at #1173, www.venicemirrors.com); and **Ca' Macana,** a mask shop that proudly designed masks for Stanley Kubrick's *Eyes Wide Shut* (they also offer mask-painting classes—arrange in advance; open daily, at #3172, www.camacana.com). The street leads straight to the delightful Campo San Barnaba.

Right on the square are two of my favorite shops. Next to Grom *gelateria* is **Madera,** a wonderful boutique that collects beautiful and practical items from around the world, with an emphasis on high-quality materials and smart design. It injects a bit of slick modernity to ye olde Venice (closed Sun, right on Campo San Barnaba at #2762, www.maderavenezia.it). To see more, check out their bigger showroom, just a few short blocks down Calle Lunga San Barnaba. At the bottom corner of the square, overlooking the canal, is **Signor Blum,** which makes and sells delightfully colorful wood-carved letters, symbols, mobiles, and scenes of Venice—fun for kids and grown-ups (open daily, at #2840, www.signorblum. com).

From here, consider crossing the bridge and continuing up Rio Terà Canal one block to the vast and lively Campo Santa Margarita. Along the way you'll pass **Gualti** boutique on the left (at #3111), worth a peek for its cutting-edge-contemporary accessories and shoes. After shopping 'til you drop, reward yourself with a gelato from **Il Doge,** located on the square (described on page 311).

West of Rialto

Here are a few other shopping neighborhoods to consider:

Santa Croce: Shoppers interested in getting off the beaten path should poke around the Santa Croce district, northwest of Rialto. Because this neighborhood is less touristed than those listed above, the rents are lower, and local artisans can afford to keep their workshops open. To explore this zone, head northwest of the Rialto Market action, passing through Campo San Cassiano and Campo Santa Maria Mater Domini, then heading west toward Campo San Giacomo de l'Orio. To visit this area with a guide, contact Walks Inside Venice, which specializes in this less-discovered zone (www.walksinsidevenice.com; for details, see page 39).

San Polo: The neighborhood on the west side of Rialto Bridge offers plenty of inviting shops. While many sell typical Venetian souvenirs, they have fewer crowds and better prices. For starters, wander Ruga Vechia San Giovanni (a.k.a. Ruga), which runs from the Rialto Market action west, toward Campo San Polo and eventually to the Frari Church.

What to Buy

Popular souvenirs and gifts include Murano glass, Burano lace (fun lace umbrellas for little girls), Carnevale masks (fine shops and artisans all over town), art reproductions (posters, postcards, and books), prints of Venetian scenes, traditional stationery (pens and marbled paper products of all kinds), calendars with Venetian scenes (and sexy gondoliers), silk ties, scarves, and plenty of goofy knick-knacks (Titian mouse pads, gondolier T-shirts, and little plastic gondola condom holders).

SHOPPING

Mask Making

In the 1700s, when Venice was Europe's party town, masks were popular—sometimes even mandatory—to preserve the anonymity of visiting nobles doing things forbidden back home. At Carnevale (the weeks-long Mardi Gras leading up to Lent), everyone wore masks. The most popular were based on characters from the lowbrow comedic theater called commedia dell'arte. We all know Harlequin (simple, Lone Ranger-type masks), but there were also long-nosed masks for the hypocritical plague doctor, pretty Columbina masks, and so on.

Masks are made with the simple technique of papier-mâché. You make a mold of clay, smear it with Vaseline (to make it easy to remove the finished mask), then create the mask by draping layers of paper and glue atop the clay mold.

You'll see mask shops all over town. Just behind St. Mark's Square, on a quiet canal just inland from the Church of San Zaccaria (on Fondamenta de l'Osmarin), is a corner with two fascinating mask and costume shops: **Ca' del Sol** at #4964 (two showrooms connected by a little bridge) and **Atelier Marega** at #4968 (two other locations near the Frari Church on Campo San Rocco at #3046 and around the corner on Calle Larga at #2940b). After you cross the bridge to the second Ca' del Sol shop, head to the next door farther on to the wood-carving shop of **Paolo Brandolisio** (described in the sidebar on page 336).

Just a bit north, a block off Campo Santa Maria Formosa (next to Acqua Alta bookstore—see listing under "Services" on page 29), is the **Papier Maché Mask Shop,** where Stefano Gottardo proudly sells only masks made in his store. The masks are both traditional and modern, and you're welcome to watch the artisans at work (daily 9:00-19:30, at the end of Calle Lunga Santa Maria Formosa, Castello 5174b, tel. 041-522-9995).

Out near the Frari Church, the **Tragicomica Mask Shop** is highly respected and likely to have artisans at work (workshop open to customers who've bought a mask). You'll pass this shop if you take my ✪ Rialto to Frari Church Walk (daily 10:00-19:00, 200 yards past Church of San Polo on Calle dei Nomboli at #2800, tel. 041-721-102). Another good option is **Ca' Macana,** near Campo San Barnaba (for details, see "Dorsoduro, Across the Accademia Bridge," earlier).

SHOPPING

But beyond the typical souvenirs, Venice has a wealth of unique and locally made items, such as artisan jewelry, handcrafted fabrics, and made-to-order shoes. Note that many shops selling artisan goods can be quite expensive. But they are still atmospheric, engaging places to window-shop and daydream. If you're curious about the product, dip into a shop and ask a few questions. The vendor never knows when browsing might turn to buying...and neither do you.

Venetian Glass

Popular Venetian glass is available in many forms: vases, tea sets, decanters, glasses, jewelry, lamps, mod sculptures (such as solid-glass aquariums), and on and on. Shops will ship it home for you, but you're likely to pay as much or more for the shipping as you are for the item(s), and you may have to pay duty on larger purchases. Make sure the shop insures their merchandise *(assicurazione)*, or you're out of luck if it breaks. If your item arrives broken and it has been insured, take a photo of the pieces, send it to the shop, and they'll replace it for free.

Some visitors feel that because they're in Venice, they ought to grab the opportunity to buy glass. Remember that you can buy fine glass back home, too (Venice stopped forbidding its glassblowers from leaving the republic a few centuries ago)—and under less time pressure.

Also be aware that much of the cheap glass you'll see in Venice is imported (a sore point for local vendors dealing in the more expensive, authentic stuff). Venetian glass producers, up in arms about the influx of Chinese glass, claim that a big percentage of the glass tourists buy is actually not Venetian. Genuine Venetian glass comes with the Murano seal.

If you'd like to watch a quick glassblowing demonstration, try **Galleria San Marco,** a tour-group staple on St. Mark's Square at #139, which offers great demos every few minutes. They let individual travelers flashing this book sneak in with tour groups to see the show (and sales pitch). If you buy anything, show this book and they'll take 20 percent off the listed price. The gallery faces the square behind the orchestra nearest to the church; come to the door at #139, go through the shop, and climb the stairs (daily 9:00-18:00, tel. 041-271-8671, info@galleriasanmarco.it, manager Marino Busetto).

If you're serious about glass, visit the island of **Murano,** its glass museum, and many shops (see page 60). You'll find greater variety on Murano, but prices are usually the same as in Venice.

SHOPPING

Jewelry

Jewelers abound in Venice. Not surprisingly, glass jewelry and beadwork are particularly popular—you'll see references to *perle de Venezia* or *perle veneziane,* colorfully speckled glass beads. In addition to buying premade pieces, at many shops you can select the beads you like to create your own masterpiece. As with other glass, you can assume that cheap beads are imported, not local.

Because jewelry is such a subjective taste, I recommend that you browse around to find the styles and prices that suit you. But if you need help, here are some places to start: Several jewelers can be found under the arcades (behind the chintzy souvenir stands) on the west (market) side of the Rialto Bridge, including **Attombri,** selling pieces with a classic, filigree-plus-beads look (Sotoportego dei Orafi, San Polo 74; another location in San Marco on Campo San Maurizio, San Marco 2668a; www.attombri.com). **Marina e Susanna Sent** sells contemporary designs in two upscale-feeling showrooms (near St. Mark's next to Campo San Moisè at San Marco 2090, and near the Accademia on Campo San Vio at Dorsoduro 669, www.marinaesusannasent.com).

Lace

Lace, made from cotton or silk thread, is another Venetian specialty. Prior to the Industrial Revolution, the city was a major trading point for luxury fabrics like lace, silk, and satin. Venice was a European fashion hot spot, and Venetian Burano lace adorned the clothing of royalty. Venice is particularly known for "needle lace," with intricate flowers, leaves, and curling stems, which was used for cuffs, gowns, and frilly collars.

In recent decades the lace industry has been on life support as cheap imitations flood the market. But lately Venetians are attempting to revive the art. Today, popular lace goods include tablecloths, doilies, clothing, and even lace pictures suitable for framing.

But buyer beware. Note that much of the lace sold in Venice (and on the island of Burano) is cheap, machine-made, and imported—so stick to reputable shops to ensure that you are buying an authentic product.

The **Il Merletto** shop just off St. Mark's Square (see page 83) is the most convenient. **Annelie,** in the Dorsoduro district, is another well-respected shop (on Calle Lunga San Barnaba, Dorsoduro 2748). Lace lovers will find the journey out to Burano worthwhile. Here you'll find many shops such as **Merletti d'arte dalla Lidia** and the **Lace Museum** (both described under the "Burano" section, page 218).

Textiles

Venetia Studium carries on the Venetian tradition for hand-painted and woodblock-printed fabrics. In addition to velvet cushions

Beware of Cheap Knockoff Bags

Along Venice's many shopping streets, you'll notice fly-by-night street vendors selling knockoffs of famous designer

handbags (Louis Vuitton, Gucci, etc.). These vendors are willing to bargain. Beware: If you're caught purchasing fakes, you could get hit with a fine. Legitimate manufacturers are raising a stink about these street merchants, and the government is trying to rid the city of them. Caught up in a city-wide game of cat and mouse (with the police playing the role of cat), the vendors spend as much time lurking in alleys waiting for the coast to clear as they do selling. Authorities, frustrated in their attempts to actually arrest the merchants, have made it illegal to buy counterfeit items. Their hope: The threat of a huge fine will scare potential customers away—so unlicensed merchants will be driven out of business and off the streets.

and runners, they specialize in hanging lamps decorated with delicate hand-painted silk shades (Mon-Sat 10:00-19:30, Sun 10:30-19:00, just east of Campo Santa Maria Zobenigo, San Marco 2445, tel. 041-523-6953, www.venetiastudium.com).

Bevilacqua is a big and well-established producer of velvet cushions, tapestries, and so on. Mario and Paola have a few high-profile shops around Venice, as well as an 18th-century, hand-operated loom that they still use. For the budget-conscious, they also sell equally fine machine-made products (easiest to find at the Canonica Bridge behind St. Mark's Basilica at San Marco 337b, another location just to the right as you look at the Church of Santa Maria Zobenigo at San Marco 2520, both open daily 10:00-19:00, tel. 041-528-7581, www.bevilacquatessuti.com).

Stationery

Several shops sell handmade paper, colorfully bound books, and fine prints. **Il Pavone** is known for its marbleized paper and custom stamps (locations at Campiello dei Meloni, San Polo 1478, near the Rialto Bridge; and at Fondamenta Venier, Dorsoduro 721, near the Guggenheim). **Il Prato,** on a side corner of Campo Santa Maria Zobenigo west of St. Mark's Square, specializes in vividly bound books, trays, and other items, as well as glass (daily, on Calle de

SHOPPING

le Ostreghe, San Marco 2456, www.ilpratovenezia.com). A couple
of blocks away is a branch of the Italy-wide chain **Il Papiro** (daily,
Calle del Piovan, San Marco 2764, www.ilpapirofirenze.it).

Handmade Shoes

Fashion-conscious travelers may find it worth the splurge to indulge in custom-made shoes from a trained Venetian cobbler. Some
of the well-regarded options include **Daniela Ghezzo** (tucked in
an adorably cluttered hole-in-the-wall on Calle dei Fuseri near
St. Mark's Square, San Marco 4365, www.danielaghezzo.it) and
Giovanna Zanella (closed Sun, Castello 5641, www.giovanna-
zanella.it). For something distinctly Venetian, check out **Dittura,**
which makes and sells velvet gondolier's slippers (on the main drag
between the Accademia and Guggenheim, Dorsoduro 871).

NIGHTLIFE IN VENICE

You must experience Venice after dark. The city is quiet at night, as tour groups stay in the cheaper hotels of Mestre on the mainland, and the masses of day-trippers return to their beach resorts and cruise ships.

Do what you must to reserve energy for evening: Take a nap, or skip a few sights during the day. When the sun goes down, a cool breeze blows in from the lagoon, the lanterns come on, the peeling plaster glows in the moonlight, and Venice resumes its position as Europe's most romantic city.

Though Venice comes alive after dark, it does not party into the wee hours. By 22:00, restaurants are winding down; by 23:00, many bars are closing; and by midnight, the city is shut tight. Evenings are made for wandering—even Venice's dark and distant back lanes are considered safe after nightfall. Enjoy the orchestras on St. Mark's Square. Experience Vivaldi's *Four Seasons* in a candlelit 17th-century church. Pop into small bars for an appetizer and a drink. Lick gelato. As during the day, it's the city itself that is the star. But Venice under a cloak of darkness has an extra dose of magic and mystery—the ambience that has attracted visitors since the days of Casanova.

Gondola Rides

Riding a gondola is simple, expensive, and one of the great experiences in Europe. Gondoliers hanging out all over town are eager to have you hop in for a ride. A rip-off for some, this is a traditional must for romantics.

The price for a gondola starts at €80 for a 40-minute ride during the day. You can divide the cost—and the romance—among up to six people per boat, but only two get the love seat. Prices jump about 30 percent after 19:00—when it's most romantic and relaxing. Adding a singer and an accordionist will cost an additional €120. If you value budget over romance, you can save money by recruiting fellow travelers to split a gondola. Prices are standard and listed on the gondoliers' association website (go to www.gondolavenezia.it, click on "Using the Gondola," and look under "*charterage*").

Dozens of gondola stations *(servizio gondole)* are set up along canals all over town. Because your gondolier might offer narration or conversation during your ride, talk with several and choose one you like. You're welcome to review the map and discuss the route. Doing so is also a good way to see if you enjoy the gondolier's personality and language skills. Establish the price, route, and duration of the trip before boarding, enjoy your ride, and pay only when you're finished. While prices are pretty firm, you might find them softer during the day. Most gondoliers honor the official prices, but a few might try to scam you out of some extra euros, particularly by insisting on a tip. (While not required or even expected, if your gondolier does the full 40 minutes and entertains you en route, a 5-10 percent tip is appreciated; if he's surly or rushes through the trip, skip it.)

If you've hired musicians and want to hear a Venetian song *(un canto Veneziano)*, try requesting "*Venezia La Luna e Tu.*" Asking to hear "*O Sole Mio*" (which comes from Naples) is like asking a lounge singer in Cleveland to sing "The Eyes of Texas."

Glide through nighttime Venice with your head on someone's shoulder. Follow the moon as it sails past otherwise unseen buildings. Silhouettes gaze down from bridges while window glitter spills onto the black water. You're anonymous in the city of masks, as the rhythmic thrust of your striped-shirted gondolier turns old crows into songbirds. This is extremely relaxing (and, I think, worth the extra cost to experience at night). Suggestion: Put the camera down and make a point for you and your partner to enjoy a threesome with Venice. Warning: Women, beware...while gondoliers can be extremely charming, local women say that anyone who falls for one of these Venetian Romeos "has slices of ham over her eyes."

For cheap gondola thrills during the day, stick to the €2 one-minute ferry ride on a Grand Canal *traghetto*. At night, *vaporetti* are nearly empty, and it's a great time to cruise the Grand Canal on the slow boat #1. Or hang out on a bridge along the gondola route and wave at romantics.

St. Mark's Square

For tourists, St. Mark's Square is the highlight, with lantern light and live music echoing from the cafés. Just being here after dark is a thrill, as **dueling café orchestras** entertain (see sidebar on page 81). Every night, enthusiastic musicians play the same songs, creating the same irresistible magic. Hang out for free behind the tables (allowing you to move easily on to the next orchestra when the musicians take a break), or spring for a seat and enjoy a fun and gorgeously set concert. If you sit a while, it can be €12-22 well spent (for a drink and the cover charge for music). Dancing on the square is free—and encouraged.

Several venerable cafés and bars on the square serve expensive drinks outside but cheap drinks inside at the bar. The scene

in a bar like **Gran Caffè Lavena** (in spite of its politically incorrect chandelier) can be great. The touristy **Bar Americano** is lively until late (under the Clock Tower). You'll hear people talking about the famous **Harry's American Bar,** which sells overpriced food and American cocktails to dressy tourists near the San Marco-Vallaresso vaporetto stop. But it's a rip-off...and the last place Hemingway would drink today. It's far cheaper to get a drink at any of the bars just off St. Mark's Square; you can get a bottle of beer or even prosecco-to-go in a plastic cup.

Wherever you end up, streetlamp halos, live music, floodlit history, and a ceiling of stars make St. Mark's magic at midnight. You're not a tourist, you're a living part of a soft Venetian night...an alley cat with money. In the misty light, the moon has a golden hue. Shine with the old lanterns on the gondola piers, where the sloppy lagoon splashes at the Doge's Palace...reminiscing.

Entertainment

Venice has a busy schedule of events, church concerts, festivals, and entertainment. Check at the TI or the TI's website (www.turismo-venezia.it) for listings. The free monthly *Un Ospite di Venezia* lists all the latest happenings in English (free at fancy hotels, or check www.unospitedivenezia.it).

Baroque Concerts

Venice is a city of the powdered-wig Baroque era. For about €25, you can take your pick of traditional Vivaldi concerts in churches throughout town. Homegrown  Vivaldi is as ubiquitous here as Strauss is in Vienna and Mozart is in Salzburg. In fact, you'll find frilly young Vivaldis hawking concert tickets on many corners. Most shows start at 20:30 and generally last 1.5 hours. You'll see posters in hotels all over town (hotels sell tickets at face-value).

Tickets for Baroque concerts in Venice can usually be bought the same day as the concert, so don't bother with websites that sell tickets with a surcharge. The general rule of thumb: Musicians in wigs and tights offer better spectacle; musicians in black-and-white suits are better performers.

The **Interpreti Veneziani orchestra**, considered the best group in town, generally performs 1.5-hour concerts nightly at 21:00 inside the sumptuous San Vidal Church (€26, church ticket booth open daily 9:30-21:00, north end of Accademia Bridge, tel. 041-277-0561, www.interpretiveneziani.com).

If you just want a quick, free Vivaldi moment, stop by the **Music Museum** inside the San Maurizio Church, which Interpreti Veneziani has turned into a bilingual exhibition on the music and instruments of Vivaldi's time (free, daily 9:30-19:00, between St. Mark's Square and the Accademia on Campo San Maurizio).

Other Performances

Venice's most famous theaters are **La Fenice** (grand old opera house, box office tel. 041-2424, see page 45), **Teatro Goldoni** (mostly Italian live theater), and **Teatro della Fondamenta Nuove** (theater, music, and dance).

Musica a Palazzo is a unique evening of opera at a Venetian palace on the Grand Canal. You'll spend about 45 delightful minutes in each of three sumptuous rooms (about 2.25 hours total) as eight musicians (generally four instruments and four singers) perform. They generally present three different operas on successive nights—enthusiasts can experience more than one. With these kinds of surroundings, under Tiepolo frescoes, you'll be glad you dressed up. As there are only 70 seats, you must book by phone or online in advance (€60, nightly at 20:30, Palazzo Barbarigo Minotto, Fondamenta Duodo o Barbarigo, vaporetto: Santa Maria del Giglio, San Marco 2504, mobile 340-971-7272, www.musicapalazzo.com).

NIGHTLIFE

Venezia is advertised as "the show that tells the great story of Venice" and "simply the best show in town." I found the performance to be slow-moving and a bit cheesy, and the venue was disappointing (€39, nightly May-Oct at 20:00, Nov-April at 19:00; 80 minutes, just off St. Mark's Square on Campo San Gallo, San Marco 1097, tel. 041-241-2002, www.teatrosangallo.net).

Movies
Venetian cinema is rarely in the original language; expect to hear it in Italian. Every September, Venice's **film festival** (with some English-language films, www.labiennale.org) doubles the viewing choices and brings the stars out to Venice's Lido, a 10-minute vaporetto ride from St. Mark's Square.

Pubs, Clubs, and Late-Night Spots

Venice doesn't have a good dance scene, unlike other Italian cities. The close proximity of apartments means loud music isn't tolerated late at night. The few *discoteche* are overpriced and exclusive (not tourist-friendly), with expensive drinks and little actual dancing. But there are plenty of zones where people gather to enjoy the late hours. The scene in front of St. Mark's Basilica is seductive (described earlier), but also consider the following options.

Near the Rialto Market
Each night, but especially on weekends, young Venetians and local night owls congregate in bars near the Rialto Market and along a nearby section of the Grand Canal. A strip of canalside restaurants I've dubbed the "Bancogiro Stretch" is a great place to enjoy a drink and the scene late at night (see page 300).

West of the Rialto Bridge
For locations, see the map on page 263.

Perhaps the best place to drink beer with an Italian is in an Irish pub—and Venice has several near the Rialto Bridge, including **Devil's Forest Pub** (daily 11:00-24:00, a block off Campo San Bartolomeo on Calle dei Stagneri at #5185, tel. 041-520-0623) and **Inishark Pub** (closed Mon, on Calle del Mondo Novo, just west of Campo Santa Maria Formosa off Salizada San Lio, at #5787, tel. 041-523-5300).

Planet Restaurant shows sports coverage on TV while serving up pizzas, expensive pastas, and drinks until very late (no cover, between Campo Santa Maria Formosa and St. Mark's Square on Calle Casellerie at #5281, tel. 041-522-0808).

NIGHTLIFE

Gondolas

Two hundred years ago, there were 10,000 gondolas in Venice. Although the aristocracy preferred horses to boats through the early Middle Ages, beginning in the 14th century, when horses were outlawed from the streets of Venice, the noble class embraced gondolas as a respectable form of transportation.

The boats became *the* way to get around the lagoon's islands. To navigate over the countless shifting sandbars, the boats were flat (no keel or rudder) and the captains stood up to see. During the Age of Decadence, wannabe Casanovas would enjoy trysts in gondolas. Part of the gondolier's professional code was to never reveal what happened under the canopy of his little love boat.

Today, there are about 400 gondolas in service, used only for tourists. The boats are prettier now, but they work the same way they always have. Single oars are used both to propel and to steer the boats, which are built curved a bit on one side so that an oar thrusting from that side sends the gondola in a straight line.

These sleek yet ornate boats typically are about 35 feet long and five feet wide, and weigh about 1,100 pounds. They travel about three miles an hour (same as walking) and take the same energy to row as it does to walk. They're always painted black (six coats)—the result of a 17th-century law a doge enacted to eliminate competition between nobles for the fanciest rig. But each has unique upholstery, trim, and detailing, such as the squiggly shaped, carved-wood oarlock *(fórcola)* and metal "hood ornament" *(ferro)*. The six horizontal lines and curved top of the *ferro* represent Venice's six *sestieri* (districts) and the doge's funny cap. All in all, it takes about two months to build a gondola.

The boats run about €35,000-50,000, depending on your options (air-con, cup holders, etc.). Every 40 days, the boat's hull

Zattere

At the south end of Dorsoduro, a canalfront strip called Zattere (near the Zattere vaporetto stop) has a youthful vibe, with fun-loving pizzerias, *gelaterie*, and bars open late. While a pub-crawl dinner is fun and colorful, most serious eating is finished early to make way for drinking. **El Chioschetto alle Zattere** is a simple outdoor bar right on the promenade (live music on some good-weather Sun in summer, 18:00-21:00, just west of Zattere vaporetto dock—see map on page 267; mobile 348-396-8466).

must be treated with a new coat of varnish to protect against a lagoon-dwelling creature that eats into wood. A gondola lasts about 15 years, after which it can be refinished (once) to last another 10 years.

You can see Venice's most picturesque gondola workshop (from the outside; it's not open to the public) in the Accademia neighborhood. (Walk down the Accademia side of the canal called Rio San Trovaso; as you approach Giudecca Canal, you'll glimpse the beached gondolas on your right across the canal.) The workmen, traditionally from Italy's mountainous Dolomite region (because they need to be good with wood), maintain this refreshingly alpine-feeling little corner of Venice.

Carving the oarlock is an art form. To see the work in action, visit the wood-carving shop of **Paolo Brandolisio**. His shop is just behind St. Mark's Square, inland from the Church of San Zaccaria on Fondamenta de l'Osmarin—look for it next door to a corner with two mask shops (Ca' del Sol and Atelier Marega). You can pop in to watch Paolo carving traditional oars and *fórcole*, the oarlocks of the gondola (workshop open Mon-Fri 9:30-13:00 & 15:30-19:00, closed Sat-Sun, on Calle Corte Rota at #4725, tel. 041-522-4155, www.paolobrandolisio.altervista.org). Search for "*fórcole e remi*" on YouTube to watch Paolo at work. You can also visit the workshop of a different *fórcole* maker, **Saverio Pastor**, in the Dorsoduro district (near the Peggy Guggenheim Collection; for details, see page 324).

There are about 400 licensed gondoliers. When one dies, the license passes to his widow. And do the gondoliers sing, as the popular image has it? My mom asked our gondolier that very question, and he replied, "Madame, there are the lovers and there are the singers. I do not sing."

Campo Santa Margarita

For locations, see the map on page 267.

The university student zone of Campo Santa Margarita, near the Accademia Bridge, is popular with young Venetians. It has a good restaurant, café, and bar scene—especially from May through September. **Caffè Rosso** is a favorite (unsigned at #2965—with a tiny interior and tons of outdoor seating). A few doors down (at #2944), **Pizza al Volo** sells cheap, hearty slices to go until 2:00 in the morning. Across the square, find the excellent **Il Doge** *gelateria* (see page 311).

NIGHTLIFE

A block away, facing the canal (across Campo San Barnaba), the **Venice Jazz Club** has live music from 21:00 to 23:00 (nightly except Thu and Sun). Doors open at 19:00 and light meals are served before the music starts (€20 includes first drink, no smoking, near Ponte dei Pugni, Dorsoduro # 3102, tel. 041-523-2056, www.venicejazzclub.com, Federico).

Cannaregio

Il Paradiso Perduto ("Paradise Lost"), on Fondamenta de la Sensa in Cannaregio, is notorious for being noisy late at night. When locals complain, night owls say there's got to be someplace in Venice that stays open late. It's a restaurant and bar with a huge following for its good casual food and ambience (Cannaregio 2540, tel. 041-720-581, http://ilparadisoperduto.wordpress.com).

VENICE
CONNECTIONS

This chapter addresses your arrival and departure from Venice—by train, plane, car, bus, and cruise ship.

A two-mile-long causeway (with highway and train lines) connects Venice to the mainland. Mestre, the sprawling mainland section of Venice, has fewer crowds, cheaper hotels, and plenty of inexpensive parking lots, but zero charm. Don't stop in Mestre unless you're sleeping there (to save on the high cost of Venice hotels—see recommendations on page 274), parking your car, or changing trains.

By Train

Santa Lucia Train Station

All trains to "Venice" stop at Venezia Mestre (on the mainland). Most continue on to Santa Lucia Station (a.k.a. Venezia S.L. or Ferrovia) on the island of Venice itself. If your train only stops at Mestre, worry not. Your train ticket to Venice will get you to Santa Lucia. Just hop any train coming by and finish your journey (6/hour, 10 minutes). If, for some reason, you need a ticket from Mestre to Santa Lucia, you can buy one at a machine for €1.20.

Santa Lucia train station plops you right into the old town on the Grand Canal, an easy vaporetto ride or fascinating 45-minute walk to St. Mark's Square. As the station has just been renovated, you may find things are different than described here.

For most of the year, you'll find the **TI** in a white kiosk out front, next to the dock for vaporetto #2; a TI desk is also open inside the station on summer afternoons and all day in winter (see page 23 for exact hours). If the station TI is crowded when you arrive, skip it and visit one of the two TIs at St. Mark's Square in-

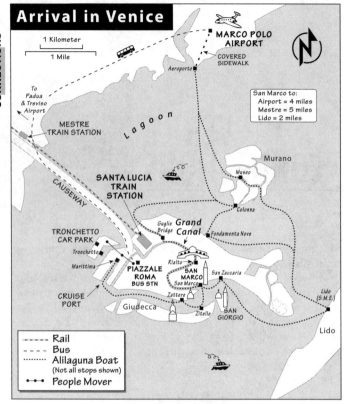

Arrival in Venice

1 Kilometer

1 Mile

MARCO POLO
AIRPORT

COVERED
SIDEWALK

Aeroporto

To
Padua
& Treviso
Airport

MESTRE
TRAIN STATION

Lagoon

Murano

Museo

San Marco to:
Airport = 4 miles
Mestre = 5 miles
Lido = 2 miles

SANTA LUCIA
TRAIN
STATION

Colonna

CAUSEWAY

Guglie Grand
Bridge Canal

Fondamenta Nove

TRONCHETTO
CAR PARK

Tronchetto

Rialto

Marittima

PIAZZALE
ROMA
BUS STN

SAN
MARCO

San Zaccaria

San Marco

CRUISE
PORT

Zattere

Giudecca

Zitelle

SAN
GIORGIO

Lido
(S.M.E.)

Lido

Rail
Bus
Alilaguna Boat
(Not all stops shown)
People Mover

stead. It's not worth a long wait for a minimal TI map (buy a good one from a newsstand or pick up a free one at your hotel).

The station has a **baggage check** (€5/5 hours, €11/24 hours, daily 6:00-23:50, no lockers; likely at track 1 but may move after renovation). **WCs** (€1) are at track 1 and in the back of the big bar/cafeteria area inside the station.

Before heading into town, confirm your departure plan (use the ticket machines or just study the *partenze*/departures posters on walls). Minimize your time in the station—the banks of user-friendly ticket machines are handy but cover Italian destinations only. They take euros and credit cards, display schedules, and issue tickets. Be aware that there are two train companies: TrenItalia, with most connections, has green-and-white machines (toll tel. 892-021, www.trenitalia.it); the red machines are for the new high-speed Italo service (no railpasses accepted, cheaper the further in advance you book, tel. 06-0708, www.italotreno.it). Ticket offices (for both TrenItalia and Italo) are in the corner, near track 14.

If you need international tickets or live help, the ticket windows are open from 6:00 to 20:30. Or you could take care of these tasks online or at a downtown travel agency (€4 fee per ticket, see page 29).

For more on train travel in Italy—including your ticket-buying options—see page 435.

Getting from the Train Station to Downtown: Walk straight out of the station to the canal. You'll see vaporetto docks and ticket booths on both sides. For vaporetto #2 (fast boat down Grand Canal), go left. For vaporetto #1 (slow boat down Grand Canal), go right. See page 31 for details on vaporetto tickets and passes. A water taxi from the train station to a hotel in central Venice will cost about €60-70 (the taxi dock is straight ahead).

From Venice by Train to: Padua (2/hour, 30-50 minutes), **Vicenza** (2/hour, 45-75 minutes), **Verona** (2/hour, 1.25-1.75 hours), **Ravenna** (roughly hourly, 3-3.5 hours, transfer in Ferrara or Bologna), **Florence** (hourly, 2 hours, often crowded so make reservations), **Bolzano/Dolomites** (to Bolzano about hourly, 3-3.5 hours, transfer in Verona; catch bus from Bolzano into mountains), **Milan** (hourly, 2.5-3.5 hours), **Cinque Terre/Monterosso** (5/day, 6 hours, change in Milan), **Rome** (roughly hourly, 3.5 hours, also 1 night train, 9 hours with change in Verona), **Naples** (almost hourly, 5.5-7 hours with changes in Bologna or Rome), **Brindisi** (5/day, 9 hours, change in Rome or Bologna). Note that the departures listed above are operated by Trenitalia; a competing private rail company called Italo offers additional high-speed connections to major Italian cities (including **Padua, Bologna, Florence,** and **Rome**). While Italo is often cheaper (particularly if you book long in advance), it doesn't accept railpasses (for details on Italo, see page 435 or visit www.italotreno.it).

International Destinations: Interlaken (5/day, 6-8.5 hours, 2-5 changes, no pleasant overnight option), **Luzern** (7/day, 6.5-7 hours, change in Milan and Arth-Goldau), **Bern** (3/day, 6 hours, change in Milan or Brig), **Munich** (4-6/day, 7 hours, change in Verona; 1 direct night train, 9 hours; most trains reservable only via www.bahn.de), **Salzburg** (5/day, 6-7 hours, 1-2 changes, 1 direct night train, 7 hours), **Paris** (2/day, 10-12 hours with change in Milan; 1 direct night train, 13.5 hours, reserve up to 4 months in advance, no railpasses accepted, www.thello.com), **Ljubljana** (2/day, 6.75 hours—buy ticket at train station, take bus from Piazzale Roma to Villach in Austria, then transfer to train; faster by direct DRD bus from Mestre—1/day, 3.75 hours, www.drd.si; also possible by private shuttle—see www.goopti.com), **Vienna** (4/day, 8-9 hours—same bus-to-train connection system as Ljubljana; 1 direct night train, 11 hours).

By Plane

Marco Polo Airport

Venice's small, modern airport is on the mainland shore of the lagoon, six miles north of the city (airport code: VCE). There's one sleek terminal, with a TI (daily 9:00-20:00), car-rental agencies, ATMs, a bank, and a few shops and eateries. For flight information, call 041-260-9260, visit www.veniceairport.com, or ask your hotel.

Getting Between the Airport and Venice

Here are four ways to transfer between the airport and downtown Venice:

- Alilaguna boats—Slowest trip, medium cost
- Water taxis—Fastest trip, most expensive
- Airport shuttle buses to Piazzale Roma (Venice's bus station)—Faster than Alilaguna, slower than water taxi, least expensive, requires change to vaporetto to reach most hotels
- Land taxi or private minivan to Piazzale Roma—Medium speed, medium cost, requires change to vaporetto to reach most hotels

Each of these options is explained in detail here. An advantage of the Alilaguna boats is that you can reach most of this book's recommended hotels very simply, with no changes—except hotels near the train station, which are better served by the bus to Piazzale Roma.

Both Alilaguna boats and water taxis leave from the airport's boat dock, an eight-minute walk from the terminal. Exit the arrivals hall and turn left, following signs along a paved, level, covered sidewalk (easy for wheeled bags).

When flying out of Venice, allow yourself plenty of time to get to the airport. Water transport can be slow. Plan to arrive at the airport two hours before your flight, and remember that getting there can easily take up to two hours. Alilaguna boats are small and can fill up. In an emergency, you can always hop in a water taxi and get to the airport in 30 minutes.

Alilaguna Airport Boats

These boats make the scenic (if slooooow) journey across the lagoon, each shuttling passengers between the airport and a number of different stops on the island of Venice (€15, €27 round-trip, €1 surcharge if bought on boat, roughly 2/hour, 1-1.5-hour trip depending on destination). Alilaguna boats are not part of the ACTV vaporetto system, so they aren't covered by city transit passes. But they do use the same docks and ticket windows as the regular *vaporetti*.

There are two Alilaguna lines—blue and orange—which take about the same amount of time to reach St. Mark's Square. From the airport, the **blue line** *(linea blu)* heads first to Fondamente Nove (on the "back" of Venice's fish, 40 minutes), then loops around the "tail" of the fish to San Zaccaria and San Marco (about 1.5 hours) before continuing on to Zattere and the cruise terminal (almost 2 hours). The **orange line** *(linea arancio)* runs down the Grand Canal, reaching Guglie (handy for Cannaregio hotels, 45 minutes), Rialto (1 hour), and San Marco (1.25 hours). For a full schedule, visit the TI, see the website (www.alilaguna.it), call 041-240-1701, ask your hotelier, or scan the schedules posted at the docks.

From the Airport to Venice: You can buy Alilaguna tickets at the airport's TI, the ticket desk in the terminal, and at the ticket booth at the dock. Any ticket seller can tell you which line to catch to get to your destination. Boats from the airport run roughly twice an hour (blue line from 6:10, orange line from 8:00, both run until about midnight).

From Venice to the Airport: Ask your hotelier which dock and which line is best. Blue line boats start leaving Venice as early as 3:40 in the morning for passengers with early flights. Scope out the dock and buy your ticket in advance to avoid last-minute stress.

Water Taxis

Luxury taxi speedboats zip directly between the airport and the closest dock to your hotel, getting you to within steps of your final destination in about 30 minutes. The official price is €115 for up to four people; add €10 for every extra person (10-passenger limit). You may get a higher quote—politely talk it down. A taxi can be a smart investment for small groups and those with an early departure.

From the airport, arrange your ride at the water-taxi desk or with the boat captains lounging at the dock. From Venice, book your taxi trip the day before you leave. Your hotel will help (since they get a commission), or you can book directly with the Consorzio Motoscafi water taxi association (tel. 041-522-2303, www.motoscafivenezia.it).

Airport Shuttle Buses

Buses between the airport and Venice are fast, frequent, and cheap. They take you across the bridge from the mainland to the island, dropping you at Venice's bus station, at the "mouth" of the fish on a square called Piazzale Roma. From there, you can catch a vaporetto down the Grand Canal—convenient for hotels near the Rialto Bridge and St. Mark's Square. If you're staying near the train station, you can walk from Piazzale Roma to your hotel.

Two bus companies run between Piazzale Roma and the airport: ACTV and ATVO. ATVO buses take 20 minutes and go nonstop. ACTV buses make a few stops en route and take slightly longer (30 minutes). They are equally good; just jump on whichever one's leaving next (either bus: €6, runs about 5:00-24:00, 2/hour, drops to 1/hour early and late, check schedules at www.atvo.it or www.actv.it).

From the Airport to Venice: Both buses leave from just outside the arrivals terminal. Buy tickets from the TI, the ticket desk in the terminal, ticket machines, or the driver. ATVO tickets are not valid on ACTV buses and vice versa. Double-check the destination; you want Piazzale Roma. If taking ACTV, you want bus #5.

From Venice to the Airport: At Piazzale Roma, buy your ticket from the ACTV windows or ATVO office before heading out to the platforms. The newsstand in the center of the lot also sells tickets. ACTV buses leave from platform A1; ATVO buses leave from platforms near the center of the lot and are well-signed.

Land Taxi or Private Minivan

It takes about 20 minutes to drive from the airport to Piazzale Roma. A **land taxi** can get you from the airport to Piazzale Roma for about €40. **Treviso Car Service** offers a private minivan service between the airport and Piazzale Roma or the cruise port (minivan-€55, seats up to 8; car-€50, seats up to 3; mobile 348-900-0700 or 333-411-2840, www.tourleadervenice.com, info@tourleadervenice.com). They also offer transfers to Treviso airport (see below), as well as guided tours (see page 39).

Treviso Airport

Several budget airlines, such as Ryanair, Wizz Air, and Germanwings, use Treviso Airport, 12 miles northwest of Venice (airport code: TSF, tel. 042-231-5111, www.trevisoairport.it). The fastest option into Venice (Tronchetto parking lot) is on the **Barzi express bus,** which does the trip in just 40 minutes (€7, buy tickets on board, 1-2/hour, www.barziservice.com). From Tronchetto, hop on the People Mover monorail to Piazzale Roma for €1. **ATVO buses** are a bit more frequent and drop you right at Piazzale Roma (saving you the People Mover ride), but take nearly twice as long because they make more stops (€7, about 2/hour, 1.25 hours, www.atvo.it; buy tickets at the ATVO desk in the airport and stamp them on the bus). **Treviso Car Service** offers minivan service to Piazzale Roma (minivan-€75, seats up to 8; car-€65, seats up to 3; for contact info, see listing above).

By Bus

Piazzale Roma Bus Station

Venice's "bus station" is actually an open-air parking lot called Piazzale Roma. The square itself is a jumble of different operators, platforms, and crosswalks over busy lanes of traffic. But bus stops are well-signed. The ticket windows for ACTV (local public buses, including #5 to Marco Polo Airport) are by the vaporetto stop. The ATVO ticket office (for express buses to Marco Polo and Treviso airports and to Padua) is in the big, white building, on the right side of the square as you face away from the canal (office open daily 6:40-19:35).

Piazzale Roma also has two big parking garages and the People Mover monorail (€1, links to the cruise port and then the parking-lot island of Tronchetto). A baggage-storage office is next to the monorail at #497m (€7/24 hours, daily 6:00-21:00).

If you arrive here, find the vaporetto docks (just left of the modern bridge) and take #1 or the faster #2 down the Grand Canal to reach the Rialto, Accademia, or San Marco (St. Mark's Square) stops. Electronic boards direct you to the letter of the dock you want. Before buying a single-ride vaporetto ticket, consider getting a transit pass (see page 31). If your hotel is near the train station, you can walk there by crossing the modern Calatrava Bridge.

By Car

Parking in Venice

The freeway dead-ends after crossing the causeway to Venice. At the end of the road you have two parking choices: garages at Tronchetto or Piazzale Roma. As you drive into the city, signboards with green and red lights indicate which lots are full. (You can also park in Mestre, on the mainland, but this is less convenient.)

Parking at Tronchetto: This garage is much bigger, a bit farther out, a bit cheaper, and well-connected by vaporetto (€3-4/hour, €21/24 hours, discounts for longer stays, tel. 041-520-7555, www.veniceparking.it).

After parking in the big Tronchetto garage, cross the street. While you can head left for a long walk to the People Mover monorail (described later), it's easiest to go right to the vaporetto dock (not well-signed, look for *ACTV*). At the dock, catch vaporetto #2 in one of two directions: via the Grand Canal (more scenic, stops at Rialto, 40 minutes to San Marco), or via Giudecca (around the city, faster, no Rialto stop, 30 minutes to San Marco).

Don't be waylaid by aggressive water taxi boatmen. They charge €100 to take you where the vaporetto will take you for €7. Also avoid the travel agencies masquerading as TIs; deal only with the ticket booth at the vaporetto dock or the HelloVenezia public transport office. If you're going to buy a local transport pass, do it now.

If you're staying near the train station and don't mind a walk, you can take the €1 **People Mover** instead of paying €7 for the two-stop vaporetto ride. The monorail brings you from Tronchetto to the bus station at Piazzale Roma, from which it's a five-minute walk across the Calatrava Bridge to the train station (buy monorail tickets with coins from machine, 3-minute trip, runs Mon-Sat 7:00-23:00, Sun 8:30-21:00).

Parking at Piazzale Roma: The two garages here are closer in and more convenient—but a bit more expensive and likelier to be full. Both garages face the busy square (Piazzale Roma) where the road ends. The big white building on your right is a 2,200-space public parking garage, the Autorimessa Communale (€26/24 hours, TI office in payment lobby, tel. 041-272-7211, www.asmvenezia.it). In a back corner of the square is the private Garage San Marco (€30/24 hours, tel. 041-523-2213, www.garagesanmarco.it). At either of these, you'll have to give up your keys. Near the Garage San Marco, avoid the Parcheggio Sant'Andrea, which charges obscene rates (€72/24 hours).

Parking in Mestre: Parking in the Parcheggio Stazione garage across from the train station in Mestre (on the mainland) only makes sense if you have light bags and are staying within walking distance of Santa Lucia Station (€10/day Mon-Fri, €14-16/day Sat-Sun; www.sabait.it).

By Cruise Ship

More than 1.5 million passengers visit Venice via cruise ship every year. If your trip includes cruising beyond Venice, consider my guidebook, *Rick Steves' Mediterranean Cruise Ports*.

Venice Cruise Ship Terminals

Most cruise ships visiting Venice dock at Stazione Marittima (also called Terminal Crociere, Venezia Terminal Passeggeri, or VTP), which is roughly between the Tronchetto parking garage and Santa Lucia train station. The terminal forms "the fish's mouth" of Venice. Some smaller ships also tie up at the Santa Marta and San Basilio docks, to the south of the main port. The Venice port website has a map of the different docks (www.port.venice.it/en/terminals.html).

The main cruise port consists of one long, wide, rectangular pier and a narrower, adjacent pier; together these form a harbor. There are six terminal buildings: #117 (along the north side of the main pier), #107 and #108 (along the south/harbor side of the main pier), #103 (at the top of the harbor), and Isonzo 1 and Isonzo 2 (along the narrower pier, used mostly by the MSC cruise line).

Wherever you arrive, the best strategy is to make your way to terminal #103 (the long, low-slung, modern, red building with the tall gray tower in the middle) at the top of the harbor. The waterfront strip in front of this terminal includes the dock for both *vaporetti* and taxi boats; the People Mover monorail is a five-minute walk beyond this building.

Getting into Town

The handy Alilaguna express boat (blue line) conveniently connects the cruise port directly to St. Mark's Square (San Marco-Giardinetti dock) in just 30 minutes (€8 one-way, €15 round-trip, €3/big bag, 2/hour in each direction; before boarding at the cruise terminal, buy ticket at kiosk in front of building #103; www.alilaguna. it). Because this service is understandably popular, the boats can fill up; if you're arriving on a cruise ship, get to this dock as quickly as possible.

To reach the Grand Canal (and the start of my self-guided Grand Canal Cruise) from Stazione Marittima, take your cruise line's free shuttle bus, if offered, or hop on the People Mover (€1) to Piazzale Roma. The People Mover station is a five-minute walk inland from the port (you'll see its elevated platform).

If money is no object, you can spring for a water taxi to anywhere in town (€70-80).

If all of these options are jammed up (as can happen when multiple cruise ships arrive all at once), you can walk to the Grand Canal in about 15 minutes, or all the way to St. Mark's Square in about 45 minutes.

If your ship arrives at the Santa Maria or San Basilio docks, take vaporetto #2 from San Basilio to get downtown.

Getting to Marco Polo Airport

Buses between Piazzale Roma and the airport are quick and inexpensive (described earlier). From the cruise port, take the People Mover to Piazzale Roma to catch the airport bus. To go from Stazione Marittima to the airport, you can also take a land taxi (€40) or the Alilaguna blue line (€15, 1.25 hours). From the Santa Marta or San Basilio docks, you can take a land taxi to the airport (€40).

DAY TRIPS FROM VENICE

Venice is just one of many towns in the Italian region of Veneto (VEN-eh-toh), but few visitors venture off the lagoon. That's a shame, as there's much to see within a very short hop of Venice. The trip from Venice westward to Milan is a route strewn with temptations: the Dolomite peaks, Italy's famous lakes, and—closest to Venice—the important and worthwhile towns of Padua, Verona, and Vicenza. While any of these towns merits an overnight (or longer), they're all within an hour of Venice—made to order for a day trip.

This trio of towns gives visitors a low-key slice of Italy that complements the intensity and earthshaking (yet exhausting) sightseeing thrills of Venice, Florence, and Rome. **Padua** is famous for its pilgrimage-site Basilica of St. Anthony (where the patron saint of travelers awaits your homage) and for its top artistic treasure, Giotto's frescoes in the Scrovegni Chapel. It's also known for its historic university, which still has students packing its cobbles,

presenting a never-ending seminar on the joys of sipping coffee on floodlit piazzas. **Verona,** while best-known for its melodramatic Romeo and Juliet connection, is so much more than a tragic love story, with its remarkably intact Roman arena, delightful pedestrian streets, and linger-a-while squares. And architecture fans could consider a quick trip to **Vicenza,** located about halfway between Padua and Verona, showcasing the seminal works of Andrea Palladio, whose style was so influential to our own founding fathers (among others).

Spending a day as a side-trip from Venice or town-hopping between Venice and Milan is exciting and efficient. Padua and Verona are on the same train line and only 40-60 minutes apart. Connected by at least two trains per hour, they're easy to visit.

If you're Padua-bound, remember that you need to reserve ahead to see the Scrovegni Chapel. Don't bother visiting Vicenza on a Monday, when many of the top sights are closed; in Verona, several sights don't open until 13:30 on Mondays.

PADUA

Padova

Living under Venetian rule for four centuries seemed only to sharpen Padua's independent spirit. Nicknamed "The brain of Veneto," Padua (*Padova* in Italian) is home to the prestigious university (founded in 1222) that hosted Galileo, Copernicus, Dante, and Petrarch. Pilgrims know Padua as the home of the Basilica of St. Anthony, where the reverent line assembles to touch his tomb and ogle his remarkably intact lower jaw and tongue. And lovers of early-Renaissance art come here to make a pilgrimage of their own: to gaze at the remarkable frescoes of Giotto in the Scrovegni Chapel. But despite the fact that Padua's museums and churches hold their own in Italy's artistic big league, its hotels are reasonably priced, and the city doesn't feel touristy. Padua's old town center is elegantly arcaded, filled with students, and sprinkled with surprises, including some of Italy's most inviting squares for lingering over an *aperitivo* as the sun slowly dips low in the sky.

Planning Your Time: Padua in Six Hours

Day-trippers can do a quick but enjoyable blitz of Padua—including a visit to the Scrovegni Chapel—in six hours. Trains from Venice are cheap, take 30-50 minutes, and run frequently. Once in Padua, everything is a 10-minute walk or a quick tram ride apart.

Your Scrovegni Chapel reservation will dictate the order of your sightseeing (see "Reservations" on page 362). When planning your day, also consider these factors: The station has a reliable baggage check desk; the open-air markets are vibrant in the morning, dead in the evening; student life is best at the university late in the day; and the Basilica of St. Anthony is open all day, but the reliquary chapel closes midday, from 12:45 to 14:45.

Ideally, I'd do it this way: 9:00—market action and sightseeing in town center, 11:00—Basilica of St. Anthony, 13:00—lunch, 15:00—Scrovegni Chapel tour.

Orientation to Padua

Padua's main tourist sights lie on a north-south axis through the heart of the city, from the train station to Scrovegni Chapel to the market squares (the center of town) to the Basilica of St. Anthony. It's roughly a 10-minute walk between each of these sights, or about 30 minutes from end to end. I've designed this chapter around Padua's wonderful, single tram line, which makes lacing things together quick and easy (see "Getting Around Padua," later).

Tourist Information

Padua has two TIs: in the **center** (in the alley behind Caffè Pedrocchi at Vicolo Cappellatto Pedrocchi 9, Mon-Sat 9:00-13:30 & 15:00-19:00, closed Sun, tel. 049-876-7927) and at the **train station** (Mon-Sat 9:15-19:00, Sun 9:00-12:30, tel. 049-875-2077). Be aware that one or both of these TIs may close in 2014 due to Italy's budget problems.

At any TI, pick up a map and the seasonal *Padova Today* entertainment listing (with a list of sights in the back). The TI's free I-PADova audio tour is creative and works well; you can download it to your smartphone or tablet for free from their website and follow any of the five routes in town (www.turismopadova.it; smart to print out audio tour map ahead of time). You can also borrow a device preloaded with the tour (leave ID as deposit).

The **Padova Card** includes entry to all the recommended sights in this chapter—except the university's Anatomy Theater and the Oratory of St. George—and unlimited tram rides (€16/48 hours, €21/72 hours). The card covers the Scrovegni Chapel and Civic Museums, but you still need to make a reservation in advance to enter (€1 extra reservation fee). This pass only makes sense if you're visiting a covered sight in addition to the Scrovegni Chapel (for example, the Palazzo della Ragione)—and even then, it may only save you a euro or two. You can buy the card at TIs, at participating sights, and at the Scrovegni Chapel website (www.cappelladeglis-crovegni.it; consider buying card when reserving chapel entry, then picking it up when checking in at chapel's ticket office).

Arrival in Padua

By Train: The efficient station is a user-friendly shopping mall with whatever you may need (Despar supermarket open daily 7:00-21:00). Along track 1 are WCs and baggage deposit (€3.87—yes, that's right, they're stubbornly sticking with the exact lire-to-euro conversion from 2002; daily 6:30-18:00, bring photo ID).

For a travel agency, go to **Leonardi Viaggi-Turismo,** which is only a block from the station and offers ticketing services for trains, planes, and boats for a small fee (Mon-Fri 9:00-13:00 & 14:30-19:00, Sat 9:00-13:00, closed Sun, up the main drag, Corso del Popolo 14, tel. 049-650-455).

To get downtown, simply hop on Padua's handy **tram** (see "Getting Around Padua," below). Purchase your ticket (€1.20) at one of the shops inside the station. Leaving the station, the tram stop is 100 yards to the right at the foot of the bridge. A **taxi** into town (a good option after dark) costs about €8-10.

By Bus: The bus station is 100 yards east of the train station. Buses arrive here from Venice's Piazzale Roma and Marco Polo Airport.

Helpful Hints

Pronunciation: You say Padua (PAD-joo-wah), they say Padova (PAH-doh-vah). The city's top sight, Scrovegni Chapel, is pronounced skroh-VEHN-yee.

Internet Access: All of the hotels I list offer free Wi-Fi. Padua has few Internet cafés (ask your hotel for the nearest). The central TI has an Internet point where you can get online for 15 minutes (free, fill out a form and show your passport).

Bookstore: Feltrinelli's International Bookstore, with books in English, is one block from the main university building (Mon-Sat 9:00-19:30, Sun 10:00-13:00 & 15:30-20:00, Via San Francesco 7, tel. 049-875-4630).

Launderette: Lavami is modern and entirely automated (€5/wash, €4/dry, daily 7:00-22:00, Via Marsala 22 near intersection with Via dell'Arco, tel. 049-876-4532).

Local Guide: Charming and helpful **Cristina Pernechele** is a great teacher (€110/half-day, mobile 338-495-5453, cristina@pernechele.eu).

Getting Around Padua

Ignore the city buses; pretend there is only the **tram** and rely on it. There's just one line, which efficiently and without stress connects everything you care about (€1.20 ticket good for 1.25 hours; buy tickets from machines at stops, tobacco shops, or newsstands; departs every 8 minutes during the day Mon-Sat, every 20 minutes evenings and Sun). The rubber-wheeled trams run on a single rail.

Before boarding, note the tram direction on posted schedules and above the front window (Pontevigodarzere is northbound, Capolinia Sud is southbound). Stops that matter to tourists include: Stazione FS (train and bus stations), Eremitani (Scrovegni Chapel), Ponti Romani (old town center, market squares, university), Tito Livio (ghetto, old town center, Hotel Majestic Toscanel-

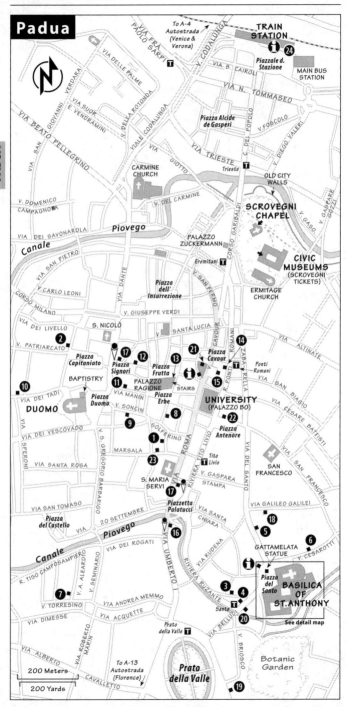

Padua

See detail map

PADUA

Padua Key

❶ Hotel Majestic Toscanelli
❷ Albergo Verdi
❸ Hotel Al Fagiano
❹ Hotel Belludi 37
❺ Hotel Al Santo & Antica Trattoria dei Paccagnella
❻ Hotel/Rist. Casa del Pellegrino
❼ Ostello Città di Padova
❽ Osteria dei Fabbri
❾ Osteria L'Anfora
❿ Enoteca dei Tadi
⓫ Rist. Dante alle Piazze
⓬ La Lanterna Ristorante
⓭ Bar dei Osei
⓮ Brek Cafeteria
⓯ PAM Supermarket & Brek
⓰ Gelato Pretto
⓱ Gelateria Grom (2)
⓲ Pizzeria Pago Pago
⓳ Zairo Rist./Pizzeria
⓴ Pollodoro la Gastronomica
㉑ Caffè Pedrocchi
㉒ Feltrinelli's Int'l Bookstore
㉓ Launderette
㉔ Buses to Venice & Marco Polo Airport

PADUA

li), Santo (Basilica of St. Anthony and neighborhood hotels), and Prato della Valle (hostel).

Padua's **hop-on, hop-off tour buses** are not worth the time or money.

Sights in Padua

Sights in the Center

Padua's two main sights (Basilica of St. Anthony and Scrovegni Chapel) are, respectively, at the southern and northern reaches of downtown. But its atmospheric, cobbled core—with bustling markets, vibrant student life, and inviting sun-and-café-speckled piazzas—is its own ▲▲▲ attraction. You could simply stroll the area aimlessly, or seek out some of the following spots.

▲▲Market Squares: Piazza delle Erbe, Piazza della Frutta, and Piazza dei Signori

The stately Palazzo della Ragione (described later) provides a dramatic backdrop for Padua's almost exotic-feeling produce market that fills the surround-ing squares—**Piazza delle Erbe** and **Piazza della Frutta**—each morning and all day Saturday (Mon-Fri roughly 8:00-13:00, Sat 8:00-19:00 but a bit quieter in the afternoon, closed Sun). Second only to

the produce market in Italy's gastronomic capital of Bologna, this market has been renowned for centuries as having the freshest and greatest selection of herbs, fruits, and vegetables. The presentation is an art in itself. As you wander, appreciate the local passion for good food: Residents can tell the month by the seasonal selections, and merchants share recipe tips with shoppers. You'll notice quite a few Sri Lankans working here (Italy took in many refugees from Sri Lanka's civil war).

Don't miss the **indoor market** zone on the ground floor of the Palazzo della Ragione. Wandering through this H-shaped arcade—where you'll find various butchers, *salumerie* (delicatessens), cheese shops, bakeries, and fishmongers at work—is a sensuous experience. For centuries, this was a market for luxury items (furs, fine fabrics, silver, and gold—notice the imposing iron gates used to lock it up each evening). Then, the devastating loss to the French in 1797 marked the end of good times, and with no market for luxury items, the arcade was used to sell perishables—meat and cheese—out of the sun.

Students gather in the squares after the markets have closed, spilling out of colorful bars and cafés, drinks in hand. Pizza by the slice is dirt-cheap. For pointers on a recommended local sandwich stand, **Bar dei Osei,** and a neighboring seafood-snack stand, see page 380. Just a few steps away from these is a classic old pharmacy that dates to 1841: The licorice-perfumed **Ai Due Cantini d'Oro,** which stocks retail items like it did before World War II, sells odd foods and specialty items for every dietary need (Piazza della Frutta 46, tel. 049-875-0623).

Piazza dei Signori, just a block away, is a busy clothing market in the morning and the most popular gathering place in the evening for students out for a drink (see next listing). The circa-1400 clock decorates the former palace of the ruling family. The aggressive lion with unfurled wings on the column was a reminder of the Venetian determination to assert its control. Today that lion can be seen as

representing the Veneto region's independence from Rome: Italy's North (Veneto and Lombardy) is tired of subsidizing the South. Grumbling about this issue continues to stir talk of splitting the country.

Drinking a *Spritz* with the Student Crowd

Each early evening, before dinner, students enliven Padua by enjoying a convivial drink in their favorite places. Piazza dei Signori is trendier, with people of all ages, while the scene on Piazza della Erbe is more bohemian and alternative. Or you could sit in front of the university, nurse your drink, and watch the graduates get roasted with their crazy gangs of friends (see "Graduation Antics in Padua" sidebar, later).

The drink of choice is a *spritz,* an aperitif generally made with Campari (a red liqueur infused with bitter herbs), white wine, and sparkling water, and garnished with a blood-orange wedge. Traditionally, men opt for the heavier and bitterer Campari *spritz,* while women prefer a sweeter and lighter *spritz* made with Aperol (an orange-flavored liqueur with less alcohol content).

Grab a table and be part of the scene. This is a classic opportunity to enjoy a real discussion with smart, English-speaking students who see tourists not as pests, but as interesting people from far away. For an instant conversation starter, ask about the current political situation in Italy, the right-wing party's policy on immigrants, or the cultural differences between Italy's North and South.

PADUA

Palazzo della Ragione

Looming over Padua's two big central market squares (Piazza delle Erbe and Piazza della Frutta), this grand 13th-century palazzo—commonly called *il Salone* (the great hall)—once held the medieval law courts. Its first floor consists of a huge hall—265 feet by 90 feet—that was at one time adorned with frescoes by Giotto. A fire in 1412 de-

stroyed those paintings, and the palazzo was redecorated with the 15th-century art you see today: a series of 333 frescoes depicting the signs of the zodiac, labors of the month, symbols representing characteristics of people born under each sign, and, finally, figures of saints to legitimize the power of the courts in the eyes of the Church.

The hall is topped with a hull-shaped roof, which helps to support the structure without the use of columns—quite an architectural feat in its day, considering the building's dimensions. The biggest thing in the hall is the giant, very anatomically correct horse. Its prominent placement represents the pride locals feel for the Veneto's own highly respected breed of horse. (After the bronze ones in St. Mark's Basilica, these are the favorite horses in the region.) The curious black stone in the corner opposite the big wooden horse is the "Stone of Shame," which was the seat of debtors being punished during the Middle Ages. It was introduced as a compassionate alternative to prison by St. Anthony in 1230. Instead of being executed or doing prison time, debtors sat upon this stone, surrendered their possessions, and denounced themselves publicly before being exiled from the city. The computer kiosks provide excellent information with entertaining videos.

Cost and Hours: €4, more during special exhibitions; Feb-

Oct Tue-Sun 9:00-19:00, Nov-Jan Tue-Sun 9:00-18:00, closed Mon year-round; enter through the east end of Piazza delle Erbe and go up the long staircase, Ponti Romani tram stop, tel. 049-820-5006. The WCs are through the glass doors at the opposite end of the hall from the wooden horse.

Caffè Pedrocchi

The white-columned, Neoclassical Pedrocchi building is much more than just a café on the ground floor. A complex of meeting rooms and entertainment venues, it stirs the Italian soul (or the patriotic Italian soul, at least). Built in 1831 during the period of Austrian rule, Caffè Pedrocchi was inaugurated for the fourth Italian Congress of Scientists, which convened during the mid-19th century to stir up nationalistic fervor as Italy struggled to become a united nation. As a symbol of patriotic hope, it was the target (no surprise) of a student uprising plot in 1848.

Each of the café's three dining rooms is decorated and furnished in a different color (denoted by the hue of velvet on the chairs): red, white, or green—representing the colors of the Italian flag. In the outer, unheated Sala Verde (Green Room), people are welcome to sit and relax without ordering anything or having to pay. This is where Italian gentlemen read their newspapers and gather with friends to chat about the old days. In the Sala Rossa (Red Room), the clock over the bar is flanked by marble reliefs of morning and night, signaling that it was once open 24 hours a day (in the 19th century). In the rooms on either side, the maps of the hemispheres with south  up top reflect the anti-conventional spirit of the place. The menu offers teahouse fare, including €13 salads, €7.50 sandwiches, and the writer Stendhal's beloved *zabaglione*, a creamy custard made with *marsala* wine. Remember that in Italy, you can order a basic coffee standing up at the bar of any place, no matter how fancy, and pay the same low, government-regulated price. In the Sala Bianca (White Room), you can still see a bullet hole (framed in tarnished silver) in the wall, where one of the insurgents in that ill-fated 1848 uprising was killed.

Cost and Hours: Café interior free, Sun-Tue 9:00-21:00, Wed-Sat 9:00-23:00, two entrances across from Via VIII Febbraio 14 and 20 near Ponti Romani tram stop, tel. 049-878-1231.

Piano Nobile: To see the café's even more elaborate upstairs, you can pay to enter this "noble floor" of the Pedrocchi building (€4, Tue-Sun 9:30-12:30 & 15:30-18:00, closed Mon; to find entrance, head outside to Piazza Cavour, face café, and go through the door on the right; tel. 049-878-1231). The rooms are all in different styles, such as Greek, Etruscan, or Egyptian, with good English descriptions throughout. These rooms were intended to evoke memories of the glory of past epochs, which a united Italy had hopes of reliving.

The Piano Nobile also hosts the small **Museum of the Risorgimento,** which traces Padua's role in Italian history, from the downfall of the Venetian Republic (1797) to the founding of the Republic of Italy (1948). Exhibits, a few with English descriptions, include uniforms, medals, weaponry, old artillery, Fascist propaganda posters, and a 30-minute propagandistic video (in Italian, but mostly fascinating footage without narration). The video, played on demand, is a "Luce" production (meaning a Mussolini production) and features great scenes of the town in the 1930s, including clips of Il Duce's visit and later WWII bombardments. The war and propaganda posters in the last room are haunting. An old woman pleads to those who question the Fascist-driven war effort: "Don't betray my son." Another declares, "The Germans are truly our friends." And another asks, "And you...what are *you* doing?"

University of Padua

The main building of this prestigious university, known as Palazzo Bò, is adjacent to Caffè Pedrocchi. Founded in 1222, it's one of the first, greatest, and most progressive universities in Europe. Back when the Church controlled university curricula, a group of professors and students broke free from the University of Bologna to create this liberal school, which would be independent of Catholic constraints and accessible to people of alternative faiths.

A haven for free thought, the university attracted intellectuals from all over Europe, including the great astronomer Copernicus, who realized here that the universe didn't revolve around him. And Galileo—notorious for disagreeing with the Church's views on science—called his 18 years on the faculty here the best of his life.

Cost and Hours: While it's free to visit the university (weekdays and Sat mornings only), you must sign up for a 30-minute tour (€5) to see the Anatomy Theater. Only 30 people may enter at a time. Tours run three times a day (March-Oct Mon, Wed, and Fri at 15:15, 16:15, and 17:15; Tue, Thu, and Sat at 9:15, 10:15, and 11:15; no tours on Sun, reduced schedule Nov-Feb—call number below, Ponti Romani tram stop, www.unipd.it). School groups often book the entire visit, and many of the guides do not speak English.

Confirm tour times and availability by calling 049-827-3047 or stopping by the ticket window (opens 15 minutes before each tour, located just inside the palace, in the hall reached from the Fascist-era courtyard described next). The bar there is fun for a cheap drink and to see photos of university life.

Visiting the University: The gawking public is not really wel-

comed in the university, but on weekdays and Saturday mornings, you can poke into two **courtyards** (when closed, just peer through the gate). Find the entrance at Via VIII Febbraio 7, under the "Gymnasium" inscription (30 yards from Caffè Pedrocchi, facing City Hall). You'll pop into a 16th-century courtyard, the school's historic core. It's littered with the coats of arms of important faculty and leaders of the university over the ages. Classrooms, which open onto the square, are still used. Today, students gather here, surrounded by memories of illustrious alumni, including the first woman in the world to receive a university degree (in 1678).

A passageway leads from here to an adjacent second courtyard from the Fascist era (c. 1938). The relief celebrates heroic students in World War I. Off of this courtyard, notice the richly decorated stairway, frescoed Fascist-style in the 1930s with themes celebrating art, science, and the pursuit of knowledge.

The exciting attraction among tourists is Europe's first great **Anatomy Theater** (from 1594), which you can visit only on a guid-

ed tour. Try to get a ticket, but keep in mind that it's not worth any heroics to see. The first two rooms of the tour are underwhelming: One features the supposed "pulpit of Galileo" (c. 1550) and portraits of 40 famous alums. The second is the Aula Magna, a ceremonial room for festivities. The historic Anatomy Theater itself is more impressive. Despite the Church's strict ban on autopsies, more than 300 students would pack this theater to watch professors dissect human cadavers (the bodies of criminals from another town). This had to be done in a "don't ask, don't tell" kind of way, because the Roman Catholic Church only started allowing the teaching of anatomy through dissection in the late 1800s.

▲Baptistery

This richly frescoed little building was originally the private chapel of Padua's ruling family. Then, in 1405, Venice took over, killing the family, and making the building a baptistery. Located next to Padua's skippable Duomo, the Baptistery was frescoed (c. 1370) by Giusto de' Menabuoi.

Graduation Antics in Padua

With 60,000 students, Padua's university always seems to be hosting graduation ceremonies. There's a constant trickle

of happy grads and their friends and families celebrating the big event.

During the school year, every 20 minutes or so, a student steps into a formal room (upstairs, above the university courtyard) to officially meet with the leading professors of his or her faculty. When they're finished, the students are given a green laurel wreath. They pose for ceremonial group photos and family snapshots. It's a sweet scene. Then, craziness takes over.

The new graduates replace their somber clothing with raunchy outfits, as gangs of friends gather around them on Via VIII Febbraio, the street in front of the university. The roast begins. The gang rolls out a giant butcher-paper poster with a generally obscene caricature of the student and a litany of *This Is Your Life* photos and stories. The new grad, subject to various embarrassing pranks, reads the funny statements out loud. The poster is then taped to the university wall for all to see. (Find the plastic panels to the right of the main entry, facing Via VIII Febbraio. Graduation posters are allowed to stay there for 24 hours. The panels are emptied each morning, but by nighttime a new set of posters is affixed to the plastic shields.)

During the roast, the friends sing the catchy but obscene local university anthem, reminding their newly esteemed friend not to get too huffy: *Dottore, dottore, dottore del buso del cul. Vaffancul, vaffancul* (loosely translated: "Doctor, doctor. You're just a doctor of the a-hole...go f-off, go f-off"). After you've heard this song (with its fanfare and oom-pah-pah catchiness) and have seen all the good-natured fun, you can't stop singing it.

The crazy show is usually staged late in the afternoon. Outdoor café tables afford great seats to enjoy the spectacle.

While the Baptistery was created 70 years after Giotto, it feels older. Because de' Menabuoi was working for a private family, he needed to be politically correct and not threaten or offend the family's allies—especially the Church. While still mind-blowing, the Baptistery's art seems relatively conservative compared to Giotto's Scrovegni Chapel. Giotto, supported by the powerful Scrovegni family and the Franciscans, could get away with being more progressive and bold.

The Baptistery's complex design must have made perfect and cohesive sense to the faithful in centuries past. Almighty Christ is in majesty on top, while approachable Mary and the multitude of saints provide the devout with access to God. Find the world as it was known in the 14th century (the disk below Mary's feet). It kicks off a cycle of scenes illustrating creation (clockwise from the creation of Adam). The four evangelists (Matthew, Mark, Luke, and John) with their books and symbols fill the corners. A vivid crucifixion scene faces a gorgeous annunciation. And the altar niche features a dim, blue-toned, literal Apocalypse from the book of Revelation.

Cost and Hours: €2.80, daily 10:00-18:00, on Piazza Duomo.

▲▲▲Scrovegni Chapel (Cappella degli Scrovegni) and Civic Museums

Wallpapered with Giotto's beautifully preserved cycle of nearly 40 frescoes, the glorious, renovated Scrovegni Chapel holds scenes depicting the lives of Jesus and Mary.  You must make reservations in advance to see the chapel. Scrovegni Chapel tickets also cover the Civic Museums, featuring the worthwhile Pinacoteca and Multimedia Room, as well as the skippable Archaeological Museum and the little-visited Palazzo Zuckermann.

Cost and Hours: The €13 ticket covers the Scrovegni Chapel and Civic Museums. Chapel tickets drop to €8 when most of the museums are closed (after 19:00 and on Monday). It's €10 for just the museums. The **chapel** is open March-Oct Mon 9:00-19:00, Tue-Sun 9:00-22:00; Nov-Feb daily 9:00-19:00; tel. 049-201-0020, www.cappelladegliscrovegni.it. The **Pinacoteca** and **Archaeological Museum** are open Tue-Sun 9:00-19:00, closed Mon; the **Multimedia Room** is open daily 9:00-19:00; **Palazzo Zuckermann** is open Tue-Sun 10:00-19:00, closed Mon; museums tel. 049-820-4551, palazzo tel. 049-820-5664.

Chapel Entry Times: To protect the paintings from excess humidity, only 25 people are allowed in the chapel at a time. Every 15 minutes (on the quarter-hour), a new group is admitted for a 15-minute video presentation in an anteroom, followed by 15 minutes in the chapel itself. After 19:00, visitors can enter every 20 minutes and get 20 minutes inside (last entry at 21:40).

Reservations: Prepaid reservations are required. It's wise to reserve at least two days in advance. It's easiest to reserve online at www.cappelladegliscrovegni.it (website also sells Padova Cards—described on page 352, tel. 049-201-0020).

PADUA

Without a reservation, it's sometimes possible to buy a ticket for the same day at the ticket office (especially for single visitors), but don't count on it. If you neglected to make a reservation and really want to see the chapel, drop by and see if anything is available (a Post-it note stuck to the desk indicates the next available entry time). Tickets for daytime visits are generally released at 9:00, and for evening visits at 17:00 (or at 16:00 on Sun); showing up at one of these times will increase your chances of getting a slot (likely for later in the day). You can't book next-day reservations in person—only online or by phone. Local tour guides, who have to book blocks of tickets, are generally happy to unload unneeded tickets to those who ask.

Helpful Hint: If you packed binoculars, bring them along for a better—and more comfortable—view of the uppermost frescoes. No photos are allowed.

Getting There: From the train station, it's a 10- to 15-minute walk, or a quick, two-stop tram ride to the Eremitani stop.

Getting In: To reach the chapel, enter through the Eremitani building, where you'll find the museums, ticket office, and a free but mandatory bag check. Though you're instructed to pick up your tickets at the ticket office at least one hour before your visit, in practice, I've found that you can arrive later. Still, give yourself a minimum of 30 minutes to weather any commotion at the desk. Present your confirmation number at the ticket desk, verify your time, pick up your ticket, and check any bags or purses.

While waiting for your reserved time, blitz the Pinacoteca and Multimedia Room (described later). Read the chapel description before you enter, since you'll only have a short time in the chapel itself.

The chapel is well-signed: From the ticket office, go outside and walk 100 yards down the path, passing some ruins of Roman Padua (described later). Be at the chapel doors at least five minutes before your scheduled visit. The doors are automatic, and if you're even a minute late, you'll forfeit your visit and have to rebook and repay to enter.

At your appointed time, you first enter an anteroom to watch a very instructive 15-minute video (with English subtitles) and to establish humidity levels before continuing into the chapel. Although you have only a short visit inside the chapel, it is divine. You're inside a Giotto time capsule, looking back at an artist ahead of his time.

Scrovegni Chapel

Painted by Giotto and his assistants from 1303 to 1305 and considered by many to be the first piece of modern art, this work makes it clear: Europe was breaking out of the Middle Ages. A sign of the

PADUA

Giotto di Bondone (c. 1267-1337)

Although details of his life are extremely sketchy, we know that the 12-year-old shepherd Giotto was discovered painting pictures of his father's sheep on rock slabs. He grew to become the wealthiest and most famous painter of his day. His achievement is especially remarkable because painters at that time weren't considered anything more than craftsmen—and weren't expected to be innovators.

After making a name for himself by painting frescoes of the life of St. Francis in Assisi, the Florentine tackled the Scrovegni Chapel (c. 1303-1305). At age 35, he was at the height of his powers. His scenes were more realistic and human than anything that had been done for a thousand years. Giotto didn't learn technique by dissecting corpses or studying the mathematics of 3-D perspective; he had innate talent. And his personality shines through in the humanity of his art.

The Scrovegni frescoes break ground by introducing nature—rocks, trees, animals—as a backdrop for religious scenes. Giotto's people, with their voluminous, deeply creased robes, are as sturdy and massive as Greek statues, throwbacks to the Byzantine icon art of the Middle Ages. But these figures exude stage presence. Their gestures are simple but expressive: A head tilted down says dejection, an arm flung out indicates grief, clasped hands indicate hope. Giotto created his figures not just by drawing outlines and filling them in with single colors; he filled the outlines in with subtle patchworks of lighter and darker shades, and in doing so pioneered modern modeling techniques. Giotto's storytelling style is straightforward, and anyone with knowledge of the episodes of Jesus' life can read the chapel like a comic book.

The Scrovegni represents a turning point in European art and culture—away from scenes of heaven and toward a more down-to-earth, human-centered view.

Renaissance to come, Giotto placed real people in real scenes, expressing real human emotions. These frescoes were radical for their 3-D nature, lively colors, light sources, emotion, and humanism.

The chapel was built out of guilt for white-collar crimes. Reginaldo degli Scrovegni (skroh-VEHN-yee) charged sky-high interest rates at a time when the Church forbade the practice. He even caught the attention of Dante, who placed him in one of the levels of hell in his *Inferno*. When Reginaldo died, the Church denied

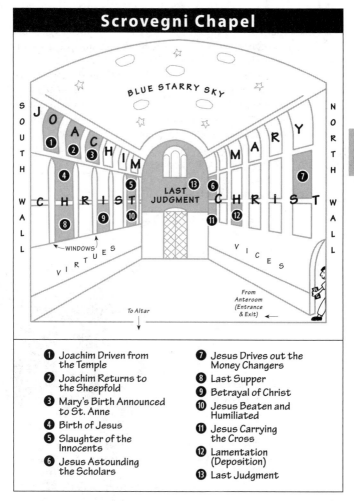

Scrovegni Chapel

- ❶ Joachim Driven from the Temple
- ❷ Joachim Returns to the Sheepfold
- ❸ Mary's Birth Announced to St. Anne
- ❹ Birth of Jesus
- ❺ Slaughter of the Innocents
- ❻ Jesus Astounding the Scholars
- ❼ Jesus Drives out the Money Changers
- ❽ Last Supper
- ❾ Betrayal of Christ
- ❿ Jesus Beaten and Humiliated
- ⓫ Jesus Carrying the Cross
- ⓬ Lamentation (Deposition)
- ⓭ Last Judgment

him a Christian burial. His son Enrico tried to buy forgiveness for his father's sins by building this superb chapel. After seeing Giotto's frescoes for the Franciscan monks of St. Anthony, Enrico knew he'd found the right artist to decorate the interior (and, he hoped, to save his father's soul). The Scrovegni residence once stood next to the chapel, but was torn down in 1824.

Giotto's Frescoes in the Scrovegni Chapel

Giotto painted the entire chapel in 200 working days over two years, but you'll get only 15 minutes to see it.

As you enter the long, narrow chapel, look straight to the far end—the rear wall is covered with Giotto's big *Last Judgment*.

Christ in a bubble is flanked by crowds of saints and by scenes of heaven and hell. This is the final, climactic scene of the story told in the chapel's 38 panels—the three-generation history of Jesus, his mother Mary, and Mary's parents.

The story begins with Jesus' grandparents, on the long south wall (with the windows) in the upper-left corner. ❶ In the first frame, a priest scolds the man who will be Mary's father (Joachim, with the halo) and kicks him out of the temple for the sin of being childless. ❷ In the next panel to the right, Joachim returns dejectedly to his sheep farm. ❸ Meanwhile (next panel), his wife is in the bedroom, hearing the miraculous news that their prayers have been answered—she'll give birth to Mary, the mother of Jesus.

From this humble start, the story of Mary and Jesus spirals clockwise around the chapel, from top to bottom. The top row (both south and north walls) covers Mary's birth and life.

Jesus enters the picture in the middle row of the south (windowed) wall. ❹ The first frame shows his birth in a shed-like manger. In the next frame, the Magi arrive and kneel to kiss his little toes. Then the child is presented in the tiny temple. Fearing danger, the family gets on a horse and flees to Egypt. ❺ Meanwhile, back home, all the baby boys are slaughtered in an attempt to prevent the coming of the Messiah *(Slaughter of the Innocents)*.

Spinning clockwise to the opposite (north) wall, you see (in a badly damaged fresco) ❻ the child Jesus astounding scholars with his wisdom. Next, Jesus is baptized by John the Baptist. His first miracle, at a wedding, is turning jars of water into wine. Next, he raises a mummy-like Lazarus from the dead. Riding a donkey, he enters Jerusalem triumphantly. ❼ In the temple, he drives out the wicked money changers.

Turning again to the south wall (bottom row), we see scenes

from Jesus' final days. ❽ In the first frame, he and his followers gather at a table for a Last Supper. Next, Jesus kneels humbly to wash their feet. ❾ He is betrayed with a kiss and arrested. Jesus is tried. ❿ Then he is beaten and humiliated.

⓫ Finally (north wall, bottom row), he is forced to carry his own cross, is crucified, and prepared for burial, while his followers mourn (**⓬** *Lamentation*). Then he is resurrected and ascends to heaven, leaving his disciples to carry on.

⓭ The whole story concludes on the rear wall, where Jesus reigns at the Last Judgment. The long south wall (ground level) features the Virtues that lead to heaven, while the north wall has the (always more interesting) Vices. And all this unfolds beneath the blue, starry sky overhead on the ceiling.

Some panels deserve a closer look:

Joachim Returns to the Sheepfold (south wall, upper left, second panel): Though difficult to appreciate from ground level, this oft-reproduced scene is groundbreaking. Giotto—a former shepherd himself—uses nature as a stage, setting the scene in front of a backdrop of real-life mountains, and adding down-home details like Joachim's jumping dog, frozen in midair.

Betrayal of Christ, a. k. a. *Il Bacio*, "The Kiss" (south wall, bottom row, center panel): Amid the crowded chaos of Jesus' arrest, Giotto skillfully creates a focus upon the central action, where Judas ensnares Jesus in his yellow robe (the color symbolizing envy), establishes meaningful eye contact, and kisses him.

Lamentation, a.k.a. *Deposition* (north wall, bottom row, middle): Jesus has been crucified, and his followers weep and wail over the lifeless body. John the Evangelist spreads his arms wide and shrieks, his cries echoed by anguished angels above. Each face is a study in grief. Giotto emphasizes these saints' human vulnerability.

Last Judgment (big west wall): Christ in the center is a glorious vision, but the real action is in hell (lower right). Satan is a Minotaur-headed ogre munching on sinners. Around him, demons give sinners their just desserts in a scene right out of Dante...who was Giotto's friend and fellow Florentine. Front and center is Enrico Scrovegni, in a violet robe (the color symbolizing penitence), donating the chapel to the Church in exchange for forgiveness of his father's sins.

Before the guard scoots you out, take a look at the actual altar. Though Enrico's father's tomb is lost, Enrico Scrovegni himself is in the tomb at the altar. The three statues are by Giovanni Pisano—Mary (in the center) supports baby Jesus on her hip with a perfectly natural, maternal, S-shape. She's flanked by anonymous deacons.

Nearby: Between the museum and the chapel are the scant remains of **Roman Padua**. The remnants are from the wall of an arena and nicely fitting pipes that once channeled water so that the arena could be flooded for special spectacles.

Civic Museums (Musei Civici Agli Eremitani)

The Eremitani, the building next to the Scrovegni Chapel, was once an Augustinian hermit's monastery and now houses several museums. While you can skip the ground-floor Archaeological Museum (with Roman and Etruscan artifacts and no English descriptions), the Pinacoteca and the Multimedia Room are worth visiting. Another part of the museum, Palazzo Zuckermann, is across the street.

Pinacoteca

The museum's highlight is upstairs, in the Pinacoteca (picture gallery). The collection has 13th- to 18th-century paintings by Titian, Tintoretto, Giorgione, Tiepolo, Veronese, Bellini, Canova, Guariento, and other Veneto artists. But I'd make a beeline for the room with the Giotto crucifix (upstairs and to the right, through the upper gallery). Ask for *"La Croce di Giotto?"* (lah KROH-cheh dee JOH-toh?)

Originally hung in the Scrovegni Chapel between the Scrovegni family's private zone and the public's worshipping zone, this crucifix is painted on wood by Giotto. If you actually sit on the floor and look up, the body really pops. The adjacent "God as Jesus" piece *(L'Eterno)* was the only painting in the otherwise frescoed chapel. (This is hung here because of preservation concerns. Its copy is the only non-original art in the chapel.) Studying these two masterpieces affirms Giotto's greatness.

Behind the crucifix room is a collection of 14th- and 15th-century art. While the works here are exquisite—and came well after Giotto—they're clearly not as modern.

Multimedia Room

Dedicated to taking a closer look at the Scrovegni Chapel, this small but interesting exhibit is downstairs. To head straight from the museum entrance to the Multimedia Room, use the entrance to the right of the main entry, step into the courtyard, make a sharp right, go through the glass doors at the end of the corridor, and head down the stairs.

Rows of computer screens offer a virtual Scrovegni Chapel visit and provide cultural insights into daily life in the Middle Ages. There are explanations of the individual panels, Giotto's fresco technique, close-ups of the art, and a description of the restoration. You'll also see a life-size re-creation of the house of Mary's mother, St. Anne, as depicted in Giotto's fresco. They show a 12-minute video (English headphones available) about the history of the chapel that is similar—but not identical—to the one that precedes your chapel visit. For me, it's worth just taking some time to enjoy a second video that features a mesmerizing, slow montage of close-ups of the Giotto frescoes.

Palazzo Zuckermann

This overlooked wing of the Civic Museum is just across a busy street. Its first two floors offer a commotion of applied and decorative arts—such as clothes, furniture, and ceramics—from the

Venetian Republic (1600s-1700s). On the top floor, the Bottacin collection takes you to the 19th century with coins and delightful (but no-name) pre-Impressionist paintings.

▲▲▲Basilica of St. Anthony

Friar Anthony of Padua, "Christ's perfect follower and a tireless preacher of the Gospel," is buried here. Construction of this impres-

sive Romanesque/Gothic church (with its Byzantine-style domes) started immediately after St. Anthony's death in 1231. As a mark of his universal appeal and importance in the medieval Church, he was sainted within a year of his death. Speedy. And for nearly 800 years, his remains and this glorious church have attracted pilgrims to Padua.

Cost and Hours: The **basilica** is free and open April-Oct daily 6:20-19:45; Nov-March Mon-Fri 6:20-19:00, Sat-Sun 6:20-19:45. The various sights within the basilica have slightly different hours: The important **Chapel of the Reliquaries** (free) is open when the basilica is, except that it closes for lunch (12:45-14:45). Other, less important sights include a **museum** (€2.50, Tue-Fri 9:00-13:00, Sat-Sun 9:00-13:00 & 14:00-18:00, closed Mon), a **multimedia exhibit** (free, daily 9:00-12:30 & 14:00-17:30), and the **Oratory of St. George and Scuola del Santo** (€3 apiece or €5 together, same hours as basilica but closed 12:30-14:30). The nearest tram stop is Santo.

Dress Code: A modest dress code is enforced.

Information: Information desks are at both entrances to the cloisters. Each desk has a free pamphlet in English on the saint's life and the basilica; make a donation in the Chapel of the Reliquaries to get a more detailed booklet. Tel. 049-822-5652, www.basilicadelsanto.org.

Church Services: The church hosts six separate Masses each morning (all before 10:00), as well as ones at 11:00, 17:00, and 18:00; on Sundays, additional services are at 12:15, 16:00, and 19:00.

Services: WCs and a picnic area are inside the cloisters.

Basilica Exterior

St. Anthony looks down from the red-brick facade and blesses all. He holds a book, a symbol of all the knowledge he had accumulated as a quiet monk before starting his preaching career.

A golden angel—the weathervane atop the spire—points her

St. Anthony of Padua (1195-1231)

One of Christendom's most popular saints, Anthony is known as a powerful speaker, a miracle worker, and the finder of lost articles.

Born in Lisbon to a rich, well-educated family, his life changed at age 25, when he saw the mutilated bodies of some Franciscan martyrs. Their sacrifice inspired him to join the poor Franciscans and dedicate his life to Christ. He moved to Italy and lived in a cave, studying, meditating, and barely speaking to anyone.

One day, he joined his fellow monks for a service. The appointed speaker failed to show up, so Anthony was asked to say a few off-the-cuff words to the crowd. He started slowly, but, filled with the Spirit, he became more confident and amazed the audience with his eloquence. Up in Assisi, St. Francis heard about Anthony and sent him on a whirlwind speaking tour.

Anthony had a strong voice, he knew several languages, had an encyclopedic knowledge of theology, and could speak spontaneously as the Spirit moved him. It's said that he even stood on the shores of the Adriatic Sea in Rimini and enticed a school of fish to listen. Anthony also was known as a prolific miracle worker.

In 1230, Anthony retired to Padua, where he founded a monastery and initiated reforms for the poor. An illness cut his life short at age 36. Anthony said, "Happy is the man whose words issue from the Spirit and not from himself!"

trumpet into the wind. (While you can never really be sure with angels, locals say they know it's a woman because she always tells the truth.)

Guarding the church is Donatello's life-size equestrian statue of the Venetian mercenary general, Gattamelata. Though it looks like a thousand other man-on-a-horse statues, it was a landmark in Italy's budding Renaissance—the first life-size, secular, equestrian statue cast from bronze in a thousand years.

The church is technically outside of Italy. When you pass the banisters that mark its property line, you're passing into Vatican territory.

• *Enter the basilica.*

Interior

Grab a pew in the center of the nave and let your eyes adjust. Sit and appreciate the space. Gaze past the crowds and through the incense haze to Donatello's glorious crucifix rising from the altar, and realize that this is one of the most important pilgrimage sites in Christendom.

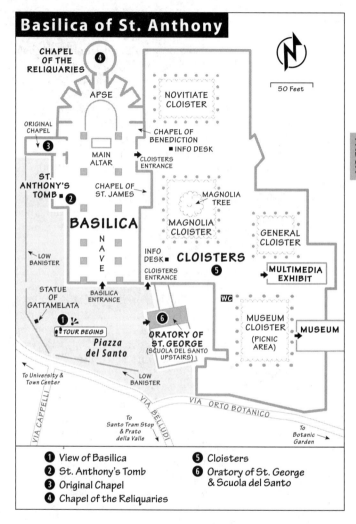

Basilica of St. Anthony

CHAPEL OF THE RELIQUARIES ④

APSE

NOVITIATE CLOISTER

50 Feet

ORIGINAL CHAPEL ③

CHAPEL OF BENEDICTION
■ INFO DESK

MAIN ALTAR

CLOISTERS ENTRANCE

ST. ANTHONY'S TOMB ■ ②

CHAPEL OF ST. JAMES

MAGNOLIA TREE

BASILICA

NAVE

MAGNOLIA CLOISTER

GENERAL CLOISTER

LOW BANISTER

INFO DESK ■

CLOISTERS ⑤

MULTIMEDIA EXHIBIT

CLOISTERS ENTRANCE

STATUE OF GATTAMELATA

BASILICA ENTRANCE

WC

MUSEUM CLOISTER (PICNIC AREA)

MUSEUM ➜

① TOUR BEGINS

⑥

Piazza del Santo

ORATORY OF ST. GEORGE
(SCUOLA DEL SANTO UPSTAIRS)

To University & Town Center

LOW BANISTER

VIA CAPPELLI

VIA BELLUDI

VIA ORTO BOTANICO

To Santo Tram Stop & Prato della Valle

To Botanic Garden ➜

① View of Basilica
② St. Anthony's Tomb
③ Original Chapel
④ Chapel of the Reliquaries

⑤ Cloisters
⑥ Oratory of St. George & Scuola del Santo

PADUA

Along with the crucifix, Donatello's bronze statues—Mary with Padua's six favorite saints—grace the high altar. Late in his career, the great Florentine sculptor spent more than a decade in Padua (1444-1455), creating the altar and Gattamelata.

• *Head to the left side of the nave to find the gleaming marble masterpiece that is the focus of the visiting pilgrims—the tomb of St. Anthony.*

St. Anthony's Tomb

Pilgrims file slowly through this side chapel around the tomb, so focused on the saint that they hardly notice the nine fine marble reliefs. (While the long queue looks intimidating, these folks are just waiting their turn to touch the tomb; you can easily skirt around the side of this group for a closer look at each panel.) These Renaissance masterpieces were carved during the 16th century, and show scenes and miracles from the life of the saint. As you enjoy each scene, notice the Renaissance mastery of realism and 3-D perspective and the intricate frames, which celebrate life with a burst of exuberance. Note also the vivid faces with their powerful emotions.

First Relief: This depicts St. Anthony receiving the Franciscan tunic. The architectural setting (such as the perspective of the arches on the left and the open door) illustrates the new ability to show depth by using mathematics. The cityscape above is Padua in about 1500.

Second Relief: A jealous husband has angrily stabbed his wife. Notice the musculature, the emotion, and the determination in the faces of loved ones. Above, Anthony intercedes with God to bring the woman back to life.

Third Relief: This panel shows Anthony bringing a young man back to life. Above is the Palazzo della Ragione looking as it still does today.

Fourth Relief: This scene, by the famous Florentine sculptor Jacopo Sansovino, shows three generations: a dead girl, her distraught mom, and a grandmother who's seen it all. A boy on the right realistically leans on his stick. Of course, Anthony will eventually change the mood, but right now it's pretty dire. Above is a relief of this basilica.

Fifth Relief: A fisherman holds a net, sadly having retrieved a drowned boy. The mother looks at Anthony, who blesses and revives the boy. Across from here is the saint's actual tomb. Under thoughtful lighting, it reads *Corpus S. Antonii.* Prayer letters are dropped behind the iron grill.

Sixth Relief: This shows "the miracle of the miser's heart." Anthony's helper dips his hand into a moneylender's side to demonstrate the absence of his heart. At his foot, the square tray with coins and a heart illustrates the scriptural verse "for where your treasure is, there your heart will be also."

Seventh Relief: Anthony holds the foot of a young man who confessed to kicking his mother. Taking a lesson from the saint about respecting your mother a little too literally, the man had cut off his own foot. The hysterical mother implores Anthony's help, and the saint's prayers to God enabled him to reattach the foot.

Stand in the corner for a moment, observing the passionate devotion that pilgrims and Paduans alike have for Anthony. Touching his tomb or kneeling in prayer, the faithful believe Anthony is their protector—a confidant and intercessor for the poor. And they believe he works miracles. Believers leave offerings, votives, and written prayers to ask for help or to give thanks for miracles they believe Anthony has performed. By putting their hands on his tomb while saying silent prayers, pilgrims show devotion to Anthony and feel the saint's presence.

Popular Anthony is the patron saint of dozens of things: travelers, amputees, donkeys, pregnant women, infertile women, and flight attendants. Most pilgrims ask for his help in his role as the "finder of things"—from lost car keys to a life companion. You'll see dozens of photos posted on his tomb in prayer or as thanks, including many of fervently wished-for newborns.

Eighth Relief: This scene makes the point that—unlike St. Francis, who was a rowdy youth—Anthony was holy even as a toddler. He tosses the glass (representing his faith), which, rather than shattering, breaks the marble floor.

Ninth Relief: A jealous husband (the bearded man behind Anthony) accuses his wife of cheating. The wife asks Anthony to identify her baby's father. Anthony asks the child, who speaks and says that the husband is his real dad and his mother was not messing around. Everyone is relieved—whew!

Before leaving, stand in the corner and take a moment to appreciate how the entire chapel is an integrated artistic wonder.

• *Leave the chapel (between scenes eight and nine) and step into the oldest part of the church. This is the...*

Original Chapel

This is where Anthony was first buried in 1231. To the left of the altar, note the fine (and impressively realistic for the 14th century) view of medieval Padua, with this church outside the wall (finished by 1300 and looking like it does today). Below the cityscape, in a circa-1380 fresco, Anthony on his cloud promises he'll watch over Padua.

As you exit this chapel, you'll notice many tombs nearby. People wanted to be buried near a saint. If you could afford it, this was about the best piece of real estate a dead person could want. (The practice was ended with Napoleonic reforms in 1806.)

• *Continue your circuit of the church by going behind the altar into the apse, to the Chapel of the Reliquaries. (At busy times, you may have to line up and trudge slowly up the stairs past the reliquaries.)*

Chapel of the Reliquaries

The most prized relic is in the glass case at center stage—Anthony's tongue. When Anthony's remains were exhumed 32 years after his death (in 1263), his body had decayed to dust, but his tongue was found miraculously unspoiled and red in color. How appropriate for the great preacher who, full of the Spirit, couldn't stop talking about God.

Entering the chapel, join the parade of pilgrims working their way clockwise around the chapel and up the stairs. First, on the left, look for the red, triangular vestment in which Anthony's body was wrapped. Next is his rough-hewn wood coffin. Then, up the stairs, is his pillow—a comfy rock (chest level in first glass case). The center display case contains (top to bottom) the saint's lower jaw with all his teeth impressively intact *(il mento,* located about 8 feet high), his uncorrupted tongue *(lingua,* at about eye level), and, finally, his vocal chords *(apparato vocale,* at about waist level) discovered intact when his remains were examined in 1981. In the last display case, a fragment of the True Cross *(la croce)* is held in a precious cross-shaped reliquary. Finally, descend the stairs and pass St. Anthony's holy, and holey, tunic *(tonaca).*

Above the relics, decorating the cornice, is the *Glorification of St. Anthony.* In this Baroque fantasy—made in 1691 of carved marble and stucco, a cloud of angels and giddy *putti* tumble to the left and right in jubilation as they play their Baroque-era musical instruments to celebrate Anthony's arrival in heaven.

• *Leaving this relic chapel, continue circling the apse. You'll come to the* **Chapel of Benediction.** *Here, under a powerful modern fresco of the Crucifixion (by Pietro Annigoni, who died in 1982), a priest is waiting to bless anyone who cares to be blessed.*

Next, past the sacristy (where you can peek in at priests preparing for Mass), is a door leading to the cloisters. But before heading out, walk just beyond this passage to the...

Chapel of St. James

Exactly opposite the tomb of St. Anthony, this chapel features an exquisite 14th-century fresco by Altichiero da Zevio. Study the vivid commotion around the Crucifixion, clearly inspired by Giotto (this was created 70 years after the Scrovegni Chapel). The faces are real—right off the streets of 14th-century Padua.

• *Next, head out into the cloisters. From the right side of the nave as you face the altar, follow signs to* chiostro; *from outside, find signs on the right side of the church.*

Cloisters

The main cloister is dominated by an exceptionally bushy magnolia tree, planted in 1810 (the magnolia tree was exotic for Europe when it was imported from America in 1760). Also in the cloister are the graves of the most illustrious Paduans, such as Gabriel Fallopius, the scientist who gave his name to his discovery, the Fallopian tube. When Napoleon decreed that graves should be moved out of cities, this once grave-covered courtyard was cleared of tombstones. But the bodies were left in the ground, perhaps contributing to the magnolia tree's fecundity. Today the tree remains an explosion of life.

Wander around the series of three cloisters. Picnic tables invite pilgrims and tourists to enjoy meals within the solitude of one of the cloisters (it's covered and suitable even when rainy, also has WCs).

The **multimedia exhibit** on the life of St. Anthony is kitschy, as pilgrimage multimedia exhibits tend to be (30 minutes, free, you move three times as you use headphones to listen to the story of each tableau).

At the far end, a fascinating little **museum** is filled with votives and folk art recounting miracles attributed to Anthony. The abbreviation *PGR* that you'll see on many votives stands for *per grazia ricevuta*—for answered prayers.

Oratory of St. George and Scuola del Santo

The small but sumptuous **Oratory of St. George** faces the little square in front of the basilica. The oratory ("ora" means prayer) is not actually a church, though it's certainly a fine place to pray—it's filled with vivid, circa-1370 frescoes showing scenes not of Anthony, but from the life of St. Catherine. Because many lovers credit St. Anthony with finding them their partners—and this is the closest place to St. Anthony where you can be married—it's popular for weddings. While you can see it all from the door, paying the entry fee lets you sit and enjoy this peaceful spot.

Next door and upstairs (buy ticket and get info sheet in the oratory) is the skippable **Scuola del Santo** (a.k.a. La Scoletta), the former meeting hall of the Confraternity of Anthony, with frescoes and paintings by various artists—including some by Titian.

Near the Basilica

Prato della Valle

The square is 150 yards southwest of the basilica (down Via Luca Belludi). Once a Roman theater and later Anthony's preaching grounds, this square claims to be the largest in Italy. It's a pleasant, 400-yard-long, oval-shaped piazza with fountains, walkways, dozens of statues of

Padua's eminent citizens, and grass. It's also a lively **market** scene: fruit and vegetables (Mon-Fri 8:00-13:00), clothing, shoes, and household goods (Sat 8:00-19:00), and antiques (third Sun 8:00-

19:00). This place is often busy with special events and festivals. Ask at the TI or your hotel if anything's going on at Prato della Valle.

Botanic Garden (Orto Botanico)
Green thumbs appreciate this nearly five-acre botanical garden, which contains the university's vast collection of rare plants. Founded in 1545 to cultivate medicinal plants, it's the world's oldest academic botanical garden still in its original location. A visitors center—in a little cottage to the right of the garden's entrance—houses models of the garden's layout and computer terminals that describe the history and composition of the garden in English.

Cost and Hours: Garden—€5; April-Oct Mon-Sat 9:00-19:00, Sun 10:00-19:00; Nov-Feb Mon-Sat 9:00-15:00, closed Sun; March Mon-Sat 9:00-15:00, Sun 10:00-16:00; entrance 150 yards south of Basilica of St. Anthony—with your back to the facade, take a hard left; Santo tram stop, tel. 049-827-2119, www.ortobotanico.unipd.it.

Sleeping in Padua

Rooms in Padua's hotels are more spacious and a better value than those in Venice. Keep in mind that when large conventions take over the town—several times a year—all hotels raise prices. Generally, prices are very flexible and are often lower than what I've written here; check hotel websites for *offerti* (specials). I've listed two hotels in the center and a group of accommodations near the basilica. All are reachable from the station by the tram; only Albergo Verdi is more than a five-minute walk from the nearest tram stop.

In the Center
$$$ Hotel Majestic Toscanelli, an old-fashioned, borderline-gaudy, family-run, 34-room hotel, owns a perfectly convenient location right in the town center—buried in the characteristic ghetto with wonderful cobbled ambience. At night, this area is popular with noisy students; request a quiet room on the back side (Sb-€95-110 depending on size, Db-€149, ask for 10 percent Rick Steves discount, book direct for the best rates, check their website for routine special discounts, spacious attic "loft" rooms with kitchenettes and low beams, air-con, elevator, free Wi-Fi, parking-€12/day for Rick Steves readers, Via dell'Arco 2, Tito Livio tram stop, tel. 049-663-244, www.toscanelli.com, majestic@toscanelli.com, Mario Morosi and family). From the tram stop, follow the passageway next to #26, then jog left down Via Marsala and turn right on Via dell'Arco.

$$ Albergo Verdi, an Ikea-mod little place, is crammed into

Sleep Code

(€1 = about $1.30, country code: 39)
S = Single, **D** = Double/Twin, **T** = Triple, **Q** = Quad, **b** = bathroom,
s = shower only. Unless otherwise noted, credit cards are accepted, breakfast is included, and English is spoken. Padua levies a hotel tax of about €2 per person, per night, which must be paid in cash (not included in the rates I've quoted).

To help you easily sort through these listings, I've divided the accommodations into three categories based on the price for a standard double room with bath:

$$$ **Higher Priced**—Most rooms €125 or more.
$$ **Moderately Priced**—Most rooms between €90-125.
$ **Lower Priced**—Most rooms €90 or less.

Prices can change without notice; verify the hotel's current rates online or by email. For the best prices, always book direct.

an old building on a small back street beyond Piazza dei Signori. While public spaces are tight, the 14 rooms are comfortable (Sb-€80, Db-€110, extra person-€30, air-con, tiny elevator, free guest computer, free Wi-Fi, Via Dondi dall'Orologio 7, Ponti Romani tram stop, tel. 049-836-4163, www.albergoverdipadova.it, info@ albergoverdipadova.it). From Piazza dei Signori, walk through the arch under the clock tower and go to the far end of Piazza del Capitaniato; the hotel is on the side street to your right.

Near Basilica of St. Anthony

Santo is the nearest tram stop for the following hotels. Use the Prato della Valle tram stop for the hostel.

$$ Hotel Al Fagiano feels like an art gallery with crazy, sexy, modern art everywhere. The hotel is all about the union of a man and a woman (quite romantic). They rent 40 bright and cheery air-conditioned rooms, each uniquely decorated with Rossella Fagiano's canvases (Sb-€64, Db-€100, Tb-€115, 10 percent Rick Steves discount if you book direct, €7/person less without breakfast, air-con, elevator, free Wi-Fi, parking-€10/day, 50 yards from the Santo tram stop at Via Locatelli 45, tel. 049-875-3396, www. alfagiano.com, info@alfagiano.com; Anita, artist Rossella, and husband Amato).

$$ Hotel Belludi 37 is a slick, stylish, borderline-pretentious place renting 15 modern rooms shoehorned into an old building. The decor is dark, woody, and fresh (S-€57, Sb-€80, Db-€125, bigger Db-€145, ask for 10 percent Rick Steves discount, €7/person less without breakfast, air-con, lots of stairs with no elevator, free Wi-Fi, a block from the Santo tram stop at Via Beato Luca Belludi 37, tel. 049-665-633, www.belludi37.it, info@belludi37.it).

$ Hotel Al Santo, run with charm by Valentina and Antonio, offers 15 spacious rooms with all the comforts on two floors above their restaurant, a few steps from the basilica. Given the warm welcome and pleasant location, it's a fine value (Sb-€60, Db-€85, Tb-€110, Qb-€130, double-paned windows, quieter rooms off street, some rooms have views of basilica, air-con, elevator, free Wi-Fi, parking-€14/day, Via del Santo 147, tel. 049-875-2131, www.al-santo.it, alsanto@alsanto.it).

$ Hotel Casa del Pellegrino, with 147 spotless, cheap, institutional rooms and straight pricing, is owned by the friars of St. Anthony. It's home to the pilgrims who come to pay homage to the saint in the basilica next door. Any visitor to Padua is welcome, making it popular with professors and students. "Superior" rooms cost €5 extra; some of these are regular rooms with basilica views (but these also come with more noise—both from the street, and starting at 6:00 in the morning, the church bells), while others are in *dipendenza,* the hotel's modern wing (S-€44, Sb-€59, D-€58, Db-€71, Tb-€85, Qb-€100, Quint/b-€110, ask for a room off the street, breakfast-€5, air-con, elevator, free Wi-Fi, parking-€5/day, Via Cesarotti 21, tel. 049-823-9711, www.casadelpellegrino.com, info@casadelpellegrino.com).

Hostel: **$ Ostello Città di Padova,** near Prato della Valle, is well-run and has 90 beds in 6-bed rooms (beds with sheets and breakfast-€19, family rooms-€88, free Wi-Fi, laundry-€5.50/load, lockers, reception open 7:00-9:30 & 15:30-23:00, rooms locked during afternoon but reception staffed if you need to leave bags, 23:30 curfew, Via Aleardi 30, Prato de Valle tram stop, tel. 049-875-2219, www.ostellopadova.it, ostellopadova@ctgveneto.it). From the tram stop, exit the square ahead of you to the right and make an immediate left down Via Memmo; after the church, continue straight one block on Via Torresini and turn right on Via Aleardi.

Eating in Padua

The university population means cheap, good food abounds. My recommended restaurants are all centrally located in the historic core. You'd think there would be fine dining on the charming market squares, but on the piazzas it's a take-out-pizza-and-casual-bar scene (dominated by students after dark). La Lanterna, at the neighboring Piazza dei Signori, is the best on-square option—but they only offer functional Italian classics. The dreamily atmospheric ghetto neighborhood (just two blocks off the market squares) thrives after dark with trendy bars and a lively student *spritz* scene.

Dining near the Center

Osteria dei Fabbri, with shared rustic tables, offers a good mix of class and accessibility, quality, and price. The dining room is spacious, and the dishes are traditional Venetian and Paduan. Ask to peek into their back courtyard, where you can see the door of an old synagogue (€9 pastas, €15-17 *secondi,* Mon-Sat 12:30-14:30 & 19:30-22:30, closed Sun except sometimes open for lunch in the springtime, Via dei Fabbri 13, on a side street on south side of Piazza Erbe, tel. 049-650-336).

Osteria L'Anfora is a classic place serving classic dishes in an informal, fun-loving space. Don't be put off by the woody, ruffian decor and the fact that it's a popular hangout for a pre-meal drink. They take food seriously and serve it at good prices, and the energy and commotion add to a great dining experience (€8-10 pastas, €14-16 *secondi,* meals served Mon-Sat 12:30-15:00 & 19:30-22:30, closed Sun, reservations smart for dinner, Via dei Soncin 13, tel. 049-656-629).

Enoteca dei Tadi is a small place with seven tables filling a cozy back room behind a convivial little bar (avoid their basement). Roberta and Anna serve traditional Paduan dishes and have earned a local following for their small but tasty menu. The selection is driven by what's fresh and in season, and they offer good wines by the glass (€7-10 dishes, Tue-Sun 18:00-24:00, closed Mon, Via dei Tadi 16, mobile 338-408-3434).

Ristorante Dante alle Piazze is a respected fixture in town for its dressy white-tablecloth dining. They are passionate about their meat and fish dishes. Reservations are smart at night (€9-11 pastas, €16-18 *secondi,* Tue-Sat 12:00-15:00 & 18:30-24:00, Sun 12:00-15:00, closed Mon, Via Daniele Manin 8, tel. 049-836-0973, www.dadantealle piazze.com).

Cheap Eats near the Center

Affordable Meals in Padua's Living Room, Piazza dei Signori: **La Lanterna** has a forgettable interior and a predictable menu of pizzas, pastas, and *secondi.* But its prime location on Piazza dei Signori provides a rare-in-Padua chance to sit in a grand square under the stars, surrounded by great architecture. Its pizzas are a local favorite—takeaway available—and reservations are recommended (€6-9 pizzas, €8-11 pastas, €15-20 *secondi,* Fri-Wed 12:00-14:30 & 18:00-24:00, closed Thu, Piazza dei Signori 39, tel. 049-660-770, www.lalanternapadova.it).

PADUA

Light Local Meals on Piazza della Frutta: **Bar dei Osei,** on Piazza della Frutta, is a very simple sandwich bar with some of the best outdoor seats in town. While Paduans love their delicate *tramezzini*—white bread sandwiches with crusts cut off (€1.50/€1.80 with table service), I'd choose their *porchetta*—savory roasted pork sandwiches (€3.50/€3.80). You'll find a two-foot-long mother lode waiting on the counter for you; tell friendly Marco how big a slice you'd like. Wines are listed on the board (Mon-Sat 7:00-21:00, closed Sun, Piazza della Frutta 1, tel. 049-875-9606). In the evenings, just a few feet away, a typical **snack stand** selling all kinds of fresh, hot, and ready-to-eat seafood appetizers sets up between 17:00 and 20:30 (daily except Sun). Belly up to the bar with your drink and try whatever Massimiliano's serving.

Fast Food: **Brek,** with one entrance next to the Ponti Romani tram stop and another tucked into a corner of Piazza Cavour at #20, is an easy self-service chain *ristorante* with healthy and affordable choices. It's big, bright, practical, and family-friendly (€4-7 pastas, €5-9 *secondi,* daily 11:30-15:00 & 18:30-22:00, tel. 049-875-3788). **Brek Foccacceria** (part of the same chain), across from Caffè Pedrocchi and next door to the PAM supermarket, is a café selling big €3-5 sandwiches and slices of pizza that you can eat at outdoor tables. During happy hour (18:30-20:30), you can buy a drink and pay €1 more to fill a plate at their *antipasti* buffet, which can easily turn into a light dinner (open daily 8:00-22:00, Piazzetta della Garzeria 6, tel. 049-876-1651).

Groceries: Stock up on picnic items at the outdoor markets, or visit the **PAM supermarket,** in the tiny *piazzetta* east of Caffè Pedrocchi (Mon-Sat 8:00-21:00, Sun 9:00-19:00, Piazzetta Garzeria 3).

Gelato: If eating dinner out, consider skipping dessert and instead licking a gelato while strolling the wonderful streets and piazzas of Padua. My favorite *gelateria* is **Gelato Pretto,** the creation of Michelin three-star chefs who wanted to bring gourmet to gelato. Their exclusive taste creations cost a bit more than the already expensive standard flavors. Ask for several tastes before choosing your favorite (daily 12:00-23:00, Via Umberto 1, tel. 049-875-0776). **Grom** is also popular for its unusual flavors and exotic ingredients. While it's tasty, organic, and green, it's also part of a big chain—the Starbucks of Italian gelato joints (two locations: Via Roma 101, tel. 049-876-4262; and Piazza dei Signori 33, tel. 049-875-4373).

Near the Basilica of St. Anthony

Antica Trattoria dei Paccagnella, the most serious restaurant near the basilica, serves up nicely presented, seasonal local dishes with modern flair and an impressive attention to ingredients. The place has friendly service, modern art on the walls, and no pretense. It's thoughtfully run by two brothers, Raffaele and Cesare, who happily explain why they are so excited about local hen (€8-10 pastas, €13-18 *secondi*, daily 12:00-14:30 & 19:00-22:00, Via del Santo 113, tel. 049-875-0549).

Pizzeria Pago Pago dishes up wood-fired Neapolitan pizzas (a local favorite) and daily specials depending on what's in season. Get there early for dinner or wait (€5-8 pizzas, €9 salads, Wed-Mon 12:00-14:00 & 19:00-24:00, closed Tue; 2 blocks from Basilica of St. Anthony, up Via del Santo and right onto Via Galileo Galilei to #59; tel. 049-665-558, Gaetano and Modesto).

Casa del Pellegrino Ristorante caters to St. Anthony pilgrims with simple, basic, and hearty meals, served in a cheery dining room just north of the basilica (€5-8 pastas, €9-10 *secondi*, €15 fixed-price meal, €2 cover, daily 12:00-14:00 & 19:30-21:30, Via Cesarotti 21, tel. 049-876-0715).

Zairo is a huge indoor/outdoor *ristorante*/pizzeria with reasonable prices, delicious homemade pastas, Veneto specialties, snappy service, and a local clientele. As it's next to the vast and inviting Prato della Valle square/park, consider combining dinner here with a relaxing stroll through the park (€5-10 pizzas, €7-8 pastas, €9-16 *secondi*, Tue-Sun 11:30-15:00 & 19:00-24:00, closed Mon, east side of Prato della Valle at #51, tel. 049-663-803).

Pollodoro la Gastronomica, my pick of the take-out delis near the basilica, sells roast chicken, pastas, pizza, and veggies. They'll also make sandwiches (Wed-Sat and Mon 8:30-20:00, Sun 8:30-14:00 only, closed Tue, 100 yards from basilica at Via Belludi 34, tel. 049-663-718). You can picnic at the nearby cloisters of the basilica.

Padua Connections

From Padua by Train to: Venice (at least 2/hour, 30-50 minutes), **Vicenza** (at least 2/hour, fewer on weekends, 15-25 minutes), **Milan** (1-2/hour, 2-3 hours), **Verona** (at least 2/hour, 40-60 minutes), **Ravenna** (roughly hourly, change in Bologna or Ferrara, 2.5-3.5 hours).

Note that the departures listed above are operated by Trenitalia; a competing private rail company called Italo offers additional high-speed connections to major cities (including **Venice, Bologna, Florence,** and **Rome**). While Italo is often cheaper (particularly if you book long in advance), it doesn't accept railpasses (for details on Italo, see page 435 or visit www.italotreno.it).

By Bus to: Venice (45 minutes, hourly at :25 past the hour from 5:25 to 20:25), and Venice's **Marco Polo Airport** (65 minutes, €8, €10 if bought on board, buses depart at :25 past each hour from platform 11 at Padua's bus station, next to the train station; recheck times at www.fsbusitalia.it). If flying into the airport, take this bus to get directly to Padua (buy tickets at windows in arrivals hall or at airport TI).

By Minibus to Airports: A minibus service runs from Padua to **Marco Polo Airport** (€32/person) or **Treviso Airport** (€41/person), reservations required, tel. 049-870-4425, www.airservicepadova.it).

Near Padua: Vicenza

To many architects, Vicenza (vih-CHEHN-zah) is a pilgrimage site. Entire streets look like the back of a nickel. This is the city of Andrea Palladio (1508-1580), the 16th-century Renaissance architect who defined the Palladian style that is now so influential in countless British country homes. But as grandiose as Vicenza's Palladian facades may feel, there is little marble here because the city lacked the wealth to build with much more than painted wood and plaster.

If you're an architecture buff, Vicenza merits a quick day trip on any day but Monday, when major sights are closed. If you're packing light, it's an easy stop, located on the same train line as Padua, Verona, and Venice. However, because you can't store bags at the train station, it's not worth stopping here if you have lots of luggage.

Tourist Information: The TI is next to the Olympic Theater at Piazza Matteotti 12 (daily 9:00-13:30 & 14:00-17:30, tel. 0444-320-854, www.visitvicenza.org). Ask for the free brochure on Palladio's buildings. Architecture fans appreciate the €2.50 *Vicenza and the Villas of Andrea Palladio.*

Arrival in Vicenza: From the **train station,** I'd head straight for the most distant sight, the Olympic Theater (with a TI next door), and then see other sights on the way back. Go straight out the train station's front door, and use the crosswalk on the right side of the roundabout. From here, it's a five-minute walk straight ahead up wide Viale Roma to the PAM supermarket at the bottom of Corso Palladio; turn right through the gate, and then it's a good 10 minutes more down the Corso to the Olympic Theater (a taxi costs €8). **Drivers** can park in one of the cheap parking lots (Parcheggio Bassano and Parcheggio Cricoli) and catch a free shuttle bus to the center.

Helpful Hints: All of the sights mentioned (except the villas

outside of town) are covered by the **Museum Card** combo-ticket (€10, €14 family pass, good for 3 days, sold at Olympic Theater and Palazzo Leoni Montanari). In a pinch, the TI may be willing to store bags for you while you walk around town.

Sights in Vicenza

Helpful bilingual signs in front of Palladio's buildings explain their history. Arrows around town point you to his major works, and you can also pick up a map from the TI.

▲▲Olympic Theater (Teatro Olimpico)

Palladio's last work, one of his greatest, shouldn't be missed. This indoor theater is a wood-and-stucco festival of classical columns, statues, and an oh-wow stage bursting with perspective tricks. When you step back outside, take another look at the town's main drag—named after Palladio. It's the same main street you saw on the stage of his theater.

Cost and Hours: Entry only with €10 Museum Card, which also covers other Vicenza sights; Tue-Sun 9:00-17:00, closed Mon, last entry 30 minutes before closing, very occasionally closed when theater is in use, audioguide available, entrance to left of TI at Piazza Matteotti 11, tel. 0444-222-800, www.olimpicovicenza.it.

▲Church of Santa Corona and Diocesan Museum

A block away from the Olympic Theater, this "Church of the Holy Crown" was built in the 13th century to house a thorn from the Crown of Thorns, given to the Bishop of Vicenza by the French King Louis IX. The church has two artistic highlights: the art embellishing its high altar and Giovanni Bellini's fine painting, *Baptism of Christ*.

Cost and Hours: €5, Tue-Sun 9:00-12:00 & 15:00-18:00, closed Mon, Piazza Duomo 12, tel. 0444-226-400, www.museodiocesanovicenza.it.

Archaeological and Natural History Museum

Located next door to the Church of Santa Corona, this museum's ground floor features Roman antiquities (mosaics, statues, and artifacts excavated from Rome's Baths of Caracalla, plus swords) and a barbarian warrior skeleton complete with sword and helmet. Prehistoric scraps are upstairs. Look for English description sheets near exhibit entryways throughout.

Cost and Hours: Covered by Museum Card, Tue-Sun 9:00-17:00, closed Mon, Contrà Santa Corona 4, tel. 0444-222-815, www.museicivicivicenza.it.

Palazzo Leoni Montanari

Across the street from the Church of Santa Corona, this small museum is a palatial riot of Baroque, with cherub-cluttered ceilings jumbled like a preschool in heaven. A quick stroll shows off Venetian paintings and a floor of Russian icons.

Cost and Hours: €5, Tue-Sun 10:00-18:00, closed Mon, last entry 30 minutes before closing, Contrà Santa Corona 25, tel. 800-578-875, www.palazzomontanari.com.

Piazza dei Signori

Vicenza's main square has been the center of town ever since it was the site of the ancient Roman forum. The commanding **Basilica Palladiana,** with its 270-foot-tall, 13th-century tower, dominates the square. This was once the meeting place for local big shots. It was young Palladio's proposal—to redo Vicenza's dilapidated Gothic palace of justice in the Neo-Greek style—that established him as the city's favorite architect. The rest of Palladio's career was a one-man construction boom. The basilica hosts special exhibitions that sometimes involve a fee, but you can often pop in for a free look.

Villas on the Outskirts of Vicenza

Vicenza is surrounded by dreamy Venetian villas. Venice's commercial empire receded in the 1500s when trade began to pick up along the Atlantic seaboard and dwindle in the Mediterranean. Venice redirected its economic agenda to agribusiness, which led to the construction of lavish country villas, such as **Villa la Rotonda,** the inspiration for Thomas Jefferson's Monticello (www.villalarotonda.it) and **Villa Valmarana ai Nani** (www.villavalmarana.com). Located southeast of the town center, both houses are furnished with period pieces and come with good English descriptions (closed Mon). Pick up the free English brochure on Palladio's villas from the TI if you plan to visit.

Vicenza Connections

From Vicenza by Train to: Venice (at least 2/hour, 45-75 minutes), **Padua** (at least 2/hour, fewer on weekends, 15-25 minutes), **Verona** (at least 2/hour, 25-60 minutes), **Milan** (1-2/hour, 1.75-2 hours). Unless you crave speed or need to burn a railpass day, you'll save a lot of money by taking the slow *R* trains to Vicenza instead of the fast *Freccia* trains.

VERONA

Romeo and Juliet made Verona a household word. Alas, a visit here has nothing to do with those two star-crossed lovers. You can pay to visit the house that falsely claims to be Juliet's (with an almost believable balcony and a courtyard swarming with tour groups), join in the tradition of rubbing the breast of Juliet's statue to help find a lover (or to pick up the sweat of someone who can't), and even make a pilgrimage to what isn't "La Tomba di Giulietta."

Fiction aside, Verona has been an important crossroads for 2,000 years and is, therefore, packed with genuine history. R&J fans will take some solace in the fact that two real feuding families, the Montecchi and the Cappellos, were the models for Shakespeare's Montagues and Capulets. And, if R&J had existed and were alive today, they would still recognize much of their "hometown."

Verona's main attractions are its wealth of Roman ruins; the remnants of its 13th- and 14th-century political and cultural boom brought about by its leading family, the Scaligeri; its 21st-century, pedestrian-only ambience; and its world-class opera festival, held each summer. After Venice's festival of tourism, the Veneto region's second city is a cool and welcome sip of pure Italy, where dumpsters are painted by schoolchildren as class projects and public spaces are primarily the domain of locals, not tourists. If you like Italy but don't need blockbuster sights, this town is a joy.

Orientation to Verona

Verona's old town fills an easy-to-defend bend in the River Adige. The vibrant and enjoyable core of Verona lies along Via Mazzini between Piazza Brà (pronounced "bra") and Piazza Erbe, Verona's market square since Roman times. Each evening the two main streets from Piazza Brà to Piazza Erbe, Via Mazzini and Corso Porta Borsari, are enlivened by a wonderful *passeggiata*...bustling with a slow and elegant parade of strollers. For a good day trip to Verona, take my self-guided walk, beginning with a visit to the Roman Arena.

Tourist Information

Verona's helpful TI is just off **Piazza Brà**—from the square, head to the big yellow building with columns and cross the street to Via degli Alpini 9 (Feb-Nov Mon-Sat 9:00-19:00, Dec-Jan Mon-Sat 9:00-18:00; Sun 10:00-16:00 year-round; tel. 045-806-8680, www.tourism.verona.it). Pick up the free city map and confirm the walking-tour schedule.

Verona Card: This tourist card covers entrance to all the recommended Verona sights (€15/2 days, €20/5 days, sold at the TI and at participating sights). If you visit the Roman Arena (€6), climb Torre dei Lamberti (€6), explore Castelvecchio (€6), and tour two churches (€5), you'll pay €23. At €15, the card saves day-trippers intent on blitzing the city almost a third off their sightseeing costs. (However, the card does not cover city transportation, nor does it include the expensive ArenaMuseOpera museum.)

The €6 **Church Card,** sold at four churches that require admission (San Zeno, Duomo, Sant'Anastasia, and San Fermo, normally €2.50 each), pays off if you visit three (www.chieseverona.it). There's no need to get both tourist cards.

If you're staying the night, ask the TI about concerts, or stop by a newsstand to pick up the €2 monthly entertainment guide, *Carnet Verona*.

Arrival in Verona

By Train: Verona's main train station is called Verona Porta Nuova. In the main hall, you'll find WCs (€0.80) and a baggage check office (€5/5 hours, €12.50/24 hours, daily 8:00-20:00). Buses and taxis are immediately outside.

Avoid the boring 15-minute walk from the station to Piazza Brà. Buses are cheap, easy, and leave every few minutes. Buy a ticket from the tobacco shop inside the station (€1.30/90 minutes, €4 day pass valid until midnight), or buy one from the driver for €0.20 more. Leaving the station, angle right across the street to the bus stalls, find platform A, and hop on a bus: #11, #12, and #13 run Monday-Saturday before 20:00; #90, #92, and #98 run after 20:00 and all day Sunday; and #510 runs daily, even after 20:00. If in doubt, confirm that your bus is headed to the city center by asking, *"Per il centro?"* (pehr eel CHEN-troh). Validate your ticket by stamping it in the machine on the bus.

Drivers don't announce stops, but you'll know Piazza Brà because of the mass exodus and the can't-miss-it Roman Arena (bus stops in front of big, yellow, Neoclassical building). The TI is just a few steps beyond the bus stop, against the medieval wall. You can catch return buses to the station (same numbers) from the stop on the piazza side of the street, or from another bus stop just outside the city wall on Corso Porta Nuova (on the right, in front of Mc-Donald's).

Taxis pick up only at taxi stands (at Piazza Brà, Piazza Erbe, and the train station) and cost about €8 for the quick ride between the train station and the center of town (€3 more on Sundays and after 22:00, €1/big bag).

If you're in downtown Verona and need train tickets or reservations, drop by World Travel (see "Helpful Hints," below).

By Car: The old town center (where nearly all my recommended hotels are located) is closed to traffic. Your hotel can get you permission to drive in—ask when you book. Otherwise your license plate will be photographed, and a €100 ticket might be waiting in the mail when you get home.

Drivers will find reasonably priced parking in well-marked lots and garages just outside the center. The underground **Cittadella garage,** at Piazza Cittadella (a block off Piazza Brà, behind the TI), is huge, convenient, and easy to find (€2/hour, €15/24 hours). The lot in front of the **train station** costs less (€8.50/24 hours), but you'll spend your savings on the bus to the center. The **Città di Nimes** parking lot (a 5-minute walk from the train station, near the wall) costs €5/day. **Street parking** is limited to two hours and costs €1/hour (spaces marked with blue lines, buy ticket at a tobacco shop or ticket machine, place ticket on dashboard; some hotels can give you a free street-parking permit—ask).

By Plane: Efficient buses connect Verona's airport (known as Catullo or Verona-Villafranca, 12 miles southwest of the city, airport code: VRN, tel. 045-809-5666, www.aeroportoverona.it) with its train station (€6, buy tickets on board or at tobacco shop, daily about 5:15-23:00, 3/hour, 15 minutes, bus stop is by front door of train station).

Helpful Hints

Sightseeing Schedules: Most sights (except churches) are closed on Monday mornings, and typically open at 13:30.

Opera: From mid-June through early September, Verona's opera festival brings the city to life, with 15,000 music fans filling the Roman Arena for almost nightly performances. The city is packed and festive—restaurants have prescheduled seatings for dinner, and hotels jack up their prices (cheap upper-level seats-€25, day-of-show tickets often available). You can book tickets at the TI (no extra charge) or through the official box office (buy online at www.arena.it or call 045-800-5151; box office open Mon-Fri 9:00-12:00 & 15:15-17:45, Sat-Sun 9:00-12:00; during opera season, open daily 10:00-17:45, or until 21:00 on performance days; Via Dietro Anfiteatro 6B). If you're not here for the festival, you can still explore the arena (at the start of my self-guided walk) and/or visit Verona's opera-focused ArenaMuseOpera museum (described later, under "Sights in Verona").

Internet Access: Just outside the wall from Piazza Brà is **Play Internet Point** (20 Internet terminals inside a casino, €2/hour, daily 10:00-24:00, to the left of the TI at 49 Via Adigetto, follow signs for *Piazza Cittadella*).

Travel Agency: If you need train tickets or reservations, stop by **World Travel** (small fee added to tickets but saves a trip to the station, Mon-Fri 9:00-19:00, Sat 9:30-12:30 & 15:00-18:00, closed Sun, Corso Porta Nuova 11, tel. 049-806-0111).

Tours in Verona

Walking Tours

The TI organizes 1.5-hour tours in English (March-Oct Sat-Sun 11:30, no tours off-season, €10/person). Tours meet inside the Piazza Brà TI and stroll all the way through the old town (call to confirm schedule, no reservation necessary, tel. 045-806-8680).

Private Guides

Two excellent and enthusiastic Verona guides enjoy giving private tours of the town and region to readers of this book (€115/2 hours, €230/5 hours, prices are per group, tours tailored to your interests—villas, wine tasting, and so on). They are **Marina Menegoi** (mobile 328-958-1108, www.marinamenegoi.com, mmenegoi@gmail.com) and **Valeria Biasi** (mobile 348-903-4238, www.aguideinverona.com or www.veronatours.com for small groups, valeria@aguideinverona.com). For families with children, Valeria offers an interactive game in the city called Safari (€130/2.5 hours).

Self-Guided Walk

Welcome to Verona

This walk covers the essential sights in the town core, starting at Piazza Brà and ending at the cathedral. Allow two hours (including the tower climb and dawdling).

❶ Piazza Brà

If you're wondering about the name, it comes from the local dialect and means "big open space." A generation ago this piazza was noisy with cars. Now it's open and people friendly—it's become the community family room and natural festival grounds.

Grab a bench near the central **fountain** called "The Alps." This was a gift from Verona's sister city Munich, which is just over the mountains to the north. You'll see in the middle of the fountain the symbols of the two cities separated by the Alps, carved out of pink marble from this region. In general, Verona has a bit of an alpine feel; historically it was the place where people rested and prepared before crossing the mountains, and to this day it's the

place where the main west-east, Milan-Venice train line meets the north-south line up to Bolzano, the Dolomites, and Austria.

The ancient **arena** looming over the piazza is a reminder that the city's history goes back to Roman times. On this walk, we'll meander across what was the ancient city, from the arena on this side to the theater across the river.

With the fall of Rome in the fifth century, Verona became a favored capital of barbarian kings. In the Middle Ages, noble families had to choose sides in the civil struggles between emperors (Ghibellines) and popes (Guelphs). During this time (1200s), the town bristled with several hundred San Gimignano-type towers, built by different families to symbolize their power. When the Scaligeri family rose to power here in the 14th century, they established stability on their terms and made the other noble families lop off their proud towers—only the Scaligeri were allowed to keep theirs. To add insult to injury, the Scaligeri paved the city's roads with bricks from the other families' toppled towers. But inter-family feuds made it impossible for the Scaligeri to maintain a stable government, and in 1405 the town essentially gave itself to Venice, which ruled Verona until Napoleon stopped by in 1796. During the 19th century, a tug-of-war between France and Austria actually divided the city for a time, with the river marking the border of each country's domain. Eventually Verona, like Venice, fell into Austrian hands. Reminders of Austrian rule remain: The huge yellow Neoclassical **city hall** facing Piazza Brà (look for the flags) was built by the Austrians to serve as their 19th-century military headquarters. Their former arsenal stands just across the river, and an Austrian fortress caps the hill looking over the city. But the big **equestrian statue** is of Italy's first king, Victor Emmanuel II, celebrating Italian independence and unity, won in the 1860s. The **statue of a modern soldier** striking a *David* pose, with a machine gun instead of a sling over his shoulder, honors Verona's war dead.

Apart from all its history, Piazza Brà is about strolling—the

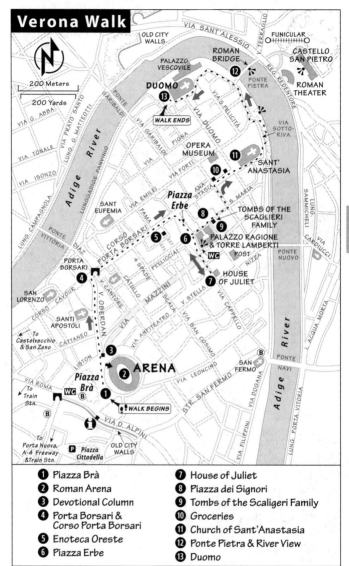

Verona Walk

200 Meters
200 Yards

VERONA

1 Piazza Brà
2 Roman Arena
3 Devotional Column
4 Porta Borsari & Corso Porta Borsari
5 Enoteca Oreste
6 Piazza Erbe
7 House of Juliet
8 Piazza dei Signori
9 Tombs of the Scaligeri Family
10 Groceries
11 Church of Sant'Anastasia
12 Ponte Pietra & River View
13 Duomo

evening *passeggiata* is a national sport in Italy. The broad, shiny sidewalk (named "Liston" after a Venetian promenade; note the fine Venetian-style marble pavement slabs) was built by 17th-century Venetians, who made it big and wide so that promenading socialites could see and be seen in all their finery.

❷ Roman Arena

The Romans built this stadium outside their town walls, just as modern stadiums are usually located outside downtown districts.

With 72 aisles, this elliptical 466-by-400-foot amphitheater is the third largest in Italy (and it was originally 50 percent taller). Most of the stone you see is original. Dating from the first century A.D., it looks great in its pink marble. Over the centuries, crowds of up to 25,000 spectators have cheered Roman gladiator battles, medieval executions, rock concerts, and modern plays, all taking advantage of the arena's famous acoustics. This is also where the popular opera festival is held every summer. Started in 1913, the festival has run continuously ever since, except for brief breaks during both World Wars, when the arena was used as a bomb shelter. While there's little to see inside except the impressive stonework, it's memorable to visit a Roman arena that is still a thriving concert venue. If you climb to the top, you'll enjoy great city views.

The gladiators posing with tourists out front are mostly from Albania, and part of a local gang; they're notorious for overcharging for photos. While they're a nuisance, the police say it's better that they're scamming a living here than finding even more disreputable ways to get by.

Cost and Hours: €6, don't bother with the combo-ticket that includes the unimpressive Maffei Museum, Tue-Sun 8:30-19:30, Mon 13:30-19:30, closes earlier—likely around 16:00—during mid-June-early Sept opera season, last entry one hour before closing, WC near entry, tel. 045-800-3204.

• *As you exit the arena, look to your right. Where the street splits you'll see a column.*

❸ Devotional Column

In the Middle Ages, this column blessed a marketplace held here. Ten yards in front of it, a bronze plaque in the sidewalk shows the Roman city plan—a town of 20,000 placed strategically in the bend of the river, which provided protection on three sides. A wall enclosed the peninsula. The center of the grid was the forum, to-day's Piazza Erbe. (Look down Via Mazzini, the busy main pedestrian drag—the bell tower in the distance marks Piazza Erbe.)

• *After viewing the bronze plaque, turn around so your back is to the arena. Head straight down Via Oberdan (bearing left at the fork) and continue a couple of blocks (passing a derelict Fascist-era theater, the Astra, set back from the street on the left, at #13) until you see an ancient gate to your right, the Porta Borsari. Walk up to it.*

❹ Porta Borsari and Corso Porta Borsari

You're standing before the main entrance to Roman Verona; back then, this gate functioned as a tollbooth (*borsari* means purse, re-

ferring to the collection of tolls here). Below the spiral, fluted columns (which parents nickname *"tortiglioni"*—a pasta kids can relate to), carved into the rock, is a tribute to the emperor who restored this gate. Outside the adjacent Caffè Rialto, the stone on the curb is from a tomb: In Roman times, the roads outside the walls

were lined with tombstones, because burials were not allowed within the town itself. Turn around, look down Corso Cavour, and imagine it in Roman times, leading away from the city gate and lined with tombs. Step into the café. A glass panel in the floor shows the original Roman foundations and pavement stones.

Back outside, cross under the Roman gate and head into the ancient city. Walk down Corso Porta Borsari, the Roman main drag, toward what was the forum. Make it a scavenger hunt. As you walk, discover bits of the town's illustrious past—chips of Roman columns, medieval reliefs, fine old facades, fossils in marble—as well as its elegant present of fancy shops, in a setting that prioritizes pedestrians over cars. On the right, you'll pass the recommended Osteria del Bugiardo, at #17, a popular wine bar and a good place to take a break and hang out with Verona's young and trendy.

• *Between Corso Porta Borsari 13 and 15, detour right down Vicolo San Marco in Foro, following the* Pozzo dell'Amore *sign. Twenty yards ahead on your right, you'll find...*

❺ Enoteca Oreste

This funky wine-and-grappa bar is still run by Oreste (with his Chicagoan wife, Beverly) like a 1970s, old-style *enoteca*. Browse and sample and clown around with Oreste. This historic *enoteca* was once the private chapel of the archbishop of Verona. Traces of the past hide between the bottles—ask Beverly to tell you the story (light food, Tue-Sun 9:00-22:00, closed Mon, Vicolo San Marco in Foro 7, tel. 045-803-4369).

• *Return to Corso Porta Borsari and continue one block until you hit a big square.*

❻ Piazza Erbe

This bustling market square is a photographer's delight. Its pastel buildings corral the fountains, pigeons, and people who have congregated here since Roman times, when this was a forum. Notice the Venetian lion hovering above the square atop a column, reminding locals of the conquest of 1405. Wander into the market, to the fountain in the middle. A fountain has bubbled here for 2,000 years. The original Roman statue lost its head and arms. After a sculptor added a new head and

arms, the statue became Verona's Madonna. She holds a small banner that reads, roughly, "The city of Verona deserves respect and justice." During medieval times, the stone canopy in the center of the square (past the fountain) held the scales where merchants measured the weight of goods they bought and sold, such as silk and wool.

If you were standing here in the Middle Ages, you would have been surrounded by proud noble family towers. Medieval nobles showed off with towers. Renaissance nobles showed off with finely painted facades on their palaces. Find remnants of the 16th-century days when Verona was nicknamed "the painted city."

Locals like to start their evening with an *aperitivo* here. Each bar caters to a different market segment. Survey the scene and, if or when the time is right, choose the terrace that suits you and join in the ritual. It's simple: Grab a spot, adjust your seat for the best view, and order a *spritz* to drink (€4 with a plate of olives and chips).

• *At the far end of Piazza Erbe is a market column featuring St. Zeno, the patron of Verona, who looks at the crazy crowds flushing into the city's silly claim to touristic fame: the House of Juliet (100 yards down Via Cappello to #23, on the left—just follow the crowds). Side-trip there now (but watch your wallet—it's a pickpocket's haven).*

❼ House of Juliet

The tiny, admittedly romantic courtyard is a spectacle: Tourists from all over the world pose on the balcony, while those hoping for love

VERONA

wait their turn to polish Juliet's bronze breast. Residents marvel that each year, about 1,600 Japanese tour groups break their Venice-Milan ride for an hour-long stop in Verona just to see this courtyard (free, gates open roughly 9:00-19:30 or longer). It's fun to stand in the corner and observe the scene, knowing that all of this commotion was started by a clever tour guide in the early 1970s as a way to attract visitors to Verona.

The courtyard walls have long been filled with amorous graffiti. The latest trend is to affix a paper note to the gates or walls with chewing gum. The wall of padlocks is another gimmick, enabling lovers to blow money in an attempt to prove that their hearts are thoroughly locked up. (The shop that sells the locks also sells pens to write on them.) The red mailbox is for love letters to Juliet. There's actually a Juliet Club that reviews these—and all the letters mailed from around the world to "Juliet, Verona, Italy." Each year, the club awards the author of the sweetest letter a free vacation to Verona.

Even those who milk their living out of this sight freely admit, "While no documentation has been discovered to prove the truth of the legend, no documentation has disproved it either." The "museum," which displays art inspired by the love story, plus costumes and the bed from Franco Zeffirelli's film *Romeo and Juliet*, is certainly not worth the €6 entry fee.

Was there ever a real Juliet Capulet? You just walked down Via Cappello, the street of the cap makers. Above the courtyard entry (looking out) is a coat of arms featuring a hat—representing a family that made hats and which would be named, logically, Capulet.

The public's interest in a fictional Romeo and Juliet—or at least Juliet—is a sign that there's a hunger for a Juliet in our world. Observing the mobs clamoring to polish her breast or blow kisses from her bogus balcony, I try to appreciate what she means to people, and to psychoanalyze what she provides to those who come to Verona specifically for this: the message that love will prevail. In love, you can lose, and still be a winner. Juliet is brave, tragic, honest, outspoken, timeless, and passionate. She's a mover and a shaker, a dreamer and a fighter. In a way, this is a pagan temple where the spirit of Juliet gives people something to believe in...or maybe it's just a bunch of baloney appreciated by a simple-minded crowd.

• *Return to Piazza Erbe. From the middle of the piazza, head right on Via della Costa. Walk down Via della Costa, into the big square.*

❽ Piazza dei Signori

Literally the "Lords' Square," this is Verona's sitting room, quieter and more harmonious than Piazza Erbe. The buildings—which span five centuries—define the square and are all linked by arches. From one arch dangles a whale's rib. It was likely a souvenir brought home by a traveling merchant from a trip to the Orient, reminding the townspeople that there was a big world out there. The long portico on the left is inspired by a building in Florence: Brunelleschi's Hospital of the Innocents, considered the first Renaissance building.

Locals call the square Piazza Dante for the statue of the Italian poet **Dante Alighieri** that dominates it. Dante—always pensive,

never smiling—seems to wonder why the tourists choose Juliet over him. Dante was expelled from Florence when that city sided with the pope (who didn't appreciate Dante's writing) and banished its greatest poet. Verona and its ruling Scaligeri family, however, were at odds with the pope (siding instead with the Holy Roman Emperor), and granted Dante asylum.

With the whale's rib behind you, you're facing the brick, crenellated, 14th-century Scaligeri residence. Behind Dante is the yellowish, 15th-century Venetian Renaissance-style Portico of the Counsel. At Dante's two o'clock is the 12th-century Romanesque **Palazzo della Ragione** (closed to the public, except for its tower).

Looking back the way you came, follow the white *toilette* signs into the courtyard of the Palazzo della Ragione. The impressive stairway is the only surviving Renaissance staircase in Verona. For a grand city view, you can climb to the top of the palazzo's 13th-century **Torre dei Lamberti** (€6 for stairs or elevator, daily June-Sept 8:30-20:30, Oct-May 8:30-19:30, ticket office next to staircase). The elevator saves you 243 steps—but you'll still need to climb 46 more to get to the first viewing platform. It's not worth continuing up 79 more spiral stairs to the second viewing platform.
• *Exit the courtyard the way you entered and turn right, continuing downhill. Within a block, you'll find the...*

❾ Tombs of the Scaligeri Family

These exotic and very Gothic 14th-century tombs, with their fine, original, wrought-iron protective cages, evoke the age when one family ruled Verona. The Scaligeri were to Verona what the Medici family was to Florence. These were powerful people. They changed the law so that they could be buried within the town. They forbade

the presence of any noble family's towers but their own. And, by building tombs atop pillars, they arranged to be looked up to, even in death.

• *Continue 15 yards to the next corner and take a left on Vicolo Cavalletto. At the first corner, turn right along Corso Sant'Anastasia toward the big, unfinished brick facade of Verona's largest church. For a fragrant and potentially tasty diversion, pop into* ❿ *two classic grocery stores: Gastronomia (on the opposite corner at the start of the street, at #33, closed Sun afternoon) and Albertini, located on your left in the next block. Gastronomia can rustle up tasty sandwiches (about €3-4).*

VERONA

⓫ Church of Sant'Anastasia

This church was built from the late 13th century through the 15th century. Although the facade was never finished (the builders ran

out of steam), the interior was—and still is—brilliant. Step inside to see the delightful way this region's medieval churches were painted. Note the grimacing hunchbacks holding basins of holy water on their backs (near main entrance at base of columns). And don't miss Pisanello's fresco of *St. George and the Princess of Trebizond* (1438; at the tip of the arch, high above chapel to right of altar). Once colorful, it has oxidized over time to its current monochrome state. For a closer look at its wonderful detail, check out the images on the computer terminal below the fresco. Ask for the English brochure, which describes the story of the church.

Cost and Hours: €2.50; March-Oct Mon-Sat 9:00-18:00, Sun 13:00-18:00; Nov-Feb Mon-Sat 9:00-13:00 & 13:30-17:00, Sun 13:00-17:00; www.chieseverona.it.

• *Leaving the church, make two lefts, and walk along the right side of the church to Via Sottoriva. To the right, the Sottoriva arcade was once busy with colorful wine bars and osterie, some of which still exist (see "Eating in Verona," later). But for now, head to the left on Via Sottoriva. In a block, you'll reach a small riverfront area with stone benches that usually have a few modern-day Romeos and Juliets gazing at each other rather than at the view. Belly up to the river view.*

VERONA

⑫ Ponte Pietra and River View

The white stones of the Ponte Pietra footbridge are from the original Roman bridge that stood here. After the bridge was bombed in World War II, the Veronese fished the marble chunks out of the river to rebuild it. From here, you can see across the river to the Roman Theater, built into the hillside behind the green hedge (see page 401). Way above the theater (behind the cypress trees) is the fortress, Castello San Pietro.

The wide spot in the river here was called the "Millers' Widening," where boats stopped and unloaded grain to be milled. Water wheels once lined the river and powered medieval Verona, employing technology imported from the Holy Land by 10th-century Crusaders.

Continue up the river toward the bridge. You'll pass the recommended **Gelateria Ponte Pietra,** where Mirko, Mariam, and Stefano dish out fine gelato. Walk to the high point on the bridge and enjoy the view.

• *From the bridge, look back 200 yards at the tall white spire...that's where you're heading. Walk back off the bridge, then turn right, keeping an eye on the left for the steeple of the...*

⑬ Duomo

Started in the 12th century, this church was built over a period of several hundred years. Before entering, note the fine Romanesque carvings on its facade.

Step inside, pick up the leaflet that explains the church's highlights, and head to the back-left corner of the church. In the last chapel on the left is Titian's 16th-century *Assumption of the Virgin.* Mary calmly rides a cloud—direction up—to the shock and bewilderment of the crowd below. Notice a handful of tombs embedded in the walls about 15 feet above floor level—an unusual feature. (Generally, tombs are found in the floor of the church or in crypts below.)

Now head up the aisle to the last door on the left (left of high altar), where you'll find the **ruins** of an older church. These are the 10th-century foundations of the Church of St. Elena, turned intriguingly into a modern-day chapel featuring exposed fourth-century mosaic floors from the Roman church that originally stood here.

From there, pass through the little open-air courtyard into the adjacent **baptistery,** with its clean Romanesque lines, hanging 14th-century crucifix, and fine marble font. Try to identify the eight biblical scenes carved on its panels before referring to my answers. (Answers, starting with the panel just to the right of center and working counterclockwise: Annunciation; first Christmas, with animals licking baby Jesus and giving him a barnyard welcome; announcement to shepherds of Jesus' birth, with their flock stacked on one side; Epiphany, with the Three Kings giving their gifts to Baby Jesus; Herod commanding that all male infants be killed; Slaughter of the Innocents; flight to Egypt; and finally, facing the entry door, John the Baptist baptizing Christ.)

Finally, after leaving the church, circle around its left side (as you face the main facade) to find the peaceful Romanesque **cloister** *(chiostro),* with mosaics from a fifth-century Christian church exposed below the walk.

Cost and Hours: €2.50; March-Oct Mon-Sat 10:00-17:30, Sun 13:30-17:30; Nov-Feb Mon-Fri 10:00-13:00 & 13:30-17:00, Sat 10:00-16:00, Sun 13:30-17:00.

Sights in Verona

In the Town Center

▲▲Evening *Passeggiata*

For me, the highlight of Verona is the *passeggiata* (stroll)—especially in the evening. Make a big circle from Piazza Brà through the old town on Via Mazzini (one of Europe's many "first" pedestrian-only streets) to the colorful Piazza Erbe, and then back down Corso Porta Borsari to Piazza Brà. This is a small town, where people know each other, and they're all out on parade. Like peacocks, the young and nubile spread their wings. The classy shop windows are integral to the *passeggiata* as, for the ladies, shopping is a sport. Their never-finished wardrobes are considered a work in progress, and this is when they gather ideas. If you're going to complement your stroll with a stop in a café or bar, the best plan is to enjoy a *spritz* drink—not on Piazza Brà, but on Piazza Erbe (the oldest and most elegant bars are on the end farthest from Juliet's balcony).

ArenaMuseOpera (AMO)

This slick museum, which opened in 2013 to celebrate the 100th anniversary of the city's renowned opera festival, fills the old Palazzo Forti in the sleepy streets at the northern edge of downtown. The underwhelming permanent exhibit, swaddled in red velvet, uses a few scant artifacts, sparse descriptions, and a handful of interactive touchscreens to trace the creation of an opera from words *(libretto)* to score *(partitura)* to staging *(rappresentazione,* including designers' sketches, along with actual sets and costumes from some of the performances that have graced the arena's stage). While the museum is vastly overpriced, opera lovers may enjoy it—particularly if the temporary exhibits, which can be excellent, are of interest.

Cost and Hours: €10-15 depending on special exhibits, daily 9:00-19:30, Via Massalongo 7, tel. 045-803-0461, www.arena-museopera.com.

West of Piazza Brà and the Arena

▲Castelvecchio

Verona's powerful Scaligeri family built this castle (1343-1356) as both a residence and a fortress. The castle has two parts: the fam-

ily palace and the quarters for their private army (separated, for the nervous family's security, by a fortified wall and an internal moat). Today, it houses the city's art gallery, with an extensive, enjoyable collection of sculpture and paintings. (Religious statues were Verona's medieval forte, while paintings were the city's Renaissance forte.) Meanwhile, kids (and kids at heart) enjoy the chance to scramble across the delightfully crenellated parapets, with fine views over Verona.

From the entrance, you'll head right toward the **statues,** once brightly painted. Cross to the next wing and head upstairs to walk through two floors that trace the evolution of **painting** from the 13th through the 17th centuries, including minor works by many major masters (such as Bellini, Mantegna, and Veronese). You'll also pass by a small armory collection; en route, watch for the chance to roam the **ramparts** with fine views of the city, river, and Ponte Scaligero (described next). Verona was an independent city-state from 1176 to 1387. Then came a long period of subjugation under other powers which, in more modern times, included the Austrians. From the ramparts you can see remnants of Austrian rule: the arsenal across the river and the castle atop the distant hill.

Cost and Hours: €6, Tue-Sun 8:30-19:30, Mon 13:30-19:30, last entry 45 minutes before closing, Corso Castelvecchio 2, tel. 045-806-2611, see map on page 403 for location. Info sheets with good English descriptions are available throughout, but the €4 audioguide (€6/2 people) is still worthwhile.

Nearby: Next to Castelvecchio, the picturesque red-brick bridge called **Ponte Scaligero**—fortified and crenellated, as if a continuation of the castle—is free, open to the public, and fun to stroll across. Destroyed by the Germans in World War II, it was rebuilt in the 1950s using many of its original bricks, which were dredged out of the river. Today it's understandably a favorite for wedding-day photos.

▲Basilica of San Zeno Maggiore

This church, outside the old center, is dedicated to the patron saint of Verona, whose remains are buried in the crypt under the main altar. In addition to being a fine example of Italian Romanesque, the basilica features Mantegna's *San Zeno Triptych* (1456-1459) with its marvelous perspective, peaceful double-columned cloisters, and a set of 48 paneled 11th-century bronze doors nicknamed "the poor man's Bible." Pretend you're an illiterate medieval peasant and do some reading. Facing the altar, on the walls of the right-side aisle, you can see frescoes painted on top of other frescoes and graffiti dating from the 1300s. These were done by people who fled into the church in times of war or flooding and scratched prayers into the walls. Druidic-looking runes are actually decorated letters typical of the Gothic period, like those in illuminated manuscripts.

Cost and Hours: €2.50, March-Oct Mon-Sat 8:30-18:00, Sun 12:30-18:00; Nov-Feb Mon-Sat 10:00-13:00 & 13:30-17:00, Sun 13:00-17:00; located on Piazza San Zeno, a 15-minute walk upriver beyond Castelvecchio, www.chieseverona.it.

Across the Roman Bridge, North of the Center

Roman Theater (Teatro Romano)

Dating from about the time of Christ, this ancient theater was discovered in the 19th century and restored. Admission includes the Roman

Museum, located high in the building above the theater (reach it via elevator—start at the stage and walk up the middle set of stairs, then continue straight on the path through the bushes).

The museum displays a model of the theater, a small chapel, and Roman artifacts, including mosaic floors, busts and other statuary, clay and bronze votive figures, and architectural fragments. There's not much to see. Unless you've never seen a Roman ruin, I'd skip it.

Cost and Hours: €4.50, Tue-Sun 8:30-19:30, Mon 13:30-19:30, last entry one hour before closing, theater located across the river near Ponte Pietra footbridge, tel. 045-800-0360. From mid-June through August, the theater stages Shakespeare plays—only a little more difficult to understand in Italian than in Elizabethan English.

VERONA

Giusti Garden (Giardino Giusti)

You'll see this picturesque Renaissance garden capping the steep hilltop just across the Roman Bridge at the northern edge of the city. It's a little oasis with manicured box hedges, towering cypress trees, and a city view from the top of its hill. For most people, however, it's not worth the hike, time, or money.

Cost and Hours: €6, daily April-Sept 9:00-20:00, Oct-March 9:00-17:00, across the river, beyond Ponte Nuovo.

Sleeping in Verona

VERONA

I've listed rates you'll pay in the regular season—most of April through May, and September through October. Prices soar (at least €20-30 more per night) from mid-June through early September (opera season), in early April (during the Vinitaly wine festival—see "The Wines of Verona" sidebar, later), and during big trade fairs or major holidays. Unless your goal is opera, consider coming before mid-June or after early September. Prices are lower from November to March. Hotel websites clearly explain their rates.

Near Piazza Erbe

$$$ Hotel Aurora, at the corner of Piazza Erbe and Via Pelliciai, has friendly family management, attention to detail, a welcoming terrace with wonderful piazza views, and 18 fresh, modern rooms (Sb-€140, Db-€170, Tb-€200, Qb-€300, Db rates can peak at €240 during opera season, elevator, air-con, free Wi-Fi, Piazzetta XIV Novembre 2, tel. 045-594-717, www.hotelaurora.biz, info@ hotelaurora.biz, Rita). Coming from the train station, you can hop off at Piazza Brà, cross the square, and walk 10 minutes up the main pedestrian street; or, for a slightly shorter walk, stay on the bus two stops longer until the San Fermo stop (from here, walk away from the river, following signs for *Piazza Erbe*).

$ Casa della Giovane, run by an association that houses poor women, also rents rooms and dorm beds to female tourists (and their children up to age 10). Buried deep in the old town and up several flights of stairs, this place offers 20 cheap beds in a clean, institutional, and peaceful setting (women only, €22/bed in 11-bed dorm, Sb-€35, Db-€60, Tb-€90, no breakfast, 23:00 curfew, reception open 9:00-21:00, free Wi-Fi, self-service laundry, Via Pigna 7, tel. 045-596-880, www.protezionedellagiovane.it).

Verona Hotels & Restaurants

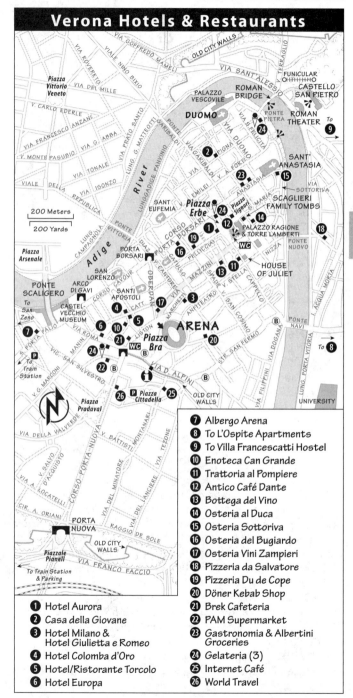

1 Hotel Aurora
2 Casa della Giovane
3 Hotel Milano & Hotel Giulietta e Romeo
4 Hotel Colomba d'Oro
5 Hotel/Ristorante Torcolo
6 Hotel Europa
7 Albergo Arena
8 To L'Ospite Apartments
9 To Villa Francescatti Hostel
10 Enoteca Can Grande
11 Trattoria al Pompiere
12 Antico Café Dante
13 Bottega del Vino
14 Osteria al Duca
15 Osteria Sottoriva
16 Osteria del Bugiardo
17 Osteria Vini Zampieri
18 Pizzeria da Salvatore
19 Pizzeria Du de Cope
20 Döner Kebab Shop
21 Brek Cafeteria
22 PAM Supermarket
23 Gastronomia & Albertini Groceries
24 Gelateria (3)
25 Internet Café
26 World Travel

VERONA

Sleep Code

(€1 = about $1.30, country code: 39)
S = Single, **D** = Double/Twin, **T** = Triple, **Q** = Quad, **b** = bathroom, **s** = shower only. Hotels accept credit cards and provide breakfast unless otherwise noted. Everyone speaks English. Many towns in Italy levy a hotel tax of about €2 per person, per night, which must be paid in cash (not included in the rates I've quoted).

To help you easily sort through these listings, I've divided the accommodations into three categories, based on the price for a standard double room with bath:

$$$ **Higher Priced**—Most rooms €125 or more.
$$ **Moderately Priced**—Most rooms between €90-125.
$ **Lower Priced**—Most rooms €90 or less.

Prices can change without notice; verify the hotel's current rates online or by email. For the best prices, always book direct.

Near Piazza Brà

You'll find several options in the quiet streets just off Piazza Brà, within 200 yards of the bus stop. From the square, white or yellow signs point you to the hotels. Most of these are big, fairly impersonal business-class places; the Torcolo is more homey and friendly.

$$$ Hotel Milano is an arty hotel with 52 rooms. The lobby and fancier rooms are tricked out in black and chrome (rates vary wildly—see website—generally about Sb-€75-100, Db-€120-150, up to €280 during opera season, air-con, elevator, free Wi-Fi, garage-€20, Vicolo Tre Marchetti 11, tel. 045-596-011, www.hotelmilano-vr.it, info@hotelmilano-vr.it).

$$$ Hotel Colomba d'Oro is a sprawling, stately, elegant place renting 51 spacious rooms with Baroque flourishes. It has generous public spaces and overlooks a quiet and central street (prices vary but generally Sb-€110-130, Db-€150-170, higher during opera season, extra bed-€30, air-con, elevator, pay Wi-Fi, Via C. Cattaneo 10, tel. 045-595-300, www.colombahotel.com, info@colombahotel.com).

$$$ Hotel Giulietta e Romeo is on a quiet side street just 50 yards behind the Roman Arena. It's stylish and well-managed; nine of its 40 sexy, ultra-modern rooms have balconies (Sb-€110, Db-€130, bigger "superior" Db-€30 more, prices shoot up to €200/€260 during opera season, air-con, elevator, free Wi-Fi, free loaner bikes, fitness room, garage-€20 or ask for free street parking permit, Vicolo Tre Marchetti 3, tel. 045-800-3554, www.hotelgr. it, info@hotelgr.it).

$$$ Hotel Europa offers 46 slightly dated rooms with spring-time colors. Try to request a balcony overlooking the *piazzetta* below (Sb-€90-100, Db-€130-150, prices up to €206 during opera season, 10 percent discount if you mention this book when reserving direct, air-con, elevator, free Wi-Fi, a couple of blocks off Piazza Brà at Via Roma 8, tel. 045-594-744, www.veronahoteleuropa. com, info@veronahoteleuropa.com).

$$ Hotel Torcolo offers 19 comfortable, lovingly maintained rooms with Grandma's furnishings (Sb-€75, Db-€100 most of the year but up to €150 during opera season, breakfast-€14, air-con, fridge in room, elevator, Wi-Fi, garage-€16; from Piazza Brà promenade, head down the alley to the right of #16 and walk to Vicolo Listone 3; tel. 045-800-7512, www.hoteltorcolo.it, hoteltorcolo@virgilio.it, well-run by Silvia, Diana, and helpful Caterina).

Near Castelvecchio

$ Albergo Arena, while dreary, is a good value for those on a budget. Located in a peaceful courtyard off a busy street a few blocks from Piazza Brà, it offers 15 very basic, quiet rooms (S-€45, Sb-€60, Db-€85, air-con, elevator, free Wi-Fi, just west of Castelvecchio at Stradone Porta Palio 2, tel. 045-803-2440, www.albergoarena.it, info@albergoarena.it, Francesco and Elena).

Across the River

$$ L'Ospite, a 10-minute walk across the river from Piazza Erbe, has six cozy, immaculate, fully equipped apartments and lots of stairs. The rooms, warmly managed by English-speaking Federica De Rossi, sleep from two to four, with air-conditioning and free Wi-Fi (Db-€95, Tb/Qb-about €40-55/person, discounts for cash and longer stays, no reception or daily cleaning; Via XX Settembre 3; tel. 045-803-6994, mobile 329-426-2524, www.lospite.com, info@lospite.com). Coming from the station by bus (ride same buses as those headed downtown—see "Arrival in Verona," earlier), get off three stops past Piazza Brà, just after crossing the bridge, at the XX Settembre stop (across the street from the apartments).

$ Villa Francescatti is a good, church-affiliated hostel in a pretty hillside setting (€18/bed in 6- or 8-bed sex-segregated rooms with hall bath, €20/bed in family rooms with private bathrooms, cash only, includes breakfast and sheets, €8 dinners, laundry €5/load, free Wi-Fi in common areas, rooms closed from 9:00 to 17:00 but reception open all day, 24:00 curfew; Salita Fontana del Ferro 15, bus #73 or #91 from station to Piazza Isolo plus short steep walk, tel. 045-590-360, www.ostelloverona.it, info@villafrancescatti.it).

Eating in Verona

Every restaurant listed here is within a 10-minute walk of the others. They're mostly small and intimate, and found along side streets. It's tempting to grab a table next to the *passeggiata* action along Piazza Brà, but you'll be sacrificing service, value, and quality for your view of the floodlit Roman Arena and Verona on parade (perhaps a fair trade-off). Except for Brek Cafeteria, restaurants on the piazza tend to charge a cover and service fee, making even pizza a pricey choice.

Fine Dining

Enoteca Can Grande is enthusiastically run by Giuliano and Corrina, who enjoy turning people on to great, well-matched food and wine. You can sit on a quiet street or in a plush little dining area inside. Their star offering is a €40 set menu, a festival of *antipasti* treats, an imaginative pasta, your choice of a meat or fish course, and dessert. They also offer a junior version at lunch for €20: a pasta and your choice of salad or dessert (Wed-Mon 12:00-15:30 & 18:00-22:30, closed Tue, closed Mon instead of Tue during opera season; a block off Piazza Brà at Via Dietro Liston 19D—if the equestrian statue jogged slightly right, he'd head straight here; tel. 045-595-022).

Trattoria al Pompiere, which has a commitment to regional traditions, is bigger, with formal waiters weaving among its tight tables and walls plastered with photos of big shots from the area. This bustling place is a favorite of local foodies. Marco and his gang serve gourmet meats and cheeses as *antipasti* from their larger-than-life back counter, ideal for a mixed plate to complement the huge selection of fine wines. Reservations are wise (€10-14 pastas, €16-19 *secondi*, Mon-Sat 12:40-14:00 & 19:40-22:30, closed Sun, chivalry lives—ladies' menus come without prices; halfway between Piazza Erbe and Juliet's courtyard—head down narrow side street next to Via Cappello 8 to Vicolo Regina d'Ungheria 5; tel. 045-803-0537, www.alpompiere.tv).

Antico Café Dante is a high-end place with a 19th-century pedigree and elegant service on the coziest and classiest square in town. You can enjoy a memorable meal of classic Veneto cuisine either at romantic tables on the square, or inside. While it's not cheap, if you want to dress up and enjoy a slow, romantic, memorable meal, this can be a good value (€15-16 pastas, €22-25 *secondi*, daily 12:30-14:30 & 19:30-23:00, Piazza dei Signori 2, tel. 045-800-0083, www.caffedante.it). For something a little more affordable, duck into their shaded alley next door to order from a more casual menu (from lunchtime through 18:00).

The Wines of Verona

Wine connoisseurs love the high-quality wines of the Verona area. The hills to the east are covered with grapes to make Soave; to the north is Valpolicella country; and Bardolino comes from vineyards to the west.

Valpolicella grapes, which are used to make the fruity, red Valpolicella table wine (found everywhere), are also the basis for full-bodied red Amarone and the sweet dessert wine Recioto. To produce Amarone, grapes are partially dried (*passito*) before fermentation, then aged for a minimum of four years in oak casks, resulting in a rich, velvety, full-bodied red. Recioto, which in local dialect means "ears," uses only the grapes from the top of the cluster (so they sort of look like the "ears" of the cluster's "head"). Because these grapes get the most sun, they mature the fastest and have the highest concentration of sugar. Before pressing, the grapes are dried for months until all moisture has gone out; the wine is then aged for one to three years.

Bardolino, from the vineyards near Lake Garda, is a light, fruity wine, like a French Beaujolais. It's a perfect picnic wine.

Soave, which might be Italy's best-known white wine, goes well with seafood and risotto dishes. While Soave can vary widely in quality, the best are called "Soave Classico" and come from the heart of the region, near the Soave Castle. Soave is sometimes aged in oak casks, giving it a mellow, rounded flavor.

Sample these and many others at the numerous *enoteche* (wine-tasting bars) or at any restaurant around town. In early April, Verona hosts Vinitaly, the most important international convention of domestic and international wines. Vintners vie for prestigious awards for the past year's vintage. Tourists are welcome to attend at the end of the week, and are shuttled to the convention hall from Piazza Brà. Hotels book up months in advance. Check with the TI and www.vinitaly.com for details.

If you're visiting the area in the fall, consider a day trip to nearby Monteforte d'Alpone, east of Verona. The town hosts a fun, raucous wine festival in September—ask at the TI for more information on this and other regional wine festivals.

VERONA

Bottega del Vino is pricey, venerable, and a bit pretentious. Under a high ceiling and walls of wine bottles, brisk black-vested waiters match traditional dishes (polenta, duck, game) with glasses of fine wine. Choose from 20 open bottles. The waitstaff, ambience, and food have deep roots in local culture. I like their front room best. Reservations are smart for dinner (€16 pastas, €20-24 *secondi*, good daily specials, daily 12:00-23:00, off Via Mazzini at Via Scudo di Francia 3, tel. 045-800-4535, www.bottegavini.it).

Budget Restaurants

Osteria al Duca is a fun, family-run place with a lively atmosphere and good traditional dishes. Locals line up for its affordable, two-course, €17 fixed-price meal with lots of choices. I much prefer their ground floor (*piano terra*—worth requesting). Reservations are advised (Mon-Sat 12:00-15:00 & 18:30-22:30, closed Sun, half-block east of Scaligeri family tombs at Via Arche Scaligere 2, tel. 045-594-474, Alessandro or Daniela).

Ristorante Torcolo is a family restaurant, with mom (Paola) running the kitchen, and father and son (Roberto and Luca) serving the meals. While it feels a bit dressy, it lacks pretense. They serve all the classic dishes, with an accessible menu and an extensive wine list. Eat in their dining hall or on the tiny courtyard outside (€9-12 pastas, €15-18 *secondi*, €35 fixed-price meal featuring traditional Verona dishes, Tue-Sun 12:00-15:00 & 19:00-22:30, closed Mon, just behind the Piazza Brà scene on a quiet street, Via Carlo Cattaneo 11, tel. 045-803-3730).

Eating in *Osterie* (Old Bars)

Wandering around the old town, you'll see plenty of Verona's thriving little watering holes. While these characteristic old bars focus more on wine than on food, most serve memorable, characteristic, and affordable plates. Menus are simple and rustic—sometimes just bar munchies and the daily pasta. Service is relaxed and the clientele is young and local. For drinks it's mostly wine or water—fine wines are served by the glass, with bottles open and prices listed on blackboards. (I saw one sign suggesting that patrons "don't drive too much to drink.")

I've listed three places below: a classic antique *osteria* with more of a menu; a trendy, more modern place in the old center; and a small one-man show just off Piazza Brà, where you're most likely to make a new friend.

Osteria Sottoriva survives from an era when Verona's river served as the town thoroughfare, and business deals could be made over a glass of wine at rustic riverside eateries. Located in a fine old covered arcade (the portico of Via Sottoriva), Sottoriva offers simple soups and pastas, with both cozy indoor and outdoor seating (€7-13 dishes, Thu-Tue 11:00-15:00 & 18:30-22:30—but open all day long in summer, closed Wed, behind the Church of Sant'Anastasia at Via Sottoriva 9, tel. 045-801-4323).

Osteria del Bugiardo is jammed with a hip young crowd that spills out into the pedestrian-filled Corso Porta Borsari. They have a buffet of little sandwiches, can whip up a plate of top quality cheeses, and serve a good pasta-of-the-day. They showcase their own Buglioni wines and are proud to tell you more about them (€7 pastas, €11 *secondi*, daily 10:00-23:00, Corso Porta Borsari 17, tel. 045-591-869).

A Mobile Feast Through Verona

Verona is a great town to sample the *aperitivo* ritual. All over town, locals enjoy a refreshing *spritz*, ideally on Piazza Erbe between 18:00 and 20:00. Choose a nice perch, and then, for about €4, you'll get the drink of your choice and a few nibbles (olives and/or potato chips) and a chance to feel very local as you enjoy the *passeggiata* scene.

Consider this for a fun sampling of many dimensions of the Verona eating and socializing scene: Start with an *aperitivo* on **Piazza Erbe** (the most refined bars are the farthest from Juliet's balcony), then walk across Ponte Nuovo to **Pizzeria da Salvatore** and enjoy the town's best pizza. If you have to wait for a table, have another *spritz* at the neighboring bar. Then stroll along the river to **Osteria Sottoriva,** and enjoy a little sampling of bar food with a glass of Amarone (wine to meditate with) under the old arcade. Finish by meandering through the old center back to Piazza Brà for a gelato at **Gelateria Savoia.** *Buon appetito!*

VERONA

Osteria Vini Zampieri, with a tiny bar and five tables, keeps a tradition of stoking conviviality with good wine since 1937. Its young and energetic manager, Leo, is passionate about organic wines, slow food, and his own home-brewed beer. As the drinks are their priority, they don't serve much food—just some bar munchies and a nice *antipasti* plate—but at lunchtime, Leo can whip up a simple pasta to complement your wine (daily 11:00-late, a few steps off Piazza Brà and next to Via Mazzini at Via Alberto Maria 23, tel. 045-597-053). You're welcome to play foosball downstairs on what Italians call the *calcio balilla* ("the little boy soldiers of Mussolini").

Pizza
Pizzeria da Salvatore, Verona's first pizzeria, opened in 1961, when pizza was considered a foreign food...from Naples. They serve the best pizza in town, and a visit here gives a nice excuse to stroll across the river into a part of town with no tourists. It's family-friendly, not fancy or romantic, and you'll squeeze into a tight row of tiny tables, rubbing elbows with your neighbors. While it's not quite Naples, it's justifiably popular—come early, or plan to leave your name on the list and wait a while (no reservations, €6-10 pizzas, Mon-Sat 12:30-14:30 & 19:00-23:00, Sun 19:00-23:00 only, across Ponte Nuovo to Piazza San Tomaso 6, tel. 045-803-0366).

Pizzeria Du de Cope is a colorful, high-energy, informal place (with paper placemats) that buzzes with smartly attired young waiters and locals who keep coming back for the pizza (€10-14 pizzas, big €10-16 salads, daily 12:00-14:30 & 19:00-23:00, flamboyant desserts, families welcome, no reservations, at Galleria Pelliciai 10, tel. 045-595-562).

Cheap Eats

Döner kebab shops all over town serve hearty, cheap kebabs to munch on from a stool or to take out (most open daily roughly noon-midnight). *Piadine* (pita-bread) kebabs are worth the €4, and the super-sized kebabs can fill a couple on a very tight budget for a total of €6. The best kebabs, according to local assessments, are behind the Roman Arena at Via Leoncino 44. There's another good place on the other side of Piazza Brà, near Hotel Europa, at Via Teatro Filarmonico 6. The benches in the center of Piazza Brà are handy for a scenic place to munch your cheap meal.

Brek Cafeteria, a well-run and modern chain right on Piazza Brà, offers a cheap and easy self-serve option inside (€5 pastas, €7 *secondi*, cheap salad plates). Or, if you want to sit out on the square, you can order off the pricier menu (€9 pastas, €13 *secondi)*—and enjoy a view that's worth paying a little extra for (daily 11:30-15:00 & 18:30-22:00, longer hours for outdoor seating during summer, facing equestrian statue at Piazza Brà 20).

Groceries: **PAM supermarket** is just outside the historic gate on Piazza Brà (Mon-Sat 8:00-21:00, Sun 9:00-20:00, exit Piazza Brà through the gate and take the first right to Via dei Mutilati 3). Near the Church of Sant'Anastasia are two classic grocery stores, **Gastronomia** and **Albertini** (described on page 397).

Gelato: The venerable **Gelateria Savoia** has been a local favorite since 1939. It's in an arcade just off Piazza Brà, marked by a happy crowd licking their distinctive *semi-freddo*—a specialty of bitter-almond amaretto, cream, and cookie (open long hours daily, just off Piazza Brà at Via Roma 1). On the other side of town, near Ponte Pietra and the Duomo, is **Gelateria Ponte Pietra** (Tue-Sun 14:30-19:30, until 23:00 in summer, closed Mon, at #23; see the end of my self-guided walk, earlier). **Gelato Pretto,** the pricey gourmet *gelateria* from Padua, also has a prime location here in Verona—right on Piazza Erbe (at #40; see description on page 380).

Verona Connections

You have three options for getting train tickets in the Verona station: the standard station ticket office (with slow-moving lines, daily 6:00-21:00), a bank of modern machines (good English descriptions, cash and credit cards accepted), and the Deutsche Bahn ticket office (20 yards from baggage check office in the tunnel, offering tickets at the same cost as the station office but with German efficiency and no lines, Mon-Sat 8:00-18:00, closed Sun).

Every hour, at least two trains connect Verona with Venice, Padua, and Vicenza: One's a slow, cheap, regional train; the other gets you to Venice faster but costs twice as much and requires reservations—meaning you need to choose a particular departure when you buy your ticket.

From Verona by Train to: Venice (at least 2/hour, 1.25-1.75 hours), **Padua** (at least 2/hour, 40-60 minutes), **Vicenza** (at least 2/hour, 25-60 minutes), **Florence** (*Firenze,* about hourly, 1.5 hours direct or 2.5 hours with transfer in Bologna), **Bologna** (hourly, 1.25-1.5 hours), **Milan** (about 2/hour, 1.5-2 hours), **Rome** (at least hourly, 4-5 hours, often with transfer in Bologna, also 1 direct night train, 6.5 hours), **Bolzano** (hourly, 1.75-2.25 hours, avoid "fast" trains that take the same amount of time but cost much more). For more information, visit www.trenitalia.com.

VERONA

VENETIAN HISTORY

In the Middle Ages, the Venetian aristocracy became Europe's clever middlemen for East-West trade, creating a great trading empire presided over by a series of elected dukes, or doges. By smuggling in the bones of St. Mark, Venice gained religious importance as well. But after the discovery of America and new trading routes to the Orient, Venetian power ebbed. Yet as Venice fell, her appetite for decadence grew. Throughout the 17th and 18th centuries, Venice partied on the wealth accumulated in earlier centuries as a trading power.

That's Venetian history in a seashell. Want more? Read on.

500: Rome Falls, Venice Rises

In A.D. 476, the last Roman emperor abdicated, the infrastructure was crumbling, and Italy was crawling with barbarians. Hoping these Visigoths, Huns, and Lombards didn't like water, mainland farmers took refuge on the marshy, uninhabited islands of the lagoon.

The refugees squatted on this wet and miserable land. Eventually, they sank pilings in the mud to build on, channeled water into canals, and constructed bridges to lace together the motley collection of more than 100 natural islands that would eventually become Venice.

500-1000: Medieval Growth

These former farmers, the first Venetians, now harvested salt and fish for their livelihood, and traded it on the mainland. Though

Venice's islands were desolate, the area—known to the Romans as the "Seven Seas"—was strategically important. In 540 A.D., the Byzantine Emperor Justinian reconquered Italy from the barbarians and briefly reunited the Roman Empire. He established a capital at Ravenna, bringing the Venetian islands under Byzantine influence.

In 726, Venice elected a local ruler, a "doge"—the first of many who would rule for the next 1,100 years. (Though "doge" is linguistically related to our word "duke," Venetian rulers were more like constitutional monarchs, elected by their fellow nobles and expected to govern according to the rule of law.) In 610 a doge established his capital in the settlement of Rivo Alto ("High Bank"), near today's Rialto Bridge.

Under Byzantine protection, Venetians became prosperous seagoing merchants. Acting as middlemen, they bought goods from the sophisticated Byzantine and Islamic lands to the East and sold them to consumers in the West.

Venice's merchant economy boomed while the rest of Europe languished under land-based feudalism. Charlemagne, the Holy Roman Emperor who'd conquered much of Italy (c. 800), eyed the region hungrily. But Venetians, wanting to keep their independence, deposed Charlemagne's bishop and chose one who was loyal to (distant) Byzantium.

To legitimize their new bishop, the Venetians managed to smuggle the holy relics of St. Mark from Egypt in 828, thus becoming a religious power overnight. To seal the city's oriental orientation, Venetian leaders had the grand St. Mark's Basilica built in a distinctly Eastern style.

Representative Sights
- Gondolas and the network of canals
- Old crypt under San Zaccaria Church
- Santa Maria Assunta Church on Torcello Island

1000-1500: A Seafaring Power

Well-located between northern Europe and the eastern Mediterranean, Venetian sea traders established trading outposts in Byzantine and Muslim territories to the east. At home, a stable, constitutional government ran an efficient, state-operated multinational corporation. The shallow lagoon was easily defended against attack, making fortifications unnecessary. Grand buildings reflected Venice's wealth.

Venetian merchants ran a profitable trading triangle: timber

Venice's Empire

London
•Amsterdam
•Bruges
Paris
Atlantic
Ocean
•Vienna
Verona
Milan• Venice
Genoa   DALMATIA
Ravenna   Adriatic Sea
Pisa
Florence
Rome
Amalfi• Corfu
Black
Sea
Constantinople
To China →
Aegean
Sea
Gibraltar Mediterranean
Sea
BATTLE OF
LEPANTO
(1571)
Nafplio
Crete
Rhodes
Cyprus
HOLY
LAND
Alexandria

Lands united with or linked to the
Venetian Empire over the centuries

Current National Borders

from Venice's mainland to Egypt for gold to
Byzantium for luxury goods to Venice. Its
merchant fleet was the biggest in the Mediterranean, backed by powerful warships.

By the 12th century, tiny Venice had effectively established itself as an independent,
self-ruling country and was running Europe's
first industrial complex, the Arsenale (1104).
With more than 1,000 workers using an early
form of assembly-line production, the Arsenale could produce about one warship a day.
This put the "fear of Venice" into visiting rulers. When France's King Henry III dropped
by the Arsenale, Venice entertained him with a
shipbuilding spectacle: from ribs to finished product in four hours.

When Europe launched its Crusades to the Holy Land (1095-
1272), Venice transported soldiers and defended Byzantine and
Crusader ports in return for free-trade privileges. This made the
eastern Mediterranean a virtual free-trade zone for a very aggressive Venetian trading community to exploit.

Wealthy Venetian nobles built lavish palaces. With a natural
lagoon defense, these were not fortified castles like the rest of Europe but luxurious palazzos, complete with loading docks, ware-
houses, and chandeliered ballrooms. The streets were paved. The

government provided oil and required that streets be lit—a first in Europe.

Besides sea trade, Venice established strong local industries. Having mastered the art of making glass, Venice was on the cutting edge of the new science of grinding lenses for eyeglasses and telescopes. Understanding medicine as a chemical rather than an herbal pursuit, Venetians developed Europe's first real pharmaceutical industry. They made Europe's first affordable paper, from rags rather than from sheepskin (parchment). As the city offered the world's first copyright protection, its printing and bookmaking industry boomed. With mountains of capital and a sophisticated trade system of insurance, joint ventures, and money drafts, Venice's merchants eventually became bankers, loaning money at interest—making them early capitalists.

Rather than being ruled by a king—as was standard in feudal Europe—Venice developed a sophisticated government run by voting aristocrats. By the 13th century, Venice was fast becoming a Mediterranean superpower. During the Fourth Crusade (1204), Venetian troops joined other Crusaders in attacking and looting Christian Constantinople. The haul of booty enriched the city, and Venice could now stand up to its former Byzantine protectors. When Venetian ships routed the fleet of their Genoan rivals at Chioggia (on the south end of the lagoon, 1381), Venice became the undisputed master of the eastern Mediterranean. Next, they launched attacks on the mainland, conquering much of northern Italy. By 1420, Venice was at the height of its power, with mainland possessions and a powerful overseas trading empire to the east.

Representative Sights
- Doge's Palace
- St. Mark's Basilica
- Frari Church
- Buildings decorated in ornate Venetian Gothic style
- Doge paraphernalia and city history at Correr Museum
- Glass and lace industries (including the Murano glassworks)
- Arsenale shipbuilding complex

Noteworthy Residents
Enrico Dandolo (r. 1192-1205): Doge during the Fourth Crusade, when Venetian crusaders looted Constantinople, helping to enrich Venice.

Marco Polo (1254-1324): Traveler to faraway China whose journal, *The Book of Marvels*, was dismissed by many as fiction.

Paolo Veneziano (1310-1358): Painter who mastered the Byzantine gold-icon style, then added touches of Western realism.

Francesco Foscari (1373-1457): Doge at Venice's peak of

Church Architecture

History comes to life when you visit a centuries-old church. Even if you wouldn't know your apse from a hole in the ground, learning a few simple terms will enrich your experience. Of course, not every church has every feature. It's worth noting that a "cathedral" (*duomo* in Italian) isn't a type of church architecture, but rather a designation for a church that's a governing center for a local bishop.

Aisles: The long, generally low-ceilinged arcades that flank the nave.

Altar: The raised area with a ceremonial table (often adorned with candles or a crucifix), where the priest prepares and serves the bread and wine for Communion.

Apse: The space beyond the altar, generally bordered with small chapels.

Barrel Vault: A continuous round-arched ceiling that resembles an upside-down "U."

Choir: A cozy area, often screened off, located within the church nave and near the high altar, where services are sung in a more intimate setting.

Cloister: Covered hallways bordering a (usually square-shaped) open-air courtyard, traditionally where monks and nuns got fresh air.

Facade: The outer wall of the church's main (west) entrance,

power, whose ill-advised wars against Milan and the Ottoman Turks started the Republic's slow fade.

Jacopo Bellini (c. 1400-1470): Father of painting family. His training in Renaissance Florence brought 3-D realism to Venice.

Gentile Bellini (c. 1429-1507): Elder son of painting family, known for straightforward, historical scenes of Venice.

1500-1600: Renaissance and Seeds of Decline

In 1500, Venice was a commercial powerhouse—among the six biggest cities in Europe. Of its estimated 180,000 citizens, nearly 1,000 were of Rockefeller-esque wealth and power. Europe's richest city-state poured money into the arts. Titian, Tintoretto, Sansovino, the Bellini family, and Palladio called Venice  home. St. Mark's Square became the gathering place for merchants and nobles from Venice's vast trading empire. Across Europe, Venice had a reputation as a luxury-loving, exotic, cosmopolitan playground.

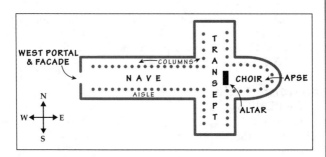

viewable from outside and generally highly decorated.

Groin Vault: An arched ceiling formed where two equal barrel vaults meet at right angles. Also: a medieval jock strap.

Narthex: The area (portico or foyer) between the main entry and the nave.

Nave: The long, central section of the church (running west to east, from the entrance to the altar) where the congregation stood through the service.

Transept: The north-south part of the church, which crosses (perpendicularly) the east-west nave. In a traditional Latin cross-shaped floor plan, the transept forms the "arms" of the cross.

West Portal: The main entry to the church (on the west end, opposite the main altar).

But Venice's power was declining. The seeds had been sown in the 15th century. In 1492, Columbus sailed the ocean blue, and established trade in a World that was New. In 1498, Vasco da Gama circled Africa's Cape of Good Hope, finding a new sea-trade route to eastern markets. Venice's sea-trade monopoly was broken.

On the Italian mainland, Venice became locked in draining wars against its rival Milan. Meanwhile, Ottomans were expanding in the East, encroaching on Venice's former monopoly on trade. Venetians and Ottomans became wary trade partners, sometimes dealing peacefully but sometimes battling over strategic ports. In 1453, the Ottomans took Constantinople, and Venice suddenly lost one of its best customers. Venice (and its European allies) scored a temporary victory over the Ottomans at the Battle of Lepanto (1571), but Venice's navy suffered major damage, and the city lost more trading rights. Spain, England, and Holland, with their oceangoing vessels, emerged as superior traders in a more global economy.

Representative Sights
- St. Mark's Square facades and other work by Sansovino

- Palladio's classical facades (San Giorgio Maggiore and Il Redentore churches)
- Masterpiece paintings by Titian, Giovanni Bellini, Giorgione, and Tintoretto (Accademia, Frari Church, Doge's Palace, San Zaccaria Church, Correr Museum, Scuola San Rocco)
- Jewish Ghetto and Jewish Museum

Noteworthy Residents

Giovanni Bellini (c. 1430-1516): The most famous son in the painting family, whose glowing, colorful, 3-D Madonna-and-Childs started the Venetian Renaissance. Teacher of Titian and Giorgione.

Vittore Carpaccio (c. 1460-1525): Painter of realistic, secular scenes and the impressive Scuola Dalmata di San Giorgio.

Giorgione (c. 1477-1511): Innovative painter whose moody realism influenced Bellini (his teacher) and Titian (his friend and fellow painter).

Jacopo Sansovino (1486-1570): Renaissance architect who redid the face of Venice (especially St. Mark's Square), introducing sober, classical columns and arches to a city previously full of ornate Gothic.

Titian (Tiziano Vecellio, 1488-1576): Premier Venetian Renaissance painter. Master of many styles, from teenage Madonnas to sober state portraits to exuberant mythological scenes to centerfold nudes.

Andrea Palladio (1508-1580): Influential architect whose classical style was much imitated around the world, resulting in villas, government buildings, and banks that look like Greek temples.

Tintoretto (Jacopo Robusti, c. 1518-1594): Painter of dramatic religious scenes, using strong 3-D, diagonal compositions, twisting poses, sharp contrast of light and shadow, and bright, "black velvet" colors (late Renaissance/Mannerist style).

Paolo Veronese (1528-1588): Painter of big, colorful canvases, capturing the exuberance and luxury of Renaissance Venice.

1600-1800: Elegant Decline

New trade routes, new European powers, and belligerent Ottomans drained Venice's economy and shrank its trading empire. At home, however, Venice's reputation for luxury—and decadence—still made it a popular tourist destination for Europe's gentry. In some ways, this is the period that most defines Venice: the city of Baroque monuments, masked balls at Carnevale, velvet-dressed nobles at opera debuts, and the roguish debauchery of Casanova.

Venice dwindled economically and politically. In 1669, its last major outpost, Crete, fell to the Ottomans. Several devastating plagues gutted the population at home. The once-enlightened government gained a nasty reputation for corruption and for locking away dissidents in the notorious prisons in the Doge's Palace. In 1797, Napoleon Bonaparte rolled into Venice and toppled the final doge. A thousand-year era of independent rule was over.

Representative Sights
- Ca' Rezzonico (Museum of 18th-Century Venice)
- La Salute Church
- Masks of the Carnevale tradition
- Old cafés (e.g., the Florian and the Quadri, both on St. Mark's Square)
- La Fenice Opera House
- Baroque interiors in many churches
- Canova sculptures (Correr Museum, Frari Church)
- G. B. Tiepolo paintings (Accademia, Doge's Palace, Ca' Rezzonico)
- Paintings of Canaletto, Guardi, and G. D. Tiepolo (Ca' Rezzonico)

Noteworthy Residents
Claudio Monteverdi (1567-1643): The composer and *maestro di capella* at St. Mark's Basilica who wrote in a budding new medium—opera.

Baldassare Longhena (1598-1682): Architect of the Baroque La Salute Church.

Antonio Vivaldi (1678-1741): Composer of *The Four Seasons* ("Dah dunt-dunt-duh dutta dah-ah-ah").

G. B. Tiepolo (Giovanni Battista, 1696-1770): Painter of mythological subjects in colorful Rococo ceilings.

Giovanni Antonio Canal, a.k.a. Canaletto (1697-1768): Painter of photo-realist Venice views.

Carlo Goldoni (1707-1793): Comic playwright who brought refinement to commedia dell'arte buffoonery.

Francesco Guardi (1712-1793): Painter of proto-Impressionist Venice views.

Giacomo Casanova (1725-1798): Gambler, womanizer, and adventurer whose exaggerated memoirs inspired Romantics.

G. D. Tiepolo (Giovanni Domenico, 1727-1804): Painter son of the famous G. B. Tiepolo.

Lorenzo Da Ponte (1749-1838): Mozart's librettist, who popularized Venice's sophisticated and decadent high society.

Antonio Canova (1757-1822): Neoclassical sculptor whose beautiful polished-white statues were especially popular in Napoleon's France.

1800 to the Present: Modern Venice

After Napoleon was defeated at Waterloo, the European allies placed Venice under Austrian rule. Sophisticated Venetians chafed against their bourgeois masters. However, Venice was still a key stop on any traveler's Grand Tour, as Europe's young aristocrats visited the city to complete their education. Venice and Italy became a political backwater as Austrian, French, and British culture dominated.

In 1866, Austria was defeated by Prussia, and rebellious Venetians seized the moment to join Italy's Risorgimento movement, annexing itself to the newly unified, democratic nation of Italy.

Venice joined the Industrial Revolution only reluctantly. The island city became connected to the mainland with a two-mile railroad causeway (1846), which was later paralleled by a highway for cars (1932). On the mainland, unbridled industrialization produced pollution (mainly sulfuric acid) that threatened Venice's stone monuments. In 1966, Venice suffered a disastrous flood, which prompted many plans and projects to control future flooding—some have been enacted, while others are still on the drawing board.

Inside Venice proper, however, there has been little new building for centuries. Today, Venice remains a museum piece for foreigners—one increasingly threatened by mainland pollution, global warming, floods, and hordes of tourists. In the 2000s, Venice continued its role as an obligatory destination, as it became a hugely popular stop for cruise ships. Venice's leaders face the dilemma of having to pay for essential upkeep by allowing billboard advertising. Local and UNESCO regulations try to preserve Venice as a cultural landmark. When Venice's venerable La Fenice Opera House burned down in 1996, it was rebuilt gloriously in 2003 in the old style. The Punta della Doga-

na, a museum devoted to contemporary art, opened in 2009, continuing Venice's legacy as a world arts capital. The current repairs to the Rialto Bridge have been largely funded by the Diesel fashion line, whose owner pledged €5 million in response to the city's pleas for sponsorship (and in return for advertising space on the scaffolding). While keeping up with what's new, Venice remains a historic wonderland. Venice is timeless—a place where visitors can easily blink away elements of the modern world and find themselves transported back in time.

Representative Sights

- Correr Museum's Risorgimento wing
- Statue of Daniele Manin (between St. Mark's Square and Rialto Bridge)
- Motorized *vaporetti* and taxis
- Train station (1954)
- Peggy Guggenheim Collection
- Biennale International Art Exhibition (held in odd years)
- Pollution from the mainland city of Mestre
- Calatrava Bridge (2008)
- Stazione Marittima cruise port
- Burger King

Noteworthy Residents

Daniele Manin (1804-1857): Rebel who led 1848 Venetian revolt against the city's Austrian rulers, eventually allowing Venice to join a united, democratic, modern Italy.

Peggy Guggenheim (1898-1979): American-born art collector, gallery owner, and friend of modern art and artists.

APPENDIX

Contents

Tourist Information

The Italian national tourist offices **in the US** are a wealth of information. Before your trip, scan their website (www.italia.it) or contact the nearest branch to briefly describe your trip and request information. You can download many brochures free of charge or call to order a free, general Italy guide. If you have a specific problem, they're a good source of sympathy.

In New York: Tel. 212/245-5618, newyork@enit.it

In Chicago: Tel. 312/644-0996, chicago@enit.it

In Los Angeles: Tel. 310/820-1898, losangeles@enit.it

In Italy, your best first stop is generally the tourist information office (abbreviated **TI** in this book). Unfortunately, the physical TIs **in Venice** aren't all that helpful, but their shared website is good: www.turismovenezia.it (see page 23 for list of TI locations).

Other useful websites are www.hellovenezia.com (vaporetto and event schedules), www.museiciviciveneziani.it (civic museums in Venice), www.veniceexplorer.net (interactive maps), www.venice-forvisitors.com, and www.aguestinvenice.com. Worthwhile sites on Italy include the Italian Tourist Board site listed above, along with www.museionline.it (museums in Italy) and www.trenitalia.com (train info and schedules; also see "Trains—Schedules" on page 436).

TIs are good places to get a city map and information on public transit (including vaporetto, bus, and train schedules), walking tours, special events, and nightlife. While Italian TIs are about half as helpful as those in other countries, their information is twice as important. Prepare a list of questions and a proposed plan to double-check.

Be wary of the travel agencies or special information services that masquerade as TIs but serve fancy hotels and tour companies. They're in the business of selling things you don't need.

While TIs are eager to book you a room, use their room-finding service only as a last resort. They are unable to give hard opinions on the relative value of one place over another. The accommodations stakes are too high to go potluck through the TI. Even if there's no "fee," you'll save yourself and your host money by going direct with the listings in this book.

Communicating

Hurdling the Language Barrier

Many Italians—especially those in the tourist trade and in big cities such as Venice—speak English. Still, you'll get better treatment if you learn and use Italian pleasantries. In smaller, non-touristy towns, Italian is the norm. Italians have an endearing habit of talking to you even if they know you don't speak their language—and yet, thanks to gestures and thoughtfully simplified words, it somehow works. Don't stop them to say you don't understand every word—just go along for the ride. For a list of survival phrases, see page 463.

Note that Italian is pronounced much like English, with a few exceptions, such as: c followed by e or i is pronounced *ch* (to ask, *"Per centro?"*—To the center?—you say, pehr CHEHN-troh). In Italian, ch is pronounced like the hard *c* in Chianti (*chiesa*—church—is pronounced kee-AY-zah). Give it your best shot. Italians appreciate your efforts.

Telephones

Smart travelers use the telephone to reserve or reconfirm rooms, get tourist information, reserve restaurants, confirm tour times, or phone home. This section covers dialing instructions, phone cards, and types of phones (for more in-depth information, see www.ricksteves.com/phoning).

How to Dial

Calling from the US to Italy, or vice versa, is simple—once you break the code. The European calling chart later in this chapter will walk you through it.

Dialing Domestically Within Italy

The following instructions apply whether you're dialing from a landline (such as a pay phone or your hotel-room phone) or an Italian mobile phone.

Italy has a direct-dial phone system (no area codes). To call anywhere within Italy, just dial the number. For example, the number of one of my recommended Venice hotels is 041-520-5764. That's the number you dial whether you're calling from Venice's train station or from Rome.

Italy's landlines start with 0, and mobile lines start with 3. The country's toll-free lines begin with 80. These 80 numbers—called *freephone* or *numero verde* (green number)—can be dialed free from any phone without using a phone card. Note that you can't call Italy's toll-free numbers from the US, nor can you count on reaching American toll-free numbers from Italy. Any Italian phone number that starts with 8 but isn't followed by a 0 is a toll call, generally costing €0.10-0.50 per minute.

Italian phone numbers vary in length; a hotel can have, say, an eight-digit phone number and a nine-digit fax number.

If you're dialing within Italy using your US mobile phone, you may need to dial as if it's a domestic call, or you may need to dial as if you're calling from the US (described next). Try it one way, and if it doesn't work, try it the other way.

Dialing Internationally to or from Italy

If you want to make an international call, follow these steps:

• Dial the international access code (00 if you're calling from Europe, 011 from the US or Canada). If you're dialing from a mobile phone, you can replace the international access code with +, which works regardless of where you're calling from. (On many mobile phones, you can insert a + by pressing and holding the 0 key.)

• Dial the country code of the country you're calling (39 for Italy, or 1 for the US or Canada).

• Dial the local number. Note that in most European countries, you have to drop the zero at the beginning of the local number—but in Italy, you dial it. (For specifics per country, see the European calling chart in this chapter.)

Calling from the US to Italy: To call the Venice hotel from the US, dial 011 (US access code), 39 (Italy's country code), then 041-520-5764.

Calling from any European country to the US: To call my office in Edmonds, Washington, from anywhere in Europe, I dial 00 (Europe's access code), 1 (US country code), 425 (Edmonds' area code), and 771-8303.

Mobile Phones

Traveling with a mobile phone is handy and practical. There are two basic options: roaming with your own phone (expensive but easy) or buying and using SIM cards with an unlocked phone (a bit more hassle, but potentially much cheaper).

Roaming with Your US Mobile Phone: This pricier option can be worthwhile if you won't be making or receiving many calls, don't want to bother with SIM cards, or want to stay reachable at your US number. Start by calling your mobile-phone service provider to ask whether your phone works in Europe and what the rates are (likely $1.29-1.99 per minute to make or receive calls, and 20-50 cents to send or receive text messages). Tell them to enable international calling on your account, and if you know you'll be making multiple calls, ask your carrier about any global calling deals to lower the per-minute costs. When you land in Europe, turn on your phone and—bingo!—you have service. Because you'll pay for receiving calls and texts, be sure your family knows to call only in an emergency. Note that Verizon and Sprint use a different technology than European providers, so their phones are less likely to work abroad; if yours doesn't, your provider may be able to send you a loaner phone.

Buying and Using SIM Cards in Europe: If you're comfortable with mobile-phone technology, will be making lots of calls, and want to save some serious money, consider this very affordable alternative: Carry an unlocked mobile phone, and use it with a European SIM card to get much cheaper rates.

Getting an **unlocked phone** may be easier than you think. You may already have an old, unused mobile phone in a drawer somewhere. When you got the phone, it was probably "locked" to work only with one company—but if your contract is now up, your provider may be willing to send you a code to unlock it. Just call and ask. Otherwise, you can simply buy an unlocked phone: Search your favorite online shopping site for an "unlocked quad-band phone" before you go, or wait until you get to Europe and buy one at a mobile-phone shop there. Either way, a basic model costs less than $50.

Once in Europe, buy a **SIM card**—the little chip that inserts into your phone (either under the battery or in a slot on the side)—to equip the phone with a European number. (Note that smaller "micro-SIM" or "nano-SIM" cards—used in some iPhones—are less widely available.) SIM cards are sold at mobile-phone shops, department-store electronics counters, and some newsstand kiosks for $5-10, and usually include about that much prepaid calling credit. Because SIM cards are prepaid, there's no contract and no commitment (in fact, they expire after just a few months of disuse); I buy one even if I'm in a country for only a few days.

In Italy, the major mobile providers are Wind, TIM, Vodafone, and 3 ("Tre"). The vendor will make a copy of your passport to register the SIM card with the service provider. You'll receive a *Benvenuti!* text message once your service is activated (it can take a few hours).

When using a SIM card in its home country, it's free to receive calls and texts; in Italy, domestic and international calls average 20-30 cents per minute. Rates are higher if you're roaming in another country, but as long as you stay within the European Union, these fees are capped (about 30 cents per minute for making calls or 10 cents per minute for receiving calls). Texting is cheap even if roaming in another country.

When purchasing a SIM card, besides confirming fees for domestic and international calls, ask about roaming charges, how to check your credit balance, and how to buy more time. If text or voice prompts are in another language, ask the clerk whether they can be switched to English.

Mobile-Phone Calling Apps: If you have a smartphone, you can use it to make free or cheap calls in Europe by using a calling app such as Skype or FaceTime when you're on Wi-Fi; for details, see the next section.

Calling over the Internet

Some things that seem too good to be true...actually are true. If you're traveling with a smartphone, tablet, or laptop, you can make free calls over the Internet to another wireless device, anywhere in the world, for free. (Or you can pay a few cents to call from your computer or smartphone to a telephone.) The major providers are Skype, Google Talk, and (on Apple devices) FaceTime. You can get online at a Wi-Fi hotspot and use these apps to make calls without ringing up expensive roaming charges (though call quality can be spotty on slow connections). You can make Internet calls even if you're traveling without your own mobile device: Many European Internet cafés have Skype, as well as microphones and webcams, on their terminals—just log on and chat away.

Landline Telephones

Just like Americans, these days most Europeans do the majority of their phoning on mobile phones. But you'll still encounter landlines in hotel rooms and at pay phones.

Hotel-Room Phones: Calling from your hotel room can be

Smartphones and Data Roaming

I take my smartphone to Europe, using it to make phone calls (sparingly) and send texts, but also to check email, listen to audio tours, and browse the Internet. You may have heard horror stories about people running up outrageous data roaming bills on their smartphones. But if you understand the options, it's easy to avoid these fees and still stay connected. The key is to turn off data roaming and only get online when you have access to free Wi-Fi. Here's how.

For voice calls and texting, smartphones work like any mobile phone (as described under "Roaming with Your US Mobile Phone," earlier). To avoid roaming charges, connect to free Wi-Fi, and use Skype, FaceTime, or other apps to make cheap or free calls (see "Calling over the Internet," earlier).

To get online with your phone, you have two options: Wi-Fi and mobile data. Because free Wi-Fi hotspots are generally easy to find in Europe (at most hotels, many cafés, and even some public spaces), the cheap solution is to use Wi-Fi wherever possible.

But what if you just can't get to a hotspot? Fortunately, most providers offer an affordable, basic data-roaming package for Europe: $25 or $30 buys you about 100 megabytes—enough to view 100 websites or send/receive 1,000 emails. If you don't buy a data-roaming plan in advance but use data in Europe anyway, you'll pay staggeringly high rates—about $20 per megabyte, or about 80 times what you'd pay with a plan.

While a data-roaming package is handy, your allotted megabytes can go quickly—especially if you stream videos or music. To keep a cap on usage and avoid incurring overage charges, I manually turn off data roaming on my phone whenever I'm not actively using it. (To turn off data and voice roaming, look in your phone's menu—try checking under "Cellular" or "Network," or ask your mobile-phone provider how to do it.) As I travel through Europe, I jump from hotspot to hotspot. But if I need to get online at a time when I can't easily access Wi-Fi—for example, to download driving directions when I'm on the road to my next hotel—I turn on data roaming just long enough for that task, then turn it off again. You can also limit how much data your phone uses by switching your email settings from "push" to "fetch" (you choose when to download messages rather than having them automatically "pushed" to your device). By carefully budgeting my data this way, my 100 megabytes last a long time.

If you want to use your smartphone exclusively on Wi-Fi—and not worry about either voice or data charges—simply turn off both voice and data roaming (or put your phone in "Airplane Mode" and then turn your Wi-Fi back on). By sticking with Wi-Fi wherever possible and budgeting your use of data, you can easily and affordably stay connected while you travel.

great for local calls and for international calls if you have an international phone card (described below). Otherwise, hotel-room phones can be an almost criminal rip-off for long-distance or international calls. Many hotels charge a fee for local and sometimes even "toll-free" numbers; always ask for the rates before you dial.

Metered Phones: In Italy, some call shops have phones with meters. You can talk all you want, then pay the bill when you leave—but be sure you know the rates before you have a lengthy conversation. Note that charges can be "per unit" rather than per minute; find out the length of a unit.

Public Pay Phones: Coin-op phones are becoming extinct in Europe. To make calls from public phones, you'll need a prepaid phone card, described next.

Telephone Cards

There are two types of phone cards: insertable (for pay phones) and international (cheap for overseas calls and usable from any type of phone). A phone card works only in the country where you bought it, so if you have a live card at the end of your trip, give it to another traveler to use—most cards expire three to six months after the first use.

Insertable Phone Cards: This type of card, which works only at pay phones, is sold by Italy's largest phone company, Telecom Italia. They give you the best deal for calls within Italy and are reasonable for international calls. You can buy Telecom cards (in €5 or €10 denominations) at tobacco shops, post offices, and machines near phone booths (many phone booths have signs indicating where the nearest phone-card sales outlet is located).

Rip off the perforated corner to "activate" the card, and then physically insert it into a slot in the pay phone. It displays how much money you have remaining on the card. Then just dial away. The price of the call is automatically deducted while you talk.

International Phone Cards: With these cards, phone calls from Italy to the US can cost less than a nickel a minute. The cards can also be used to make local calls, and they work from any type of phone, including your hotel-room phone or a mobile phone with a European SIM card. To use the card, dial a local or toll-free access number, then enter your scratch-to-reveal PIN code. If you're calling from a hotel, be sure to dial the *freephone* number (starts with "80") provided on your card rather than the "local access" number (which would incur a charge). Some hotels block their phones from accepting these access numbers. (Ask your hotelier about access and rates before you call.)

You can buy the cards at small newsstand kiosks, tobacco shops, Internet cafés, hostels, and hole-in-the-wall long-distance phone shops. Buy a lower denomination in case the card is a dud.

European Calling Chart

Just smile and dial, using this key:
AC = Area Code, LN = Local Number.

European Country	Calling long distance within ...	Calling from the US or Canada to ...	Calling from a European country to ...
Austria	AC + LN	011 + 43 + AC (without initial zero) + LN	00 + 43 + AC (without initial zero) + LN
Belgium	LN	011 + 32 + LN (without initial zero)	00 + 32 + LN (without initial zero)
Bosnia-Herzegovina	AC + LN	011 + 387 + AC (without initial zero) + LN	00 + 387 + AC (without initial zero) + LN
Britain	AC + LN	011 + 44 + AC (without initial zero) + LN	00 + 44 + AC (without initial zero) + LN
Croatia	AC + LN	011 + 385 + AC (without initial zero) + LN	00 + 385 + AC (without initial zero) + LN
Czech Republic	LN	011 + 420 + LN	00 + 420 + LN
Denmark	LN	011 + 45 + LN	00 + 45 + LN
Estonia	LN	011 + 372 + LN	00 + 372 + LN
Finland	AC + LN	011 + 358 + AC (without initial zero) + LN	999 (or other 900 number) + 358 + AC (without initial zero) + LN
France	LN	011 + 33 + LN (without initial zero)	00 + 33 + LN (without initial zero)
Germany	AC + LN	011 + 49 + AC (without initial zero) + LN	00 + 49 + AC (without initial zero) + LN
Gibraltar	LN	011 + 350 + LN	00 + 350 + LN
Greece	LN	011 + 30 + LN	00 + 30 + LN
Hungary	06 + AC + LN	011 + 36 + AC + LN	00 + 36 + AC + LN
Ireland	AC + LN	011 + 353 + AC (without initial zero) + LN	00 + 353 + AC (without initial zero) + LN
Italy	LN	011 + 39 + LN	00 + 39 + LN

European Country	Calling long distance within ...	Calling from the US or Canada to ...	Calling from a European country to ...
Latvia	LN	011 + 371 + LN	00 + 371 + LN
Montenegro	AC + LN	011 + 382 + AC (without initial zero) + LN	00 + 382 + AC (without initial zero) + LN
Morocco	LN	011 + 212 + LN (without initial zero)	00 + 212 + LN (without initial zero)
Netherlands	AC + LN	011 + 31 + AC (without initial zero) + LN	00 + 31 + AC (without initial zero) + LN
Norway	LN	011 + 47 + LN	00 + 47 + LN
Poland	LN	011 + 48 + LN	00 + 48 + LN
Portugal	LN	011 + 351 + LN	00 + 351 + LN
Russia	8 + AC + LN	011 + 7 + AC + LN	00 + 7 + AC + LN
Slovakia	AC + LN	011 + 421 + AC (without initial zero) + LN	00 + 421 + AC (without initial zero) + LN
Slovenia	AC + LN	011 + 386 + AC (without initial zero) + LN	00 + 386 + AC (without initial zero) + LN
Spain	LN	011 + 34 + LN	00 + 34 + LN
Sweden	AC + LN	011 + 46 + AC (without initial zero) + LN	00 + 46 + AC (without initial zero) + LN
Switzerland	LN	011 + 41 + LN (without initial zero)	00 + 41 + LN (without initial zero)
Turkey	AC (if there's no initial zero, add one) + LN	011 + 90 + AC (without initial zero) + LN	00 + 90 + AC (without initial zero) + LN

APPENDIX

- The instructions above apply whether you're calling to or from a European landline or mobile phone.

- If calling from any mobile phone, you can replace the international access code with "+" (press and hold 0 to insert it).

- The international access code is 011 if you're calling from the US or Canada.

- To call the US or Canada from Europe, dial 00, then 1 (country code for US and Canada), then the area code and number. In short, 00 + 1 + AC + LN = Hi, Mom!

Ask for an international phone card (*carta telefonica prepagata internazionale*, KAR-tah teh-leh-FOHN-ee-kah pray-pah-GAH-tah in-ter-naht-zee-oh-NAH-lay). Tell the vendor where you'll be making most calls (*"per Stati Uniti"*—to America), and he'll select the brand with the best deal.

I've had good luck with the Europa card, which offers up to 350 minutes from Italy to the US for €5. Some shops also sell cardless codes, printed right on the receipt.

US Calling Cards: These cards, such as the ones offered by AT&T, Verizon, and Sprint, are a rotten value, and are being phased out. Try any of the options outlined earlier.

Useful Phone Numbers

Emergency Needs
English-speaking police help: Tel. 113
Ambulance: Tel. 118
Road Service: Tel. 116

Embassies and Consulates
Nearest US Consulate: Tel. 02-290-351 (Via Principe Amedeo 2/10, Milan, http://milan.usconsulate.gov)
US Embassy: 24-hour emergency line—tel. 06-46741, non-emergency—tel. 06-4674-2406 (Via Vittorio Veneto 121, Rome, www.usembassy.it)
Canadian Embassy: Tel. 06-854-441 (Via Zara 30, Rome, www.italy.gc.ca)

Travel Advisories
US Department of State: Tel. 888-407-4747, from outside US tel. 1-202-501-4444, www.travel.state.gov
Canadian Department of Foreign Affairs: Canadian tel. 800-387-3124, from outside Canada tel. 1-613-996-8885, www.travel.gc.ca
US Centers for Disease Control and Prevention: Tel. 800-CDC-INFO (800-232-4636), www.cdc.gov/travel

Directory Assistance
Telephone Help: Tel. 170 (in English; free directory assistance)
Directory Assistance: Tel. 12 (€0.50, an Italian-speaking robot gives the number twice, very clearly)

Airports
Venice: Marco Polo Airport (airport code: VCE)—tel. 041-260-9260, www.veniceairport.com; **Treviso Airport** (airport code: TSF)—tel. 042-231-5111, www.trevisoairport.it

Verona: Catullo Airport (also known as Verona-Villafranca, airport code: VRN)—tel. 045-809-5666, www.aeroportoverona.it.

Internet Access

It's useful to get online periodically as you travel—to confirm trip plans, check train or bus schedules, get weather forecasts, catch up on email, blog or post photos from your trip, or call folks back home (explained earlier, under "Calling over the Internet").

Your Mobile Device: The majority of accommodations in Italy offer Wi-Fi, as do many cafés, making it easy for you to get online with your laptop, tablet, or smartphone. Access is often free, but sometimes there's a fee. At hotels that charge for a certain number of hours, save money by logging in and out of your account on an as-needed basis. You should be able to stretch a two-hour Wi-Fi pass over a stay of a day or two.

Some hotel rooms and Internet cafés have high-speed Internet jacks that you can plug into with an Ethernet cable.

Public Internet Terminals: Many accommodations offer a guest computer in the lobby with Internet access. If you ask politely, smaller places may let you sit at their desk for a few minutes just to check your email. If your hotelier doesn't have access, ask to be directed to the nearest place to get online. Italian keyboards are a little different from ours; to type an @ symbol, press the "Alt Gr" key and the key that shows the @ symbol.

Security: Whether you're accessing the Internet with your own device or at a public terminal, using a shared network or computer comes with the potential for increased security risks. If you're not convinced a connection is secure, avoid accessing any sites (such as online banking) that could be vulnerable to fraud.

Mail

You can mail one package per day to yourself worth up to $200 duty-free from Europe to the US (mark it "personal purchases"). If you're sending a gift to someone, mark it "unsolicited gift." For details, visit www.cbp.gov and search for "Know Before You Go."

The Italian postal service works fine, but for quick transatlantic delivery in either direction, consider services such as DHL (www.dhl.com).

Transportation

By Car or Public Transportation?

If your trip will cover more of Italy than just Venice, you'll need to decide whether to rent a car or take trains. Cars are best for three or more traveling together (especially families with small kids), those

Italy's Public Transportation

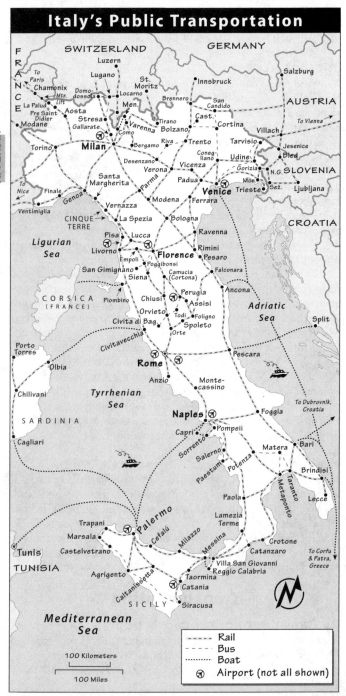

packing heavy, and those scouring the countryside. Trains and buses are best for solo travelers, blitz tourists, city-to-city travelers, and those who don't want to drive in Europe. While a car gives you more freedom, trains and buses zip you effortlessly and scenically from city to city, usually dropping you in the center, often near a TI.

Public Transportation

Trains

To travel by train cheaply in Italy, you can simply buy tickets as you go. Ticket machines in stations are easy to use (see "Buying Tickets," later), so you can usually avoid long lines at ticket windows. Pay all ticket costs in the station before you board, or you'll pay a penalty on the train.

Types of Trains: Most trains in Italy are operated by the state-run Trenitalia company (a.k.a. Ferrovie dello Stato Italiane, abbreviated *FS* or *FSI*). Since ticket prices depend on the speed of the

train, it helps to know the different types of trains: pokey R or REG *(regionali);* medium-speed RV *(regionale veloce),* IR (InterRegio), D *(diretto),* and E *(espresso);* fast IC (InterCity) and EC (EuroCity); and super-fast Frecce trains: the Frecciabianca ("White Arrow"), faster Frecciargento ("Silver Arrow"), and Frecciarossa ("Red Arrow"). (You may also see the Frecce trains marked on schedules as ES, AV, or EAV for Eurostar Italia Alta Velocità.) If you're traveling with a railpass, note that reservations are required for EC and international trains (€5) and Frecce trains (€10). Reservations are optional for railpass holders on IC trains, and you can't make reservations for regional trains.

A new, private train company called **Italo** now runs fast trains on major routes in Italy (thereby challenging Trenitalia's monopoly). Italo is focusing on two high-speed corridors: Venice-Padua-Bologna-Florence-Rome and Turin-Milan-Bologna-Florence-Rome, with additional connections onward to Naples. The trains run at more or less the same speed as Trenitalia's high-speed trains, but often with lower fares, particularly for tickets booked well in advance. In some cities (most notably Rome and Milan), its trains use a secondary station rather than the main one—if taking an Italo train, pay attention to which station you need. Italo does not currently accept railpasses, but its affordable fares make it worth considering for point-to-point tickets. You can book in person (look for Italo ticket offices or machines—tickets not sold through Trenitalia), by phone (tel. 06-0708), or on their user-friendly website (www.italotreno.it).

Schedules: At the train station, the easiest way to check schedules is at a handy ticket machine (described later, under "Buying Tickets"). Enter the desired date, time, and destination to see all of your options. Printed schedules are also posted at the station (departure—*partenzi*—posters are always yellow).

Newsstands sell up-to-date regional and all-Italy timetables (€5, ask for the *orario ferroviario*). On the Web, check www.trenitalia.it and www.italotreno.it (domestic journeys only); for international trips, use www.bahn.de (Germany's excellent all-Europe train-schedule website). Trenitalia offers a single all-Italy telephone number for train information (24 hours daily, tel. 892-021, in Italian only, consider having your hotelier call for you). For Italo trains, call 06-0708.

Be aware that Trenitalia and Italo don't cooperate at all. If you buy a ticket for one train line, it's not valid on the other. Even if you're just looking for schedule information, the company you ask will most likely ignore the other's options.

Point-to-Point Tickets

Train tickets are a good value in Italy. Fares are shown on the map on page 437, though fares can vary for the same journey, mainly depending on the time of day, the speed of the train, and more. **First-class** tickets cost 30-50 percent more than **second class.** While second-class cars go just as fast as their first-class neighbors, Italy is one country where I would consider the splurge of first class. The easiest way to "upgrade" a second-class ticket once on board a crowded train is to nurse a drink in the snack car. A *flessible* (flexible) ticket costs more than a *base* (basic) fare—but special *promo* deals can drive the cost even lower. Fares labeled *servizi abbonati* are available only for locals with monthly passes—not tourists.

Speed vs. Savings: For point-to-point tickets on mainline routes, fast trains save time, but charge a premium. For example, super-fast Venice-Rome trains run more-or-less hourly, cost €80 in second class, and make the trip in 3.75 hours, while infrequent InterCity trains (only 1-2/day) cost €50 and take 6 hours.

Discounts: Families with young children can get price breaks—kids ages 4 and under travel free; ages 4-11 at half-price.

Train Costs in Italy

Map key: Approximate point-to-point one-way second-class rail fares in US dollars. First class costs 50 percent more.

Before deciding to get a railpass, add up the approximate ticket costs for your itinerary. If you'll be making short, inexpensive trips each day, you'll probably find it's cheaper to buy tickets as you go in Italy.

Ask for the "Offerta Familia" deal when buying tickets at a counter (or, at a ticket machine, choose "Yes" at the "Do you want ticket issue?" prompt, then choose "Familia"). With the discount, families of three to five people with at least one kid (age 12 or under) get 50 percent off the child fare, and 20 percent off the adult fare. The deal doesn't apply to all trains at all times, but it's worth checking out.

Discounts for youths and seniors require purchase of a separate card (Carta Verde for ages 12-26 costs €40; Carta Argento for ages 60 and over is €30), but the discount on tickets is so minor (10-15 percent respectively for domestic travel), it's not worth it for most.

Buying Tickets: Avoid train station ticket lines whenever possible by using the ticket machines found in station halls. You'll be able to easily purchase tickets for travel within Italy (not international trains), make seat reservations, and even book a *cuccetta* (koo-CHEH-tah; overnight berth). If you do use the ticket windows, be sure you're in the correct line. Key terms: *biglietti* (general tickets), *prenotazioni* (reservations), *nazionali* (domestic), and *internazionali*.

Trenitalia's ticket machines (usually green and white, marked *Biglietto Veloce/Fast Ticket*) are user-friendly and found in all but the tiniest stations in Italy. You can pay by cash (they give change) or by debit or credit card (even for small amounts). Select English, then your destination. If you don't immediately see the city you're traveling to, keep keying in the spelling until it's listed. You can choose from first- and second-class seats, request tickets for more than one traveler, and (on high-speed Frecce trains) choose an aisle or window seat. Don't select a discount rate without being sure

APPENDIX

Open or Non-Reserved Ticket—Need to Validate

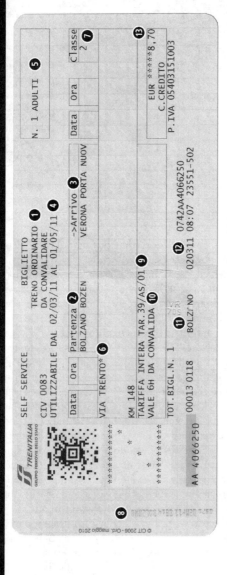

1 Open ticket for non-express trains, must be validated
2 Point of departure
3 Destination
4 Validity of ticket (use once within 2 months of purchase)
5 Number of passengers
6 Route
7 Class of travel (1 = 1st, 2 = 2nd)
8 Validation stamp
9 Full fare for non-express train
10 Once stamped, ticket is good for 1 trip within 6 hours
11 Location of ticket sale
12 Date ticket was purchased
13 Ticket cost

Reserved Ticket (Fast Train)—Need Not Validate

1. Departure date & time
2. Point of departure
3. Destination
4. "Ticket with reservation"
5. Number of passengers
6. Arrival date & time
7. Class of travel (1 = 1st, 2 = 2nd)
8. "Present to official if changing trains"
9. Train #, train car # & seat # (finestrino = window seat)
10. Fast-train fare (other types of trains can be cheaper and don't require reservations)
11. Location of ticket sale
12. Date ticket was purchased
13. Booking ID
14. Ticket cost
15. Amount of CO_2 usage reduced by this train trip

© CTT 2006 - Ord., maggio 2010

APPENDIX

that you meet the criteria (for example, Americans are not eligible for certain EU or resident discounts). Railpass holders can use the machines to make seat reservations. If you need to validate your ticket, you can do it in the same machine if you're boarding your train right away.

For nearby destinations only, you can also buy tickets from the older, gray-and-blue machines marked *Rete regionale* (cash only, push button for English).

It's possible, but generally unnecessary, to buy Trenitalia tickets in advance online at www.trenitalia.it. Because most Italian trains run frequently and there's no deadline to buy tickets, you can keep your travel plans flexible by purchasing tickets as you go. (You can buy tickets for several trips at one station when you're ready to commit.) For busy weekend or holiday travel, however, it can be a good idea to buy tickets in advance, whether online or at a station.

To buy tickets for **Italo** trains, look for a dedicated service counter (in most major rail stations) or a red ticket machine labeled *Italo.* You can also book Italo tickets by phone (tel. 06-0708) or online (www.italotreno.it).

You can't buy international tickets from machines; for this and anything else that requires a real person, you must go to a ticket window. A good alternative, though, is to drop by a local travel agency. Agencies sell domestic and international tickets and make reservations. They charge a small fee, but the language barrier (and the lines) can be smaller than at the station's ticket windows.

Validating Tickets: If your ticket includes a seat reservation on a specific train *(biglietto con prenotazione)*, you're all set and can just get on board. An open ticket with no seat reservation (it may say *da convalidare* or *convalida*) must always be validated—stamp it before you board in the machine near the platform (usually marked *convalida biglietti* or *vidimazione*). Once you validate a ticket, you must complete your trip within the timeframe shown on the ticket (within 6 hours for medium-distance trips; within 1.25 hours for short rides under 6 miles). If you forget to validate your ticket, go right away to the train conductor—before he comes to you—or you'll pay a fine.

Railpasses

The **Italy Pass** for the Italian state railway may save you money if you're taking three long train rides or prefer first-class travel, but don't count on it for hop-on convenience on every train. Use the price map on page 437 to add up your ticket costs (ticket prices on the map are for the fastest trains on a given route, many of which have reservation costs built in). Remember that railpasses are not valid on Italo-brand trains.

Railpass travelers must make separate seat reservations for the

Railpasses

Prices listed are for 2013 and are subject to change. For the latest prices, details, and train schedules (and easy online ordering), see my comprehensive *Guide to Eurail Passes* at www.ricksteves.com/rail.

"Saver" prices are per person for two or more people traveling together. "Youth" means under age 26. The fare for children 4–11 is half the adult individual fare or Saver fare. Kids under age 4 travel free.

ITALY PASS

	Individual 1st Class	Individual 2nd Class	Saver 1st Class	Saver 2nd Class	Youth 2nd Class
3 days in 2 months	$289	$237	$247	$202	$192
Extra rail days (max 7)	32-37	24-30	26-32	21-26	21-24

ITALY RAIL & DRIVE PASS

Any 3 rail days and 2 car days in 2 months.

Car Category	1st Class	2nd Class	Extra Car Day
Economy 2-Door	$367	$311	$64
Economy 4-Door	375	320	72
Compact	394	339	92
Intermediate	420	365	118
Economy Automatic	403	347	100
Premium	520	464	217
Extra rail days (max 2)	32	26	

Prices are per person, two traveling together. Solo travelers pay about 20 percent more. To order a Rail & Drive pass, call your travel agent or Rail Europe at 800-438-7245. *This pass is not sold by Europe Through the Back Door.*

FRANCE–ITALY PASS

	Individual 1st Class	Individual 2nd Class	Saver 1st Class	Saver 2nd Class	Youth 2nd Class
4 days in 2 months	$404	$345	$345	$294	$264
Extra rail days (max 6)	45-51	38-44	38-44	33-37	29-33

Be aware of your route. Direct Paris–Italy trains (day and overnight) and trains via Switzerland aren't covered by this pass.

GREECE–ITALY PASS

	Individual 1st Class	Individual 2nd Class	Saver 1st Class	Saver 2nd Class	Youth 2nd Class
4 days in 2 months	$375	$301	$319	$256	$245
Extra rail days (max 6)	38-40	31-32	33-34	26-27	25-26

Covers deck passage on overnight Superfast Ferries between Patras, Greece and Bari or Ancona, Italy (starts use of one travel day). Does not cover travel to or on Greek islands, except a 30% discount on Blue Star Ferries. Very few trains run in Greece.

SELECTPASS

This pass covers travel in three adjacent countries, not including France. Please visit **www.ricksteves.com/rail** for four- and five-country options.

	Individual 1st Class	Saver 1st Class	Youth 2nd Class
5 days in 2 months	$479	$408	$313
6 days in 2 months	529	450	345
8 days in 2 months	625	532	408
10 days in 2 months	724	616	472

fastest trains between major Italian cities (€10 each). Railpass travelers can just hop on InterCity trains (optional €5 reservation) and regional trains (no reservations possible). Making a reservation at a train station or travel agency is the same as the process to buy a ticket, so you may need to stand in line either way. Reservations for berths on overnight trains cost extra, aren't covered by railpasses, and aren't reflected on the ticket cost map.

A **Global Pass** can work well throughout most of Europe, but it's a bad value for travel exclusively in Italy. A cheaper version, the **Select Pass,** allows you to tailor a pass to your trip, provided you're traveling in three, four, or five adjacent countries directly connected by rail or ferry (excluding France). For instance, with a three-country pass allowing 10 days of train travel within a two-month period (about $730 for a single adult in 2013), you could choose Switzerland-Italy-Greece or Germany-Austria-Italy. A **France and Italy Pass** combines just those two countries. Note that none of these passes cover direct day or night trains between Italy and Paris, which require a separate ticket. Before you buy a Select Pass or France and Italy Pass, consider how many travel days you'll really need. Use the pass for travel days that involve long hauls or several trips. Pay out of pocket for tickets on days you're taking only short, cheap rides.

For a summary of railpass deals and the latest prices, check my Guide to Eurail Passes at www.ricksteves.com/rail. This guide will help you know that you're getting the right railpass for your trip.

Train Tips

This section contains more information on making seat reservations, storing baggage, avoiding theft, and dealing with strikes.

Seat Reservations: Trains can fill up, even in first class. If you're on a tight schedule, you'll want to reserve a few days ahead for fast trains (see "Types of Trains," earlier). Purchasing tickets or passholder seat reservations onboard a train comes with a nasty penalty. Buying them at the station can be a time-waster unless you use the ticket machines.

If you don't need a reservation, and if your train originates at your departure point (e.g., you're catching the Venice-Florence train in Venice), arriving at least 15 minutes before the departure time will help you snare a seat.

On the platforms of some major stations, posters showing the train composition *(composizione principali treni)* indicate where first- and second-class cars will line up when the trains arrive (letters on the poster are supposed to correspond to letters posted over the platform—but they don't always). Since most trains now allow you to make reservations up to the time of departure, conductors post a list of the reservable and non-reservable seat rows (sometimes in English) in each train car's vestibule. This means that if

Deciphering Italian Train Schedules

At the station, look for the big yellow posters labeled *Partenze*—Departures. (The white posters show arrivals.)

Schedules are listed chronologically, hour by hour, showing the trains leaving the station throughout the day. Each schedule has columns:

- The first column *(Ora)* lists the time of departure.
- The next column *(Treno)* shows the type of train.
- The third column *(Classi Servizi)* lists the services available (first- and second-class cars, dining car, *cuccetta* berths, etc.) and, more importantly, whether you need reservations (usually denoted by an R in a box). All Frecce trains, many EuroCity (EC) trains, and most international trains require reservations.
- The next column lists the destination of the train *(Principali Fermate Destinazioni)*, often showing intermediate stops, followed by the final destination, with arrival times listed throughout in parentheses. Note that your final destination may be listed in fine print as an intermediate destination. For example, if you're going from Venice to Verona, scan the schedule and you'll notice that regional trains that go to Milan usually stop in Verona en route. Travelers who read the fine print end up with a far greater choice of trains.
- The next column *(Servizi Diretti e Annotazioni)* has pertinent notes about the train, such as "also stops in..." *(ferma anche a...)*, "doesn't stop in..." *(non ferma a...)*, "stops in every station" *(ferma in tutte le stazioni)*, "delayed..." *(ritardo...)*, and so on.
- The last column lists the track *(Binario)* the train departs from. Confirm the *binario* with an additional source: a ticket-seller, the electronic board that lists immediate departures, TV monitors on the platform, or the railway officials who are usually standing by the train unless you really need them.

For any odd symbols on the poster, look at the key at the end. Some of the phrasing can be deciphered easily, such as *servizio periodico* (periodic service—doesn't always run). For the trickier ones, ask a local or railway official, try your *Rick Steves' Italian Phrase Book & Dictionary*, or simply take a different train.

You can also check schedules—for trains anywhere in Italy, not just from the station you're currently in—at the handy ticket machines. Enter the date and time of your departure (to or from any Italian station), and you can view all your options.

you board a crowded train and get one of the last seats, you may be ousted when the reservation-holder comes along.

Baggage Storage: Many stations have *deposito bagagli* where you can safely leave your bag for about €8 per 12-hour period (payable when you pick up the bag, double-check closing hours). Because of security concerns, no Italian stations have lockers.

Theft Concerns: Italian trains are famous for their thieves. Never leave a bag unattended. Police do ride the trains, cutting down on theft. Still, for an overnight trip, I'd feel safe only in a *cuccetta* (a bunk in a special sleeping car with an attendant who keeps track of who comes and goes while you sleep—approximately €20 in a six-bed compartment, €26 in a less-cramped four-bed compartment, €50 in a more-private double compartment).

Strikes: Strikes, which are common, generally last a day. Train employees will simply explain, *"Sciopero"* (strike). But in actuality, sporadic trains, following no particular schedule, lumber down the tracks during most strikes. When a strike is pending, travel agencies (and hoteliers) can check online for you to see when the strike goes into effect and which trains will continue to run. Revised schedules may be posted in Italian at stations, and station personnel still working can often tell you what trains are expected to run. If I need to get somewhere and know a strike is imminent, I leave early (before the strike, which often begins at 9:00), or I just go to the station with extra patience in tow and hop on anything rolling in the direction I want to go.

Buses

You can usually get anywhere you want to in Italy by bus, as long as you're not in a hurry, and plan ahead using bus schedules (pick up at local TIs). For reaching small towns, buses are sometimes the only option if you don't have a car.

Larger towns have a long-distance bus station *(stazione degli autobus)*, with ticket windows and several stalls (usually labeled *corsia*, *stallo*, or *binario*). Smaller towns—where buses are more useful—just have a central bus stop *(fermata)*, likely along the main road or on the main square, and maybe several more scattered around town. In small towns, buy bus tickets at newsstands or tobacco shops (with the big *T* signs). When buying your ticket, confirm the departure point *("Dov'è la fermata?")*, and once there, double-check that the posted schedule lists your destination and departure time. In general, orange buses are local city buses, and blue buses are for long distances.

Once the bus arrives, confirm the destination with the driver. You are expected to stow big backpacks underneath the bus (open the luggage compartment yourself if it's closed).

Sundays and holidays are problematic; even from large cities schedules are sparse, departing buses are jam-packed, and ticket offices are often closed. Plan ahead and buy your ticket in advance. Most travel agencies book bus (and train) tickets for just a small fee.

Renting a Car

If you're renting a car in Italy, bring your driver's license. You're also required to have an International Driving Permit—an official translation of your driver's license (sold at your local AAA office for $15 plus the cost of two passport-type photos; see www.aaa. com). While that's the letter of the law, I've often rented cars in Italy without having this permit. If all goes well, you'll likely never be asked to show the permit—but it's a must if you end up dealing with the police.

Rental companies require you to be at least 21 years old and to have held your license for one year. Drivers under the age of 25 may incur a young-driver surcharge, and some rental companies do not rent to anyone 75 or older. If you're considered too young or old, look into leasing (covered later), which has less-stringent age restrictions.

Research car rentals before you go. It's cheaper to arrange most car rentals from the US. Call several companies and look online to compare rates, or arrange a rental through your hometown travel agent.

Most of the major US rental agencies (including Avis, Budget, Enterprise, Hertz, and Thrifty) have offices throughout Europe. Also consider the two major Europe-based agencies, Europcar and Sixt. It can be cheaper to use a consolidator, such as Auto Europe (www.autoeurope.com) or Europe by Car (www.ebctravel.com), which compares rates at several companies to get you the best deal. However, my readers have reported problems with consolidators, ranging from misinformation to unexpected fees; because you're going through a middleman, it can be more challenging to resolve disputes that arise with the rental agency.

Regardless of the car-rental company you choose, always read the fine print carefully for add-on charges—such as one-way drop-off fees, airport surcharges, or mandatory insurance policies—that aren't included in the "total price." You may need to query rental agents pointedly to find out your actual cost.

For the best deal, rent by the week with unlimited mileage. To save money on fuel, ask for a diesel car. I normally rent the smallest, least-expensive model with a stick shift (generally much cheaper than an automatic). Almost all rentals are manual by default, so if you need an automatic, request one in advance; be aware that these cars are usually larger models (not as maneuverable on narrow, winding roads). Roads and parking spaces are narrow in Italy, so you'll do yourself a favor by renting the smallest car that meets your needs.

For a one-week rental, allow roughly $400. Allow extra for insurance, fuel, tolls, and parking. For trips of three weeks or more, look into leasing; you'll save money on insurance and taxes.

You can sometimes get a GPS unit with your rental car or leased vehicle for an additional fee (around $15/day; be sure it's set to English and has all the maps you need before you drive off). Or, if you have a portable GPS device at home, consider taking it with you to Europe (buy and upload European maps before your trip). GPS apps are also available for smartphones, but downloading maps in Europe could lead to an exorbitant data-roaming bill (for more details, see the sidebar on page 428).

Big companies have offices in most cities; ask whether they can pick you up at your hotel. Small local rental companies can be cheaper but aren't as flexible.

Compare pickup costs (downtown can be less expensive than the airport) and explore drop-off options. Always check the hours of the location you choose: Many rental offices close from midday Saturday until Monday morning and, in smaller towns, at lunchtime.

When selecting a location, don't trust the agency's description of "downtown" or "city center." In some cases, a "downtown" branch can be on the outskirts of the city—a long, costly taxi ride from the center. Before choosing, plug the addresses into a mapping website. You may find that the "train station" location is handier. But returning a car at a big-city train station or downtown agency can be tricky; get precise details on the car drop-off location and hours, and allow ample time to find it.

When you pick up the rental car, check it thoroughly and make sure any damage is noted on your rental agreement. Find out how your car's lights, turn signals, wipers, and fuel cap function, and know what kind of fuel the car takes. When you return the car, make sure the agent verifies its condition with you.

If you want a car for only a couple of days, a rail-and-drive pass (such as a Select Pass Drive or Italy Rail and Drive) can be put to thoughtful use. The basic Italy Rail and Drive Pass comes with two days of car rental and three days of rail travel in two months. While rail-and-drive passes are convenient, they're also pricey, particularly for solo travelers.

Car Insurance Options

Accidents can happen anywhere, but when you're on vacation, the last thing you need is stress over car insurance. When you rent a car, you're liable for a very high deductible, sometimes equal to the entire value of the car. Limit your financial risk with one of these two options: Buy Collision Damage Waiver (CDW) coverage from the car-rental company (figure roughly 30 percent extra), or get coverage through your credit card (free, but more complicated).

In Italy, most car-rental companies' rates automatically include CDW coverage. Even if you try to decline CDW when you reserve your Italian car, you may find when you show up at the counter that you must buy it after all.

While each rental company has its own variation, basic CDW costs $15-35 a day and reduces your liability, but does not eliminate it. When you pick up the car, you'll be offered the chance to "buy down" the deductible to zero (for an additional $10-30/day; this is sometimes called "super CDW").

If you opt for credit-card coverage, there's a catch. You'll technically have to decline all coverage offered by the car-rental company, which means they can place a hold on your card for up to the full value of the car. In case of damage, it can be time-consuming to resolve the charges with your credit-card company. Before you decide on this option, quiz your credit-card company about how it works.

For more on car-rental insurance, see www.ricksteves.com/cdw.

Theft Insurance: Note that theft insurance (separate from CDW insurance) is mandatory in Italy. The insurance usually costs about $15-20 a day, payable when you pick up the car.

Leasing

For trips of three weeks or more, consider leasing (which automatically includes zero-deductible collision and theft insurance). By technically buying and then selling back the car, you save lots of money on tax and insurance. Leasing provides you a new car with unlimited mileage and a 24-hour emergency assistance program. You can lease for as little as 21 days to as long as six months. Car leases must be arranged from the US. One of many companies offering affordable lease packages is Europe by Car (US tel. 800-223-1516, www.ebctravel.com).

Driving

Driving in Italy can be scary—a video game for keeps, and you only get one quarter. Italian drivers can be aggressive. They drive fast and tailgate as if it were required. They pass where Americans are taught not to—on blind corners and just before tunnels. Roads have narrow shoulders or none at all. Driving in the countryside is less stressful than driving through urban areas, but stay alert. On one-lane roads, larger vehicles have the right-of-way. If you're on a

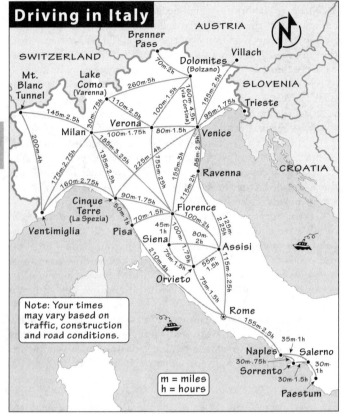

Driving in Italy

Note: Your times may vary based on traffic, construction and road conditions.

m = miles
h = hours

truckers' route, stifle your Good Samaritan impulse when you see provocatively dressed women standing by camper-vans at the side of the road; they're not having car trouble.

Road Rules: Stay out of restricted traffic zones or you'll risk huge fines. Car traffic is restricted in many city centers. Don't drive or park anywhere with signs reading *Zona Traffico Limitato* (ZTL, often shown above a red circle, see image). If you do, your license

plate will likely be photographed and a hefty (€100-plus) ticket mailed to your home without your ever having met a cop. Bumbling in and out of these zones can net you multiple fines. If your hotel is within a restricted area, it's best to ask your hotelier to direct you to parking outside the zone. (Although your hotelier can register your car as an authorized vehicle permitted to enter the zone, this usually isn't worth the hassle.) If you get a ticket, it could take months to show up (see www.bella-toscana. com/traffic_violations_italy.htm for details).

Be aware of typical European road rules; for example, many countries require headlights to be turned on at all times, and it's generally illegal to drive while using your mobile phone without a hands-free headset. Seatbelts are mandatory and children under age 12 must ride in child-safety or booster seats. In Europe, you're not allowed to turn right on a red light, unless there is a sign or signal specifically authorizing it. Ask your car-rental company about these rules, or check the US State Department website (www. travel.state.gov, click on "International Travel," then specify your country of choice and click "Traffic Safety and Road Conditions").

Tolls: Italy's freeway system, the *autostrada*, is as good as our interstate system, but you'll pay a toll (for costs, use the trip-planning tool at www.autostrade.it or search "European Tolls" on www. theaa.com). While I favor the freeways because I feel they're safer and less nerve-racking than smaller roads, savvy local drivers know which toll-free *superstradas* are actually faster and more direct than the *autostrada*.

Fuel: Gas is expensive—often about €2/liter ($8.50/gallon). Diesel cars are more common in Europe than back home, so be

sure you know what type of fuel your car takes before you fill up. Gas pumps are color-coded for unleaded *(senza piombo)* or diesel *(gasolio).* Autostrada rest stops are self-service stations open daily without a siesta break. Many 24-hour-a-day stations are entirely automated. Small-town stations are usually cheaper and offer full service but shorter hours.

Maps and Signage: A good map is essential. Learn the universal road signs (see illustration on this page). Although roads are numbered on maps, actual road signs often give just a city name (for example, if you were heading east out of Venice, the map would be marked "route S-11"—but you'd follow signs to Padua, the next town along this road).

The signs are inconsistent: They may direct you to the nearest big city or simply the next town along the route.

Theft: Cars are routinely vandalized and stolen. Thieves easily recognize rental cars and assume they are filled with a tourist's gear. Try to make your car look locally owned by hiding the "tourist-owned" rental-company decals and putting an Italian newspaper in your back window. Be sure all of your valuables are out of sight and locked in the trunk, or even better, with you or in your room.

Parking: White lines generally mean parking is free. Yellow lines mean that parking is reserved for residents only (who have permits). Blue lines mean you'll have to pay—usually around €1.50 per hour (use machine, leave time-stamped receipt on dashboard). If there's no meter, there's probably a roving attendant who will take your money. Study the signs. Often the free zones have a 30- or 60-minute time limit. Signs showing a street cleaner and a day of the week indicate which day the street is cleaned; there's a €100 tow-fee incentive to learn the days of the week in Italian.

Zona disco has nothing to do with dancing. Italian cars come equipped with a time disc (a cardboard clock), which you can use in a *zona disco*—set the clock to your arrival time and leave it on the dashboard. (If your rental car doesn't come with a *disco*, pick one up at a tobacco shop or just write your arrival time on a piece of paper and place it on the dashboard.)

Garages are safe, save time, and help you avoid the stress of parking tickets. Take the parking voucher with you to pay the cashier before you leave.

Cheap Flights

If you're considering a train ride that's more than five hours long, a flight may save you both time and money. When comparing your options, factor in the time it takes to get to the airport and how early you'll need to arrive to check in.

The best comparison search engine for both international and intra-European flights is www.kayak.com. For inexpensive flights within Europe, try www.skyscanner.com or www.hipmunk.com. If you're not sure who flies to your destination, check its airport's website for a list of carriers.

Well-known cheapo airlines include easyJet (www.easyjet.com) and Ryanair (www.ryanair.com). Both serve Venice (airport code: VCE).

Be aware of the potential drawbacks of flying on the cheap: nonrefundable and nonchangeable tickets, minimal or nonexistent customer service, treks to airports far outside town, and stingy baggage allowances with steep overage fees. If you're traveling with lots of luggage, a cheap flight can quickly become a bad deal. To avoid unpleasant surprises, read the small print before you book.

Resources

Resources from Rick Steves

Books: *Rick Steves' Venice 2014* is one of many books in my series on European travel, which includes country guidebooks, city guidebooks (Rome, Florence, Paris, London, etc.), Snapshot guides (excerpted chapters from my country guides), Pocket Guides (full-color little books on big cities, including Venice), and my budget-

travel skills handbook, *Rick Steves' Europe Through the Back Door*. Most of my titles are available as ebooks. My phrase books—for Italian, French, German, Spanish, and Portuguese—are practical and budget-oriented. My other books include *Europe 101* (a crash course on art and history designed for travelers); *Mediterranean Cruise Ports* and *Northern European Cruise Ports* (how to make the most of your time in port); and *Travel as a Political Act* (a travelogue sprinkled with tips for bringing home a global perspective). A more complete list of my titles appears near the end of this book.

Video: My public television series, *Rick Steves' Europe,* covers European destinations in 100 shows, with 17 episodes on Italy, including two on Venice. To watch episodes online, visit www.hulu.com; for scripts and local airtimes, see www.ricksteves.com/tv.

Audio: My weekly public radio show, *Travel with Rick Steves,* features interviews with travel experts from around the world. I've also produced free, self-guided **audio tours** of the top sights in Venice. All of this audio content is available for free at Rick Steves Audio Europe, an extensive online library organized by destination. Choose whatever interests you, and down-

load it for free via the Rick Steves Audio Europe smartphone app, www.ricksteves.com/audioeurope, iTunes, or Google Play.

Maps

The black-and-white maps in this book are concise and simple, designed to help you locate recommended places and get to local TIs, where you can pick up more in-depth maps of cities and regions (usually free). Better maps are sold at newsstands and bookstores. Before you buy a map, look at it to be sure it has the level of detail

APPENDIX

Begin Your Trip at www.ricksteves.com

At our travel website, you'll discover a wealth of free information on European destinations, including fresh monthly news and helpful tips from thousands of fellow travelers. You'll find my latest guidebook updates (www.ricksteves.com/update), a monthly travel enewsletter, my personal travel blog, and my free Rick Steves Audio Europe smartphone app (if you don't have a smartphone, you can access the same content via podcasts). You can also follow me on Facebook and Twitter.

Our **online Travel Store** offers travel bags and accessories that I've designed specifically to help you travel smarter and lighter. These include my popular bags (rolling carry-on and backpack versions), money belts, totes, toiletries kits, adapters, other accessories, and a wide selection of guidebooks, planning maps, and DVDs.

Choosing the right **railpass** for your trip—amid hundreds of options—can drive you nutty. We'll help you choose the best pass for your needs and ship it to you for free.

Want to travel with greater efficiency and less stress? We organize **tours** with more than three dozen itineraries and more than 500 departures reaching the best destinations in this book...and beyond. Our Italy tours include "the best of" in 17 days, Village Italy in 14 days, South Italy in 13 days, Sicily in 10 days, Venice-Florence-Rome in 10 days, the Heart of Italy in 9 days, My Way: Italy "unguided" tour in 13 days, and a week-long Rome tour. You'll enjoy great guides, a fun bunch of travel partners (with small groups of 24 to 28 travelers), and plenty of room to spread out in a big, comfy bus. You'll find European adventures to fit every vacation length. For all the details, and to get our Tour Catalog and a free Rick Steves Tour Experience DVD (filmed on location during an actual tour), visit www.ricksteves.com or call us at 425/608-4217.

you want. Drivers will want to pick up a good, detailed map in Europe (I'd recommend a 1:200,000- or 1:300,000-scale map).

Other Guidebooks

If you're like most travelers, this book is all you need. But if you're heading beyond my recommended neighborhoods and destinations, $40 for extra maps and books can be money well spent. If you'll be traveling elsewhere in Italy, consider *Rick Steves' Italy*, *Rick Steves' Florence*, or *Rick Steves' Rome*.

The following books are worthwhile, though most are not updated annually; check the publication date before you buy. Focusing mainly on sights, Eyewitness' colorful *Venice and the Veneto* guide is fun for its great graphics and photos, but it's relatively skimpy on content and weighs a ton. (Their *Top 10 Venice* book, which features top-10 lists, is lighter, as is Rough Guides' *Pocket Rough Guide Venice*.) Frommer's publishes *24 Great Walks in Venice*, and Lonely Planet offers *Venice Encounter*. You can buy these in Venice (no more expensive than in the US) or simply borrow them for a minute from other travelers at certain sights to make sure you're aware of that place's highlights. In Venice, local guidebooks (sold at kiosks) are cheap and give you a map and a decent commentary on the sights.

Recommended Books and Movies

To learn more about Venice past and present, check out a few of these books or films.

Nonfiction

A History of Venice (Norwich) covers the city from its beginnings until Napoleon ended the Republic's independence. *Venice: A Maritime Republic* (Lane) explains how dominance on the high seas brought in piles of riches. *Venice: Lion City* (Wills), another city history, has a more academic tone. *Francesco's Venice* (da Mosto), based on a BBC series, balances history with coffee table-book illustrations. *The Venetian Empire* (Morris) is an easy read and shows the city's place on a larger historical canvas.

Filled with stories of a woman abroad, *Venice Observed* rings with Mary McCarthy's engaging voice. *The City of Falling Angels*, by best-selling author John Berendt, hinges on a devastating fire at La Fenice Opera House. Based on once-hidden letters found in a palazzo, *A Venetian Affair* (di Robilant) tells a true love story. *Venice: A Cultural and Literary Companion* (Garrett) also covers the nearby islands, while *A Literary Companion to Venice* (Littlewood) includes walking tours of the city, as does *Strolling Through Venice* (Freely). For a traveler's insight into Venice, consider picking up Barrie Kerper's *Venice: The Collected Traveler*. Kids of all ages enjoy the whimsical impressions of the city in Miroslav Sasek's classic picture-book *This is Venice*.

For a fun, critical perspective on tourism in Venice, get *Venice: The Tourist Maze* (Davis and Martin). Jane da Mosto's *The Science of Saving Venice* is a readable introduction to the ecology and future of Venice's lagoon.

Fiction

Henry James set many of his best books in Venice, including *The Wings of the Dove*, *Italian Hours*, and *The Aspern Papers and Other Stories*. Thomas Mann also chose this city for his doomed tale *Death in Venice*.

In *Invisible Cities* (Calvino), "Marco Polo" tells of the fantastical cities he's seen...or is he just describing the many facets of his beloved Venice? *The Palace: A Novel* (St. Aubin de Terán) has the Italian Risorgimento as its backdrop. Set in the Napoleonic era, *The Passion* (Winterson) is both a complex love story and a work of magical realist fiction. *In the Company of the Courtesan* (Dunant), *The Glassblower of Murano* (Fiorato), and *The Rossetti Letter* (Phillips) novelize the drama and romance of Venice.

Venice's murky waters make a perfect setting for intrigue. Mystery fans will enjoy *Dead Lagoon* (Dibdin), *Dirge for a Doge* (Eyre), *Stone Virgin* (Unsworth), and *The Haunted Hotel* (Collins). In *Death at La Fenice,* one of a dozen of her novels set in Venice, Donna Leon chronicles the adventures of detective Guido Brunetti and his wife Paola. Fans of the series will enjoy *Brunetti's Venice* (Sepeda), which leads visitors on intimate walks through the city, highlighting Brunetti's haunts and settings from Leon's novels.

Films

Summertime (1955) sends melancholy Katherine Hepburn to Venice for romance. *Death in Venice* (1971), based on the book (see above), shows the devastating impact of a troubling infatuation. *Don't Look Now* (1973), based on a novel by Daphne du Maurier, uses Venice as a mysterious backdrop for a haunting tale.

Only You (1994) is a cute (and even sappy) love story, while *Bread and Tulips* (2000)—equally romantic, but firmly grounded in reality—shows the power of Venice in reviving a wounded soul. *Dangerous Beauty* (1998), meanwhile, keeps love out of the picture in the story of a 16th-century prostitute. *The Wings of the Dove* (1997), based on the Henry James novel, is a tale of desire that takes full advantage of its Venetian locale.

The 2003 version of *The Italian Job* begins its fluffy, fun crime caper in Venice. Shakespeare fans will appreciate *The Merchant of Venice* (2004), which won raves for Al Pacino. The Woody Allen musical *Everyone Says I Love You* (1997) is partially set in Venice.

And the climax of the James Bond thriller *Casino Royale* (2006) takes place along—and under—the canals of Venice. For more lightweight Venetian eye-candy, try *Casanova* (2005), starring Heath Ledger as the master of *amore*, or *The Tourist* (2010), with Johnny Depp and Angelina Jolie.

If you're visiting Verona, try *Letters to Juliet* (2010) for a romance woven around the letter-writing tradition.

Holidays and Festivals

This list includes selected festivals in Venice in 2014, plus national holidays observed throughout Italy. Many sights and banks close on national holidays—keep this in mind when planning your itinerary. Before planning a trip around a festival, verify its dates by checking the festival's website or TI sites (www.italia.it and www.turismovenezia.it).

In Venice, hotels get booked up on Carnevale, Easter weekend, Liberation Day/St. Mark's Day, Labor Day, Feast of the Ascension Day, the Feast and Regatta of the Redeemer, the Historical Regatta, All Saint's Day, the Feast of our Lady of Good Health, Christmas, and New Year's Eve, and on Fridays and Saturdays year-round. Some hotels require you to book the full three-day weekend around a holiday.

Jan 1	New Year's Day
Jan 6	Epiphany
Feb 22-March 4	Carnevale
April 20	Easter Sunday
April 21	Easter Monday
April 25	Italian Liberation Day, St. Mark's Day (Venetian patron saint)
May 1	Labor Day
May 29	Feast of the Ascension Day
Late May-Early June	Vogalonga Regatta (www.vogalonga.it)
June 2	Anniversary of the Republic
June 19	Feast of Corpus Christi
Third Weekend in July	Feast and Regatta of the Redeemer (Festa del Redentore)
Aug 15	Assumption of Mary (Ferragosto)
First Sat-Sun of Sept	Historical Regatta
Nov 1	All Saints' Day
Nov 21	Feast of Our Lady of Good Health
Dec 8	Feast of the Immaculate Conception
Dec 25	Christmas
Dec 26	St. Stephen's Day

2014

JANUARY
S	M	T	W	T	F	S
			1	2	3	4
5	6	7	8	9	10	11
12	13	14	15	16	17	18
19	20	21	22	23	24	25
26	27	28	29	30	31	

FEBRUARY
S	M	T	W	T	F	S
						1
2	3	4	5	6	7	8
9	10	11	12	13	14	15
16	17	18	19	20	21	22
23	24	25	26	27	28	

MARCH
S	M	T	W	T	F	S
						1
2	3	4	5	6	7	8
9	10	11	12	13	14	15
16	17	18	19	20	21	22
23/30	24/31	25	26	27	28	29

APRIL
S	M	T	W	T	F	S
		1	2	3	4	5
6	7	8	9	10	11	12
13	14	15	16	17	18	19
20	21	22	23	24	25	26
27	28	29	30			

MAY
S	M	T	W	T	F	S
				1	2	3
4	5	6	7	8	9	10
11	12	13	14	15	16	17
18	19	20	21	22	23	24
25	26	27	28	29	30	31

JUNE
S	M	T	W	T	F	S
1	2	3	4	5	6	7
8	9	10	11	12	13	14
15	16	17	18	19	20	21
22	23	24	25	26	27	28
29	30					

JULY
S	M	T	W	T	F	S
		1	2	3	4	5
6	7	8	9	10	11	12
13	14	15	16	17	18	19
20	21	22	23	24	25	26
27	28	29	30	31		

AUGUST
S	M	T	W	T	F	S
					1	2
3	4	5	6	7	8	9
10	11	12	13	14	15	16
17	18	19	20	21	22	23
24/31	25	26	27	28	29	30

SEPTEMBER
S	M	T	W	T	F	S
	1	2	3	4	5	6
7	8	9	10	11	12	13
14	15	16	17	18	19	20
21	22	23	24	25	26	27
28	29	30				

OCTOBER
S	M	T	W	T	F	S
			1	2	3	4
5	6	7	8	9	10	11
12	13	14	15	16	17	18
19	20	21	22	23	24	25
26	27	28	29	30	31	

NOVEMBER
S	M	T	W	T	F	S
						1
2	3	4	5	6	7	8
9	10	11	12	13	14	15
16	17	18	19	20	21	22
23/30	24	25	26	27	28	29

DECEMBER
S	M	T	W	T	F	S
	1	2	3	4	5	6
7	8	9	10	11	12	13
14	15	16	17	18	19	20
21	22	23	24	25	26	27
28	29	30	31			

Festivals in Venice

Venice's most famous festival is **Carnevale,** the celebration Americans call Mardi Gras (Feb 22-March 4 in 2014, www.carnevale.venezia.it). Carnevale, which means "farewell to meat," originated centuries ago as a wild two-month-long party leading up to the austerity of Lent. In Carnevale's heyday—the 1600s and 1700s—you could do pretty much anything with anybody from any social class if you were wearing a mask. These days it's a tamer 18-day celebration, culminating in a huge dance lit with fireworks on St. Mark's Square. Sporting masks and costumes, Venetians from kids to businessmen join in the fun. Drawing the biggest crowds of the year, Carnevale has nearly been a victim of its own success, driving away many Venetians (who skip out on the craziness to go skiing in the Dolomites).

Every year, the city hosts the **Venice Biennale International Art Exhibition,** a world-class contemporary fair, alternating between art in odd years and architecture in even years. The exhibition spreads over the Arsenale and Giardini park. When the Biennale focuses on visual art, representatives from 70 nations offer the latest in contemporary art forms: video, computer art, performance art, and digital photography, along with painting and sculpture (take vaporetto #1 or #2 to Giardini-Biennale; for details and an events calendar, see www.labiennale.org). The actual exhibition usually runs from June through November, but other events—film, dance, theater—loosely connected with the Biennale are held throughout the year (starting as early as Feb) in various venues on the island.

Other typically Venetian festival days filling the city's hotels with visitors and its canals with decked-out boats are **Feast of the Ascension Day** (May 29 in 2014), **Feast and Regatta of the Redeemer** (Festa del Redentore) on the  third weekend in July (with spectacular fireworks show Sat night), and the **Historical Regatta** (old-time boats and pageantry, first Sat and Sun in Sept). **Vogalonga** is a colorful regatta that attracts more than 1,500 human-powered watercraft; teams of often-costumed participants follow a 20-mile course through the canals and lagoon (late May-early June, www.vogalonga.it). Smaller regattas include the **Murano Regatta** (early July) and the **Burano Regatta** (mid-Sept).

Venice's patron saint, **St. Mark,** is commemorated every April 25. Venetian men celebrate the day by presenting roses to the women in their lives (mothers, wives, and lovers).

Every November 21 is the **Feast of Our Lady of Good Health.** On this local "Thanksgiving," a bridge is built over the Grand Canal so that the city can pile into La Salute Church and remember how Venice survived the gruesome plague of 1630. On this day, Venetians eat smoked lamb from Dalmatia (which was the cargo of the first ship admitted when the plague lifted).

APPENDIX

Conversions and Climate

Numbers and Stumblers

- Europeans write a few of their numbers differently than we do. 1 = 1, 4 = 4, 7 = 7.
- In Europe, dates appear as day/month/year, so Christmas is 25/12/14.
- Commas are decimal points and decimals are commas. A dollar and a half is 1,50, one thousand is 1.000, and there are 5.280 feet in a mile.
- When counting with fingers, start with your thumb. If you hold up your first finger to request one item, you'll probably get two.
- What Americans call the second floor of a building is the first floor in Europe.
- On escalators and moving sidewalks, Europeans keep the left "lane" open for passing. Keep to the right.

Metric Conversions

A kilogram is 2.2 pounds, and 1 liter is about a quart, or almost four to a gallon. A kilometer is six-tenths of a mile. I figure kilometers to miles by cutting them in half and adding back 10 percent of the original (120 km: 60 + 12 = 72 miles, 300 km: 150 + 30 = 180 miles).

1 foot = 0.3 meter	1 square yard = 0.8 square meter
1 yard = 0.9 meter	1 square mile = 2.6 square kilometers
1 mile = 1.6 kilometers	1 ounce = 28 grams
1 centimeter = 0.4 inch	1 quart = 0.95 liter
1 meter = 39.4 inches	1 kilogram = 2.2 pounds
1 kilometer = 0.62 mile	32°F = 0°C

Roman Numerals

In the US, you'll see Roman numerals—which originated in ancient Rome—used for copyright dates, clocks, and the Super Bowl. In Italy, you're likely to observe these numbers chiseled on statues and buildings. If you want to do some numeric detective work, here's how: In Roman numerals, as in ours, the highest numbers (thousands, hundreds) come first, followed by smaller numbers. Many numbers are made by combining numerals into sets: V = 5, so VIII = 8 (5 plus 3). Roman numerals follow a subtraction principle for multiples of fours (4, 40, 400, etc.) and nines (9, 90, 900, etc.); the number four, for example, is written as IV (1 subtracted from 5), rather than IIII. The number nine is IX (1 subtracted from 10).

Rick Steves' Venice 2014—written in Roman numerals—would translate as *Rick Steves' Venice MMXIV*. Big numbers such as dates can look daunting at first. The easiest way to handle them is to read the numbers in discrete chunks. For example, Michelangelo was born in MCDLXXV. Break it down: M (1,000) + CD (100 subtracted from 500, or 400) + LXX (50 + 10 + 10, or 70) + V (5) = 1475. It was a very good year.

M = 1000	XL = 40
CM = 900	X = 10
D = 500	IX = 9
CD = 400	V = 5
C = 100	IV = 4
XC = 90	I = duh
L = 50	

Clothing Sizes

When shopping for clothing, use these US-to-European comparisons as general guidelines (but note that no conversion is perfect).

- Women's dresses and blouses: Add 30 (US size 10 = European size 40)
- Men's suits and jackets: Add 10 (US size 40 regular = European size 50)
- Men's shirts: Multiply by 2 and add about 8 (US size 15 collar = European size 38)
- Women's shoes: Add about 30 (US size 8 = European size 38-39)
- Men's shoes: Add 32-34 (US size 9 = European size 41; US size 11 = European size 45)

Venice's Climate

First line, average daily high; second line, average daily low; third line, average days without rain. For more detailed weather statistics for destinations in this book (as well as the rest of the world), check www.wunderground.com.

J	F	M	A	M	J	J	A	S	O	N	D
42°	46°	53°	62°	70°	76°	81°	80°	75°	65°	53°	46°
33°	35°	41°	49°	56°	63°	66°	65°	61°	53°	44°	37°
25	21	24	21	23	22	24	24	25	24	21	23

Temperature Conversion: Fahrenheit and Celsius

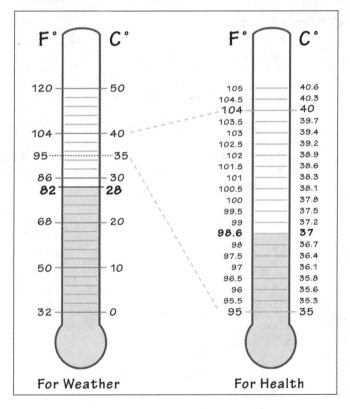

Europe takes its temperature using the Celsius scale, while we opt for Fahrenheit. For a rough conversion from Celsius to Fahrenheit, double the number and add 30. For weather, remember that 28°C is 82°F—perfect. For health, 37°C is just right.

APPENDIX

Packing Checklist

Whether you're traveling for five days or five weeks, here's what you'll need to bring. Pack light to enjoy the sweet freedom of true mobility. Happy travels!

❏ 5 shirts: long- & short-sleeve
❏ 1 sweater or lightweight fleece
❏ 2 pairs of pants
❏ 1 pair of shorts
❏ 5 pairs of underwear & socks
❏ 1 pair of shoes
❏ 1 rainproof jacket with hood
❏ Tie or scarf
❏ Swimsuit
❏ Sleepwear
❏ Money belt
❏ Money—your mix of:
  ❏ Debit card
  ❏ Credit card(s)
  ❏ Hard cash ($20 bills)
❏ Documents plus photocopies:
  ❏ Passport
  ❏ Printout of airline eticket
  ❏ Driver's license
  ❏ Student ID, hostel card, etc.
  ❏ Railpass/train reservations/ car-rental voucher
  ❏ Insurance details
❏ Guidebooks & maps
❏ Address list (for sending emails & postcards)
❏ Notepad & pen
❏ Journal
❏ Daypack
❏ Toiletries kit:
  ❏ Toiletries
  ❏ Medicines & vitamins
  ❏ First-aid kit
  ❏ Glasses/contacts/ sunglasses (with prescriptions)
❏ Small towel/washcloth
❏ Laundry supplies:
  ❏ Laundry soap
  ❏ Clothesline
❏ Sewing kit

❏ Electronics—your choice of:
  ❏ Camera (& related gear)
  ❏ Mobile phone
  ❏ Portable media player (iPod or other)
  ❏ Laptop/netbook/ tablet
  ❏ Ebook reader
  ❏ Headphones or earbuds
  ❏ Chargers for each of the above
  ❏ Plug adapter(s)
❏ Alarm clock
❏ Earplugs
❏ Sealable plastic baggies
❏ Empty water bottle
❏ Postcards & photos from home

If you plan to carry on your luggage, note that all liquids must be in 3.4-ounce or smaller containers and fit within a single quart-size sealable baggie. For details, see www.tsa.gov/travelers.

Italian Survival Phrases

English	Italian	Pronunciation
Good day.	Buon giorno.	bwohn **jor**-noh
Do you speak English?	Parla inglese?	**par**-lah een-**glay**-zay
Yes. / No.	Sì. / No.	see / noh
I (don't) understand.	(Non) capisco.	(nohn) kah-**pees**-koh
Please.	Per favore.	pehr fah-**voh**-ray
Thank you.	Grazie.	**graht**-seeay
You're welcome.	Prego.	**pray**-go
I'm sorry.	Mi dispiace.	mee dee-spee**ah**-chay
Excuse me.	Mi scusi.	mee **skoo**-zee
(No) problem.	(Non) c'è un problema.	(nohn) cheh oon proh-**blay**-mah
Good.	Va bene.	vah **behn**-ay
Goodbye.	Arrivederci.	ah-ree-vay-**dehr**-chee
one / two	uno / due	**oo**-noh / **doo**-ay
three / four	tre / quattro	tray / **kwah**-troh
five / six	cinque / sei	**cheeng**-kway / **seh**ee
seven / eight	sette / otto	**seht**-tay / **ot**-toh
nine / ten	nove / dieci	**nov**-ay / dee**ay**-chee
How much is it?	Quanto costa?	**kwahn**-toh **kos**-tah
Write it?	Me lo scrive?	may loh **skree**-vay
Is it free?	È gratis?	eh **grah**-tees
Is it included?	È incluso?	eh een-**kloo**-zoh
Where can I buy / find...?	Dove posso comprare / trovare...?	**doh**-vay **pos**-soh kohm-**prah**-ray / troh-**vah**-ray
I'd like / We'd like...	Vorrei / Vorremmo...	vor-**reh**ee / vor-**ray**-moh
...a room.	...una camera.	**oo**-nah **kah**-meh-rah
...a ticket to ____.	...un biglietto per ____.	oon beel-**yeht**-toh pehr
Is it possible?	È possibile?	eh poh-**see**-bee-lay
Where is...?	Dov'è...?	**doh**-veh
...the train station	...la stazione	lah staht-seeoh-nay
...the bus station	...la stazione degli autobus	lah staht-seeoh-nay **dayl**-yee ow-toh-boos
...tourist information	...informazioni per turisti	een-for-maht-seeoh-nee pehr too-**ree**-stee
...the toilet	...la toilette	lah twah-**leht**-tay
men	uomini, signori	**woh**-mee-nee, seen-**yoh**-ree
women	donne, signore	**don**-nay, seen-**yoh**-ray
left / right	sinistra / destra	see-**nee**-strah / **dehs**-trah
straight	sempre diritto	**sehm**-pray dee-**ree**-toh
When do you open / close?	A che ora aprite / chiudete?	ah kay **oh**-rah ah-**pree**-tay / keeoo-**day**-tay
At what time?	A che ora?	ah kay **oh**-rah
Just a moment.	Un momento.	oon moh-**mayn**-toh
now / soon / later	adesso / presto / tardi	ah-**dehs**-soh / **prehs**-toh / **tar**-dee
today / tomorrow	oggi / domani	**oh**-jee / doh-**mah**-nee

In an Italian-speaking Restaurant

English	Italian	Pronunciation
I'd like...	Vorrei...	vor-**rehee**
We'd like...	Vorremmo...	vor-**ray**-moh
...to reserve...	...prenotare...	pray-noh-**tah**-ray
...a table for one / two.	...un tavolo per uno / due.	oon **tah**-voh-loh pehr **oo**-noh / **doo**-ay
Non-smoking.	Non fumare.	nohn foo-**mah**-ray
Is this seat free?	È libero questo posto?	eh **lee**-bay-roh **kwehs**-toh **poh**-stoh
The menu (in English), please.	Il menù (in inglese), per favore.	eel may-**noo** (een een-**glay**-zay) pehr fah-**voh**-ray
service (not) included	servizio (non) incluso	sehr-**veet**-seeoh (nohn) een-**kloo**-zoh
cover charge	pane e coperto	**pah**-nay ay koh-**pehr**-toh
to go	da portar via	dah **por**-tar **vee**-ah
with / without	con / senza	kohn / **sehn**-sah
and / or	e / o	ay / oh
menu (of the day)	menù (del giorno)	may-**noo** (dayl **jor**-noh)
specialty of the house	specialità della casa	spay-chah-lee-**tah** dehl-lah kah-zah
first course (pasta, soup)	primo piatto	**pree**-moh peeah-toh
main course (meat, fish)	secondo piatto	say-**kohn**-doh peeah-toh
side dishes	contorni	kohn-**tor**-nee
bread	pane	**pah**-nay
cheese	formaggio	for-**mah**-joh
sandwich	panino	pah-**nee**-noh
soup	minestra, zuppa	mee-**nehs**-trah, **tsoo**-pah
salad	insalata	een-sah-**lah**-tah
meat	carne	**kar**-nay
chicken	pollo	**poh**-loh
fish	pesce	**peh**-shay
seafood	frutti di mare	**froo**-tee dee **mah**-ray
fruit / vegetables	frutta / legumi	**froo**-tah / lay-**goo**-mee
dessert	dolci	**dohl**-chee
tap water	acqua del rubinetto	**ah**-kwah dayl roo-bee-**nay**-toh
mineral water	acqua minerale	**ah**-kwah mee-nay-ray-**rah**-lay
milk	latte	**lah**-tay
(orange) juice	succo (d'arancia)	**soo**-koh (dah-**rahn**-chah)
coffee / tea	caffè / tè	kah-**feh** / teh
wine	vino	**vee**-noh
red / white	rosso / bianco	**roh**-soh / beeahn-koh
glass / bottle	bicchiere / bottiglia	bee-keeay-ray / boh-**teel**-yah
beer	birra	**bee**-rah
Cheers!	Cin cin!	cheen cheen
More. / Another.	Ancora un po.' / Un altro.	ahn-**koh**-rah oon poh / oon **ahl**-troh
The same.	Lo stesso.	loh **stehs**-soh
The bill, please.	Il conto, per favore.	eel **kohn**-toh pehr fah-**voh**-ray
tip	mancia	**mahn**-chah
Delicious!	Delizioso!	day-leet-seeoh-zoh

For more user-friendly Italian phrases, check out *Rick Steves' Italian Phrase Book & Dictionary* or *Rick Steves' French, Italian, and German Phrase Book.*

INDEX

MAP INDEX

MAP INDEX